LATIN AMERICA
A Social History of the Colonial Period

LATIN AMERICA
A Social History of the Colonial Period

Jonathan C. Brown
The University of Texas at Austin

HARCOURT COLLEGE PUBLISHERS

Fort Worth   Philadelphia   San Diego   New York   Orlando   Austin   San Antonio

Toronto   Montreal   London   Sydney   Tokyo

Publisher	**EARL MCPEEK**
Executive Editor	**DAVID TATOM**
Developmental Editor	**STEVE NORDER**
Project Editor	**JOYCE FINK**
Art Director	**BURL SLOAN**
Production Manager	**SERENA BARNETT**

Cover: Nettie Lee Benson Latin American Collection, The University of Texas at Austin

ISBN: 0-03-055387-3
Library of Congress Catalog Card Number: 99-067138

Address for Domestic Orders
Harcourt College Publishers, 6277 Sea Harbor Drive, Orlando, FL 32887-6777
800-782-4479

Address for International Orders
International Customer Service
Harcourt, Inc., 6277 Sea Harbor Drive, Orlando, FL 32887-6777
407-345-3800
(fax) 407-345-4060
(e-mail) hbintl@harcourtbrace.com

Address for Editorial Correspondence
Harcourt College Publishers, 301 Commerce Street, Suite 3700, Fort Worth, TX 76102

Web Site Address
http://www.harcourtcollege.com

Printed in the United States of America

9 0 1 2 3 4 5 6 7 8 039 9 8 7 6 5 4 3 2 1

Harcourt College Publishers

PREFACE

In the last two decades, historians of Latin America have produced many fine monographs on ethnohistory, landlords and peasants, employers and workers, governors and the governed, missionaries and converts, clergy and parishioners, and the family. Yet the full panorama of their findings, up to now, has not been synthesized. Most textbooks highlight the area of the authors' specialties, so that Mexico, Peru, and Brazil receive greater treatment than the countries of the Caribbean and northern and southern South America. Such textbooks tend to also neglect the active role taken by Native and African Americans in the making of their own history. Many authors treat peasants and workers as mere appendages to the top-down story of European conquest and economic expansion. Though these works may convey an accurate portrait of political events and economic structure, they do not reflect the richness of the recent research on social history and how ordinary people have shaped their own lives.

In contrast, my goals in writing this new textbook remain close to the objectives of social history. In *Latin America: A Social History of the Colonial Period* I place the emphasis on a bottom-up approach to the evolution of colonial institutions and focus on the popular classes; that is, the indigenous peoples, African Americans, persons of mixed race, peasants, and workers. Not only did members of the popular classes influence employers in subtle ways, but their rebellions and defiance rerouted the trajectory of economic and political developments. How did the Revolutions for Independence, for example, result in social reforms such as termination of the slave trade and an end to forced labor for the native peoples? According to this analysis, they emanated from the acquiescence of the leaders to the demands of their followers.

In pursuing these goals, I have not neglected to bring to the discussion the great personalities, such as Hernán Cortés, Sor Juana, Túpac Amaru, and Simón Bolívar. These men and women add human interest and drama to the story. Neither do I ignore the church, the state or, especially, the economic organization of colonialism. Nevertheless, social relations remain more important to my interpretation of colonial history as I always attempt in this narrative to uncover the visible hand of the popular classes in shaping outcomes.

Latin America is made up of variegated mixtures of indigenous, African, and European cultures. Each region and nation has inherited a varied and localized blend of these three influences. Today, the casual traveler cannot help but notice the "European" milieu of cities like Buenos Aires, Bogotá, and Santiago de Chile. Yet other cities retain a Native American flavor—Cuzco and Oaxaca come to mind. No one who experiences the songs and dances of Carnival, the great pre-Lenten celebrations of Cartagena and Salvador, can escape the contributions of Africa. And the food differs in all these localities as well. Latin America is a celebration of cultural diversity.

Latin America: A Social History of the Colonial Period seeks to explain the origins of this diversity and to explore how persons of different races, ethnicity, and social rank related to one another. Rather than attempting a static description of colonial society, the narrative and the statistical tables appearing in this textbook deal with the diversity of social actors and depict how their inter-relationships were changing over time. This analysis includes gender relationships as well. I explain how colonialism forged new associations between men and women of the same and of different social rank. The reader will discover that, for women, privilege and personal mobility seldom coincided. These gender relationships had a great deal to do with another singular feature of Latin America— namely racial miscegenation.

It has been my intention throughout to make this book accessible to a wide audience of students and professionals, avoiding trendy paradigms and ideologically charged jargon. Its extensive chapter bibliographies will give the reader ample opportunity independently to pursue many facets of the story. This book provides insights into the craft of history as well, discussing the evidence and documentation from which we draw conclusions about social relationships. For this purpose, I have added illustrations and excerpts from original manuscripts that demonstrate how common people lived and acted. All terms are defined in the text. The glossary and maps serve to keep the reader on course just as Portuguese mariners used the astrolabe (for calculating the latitude) and sailing charts for much the same purpose. Like them, I try to steer the readers between the shoals of misunderstanding and the reefs of confusion.

The writer of a textbook incurs many debts. I could not have attempted a bottom-up approach to Latin American social history without the skillful and dedicated work of hundreds of my colleagues in Latin America, Britain, and the United States. I have also benefited from the advice and wise counsel of John Tutino, Mariano Díaz-Miranda, Alida Metcalf, Louisa Hoberman, Sandra Lauderdale-Graham, Pablo Picatto, and Xóchitl Medina. Additional help came from Adrian A. Bantjes (University of Wyoming), Donald S. Castro (California State University, Fullerton), Wayne M. Clegern (Colorado State University), Kathleen Higgins (University of Iowa), Robert Himmerich y Valencia (University of New Mexico), Daniel Masterson (United States Naval Academy), Ronn Pineo (Towson State University), F. Arturo Rosales (Arizona State University), Terry Rugeley (University of Oklahoma), Eric Van Young (University of California, San Diego), and Ralph Lee Woodward Jr. (Tulane University). In Mexico City, Marcos Tonatiuh Aguila M. lent me his apartment and use of his impressive library. I learned of the Brazilian frontier from Hal Langford and slave rebellions from Matt Childs. Teresa Van Hoy and Soraya González cheerfully translated some of the manuscripts that appear within the chapters. Susan Long composed some of the most informative maps to be found in any textbook.

In addition, I would like to acknowledge my gratitude to the staff of the Nettie Lee Benson Collection of the University of Texas at Austin. Director Laura Gutiérrez-Witt, Carmen Sacomani, Michael Hironymous, Jane Garner, and Ann Lozano were especially helpful and patient with my requests for illustrations, manuscripts, and rare books. I am fortunate in my department to work with some of the best scholars of Latin America: Susan

Deans-Smith, Aline Helg, Virginia Garrard Burnett, and Mauricio Tenorio. Knowledgeable and talented graduate students give our program at the University of Texas its top ranking, and their research has influenced my own understanding over the years.

Lynore Brown has been an indispensable collaborator and muse for my entire academic career. She read nearly every word of this manuscript and convinced me to correct my errors and conceits—or at least some of them. Many undergraduate students are also developing an enthusiasm for Latin America, finding in its history a counterpoint to their own heritage. It is for them that I wrote this book.

Jonathan C. Brown
Austin, Texas

BRIEF CONTENTS

Contents

Manuscripts

MAPS

TABLES

FIGURES

PART I

PART I

THE ENCOUNTER BETWEEN NATIVE AMERICANS AND EUROPEANS

When the Europeans arrived in the Americas in 1492, they discovered numerous flourishing civilizations that both amazed and repelled them. The Native Americans then inhabiting these two vast continents—about which Europeans had no previous knowledge—existed in a dizzying variety of ethnic cultures and language groups. Conquest overtook some indigenous peoples rapidly and progressed very slowly over others. The forest and prairie hunters who lived in decentralized groupings would hold out against the Europeans for centuries. The great civilizations of Mexico and Peru, on the other hand, became victims of their political centralization and accumulated wealth. These sophisticated agriculturists also made good workers. Densely populated agricultural zones attracted European colonization more than the sparsely populated forests and prairies, and the conquerors utilized their technological and commercial innovations to subdue the Stone Age empires of what they called the New World. Furthermore, the indigenous Americans did not have immunities to the diseases of the Old World, an important factor in conquest. The ethnic and political diversity of the American peoples also aided the European conquerors. Because of internecine warfare among different indigenous communities and groups, native peoples actively assisted the Europeans in conquering their traditional rivals and foes—only to be subsequently conquered themselves.

But the new colonial society created by the conquests of the sixteenth century did not emerge as a mirror copy of the Spain and Portugal whence

came the settlers. Native peoples preserved their ancient institutions and beliefs throughout the colonial period right up until today. They merely grafted new foreign practices onto the branches of their own culture, which were supported by deep roots that defied Europeanization.

Therefore, consideration of the isolated and autonomous development of the prehistoric Native Americans is important to the present study. Unless students and scholars appreciate the origins of Native American culture during the millennia before the Europeans arrived, they can understand neither the present nor the colonial past of the descendants of the Inka, Aztec, and Tupí. Today 10 million people still speak native languages in the Andean nations of Ecuador, Peru, and Bolivia. Indeed, the absolute numbers of indigenous ethnic groups are growing in many parts of Latin America. Nearly three times as many indigenous people live in Guatemala today as did at the time of conquest. The Pan-Maya movement in this country and in southern Mexico today seeks to rescue the native languages and to preserve ancient traditions. During colonial times in these same areas, the indigenous peoples remained the majority of the population; for this reason alone, we must delve into their prehistory. The European conquest did not destroy the culture of the Native Americans any more than slavery obliterated the customs of African Americans.

Yet no matter how strong Native American traditions were, the Conquest certainly ended their independent evolution. The Spaniards and Portuguese seized indigenous peoples and forced them to adapt to new social norms and work habits. As shall be seen, the conquerors did not succeed in their designs to Europeanize the Native Americans. However, the conquered people did adopt certain social institutions and new technologies brought by the Europeans—especially those that helped them retain their separate identities and survive independently. But the European settlers, too, had to change to survive in the Americas. Even in conquest, the Europeans had to respond to those they aimed to vanquish. The variegated nature of pre-Columbian civilizations determined where the conquerors went and how they behaved when they got there. Indeed, the conquerors themselves adapted to selected indigenous lifestyles and social institutions to dominate the new colonial societies being created. What ultimately emerged, therefore, was neither European nor Native American but a localized amalgam of their numerous cultures—which subsequently combined with strong cultural contributions from enslaved Africans.

In this section, two of the most profound developments in the lives of Americans are considered: first, the gradual evolution of agriculture over a period of two millennia, and second, the relatively sudden European conquest, whose principal accomplishments took less than a century. Both developments left indelible imprints on the panorama of Latin American history.

CHAPTER I

THE ANCIENT MESOAMERICANS

No account of colonial Latin America can fully explain what changed and what remained the same as a result of the European conquest without first examining the development of American civilization in the prehistoric period, that is, before the arrival of Europeans. The indigenous population to this day has preserved languages, tools, beliefs, family practices, and social institutions whose origins go back thousands of years. More than that, the native peoples have contributed their labor and capital to build the often lavish buildings and monuments of Latin America, adding their unique artistic flourishes to the finished product. They also offered to Europe their arts, crafts, and agricultural products. The entire world has been enriched by the centuries of independent development of civilization and cultures that occurred in the Americas prior to 1492. Moreover, how Latin America has grown and evolved in the five centuries since then has been determined, in varying degrees, by what the indigenous peoples had created prior to that watershed date. All those many and diverse peoples whom we now call "Indians" had accomplished more than merely living in harmony with nature. They were actively involved in manipulating and altering the environment as well. What they learned has endured.

Although their achievements should not be diminished, their shortcomings should not be exaggerated either. Despite having created impressive empires, these prehistoric

Map 1.1   Ancient Mesoamerica

Americans found no solution to warfare among themselves. They practiced ritual cruelties upon their enemies, ate human flesh, and acted exploitatively and unjustly toward the weak. In other words, they were human. Their social institutions suffered some of the same defects and strengths as those being created separately and coterminously in Africa, Asia, and Europe: The elite reaped the wealth and power created or supported by the commoners' work and tax revenue, yet bonds of social obligation and religion nevertheless united these two disparate classes. This chapter chronicles the rise of indigenous civilizations in Mesoamerica, which consists of Mexico and Central America (see Map 1.1); the next chapter treats the civilizations that developed in South America. We will see that the centrifugal force of ethnic diversity and the unifying pressure of imperial domination were engaged in a dynamic competition long before the Europeans arrived in America. In fact, this struggle between domination and decentralization among the ancient peoples resulted in the spread of culture among them.[1] Few ancient inhabitants of what we now call Latin America were isolated from these cultural advances.

THE ORIGINS OF AGRICULTURE

How long has humankind inhabited the Western Hemisphere? Conjecture on this point still persists, but scholars generally agree that humans have existed in the Americas for thirty-five thousand to fifty thousand years. During the Wisconsin Ice Age, huge glaciers formed over what is now Canada and the midwestern United States. Buildup of the ice cap actually lowered sea levels worldwide, exposing a land bridge across the Bering Strait between Asia and Alaska. Several different Asian peoples crossed the land bridge over a period of many centuries, with successive waves of migration spreading southward and eastward. Climatic changes then melted the glaciers and caused sea levels to rise, once again inundating the Bering passage. Those peoples who had migrated in the interim were now cut off from Asia, although some scholars acknowledge that sporadic contact may have continued across the Pacific Ocean via small watercraft.

In the intervening millennia, the emerging cultures of the Americas took a different course from those of the so-called Old World. Asia, Europe, and Africa shared developments such as the domestication of draft animals; the invention and use of the wheel, the cart, the plow, the potter's wheel, glass, iron, stringed instruments, and the true arch in construction; and the cultivation of rice and wheat. Cultures in the Americas developed not only different tools and foodstuffs but also distinct political and religious structures. By 9000 B.C., these peoples inhabited all the lands down to the southernmost tip of South America, known today as Tierra del Fuego (Land of Fire). By then, they were divided into thousands of different language groups, many unrelated. Their physical appearances varied markedly from region to region, and they adapted themselves to many different geographical niches to survive. But these early peoples all had one thing in common: They lived by hunting, fishing, and gathering nuts, berries, and roots. Except for those groups or tribes that subsisted largely on fish, all were nomadic and followed the seasonal migrations of game. They hunted larger horses and mammoths that died out during dramatic climatic changes that occurred around 7000 B.C., and a gradual but momentous innovation soon came about as a result: agriculture.

The beginnings of organized plant cultivation permitted many—but not all—of the American peoples to settle in villages. In certain areas, agriculture supported a significant rise in population, necessitating more advanced forms of political and social control and leading to primitive commercial exchange. At least four different places gave rise to this agricultural revolution simultaneously. Pumpkins were cultivated in the region we now call Mexico as early as 8,000 years ago; sunflowers, in the southwest of the present-day United States; and nuts, on the coast of what is now Peru. The cultivation of amaranth (a weedlike plant yielding tiny seeds rich in starch and oil) appeared in south central Mexico, and peppers seem to have been grown in all these areas. At first, agriculture produced no dramatic differences in the lives of these peoples; it merely supplemented

---

[1] Anthropologists define *culture* as an integrated system of socially acquired beliefs, values, and rules of conduct that determine the range of accepted behaviors in society. In this chapter, we are interested in *material culture*, the remains of extinct human cultures such as pottery and buildings, in order to decipher something of the way the people in question lived.

Planting, harvesting, and storing corn. (Florentine Codex, ca. 1575)

hunting and fishing, which remained the primary sources of food. During this long transition, gender specialization was applied to food production. Men took care of hunting and fishing, while women added cultivation to their duties of cooking and child care.

The birth of agriculture can easily be underestimated as an achievement if one neglects the considerable geographical disadvantages of the Americas. Cultivation of food plants did not begin in the modern breadbaskets of the Argentine Pampas or the North American Midwest until the advent of the steel plow in the nineteenth century. Instead, agriculture began in Mesoamerica and the Andean region. (The term *Andean* refers to all the territories bounded by the Andes Mountains of South America but especially Peru, Ecuador, and Bolivia; see Chapter 2.) Crisscrossed by mountain chains, both Mesoamerica and the Andean region had but a fraction of their total area—not much more than 2 percent—that was suitable for cultivation. Therefore, the ancient inhabitants had to actively engage their environment. Where rainfall was abundant, they had to burn the resultant dense vegetation to work the soil and rotate planting between the cleared fields. The resourceful farmers of the Mesoamerican tropical jungles were the first to perfect the cultivation of maize, or corn. The coastal lowlands of Peru hardly get any rainfall at all, and irrigation systems had to be devised to make them productive. On the other hand, certain temperate locations in the highland valleys of Mexico and Peru were well suited to agriculture. With sufficient rainfall, a farming family in Mesoamerica could raise about twice as much corn as it needed to subsist. And in the fertile Andean valleys of Peru, peasant producers developed several varieties of hearty potatoes. Moreover, the indigenous cultivators found ways to store corn and potatoes for months. In highland Peru, freeze-dried potatoes known as *ch'uño* remained palatable for years and are still produced today.

Eventually, surplus production and the organization of labor needed for irrigation projects and food distribution gave rise first to population growth and then to sophisticated political systems and social differentiation among agricultural peoples. Cotton garments began to replace clothes made from animal skins. The first permanent houses appeared. Pottery began to be used in food preparation around 2000 B.C., and pressure-flaked obsidian was used in place of the older, cruder stone tools and weapons in the settled agricultural villages. Gender relationships also changed. Men no longer had to hunt and now joined women in cultivation. However, male cultivators specialized in the heavy work such as turning up the land with digging sticks. Women toiled in the lighter agricultural tasks and participated in planting and harvesting in addition to performing their household chores. Task specialization among agricultural peoples also relieved the men from their duties as warriors; a professional military caste emerged and joined the new priestly class in becoming a protonobility that gave rise to the production of luxury goods—jewelry, arts and crafts, and fine clothing. By 1500 B.C., the agricultural peoples of Mesoamerica and the Andean region were simultaneously yet separately poised to create advanced civilizations.

THE PRECLASSICAL PERIOD

Before beginning our discussion of ancient Mesoamerican and Andean social evolution and accomplishments in earnest, we would do well to define *civilization*. Civilization consists of the following hallmarks:

1. Subsistence based on intensive agriculture
2. Relatively large, dense populations
3. Distribution of foodstuffs and luxury goods over large areas
4. A diversity of settlement types, from rural villages to urban centers
5. Central governments exerting control over peoples in widespread settlements
6. Intensive social stratification
7. Occupational specialization in agriculture and crafts, administration, commerce, and religion

Civilization introduced advantages and disadvantages to life. Simple tribal hunting societies enjoyed more freedom than their civilized counterparts but were less secure against famine and enemies. To look at it another way, civilized societies extended protection from enemies and allowed for a more stable and ensured food supply in exchange for the loss of personal freedom and a much longer workday.

A people of the tropical lowlands, the Olmec generated the region's "mother culture" beginning around 1400 B.C. during what is called the Preclassical Period (see Table 1.1). This group devised complex political, social, and religious institutions that set them apart from the simple clan-based organization of previous hunters and agricultural peoples. Not only did the Olmec begin civilization in this region, but they also sustained it for a long period of time—eight centuries. Because the Olmec reigned at such a remote time in prehistory, scholars have found it more difficult to study them than the more recent Aztec and Inka. Both of these civilizations had flourished for a mere century immediately preceding the arrival of the Europeans. But the Aztec and Inka had benefited from the numerous precedents established by several previous civilizations. The Olmec initiated this accretionary process in Mesoamerica.

It is remarkable that the Olmec accomplished this initial cultural florescence because their system of cultivation consisted primarily of slash-and-burn farming on the fragile soil base of the Mexican rain forest. A peasant farmer would begin by cutting down and setting fire to the thick tropical underbrush. Then he planted squash, peppers, and corn up to four times over a two-year period, by the end of which all the nutrients

Table 1.1   Mesoamerican Timeline

MESOAMERICAN DEVELOPMENTS	DATES	WORLD DEVELOPMENTS
Postclassical Period		
Spanish Conquest of the Aztec Empire	1521	Spanish, Portuguese Expansion
Mexica found Tenochtitlán	1345	Renaissance in Italy
Toltec Empire		The Crusades
Classical Period	1000	
Tikal, last Maya center, falls	900	Vikings reach Newfoundland
Copán in Honduras is destroyed		Holy Roman Empire
Destruction of Teotihuacán	600	
Height of Teotihuacán civilization		Birth of Mohammed
Maya hieroglyphic writing		Great Wall in China
Preclassical Period	150	
		Roman Empire
Great Pyramids at Teotihuacán	A.D.	Birth of Christ
	B.C.	
Olmec center of La Venta is sacked		Han Dynasty in China
	400	Alexander the Great
Construction of Monte Albán		Birth of Buddha
San Lorenzo (Olmec) destroyed	1200	Trojan War
Spread of Olmec influence		Shang Dynasty in China
Archaic Period	1800	
		Egyptians construct pyramids
Origins of village life		Walled cities in Sumer
Agriculture is developed	6000	Farming in Asia, Near East

had been depleted from the thin top soil. The farmer then moved on to a second site and repeated the process. He did not return to prepare the first field again until it had fully recovered its rain forest growth and replenished the nutrients in the soil. Therefore, an Olmec family of five probably needed a large area on which to subsist, effectively dispersing the peasant population.

Olmec civilization and influence owed their existence more to several agricultural innovations that supported a relatively large population in rather inhospitable environs. People along rivers and swamps established elaborate drainage systems and piled up the alluvial muck into raised fields. Farmers planted every season on these raised fields, harvesting two crops per year. The first cultivation took place from November to February, with its harvest beginning in May; then a June planting was followed by a second harvest in November. Yearly floods renewed and enriched the soil. The final result of Olmec agricultural ingenuity was the creation of a significant surplus. In turn, agricultural production generated population growth and the division of society into rulers and the ruled. The first clans that arose to become the religious and political elite were able to do so because of their control of the river and swamplands that yielded abundant yearly harvests.

Creation of the Olmec civilization by force of arms and by commerce marked the first time that one Mesoamerican group successfully dominated others. Most of the rest of the region was settled rather sparsely at this time, and one of the greatest Olmec contributions to the progression of culture in Mesoamerica was spreading their agricultural refinements to other peoples. The newly created elite groups sought material possessions to reinforce their status and power, thus encouraging trade and some military domination. The resources for these prestige goods came from other parts of Mesoamerica, most of whose peoples continued to live in small villages beyond Olmec military control. Now hunting became the recreational pastime of the elites and forbidden to the peasants. The class of priests developed and directed construction of the great Olmec religious centers at San Lorenzo from 1150 to 900 B.C. and at La Venta from 900 to 400 B.C. The cult of the jaguar developed imperial importance. Olmec proselytizers and military expeditions spread this cult north, south, and west to adjacent agricultural peoples. The temple platforms at La Venta attracted pilgrims from all over Mesoamerica. The jaguar cult influenced peoples who never submitted to Olmec rule, even as far away as the Andean region. Scholars also credit the Olmec priests for elaborating a sophisticated calendar to govern the agricultural cycle and fix the dates of religious observances. They also laid the basis for a system of hieroglyphic writing.

Olmec rulers developed state power to the extent that they were able to equip and direct armed forces on campaigns throughout Mesoamerica as well as to enlist large numbers of workers for public works. Military craftsmen fashioned projectile points from imported obsidian, making Olmec weapons particularly deadly. With their specialized obsidian-tipped clubs and spears, Olmec warriors were able to defeat other peoples who still fought with wooden hunting tools. Warfare became the exclusive pursuit of trained and privileged warriors. Whereas nearly every male in hunter-gatherer bands had counted himself a warrior, the peasant commoners among the Olmec no longer had to engage in offensive warfare.

Nevertheless, the dense population of 350,000 in the Olmec heartland of Veracruz and Tabasco supported the warriors, whose sparse numbers sufficed to spread Olmec influence without having to create an empire of military occupation. An occasional show of force sufficed to convince local leaders of the virtue of adopting Olmec practices, values, and religion more effectively than the mere posting of garrisons. In fact, this strategy proved powerful enough that villages in Oaxaca, which had been among the first to be influenced by Olmec culture, eventually consolidated themselves into a rival trade zone. Thereafter, San Lorenzo, the Olmec gateway to the Oaxaca Valley, went into decline. In 900 B.C., it was replaced in importance by La Venta because the latter faced south across the lowland routes to important jade and cacao production areas. Outside of Oaxaca, most Mesoamerican peoples found advantage in cooperating with the Olmec.

The political and priestly authorities' ability to mobilize labor is evidenced by ruins of massive temples at Olmec archaeological sites. From 1500 to 400 B.C., the Olmec and their allies built more than twenty-four monuments and cities that served as commercial centers and military outposts. Artisans at San Lorenzo were responsible for producing some of the most spectacular sculptures ever discovered in the Americas. Huge blocks of basalt were quarried at a distant volcano and carried down to the lowland settlement on rafts and rollers. There artists sculpted eight huge heads with flat-faced, thick-lipped features, each of which represents a mighty ruler and weighs several tons. Archaeologists have also uncovered stone drainage systems and delicate figurines, suggesting a developed aesthetic sensibility. Moreover, the quality of Olmec jade carving, pottery, and figurines suggests complex occupational specialization within a well-defined artisan class.

Trade preceded conquest, and the Olmec oversaw commercial exchange between the more settled population centers of the region. All ancient commerce was conducted by long-distance traders and carried on the backs of human bearers. However, trade did not provide basic foodstuffs for peasant consumption. Long-distance commerce remained very much a means for the elites of the communities to exchange goods. Artisans specialized in high-value crafts and exotic foodstuffs destined for upper-class consumption. Fine jewelry, featherwork, cotton linens, cacao beans, dried fish, wild game, and ceramics and figurines loomed large in Olmec commercial networks.

The influence of Olmec cultural motifs followed their soldiers and merchants down to Guatemala and up to the highlands of central Mexico. Olmec centers were established in the Valley of Mexico and on the Gulf of Tehuantepec, whence they traded with South America (see Chapter 2). Local elites in these areas of Mesoamerica willingly participated in the system because it enhanced their lifestyles and prestige. The trade routes between population centers were lengthy, and travel for merchants, bearers, and warriors lasted for days, taxing the food storage technology of the day. A breakthrough came with the invention of the tortilla, the thin cornmeal pancake that women prepared on a ceramic griddle called the *comal*. Its use spread widely and has continued to the present day. The tortilla reduced the time needed for food preparation, prolonged freshness, and permitted extended travel. Even so, corn grinding consumed a great deal of the women's time. To grind enough corn to feed a family of four would typically take a woman six hours every day.

The decline of the Olmec was a manifestation of their own success. Elite groups at the other population centers in Mesoamerica had adopted the Olmec innovations in religious observance, the calendar and knowledge of the priests, agricultural and food technologies, commercial circuits, and weaponry. They slowly dispensed with Olmec leadership, and the direct heirs of the mother culture retreated to their forest centers and slowly faded away. But the cultural influence lived on in the adoption of Olmec religious practices and artistic styles by generations of Mesoamericans. More than one thousand years later, the Aztec temple builders were preserving jade masks and other Olmec artifacts. Until the archaeological discoveries of the twentieth century, however, Mesoamericans had only a vague knowledge of their Olmec heritage despite the fact that Olmec religious and political institutions were passed on to others in Mesoamerica such as the Teotihuacán and the Maya, each of whom created even more splendor and glory.

THE CLASSICAL PERIOD

The Classical Period, from A.D. 150 to 900, was characterized by a long period of culture building based on agricultural surplus and rule by a theocratic elite. It had many foci of dynamism, one following upon another, in which indigenous groups sought to discover the secret of security and permanence. Several succeeded remarkably well given the prevailing Stone Age technology and the paucity of resources. We refer to these epochs as prehistoric because history is defined by what scholars can reconstruct from the written documents of the age. Only a few, tantalizing written manuscripts have survived from the ancient Americans. What we understand of these civilizations comes not from history but principally from archaeology, the study of the material remains of the past such as artifacts, fossils, and ruins. Tourists may visit the ruins of these great prehistoric city-states, and museums throughout the world have collected their treasures. Although the Maya developed a system of writing, only recently have scholars begun to decipher their hieroglyphics.

Teotihuacán

In the highland valleys of Mesoamerica, agricultural development reached a high level of sophistication based on the manipulation of rainfall, soil fertility, and water resources. There a peasant family of five might have been able to subsist (and even produce a surplus) on six or seven hectares (16 acres). As the population expanded during Olmec times, some permanent agricultural villages grew into larger cities, many taking on commercial and religious significance. Their inhabitants constructed a complex water distribution system consisting of reservoirs, channels, and drainage and irrigation ditches that was linked to a series of natural springs that graced the area. At the northern extremity of this highland zone, Teotihuacán rose as the most spectacular city-state of the Classical Period, uniting important population centers of Mesoamerica under its suzerainty from approximately A.D. 100 to 600.[2]

The population of Teotihuacán at its early stage reached an estimated seventy thousand inhabitants (some experts say the number might have been as high as one hundred fifty thousand) living in more than two thousand permanent compounds of adobe huts that surrounded a magnificent religious and ceremonial center. What Mexicans today call the great Pyramid of the Sun measures 210 meters on each side, reaches 64 meters into the sky, and contains approximately one million cubic meters of earth. Ten thousand workers labored on its construction over a period of two decades. The surface of this pyramid was stuccoed and covered with brightly colored frescoes of religious symbols that connected the people of Teotihuacán to the cosmos and to the natural world. A second pyramid was also constructed later. These two large pyramids were misconstrued later by Aztec scholars as temples to the sun and moon; they actually commemorated the water gods, an indication of how that commodity contributed to life on the high, semiarid plateau.

Buildings housing the commoners were much less ostentatious than the great religious temples. The typical dwelling had one story and no windows, and its door opened onto a patio surrounded by a complex of similar apartments. Several urban complexes included a larger dwelling, perhaps reserved for the clan leaders of a particular social grouping. A true city, Teotihuacán became home to more than just the warrior and priestly classes; merchants and artisans took up residence there as well. Merchants lived in dwellings separate from those of craftspersons and farmers, and evidence indicates that many merchant clans had foreign origins. Its large marketplace drew merchants of many

---

[2] The term *city-state*, refers to an independent political unit consisting of a city and surrounding countryside.

ethnicities and regional origins, each of which maintained their compounds within the multi-ethnic city. Oaxacan, Maya, and Huastec peoples (the latter from the Gulf Coast) spoke their native languages, adding a cosmopolitan air to the city that one did not find in the countryside. These foreigners at Teotihuacán served the important purpose of linking the theocratic rulers to sources of luxury goods from other regions of Mesoamerica.

But Teotihuacán fostered a theocratic polity; that is, it was governed by religious leaders. An elite stratum of priests directed the people by systematizing the cosmos, preserving knowledge, and making the universe predictable. Priests maintained the agricultural calendar, organizing festivals and rites prior to planting and dictating when fields should be weeded and when they should be harvested. And the peasants congregated around the religious temples voluntarily; they sought the protection of the gods and the priests for the exchange of goods. Many long-distance merchants also traveled under the patronage of one group of priests or another. At Teotihuacán, the professional priesthood developed the cult of the Feathered Serpent, Quetzalcóatl, a god who was responsible for teaching crafts and farming to his peoples. A second important cult formed to appease the rain god Tláloc. Other gods, perhaps adopted from subject peoples, were worshipped as a method of uniting diverse ethnic and linguistic groups of the Valley of Mexico into a loose political and commercial federation dominated by Teotihuacán.

This city owed its hegemony partly to the obsidian industry. At its height, Teotihuacán had as many as four hundred to five hundred workshops specializing in the manufacture of obsidian weapons and wares for distribution throughout Mesoamerica. Craft specialists made up more than one-quarter of the city's residents; like the merchants, they lived in special housing compounds. The reign of the great city also witnessed stunning advances in irrigation and cultivation. Knowledge of agriculture spread northward to the frontier of the Chichimec hunters. Protected by military garrisons, cultivation had extended up to present-day Zacatecas and Sonora. Irrigation played a large role in expanding this agricultural boundary northward.

Teotihuacán's population growth served its imperial interests as well, as it was thus able to settle military and merchant colonists in the far reaches of Mesoamerica. As always, commerce preceded conquest, because commercial successes led to the establishment of a military presence to protect merchants and trade routes. These colonists then entered into alliances with the nobility of selected local city-states in order to dominate a particular region both militarily and economically. Colonists also obviated the need for developing an expensive, centralized bureaucracy to govern far-off dependencies. Instead, these vassal states retained a measure of political and cultural autonomy in exchange for military cooperation and economic exchange with Teotihuacán. Areas once conquered in warfare thus regained a measure of status within the *pax teotihuacana*. The dependent regions benefited by receiving not only the finest luxury items but also the latest knowledge and innovations. Teotihuacán's commercial routes reached south to the Guatemalan highlands and north to what is now New Mexico.

The warriors of Teotihuacán developed military tactics based on the *atlatl*. An ancient hunting weapon redesigned with obsidian tips, the *atlatl* featured a dart propelled by a stick. It had an effective range of forty to seventy meters and contained nearly twice the thrust of a hand-thrown spear, and its firing usually preceded a charge by the spearmen. The professional warriors of Teotihuacán came to dominate the battlefields of the Classical Period because they had learned to integrate their military formations with specialists in slings, spears, and the *atlatl*.

Teotihuacán reached its peak in A.D. 500, when it boasted a population of 200,000. From this time until its collapse, the empire entered a very militaristic stage of development. Other groups had adopted their weapons and tactics, so the warriors of Teotihuacán had to devise new defensive equipment such as heavy shields and body armor made of thick, quilted cotton. Formal military orders were established to enhance the esprit de corps among the warrior elite. Each order marched into battle in suits representing eagles, jaguars, coyotes, and other mascots. Despite this emphasis on warfare, the far-flung dependencies among the lowlands and in Guatemala drifted away from the economic sphere of this northern city.

Teotihuacán fell in the middle of the seventh century. Parts of the ceremonial center of the city were burned, apparently in an internal dispute among the rulers. Archaeologists have found evidence of systematic looting, perhaps by the city's own inhabitants, and deliberate defacing of religious symbols. Many persons buried their valuables to preserve them in the turmoil. However, not everyone abandoned the city immediately. The urban centers that once had paid homage to the empire now became more independent militarily and economically. Teotihuacán simply could not manage the distant dependencies when they began to create alternative sources for production and commerce. Its former vassal states fragmented into numerous semi-autonomous areas, and the colonies on the northern rim of the Valley of Mexico collapsed under the raids of northern tribes of hunters and gatherers. Thus, one of the great cities of ancient America came to an end—but its culture passed on to enrich a number of successor states.

Monte Albán

In the highland valley of Oaxaca, several hundred kilometers south of Teotihuacán, lay the great ceremonial center of Monte Albán. It was built by the Zapotec peoples who still live in the region, but archaeological evidence points to much Olmec and Teotihuacán influence (and later, Maya influence as well) in its temples, tombs, pottery, and pictographs. Monte Albán, which flourished between 200 B.C. and A.D. 900, was the burial site of many important rulers and members of the nobility and was also a great ceremonial center, yet it did not have a source of water. It had to be delivered daily to the numerous priests and nobles in residence there.

Monte Albán was not a true city but rather an elite center of warriors and priests who made up the nobility. The vast peasantry of Oaxaca still lived a scattered existence though dominated by its military and religious power. Although basically a religious center, Monte Albán also played an important role as a conduit for trade between Mexico and Central America. The functions of religion and commerce, in fact, coincided because the religious and political elites of Monte Albán collected the trappings of their rank and authority in society—namely, the scarce goods produced in other regions of Mesoamerica. The surrounding countryside itself produced a commodity that was not found elsewhere and was thus a valuable source of trade and wealth for Monte Albán: cochineal, a dye obtained from boiling scale insects that flourished on cacti in Oaxaca and only a few other places. Upper-class consumers from throughout the region greatly admired cotton cloth colored scarlet with this dye. Village agriculturists supplemented their livelihoods by supplying cochineal to merchants. The valley of Oaxaca must have been extremely productive in foodstuffs, too, for archeologists have uncovered a large dam that probably provided water for an irrigation system.

Monte Albán united the other urban centers of the valley into a pan-Oaxacan tribute system, and in 200 B.C. it served as capital of a Oaxacan federation defending the valley from incursion by the Olmec and later by various outside successor states; its population increased to 16,000 during this period. Military conquest was central to the existence of Monte Albán, as evidenced by its many monuments depicting bound captives of war. A series of famous sculptures set into the walls of a stone platform attest to this city's military past even today. Misnamed the Danzantes (Dancers) by later Spanish colonists because of their contorted figures, these carvings depict human forms, all nude and some sexually mutilated, who may represent dead and tortured enemies; some of them are identified by hieroglyphic inscriptions as leaders. The authorities had a great fortification built and a water reservoir constructed to protect this political and religious center from military siege. Around the hillside perch of Monte Albán, farmers constructed more than two thousand terraces for cultivation and dwellings.

After A.D. 200, this dominant center of Oaxaca entered into a beneficial relationship with the larger Teotihuacán. Trade with the superior economy to the north increased the power and prestige of the local nobility at Monte Albán by aiding them in maintaining and tightening control over neighboring population centers in the Valley of Oaxaca. By A.D. 500, its population had risen to 24,000 persons, while an additional 31,000 resided in more than three hundred villages interspersed throughout the valley. But as Teotihuacán began to decline, Monte Albán could no longer sustain the distribution of goods that had maintained elite unity. Other political centers in Oaxaca withheld tribute and allegiance, and Monte Albán's nobility fell to bickering and political intrigues. The city was depopulated by A.D. 700, and rival city-states in the region came to divide political and economic power among themselves. A second powerful ethnic group, the Mixtec, arose in Oaxaca from under the thumb of the Zapotec. When the Europeans arrived seven centuries later, the ruins of Monte Albán and many other city-states of the Classical Period were overgrown, their significance all but forgotten. However, the Zapotec and Mixtec remain even today as reminders of these civilizations' cultural heritage.

The Classical Maya

One other focus of Mesoamerican civilization developed during the Classical Period in the first millennium A.D.. The term *Maya* denotes several linguistic groups that inhabited (and still inhabit) present-day Honduras, Belize, Guatemala, El Salvador, and the Mexican states of Campeche, Chiapas, Tabasco, Quintana Roo, and Yucatán. In its heyday, Maya civilization had several centers, with some cities succeeding others in influence but all nurturing similar cultural and intellectual patterns. Building on the work of the Olmec, the Maya developed an accurate calendar and sophisticated systems of mathematics and hieroglyphic script.

The ancient Maya created great cities out of the lowland jungles in much the same fashion as the Olmec before them. Maya cities carried on a flourishing trade with Teotihuacán and other highland city-states of Mexico. But at the base of this remarkable achievement were the peasants, who produced enough surplus to support dense populations, including the ruling classes made up of priests and warriors, in areas that are today relatively underpopulated. Like the Olmec, they built their civilizations on slash-and-burn agriculture and raised fields. Only in the highland valleys of Guatemala did the Maya create a more conventional, temperate-climate agriculture, and on the Pacific slopes of the mountains, cacao was cultivated. The raw chocolate beans served as the currency of trade and exchange for all of Mesoamerica. Some of the first great Mayan monuments were erected in the Guatemalan highlands, perhaps to control and regulate the flourishing cacao trade. Centuries later, however, while Teotihuacán dominated highland Mesoamerica, the locus of autonomous Maya power shifted to the lowlands.

By 200 B.C., the Maya had developed the institutions of divine kingship and hierarchical societies that would dominate their political lives for the next millennium. In the north, peasant villages joined together in relatively egalitarian confederacies for defensive purposes. But in the extreme south of the Maya territory, from Honduras to Guatemala and El Salvador, several great political centers arose from the jungle growth, complete with public buildings and elaborate graves for important leaders.

The world of the Maya during the Classical Period was a constellation of fifty or more independent city-states encompassing more than one hundred seventy thousand square kilometers of forest and plain. The kings of these city-states ruled over thousands of farmers, craftspeople, merchants, warriors, and members of the nobility. Their capitals were graced with pyramids, temples, palaces, and vast open plazas. The Maya traded, negotiated, and battled with each other and with other great states of Mesoamerica, attempting to deal with problems of war, drought, famine, trade, food production, and the transition of political power. The Maya also had a tribute system, but the peasants' deference and show of obsequiousness seemed to have been equally as important to the elite as the donation of material goods and labor. For the commoners, however, reciprocity—the assurance of a steady and adequate food supply, religious observation, and protection—was worth their show of deference, whether real or feigned, to the elite.

Together with the other peoples of Mesoamerica, the Maya lived their lives according to their dominant cultural traditions. These consisted of the 260-day religious or sacred calendar, common religious beliefs and rituals centered around a pantheon of gods, with bloodletting as central act of piety; the cultivation of corn; the use of cacao as a drink as well as a medium of exchange; the playing of a game with a rubber ball; the development of screen-fold books; the building of pyramids and plazas; and a sense of common identity. As they progressed, the ancient Maya developed a type of writing to record their political history. However, they did not use an alphabet; instead, their writing was made up of a combination of syllabic signs and graphic representations, which often carried more than one meaning. The same word could be written in several different ways (see Manuscript 1.1). Maya numbers from 1 to 10, for instance, could be represented with bars and dots for 5 and 1 or by pictures of the various gods and goddesses they represented.

Religion played an important role in the lives of the ancient Maya; they came to embody their understanding and manipulation of the world around them entirely in religious terms. The Maya religion spoke to central problems of human existence: power, justice, individual purpose, and group destiny. Ritual and myth explained the creation of the world and provided guidelines to the relationship of the individual to family, society, and the gods. Bloodletting permeated Maya religious life. For kings, every stage in life and every event of political or religious importance required sanctification through bloodletting. Blood was given to express devotion and call the gods into attendance. Ceremonies involving blood sacrifice were held when buildings were dedicated, crops planted, children born, couples married, or the dead buried.

Additional religious practices would be enormously influential. Like many other Mesoamericans, the Maya believed that time was cyclical, that the end was also the

MANUSCRIPT 1.1

Maya Books and Writing

A basic source for the study of the prehistoric peoples of the Americas has always been the treatises on the "Indians" written by European priests in the sixteenth century. The friars learned the language of the indigenous people in their parish or mission (the better to convert them) and recorded the memories and oral traditions of their new minions. These sources of information contain many biases, both of the indigenous collaborators and of the priests themselves. One problem for the study of the Maya has been the absence of their own manuscripts, despite the fact that the priestly class was literate during the Classical Period. The Franciscan missionary Diego de Landa, who became bishop of Yucatán, explains why today's scholars have few manuscript sources on the ancient Maya besides his own.

[The high priest of the ancient Maya] also taught the children of the other priests and the second sons of the lords, who were reared for the office from infancy if they showed any inclination to it.

The sciences which they taught were the reckoning of the years, months, and days, and of their feasts and ceremonies; the administration of their sacraments, and of the fateful days and seasons; their manner of divination, and their prophecies, incidents, and cures for sickness, as well as their antiquities and method of reading and writing where by means of the letters and characters they wrote in glyphs which represented the meaning of the writings.

They wrote their books on a large sheet doubled several times. This closed together between two boards which were highly decorated. They wrote on both sides of the sheet in columns, following the folds; and the paper they made from the roots of a tree, giving it a white gloss on which it was easy to write. Some of the principal lords out of diligence had also acquired these sciences, and although they never used them in public, they were held in great esteem for having done so.

• • •

These people also used certain glyphs or letters in which they wrote down their ancient history and sciences in their books; and by means of these letters and figures and by certain marks contained in them, they could read about their affairs and taught others to read about them too. We found a great number of these books in Indian characters and because they contained nothing but superstition and the Devil's falsehoods, we burned them all; and this they felt most bitterly and it caused them great grief.

SOURCE: A. R. Pagden, ed. and trans., *The Maya: Diego de Landa's Account of the Affairs of Yucatán* (Chicago: J. Philip O'Hara, 1975), 41, 124.

beginning. Their conception of the earth's axis had been depicted for more than a millennium in the form of the cross, which represented the World Tree. Their shamans had repeated the words of the prophecy of the Chilam Balam, a sacred text:

Let us exalt his sign on high, let us exalt it that we may gaze upon it today with the raised standard. Great is the discord that arises today. The First Tree of the World is restored; it is displayed to the world. This is the sign of Hunab-Ku on high. Worship it, Itzá [Yucatán Maya]. You shall worship today his sign on high.

You shall worship it furthermore with true goodwill, and you shall worship the true god today, lord. You shall be converted to the word of Hunab-Ku. You shall be converted to the word of Hunab-Ku, lord; it came from heaven.[3]

Thus, the cross was already a very powerful symbol to the Maya and later would assist their nominal conversion to Christianity.

Maya Society

In terms of social organization, the Maya shared many traditions with other Mesoamerican peoples. Peasant hamlets were made up of several household compounds, each of which was occupied by an extended family. These family compounds housed related adults, several unmarried adolescents, numerous children, and perhaps a senior couple or grandparents. The standard peasant living arrangement had a rationale. Many hands were needed for the labor-intensive process of farming—preparing the fields, planting, cultivating, harvesting, and processing and storing the harvests. The extended households also provided labor for other demanding tasks unrelated to agriculture such as building and repairing houses, kitchens, and storerooms; collecting firewood; weaving and decorating cloth; and making pottery.

Since the first millennium B.C., Maya commoners had been building wattle-and-daub houses for their nuclear families. They built the basic structure over a platform of earth and stone, which served as the floor, and oriented the house in line with the prevailing winds. Thus, the openings at the ends permitted natural ventilation by the tropical breezes. A stone foundation supported the walls, which consisted of four to eight main posts joined by numerous cross-poles, or wattles. The builders then mixed mud, sand, and grass together and daubed this substance like plaster over the superstructure. The roofs were made of palm fronds. A clan of related families might connect their houses into a compound surrounding a central courtyard. This basic structure can still be seen in the tropical lowlands of southern Mexico and Central America.

Maya peasants also observed a gender-based division of labor within the family, and they were uncomfortable with nonconformity in their communities. Men raised the crops, and women prepared the food. Maya families promoted this gender identification from infancy, as girls received toy household utensils and boys were given toy field tools.[4] Peasants practiced monogamy, as only male nobles were allowed to have several wives, and women were influential in family decisions within the peasant communities. Senior men carried the authority to engage in the public affairs of their villages, especially in organizing the local religious festivals and other civic matters. In their negotiation and adjudication of local conflicts, these village elders promoted reconciliation and compromise. The shaman served as religious leader and public relations expert, and his job was to conserve tradition within the community. He preserved his village's oral traditions, led prayers and rituals, and treated the sick.

---

[3] As quoted in Linda Schele and David Freidel, *A Forest of Kings: The Untold Story of the Ancient Maya* (New York: William Morrow, 1990), 378.

[4] This practice continues even today in traditional rural families. A boy receives a small machete with due ceremony at age 6 and then a full-sized one in a rite of passage at age 13. Commonly, this machete serves the man for his lifetime, as village patriarchs often have well-worn machetes still in use. Of course, the steel-bladed machete did not come into use until the arrival of the Europeans.

The family and clan provided the basic structure for labor exchange among the Maya; in the absence of any other convenient medium of exchange or of a labor market, the heads of household traded work among themselves. They built each other's houses this way and often helped each other with the planting and harvests. Important village and lineage leaders received the labor of their clan subordinates but were expected to reciprocate—not with money but with food, favors, gifts, and festive occasions. Village leaders repaid the followers by providing administrative and judicial services.

The ruling elites also commanded the labor of the peasants on a rotational or draft basis. For example, gangs of hundreds of workers built the temples and palaces of the great ceremonial city of Copán in Honduras between A.D. 600 and 700. These work gangs consisted of male heads of household, each of whom owed an extended period of labor each decade or so to the king and the priests. In exchange, Copán's elite bestowed military protection, usufruct of land, religious services, and gifts of food and clothing. At the time, the area ruled by Copán probably took in 25,000 persons, most of whom lived in dispersed agricultural villages. This system of reciprocity became the norm among other ancient peoples although it was open to abuse by the selfish elite.

Although quite advanced in terms of their remarkable social discipline and city building, the Maya relied on Stone Age technology. They used no metal at all until a few centuries before contact with Europeans, and even then gold and copper were not used for tools but for jewelry and ornamentation. Neither did they use any beasts of burden. Human bearers carried all commercial cargoes on their backs. Trade moved along paths through the rain forests; no highways existed because the wheel was not in use. Canoes dug out of single hardwood logs formed the most important means of transportation on the rivers and along the coastlines, but canoe transportation was hampered both when the dry season reduced the flow of the mighty rivers and when the rainy seasons caused destructive flooding. Nevertheless, artisans in the city of Colhá in northern Belize supplied farmers with cutting tools through trade with the many city-states of the Maya world. The chert beds of Belize provided the raw materials with which Maya peasants cut back the thick roots of the rain forests and swamps.

One important task of kings was to direct the excavation of reservoirs, cisterns, and canals to control the distribution of water. Cities on the Yucatán peninsula had to be constructed near the sacred cenotes, natural sinkhole wells in the limestone, that served both as sources of water and also, in Maya belief, as the portals to the Other World beneath the earth.

The ceremonial centers of the Maya, unlike Teotihuacán at the time, could hardly be called cities. Upwards of five thousand persons occupied each one. These settlements served as residences for the elite and their servants, but peasants gathered there on market days and for religious festivals. The cities supported not only the nobility and warriors but also a class of priests, whose learning turned to astronomy and mathematics. They devised a calendar more accurate than the one used in Europe at the time to set the seasons for agricultural production. Without technical equipment, the Maya priests accurately predicted eclipses of the sun and other solar phenomena, and they devised the numeral 0 in mathematics before Arabs returning from India introduced it to Europe in 1200.

Copán became the intellectual center of the Maya world. Astronomers there worked out the length of the tropical year as well as tables predicting solar and lunar eclipses. As befitted its status, Copán hosted conferences: Priests and astronomers came from central Mexico and the Guatemalan highlands to confer on scientific matters.

Maya priests there and at other centers developed a written language based on pictographs to record the history of their kings. They made accordion-folded books of beaten bark paper surfaced with a thin layer of plaster. In these, the scribes entered the details of their lives: genealogy, history, learning, prescriptions for ritual, tribute, trade, mythology, worldviews, and even poetry.

Despite Copán's preeminence in science and learning, Tikal, in Petén, a province of Guatemala, seemed to dominate culturally the other city-states during the Classical Period. This urban center probably had a population of 10,000 persons, not large in comparison to Teotihuacán. Tikal also had a long history in the region, dating back several millennia before the common era. It was renowned for its great monuments.

Still, the greater Maya confederation apparently was not a military one in the Classical Period. Warfare apparently had always been a part of Maya life, although each center seemed to coexist autonomously with the others, carrying on trade with them and with the villages of the highlands. At least, this was the case until approximately A.D. 700. Over the next 200 years, a period of extraordinary internecine warfare, one after another of the remaining Maya centers collapsed. Copán in Honduras fell in 800; Tikal, in 900.

Maya literacy may also have ended in this Armageddon-like series of conflicts. As one kingdom after another declined, the survivors returned to the land as peasant villagers and lost the ability to decipher all that had been written in the books during the previous millennium. No longer could they read and understand the inscriptions on the ruins of the great cities. Nonetheless, hundreds of the books were preserved by village shamans as religious relics. (The Spanish priests later collected and destroyed these same Maya writings as the works of the devil; see Chapter 3.) Four of these picture books remain. Three of them that originated among the lowland Maya found their way to Europe during colonial times and turned up in Madrid, Paris, and Dresden. A fragment from a fourth book was recovered from looters who had discovered it in a cave in the present-day Mexican state of Chiapas.

Why did these societies suddenly crumble into ruin? One theory holds that the population rose to the limits of its resources and of agricultural technology, stretching the meager resources to the limit. Perhaps a series of droughts or climate changes weakened the entire social structure. Neither do scholars discount the overexpansion of the upper classes. From excavation of their burial sites, we know that members of the Maya nobility were taller and better fed, worked less strenuously, lived longer, and reproduced more quickly than the peasants. Probably this elite class made increasing demands on their kings to extend their conquests so as to provide them jobs and tribute. All the while, malnutrition, sickness, and infection afflicted the common people.

Warfare among the city-states grew vicious and ever more frequent. Military castes were founded. Dominant cities began to demand more of subordinate cities, and social convulsions and civil wars weakened the alliances of trade that stretched from Teotihuacán to Honduras. At the frontiers of culture, those hunter-gatherer groups that were learning the culture and agriculture of the great civilizations burst through the garrisons in a fury of pillage and rape. In the wake of the peasant revolts and invasion by foreign peoples, most of the heirs of these classical civilizations returned to a more primitive lifestyle. The scope and range of the collapse was staggering. Some authorities believe that the Maya population fell by as much as 80 percent, from 12 million at its height during the Classical Period to a little more than 2 million. The succeeding period of cultural fluorescence in Mesoamerica would be very militaristic indeed.

pop ↓→ beginning of military campaigns

POSTCLASSICAL CULTURES

We know more about the ancient societies in the Americas during the Postclassical Period because it immediately preceded the arrival of the Europeans. The Catholic priests who came in the sixteenth century served as the first foreign anthropologists in the region. They observed the peoples they brought into their chapels, learned the indigenous languages, and wrote down the first oral histories and founding myths of the various groups. In most cases, the names used to identify the various indigenous groupings came from the Europeans in the sixteenth century, as did the term used to describe them all—*Indian.* Later, especially in the twentieth century, archaeologists began to unravel the ancient world based on careful study of campsites, burial grounds, and ceremonial centers. Just recently, in 1978, workers uncovered one such Aztec ceremonial center, the Templo Mayor (Main Temple), as they were constructing the subway in downtown Mexico City. The artifacts found during this and other excavations reveal facts about social and political life of the ancients as well as their trade and commerce. But the fact remains that much of the information we have of pre-Columbian Americans is based on the writings of prejudiced and ethnocentric Europeans.

The Postclassical Period of American civilizations began approximately in 1000 and was characterized by the development of aggressive imperial states and large-scale warfare. At that time, Mesoamerica remained a mosaic of languages and ethnic diversity. Perhaps more than two hundred sixty major languages were spoken in the area between the northern border of Mexico down to the southern border of Guatemala. Often, inhabitants of neighboring villages could not communicate with each other unless their leaders spoke the lingua franca of some dominant imperial group. Two such powers, the Toltec and the Aztec, spread the Nahuatl language throughout the region late in the Postclassical Period. Besides the adoption of a dominant language, few new material advances were made in agriculture, technology, and culture. Rather, the new states created by the Toltec and the Aztec and others borrowed from the more creative Classical civilizations. In fact, the Postclassical city-states did not even maintain the previous level of learning in mathematics and writing. Only in one area was there significant change: The Postclassical empires were much more warlike and predatory than the city-states of the previous period.

The Toltec

The warfare attendant on the fall of Teotihuacán opened the gates to the more nomadic hunter-gatherers of northern Mexico, who began to overrun the sedentary farming groups and roll back the agricultural frontier. The rise of the militaristic city-state of Tula, the Toltec capital located north of present-day Mexico City, co-opted many of these warlike tribes by hiring them as mercenaries and finally stabilized the frontier once again, but only after the seminomadic hunters had already reclaimed land from the cultivators. In fact, many Nahuatl-speaking hunters had migrated southward as a result of the power vacuum created when Teotihuacán fell. There they learned the rudiments of cultivation and of culture, swelling the population of Tula. This rising city-state was ultimately home to 60,000 craftspeople and other specialists. Thus it was that the Toltec developed the first Postclassical empire in Mesoamerica; at its height, it stretched from present-day Zacatecas to the Yucatán peninsula. Tula commanded the region for two centuries following 950.

The Toltec worshipped Quetzalcóatl, the Feathered Serpent originally venerated in Teotihuacán, for whom they built many monuments at Tula. Among his other attributes, Quetzalcóatl was identified as the provider of culture and of agricultural abundance. The founding myth of Tula identified him with a golden age of peace and abundance:

> Under his rule maize was plentifully available, gourds were very plump, an armful in circumference, and the maize cobs were of a gigantic length. . . . Cotton of all colours was harvested, red, yellow, brown, white, green, blue and orange. These cotton colours were natural colours. So cotton flourished exceedingly . . . cocoa trees of the most diverse colours grew plentifully. . . . Quetzalcóatl's subjects were exceedingly rich and they lacked for nothing. There was no hunger, maize was not lacking, indeed it was so abundant that the small maize cobs were not consumed, but used for heating baths.[5]

As legend had it, the Feathered Serpent was ultimately banished from the city of Tula for having succumbed to human frailties. He was said to have escaped to the lowlands of the Yucatán peninsula. Worship of Quetzalcóatl continued among the successors of the Toltec, and he was expected one day to return from exile to the central highlands. This legend and the frequent depiction of the god wearing facial hair eventually led later peoples to confuse the arrival of the Spanish conquistadors with Quetzalcóatl's return.

Although a multi-ethnic city, Tula came to be dominated by the Nahuatl-speaking groups from the north. They are credited with the secularization of the polity, as the priests there lost a power struggle and the secular nobility and warrior class emerged triumphant. In fact, the myth of Quetzalcóatl's exile serves to explain this shift, as he had lost a contest with the war god. Besides the secularization of rule, the Toltec are also known for first establishing Nahuatl as the dominant language of central Mexico. This they accomplished through not only military conquest but also the migration of peoples from north to south.

The armies and allies of the Toltec in the tenth and eleventh centuries achieved remarkable military hegemony throughout Mesoamerica. Like Teotihuacán before it, Tula became the leading manufacturing center for obsidian tools and weapons. Temple frescos glorified military conquests, a rack in the temple displayed the skulls of former enemies, and captive enemies were sacrificed and eaten. The Toltec used all the weaponry of the time and also invented the short sword, a lightweight, curved club with a long cutting surface of inlaid obsidian blades. This was a slashing weapon especially useful in close combat. Evidence points to the establishment of special military orders, particularly among the mercenaries. They drove north to carry agriculture back into the land inhabited by their "cousins," the hunter-gatherers. The civilized peoples of central Mexico had called these northern tribes *Chichimec,* a term meaning "a race of dogs" or simply "barbarians." A fortress at La Quemada, near the present-day city of Zacatecas, secured Toltec power in the north. Mines in the area yielded precious stones for jewelry, although silver was not mined at all by the indigenous peoples. The fortress at La Quemada also served as a frontier trading post, introducing the northern tribes to goods from the cities of central Mexico and obtaining pelts and feathers in return. This trade extended all the

---

[5] From Bernardino de Sahagún, *Historia general de las cosas de la Nueva España* (Mexico City: Porrua, 1956), 1:278–79, as quoted in Friedrich Katz, *The Ancient American Civilizations* (New York: Praeger, 1972), 121.

way to Arizona and New Mexico, where the Pueblo and other groups provided turquoise. Carrying out their imperial mission, the Toltec brought culture to the Chichimec, incorporating them into the imperial system.

Trade followed the Toltec armies into the Valley of Mexico (where a number of existing city-states became allies or subjects), into Oaxaca, and down to the Maya lowlands. In the Yucatán, the city-state of Chichén Itzá became the southern center of the Toltec military and commercial empire. The temples and public buildings of this city hewn out of the forest displayed Toltec religious, military, and cultural influences. At Chichén Itzá as at the imperial capital of Tula, religious cults practiced human sacrifice, a trait adopted by successor militaristic states. The lowlands yielded trade goods of high demand in the highlands, such as salt, cacao, jewelry, feathers and fine featherwork, and cotton. Toltec-protected trade spread far beyond its military borders, extending into the Guatemalan highlands and Central America. Objects made of bronze constituted an important commodity in this commerce. Though these ancient advances in metallurgy never produced tools or weapons, the alloying of copper and tin to make bronze required extraordinary sophistication. Andean craftsmen had been the first to develop metallurgy, and the skill moved north through Ecuador, Colombia, and Mesoamerica. Members of the elite in Tula used bronze disks and ornaments for jewelry and decoration.

Tula fell in 1175, a victim of famine and Chichimec invasions. In the twelfth century, climatic change caused a crisis in the irrigation systems on which the peoples north of the Valley of Mexico had depended since the days of Teotihuacán. It is likely that the

MANUSCRIPT 1.2

Chronicle of the Decline of Maya Civilization

The following manuscript records the last of many invasions of northern Guatemala. At the date of the invasion, approximately 1400, the Guatemalan highlands presented a patchwork of fortified towns and wary peasant peoples, each speaking different dialects and observing separate cultural traditions. A Mexicanized group of outsiders named the Quiché conquered most of these groups beginning in 1400, but even this brief Postclassical Maya empire collapsed in rebellion and warfare several decades before the Spaniards arrived. The text is from the Popol Vuh, an indigenous history book written in the mid-sixteenth century by Quiché scribes using the Roman alphabet that the Dominican friars had taught them. They based the Popol Vuh on the oral histories of their people. The "mountain of stones" refers to the ruins of the old fortresses that the Quiché razed in their wars of conquest. These ruins were known to the Maya residents of the sixteenth century.

And [the chiefs] Quicab and Cauizimah did a great deal in their turn. They added to the greatness of the Quiché because they truly had genius. They crushed and they shattered the canyons and the citadels of the tribes, small and great—the ones that had citadels among them in ancient times. . . .

[These tribes] all hated Quicab. They made war, but in fact they were brought down, they were shattered, these canyons, these citadels of the Rabinals, Cakchiquels, White Earths. All the tribes went down on

political and military elites attempted to increase their exaction on the merchants and peasants and that the resulting internal unrest weakened the defenses against a renewal of Chichimec invasions from the north. The Toltec were cut off from the strategic obsidian mines. In the south, the Mexican hegemony over the Maya groups of the highlands also ended in violence and rebellion (see Manuscript 1.2). When Tula fell, political power in the highlands shifted south to central Mexico.

The Aztec

During the *pax tolteca,* the peoples of the Valley of Mexico had made a number of significant advances in agriculture and water control. Several cities surrounding the highland lakes, which covered the ground on which Mexico City is now located, had always been vulnerable to periodic floods, especially when Lake Tetzcoco, the only saltwater lake in the region, burst its banks. But extensive dikes and flood canals were built in the twelfth century that served to control these seasonal inundations.

Moreover, a system of *chinampa* agriculture developed in the freshwater lakes. *Chinampas* were raised gardens made of branches, roots, and brushwood covered with fertile soil from the lake bottoms. Although they have acquired the name "floating gardens," *chinampas* were firmly fixed to the shore or the lake bed, anchored by poles and cypress trees. Water circulated among the gardens on canals that divided them into grid-like patterns. *Chinampas* permitted year-round productivity of a variety of root crops, vegetables, cereals, and fruits. The exceptionally abundant harvests of the *chinampas*

their faces or flat on their backs. The warriors of Quicab kept up the killing for a long time, until there were only one or two groups, from among all the enemies, who hadn't brought tribute. Their citadels fell and they brought tribute to Quicab and Cauizimah. Their lineages came to be bled, shot full of arrows at the stake. Their day came to nothing, their heritage came to nothing.

Projectiles alone were the means for breaking the citadels. All at once the earth itself would crack open; it was as if a lightning bolt had shattered the stones. In fear, the members of one tribe after another went before the gum tree, carrying in their hands the signs of the citadels, with the result that a

mountain of stones is there today. Only a few of these aren't cut stones; the rest look as though they had been split with an axe. The result is there on the flat named Petatayub; it is obvious to this day. Everyone who passes by can see it as a sign of the manhood of Quicab. He could not be killed, nor could he be conquered. He was truly a man, and all the tribes brought tribute.

And then all the lords made plans; they moved to cordon off the canyons and citadels, the fallen citadels of all the tribes.

SOURCE: *Popol Vuh: The Definitive Edition of the Maya Book of the Dawn of Life and the Glories of Gods and Kings,* trans. Dennis Tedlock (New York: Simon & Schuster, 1985), 213–216.

Map 1.2   City-States in the Valley of Mexico

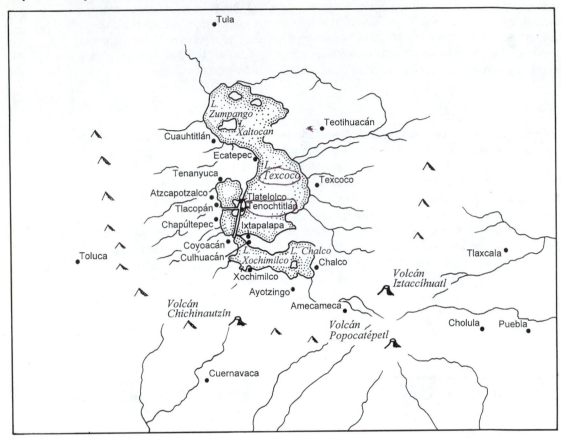

supplemented and gradually surpassed land-based agriculture in the area. The southern part of Lake Chalco contained the largest extension of *chinampas*, approximately ten thousand hectares (or twenty-five thousand acres) in 1519, worked by about one hundred thousand farmers. Each *chinampero* produced enough to support an equal number of nonfarming artisans, priests, warriors, and administrators.

Consequently, the population burgeoned in the numerous cities surrounding the lakes of the Valley of Mexico (see Map 1.2). When the Toltec empire broke up, these formerly vassal cities fell to warring among themselves over highland resources and tribute. This division provided an opening for several Chichimec groups that had been given a taste of culture and power as mercenaries and trading partners of the Toltec. Besides engaging in the ceaseless warfare, these mercenary peoples learned agriculture, cuisine, and how to build houses and speak Nahuatl. None of the competing cities that employed these mercenaries in the thirteenth century foresaw that one of these Chichimec groups, the Mexica, would eventually come to rule them. The Mexica also took the name by which they came to be known later, *Aztec,* after Aztlán, the mythical area of the group's origin in northwest Mexico.[6]

When the Mexica arrived in the central valley, they were a ragged tribe of outcasts. They attempted to settle on the hill of Chapultepec, an impoverished agricultural site but one of strategic importance. They were subsequently driven off the hill. Reverting to hunting and gathering for half a century, they were finally allowed to settle on the snake-infested lava beds of the southwestern sector of the valley, where they served as military allies to the city of Culhuacán. Known as "military maniacs" to those who hired them for their services, by 1345 the Mexica were able to move to a barren island called Tenochtitlán in the middle of the lakes. Their tribal god Huitzilopochtli, "Hummingbird on the Left," had instructed them to settle where they spied an eagle perched on a cactus with a snake in its beak. (This image has since become the national emblem of Mexico, which also takes its name from the Mexica tribe.) The meteoric rise of this people would last scarcely more than a century before they too would be overthrown—not by indigenous foes but by European invaders.

Their rise, nevertheless, was spectacular. By the time that the Mexica arrived at their island, Atzcapotzalco was the most powerful city-state in the valley. The Mexica paid tribute to Atzcapotzalco and served in the wars the latter visited on the other cities of central Mexico. But the mercenaries switched allegiance, forming the so-called Triple Alliance with the city-states of Texcoco and Tlacopán. Thereafter, they conquered Atzcapotzalco in 1433 and formed the Aztec Empire. Together, all the peoples inhabiting the Valley of Mexico, numbering about 1 million, became known collectively as Aztec. They made up many different cultural and ethnic groups and lived in some fifty small city-states, although most spoke Nahuatl. The Mexica came to dominate the Aztec peoples. At this time, Aztec warriors added new weapons to their arsenal: the thrusting spear and the broadsword, the latter of which sported obsidian-tipped edges on both sides of the blade. Eventually, their military prowess enabled the Mexica to dissolve the Triple Alliance, reduce their former allies to subordinate status, and assume direction of the Aztec Empire.

By this time, the Mexica had begun to acquire great wealth through tribute, and their leaders formed a haughty nobility. Their polity had always been a secular one, and the leader of the Aztec had been elected by the elders of the Mexica clans; now the emperor was nominated and imposed by the warrior castes. The ruler likewise became more autocratic and wealthy from receiving the tribute of conquered city-states, and the Aztec city grew important in reconstructing the Mesoamerican commercial network. Tenochtitlán and the highlands exported rich clothing, gold and precious stones, obsidian, herbs, rabbit fur, copper bells, red dyestuffs, and slaves. Luxury goods were imported from the Gulf Coast lowlands, mainly destined for elite consumers. Feathers and feather cloaks, turquoise, jade, jaguar skins, shirts, and cacao became the mark of the Aztec nobility.

The capital of Tenochtitlán was now growing in population and architectural splendor. Six major canals ran east and west through the city, and two major canals ran north and south. Tens of thousands of small canoes plied the lakes and canals, carrying people and supplies. The central religious plaza of Tenochtitlán was dominated by the main

---

[6] Today in the United States, the name *Aztlán* refers to the southwest of the United States, even Southern California, the cultural homeland of Mexican Americans.

temple topped by twin shrines, one to the Mexica patron god Huitzilopochtli and the other to the rain god Tláloc.[7] Quetzalcóatl, the god of culture, had a separate temple, a smaller round structure, in front of the larger main temple. A special temple was constructed to contain the images of gods captured from subject peoples. An extensive network of canals connected the island to the complex of *chinampa*s that surrounded it. To connect the island city to the mainland, three impressive stone causeways were constructed. The neighboring city of Tlatelolco, which featured a huge central marketplace, was annexed as a center of artisanry and commerce (see Manuscript 1.3). Although the Mexica converted themselves into a warrior and bureaucratic class with residence at Tenochtitlán, Tlatelolco attracted merchants, artisans, and farmers from many of the subject peoples. Texcoco also became a center of crafts, for its wise ruler, Netzahualcoyotl, had a house built for artisans migrating from other city-states; he was

---

[7] This is the very Templo Mayor that workers discovered in 1978 while constructing the Mexico City metro system and mentioned previously in this chapter. It is now open to view as a museum.

MANUSCRIPT 1.3

The Aztec Marketplace at Tlatelolco

Bernal Díaz del Castillo reputedly served in the expedition of Hernán Cortés, which conquered the Aztec empire in 1521. However, two years before, the Cortés expedition had entered the capital of Tenochtitlán as the guests of Emperor Moteuczoma. On this occasion, before the great battles between Spaniards and Aztec, Díaz del Castillo and some compatriots visited the marketplace at Tlatelolco, located adjacent to Tenochtitlán. He completed his remembrances of that visit nearly fifty years later as he lived in retirement on his estates in Guatemala.

On reaching the market-place, . . . we were astounded at the great number of people and the quantities of merchandise, and at the orderliness and good arrangements that prevailed, for we had never seen such a thing before. . . . Every kind of merchandise was kept separate and had its fixed place marked for it.

Let us begin with the dealers in gold, silver, and precious stones, feathers, cloaks, and embroidered goods, and male and female slaves who are also sold there. . . . Some are brought there attached to long poles by means of collars round their necks to prevent them from escaping, but others are left loose. Next there were those who sold coarser cloth, and cotton goods and fabrics made of twisted thread, and there were chocolate merchants with their chocolate. In this way you could see every kind of merchandise to be found anywhere in [Mexico]. . . . There were those who sold sisal cloth and ropes, and the sandals they wear on their feet, which are made from the same plant. All these were kept in one part of the market, in the place assigned to them and in another part were skins of tigers and lions, otters, jackals, and deer, badgers, mountain cats, and other classes of merchandise.

There were sellers of kidney-beans and sage and other vegetables and herbs in another place, and in yet another they were selling fowls, and birds with great dewlaps [turkeys], also rabbits, hares, deer, young ducks, little dogs, and other such creatures. Then there were the fruiterers; and the women who sold

himself a poet (see Manuscript 1.4), and his name is still revered in Mexico. As the second most important city of the Valley of Mexico, Texcoco also gained renown for its sophisticated and extensive public works in irrigation and flood control. Sixty thousand canoes operated on the lakes and canals connecting this complex of urban civilization. Tenochtitlán, with its population of 300,000 residents, had become the largest city in the world, bigger than Paris and Madrid at the time. Its direct descendant, Mexico City, would not again exceed this population until the twentieth century.

The disastrous famines that struck the Valley of Mexico from 1450 to 1454 caused significant changes in politics and trade throughout all of Mesoamerica. The Aztec began a series of aggressive military campaigns throughout the highlands and raised tribute quotas. The famine also had another consequence: The Mexica began to practice human sacrifice on a massive scale. According to prevailing religious beliefs, human sacrifices appeased the gods and prevented the life-giving sun from stopping its course through the skies. Militarily, the voracious appetite for human sacrifice of their war god, Huitzilopochtli, was meant to intimidate subject states into not challenging Aztec authority. Just before

cooked food, flour and honey cake, and tripe, had their part of the market. Then came pottery of all kinds, from big water-jars to little jugs, displayed in its own place, also honey, honey-paste, and other sweets like nougat. Elsewhere they sold timber too, boards, cradles, beams, blocks, and benches, all in a quarter of their own.

Then there were the sellers of pitch-pine for torches, and other things of that kind, and I must also mention, with all apologies, that they sold many canoe-loads of human excrement, which they kept in the creeks near the market. This was for the manufacture of salt and the curing of skins, which they say cannot be done without it. . . .

But why waste so many words on the goods in their great market? If I describe everything in detail I shall never be done. Paper, which in Mexico they call *amal*, and some reeds that smell of liquid amber, and are full of tobacco, and yellow ointments and other such things, are sold in a separate part.

Much cochineal is for sale too, under the arcades of that market, and there are many sellers of herbs and other such things. They have a building there also in which three judges sit, and there are officials like constables who examine the merchandise. I am forgetting the sellers of salt and the makers of flint knives, and how they split them off the stone itself, and the fisherwomen and the men who sell small cakes made from a sort of weed which they get out of the great lake, which curdles and forms a kind of bread which tastes rather like cheese. They sell axes too, made of bronze and copper and tin, and gourds and brightly painted wooden jars. . . .

Some of our soldiers who had been in many parts of the world, in Constantinople, in Rome, and all over Italy, said that they had never seen a market so well laid out, so large, so orderly, and so full of people.

SOURCE: Bernal Díaz del Castillo, *The Conquest of New Spain*, trans. J. M. Cohen (Harmondsworth, England: Penguin Books, 1963), 232–33, 235.

MANUSCRIPT 1.4

Pre-Columbian Nahuatl Poetry

Melancholy and pessimism pervade the extant poetry of the ancient Mesoamericans. What we know of their literature, which was recited and transmitted as oral tradition more than written, has come to us from the transcriptions of the early Spaniards. Shortly after the Conquest, the missionaries wrote down what they were told of the ancient literature by surviving members of the indigenous nobility. The elite of the Valley of Mexico apparently delighted at reciting the poetry ascribed to Netzahualcoyotl, the cultured ruler of Texcoco. The scholar suspects that the oral traditions dating back to the times of the Olmec and Teotihuacán may have been lost to us, but we can only surmise that the fatalism expressed by this sixteenth-century poet was shared by his predecessors.

All the earth is a grave and nothing escapes it;
nothing is so perfect that it does not descend to
its tomb.
Rivers, rivulets, fountains and waters flow,
but never return to their joyful beginnings;
anxiously they hasten on to the vast realms of
the rain god.
As they widen their banks, they also fashion
the sad urn of their burial.
Filled are the bowels of the earth with
pestilential dust
once flesh and bone, once animate bodies
of men
who sat upon thrones, decided cases, presided
in council,
commanded armies, conquered provinces,
possessed treasure,
destroyed temples,
exulted in their pride, majesty, fortune, praise
and power.

Vanished are these glories, just as the fearful
smoke vanishes
that belches forth from the infernal fires of
Popocatepetl.
Nothing recalls them but the written page.

• • •

With flowers You paint,
O giver of life!
With songs You give color,
those who will live on earth.
Later You will destroy eagles and jaguars:
we live only in Your painting
here, on the earth.
With black ink You will blot out
all that was friendship,
brotherhood, nobility.
You give shading
to those who will live on the earth.
We live only in your book of paintings,
here on the earth.

• • •

I, Netzahualcoyotl, ask this:
Is it true one really lives on the earth?
Not forever on earth,
only a little while here.
Though it be jade it falls apart,
though it be gold it wears away,
Not forever on earth,
only a little while here.

HUNGRY COYOTE (NETZAHUALCOYOTL)
King of Texcoco (1431–72)

SOURCES: As published in Eric R. Wolf, *Sons of the Shaking Earth* (Chicago: University of Chicago Press, 1959), ix; and Michael D. Coe, *Mexico: From the Olmecs to the Aztecs,* 4th ed. (New York: Thames and Hudson, 1994), 193–194.

the arrival of the Spaniards, Aztec priests were sacrificing thousands of persons each year, most of them prisoners of war. The commoners themselves were implicated in the care and preparation of the victims, their delivery to the place of death, and then in the elaborate processing of the bodies: the dismemberment and distribution of heads and limbs, flesh and blood, and flayed skins. Elite households participated in the ritual cannibalism that accompanied these sacrifices.[8]

Among the other gods who received homage among the Aztec were Tláloc, the rain god, and Xipe Totec, a deity originating in the lowlands who represented springtime. The rites ascribed to Xipe Totec demanded ferocious human sacrifice, the priests often dressing themselves in flayed human skins. At least one Aztec goddess might still be worshipped today under another name. Tonantzín, the mother of the gods, had a temple east of the capital city. Her temple was destroyed by the Spaniards, but on that site now stands the church of Our Lady of Guadalupe, the patron saint of Mexico who is associated with the Virgin Mary, Mother of God. In any case, the religion of the Aztec was extremely gloomy, filled with predictions of a climactic and universal final battle and conceiving that only those who died honorably in battle, religious sacrifice, or childbirth would have an afterlife. However, the Aztec may not have believed that the afterlife, for those who got it, would be an improvement over life on earth, and it was very difficult for even the most devout to gain divine help, because the gods were held to be in everlasting conflict among themselves. In the hope of gaining assistance, supplicants could only chart on the calendar exactly when each deity's powers might be most potent and offer a prayer or sacrifice at the appointed time.

The Aztec Empire embraced a diversity of peoples, cultures, and language groups that, centuries before, had been under the suzerainty of the Toltec and before that, Teotihuacán. Once again, trade and tribute seem to have been the organizing principles of empire. Based on pictographic orders from the emperor, Aztec tax collectors brought in foodstuffs and artisan goods from subject states at least once a year. Whole caravans of human bearers were organized to deliver these goods to the Valley of Mexico. More than one hundred twenty-three thousand cotton blankets were delivered annually to Tenochtitlán, in which great warehouses were built to store the tribute. The emperor then took charge of distributing these goods to his bureaucrats and warriors during great banquets held for just that purpose. According to ancient custom, the emperor was not to forget the widows, the elderly, and the sick among his Mexica subjects. But the perfection of the authoritarian state spawned pernicious traits as well. Aztec tax collectors were hated by the subject peoples for their greedy personal exaction and their demand for sexual favors from local women. A merchant class also developed, although most merchants were not Mexica but from Texcoco, Tlatelolco, and other subject cities. They worshipped their own gods, observed their own laws, and controlled the markets and imperial trade. Because commerce was so important, the Aztec protected the merchants, and their warriors punished those who interrupted trade.

Nevertheless, the Aztec Empire did not create an imperial bureaucracy to unify the administration of the subject territories. Local elites were left to rule over the subject peoples and collect the allotted local tribute, which could be an onerous task in itself.

---

[8] It is said that the Mexica especially enjoyed eating pork, which the Spaniards introduced after the Conquest, because it tasted similar to human flesh.

The Aztec tax collectors merely dealt with the local rulers. Garrisons were established throughout the realm, and the fear of a punishing expedition by the Aztec army, followed by human sacrifices, sufficed to entice local rulers to pay their tributes on time. Aztec administration did not spread into the territories, and neither did its culture and architecture; the Aztec did not resettle sizable communities of their citizens anywhere outside of the Valley of Mexico. Except for a few poor warriors, who went with their families to live in the scattered garrisons, the Aztec were not colonizing peoples.

The Aztec were obviously quite militaristic, and some became aristocratic, too. Many of the Mexica, with the support of the state, gave up working in agriculture to devote themselves full time to military training. "Are not war and victory the true profession of a Mexican," asks a typical Aztec proverb, "and is it not more worthwhile to win victory even against a thousand perils than sit at home like a woman and work?" Several elite military orders formed to which only the aristocracy could belong, and two others that commoners who had distinguished themselves in battle could join were founded as well. The aristocracy had its own schools, which turned out upper-class soldiers as well as priests. The latter staffed the extensive temple complexes at Tenochtitlán, maintained the calendars, and devoted their lives to appeasing the capricious gods. Supported by additional conquest and growing wealth at the capital city, the high nobility proliferated. The nobles had their own lands, held in private domain as a gift from the emperor, as well as servants to tend the fields and to care for their palatial residences. Only noblemen could practice polygamy, which also tended to swell their ranks, reinforcing the predatory acquisitiveness of the Aztec state.

However, several important peoples carried on trade within the imperial system but did not pay tribute to the Aztec. Guatemala and the Yucatán lay beyond the Aztec grasp, principally because the Mayan peoples had broken apart into mutually hostile, decentralized communities, no one of which would cooperate with the Aztec to reassemble and unite the Maya as in the times of Chichén Itzá. Also, the Mixtec and Zapotec peoples of Oaxaca remained out of direct Aztec control. In the west, the Tarascan of Michoacán remained independent by virtue of their decisive defeat of an Aztec invasion in 1480. To the north, the Aztec had not been able to reestablish the frontier posts that the Toltec had used to control the Chichimec. One major city-state of the central highlands, Tlaxcala, had also succeeded in fending off the Aztec armies. In the so-called War of the Flowers, Tlaxcala might have tacitly made a cynical agreement whereby the two sides fought not for victory but to provide each other with prisoners of war for religious sacrifices, which the Tlaxcalans also practiced with fervor. Although for the most part central Mexico was firmly in the grasp of the Aztec, with more than five million persons living under their rule, most Mesoamericans at the time resided outside the empire.

Aztec Society

Among the Mexica and other Nahuatl-speaking peoples of the Valley of Mexico, the *calpolli* was the basic unit of social organization; it lent a degree of democratic decision making and participation to an autocratic, imperial political system in which the emperor was practically deified. A *calpolli* was a community whose members, related by birth and kinship, lived in one place. It could be a small peasant enclave or a section of a large city. Land did not belong to individuals per se but to the *calpolli* whose members were duty bound to work the land. The Aztec state forged a political linkage to the *calpolli* by confirming or reconfirming the community members' titles and usufruct to the land, thus binding the peasants to work that land. Besides administering the land, the *calpolli* organized the community's participation in military campaigns. Each *calpolli* identified with its patron god, and the local temple was the center of local life and even of the local economy, as markets were always located adjacent to temples. In theory, the local god gave the people the land to use, if not to own, and rules by which they lived. Thus, resident farmers did not believe that they owned the land so much as that the gods had lent it to them.

The leader of the *calpolli* usually came from a local noble family, but he was elected to serve in this post. Assisted by a council of elders, the community leader distributed land and settled disputes, a responsibility that exempted him from having to till fields and construct public works. The leader was granted land for his family's subsistence, and other members of the community worked it for him. Social inequalities eventually developed, for this was not peasant socialism. At some point, as the result of military victory, a *calpolli* might come into possession of land and divide it equally among all its member households. But then land became vested in a family and could change hands between peasant farmers. Social differentiation among families within the community did develop based on possessing—though not owning—more or less land.

The *calpolli* served as a building block for a higher institution, the *altepetl*, and these together became the constituent elements of ethnic confederations and empire among the Nahuatl-speaking peoples of central Mexico. The political organization of the *altepetl* governed the civic obligations of its member *calpolli*, such as tribute collection, provision of troops, and rotational labor drafts. The heads of the *calpolli* served on the ruling council of the *altepetl* and took turns at being head of the council. Therefore, each *altepetl* was composed of a fluid group of leaders and leading families that served as a local nobility. Fratricidal vendettas and political struggles often broke out between rival families within this local nobility, especially as political alliances within the empire shifted. The *altepetl* also organized the local markets and arranged the basis for exchange with neighboring *altepetl* and other, more distant trading partners.

Life for the commoners in the Aztec empire paralleled that of their counterparts elsewhere in Mesoamerica. In the rural areas, they lived in dwellings made of wattle and daub and thatched roofs. Only those in the city had a likelihood of living in stone buildings. Nonetheless, extended families lived in cramped quarters that could be chilly at night, especially in the highlands and in the Valley of Mexico. As there were no heating systems, families huddled together at night. In the absence also of illumination, most people set their daily schedules according to the sunrise and the sunset. They spent most of their time outside, cooking and eating in the patio and working in the fields or in nearby workshops. No animal fats were used in cooking, so women did not fry their food. Commoners ate corn and beans spiced with chili. Women also made a porridge of corn known as *atole* and stuffed vegetables and meat into corn dough to make tamales. They rolled spicy meat and vegetables into tortillas to make tacos. Sources of animal protein consisted of rabbit, frogs, iguanas, freshwater shrimps, water flies and their eggs, and even worms. Commoners dressed mainly in clothes made of maguey (a form of cactus) fiber and rabbit fur. Men wore a simple loincloth, and women dressed in skirts reaching to the ankles with a top garment or rectangular cloak draped over the torso.

These commoners punctuated their monotonous lives with enthusiastic participation in great religious festivals that involved dressing up, dancing, and singing. These rites linked everyone to the cycle of seasons and fertility, so honoring the gods who governed these life cycles became indispensable to sowing and reaping as well as to having good harvests. Public celebrations of this type bound the commoners to the priesthood and the ruling elite, who bore the responsibility of sponsoring the festivities. However, commoners seldom if ever engaged in drinking alcoholic beverages. Only priests, warriors, and the nobility could imbibe pulque, a fermented drink distilled from the maguey cactus, which held religious significance. Only after the Conquest did pulque and other spirits become available to commoners.

As elsewhere in Mesoamerica, Aztec society strictly defined the roles of women. Adult females helped in the fields, but their main tasks centered on tending to the children, weaving cloth for family garments, shopping in the market, and preparing meals. Mothers instructed their young daughters on sweeping under the spirit house (the family shrine), making religious offerings, and preparing incense from copal resin. Young girls learned that it fell to them to prepare the beverages and meals and to learn about the use of the spindle, weaving stick, and loom as well as how to create featherwork and colorful embroidery. Mothers also lectured their daughters on sexual matters, emphasizing virginity before marriage and monogamy afterwards. Beware not to be an adulteress, warned one mother, "[b]ecause, my little daughter, my little girl, if this transpires, if this takes place, there is no remedy, there is no going back. . . . [Y]ou will be dragged through the streets, they will break your head with stones, they will turn it into pulp."

Parents arranged for the courtship and marriage of their children. The boy's parents would formally approach those of the girl, delivering a set speech full of rhetorical flourishes and fine words. At first, the girl's parents would decline the offer, stating that their daughter was unworthy of so fine a young man and unfit for marriage. Later, they would accept with feigned reluctance. The wedding took place in the bridegroom's home, after which the couple would spend four days praying in seclusion before the marriage was consummated.

Although the *calpolli* and *altepetl* in some form remained the basic units of society among most other agricultural peoples of Mesoamerica, the Aztec followed previous imperial patterns to form additional social differentiation. The creation of an aristocracy made up of the military and priestly castes and of the merchant and artisan communities have already been discussed. Slaves existed among the Aztec and other peoples, although they made up only 5 percent of the population of Tenochtitlán. Slaves served primarily as bearers and household servants for the aristocracy. However, slavery was not hereditary. Many persons entered into slavery during famine, selling themselves or their children to a wealthy family to obtain food and shelter. Merchants owned slaves because of the demand for human carriers in long-distance trade. A more important group of dependents were known as *mayeque*s (bondspersons). Originally made up of recent immigrants to the valley, the *mayeque*s came to be a hereditary group tied to the lands and *chinampa*s owned by the nobility, farming for the latter's benefit. Although free from tribute exaction, they were nonetheless made to perform military services and probably contributed to public works and other construction projects. This group made up 35 percent of the population of Tenochtitlán.

When Moteuczoma II ascended the imperial throne at Tenochtitlán in the year 1502, the Aztec empire may already have been entering into crisis.[9] He finally subdued

---

[9] Moteuczoma II is popularly known in the United States as Montezuma, as in "the halls of Montezuma" mentioned in the U.S. Marine Corps anthem. His name may also appear as Motecuhzoma.

The backstrap loom. (Florentine Codex, ca. 1575)

the Mixtec of Oaxaca, but the lack of other new conquests severely reduced the amount of booty coming into the Valley of Mexico. The famine of 1505, an indication that population growth had once again pushed against the limits of agriculture, forced many in the valley to sell themselves into slavery to survive. Moteuczoma doubled the tribute schedules for the subject cities. Taxes on merchants and artisans were increased, as did the unpaid toil of the *mayeque*s who worked for the nobility. Still, tribute collections fell off, and the expansion of the aristocracy ceased. Dissension and rebellion loomed everywhere in the Aztec Empire.

It appeared that the limits of Aztec power had already been exhausted in 1519, when runners brought Moteuczoma pictographs of the strange bearded men who had just landed on the coast of Veracruz with their "sticks of thunder" and great war beasts. Could this be the long-awaited return of the god Quetzalcóatl? The end of the world that had been prophesied?

CONCLUDING REMARKS

The ancient civilizations may have risen and declined, the last having been destroyed in the early sixteenth century, but the culture of the ancient peoples has endured. Mesoamerica remains divided socially, regionally, and linguistically according to prehistoric antecedents. Even subtle local differences of temperament have persisted through the millennia to differentiate one people from another: the mobile and voluble Chichimec to the north, the imperious Aztec of the central valley, the fiercely independent Tarascan of Michoacán, the autonomous Zapotec in Oaxaca, and the stolid Maya of Chiapas and Yucatán. The ancient languages of Mesoamerica are still spoken today by millions of the modern descendants of the Mexica, Tarascan, Otomí, Huastec, Maya, and many others. Among them, however, Spanish is now the lingua franca, not Nahuatl. Regional differences are also assiduously maintained even within the several nations that now inhabit Mesoamerica. Thus, the ancient diversity persists, militating always against the unity enforced by authoritarian political power. In turn, autocratic rule justifies itself so as to enforce order and cooperation among the unruly elements—but more often degenerates into exploitation.

Elements of other social practices and lifestyles of the ancients are also still observed. The patterns that ancient Mesoamericans established to govern their lives still influence the modern phenomena of extreme social differentiation, peonage and labor practices, personal service, community organization, agricultural techniques, food and cuisine, local commerce, gender relationships, housing, tribute and taxation, political articulation, and religious practices. Even the subsequent political domination of the whole of Mesoamerica by the Valley of Mexico, featuring today's Mexico City, was presaged by the rise of Teotihuacán, Tula, and Tenochtitlán. The record of the ancient civilizations is remarkable. Indeed, their legacy has been so indelible that it has endured, in various permutations, through five centuries of European political and economic domination—not only in Mesoamerica but also in South America.

Additional Reading

Abrams, Elliot M. *How the Maya Built Their World: Energetics and Ancient Architectures.* Austin: University of Texas Press, 1994.

Adams, Richard E. W. *Prehistoric Mesoamerica.* Rev. ed. Norman: University of Oklahoma Press, 1991.

Bernal, Ignacio. *Mexico before Cortez: Art, History and Legend.* Trans. Willis Barnstone. Garden City, N.Y.: Doubleday, 1975.

Bethell, Leslie, ed. *Cambridge History of Latin America.* Vol. 1. Cambridge, Mass.: Cambridge University Press, 1984.

Clendinnen, Inga. *Aztec: An Interpretation.* Cambridge, Mass.: Cambridge University Press, 1991.

Coe, Michael D. *The Maya.* 5th ed. New York: Thames and Hudson, 1993.

———. *Mexico: From the Olmecs to the Aztecs.* 4th ed. New York: Thames and Hudson, 1994.

Collier, George A., Renato I. Rosaldo, and John D. Wirth, eds. *The Inca and Aztec States, 1400–1800: Anthropology and History.* New York: Academic Press 1982.

Davies, Nigel. *The Ancient Kingdoms of Mexico.* London: Allen Lane, 1982.

Hassig, Ross. *Trade, Tribute, and Transportation: The Sixteenth-Century Political Economy of the Valley of Mexico.* Norman: University of Oklahoma Press, 1985.

———. *War and Society in Ancient Mesoamerica.* Berkeley: University of California Press, 1992.

León-Portilla, Miguel. *The Aztec Image of Self and Society: An Introduction to Nahua Culture.* Salt Lake City: University of Utah Press, 1992.

Padden, R. C. *The Hummingbird and the Hawk: Conquest and Sovereignty in the Valley of Mexico, 1503–1541.* Columbus: Ohio State University Press, 1967.

Proskouriakoff, Tatiana. *Maya History.* Austin: University of Texas Press, 1993.

Sabloff, Jeremy A., and John S. Henderson, eds. *Lowland Maya Civilization in the Eighth Century A.D.* Washington, D.C.: Dumbarton Oaks Research Library, 1993.

Schele, Linda, and David Freidel. *A Forest of Kings: The Untold Story of the Ancient Maya.* New York: William Morrow, 1990.

Schele, Linda, and Mary Ellen Miller. *The Blood of Kings: Dynasty and Ritual in Maya Art.* New York: George Braziller, 1986.

Sharer, Robert J. *Daily Life in Maya Civilization.* Westport, Conn.: Greenwood, 1996.

Soustelle, Jacques. *Daily Life of the Aztecs.* London: Pelican, 1964.

Stark, Barbara L., and Philip J. Arnold III. *Olmec to Aztec: Settlement Patterns in the Ancient Gulf Lowlands.* Tucson: University of Arizona Press, 1997.

West, Robert C., John P. Augelli, et al. *Middle America: Its Lands and Peoples.* 3d ed. Englewood Cliffs, N.J.: Prentice-Hall, 1989.

Wilken, Gene C. *Good Farmers: Traditional Agriculture and Resource Management in Mesoamerica.* Berkeley: University of California Press, 1987.

In Spanish

Bernal, Ignacio. *El mundo olmeca.* Mexico City: Porrua, 1968.

——. *Tenochtitlán en una isla.* 3d ed. Mexico City: Utopia, 1976.

Caso, Alfonso. *El tesoro de Monte Albán.* Mexico City: Instituto Nacional de Antropología e Historia, 1969.

Kirchhoff, Paul, Lina Odena Güemes, and Luis Reyes García. *Historia tolteca-chichimeca.* Mexico City: Instituto Nacional de Antropología e Historia, 1976.

CHAPTER 2

THE ANCIENT SOUTH AMERICANS

The middle Andean region, made up of the great coastal lowlands and narrow but fertile valleys of the Andes Mountains, formed the second cradle of ancient American civilization. The highlands and coastal zones of Peru contributed different but complementary ingredients to the formation of complex societies in prehistoric times: Culture, religion, and art originated on the coast; political innovations and military power came from the highlands. The long process of development began about twelve thousand years ago. Along the coasts, fishing villages slowly learned to cultivate squash, beans, and corn while also evolving the arts of weaving cotton cloth and of making pottery. These coastal peoples effected these breakthroughs at about the same time that the Olmec peoples began to flourish. In the millennium before the common era, the ancient Peruvians were converting simple canals for watering garden plots into complex irrigation systems. As in Mesoamerica, religion served to unite peoples under theocratic authority and to spread cultural and economic advancements far and wide. Livestock developed here that had no equivalent in Mesoamerica. Finally, a century before European conquest, a people of the southern highlands succeeded in consolidating the greatest pre-Columbian empire of the Americas, that of the Inka.[1]

What evolved in South America was no mere copy of Mesoamerican civilization, although there were mutual influences. The Andean peoples developed local practices and great civilizations that paralleled Mesoamerican accomplishments but left wholly different legacies. Both centers of civilization shared certain breakthroughs in state building, warfare, physical and cultural domination, crop diversification, social differentiation, and religious interpenetration. And as in Mesoamerica, each generation of Andeans built upon the cultural contributions inherited from those preceding. While state and imperial structures came and went, hydraulic agricultural practices and reciprocity within kin groups from sea level to the Altiplano remained.

Other qualities distinguished the Andeans from the Mesoamericans. Although interregional commerce was important to all Mesoamerican civilizations, local practices of reciprocity and economic autonomy remained of greater importance to the Andean peoples. Slash-and-burn agriculture played no role in the dry coastline and cold mountain valleys of the Middle Andes. Agricultural irrigation reached impressive proportions, and the potato was more important than corn. The various camelids raised in the Andes highlands as early as 3500 B.C. such as the llama, alpaca, and vicuña (only the first two of which were domesticated) had no equivalents in Mesoamerica. Also, the late-developing Inka empire built upon the military achievements of all its predecessors, as did the Aztecs, but the Andean Empire achieved a system of bureaucracy unique to the Americas. Andean imperial systems always emphasized tribute in the form of labor rather than goods and favored imperial redistribution over the long-distance trading of the type so important in Mesoamerica.

Nevertheless, the Andeans had not solved the problem of periodic cycles of doom and destruction any better than had the Mesoamericans. The several periods of Andean civilization building—each with its cities, agricultural achievements, and cultural motifs—ended in a paroxysm of rebellion and warfare. The impressive Andean states did not succeed in curbing the rapaciousness of their own nobility, and neither could they overcome the consequences of agricultural catastrophes caused by such events as periodic drought. Even in the short-lived Inka empire, there were disquieting signs that it, too, might have eventually collapsed into chaos and depopulation.

The Andean civilizations covered but a part of South America. Other indigenous peoples—equally diverse in ethnicity and language—inhabited the vast stretches of tropical lowlands stretching from Venezuela through Brazil to Paraguay. They practiced a slash-and-burn agriculture in combination with hunting and fishing, an economic base that they carried with them as they migrated into the Caribbean Islands. Distant cousins of the ancient Brazilians also inhabited Puerto Rico, Hispaniola (today Haiti and the Dominican Republic), and Cuba. At the southern end of the continent, hunter-gatherers held sway. From the Gran Chaco, through the Pampas, and to Patagonia, these southern peoples roamed

---

[1] Some anthropologists are converting these Andean names from their Hispanicized forms back to their original Quechua spellings and pronunciations. Therefore, they use *Inka* rather than *Inca, Wari* instead of *Huari, Tiwanaku* instead of *Tiahuanaco, wak'a* instead of *huaca,* and *kuraka* instead of *curaca.* See John Murra, "Andean Societies Before 1532," *The Cambridge History of Latin America,* ed. Leslie Bethell, (Cambridge, England: Cambridge University Press, 1984), 1:59. However, we shall retain the names of several pre-Inka civilizations in their Hispanicized forms, as Chavín and Mochica, because they continue to be identified by the modern names of their locations.

Table 2.1 Estimated Indigenous Population of the Americas, 1492

Location	Estimated Population
North America	3,790,000
Mexico	17,174,000
Guatemala	2,000,000
Other Central American Countries	3,625,000
Hispaniola	1,000,000
Other Caribbean Islands	2,000,000
Venezuela	1,000,000
Colombia	3,000,000
Ecuador-Peru-Bolivia	11,696,000
Chile	1,000,000
Amazonia	5,664,000
Southern Brazil-Paraguay-Uruguay	1,055,000
Argentina	900,000
TOTAL	53,904,000

SOURCES: William D. Denevan, "Introduction," in *The Native Population of the Americas in 1492*, 2d ed., ed. William D. Denevan, (Madison: University of Wisconsin Press, 1992), xxviii; and Leslie Bethell, "A Note on the Native American Population on the Eve of the European Invasions," in *The Cambridge History of Latin America*, ed. Leslie Bethell, vol. 1 (Cambridge, England: University of Cambridge Press, 1984), 145–46.

their territories in search of game and natural fruits. Housing was temporary. Their existence and characteristics may be compared to those of the Chichimec of northern Mexico.

All these tropical agriculturists and hunter-gatherers held certain traits in common. They observed basic political and religious loyalties at the village or clan level. Although individually the clans lived harmoniously with nature, their subsistence was so precarious that they competed incessantly over resources and territory. Raiding and warfare were endemic to their societies. They may have shared some cultural and linguistic affinities with neighboring groups, but no imperial polity like the Inka ever succeeded in conquering and forcibly uniting these disparate peoples. The incessant competition among the various groups made for a very fluid history, the particulars of which we know very little. It is clear, however, that great migrations of various linguistic and cultural groups had occurred in prehistoric times. Some groups had enlarged their territories, while others retreated to the poorer lands to form a complex and fluid map of ethnic and linguistic diversity across South America. Yet some of these peoples did achieve territorial stability. In the Amazon and Orinoco Basins, impressive chiefdoms based on hereditary elite families effectively united diverse ethnic and language groups into mutually beneficial systems of exchange and protection.

Therefore, the splendor of these ancient Americans' artistic and cultural achievements and the resiliency of their political and economic innovations—many of which withstood the eventual European encounter—stand out as testimonies to their creative spirit. Not until the twentieth century did the land again support the population that the ancient Americans had nurtured up to 1492, when an estimated 53 million persons inhabited the hemisphere (see Table 2.1).

THE EARLY HORIZON

We know less about the peoples of South America than about the ancient Mesoamericans. Material remains of the ancient Andean civilizations abound in the form of stone temples, foundations of homes, elite burial sites, shards of tools and pottery, and bits of cloth. From these, archaeologists can infer the dates of various sites and gauge the spread of cultural motifs. However, ancient South Americans outside of the Andean region worked with more perishable materials, such as wood and palm fronds, that have not survived to the present day. Scholars have found cave paintings, burial mounds, campsites, and deposits of tools and pottery in Amazonia and Chile, for example, but nothing like the great platforms of earth and stone on the coast of Peru. Therefore, we cannot make as many concrete conclusions about the earliest peoples inhabiting Venezuela, Brazil, and Argentina; our knowledge of their most recent developments tends to be richer, principally because the earliest Europeans recorded their impressions of their new subjects. However, these chroniclers observed these civilizations and cultures at a time of disruption during the Conquest and not during the millennia in which they flourished without European interference.

Moreover, the voice of the Andeans did not survive with the same resonance as did that of the Mesoamericans. The Andeans did not develop hieroglyphics or pictorial scripts as did the Maya and the Aztec. The first European clerics arriving in Mexico converted the Nahuatl language to the Roman alphabet and taught indigenous scribes to record their oral traditions using it. As far as we know, no one performed the same service for the dominant Quechua language of the Andeans. Little writing by native Andeans, therefore, has been uncovered. Even the knowledge of record keeping in the famous *khipu,* the Andean system of tying knots in cores to transmit information, became lost during the turmoil that accompanied the conquest of Peru. Nevertheless, we are fairly certain about the general trajectory of development in the Andean region, if not in other parts of South America.

When the hunter-gatherers migrated through the Isthmus of Panama south to the Peruvian coastline approximately fourteen thousand years ago, they came upon a harsh environment that yet held possibilities for sustaining life. Thirty-five westward-flowing rivers drained the Andean cordillera, carving an equal number of broad valleys that spilled out onto the semi-arid coastline. Coastal forests nurtured the small game that sustained these first inhabitants of the region, who subsequently also harvested fish from the Pacific Ocean. Twelve millennia ago, those groups that wandered into the Andes Mountains found game in the temperate intermontane valleys of northern and central Peru. In southern Peru, civilization developed even on the cold, high plains surrounding Lake Titicaca, which were known as the Puno on the Peruvian side and the Altiplano on the Bolivian side. This region contained enough small and medium-sized game to sustain the heartiest hunters. Yet other migratory peoples descended the eastern slopes of the Andes into the lush rain forests of the great Amazon Basin. Although these forest dwellers adapted themselves, their culture, and their worldview to form highly stratified and densely populated societies in the tropical and subtropical environment, they did not develop civilizations, as did those who had settled in the mountains and along the coastline of Peru.

Yet civilization did not come easily or rapidly. First, the cultural and economic elements from which to construct complex societies had to be developed; this took place between 10,000 and 3000 B.C. Generation upon generation of peoples perfected the fishing industry, establishing permanent villages along the coast. They then spread the cultivation of beans, chili peppers, and squash into each of the coastal valleys. Roving bands of hunters also settled down into permanent agricultural settlements. Cotton was spun into fish lines and nets as well as coarse clothing. By 2000 B.C., the first ceremonial centers of crude platforms and buildings used for religious purposes were built. Then the pace of change quickened. The ancient Peruvians learned the art of making pottery from the peoples of Colombia and Ecuador, who had already been making it for a thousand years. Food storage now became possible, and the Andean peoples began to add new crops to their gardens, most importantly the corn brought in from Mesoamerica. Settlements and ceremonial centers became more numerous, the society more specialized. Civilization began to take hold in Peru in the millennium before the common era.

Chavín

Archaeologists who study Peru have devised their own periodization scheme for Andean prehistory based on the concept of the *cultural horizon,* which is a long period of development characterized by the diffusion of knowledge, agricultural techniques, artistic motifs, and religious concepts from a dominant cultural center (see Table 2.2). During the Early Horizon, the Andean peoples of the mountains and coast first began to develop the hallmarks of civilization. Some time around 900 B.C., contemporaneous with the spread of Olmec influence in Mesoamerica, the first of the great diffusions of ancient art and architecture spread across northern and central Peru: the Chavín cult, which obtained its name from the most impressive ceremonial center of the period, Chavín de Huántar. The Chavín cult was more akin to a movement of religious and cultural conversion than to any sort of military conquest; in fact, some scholars believe that no warfare was involved at all in its ascendancy. The most refined pottery, design, and textile innovations were adopted in the agricultural settlements of the coast and mountains. Chavín pottery became renowned for delicate styling and stirrup-shaped spouts. Only the southern

Table 2.2 Andean Timeline

	EARLY HORIZON			MIDDLE HORIZON		LATE HORIZON
	900 B.C.	*200 B.C.*	*A.D. 600*	*A.D. 1000*	*A.D. 1460*	*A.D. 1532*
Coastal Developments	Chavín		Mochica		Chimú	
Highland Developments			Tiwanaku	Wari	Inka	
Mesoamerican Comparisons	Olmec	Teotihuacán	Maya	Toltec	Aztec	
European Comparisons	Ancient Greece	Roman Empire	Middle Ages	Crusades	Renaissance	

Map 2.1 The Inka Empire and Its Andean Predecessors

region, especially around Lake Titicaca, seemed to escape the homogenizing influence of this cult.

A spectacular characteristic of this age of Chavín cultural hegemony was the growth of large towns and small cities. Chavín de Huántar, the ceremonial center, soon became the largest and most architecturally interesting city of them all (see Map 2.1). In addition to magnificent temples and pyramids, Chavín de Huántar soon boasted residences for merchants, administrators, and craftspeople. Goods were exchanged there, all under the authority and benevolent gaze of the priests. The city's resident craftspeople specialized in coppersmithing, a southern Peruvian invention, and gold work, which originated in Colombia. Advancements in textile manufacture were also made there and in other towns. Weavers produced gauze, tapestry, painted cloth, embroidery, and patterned weaves. They used the apparatus that survives today for making traditional textiles in the Andean region—the backstrap loom. It consists of two rods, one attached to a stationary support and the other wrapped around the weaver's waist, with the warps stretched between them. On the backstrap loom, the artisan wove both intricate and coarse cloth of distinctive colors and design.

The Chavín-era peoples were capable of remarkable feats of agricultural engineering. On the coast, the religious leaders of the growing towns took charge of constructing irrigation ditches, permitting the year-round cultivation of crops. Irrigation also brought more land under cultivation. Local authorities governed the distribution of water and organized the peasants during the off-season in repairing and cleaning the silt out of the ditches. The main irrigation canal watering the fields of the Chicama Valley of northern Peru was 130 kilometers in length. These same irrigation systems are still in use today. Inhabitants of highland valleys also built extensive agricultural terraces up the mountainsides. The population of Peru increased significantly during this period.

Before the Chavín culture dissipated around 200 B.C., several peoples of the coastal and intermontane valleys engaged in temple-building projects. The Chavín cult melded and intermeshed with local religious practices in infinite variety; archaeologists have excavated numerous temples dating from this period, many of which betray similar artistic motifs and pay homage to beasts of prey such as the condor, serpent, and jaguar. The presence of the jaguar, a cat of the tropical forest, on the temples of the semi-arid coastline of Peru leads scholars to speculate that the Andeans had exchanged cultural influences with the Olmec of Mesoamerica, possibly through travel by boat. No matter how impressive the artistic, religious, and agricultural achievements of the Chavín period were, however, no centralizing state apparatus developed then as in Mesoamerica or later in the Andean region. Although experts remain uncertain as to how the Chavín culture declined, archaeological evidence points to the familiar cycle of overpopulation, social upheaval, and rising warfare.

THE MIDDLE HORIZON

Mochica

At about the same time that Teotihuacán rose to prominence in Mesoamerica, the central coast of Peru was witness to a period of remarkable city and state building known for its most important city, Mochica, which dominated the Moché Valley. Between A.D. 200 and 750, arguably more people inhabited coastal Peru than at any time until the twentieth century. True cities of some size were built, and regional states formed. The new administrative and priestly classes developed valleywide irrigation systems to sustain the population. During this first millennium of the common era, warfare became a feature of life among the Andean peoples. The cities of the mountains launched invasions of the coastal valleys. Military action and coercion now performed the function of consolidating political power on a grander scale, integrating the vast irrigation projects and maintaining peace between peoples of different ethnic and linguistic identities. Under the rule of the new states, culture and craftsmanship flourished and developed new patterns.

Moché consisted of densely packed houses with stone foundations and several plazas. Open spaces within the city served to gather the citizens together for markets, religious festivals, and military maneuvers. The Mochica had fortifications surrounding the city, just like the dozen or so other cities of the northern coast of Peru. Each city, which numbered upwards of five thousand inhabitants, maintained its own religious cults, merchants, local nobility, administrators, and craftspeople. What sustained these cities was the development of large-scale hydraulic engineering. Rather than taking water directly from the coast rivers, which were dry for half the year, these city-states went straight to the head of the valley to tap the water year-round for their valleywide irrigation systems. The priests and administrators organized thousands of peasants to build the necessary stone canals and to keep them in repair and clear of silt. During this millennium, peasants cut down the remaining coastal forests and converted all arable land to agriculture. The hydraulic system within each valley served many communities and thus demanded political consolidation.

Under the Mochica, a state bureaucracy formed to administer the extensive irrigation systems and gradually extended its power over religion and the arts as well. Soon a social and economic gulf widened between the rulers and the ruled. A great ceremonial center rose at Moché, complete with large pyramids dedicated to the sun and the moon just as in the cities of their Mexican counterparts. Other buildings paid homage to the demons of war and to the spirits of agricultural plants like beans and corn. Signs of human sacrifice appear in the ruins of Moché, and apparently the priests held nocturnal rites celebrating the coca leaf. Cultivated in the wet eastern lowlands of the Andean cordillera, coca was and is still chewed by Peruvian peasants and workers as a stimulant for physical work.

The extensive irrigation systems of the Mochica provided abundant varieties of food, including corn, sweet potatoes, chili peppers, fruits, and vegetables. Fish and meat supplemented the diet, much of the latter provided by trade in llamas from the southern Andean highlands. Women were responsible for weaving colorful and patterned fabric from cotton as well as wool from alpacas and llamas, the two domesticated camelids of the highlands. Artisans worked copper, silver, gold, turquoise, and lapis lazuli into jewelry and ornaments. The cultural products of this millennium also depicted the newly bellicose milieu. Depictions of battle scenes, combatants, and trophy heads (for victorious Andean warriors were accustomed to behead the losers) came to adorn fine stirrup-spouted and bottle-necked porcelain.

Scholars cannot explain the exact process by which this culture and people declined in importance. After nearly six centuries of development, the Mochica suffered greatly during an unprecedented 32-year drought. Perhaps a major El Niño event provoked the climatic disturbance. Then as today, changes in the major trade winds of the Pacific Ocean every 25 to 40 years prevent the upwelling of colder currents, raising the temperature of the surface waters along the west coast of South America. Floods afflict some areas of the hemisphere because of this event, and in other regions, droughts occur. The great drought at the end of the sixth century may have led to the abandonment of the capital city at Moché and the building of a new one at Pampa Grande. At the same time, military pressure from rising highland city-states, particularly Wari, placed the Mochica on the defensive.

During the coastal hegemony of the Mochica state, the leaders of a separate agricultural civilization, the Nazca, constructed enormous animal and geometrical designs in the earth. These figures, subsequently forgotten until the age of the airplane, pointed to the solstices and equinoxes, but their ultimate meaning remains very much a mystery. The Nazca were agriculturists who had developed irrigation systems and built cities and monuments on the southern desert coast of Peru. Their pottery and cotton fabrics, although not as fine as those of the Mochica, displayed the fetishes they ascribed with supernatural powers: animals, birds, and cactus plants. In designs several hundred feet in length, they drew figures of these creatures in the desert crust and by piling up stones of different colors. Monkeys, hummingbirds, foxes, dogs, frigate birds, and spiders appear, several of which are not native to the region. The people of the southern coast constructed these images over two millennia. Some of the lines were meant to link their villages with distant mountain peaks, and the Nazca could watch the sun, moon, and stars rise in perfect alignment with animal figures built long before by their forebears. The figures are sufficiently huge that they cannot be seen for what they are at ground level. Scholars have discarded a recent theory that the ancient Peruvians were constructing landing strips for space travel, but they still are not satisfied with explanations linking the figures to astronomical features. Without a doubt, however, the desert images reflect religious beliefs that connected these ancient Andeans to the cosmos, to the cycles of seasons and time, to fertility, and to the supernatural world.

Just as in the decline of the Maya, which occurred at about the same time, the city states of the Andean coast deteriorated rapidly for relatively unknown reasons. Warfare seems to have become a general phenomenon in the Andes at the end of the Middle Horizon, perhaps because competition for scarce land promoted hostility between neighboring peoples. The size of the population may have finally outstripped the sustaining power of agriculture and irrigation. It is clear that social chaos accompanied the downfall of one great city after another from the central highlands down to the northern coast. We do not know if outside invasions, peasant uprisings, dynastic rivalries, or internecine warfare doomed these great cities, but the results were dramatic. Beginning around 800, the population density went into decline, and the inhabitants scattered into rural hamlets. "The towns were depopulated," Andean oral tradition reported. "Fearing war, they had to leave the good places. . . . They were forced to move from their towns to the higher places and now lived on peaks and precipices of the high mountains."

Tiwanaku and Wari

Despite its wealth and power, the Mochica state never succeeded in conquering the peoples of the highlands. Lowland combatants found it difficult to accustom themselves to the extreme weather changes common at such high altitudes. In fact, the threat of highland groups descending to disrupt the irrigation ditches caused the coastal peoples to construct protective fortress cities at the top or throat of the coastal valleys. Ultimately, the lowland Andean civilizations would be absorbed by those highland dwellers. While the people of the Moché Valley were developing and spreading culture, the warriors of the mountains were forging the political and military authority to unify the valleys of the coastal region.

labrador
pachaca

Harvesting potatoes in the Andes. (Guaman Poma de Ayala, ca. 1615)

Highland Andean civilization had its origins in breakthroughs made in two food items. First, the practice of freeze-drying the abundant potato harvests allowed this basic foodstuff to be stored for long periods of time; the resulting product was called *ch'uño.* Second, the Puno region east of Lake Titicaca, an area of high plains, rolling grasslands, and nighttime frosts, proved ideal for raising the domesticated llama and alpaca, sources of both meat and wool; the wild vicuña also provided these important commodities. The llama is not sturdy enough to be ridden or pull a cart, but as a draft animal it could carry light cargoes. Moreover, alpaca and llama wool provided the basis for a textile industry to clothe and warm the peoples of the windswept mountains.

But an organized state developed relatively late in the highlands, because potato growing and llama breeding did not produce sufficient surplus to warrant a bureaucracy, as did irrigation and the extensive agriculture on the coast. But by the second millennium of the common era, interethnic military rivalries finally spawned the powerful city-state of Wari in the highlands. Located near the present city of Ayacucho, Wari developed a formidable military system that conquered the area from Cajamarca in the north nearly to the shores of Lake Titicaca in southern Peru. Archaeologists believe that this imperial state began constructing the system of roads connecting the Andean valleys and stone storehouses; it was also an efficient method to rapidly concentrate and support Wari armed forces. Befitting its military tradition, the Wari people built their city of large walled enclosures divided into barracklike residences. However, the Wari artisans gained great facility in the fashioning and design of pottery. Even craftspersons from cities outside the area of Wari control copied their work.

The second most impressive monument of highland civilization during the Middle Horizon turned out to be a religious and cultural center rather than a political state: Tiwanaku. Situated at an altitude of 4,000 meters and 20 kilometers from Lake Titicaca in what is now Bolivia, Tiwanaku had two great pyramids, a massive platform and patio, and the famous Gateway to the Sun. This massive gate, 3 meters high and nearly 4 meters wide, was hewn out of solid rock. It was decorated with images of the sun god, pumas, condors, and animals and birds with human attributes. The god Wiraqocha (later Viracocha) resided at Tiwanaku, which flourished in the third and fourth centuries and became an important site of pilgrimages from all over the region. Apparently, the wealthy llama and wool traders from the area surrounding Tiwanaku had built the monument to impress their highland neighbors and gain markets for their produce. In fact, corn and cotton did find their way into the region in exchange for highland meat and wool, and Tiwanaku contributed to spreading the popularity of *chicha,* a beer fermented from corn. The Inka would later benefit from the religious innovations of Tiwanaku and the military tradition established by Wari.

THE LATE HORIZON

The Late Horizon in the Andes, like the Postclassical Period in Mesoamerica, is known for its economic and political centralization, features also exhibited by the Toltec and Aztec. Similarly, the civilizations of the Late Horizon displayed extraordinary cohesion. Several powerful city-states unified the coastal valleys and the cordilleras beginning in 1000, especially in northern Peru. Then, in the fifteenth century, the most centralized imperial state in all the Americas arose in the southern cordillera—that of the Inka. Whereas the Aztec consolidated power through military intimidation and tribute, the Inka lords created an administrative bureaucracy and spread their hegemony via cultural and linguistic consolidation. The Inka Empire tolerated and accommodated local customs and leadership and took care to provide for the subsistence of its subject peoples. To the Inka, the requisition of labor and redistribution of goods took precedence over tribute in goods and long-distance trade. Again, what the Inka inherited from their forerunners accounts for the difference between Andean and Mesoamerican political systems on the eve of contact with Europeans.

Chimú

Once again, coastal civilization attempted a resurrection in the Moché Valley, this time among a people known as the Chimú. Their period of warlike domination corresponded to the era of the Toltec in Mesoamerica, lasting from 1280 to 1480. The proud seat of Chimú power was their capital Chan-Chan, which eventually boasted a population of 150,000 inhabitants, making it one of the world's largest cities. The Chimú constructed public monuments and dwelling houses entirely of adobe bricks, a practice for which their artisans became noted. Political leaders made advances in public administration, even devising a severe penal code in which thieves—together with members of their family—faced hanging as a deterrent to crime. However, few other cities flourished in this period, and the rest of the Andean population remained relatively rural and autonomous. Visual art and pottery of the time was not very noteworthy, but artisans advanced their knowledge of metallurgy and fashioned silver, gold, and copper into jewelry, although metal tools were unknown. Weaving reached a high level of sophistication and quality. Textile makers, especially those serving the nobility, learned to spin delicate cotton yarn and made fine cloth of more than 200 weft per inch, whereas European handwoven cloth at that time seldom surpassed 80 weft per inch.

The cultural hegemony of the Chimú could not be sustained by political and military will. The valley states of the northern coast of Peru broke up into feuding ethnic groupings even while the spread of administrative know-how and culture invited inevitable imitation. Just as the Aztec left the wilderness to consolidate existing Mesoamerican civilization in the fifteenth century, so too did a resolute barbarian tribe from the Southern Andes.

The Inka

The Inka started out as impoverished migrants in search of a suitable place to subsist in the harsh southern highlands.[2] In 1250, they obtained some land and settled into a small village they called Cuzco. The city grew strong, apparently causing some jealousy among its neighbors. In 1438, an adjoining state attacked Cuzco, and the Inka successfully rallied allies in other regions, winning a decisive victory. The Inka quickly exploited their military success, consolidating power within the southern highlands and present-day Bolivia before striking out to overthrow the state of Cajamarca and conquer the city-states of the coastal region, beginning with the great Chan-Chan. Finally, Inka armies penetrated what is now Ecuador and took over the city of Quito. At its height at the turn of the sixteenth century, approximately 5 million subjects, nearly all the populous high cultures of the Andean region, lived within the Inka Empire, which stretched for 4,400 kilometers from Ecuador into present-day Chile and Argentina. Only the cultures of Colombia to the north, the tropical agriculturists of Venezuela and Brazil, and the hunter-gatherers of western Argentina and southern Chile lay outside Inka suzerainty.

The Inka completed their remarkable series of conquests by combining wise leadership and a capacity to incorporate conquered peoples as allies in future campaigns. Unlike the Aztec, the Inka did not maintain a professional warrior class. Members of the Inka nobility trained as officers and led mercenaries and troops provided by allied states. These new allies, who often harbored hostility toward their neighbors, willingly participated in the distribution of captured booty and land following an Inka victory. Of course, this imperial consolidation was fragile. A disastrous defeat might endanger the empire, and rebellions against the Inka did indeed occur. The Aymara-speaking peoples of the Bolivian Altiplano, the source of the Inka's gifts of camolids, were particularly rebellious, as the spread of the empire depleted their herds.

Therefore, the Inka extended economic benefit to those states incorporated into the empire. They distributed llama wool to subject peoples and even donated llama herds to those who never had them before. The empire also encouraged its subject peoples to build and maintain irrigation canals and terraces. Naturally, the Inka benefited from these improvements in the form of tribute, but scholars speculate that they also took care to avoid the arbitrary and imperious methods that made the Aztec so unpopular in Mesoamerica. As

---

[2] Inka refers both to the original people of Cuzco as well as to their emperor, as the Inca Atawallpa.

a Spanish chronicler later stated about Inka administrators, "Care would be taken that tribute should not be too high so that (subject communities) could easily pay it."

Reciprocal exchange between rulers and the ruled, however, tends to favor the former and to encourage the elite to engage in self-righteous aggrandizement through excessive taxation and corruption. During its brief reign, the Inka Empire had not yet gained the reputation for excessive abuse and corruption. Even as the Inka also practiced the long-standing imperial tactic of adopting the gods of the conquered peoples, they also constructed temples to the sun and other Inka deities throughout the empire. Moreover, the priests of the sun were probably responsible for spreading the understanding of the Quechua language among the subject peoples. Quechua came to be spoken by peasants as well as by the nobles. The brief rule of the Inka also stimulated the spread of a second common language—Aymara—principally in the area of today's Bolivia.

Finally, the Inka integrated a gigantic road system, paved with cobblestones and serviced with rest houses, that provided for rapid movement of messengers and troops

MANUSCRIPT 2.1

Native Commoners on the Road

Andean civilization before the European conquest was anything but stagnant. Across the expansive Inka road system flowed the traffic of thousands of people and hundreds of llamas. Little of this traffic, however, consisted of commerce. Instead, there were armies on the move, joined by bureaucrats and tribute carriers, laborers requisitioned by the state, and peasant families passing from one niche of their extended ayllu to another. The commoners among these travelers most often carried cargoes on their backs and heads and in their arms. We naturally lack a description of this traffic dating from the days of the Inka, but many Spaniards commented on its continuance into the sixteenth century. Much of what they described is timeless and can still be seen even today. Although due allowance must be made for the prejudices of the Spanish chroniclers, who generously added their own value judgments to their descriptions, the modern student can still gain an inkling of the relationships (especially gender relationships in these passages) within the indigenous peoples that antedated the colonial period.

It is a pitiful thing to see the excessive and unbearable loads which these unhappy people put on their shoulders. The weight that the ragamuffin peons and Moorish halfbreeds of la Palanca [in Spain] pile on themselves, is light as air compared to what these poor people carry. For the most that the porters of la Palanca do, is help in moving furniture from one house to another, or carry what cargo they can for a short distance; but these Indians, the women as well as the men, do such work without respite, and they walk four or six leagues at a stretch with loads of three *arrobas'* weight, or a two-*arroba* wine jar, or a pot of maize beer or water. [An *arroba* is equivalent to 11.4 kilograms.] They carry a load of firewood that no beast of burden would ever haul. And they are used to this work and consider it something natural . . . because they are habituated to it from the age of four years, moderating the load and the distance according to their tender age. And so the boys never walk without some load such as their little meals and bag lunches, both in town and in the fields, where, in the company

throughout the Andean region. One main road traversed the coastline, and the other passed through the highlands between Cuzco and Quito. A number of trunk roads connected the two main routes at various points, bringing the total distance of the Inka road system to an estimated sixteen thousand kilometers (see Map 2.1). The engineering proved so superb that Andean highlanders today still use several of the original wood-and-earth bridges; one of the Inka rope bridges suspended over a deep gorge serviced traffic as late as the nineteenth century. The celebrated *khipu,* strings on which knots were tied at different lengths, served to convey orders and messages over great distances. Accountants kept records of goods and services distributed throughout the empire, although no hieroglyphic writing developed in the Andes as in Mesoamerica. The vast road system served the military and communication requirements of the empire as well as the transport needs of peasant communities and public works laborers. However, long-distance commerce, being of lesser importance, did not take advantage of the system (see Manuscript 2.1).

of their parents, they work with as much vigor as if they were grown up. . . .

Those who travel with their legitimate wives or concubines walk slowly and never break their stride or double the day's march. The women are the ones who suffer and they, poor things, are the ones who work, for, besides carrying their little children on their backs, they load onto themselves a good heavy pot, nor do they leave out a drinking gourd; and finally, they pile onto their battered shoulders everything needed in a saloon, tap, and kitchen, without leaving out any known utensil. Their husbands and male friends go along tossing sticks the whole way, perfectly relaxed.

At the end of the day's journey, wherever nightfall finds them, they make their encampment, and there they lodge with their poverty and misery. Instead of tinder and flint, they take two sticks that they carry for the purpose, protected from dampness, and with them they start a fire. Meanwhile, the poor women prepare their pitiful meals, with which they refresh the men and relieve their fatigue, comforting themselves with the thought that at least by such extreme subservience they can keep [the men] happy during the time they rule over [the women]. And in case this left them too easy and careless on the road, besides carrying their heavy load, [the women] also busy themselves spinning, or they go along weaving some net bags called *gicara,* or chewing maize to make ferment for the maize beer they will drink that day. . . .

Their beds, both on the road and at home, are always the same, and do not cost them much in curtains and less in mattresses, for all they do is lie down on the ground. At most, they put under themselves an old reed mat, if they can spare one, and that serves them for a mattress. For sheets and blankets, they have only their own clothing, and for pillows, a stone or a piece of wood.

SOURCE: Lope de Atienza, "Compendio historico del estado de los indios del Perú," in *La religión del imperio de los Incas,* ed. Jacinto Jijón y Caamaño (Quito: Escuela Tipográfica Salesiana, 1931), 49–50, 113–14, as quoted by Frank Salomon, *Native Lords of Quito in the Age of the Incas: The Political Economy of North Andean Chiefdoms* (Cambridge, England: Cambridge University Press, 1986), 153–54.

Cuzco, the Inka capital, came to reflect the ethnic diversity of the empire. The rulers brought together peasants, artisans, workers, and mercenaries to build, sustain, and defend the growing city. Each ethnic group wore its traditional costumes, adding to Cuzco's image as a cosmopolitan imperial capital. At least forty thousand workers, drafted by the state under a rotational labor system called the *mit'a,* gathered each year to work on construction. Cuzco's population may have been between one hundred thousand and three hundred thousand inhabitants. The Inka nobility had a large number of *yanakona,* bonded servants who took care of the expansive households and tilled the fields belonging to the nobility. Here in the highlands, construction reached such a state of perfection that the huge stones forming the walls of great buildings fit together with unmatched tightness without the use of mortar. In contrast, the roofs consisted of straw and thatch. Commoners lived in austere one-room houses made of stone and adobe bricks, windowless but for a small entrance and furnished only with sleeping blankets woven from llama wool.

Noticeably absent in Cuzco was a large marketplace. Long-distance trade was not very important within the Inka Empire, as it had been in all previous Andean civilizations. Tribute did not become an overriding feature of Andean conquest, unlike among the Mesoamerican empires. The Inka made an initial confiscation of the lands of conquered peoples, kept one-third of them, passed out another portion to the religious hierarchy, and donated the rest to the peasants. The Inka followed precedents in establishing imperial storehouses. Here, stored goods and provisions supported the armies and requisitioned workers of the Inka and also became the source for redistributions by the state to its own bureaucratic elite and also to village leaders who passed goods on to the peasants as rewards for obedience and loyalty. This system theoretically ensured the subject peasants a minimum of subsistence and material comfort. Thereafter, the imperial court demanded only labor from the peasants, who were organized by their community leaders to work the fields of the Inka and of the religious orders. Imperial storehouses were built to provide for the needs of military expeditions and draft laborers. They were also to provide occasional drafts of labor under the *mit'a* system.

Andean Society

Besides the family, the basic unit of Andean society was the *ayllu* (pronounced AISLE-you), a community or group of households related by blood and ritual ties. In the highlands, the *ayllu* was basically a self-contained, autarchic social and economic village. The group controlled enough land for self-subsistence of all its members, usually by farming in fertile valleys or herding llamas in the Altiplano and Puno regions. The *ayllu* did not acknowledge the concept of private property, at least not in the sense Europeans did. The lands of the village were distributed according to the need of the members, and it was expected that the members would render favors and labor services to each other and to the needy and infirm within the community. Members assisted each other in mending the agricultural terraces and in planting and harvesting.

The many *ayllu* of the highlands did not carry on trade among themselves, and exchange in markets there paled in comparison to that of Mesoamerica. Instead, each *ayllu* expected to provide for its own subsistence, supplemented by gifts from the Inka. Survival called for each community to control production in different ecological zones. The *ayllu* sent out colonists to designated areas on the coast, where corn and fish could be obtained; in the mountains, where potatoes thrived and llamas provided wool; and on the semitropical eastern slopes of the cordilleras, where coca leaves were gathered. In this way, the community ensured itself of sufficient supplies of these essentials. These community members, rather than merchants, traveled frequently on Inka roads with their produce. The overarching political power of the Inka at Cuzco reinforced and regulated the entire structure. Therefore, the basic tax paid to the Inka state consisted of labor. Each year the *ayllu* members were required to render service to the Inka by working his lands or those of his gods and by assisting with his various construction projects. The Inka reciprocated for the labor with a redistribution of goods stored in the imperial warehouses. Everywhere, the *ayllu* observed the basic Andean principles of reciprocity and of community ownership of land.

The *kuraka* (clan leader) directed all this activity. Selected from among the few local noble families, the *kuraka* distributed lands and obligations equally among all members of the *ayllu;* as compensation for this administrative responsibility, the leader received his own lands for maintenance, which the peasants cultivated under reciprocal arrangements. In times of scarcity, these peasants expected the *kuraka* to provide from his reserves and make his land available to the impoverished among them. When he died, the land of the *kuraka* passed to his successor in office, usually a brother or son. But none of the noble families that traditionally provided the community's leadership actually owned land separate from the *ayllu.* Most of all, one could not sell land to others.

These community leaders were also responsible for marshaling the men and women of the community for the Inka's requirements. The *kuraka* called the men for duty in the army or for *mit'a* labor in public works. In addition, Inka bureaucrats visited peasant villages. They looked after the Inka's land and public works and mobilized the peasants for additional conquests. They might also recruit some of the young women to the Inka's palaces and temples and to serve the nobility. As "Virgins of the Sun," selected women performed specialized religious functions for the principal gods of the Inka.

The Inka conquest probably caused little change to the peasant communities of the defeated state. They merely exchanged the Inka for the old political masters, and the same community leaders continued with their customary privileges and duties. Perhaps the imposition of a *pax incaica,* the introduction of llama wool, the building of terraces on the mountainsides, and the security that allowed subjects of the Inka state to undertake production in alternate climatic zones (as described earlier) might have counted as positive benefits. However, most defeated peoples submitted uneasily to the Inka, and others continued resistance and rebellion at every opportunity, Ecuador's Caranqui people serving as a case in point.

Among the Andean peoples, religion served the same function as it did in Mesoamerica: It explained both the demonstrable logic and the randomness of the universe. Religious observances also served to unite disparate ethnic and language groups, which explains why the ancient religions were also diverse. Each *ayllu* worshipped its own founding deities, spirits thought to inhabit plants, animals, or stones. The gods of the cosmos and of civilization ranked at the top of the pantheon. Usually depicted as a circular golden disc with a human face and beams radiating in all directions, the sun god was particularly venerated among the Inka as well as other highlanders. Wiraqocha, the god of creation, was also important, having been worshipped for centuries by many peoples. Because irrigation had become so important to the Andean peoples, the Inka adopted the god Pariacaca to symbolize the earth's fecundity. Andean peoples occasionally used human sacrifice but to a much lesser extent than in Mesoamerica. The fetuses of llama and *chicha* beer served more commonly as appeasements for the arbitrary appetites of the gods.

Some archaeologists speculate that priests and even common villagers had enough knowledge of astronomy to arrange the calendar. They calculated the proper time for planting and harvesting according to the position of certain constellations in the heavens and their relation to prominent geographical features, such as mountain peaks. The priests also built special holy sites and pillars in straight lines across the Cuzco Valley to help them observe the sun and the stars and to calculate their seasonal calendars. Scholars know much less about the Andean calendar than that of the Maya because the Andean priests recorded their observations in perishable woven textiles rather than in stone.

Persons belonging to the elite consumed the sumptuous materials befitting their rank in society. Gold and silver jewelry adorned their clothes, and they also wore head-dresses, the relative elaborateness of which reflected an individual's social and political rank. Only the elite practiced polygamy. The Inka himself often presided over the marriages of upper-class males to their first wives, who were subsequently to hold the highest female status in the household. Secondary and tertiary wives entered the home without much ceremony, often as a gift from the Inka for meritorious service. As these other wives mostly came from the peasant class, they were to serve as helpers under the orders of the primary wife. They took care of the first wife's children and helped with the cooking and cleaning. Women of the nobility had *yanakona*s (servants) to help them with their chores, but they still spun thread and wove cloth.

Gender divisions within the families of commoners also corresponded to those of the elite. Normally, Andean women wore a large cloth wrapped around the body, belted at the waist. They draped a mantle over their shoulders and fastened it in front with a copper pin. The men wore a simple loincloth topped off by a poncho-like tunic. Cloaks made of llama and alpaca wool sufficed to ward off the chilly night air. When they reached the proper age, boys went into the fields with their fathers and older brothers, while the girls assisted their mothers in cooking, cleaning, making clothing, and taking care of younger siblings. Women did help work in the fields or tend the herds of llamas and alpacas during planting and harvests and also while the men were responding to a call for labor or military service. Normally rising before the men and boys, the young girls left the house in the predawn darkness to collect kindling wood. Because their ancestors had long since deforested both the coastal valleys and the highlands, the girls had to obtain firewood from bushes and brush. When the sons and daughters reached the ages of 25 and 16 to 20 years, respectively, the parents arranged for their marriages to members of other peasant families. The marriage took place at the home of the bride, after which the bride accompanied her husband to the home of his family. There they both received a lecture on the responsibilities of marriage. A feast and gift giving followed.

Women also played key roles in local religious observance. They formed the membership of the cult of the moon, which celebrated the leading female deity. Women cared for and made sacrifices to the local *wak'a*, spirits that inhabited certain places and geographical objects. Amulets also held supernatural powers and, when worn, were treated as *wak'a*. Peasant women also rendered additional religious and political services to the Inka. The Inka's bureaucrats would choose from among 10-year-old girls of conquered peoples for their beauty. Following four years of training in spinning, weaving, cooking, *chicha* making, and religion, they were presented to the Inka at Cuzco. The Inka and his advisers then singled out some of the girls for service with the

Virgins of the Sun cult and gave the others as rewards to elite men and local *kuraka*s. In this manner, women served to reward the very loyalty to the Inka that united the peoples of various ethnicities and languages into an empire. Obviously, these young women seldom had the freedom to chose their destinies.

As in Mesoamerica, the Europeans landed on the coast of Peru at a time of political crisis in the Inka empire. The Andean area may have been nearing its capacity to sustain the large population and command imperial unity through systems of redistribution and labor and military requisitions. The expanding Inka nobility faced the prospect of diminishing land and labor. Increasingly, especially in the territories closest to Cuzco, peasants were taken from villages and converted into *yanakona*. As bondspeople, they subsisted and worked in fields belonging to the nobility, which, as they grew in number, began to absorb larger and larger amounts of land at the expense of the peasant communities. In addition, local communities increasingly suffered frequent redistribution of land motivated by imperial policy. Rebellious peoples could be scattered and relocated among the loyal *ayllu,* which had to tolerate the encroachment of unwelcome new neighbors. The Inka also resettled loyal peoples on the land of the former rebels (see Manuscript 2.2). The orders to move did not often sit well with peoples who then were forced to vacate

---

MANUSCRIPT 2.2

The Inka System of Colonization

In contrast to the other late-developing American empire—that of the Aztec—the Inka overlords attempted to rule subject peoples of the Andes through accommodation and justice rather than through terror and intimidation alone. Conquered peoples were permitted a modicum of autonomy over their own affairs, being allowed, for example, to worship their own local deities as before although also required to support the cult of the Inka sun god. Moreover, the Inka rulers distributed their own knowledge of raising highland livestock throughout the Andean region and took pains to adjust tribute collections fairly. Forcible movement of peoples also became a deliberate strategy of the Inka state, as the following description of the mitimaes, or colonists, attests. The author, Pedro Cieza de León, had participated in the campaigns of conquest in Colombia and Ecuador, settling down in Peru in 1547 to research and write about the pre-Conquest Inka.

The first kind of *mitimaes,* as instituted by the Inkas, were those who were moved to other countries, after a new province had been conquered. A certain number of the conquered people were ordered to people another land of the same climate and conditions as their original country. If it was cold, they were sent to a cold region, if warm, to a warm one, where they were given lands and houses such as those they had left. This was done that order might be secured, and that the natives might quickly understand how they must serve and behave themselves, and learn all that the older vassals understood concerning their duties, to be peaceful and quiet, not hasty to take up arms. At the same time, an equal number of settlers was taken from a part which had been peaceful and civilized for a long time, and sent into the newly conquered province, and among the recently subjugated people.

There they were expected to instruct their neighbours in the ways of peace and civilization; and in this way, both by the emigration of some and the arrival of others, all was made secure under the royal governors and lieutenants.

The Inkas knew how much all people feel the removal from their country and their home associations, and in order that they might take such banishment with good will, they did honour to those who were selected as emigrants, gave bracelets of gold and silver to many of them, and clothes of cloth and feathers to the women. They were also privileged in many other ways. Among the colonists there were spies, who took note of the conversations and schemes of the natives, and supplied the information to the governors, who sent it to Cuzco without delay, to be submitted to the Inka. In this way all was made secure, for the natives feared the *mitimaes,* while the *mitimaes* suspected the natives, and all learnt to serve and to obey quietly. If there were turmoils or disturbances they were severely punished. Among the Inkas there were some who were revengeful, and who punished without moderation and with great cruelty.

The *mitimaes* were employed to take charge of the flocks of the Inka and of the Sun, others to make cloth, others as workers in silver, and others as quarrymen and labourers. Some also were sculptors and gravers of images; in short, they were required to do such service as was most useful, and in the performance of which they were most skillful. Orders were also given that *mitimaes* should go into the forests of the Andes to sow maize and to cultivate coca and fruit-trees. In this way the people of the regions where it was too cold to grow these things were supplied with them. . . .

In the course of the conquests made by the Inkas, either in the mountains, or plains, or valleys, where a district appeared to be suitable for cultivation, with a good climate and fertile soil, which was still desert and uninhabited, orders were at once given that as many colonists as would be sufficient to people it should be brought from a neighbouring province with a similar climate. The land was then divided amongst them, and they were provided with flocks and all the provisions they needed, until they had time to reap their own harvests. These colonists worked so well, and the king required their labours to be proceeded with so diligently, that in a short time the new district was peopled and cultivated, insomuch that it caused great content to behold it. In this way many valleys on the coast and ravines on the mountains were peopled, both such as had been personally examined by the Inkas, and such as they knew of from report. No tribute was required from the new settlers for some years; and they were provided with women, provisions, and *coca,* that they might, with more good-will, be induced to establish themselves in their new homes.

In this way there were very few cultivable lands that remained desert in the time of the Inkas, but all were peopled, as is well known to the first Christians who entered the country.

SOURCE: Pedro Cieza de León, *The Second Part of the Chronicle of Peru,* translated and edited by Clements R. Markham (London: The Hakluyt Society, 1883), 26–31.

lands on which their ancestors had been buried for generations. For all these reasons, peasant resentments were building.

Rivalries among the Inka nobility also threatened imperial power. One of the last Inka rulers, Wayna Qhapaq, moved his place of residence from Cuzco to Ecuador, which he had just conquered and where he surrounded himself with a mercenary guard. He died in 1525 and left two sons from different wives, Washcar in Cuzco and Atawallpa in Ecuador. The northern provinces lined up behind Atawallpa, who defeated his half brother in a series of battles, the last at Cuzco. No sooner had he consolidated his imperial rule than the first outbreak of smallpox, a European disease, struck the domains of the Inka. Native peoples exposed to the first Spanish explorers spread the sickness among the Andean peoples even before the Pizarro expedition of conquest arrived. This was the background to Atawallpa's trip in 1532 from Cuzco to Cajamarca to meet the strange visitors.

OTHER ANCIENT ANDEANS

Muisca

Although the Inka had not been a trading empire, other Andean groups maintained extensive commercial networks, including the agricultural peoples who inhabited the highland valleys of Colombia and Venezuela. In the midst of the linguistic and cultural diversity of this region, one group succeeded in beginning to develop an advanced civilization: the Muisca, a Chibcha people. The peoples of Colombia followed a different trajectory of civilization than the Aztec and Inka, one marked by more decentralization and independence in political development. They built no cities, achieved only modest craftsmanship in pottery and textiles, practiced relatively simple religious rituals with a small class of priests, and erected no stone monuments that endure. However, when the Spaniards arrived early in the sixteenth century, they found the numerous Muisca united under a sophisticated rulership and a class of elite families.

The homeland of the Muisca was in what are now the Colombian states of Boyacá and Cundinamarca, roughly the area stretching out north and south of modern-day Bogotá. Nearly 1 million Muisca lived here. They farmed their lands extensively, utilizing the universal digging stick as the principal tool and raising corn and quinoa as their staple foods.[3] However, the climate did not support the domesticated llama, and the potato was not a common item in their diet. The nobility of the Muisca and that of other highland and lowland groups in Colombia, Ecuador, and Venezuela engaged in a great deal of commerce among themselves. Several villages within the Muisca territory supported markets for the barter of goods, for these people had no currency. Dried fish arrived from Panama; exotic fruits, from the Magdalena River Valley; gold trinkets, from the area of modern Medellín; and silver ornaments, from Pasto to the south. The Muisca traded in salt obtained from salt springs. Apparently these products had ritual and symbolic as well as economic meaning to the Muisca, for to possess them denoted social and religious rank as well as wealth.

---

[3] Quinoa is one of the sixty or so species of amaranth. Grain amaranths have black, red, or white seeds about the size of a poppy seed. Each plant can produce fifty thousand or more seeds. The dried flowers of the amaranths make a tealike beverage.

As previously mentioned, the Muisca were beginning to develop the attributes of civilization but had not yet completely succeeded upon the arrival of the Europeans. The society had divided itself hereditarily into classes of elites, commoners, and slaves captured in war. There were actually two Muisca kingdoms in the early sixteenth century, the Zipa in the north and the Zaque in the south. The rulers of these two polities enjoyed enormous privilege. They were carried on litters enclosed completely in glittering curtains of gold foil, all the more remarkable because gold was imported into Muisca territory from other regions of Colombia. Each ruler was capable of collecting the tribute of thousands of subjects and of raising armies of five hundred to one thousand men. The peoples of central Colombia had never been made part of the Inka empire, principally because they never had to confront the Inka armies. The latter in fact had been stopped from entering southern Colombia by the fiercely independent chiefdoms at Pasco. Nonetheless, their military prowess and cultural resistance would soon be tested when Spaniards arrived in 1536. The Muisca put up little initial resistance, and in time their language and separate identity disappeared.

Mapuche

The opposite circumstance would be the fate of the Mapuche, an agricultural people at the other end of the Andes Mountains. The predecessors of these inhabitants of southern Chile were already living there 15,000 years ago, at the end of the last Ice Age. Archaeologists recently uncovered a campsite for about fifty persons dating from this time, complete with stone-tipped spears and remains of wild game and items traded from other regions. Among other game, these hunters lived off the hairy, long-tusked mastodon. They had already developed a hunting weapon called the *bolas*, three stones bound together by long leather thongs, that was flung to entangle the legs of fleeing prey. Soon thereafter the mastodon died off, and the Mapuche (also known as Araucano) had to develop other means of subsistence. They benefited from agricultural breakthroughs elsewhere, gradually adopting the cultivation of corn, potatoes, and peppers—each plant acclimated to conditions found in the temperate forests and valleys along the southern coasts of Chile. Game and fish supplemented their diet, so the Mapuche were able to settle in relatively permanent villages. The inhabitants of this region did not have to engage in slash-and-burn agriculture, as did tropical peoples, because the fields cleared of trees could be used annually with proper crop rotation. Their deities represented the forces of nature and the harvest, which the shamans appeased with animal sacrifices and food offerings. Masked dancers warded off evil spirits. With stone tools only, the Mapuche harvested the wood with which they constructed homes, corrals for llamas, and defensive palisades. These people occasionally carried out raids on neighboring villages, even though those villagers were of the same Mapuche cultural and linguistic family.

These same forts and warlike independence would serve the Mapuche well when the Inka armies extended their conquests into the central valley of Chile in the fifteenth century. The outside threat sufficed to unite the feuding Mapuche groups for an effective defense of the home territory. Usually, the leaders had little control over their subjects and warriors. "They had no recognized right to inflict punishment, to claim tribute or personal service, or to demand obedience from their kinsfolk or subjects," observed an early Spaniard. "The latter paid no attention to them and did as they pleased if the leaders showed themselves arrogant or domineering." Nonetheless, to stop the Inka armies, they elected war chiefs to lead several allied groups and mobilized large forces of warriors. These same Mapuche were later to aggressively and effectively maintain their independence from European conquest, not submitting to outside authority until 1882 to the independent Republic of Chile. All during this long period of resistance, they rejected European religion and even engaged in defensive expansion across the Andes into Patagonia and the Pampas of Argentina.

THE TROPICAL AGRICULTURISTS

The Ancient Brazilians

In all the territories covered by Brazil today, at the end of the fourteenth century, an estimated 6 million people lived in the area today covered by Brazil. The region drained by the Amazon River, Amazonia, dominated the landscape. The Amazon is the world's largest river, discharging fifteen times the volume of water of the Mississippi River. A dense forest canopy covered most of Amazonia, an area equivalent to the continental United States. Here lived forest peoples engaging in slash-and-burn cultivation, riverbank farming of a variety of crops, and hunting and fishing; they also collected the numerous tropical plants and fruits. As elsewhere in the Americas, these various groups existed in constant skirmishes between and among themselves. The tribes of Brazil belonged to four major language groups: The Tupí inhabited the vast stretches of the Atlantic coast; the Carib lived in the regions north of the Amazon River, spilling into Venezuela and the Guineas; the Gê peoples resided in the central plateau stretching out toward Paraguay and Bolivia; and Aruak-speaking groups inhabited the vast interior of the Amazon Basin. Moreover, via migration, the Aruak linguistic hegemony reached through Venezuela into the Caribbean islands.

Most of these tropical peoples lived in semipermanent villages spread out across the great expanses of rain forest. Although territorial, these agriculturists moved their shelters every two to three years, leaving the land to lie fallow. Councils of elders and religious shamans maintained political control among several related villages. Besides walking, the canoe provided their basic mode of transportation, and they shared similar diets (cultivated manioc, corn, pumpkins, beans, and squashes combined with wild game and freshwater fish). The starchy root plant called manioc or cassava could be stored for many months and became the basic foodstuff. It was boiled whole and ground into meal. Men cleared the land for cultivation, hunted and fished, and trained for warfare, while it fell to the women to cultivate the crops, prepare the food, and care for the children. Large huts accommodated several extended families having few possessions other than weapons, rudimentary tilling sticks, and hammocks on which to sleep.

The competition for hunting ground and subsistence kept the various tribes in conflict among themselves. Battles were fought to capture prisoners for ritual execution. They believed that by devouring their enemies, they also captured their power and strength, although human sacrifice in Amazonia never reached the systematic levels of the Aztec. Of course, the cycle of warfare and competition for space had proceeded in this fashion for generations. No imperial state arose on a base of intensive agriculture that

Native canoe in Brazil. (Johann Moritz Rugendas, ca. 1830)

could subjugate and forcibly unite the competing groups of Brazil. The rainy climate, dense forests, and fragile soil prevented organized farming, especially given the plant varieties available. There was no food surplus that could support tribute, a ruling nobility, and complex religious practices.

Archaeological evidence in the form of pottery and tools found in Brazilian caves and mounds indicate that more advanced societies had existed in 1000 B.C. than the ones that the Europeans encountered there in A.D. 1500. However, we know little of these early peoples because, unlike the Chavín and the Inka, they left few monuments. They constructed their homes, containers, tools, and artwork from perishable materials such as plants, wood, feathers, and animal parts. But what record remains of Amazonia before the common era indicates sophistication and advancement. What could account for the apparent decline? Perhaps the population had outgrown the resource base, forcing the various groups into a destructive fight for territory and resources. Perhaps there was a famine. We can only speculate.

The peoples of prehistoric Brazil certainly knew and practiced agriculture. They engaged in slash-and-burn planting, cultivating manioc on flood plains and riverbanks. But in the Amazon rain forests, heavy downpours leach the thin soils, and thick vegetation competes for dominion over food plants. There were no domesticated animals like the guinea pigs or llamas of Peru that thrived naturally in the tropics. Moreover, like other American peoples, the tribes inhabiting the tropics had no knowledge of metal tools that might have helped them fight the thick vegetation. Yet they sustained life creatively, utilizing what nature offered. The forests contained fruits and birds, and the rivers teemed with fish and manatees. Those groups strong enough to command the fertile riverbanks or sea coasts enjoyed a relatively sedentary and prosperous existence. The other groups lived more precariously—and nomadically—in the marshes and drier plateaus.

One thing is certain: These groups competed incessantly among themselves for territory and resources. Warriors became the most respected members of their societies, and they carried on raiding and warfare on a continuous basis. The military competition between contiguous groups unrelated by language and culture became so fierce that they often left buffer zones of unsettled land between themselves. But raids were even common among related groups. Populations ebbed and flowed and changed locations based not only on hunting and gathering but also on warfare. It was not without cause that the Tupí surrounded their villages with timber balustrades.

Consequently, warriors revered for their prowess at killing and capturing the enemy became the chieftains of most tribes. However, they seldom became despotic, because most decisions were made by a council of elders that consisted of warriors over 40 years of age. The constant battling, mainly a male activity, meant that women outnumbered men in most villages. Intercommunity raids also provided brides to ensure endogamy. Chieftains, shamans, and accomplished warriors had two or more wives and numerous children. Women represented wealth because they labored at fashioning the handicrafts and raising the food plants that sustained the family and the clan; moreover, clan leaders desired many children on whom to rely to sustain their leadership. But most young men, unproved in battle, started out in monogamous marriages.

Gê

In the vast upland shield of dry forests and prairies live the many tribes belonging to the Gê peoples. They may have been the original inhabitants of Brazil, for some of the oldest human remains found there exhibit Gê physical characteristics. But in the several centuries before the European encounter, they were on the defensive against the Tupí in most parts of Brazil. The Gê lived in more scattered and smaller groups than the Tupí, inhabiting the less fertile lands far from the riverbanks. The young men became magnificent runners, capable of pursuing and killing game on the savannas. As a result, the Gê peoples enjoyed races.

In their isolated locations, they proved very resistant to annihilation first by Tupí and later by Europeans. The Gê peoples fought to defend their territory with hit-and-run tactics, using stealth and camouflage to fall on unsuspecting enemies and then disappear by running across the savanna and through the forest. Women, too, escaped capture through mobility and evasion. Adept at the use of the large bow, the men could shoot arrows at their adversaries from great distances. These peoples aggressively defended their remaining territories inland from the coast from Tupí encroachment and would do the same when the Portuguese arrived. Many Gê groups survived independently in the interior of Brazil into the twentieth century, although their lifestyles would change radically because of European intrusion.

Tupí

The dominant cultural and linguistic group found along the coast from the mouth of the Amazon down nearly to the Río de la Plata—and in certain areas, extending into the hinterlands—was the Tupí. The Tupí and their linguistic cousins, the Guaraní, may have originated in the foothills of the Andes Mountains and slowly moved into present-day Paraguay and the Brazilian coasts during the first millennium B.C. They displaced the original inhabitants as they progressed. Their villages, made up of extended clans and numbering several hundred people, were organized in extended households in four thatched huts surrounding an open plaza. Within each large hut, individual families maintained an area for their cooking fires and sleeping hammocks. In the absence of material possessions, communal harmony reigned, and food was shared equally. Men hunted and fished; women tilled the soil, cooked, and cared for the children. Men made and rowed canoes and constructed bows and arrows. Women wove the baskets and maintained hammocks and households. Therefore, the job specialization among the Tupí paralleled the strictly gender-specific separation of tasks common to other American peoples.

Finally, the Tupí shared a commitment to conformity for the sake of survival. Athleticism among men was prized, and abnormal infants were killed at birth. The community frowned on nonconformity, and the council of elders could condemn individualists to death. The shamans were particularly vigilant in rooting out those who differed from the norm. Conforming behavior ensured that traditions and practices would endure almost unchanged through centuries as each group grappled with the immediate task of eking out a living from the harsh environment amidst competition from rival tribes (see Manuscript 2.3).

Guaraní

Bands of Tupí-Guaraní inhabited the tropic rain forests of present-day northeastern Argentina, Paraguay, and southern Brazil (see Map 2.2). They probably emigrated from Amazonia in 200 B.C., at the time of Teotihuacán in Mexico. These people of the rain forests and rivers developed an economy based on hunting, fishing, and slash-and-burn agricul-

MANUSCRIPT 2.3

Description of the Tupí

Much of our knowledge of the tropical agriculturists of South America comes from descriptions of early European settlers and missionaries, the first of whom accompanied the Cabral Expedition landing on the Brazilian coast in 1500. One of the passengers on that voyage was Pero Vaz de Caminha. His description of the aborigines illustrates how different they were from the Europeans, although he said that their conversion to Catholicism was desirable. Also, the nakedness of the ancient Brazilian both repelled and amused these early chroniclers, and most of their editorial comments and value judgments say more about themselves than about the people they were attempting to describe. Note that the Europeans' obsession about gold may not necessarily reflect the place of precious metals in the lives of the Tupí themselves.

They are of a dark brown, rather reddish colour. They have good well-made faces and noses. They go naked, with no sort of covering. They attach no more importance to covering up their private parts or leaving them uncovered than they do to showing their faces. They are very ingenuous in that matter. [Two native men] both had holes in their lower lips and a bone in them as broad as the knuckles of a hand and as thick as a cotton spindle and sharp at one end like a bodkin. They put these bones in from inside the lip and the part which is placed between the lip and the teeth is made like a rook in chess. They fit them in such a way that they do not hurt them nor hinder them talking or eating or drinking. . . .

For all that, one of them gazed at the admiral's [gold] collar and began to point towards the land and then at the collar as if he

ture. They cut the trees, burned off the underbrush, planted for several years, and then moved on to another area while the rain forest growth returned and replenished the fertility of the abandoned patch. The various tasks of cultivation fell to the women, who raised corn, beans, sweet potatoes, peanuts, squash, and especially manioc. Extended families resided together in their long houses, large straw-thatched huts. As many as fifty might live in the house of a more important family. Everyone slept in hammocks suspended from the poles that held up the roof. For protection from raiders, wooden palisades surrounded the villages of twenty to thirty long houses. Clothes made of feathers and animal skins warded off the winter's cold. In the summer months, men and women were accustomed to go about their chores entirely naked.

Like other peoples of ancient America, the Guaraní observed strict gender specificity as regarded social roles. Besides farming, women were in charge of preparing the meals, rearing the children, weaving baskets, and making pottery. Guaraní women also made the *chicha,* a fermented beer brewed with corn and human saliva. When it was used in religious observances, virgin girls brewed the *chicha* as a method of ensuring that no harm would befall the village. Men engaged in hunting and fishing and developed skills as warriors; in fact, the word *Guaraní* means "warrior." The more prestigious chieftains and accomplished warriors practiced polygamy, having large households of up to nine wives. Most men, however, had only one wife. Unlike the males, women faced death if caught in adultery, although they were able to separate from their husbands.

wished to tell us that there was gold in the country. And he also looked at a silver candlestick and pointed at the land in the same way, and at the candlestick, as if there was silver there, too. . . . We took it in this sense, because we preferred to. . . .

As they afterwards related, [three Portuguese men] went a good league and a half to a hamlet of nine or ten houses. They said those houses were each as big as this flagship. They were made of wooden planks sideways on, had roofs of straw, and were fairly high. Each enclosed a single space with no partitions, but a number of posts. High up from post to post ran nets, in which they slept. Down below they lit fires to warm themselves. Each house had two little doors, one at one end and one at the other. Our men said that thirty or forty people were lodged in each house. . . .

They do not plough or breed cattle. There are no oxen here, nor goats, sheep, fowls, nor any other animal accustomed to live with man. They only eat this [manioc], which is very plentiful here, and those seeds and fruits that the earth and the trees give of themselves. . . .

My opinion and every one's opinion is that these people lack nothing to become completely Christian except understanding us; for they accepted as we do all they saw us do, which makes us consider that they have no idolatry or worship. . . . Therefore, if any one is coming out here, let him not omit to bring a clergyman to baptize them.

SOURCE: E. Bradford Burns, ed., *A Documentary History of Brazil* (New York: Alfred A. Knopf, 1966), 25.

Map 2.2   Forest Agriculturists and Southern Hunters of South America

Politically, each group of Guaraní inhabited a defined area of territory, on which its allied clans could hunt, fish, and engage in slash-and-burn agriculture. Fighting between groups was common. Raiding and stealing formed part of the contest for human survival in the forests. Therefore, individual warriors came to share some of the political authority within the groups with shamans, the spiritual leaders, and the hereditary chieftains. Poison-tipped bows and arrows, wooden clubs, and spears were the weapons of choice for hunting and raiding. Few material possessions seemed to separate the Guaraní leaders from the followers, for tropical agriculture yielded much less surplus compared with field agriculture in Mexico and Peru. Notions of reciprocity were maintained, although hereditary chiefs and shamans usually enjoyed some material advantage over commoners, with whom they were expected to share gifts. Chiefs and shamans had more wives to labor for the household, which increased their wealth.

Warfare was central to the male's socialization within his kin group. Guaraní boys customarily carried bows and arrows from childhood and studied animals and hunting as a way to perfect their knowledge of combat. Raids and individual hostilities between members of neighboring clan groups were a constant feature of life in the rain forests. However, hostilities between the semisedentary Guaraní and the nomadic groups in Argentina and the Chaco proceeded on a low-intensity basis most of the time.

Local mythology maintained that Tupí and Guaraní were brothers. Tupí, the elder brother, stayed in the homeland of Amazonia, while the younger one, Guaraní, moved south to settle in the lands drained by the Paraná, Paraguay, and Uruguay rivers. Although approximately eleven different groups of Guaraní lived in the region, they all shared a common language and had similar customs and cultural beliefs. Moreover, their pottery and dress were similar, traits that they also shared with the Tupí of Brazil, who spoke a different dialect of the same language. Both the Tupí and the Guaraní were known to practice a ritual form of cannibalism that symbolically strengthened them to do battle with rival tribes. Each member of the clan cooked and tasted enemies captured in battle, a practice sustaining a kind of vendetta in which the offended group would retaliate for the loss of its individuals.

Like their Tupí cousins, the Guaraní were also animistic in religious thought and practice. They identified the natural forces such as the sun, the sky, thunder, lightning, and rain as deities. Often a deity might take on the form of animals and especially of birds, the latter of which held special sacred meanings for the peoples of the rain forests. The Guaraní often named their children for the birds and animals of the forest. Shamans might invoke these spirits in order to bring individuals success in love, battle, and the harvest. Evil, pain, and death were also associated with deities. Therefore, offerings, ritual dances, chants, and charms were used to ward off the darker forces of the universe. Male and female shamans practiced rituals and developed herbal remedies to combat sickness and injury. Special ceremonies were used by the Guaraní to venerate their ancestors, whose remains were always buried close by to give comfort and a place in the cosmos for their progeny.

Aruak[4]

The Aruak, a large linguistic and cultural group became well established in northern Brazil and Venezuela. By 5000 B.C., they were moving up from one Caribbean island to another

---

[4] Also known as Arawak and Arauá.

until they reached Florida. Other migratory waves followed, bringing new cultures and tools. These peoples were particularly at home on rivers and the sea, using their skills with the canoe to fish and trade. The Aruak were also a tropical agricultural people who grew manioc, squash, beans, and peppers on raised beds of soil called *conucos.* They lived quite simple lives without the use of clothes. However, they perfected the art of body painting and feather decorating. Also, the warriors often tattooed their bodies and wore disks in the ears and mouth in order to appear as formidable fighters to their enemies. The shamans served as intermediaries between the community and the various deities and spirits of the supernatural world. They led tribal ceremonies, dances, and healing. Shamans gained stature in being able to predict the outcomes of battles and to foresee floods. Incorrect predictions sometimes cost shamans their reputation—and their lives. The enemy of these agriculturists were the aggressive and cannibalistic Carib, who alone among the tropic people did not cultivate crops extensively and who raided the Aruak settlements in the Caribbean, Venezuela, and Brazil.

At the time of contact with Europeans, the Aruak in the Caribbean were known as Taíno. Cultural influences of the Aruak on Puerto Rico, Hispaniola, Cuba, and other Caribbean islands remained very much South American. However, they carried on trade with Mesoamerican peoples with their long canoes. They probably adopted a game they played with a rubber ball on constructed courts from the Maya. The Taíno lived in settled villages headed by a leader called a *cacique.* He took charge of the storage and distribution of goods and foodstuffs and carried on trade and political affairs with neighboring villages. All of the *cacique*s were polygamous, whereas most commoners among the Taíno were monogamous. Also there remained a clear distinction between common peasants and family members of the Taíno caciques, who supervised workers and were carried about on litters. Europeans later attempted to usurp the privileges of this upper class, adopting the Taíno term *naborío* to refer to a personal servant. Above these village leaders reigned a regional head *cacique.* He assumed responsibility for maintaining the peace and mediating disputes between villages and also coordinated military operations against the remaining pockets of non-Aruak peoples and Carib raiders.

Meanwhile, another group called the Moxo (pronounced MO-hoe) occupied the southern end of the Aruak archipelago in the tropical savannas nestled astride the Andean foothills of Bolivia. Magnificent stands of tropical trees populated the riverbanks, while the grasslands between were flooded and parched by the alternating seasons of rain and drought. True to Amazonian principles and as the dominant group in the area, the Moxo inhabited the riverbanks. Living in small, permanent settlements of up to two hundred people on riverbank deposits and planting in raised fields nearby, they cultivated manioc, squash, peanuts, beans, peppers, and yams. The lowest portions of Moxo territory remained marshy year-round. Birds, deer, armadillos, manatees, and freshwater dolphins provided additional sources of food.

Canoes served as the Moxo's main mode of transport and refuge in times of flooding, when they merely tied their hammocks higher in the trees to sleep above the rising waters. The women were particularly adept at weaving mats, baskets, and feather garments and at making ceramic vessels for cooking and food storage. Village society lacked rigid social structures, and the chieftainships were not hereditary. But the Moxo were only the most dominant of perhaps thirty other Indian groups—most of whom spoke different Aruak dialects. These groups skirmished incessantly with the Moxo and among themselves. Several smaller non-Aruak groups lived on the less hospitable savannas, having been displaced from the riverbanks when, several centuries before the time of contact with Europeans, the Moxo moved into the region.

THE SOUTHERN HUNTERS

In the forests, plains, riverbanks, and sea coasts of southern South America lived bands of primarily hunting and gathering peoples. They contrasted starkly with the agricultural peoples of the Andean highlands in that they accumulated little surplus, developed few social divisions, resided in dispersed and migratory groups, battled constantly with each other to control hunting territories, and lived within the constraints of the natural environment. Because they followed game, none of these groups built permanent towns or ceremonial centers, living instead in temporary encampments. Although as military-minded and religious as the Maya or the Aztec, the southern hunters developed no distinct warrior or priestly classes. Their chieftains do not compare in authority and grandeur with the Inka Atawallpa. Their shamans, who specialized in paying homage to and influencing the numerous spirits, did not develop the knowledge or ritual refinements, for example, of the priests of the Mexican rain god Tláloc. In many ways, the southern hunters were akin to the Chichimec of northern Mexico.

Some of these innumerable hunter bands were culturally and linguistically related to each other. However, the complete lack of imperialism among them meant that no one group ever conquered the others and imposed its common beliefs and language on them. Despite mutual hostilities and severe language differences, the hunter-gatherers of southern South America did trade among themselves and share knowledge. But in their adaptability to their often harsh environment and in their political decentralization lay the secret of their enduring autonomy. The hunter-gatherers presented no fixed target to be conquered by the Andean armies of the Inka Empire—or by each other, for that matter. These ancient Americans pursued lives of splendid, if impoverished, independence.

Chaco

The first major group of the southern hunters resided in the Gran Chaco region, which is the great depression between the Bolivian Andes Mountains, the Brazilian massif, the rocky hills along the Paraguay river, and the Cordobá mountains of present-day Argentina. It is not a region conducive to tilling. The numerous marshes of the Gran Chaco spill into and flood the surrounding grasslands during the rainy season, leaving a thin crust of salt on the land. During much of the rest of the year, the rainfall supports little vegetation, although thick tropical woodlands bound the Gran Chaco on at least two sides. Numerous cultural and linguistic groups inhabited this sparse landscape at the time of contact with Europeans. These groups are known as the Chaco only because they all were hunters occupying the same geographical location. Certainly, the Chaco groups displayed much variation among themselves. Each band had its own distinctive tattooing and body decoration, both for men and women. A group called the Payaguá lived at the headwaters of the Paraguay River. The men of the Payaguá were particularly adept at handling canoes, which they used in fishing, hunting, and raiding.

We know that the Chaco peoples came to the border villages of the Andean civilizations to barter animal skins and ostrich (rhea) and egret feathers for gold, silver, and copper ornaments. Through trade and exchange, these same Andean products found their way east and south to the peoples of the Argentine pampas. At the same time, some of the hunters who lived near the Andean kingdom even hired themselves out to the Inka as itinerant agricultural workers. Only one group in the Chaco region, the Guaná, were farmers; they cultivated root crops, especially the cassava plant, and tobacco, which they cured and crushed into a coarse powder and smoked in pipes. (Few Chaco groups chewed coca leaves like the Andeans.) But the Guaná's sedentary and peaceful nature rendered them vulnerable to attack by their neighbors. Conquered by various bands of Mbayá, another people of the Chaco, the Guaná villages paid tribute in crops to their conquerors, while also receiving their protection from the depredations of other groups.

Each of the seven major and numerous minor cultural and linguistic groups in the Gran Chaco also maintained rituals representing its own beliefs about its relation to the cosmos. Certain rites of passage related to manhood and menstruation initiated the youth into full participation in village affairs. Like all other ancient Americans, the Chaco were polytheistic. Several groups especially worshipped one mythological character, Chamacoco, whom they construed to be something like a supreme god. She was the mother of many spirits who kept the sun from burning the earth and provided water. However, good and evil spirits and ghosts were believed to exist everywhere, in nature, in animals, and in the heavens. The shaman chanted and led dances to placate the harmful spirits and bring good luck to the camp. The herbal and chanting arts of the male shamans, and, in some cases, female shamans, served also to cure the sick.

The community divided tasks by gender. Women constructed the temporary shelters, wove baskets, and made crude pottery. Only the leaders had more than one wife; otherwise, monogamy prevailed. Men honed their skills at warfare and hunted deer, peccaries, tapir, jaguars, and nutria. Boys caught fish in baskets or shot them with bows and arrows. Besides using tobacco, some groups brewed an alcoholic drink from the carob-like pods of the algarroba tree.

As among other tribes of pre-Columbian America, the typical Chaco band of fifty to one hundred people made major decisions by consensus, with the chieftain merely carrying out the decision of the band's adult males. Though individuals may have lived in concert with nature, the hunting groups never existed in peace and harmony among themselves. They were vulnerable to seasonal variations in the availability of game and to internal population growth. These factors placed the small hunting band under constant pressure to expand its living space.

To avenge some territorial encroachment, the warriors preferred to launch their raids in the early morning when the offending neighbor village would be fast asleep. The leader of the band would announce the need for a foray by saying, "It is time to avenge the death of our kinsman." Before battle, the warriors selected a young chieftain to lead the charge. Warfare seldom amounted to complete extermination. It is true that warriors killed and scalped their rivals to make war trophies for the victory dance. In some cases, an enemy's head was removed, and the skull was converted into a drinking cup. But Chaco raiders usually retreated after suffering a few casualties; they brought captured women and children into the victorious band. Slavery was not unknown among them. One group's constant raids on another, however, would cause the second group to move into marginal land or to take territory from a third group. Despite the fact that the hunters preferred to live in the vicinity of their ancestors' burial sites, the groups over time were continually moving and adjusting to each other.

Charrúa

A second major group of southern hunters inhabited the region of present-day Uruguay, southern Brazil, and northeastern Argentina. On the eve of the European conquest, the Charrúa consisted of five distinct yet linguistically related peoples. Like most other southern hunters, the Charrúa did not practice agriculture but lived on game, fish, wild fruits, and roots. They made their houses of woven mats hung between pole frames. Fond of tattooing and painting their bodies, especially for battle, the Charrúa dressed in skins during the winter and wore just a leather apron in the summer. Like many other prairie hunters, the Charrúa also placed feathers and shells in their pierced lips, ears, and noses. Large canoes facilitated fishing on the rivers and in the estuary of the Río de la Plata. In 1531, a Portuguese mariner noted that the canoes of the Charrúa "were 10 to 12 fathoms [approximately 21 meters] in length and half a fathom [1 meter] in width; the wood was cedar, very beautifully worked; they rowed them with very long paddles decorated by crests and tassels of feathers on the handles; and 40 standing men rowed each canoe." The men hunted with bows and arrows, spears, and bolas. They were very skilled at slinging jagged stones at large and small game.

These hunting groups tended to live rather dispersed lives on the grasslands of Uruguay. Eight to ten family members inhabited each hut, with eight to twelve families roaming a general hunting ground together. Two or more roving groups might band together for warfare but otherwise kept to themselves. The chiefs did not have much authority in the hunting band, and fistfights sufficed to settle individual disputes. In battle, their warriors were merciless to the opponents but also incorporated captured women and children into their bands.

Pampas and Patagonia

In the expansive prairies that make up what today is Argentina, small bands of hunter-gatherers predominated. They hunted native animals such as deer, guanacos, armadillos, prairie dogs, and South American ostriches. In the woodlands, gathering seeds and hunting deer formed the basis of existence. Peoples along the extensive Paraná, Uruguay, and Paraguay rivers fished from canoes and rafts. In the extreme south, in Patagonia, coastal peoples also hunted seals and fished from canoes. For many centuries, life had been much the same for them.

Just before the arrival of the Europeans, the larger of these cultural groups, such as the Querandí, Puelche, and Tehuelche, inhabited the Argentine Pampas and Patagonia. These Indians moved on foot and set up camps according to the seasons and hunting possibilities. They lived with little accumulation of surplus. Their tools were simple, usually bone and stone weapons and scrapers, and they lived in *toldos*, unelaborated tents. The Indians of the Argentine prairies would become known for one unique weapon—the bolas. With the bolas, they brought down ostrich, guanaco, and other large game. The hunter whirled the bolas around the head and flung them at his prey so as to entangle the legs. He then made the kill with a club or spear.

As among the Charrúa to the north, the principal groups of the Pampas and Patagonia were quite small, made up of only a few families or clans. There existed neither great confederations of tribes nor a differentiation of their simple societies into priest, warrior, and peasant classes. Families were tightly knit and patriarchal, with women subordinate to men who, for the most part, were monogamous. Women cooked, cleaned game, cared for the children and *toldos,* wove baskets, and made simple pottery. Men and women alike shared the duties of gathering and preparing food, and basic decisions within the groups were made by a council. As hunters and warriors, the men dominated the decision making and carried out raids between neighboring groups.

CONCLUDING REMARKS

The characteristics of the indigenous population mattered very much to the subsequent history of the Americas under European domination. Even the most elemental ethnography of Meso- and South America could predict at least the general outlines of the coming conquest. The following chapters will demonstrate that the relative degrees of population density, political unification, and wealth as well as settlement patterns helped determine how the European invasions of the sixteenth century would proceed. In some cases, the invaders would be able to build towns and cities directly over the ruins of indigenous settlements that they had just destroyed, and they would be able to tap into existing agricultural and commercial networks. The conquest would be dramatically quick and successful at the centers of the Aztec and Inka empires. On the other hand, where the pre-Columbian population lived in dispersed and decentralized patterns, the subsequent European settlement would demand a longer-term commitment and substantial rearrangement of social and economic relationships. The newcomers would have to take their time, settling regions over the span of several centuries and constructing towns and farms from scratch in the wilderness. Europeans here would have to settle areas that were once home to tropical agriculturists and hunter-gathers in ways that the original inhabitants never did. Brazil, Argentina, Chile, and northern Mexico come to mind.

Finally, pre-Columbian languages, gender relationships, religious beliefs, rivalries, ethnic diversity, and cultural and material contributions—all of which were already thousands of years old—would endure the coming Conquest. All indigenous peoples of the Americas were quite experienced at the arts of resistance and accommodation. As dominant groups, they had learned how to assimilate and work around the religious beliefs and local customs of subordinated peoples. As the subordinated, they had learned how to accept certain practices of their new overlords while preserving their own ways of doing things. Certain tools, foods, habits, modes of transportation, religious beliefs, and social relationships of the ancient Americans would also influence and transform the European invaders because these established native traditions suited the American environment.

These first two chapters have mentioned the effects of famine and warfare on the ancient Americans but not disease—and for good reason. Because of their isolation, the ancient Americans had escaped the ravages of African, European, and Asian epidemics that produced the historic phenomena of the Great Plague and the Black Death. Native Americans had not developed any immunities whatsoever to diseases such as measles, smallpox, mumps, typhus, and diphtheria. The arrival of the Europeans in 1492 unleashed for the first time a terrible wave of multiple epidemics upon the indigenous populations.

Most ancient Americans underwent these ravages within the first century of the European arrival; the most isolated native groups, however, would not bear the brunt of these diseases until the nineteenth and twentieth centuries. But there was to be no escape. The effects of these new diseases would be most devastating in tropical areas, where the aboriginal population faced near extinction as a result. Only in the temperate zones and in colder climates would indigenous peoples survive, eventually regain their numbers, and reconstitute their rich cultural heritage.

The resilience and adaptability of pre-Columbian people served to ensure that they might be vanquished but never subdued—and certainly never eliminated from historical importance. For this reason, the 1492 voyage of Columbus began an encounter rather than a discovery and conquest.

Additional Reading

Bauer, Brian S. *The Development of the Inca State*. Austin: University of Texas Press, 1992.

Burger, Richard L. *Chavín and the Origins of Andean Civilization*. New York: Thames and Hudson, 1992.

Classen, Constance. *Inca Cosmology and the Human Body*. Salt Lake City: University of Utah Press, 1993.

Conrad, Geoffrey W., and Arthur A. Demarest. *Religion and Empire: The Dynamics of Aztec and Inca Expansionism*. Cambridge, England: Cambridge University Press, 1984.

D'Altroy, Terence N. *Provincial Power in the Inka Empire*. Washington, D.C.: Smithsonian Institution Press, 1992.

Davies, Nigel. *The Incas*. Boulder: University Press of Colorado, 1995.

Denevan, William M. *The Native Population of the Americas in 1492*. 2d ed. Madison: University of Wisconsin Press, 1992.

Denevan, William M., et al., eds. *Pre-Hispanic Agricultural Fields in the Andean Region*. Oxford, England: B.A.R., 1987.

Garcilaso de la Vega [the Inka]. *Royal Commentaries of the Incas and General History of Peru (1609)*. Trans. Harold V. Livermore. Austin: University of Texas Press, 1970.

Hass, Jonathan, Shelia Pozorski, and Thomas Pozorski, eds. *The Origins and Development of the Andean State*. Cambridge, England: Cambridge University Press, 1987.

Hastorf, Christine Ann. *Agriculture and the Onset of Political Inequality before the Inka*. New York: Cambridge University Press, 1993.

Hyslop, John. *Inka Settlement Planning*. Austin: University of Texas Press, 1990.

———. *The Inka Road System*. Orlando, Fla.: Academic Press, 1984.

Josephy, Alvin M., Jr. *America in 1492: The World of the Indian Peoples before the Arrival of Columbus*. New York: Vintage Books, 1993.

Katz, Friedrich. *The Ancient American Civilizations*. Trans. K. M. Lois Simpson. New York: Praeger, 1972.

Malpass, Michael A. *Daily Life in the Inca Empire*. Westport, Conn.: Greenwood Press, 1996.

Moseley, Michael E. *The Incas and Their Ancestors: The Archaeology of Peru*. New York: Thames and Hudson, 1992.

Patterson, Thomas C. *The Inca Empire: The Formation and Disintegration of a Pre-Capitalist State*. New York: Berg, 1992.

Roosevelt, Anna C., ed. *Amazonian Indians from Prehistory to the Present: Anthropological Perspectives*. Tucson: University of Arizona Press, 1995.

———. *Parmana: Prehistoric Maize and Manioc Subsistence along the Amazon and Orinoco*. New York: Academic Press, 1980.

Rouse, Irving. *The Tainos: Rise and Decline of the People Who Greeted Columbus*. New Haven, Conn.: Yale University Press, 1992.

Salomon, Frank. *Native Lords of Quito in the Age of the Incas: The Political Economy of North Andean Chiefdoms*. Cambridge, England: Cambridge University Press, 1986.

Shimada, Izumi. *Pampa Grande and the Mochica Culture*. Austin: University of Texas Press, 1994.

Steward, Julian H., ed. *Handbook of South American Indians*. Vol. 1. New York: Cooper Square, 1963.

Urton, Gary. *At the Crossroads of the Earth and Sky: An Andean Cosmology*. Austin: University of Texas Press, 1981.

Wilson, Samuel M. *Hispaniola: Caribbean Chiefdoms in the Age of Columbus*. Tuscaloosa, AL: University of Alabama Press, 1990.

———, ed. *The Indigenous People of the Caribbean*. Gainesville: University Press of Florida, 1997.

Zuidema, R. Tom. *Inca Civilization in Cuzco*. Trans. Jean-Jacques Decoster. Austin: University of Texas Press, 1990.

In Spanish and Portuguese

Espinoza Soriano, Waldemar. *Los Incas: Economía, sociedad y estado en la era del Tahuantinsuyu*. La Victoria, Peru: Amaru Editores, 1987.

Fernandes, Florestan. *A organização social dos Tupinambí*. São Paulo: Editora Hucitec, 1989.

Langabaeck, Carl Henrik. *Los Muiscas*. Bogotá: Banco de la República, 1987.

Murra, John V. *La organización económica del estado Inka*. Mexico City: Siglo Veintiuno, 1987.

Pease, G. Y. Franklyn. *Del Tawantinsuyu a la historia del Perú*. Lima: Instituto de Estudios Peruanos, 1978.

Rostworowski de Diez Canseco, María. *Etnia y sociedad: costa peruana prehispánica*. Lima: Instituto de Estudios Peruanos, 1977.

———. *Historia del Tahuantinsuyu*. 4th ed. Lima: Instituto de Estudios Peruanos, 1992.

CHAPTER 3

IBERIAN CONQUEST AND SETTLEMENT

The European arrival in the Americas, heralded by Columbus's first voyage in 1492, was no mere accident. It resulted from a long history of dynastic rivalries, expansion of commerce, technological breakthroughs in navigation, religious aggression, and the systematic accumulation of practical knowledge. Christian Iberians' previous experiences at warfare, religious conversion, and economic expansion on the European continent and the Atlantic islands conditioned these conquerors and settlers to conduct themselves in certain ways. By no means would their arrival in the Americas mark the Europeans' first encounter with peoples of different races and religions. In Iberia, Christians had been interacting with Muslims and Jews for many centuries.[1] Some even had African slaves. Most importantly, the first Europeans who launched the enterprise of conquest in the Americas treated it as being both a business matter and a religious crusade—with a decisive emphasis on business. The Spanish and Portuguese had been mingling these several notions during the Reconquest of the Iberian Peninsula from Islamic forces—a four-century process completed in the very year that Columbus set sail.

---

[1] Iberians refer to residents of the Iberian peninsula, today Spain and Portugal. As a country, Portugal evolved from the Kingdom of Portugal in 1348. At the time, Spain was divided into a number of competing kingdoms, one Islamic and the rest Christian. The nation of Spain, however, did not come into being until the early sixteenth century.

But the very conceit and arrogance of the Europeans in the Americas reveals much about their underlying attitudes. They believed that European ways were superior, rejecting native accomplishments as trivial and meaningless. The religion of the Europeans in the fifteenth century was the Catholicism of the Holy Roman Church. To Iberian Christians, their religion had become political, a sign of allegiance to the Christian kings and their source of strength in the struggle with the Muslims. Before their arrival in the Americas, Europeans already believed they were engaged in a crusade to destroy all competing religions as unworthy diversions of the devil. Iberians especially had a keen sense of religious mission. They felt little compunction at mercilessly killing non-Christians in battle yet would be appalled by the human sacrifice and cannibalism of the Americas.

Nonetheless, despite the accumulation of practical knowledge gained in the Old World, the newly arrived Spanish and Portuguese men-at-arms could not substitute for hearty veterans of warfare against indigenous Americans. The expeditions into Mexico and Peru, in particular, succeeded because their leaders were seasoned fighters and entrepreneurs with many years' prior experience in the Caribbean theater. Men such as Cortés and Pizarro had learned enough of Native American political structures and military tactics to be able to exploit their weaknesses. The best "Indian fighters" in Brazil were half-breeds who spoke the native language. Moreover, other factors helped to make up for the inferior number of Spaniards and Portuguese. They had access to military technology not known to the defenders—horses, iron and steel weaponry, gun powder, artillery, and sailing warships—and infected their enemies with crippling and devastating diseases. In addition, ethnic rivalries among the indigenous groups meant that the invaders could also find local allies to assist in conquest.

The very nature of native societies dictated where and how European conquest would proceed. Spaniards succeeded rapidly in conquering preexisting empires, such as those of the Aztec and the Inka. Where no previous empire existed and Native Americans lived in a state of semi-autonomous political decentralization, the conquest bogged down. Territories dominated by hunter-gatherers and tropical agriculturists had to be settled gradually rather than quickly subdued and overrun.

Yet the true secret of Iberian success resided in the determination of the individual conquerors. To them, colonizing the Americas represented business opportunity and a means for upward social mobility. They could either return to their hometowns as noblemen or create for themselves a status-conscious society not unlike the Iberian one from which they came but with one important difference: They themselves would be the new upper class, the nobility, the privileged grandees with power to command the labor and loyalty of retainers and the respect of the political authorities. All else was incidental. The acquisition of gold, the seizure of Native Americans, and the spread of Christianity were merely means to an end—not an end in themselves. The quest to dominate other people drove the invaders.

THE IBERIAN BACKGROUND

Historical circumstances prepared the two countries of the Iberian Peninsula to explore and settle colonial possessions before other European nations. Iberians belonged to the Roman Empire and spoke a vernacular Latin. In the third and fourth centuries, they also converted to Christianity, first in defiance of and then in concert with Roman rule. The

Germanic peoples known as Visigoths overran Iberia in A.D. 409 as the Roman Empire collapsed, but their language and religion remained very much the same. Then, as a manifestation of the effervescence of the Arab world in the eighth century, the Berbers of North Africa invaded the Iberian Peninsula. The followers of Mohammed reserved political privileges for themselves but showed remarkable tolerance toward the religious diversity of their subjects. They shared the improved agricultural techniques, superior crops, scientific and medical knowledge, and metallurgical craftsmanship of the vast Islamic world of the Middle East. By the ninth century, Christian peasants living under Berber control were converting to Islam in large numbers. Some who remained Christians migrated north.

In contrast to the Berber conquest, which had been sudden and complete, the Christian Reconquest of Iberia took a much longer time. The Berbers had not succeeded in bringing the Christian north of Spain under their control, but they still held some three-quarters of the peninsula. Their political unity in Iberia shattered in 1031 with the fall of the Caliphate (Islamic political state) of Córdoba. Thereafter, the Islamic rulers formed several independent and feuding kingdoms in the southern half of Iberia. Beginning in the eleventh century, the Christian kings of the north started to wrest the peninsula from Islamic control in a long process that became known as the *Reconquista*, or Reconquest. The Christians drove the Islamic rulers out of southwestern Iberia and secured their independence under the royal House of Avis in 1385. Already, the Latin vernacular spoken in this kingdom was departing from that of Castile and would become a separate but related language, Portuguese.

In the meanwhile, the kingdoms of Castile and Aragón had become the linchpins of the Spanish Reconquest. In 1236 and 1250, Castile seized Córdoba and Cádiz in southern Iberia. Now Islamic artisans and farmers and Jewish professionals and merchants faced having to convert to Christianity or to emigrate. The middle kingdom of Castile benefited most from the Reconquest, especially when its queen, Isabella, wed King Ferdinand of Aragón, thus uniting these two most important kingdoms in Spanish Iberia. In 1492, the Castilian forces of Isabella finally removed the last bastion of non-Christian power on the peninsula by conquering the Islamic Kingdom of Granada, located in the southeastern quadrant of Iberia.

During the long struggle against the Muslims, the citizens of what would become Portugal and Spain nurtured certain traditions of combat and conquest upon which their progeny called later to continue the process abroad. The Castilian nobility combined the arts and virtues of soldiering, valor, and service to Crown and Christianity with generous measures of self-aggrandizement. Ambitious nobles raised their own forces to fight the infidels. The victors were used to dividing up the spoils of victory and resettling conquered land while setting aside portions for king and clergy. The Crown repaid them with seigniorial titles, deeds to the land they had conquered, and promotion to prestigious military orders. The church provided the moral sanction for conquest, converting the long struggle into a crusade. Over the course of four centuries, these Christian warriors created not only the nations of Portugal and Spain but also an exaggerated notion of their own destiny. The nobility, in particular, grew intolerant of those who practiced Islam and Judaism and forced their monarchs to support policies calling for the conversion of Muslims and Jews or their emigration from conquered lands. Jews faced expulsion in the eventful year of 1492; the remaining Muslims, in 1502. The experience of the Reconquest developed a crusading fervor as well as economic opportunism among the Spaniards. These traditions passed on to the following generations through diffusion of ballads and popular literature extolling the virtues of bearing arms for the Christian cause. This literature would soon inspire those who sailed to the Americas.

Aside from conquest, a second Iberian tradition just reaching fruition in the late fifteenth century concerned trade. Venice and Genoa, the titans of commerce in the Mediterranean world, were entering a time of severe economic crisis. The expansion of the Ottoman Empire had severed their trade routes through the Middle East into Asia, jeopardizing their lucrative trade in spices, gold, and gemstones. Genoa desired to promote exploration and trade by going around Africa to the Indian subcontinent, bypassing the Middle East. Therefore, the Genoese merchant community forged alliances with Spanish traders at Seville and with Portuguese merchants at Lisbon. These allied commercial interests sponsored expeditions through the Mediterranean Sea into the Atlantic Ocean. Spain occupied the Canary Islands between 1478 and 1492, while the Portuguese took the Azores. In both island colonies, the Genoese established trading posts and introduced sugarcane. The expeditions that opened these commercial opportunities were privately financed but held exclusive rights of conquest under grants from the crown.

For the Spaniards, the Canary Islands had served as a training ground for their later—and much vaster—colonization of the Americas. They found a native population on the islands that resembled the Berbers of North Africa, although without the latter's technical advancement. Though they knew about agriculture, native Canary Islanders had no knowledge of metallurgy. They lived in small bands; the Spaniards made pacts with some groups in order to defeat the others and thus bring the island under their rule. Castilian law permitted the colonists to enslave those who resisted Spanish political control and set them to work in Spanish enterprises and homes. Presaging events in the Americas, disease and epidemics ravaged the native population throughout the fifteenth century, and the Spaniards resorted to buying West African slaves as replacement workers. These slaves were put to work on the cane plantations established to supply Spain with sugar.

While Castile was more preoccupied with completing the Reconquest, the Kingdom of Portugal proved particularly supportive of opening the African trade route. Prince Henry the Navigator established a school in Lisbon to promote maritime technology and cartographic knowledge. By the time of his death in 1460, his mariners had developed a sturdy oceangoing vessel called the caravel, which combined the square rigging of northern European craft and the lateen sails of Mediterranean vessels. The school also spread the knowledge of navigation. Mariners now used the astrolabe and quadrant to measure the elevation in degrees between the ship's deck and certain stars. If the ship was not heaving and rolling too much, these readings permitted the sailors to estimate their latitude with a degree of certainty. The compass and sightings off the North Star or the Southern Cross determined their direction. On their return from voyages along the coast of Africa, these mariners reported their discoveries to Genoese cartographers, who made sophisticated sailing charts for the merchant community.

Soon the Portuguese were perfecting methods to commercially exploit the new African territories they were discovering. They set up *feitorias,* fortified trading factories, on the coast. With the introduction of *feitorias,* Portuguese traders did not have to spend time and money on conquering inland areas but merely traded with the local populace for exotic goods and raw materials. In addition, merchants introduced African slaves from these *feitorias* directly into Europe, bypassing the Arab slave traders of North Africa.

Table 3.1 depicts the long-term historical trends that developed in Iberia during this epoch of Reconquest, discovery, and trade from which emerged the ambitious Genoese

Table 3.1   Iberian Timeline

Iberian Developments	Year	American Developments
Islamic Granada falls; Jews expelled.	1492	Columbus arrives in Caribbean.
	1490	The Inka conquer Ecuador.
Spanish inquisition established.	1479	Tarascans defeat Aztec invasion.
Spaniards occupy Canary Islands.	1478	
	1472	Death of Netzahualcóyotl, poet-king of Texcoco.
Marriage of Isabella, Ferdinand.	1469	The Inka conquer north coast of Perú.
	1450	Famine in the Valley of Mexico.
Portuguese colonize the Azores.	1445	
Portuguese sell slaves from Africa.	1442	
	1438	The Inka conquer Peruvian highlands.
	1433	Triple Alliance establishes the Aztec Empire.
Portuguese colonize Madeira.	1420	
Prince Henry founds naval school.	1418	
Program against Jews, many convert.	1391	
Portugal defeats Castile.	1385	
Black Death strikes Iberia.	1348	Mexica construct Tenochtitlán.
	1280	Rise of Chimú in Peru.
Cádiz falls to Castile.	1250	The Inka build capital at Cuzco.
Córdoba falls to Castile.	1236	Chichimec invade Valley of Mexico.
Muslims defeated at Las Navas de Tolosa.	1212	
Military order of Santiago founded.	1170	Decline of the Toltec.
El Cid conquers Valencia.	1090	Wari build Andean road system.
Caliphate of Córdoba collapses.	1031	Rise of the Toltec in central Mexico.
Some Christians convert to Islam.	900	Fall of Maya cities and Monte Albán.
Advances in agriculture, science.	800	Decline of the Mochica.
Muslims invade Iberia.	711	Maya city-states flourish.
	650	Fall of Teotihuacán.
Visigoths invade Iberia.	409	Cult of Wiraqocha in Tiwanaku, Bolivia.
Iberians convert to Christianity.	200	Rise of Mochica in Perú.
Iberia is part of the Roman Empire.	202 B.C. to A.D. 409	Teotihuacán flourishes in Mexico.

merchant Christopher Columbus. Participation in several voyages down the African coast had made him familiar with the commercial expansion of the age. Nonetheless, his ambition held certain risks. The Portuguese were engaged in reaching the Far East by sailing around the African continent, but his novel plan called for reaching Asia by sailing directly westward across the Atlantic Ocean and would certainly have improved upon the circum-African route. But Columbus was also proposing to sail into uncharted waters.

CONQUEST IN THE CARIBBEAN

The encounter of the European and American civilizations, beginning in 1492, set in motion cycles of conquest that would not end until nearly all of Meso- and South America had been involved. These cycles included stages that Spaniards had already practiced and experienced, to some extent, in the Reconquest and the settlement of the Canary Islands. For the Spaniards under the command of Columbus, however, the voyage of 1492 was risky. As it turned out, two of the three ships and 52 of the 90 men did not return. The islands of the Caribbean Sea and the continents of North and South America represented "discoveries" because the Europeans had no previous knowledge of their existence. However, there was some initial confusion among the Europeans. Until his dying day, Columbus mistook the Americas for Asia. He thought the Caribbean Islands were Japan and the East Indies, so he called these lands the Indies and their inhabitants, the Indians. Yet he would be disappointed that the Indies he explored did not measure up to European conceptions of Asian wealth.

But the first step that this merchant captain needed to take was to acquire the financial underwriting and royal patronage to carry out his bold plan. Columbus demanded such titles and emoluments for his future discoveries that the sovereigns of Portugal, France, and England—one by one—all declined to finance his expedition. He wanted to be recognized as "Admiral of the Ocean Sea" and owner of all business and trade accruing from lands he would discover. Queen Isabella and King Ferdinand, even after finally defeating the Muslims at Grenada in 1492, almost balked. After all, Columbus was a commoner. Nevertheless, this commoner inherited the business acumen of his father, a master weaver with his own mill in Genoa and trading interests in the Mediterranean. These credentials, as well as his reputation as a mariner, earned Columbus venture capital from the merchant community of Seville, a port on the Guadalquivir River and Spain's most import trading center. Finally, he gained the royal sponsorship of Isabella and Ferdinand in exchange for sovereignty over any lands he discovered. They got the better of the bargain. While Columbus would ruin his health attempting to maximize his business opportunities, the Castilian monarchy acquired the largest and richest empire of any European kingdom.

Columbus and 90 men headed their three small caravels straight across the Atlantic Ocean. They sailed 33 days out of sight of land, an unusual feat at the time, landing at one of the Bahamian Islands in October 1492. He then sailed around a large island that the Aruak who lived there called Cuba. This Columbus mistook for the land that Marco Polo had called Cipangu, or Japan, although he was disappointed that Cuba did not contain any of the golden palaces described by Polo. Moreover, the Aruak of Cuba did not recognize the cinnamon and pepper said to have originated in the East. On the next large island, Hispaniola, the people were more reticent and suspicious of the foreigners than the

Aruak of Cuba. They were known for their warlike demeanor and ferocity. But the Taíno of Hispaniola did have gold jewelry, which they traded with the Spaniards. More than anything else, the gold caused Columbus to concentrate his early attentions on Hispaniola.

Here in the Caribbean, Spaniards developed the basic principles they would use thereafter for the next 300 years of warfare with the indigenous population. These first settlers at Hispaniola depended on the indigenous Taíno for food and work. Thus, the Spaniards learned about the sociopolitical organization of the host society and obtained goods through the existing tribute and redistributive systems run by chieftains. They even took the Taíno name for chieftain, *cacique,* into their own vernacular, later spreading it by conquest across the rest of the Americas. Columbus made an alliance with one Taíno *cacique,* Guacanagarí, against the other leaders. Guacanagarí's followers provided intelligence for the Spaniards and served them as guides and bearers. The Spaniards established fortifications in hostile territory from which to venture forth on expeditions throughout the island.

When the Spaniards first arrived, the Taíno of Hispaniola offered gold ornaments and food as presents to the visitors; when they returned, they demanded more gold and food. Columbus then established a tribute system that forced the *caciques* to divert labor from planting and fishing to panning for gold in the rivers. Consequently, food production declined. For the short amount of time that the tribute system functioned, the Spaniards supported the traditional political system of the Taíno because these clan leaders were key brokers in the system. They collected tribute for the Spaniards, who terrorized and punished villagers and *caciques* who resisted.

Once news of these developments circulated in Spain, more Spanish men emigrated to Hispaniola. As their numbers increased, the demand for local goods and services grew beyond the capacity of the indigenous producers. Internal factionalism soon broke out among the Europeans over the division of tribute. Occasionally, the squabbling allowed for Taíno counterattack, which only provoked additional European military campaigning and native casualties. The Taíno warriors succeeded in killing a handful of Spaniards here and there, but usually their military encounters were routs. In the first full-fledged military campaign in Hispaniola, an army of several thousand Taíno warriors fell quickly to a force of 220 Spaniards, 10 horses, war dogs, arquebuses, crossbows, and local allies. The campaign lasted just a few days in March 1495 and resulted in the enslavement of the surviving Taíno rebels, some of whom were exported to Spain.

Then began the epidemics and demographic disasters among the still vast indigenous population—and this scourge did not discriminate between those who were collaborating with the Europeans and those who were not. Epidemic disease was common among the invaders. Medieval Europe had been the common market of microbes and diseases during a period of intensive conquest and commerce with Asia and Africa from 1300 to 1600. The greatest of these periodic plagues, which lasted from 1345 to 1355, wiped out about half the population of some European cities. In the New World, indigenous Caribbean islanders suffered a veritable constellation of European diseases all at once. The intensity of the multiple pestilence caused the death of an estimated 8 of every 10 natives on the island of Hispaniola between 1495 and 1500. The sudden decline of the indigenous population there produced two results: Various groups of Taíno raised isolated and desperate rebellions, which the Spaniards quickly and brutally quelled, and factionalism arose among the Spaniards in an inverse ratio to the decline of Taíno tribute.

The final phase of the conquest cycle concerned the issue of provisions for the conquerors. With the indigenous population of Hispaniola having been destroyed by 1500, the bickering Spaniards were confronted with starvation. Few of them had come to Hispaniola expecting to engage in agriculture, and supplies sent from Spain were quickly exhausted. Therefore, the first Spanish officials sent into Hispaniola to settle the disputes between Columbus and dissenting Spaniards also had to organize European-style farming and, therefore, introduce European plants and animals. Those Spaniards who could not abide the new order of things enlisted in additional expeditions of conquest in the Caribbean. Besides searching for gold, these expeditions sought to capture slaves to sell to settlers in Hispaniola who, after all, expected to organize agricultural production but not with their own labor. Led by those experienced at fighting the Taíno in Hispaniola, these expeditions headed out for Puerto Rico, Cuba, Central America, and the northern coast of South America. There the cycle of conquest was carried out anew. Eventually, the wave of conquest would reach Mexico and Peru.

No sooner had Columbus exported enslaved Native Americans back to Spain than a debate developed in the court of Queen Isabella. Were they to be considered infidels, like the Africans, and therefore subject to "just" enslavement? Or were they merely ignorant of the superiority of Christianity and thus to be spared the degradation of slavery? In 1500, the defenders of the Native Americans won the debate, and the Crown ordered that they were not automatically to be enslaved. However, there were loopholes in the royal edict. Those who were cannibalistic as well as those who had been properly introduced to Christianity and still resisted could be reduced to slavery if captured in a "just war." The conquerors took liberal advantage of the loopholes.

The unrest among the Spaniards at Hispaniola was not put to rest until the arrival of its first royal governor, Fray Nicolás de Ovando. This agent of Queen Isabella rebuilt the city of Santo Domingo in 1502, laying out the city in a perfect grid pattern; as one chronicler reported, "for it was laid out in our time . . . it was laid out with rule and compass, and all the streets planned on regular lines." In truth, not many of the old towns and cities of Iberia conformed to this grid pattern, but it would become the norm for most new European city building in the Americas.

Ovando was also the first of many royal officials to take control of Indian labor from the conquistadores. As a means to protect and ration the dwindling number of indigenous workers, Ovando took over from Columbus control of the labor draft called *repartimiento* (reapportionment). The governor assumed responsibility for assigning workers from local villages to temporary work with Spanish employers. This system gave the Crown official the sole right of apportioning the labor of Her Majesty's new subjects to European employers in mines and farms. This system of labor distribution contained guarantees for the workers. Employers were to pay them a living wage, care for their welfare, and instruct them in the faith. But only men of substance could hope to benefit from the *repartimiento,* and Ovando encouraged the Spaniards to settle down in cities and towns and to begin raising livestock and sugarcane on farms and properties. The Queen's representative, therefore, encouraged the introduction of livestock and sugarcane. The natives, too, were resettled in villages under the governor's protection, their *caciques* still in nominal charge of their well-being. Only those who were *naboríos* (a Taíno institution of personal service) could enter Spanish households as servants. The governor had envisioned that Spaniards and Native Americans would live separately in these new

Table 3.2   The Cycle of Spanish Conquest in the Indies

Phase	Characteristics
Exploration	Reconnoitering the target area for gold and/or slaves
Organization	An experienced Indian fighter organizes an expeditionary company from pool of new Spanish arrivals
First foray	Trading base established; gold and captives acquired; indigenous allies recruited
Second foray	Spaniards venture into hinterland, subdue native resistance, set up tribute system; more Spaniards arrive
Demographic decline	Indigenous population declines precipitously from European diseases; indigenous production falls
Rebellion	Various native groups rebel in isolated and desperate circumstances; captive rebels sold into slavery
Internal dissension	Growing population of Europeans argue over diminishing receipts of native tribute
Colonization	Production established, based on a mix of European and native foodstuffs; indigenous slaves imported
Political consolidation	Arrival of King's representatives to mediate dissension among Spaniards and claim royal tax rights; African slaves imported

domains, each subservient to royal authority. These royal plans to turn Hispaniola into a prosperous and orderly colony failed for one grave reason—the indigenous population continued its precipitous decline.

The poor treatment and decline of the Taíno population on Hispaniola introduced yet another stage in the cycle of conquest and settlement. On the one hand, the disappearance of this pool of workers gave rise to a new business activity—the traffic in Hispaniola and other islands of Spanish settlement of thousands of Native American slaves captured on voyages to Central America and the shores of Colombia and Venezuela. The coastal lands stretching from the Isthmus of Panama to the mouth of the Orinoco River became famous as "The Spanish Main." These imported laborers, however, also died in large numbers from disease and overwork. Clergymen like Fray Bartolomé de las Casas were appalled at the mass death of the natives. They argued that control of these "childlike" peoples be turned over to the clergy so that they could be safeguarded and instructed in Christianity and European ways. To provide workers for Spanish colonists and also save the indigenous population, clergymen in the Caribbean counseled the authorities to import slaves from sub-Saharan Africa. The first of them arrived in Hispaniola in 1505, and several hundred more came under royal license in 1518. Thus, the African entered the Americas as a European solution to the demographic collapse of the indigenous population. Slave imports ended the first cycle of conquest in Hispaniola, but it was to be repeated in the other Caribbean islands of Cuba, Puerto Rico, and Jamaica—and then Mexico (see Table 3.2).

Spaniards unloading European goods and livestock in Mexico. (Florentine Codex, ca. 1575)

THE CONQUEST OF MEXICO

In 1519, Hernán Cortés set out from Cuba with an expedition of 11 ships, 110 sailors, 508 armed men, and 16 horses. He and his principal lieutenants all had prior experience in the Caribbean, particularly in the conquest and settlement of Cuba. Two earlier expeditions had explored the coast of the Yucatán Peninsula and the Gulf Coast of Mexico, returning to Cuba with stories of a great civilization in the mountains. Cortés fully intended to conquer this land and establish a new colony for himself and his followers there. But he was careful not to reveal his plan to his patron, the governor of Cuba, who had invested in and was expecting to benefit from Cortés's expedition. Besides borrowing capital from others, Cortés had outfitted this part of his expedition with the small fortune he had made from previous conquests, gold mining, and tribute collections in Cuba. Several of his followers owed Cortés money for financing their participation. Although they never repaid him, he would make his fortune in other ways.

Landing on the shores of the Yucatán, Cortés picked up a Spanish castaway, Gerónimo de Aguilar, who had been shipwrecked on a previous exploratory voyage and who had lived (as a slave) for some eight years among the Maya, learning their dialect. Then Cortés acquired the services of a native woman named Malinche, who, after becoming Cortés's mistress and the mother of one of his sons, was called Doña Marina. She spoke both the Nahuatl of the highlands and the Maya dialect of the coast. Thus, the Spanish expedition fortuitously acquired the ability to communicate with the indigenous peoples it was setting out to subdue: Cortés spoke Spanish to Aguilar, who translated to Maya for Malinche, who translated to Nahuatl, and vice versa.

On landing on the coast of Veracruz, Cortés revealed his plan. The expeditionaries founded the city of Veracruz, creating a corporate entity that signaled their independence from the Cuban governor and gave Cortés the right to correspond directly to his sovereign back in Spain. He had his ships burned and scuttled. His expedition was not returning to Cuba but instead marching inland to conquer the Aztec empire. Cortés and his men had learned from the Caribbean experience that by capturing the powerful ruler, they could easily take over the entire tribute system. However, the Aztec empire was to present unexpected challenges to its would-be conquerors.

The Spaniards advanced up the steep slopes of the Sierra Oriental into the Aztec Empire, which awaited the strange visitors without so much as a plan. Neither the emperor, Moteuczoma II, nor any other native leader knew from whence the strangers had come or what their intentions were. Rumors abounded that the bearded Cortés was the god Quetzalcóatl returning from his eastern exile to reclaim his land. Spanish arms and horsemen easily defeated the military resistance that single city-states mounted against them. A show of force—firing cannon and arquebuses or charging the horses—sufficed to intimidate other opponents. One group, the Tlaxcalans, saw the Spaniards as their liberators from the hated Aztec and became their principal allies, even despite Cortés having destroyed their statues of the gods and forbidden the practice of human sacrifice. Other city-states hesitated. Cholula's leaders invited the Spaniards into the city and then hatched a plan to ambush their guests. The Tlaxcalan allies of the Spaniards informed Malinche, who reported the conspiracy to Cortés. In retribution, Cortés ordered his men to launch a devastating preemptive attack upon his hosts, killing 6,000 Cholulan warriors. They also attacked the temples and priests who had offended the Europeans with their practice of human sacrifice.

On their leisurely march toward the imperial city of Tenochtitlán, not once were the Spaniards confronted by an army of fierce Aztec warriors. Instead, the emperor equivocated. Moteuczoma even invited Cortés and his followers to take up temporary residence at Tenochtitlán while he and his advisers decided what to do with them. His gifts of gold objects and gemstones only served to make these unwanted guests even more demanding. Then Cortés seized the Aztec emperor as a guarantee for the safety of him and his men (see Manuscript 3.1). During the six months they resided in Tenochtitlán, it appeared that Cortés was succeeding in conquering the Aztec Empire from the inside out, and he planned for a massive conversion to Christianity. But it was not to be so easy.

Not the least of Cortés's worries stemmed from the wrath of the governor of Cuba, who had felt betrayed by his former subordinate. He dispatched 1,000 men to arrest Cortés, but the resourceful captain departed Tenochtitlán with a small band and fell on the superior Spanish force, winning a stunning victory. He then brought most members of this punitive expedition into his venture of conquest, more than doubling his forces. Back in the Aztec capital, meanwhile, the Spaniards' demands for gold and their severe attacks against the Aztec priests and their deities had shamed many of Moteuczoma's subordinates, who planned a popular rebellion while Cortés was out of the city. When a Spanish lieutenant put to death hundreds of Aztec nobles during a religious festival, the Aztec rose up and trapped the Spaniards in their quarters.

Cortés quickly returned with 1,000 soldiers and 100 horsemen, a force the Aztec allowed back into the city without incident—and then attacked relentlessly. The Spaniards had their captive, Moteuczoma, appear to order the unruly mob to disperse, but the attackers stoned the emperor, and he died three days later. The Spaniards now had to fight their way out of the city, where Aztec warriors inflicted heavy casualties on the men of Cortés at close quarters among the houses and from canoes along the causeway. Four hundred fifty Spaniards and 4,000 of their native allies died. The others successfully escaped, but the night of July 1, 1520, would be known as the "sad evening," *la noche triste* for the Spaniards, and it would take another 14 months for them to capture Tenochtitlán.

The Spaniards' ultimately successful assault on the Aztec capital resulted as much from their ingenuity as from the diseases they had brought with them. An epidemic of smallpox broke out among the residents of Tenochtitlán that devastated the population and dispirited its defenders. The victims of disease could find little solace in their implacable gods, and a sense of doom cast a pall over the survivors. Disease claimed the Aztec emperor chosen to replace Moteuczoma, and the high nobility then selected the 18-year-old Cuauhtémoc, who immediately rallied his people to fight the Spaniards to the end. In the meanwhile, Cortés's men stripped the riggings from the captured ships of the Cuban governor, sent two back to Spain with Cortés's message to the king, and burnt the remaining ships. His men brought the ships' hardware up to the lakes surrounding Tenochtitlán, where his carpenters constructed a fleet of war barges whose cannons soon swept the lakes of Aztec war canoes. Then his Spanish combatants and

MANUSCRIPT 3.1

The Aztec Version of Conquest

Several years after conquest, one of the first clergymen to arrive in Mexico set about collecting the memoirs of the Nahua (those peoples who spoke Nahuatl) as to how the Spaniards had been able to defeat the great Aztec city of Tenochtitlán. Father Bernardino Sahagún established his headquarters at Tlatelolco, the former marketplace city adjacent to Tenochtitlán, where a cathedral and college had been built directly over the Aztec ruins. There he taught native scribes to write their own language in the Roman alphabet. His Nahuatl-speaking students then composed the Florentine Codex, a collection of descriptions of Nahua life. Alongside the script, artists rendered drawings of the subjects. Book 12 of the Florentine Codex details the story of the Conquest from the perspective of the vanquished. The following passage describes the events that transpired after the Spaniards, accompanied by their allies the Tlaxcalans, first entered the Aztec capital and met Emperor Moteuczoma.

Seventeenth chapter, where it is said how the Spaniards went with Monteucçoma to enter the great palace, and what happened there.

And when they had reached the palace and gone in, immediately they seized Monteucçoma and kept close watch over him, not letting him out of their sight, and Itzquauhtzin [governor of Tlatelolco] along with him. But the others were just [allowed to] come back out.

And when this had happened, then the various guns were fired. It seemed that everything became confused; people went this way and that, scattering and darting about. It was as though everyone's tongue were out, everyone were preoccupied, everyone had been taking mushrooms, as though who knows what had been shown to everyone. Fear reigned, as though everyone had swallowed his heart. It was still that way at night; everyone was terrified, taken aback, thunderstruck, stunned.

And when it dawned, everything [the Spaniards] needed was proclaimed: white tortillas, roast turkeys, eggs, fresh water, wood,

native allies advanced over the causeways and destroyed Tenochtitlán, house by house and temple by temple. On August 13, 1521, following a siege of three full months, the last defenders capitulated. Cortés had a Spanish-style city built directly over the ruins of the Aztec capital, which he named México (Mexico City). It was to be the capital of the Spanish colony called New Spain.

The Encomienda

As de facto Spanish governor of Mexico, Cortés expressed reluctance to apportion the Indians to the conquerors in a manner similar to what had been the practice in Hispaniola, but he realized that he would never get the restless conquistadores to settle down unless they had a source of tribute and labor (see Manuscript 3.2). That Cortés did apportion local villages to individual men on a hereditary basis attests to the strength with which these first conquerors made their demands. For the first generation of settlers after the Conquest, these grants, called *encomiendas,* served as the basis of economic prosperity,

firewood, charcoal, earthen tubs, polished bowls, water jars, large clay pitchers, vessels for frying, all kinds of earthenware. Monteucçoma himself ordered it. But when he summoned the noblemen, they would no longer obey him, but grew angry. They no longer performed their duty to him, no longer went to him; no longer was he heeded. But he was not therefore forsaken; he was given all he needed to eat and drink, and water and deer fodder [for the Spaniards].

And when [the Spaniards] were well settled, right away they interrogated Monteucçoma about all the stored treasure of the altepetl [his noble clan], the devices and shields. They greatly prodded him, they eagerly sought gold as a thing of esteem. And then Monteucçoma went along leading the Spaniards. They gathered around him, bunched around him; he went in their midst, leading the way. They went along taking hold of him, grasping him. And when they reached the storehouse, the place called teocalco, then all the [shining things] were brought out: the

quetzal-feather head fan, the devices, the shields, the golden disks, the necklaces of the devils, the golden nose crescents, the golden leg bands, the golden arm bands, the golden sheets for the forehead.

Thereupon the gold on the shields and on all the devices was taken off. And when all the gold had been detached, right away they set on fire, set fire to, ignited all the different precious things; they all burned. And the Spaniards made the gold into bricks. And they took as much of the green-stone as pleased them; as to the rest of the green-stone, the Tlaxcalans just snatched it up. And [the Spaniards] went everywhere, scratching about in the hiding places, storehouses, places of storage all around. They took everything they saw that pleased them.

SOURCE: *We People Here: Nahuatl Accounts of the Conquest of Mexico,* trans. and ed. James Lockhart (Berkeley: University of California Press, 1993), 120, 122.

for they funneled goods and services from thousands of Native American tributaries into the new cities built for the settlers. Only 506 Spaniards received these valuable grants, and the original followers of Cortés, who had much competition from late-arriving settlers, attempted to monopolize their distribution. "All the Spaniards, even the most miserable and unfortunate," wrote one early clergyman, "want to be señores and live for themselves, not as servants of anyone, but with servants of their own."

According to the terms of the grant contract, the *encomendero* was to protect the Native Americans under his care, instruct them in the Christian faith, and take up arms for the king in defense of the new land. In exchange for these obligations, the *encomendero* could live off the tribute his charges paid to him and could benefit from their labor. The natives would continue to live in their own villages, cultivate their own fields, and fulfill their obligations under the orders of their own village leaders. Most importantly, the *encomienda* carried no title to land, although the *encomendero* held land separate from his indigenous charges and obliged them to work that land. Throughout the sixteenth century, the Crown's officials increased their oversight of the *encomenderos*. Spanish officials and some of the clergy who arrived following the Conquest believed that the excessive demands of Spanish settlers threatened the indigenous population

MANUSCRIPT 3.2

The *Encomienda* System of the Sixteenth Century

A decree by Philip II defined the legal basis of the encomienda in 1571, one of the numerous adjustments to it that would lead the Crown to abolish it altogether. Despite the legal changes issued from Spain, the encomienda remained very much a local mechanism. It was established and operated by the first conquerors to establish the basis for the new relationship between Spaniards and Native Americans. Cortés's letter to the king reveals how much pressure his followers were placing on him to give them control of the natives. European social domination of colonial Latin America, therefore, had its institutional foundations in the encomienda. Though it was abolished in the core colonies of New Spain and Peru, other institutions were created to sustain that European domination. However, in the fringe areas, where Spanish settlement remained small and less complex, as in Paraguay and Venezuela, the encomienda endured for centuries because no finely tuned substitutes were needed.

Philip II. Decree of 1571

The *encomienda* is a right granted by Royal Grace to the deserving of the Indies to receive and collect for themselves the tributes of the Indians that shall be given them in trust, for their life and the life of one heir . . . with the charge of looking after the spiritual and temporal welfare of the Indians and of dwelling in and defending the Provinces where they are given them in trust and of doing homage and making personal oath to fulfill all this.

Cortés to the King of Spain, May 15, 1522

In a letter of mine I informed Your Majesty how the natives of these parts are of much greater intelligence than those of the other islands; indeed, they appeared to us to possess such understanding as is sufficient for an ordinary citizen to conduct himself in a civilized country. It seemed to me, therefore, a serious matter at this time to compel them to serve the Spaniards as the natives of the other

with extinction. The Native Americans were to be the source of tax revenues and religious converts, so the state sought increasingly to intervene in this relationship between *encomendero* and tributaries. In addition, the Castilian Crown did not wish to permit the formation of a powerful nobility so far away that might one day challenge royal authority.

Control of the natives eventually passed from the tight-fisted grip of the first conquerors. Competition for allotments of indigenous workers, spurred by the growing population of Spanish immigrants, provided the representatives of the Crown an opportunity to reduce the feudal power of the original conquerors. They removed the hereditary features of the *encomienda,* even though royal officials found it difficult at first to enforce these strictures. Decline of the indigenous population greatly assisted the process of divestiture. In stripping the conquerors of control over the Native Americans, the Crown received the support of the church, as shall be seen in subsequent chapters. With the appointment of the royal *audiencia,* the high judicial tribunal, at Mexico City in 1527, the royal encroachment on the power of Cortés and the original conquerors began. Natives with grievances against the *encomenderos* now had somebody to whom to complain. In 1535, the first Spanish viceroy was dispatched to New Spain by the king; by the mid-sixteenth century, the *encomenderos* had lost nearly all of

islands do; yet if this were not done, the conquerors and settlers of these parts would not be able to maintain themselves. In order therefore to avoid enslaving these Indians, and at the same time to provide the Spaniards with their needs, it seemed to me that Your Majesty should command that from the income which belongs to Your Majesty here we should obtain assistance for the expenses and maintenance of the settlers; and in this matter Your Majesty should decree as You saw most fitting to Your service. Since then, however, I have been almost forced to deliver the chieftains and other natives of these parts to the Spaniards in recognition of the services they have rendered to Your Majesty, because Your Majesty's expenses have been continuous and considerable, and we ought rather to try by every means to increase Royal revenues than to give cause for spending them; also we have been at war for a long time and have all contracted debts thereby

and find ourselves in difficulties. Furthermore, on account of the inevitable delay in ascertaining Your Majesty's commands on this matter, and because I was so pressed by Your Majesty's officials and the other Spaniards, I could not in any way avoid it. So until some new order is made, or this one confirmed, the aforementioned chieftains and natives will serve the Spaniards with whom they have been deposited in all that may require in their affairs. This conclusion was reached on the advice of persons who have considerable knowledge and experience in this land; moreover, nothing better or more convenient could be devised either for the maintenance of the Spaniards or for the safety and good treatment of the Indians. . . .

SOURCES: As quoted in Elman R. Service, *Spanish-Guarani Relations in Early Colonial Paraguay* (Ann Arbor: University of Michigan Press, 1954), 4; and Hernan Cortés, *Letters from Mexico,* trans. and ed. A. R. Pagden (New York: Grossman, 1971), 279–80.

their control over the indigenous population to Spanish officials, and the sons of the original conquerors now had to share social status, wealth, and privilege with a growing body of Spanish miners and merchants.

From the Spanish base at Mexico City, in the meanwhile, the conquests in Mesoamerica spread north and south. Cortés felt compelled to compete in this expansion in order to retain his authority and status as de facto governor. He had captured the Aztec emperor, Cuauhtémoc, and held him prisoner in an effort to command the obedience of the remaining Aztec. Expeditions under the auspices of Cortés took his lieutenants west into Michoacán and south to Oaxaca, the Yucatán, and eventually Guatemala. Rival expeditions were fitted out from Cuba to conquer Honduras, the latter of which sparked Cortés's own counterthrust from 1524 to 1526. Here the hostage Cuauhtémoc met his death. Accusing him of fomenting rebellion among the native bearers of the expedition, Cortés had him executed.[2] While he was gone from Mexico City, his enemies among the new post-Conquest immigrants made common cause with royal treasury officials to despoil Cortés and the original conquerors of their *encomiendas*. The Spaniards in New Spain were on the verge of civil war when Cortés returned to help his partisans recover their lost authority. The great conqueror then went to Spain to seek confirmation of his governorship from King Charles V, who instead conferred on Cortés the title of Marquis of the Valley of Oaxaca with control over more than twenty-three thousand indigenous tributaries. He never did receive what he considered "proper" recognition of his great conquests. Cortés died an embittered man in 1547. By the close of the sixteenth century, few *encomiendas* existed in the valuable colony of New Spain.

Now colonial officials were free to take official control of the native population and other affairs of the colony, including further expansion. Crown officials sponsored the remaining expeditions in Jalisco and Sinaloa and the exploration of northern Mexico and the southwest of what would become the United States, although their success fell far short of Cortés's conquest of the Aztec Empire (see Map 3.1). However, Spain laid claim to territories as far north as California, New Mexico, and Texas, which would be settled more leisurely in the next three centuries.

Of these secondary conquests in Mesoamerica, only that of Guatemala offered wealth and tribute to the conquerors. The Maya of the Guatemalan highlands were conquered after a laborious series of campaigns—not with one dramatic stroke as with the Aztec. The Spaniards had to defeat, one by one, the Quiché, the Mam, the Tzutuhil, the Pocomán, the Cakchiquel, the Ixil, the Uspantec, and the Kekchí. Pedro de Alvarado, who had been second in command to Cortés at Tenochtitlán, led the Spanish expedition. He first allied with the Cakchiquel, crushing the Quiché and Tzutuhil and, when the Cakchiquel later rebelled, he crushed them, too. The native population was divided into *encomiendas* and distributed to members of the expedition based on their rank and status in the expedition of conquest. The leader, Alvarado, received the largest number of tributaries, followed by his brother, Jorge. In 1548, six captains had pueblos of more than 500 natives; two captains had more than one thousand. The wealth of these new *encomenderos* was based on cacao production by the people of Chiapas and El Salvador. However, the epidemic of 1578 reduced the native population by as much as 90 percent, and Spanish officials stepped in to prevent worse population decline by forbidding the

---

[2] Today, the Mexican nation has enshrined the last Aztec emperor, Cuauhtémoc, in its pantheon of national heroes. Mexican leaders do not identify at all with the Spaniards nor with Cortés.

Map 3.1 The European Conquest and Settlement of the Americas

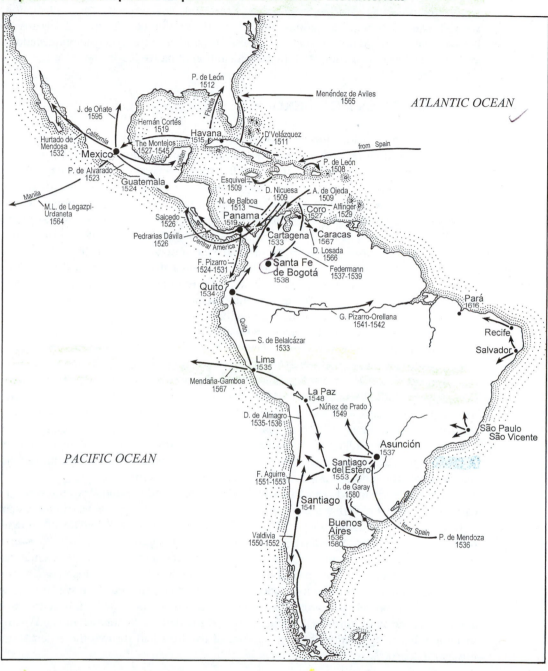

ATLANTIC OCEAN

- P. de León 1512
- Menéndez de Aviles 1565
- J. de Oñate 1595
- Hernán Cortés 1519
- Havana 1515
- D'Velázquez 1511
- from Spain
- Hurtado de Mendosa 1532
- California
- The Montejos 1527-1545
- Mexico
- Yucatan
- P. de León 1508
- P. de Alvarado 1523
- Guatemala 1524
- Esquivel 1509
- D. Nicuesa 1509
- A. de Ojeda 1509
- Manila
- M.L. de Legazpi-Urdaneta 1564
- N. de Balboa 1513
- Coro 1527
- Alfinger 1529
- Salcedo 1526
- Panama 1519
- Cartagena 1533
- Caracas 1567
- Pedrarias Dávila 1526
- Central America
- Santa Fe de Bogotá 1538
- D. Losada 1566
- Federmann 1537-1539
- F. Pizarro 1524-1531
- Quito 1534
- Pará 1616
- G. Pizarro-Orellana 1541-1542
- Quito
- S. de Belalcázar 1533
- Recife
- Salvador
- Lima 1535
- Mendaña-Gamboa 1567
- La Paz 1548
- Núñez de Prado 1549
- D. de Almagro 1535-1536
- São Paulo São Vicente
- **PACIFIC OCEAN**
- Asunción 1537
- Santiago del Estero 1553
- F. Aguirre 1551-1553
- J. de Garay 1580
- Santiago 1541
- Buenos Aires 1536 1580
- Valdivia 1550-1552
- from Spain
- P. de Mendoza 1536

conquerors from using workers from the Guatemalan highlands in the hot lands. Cacao production in Central America plummeted after 1590, as Venezuelan cacao plantations with African slaves began to capture Mexican markets. When the king's officials arrived in Guatemala, they did not so much dispossess the families of the original conquistadores as they did take gradual control of the administration of native labor.

THE CONQUEST OF PERU

Once the Spaniards had subdued most of the original inhabitants of Central America, word arrived at their base in Panama, the first European city built on the Pacific coast, that a rich and powerful native state lay to the south. Several exploratory expeditions down the west coast of South America confirmed the rumors. Two long-standing business partners in the Caribbean, Francisco Pizarro and Diego de Almagro, drew up a partnership to outfit an expedition, which they financed with their previous business profits as well as by attracting new capital investments. No doubt they were envious of the success and riches of Cortés in Mexico. Pizarro had even gone to Spain to gain the king's permission for the conquest and to recruit men from his native province of Estremadura. Back in Panama, he assembled other seasoned fighters and finally set sail for Peru in 1531 with 180 men and 30 horses. There he found that fate had already intervened.

The measles and smallpox had arrived in Peru before Pizarro did, in 1524 and 1526, spread by infected Native Americans who had had contact with Europeans in the Caribbean. Emperor Wayna Qhapaq (Huayna Cápac in Spanish) fell sick and died in Quito, as did his designated heir, opening the way for the dynastic struggles that facilitated Spanish conquest. Atawallpa (Atahualpa in Spanish) won the civil war, but the kingdom still seethed with dissension. The victor did not concern himself too much with these strange humans who had just landed on the coast, for the new Inka knew that Andean political power lay in the highlands. He allowed the invaders to marshal their strength and gather intelligence and local allies for more than a year. Finally, in November 1532, the Spaniards under Pizarro were ready. They advanced to the high plains of Cajamarca, where the emperor and an army of 5,000 awaited them.

By now, the Spaniards had a time-tested battle plan and the audacity and means to carry it out. They knew that they could take control of the existing native tribute system if they captured the native political leader. They were not wrong. While Spanish horsemen waited in ambush, Atawallpa entered the Inka town of Cajamarca in order to receive the expected homage of these visitors. However, the priest and an interpreter went to demand Atawallpa's conversion to Christianity and his submission to the king of Spain. The mere suggestion outraged the Inka, and the priest hastily retreated. That was the signal for the Spanish horsemen to rush forward and seize the emperor, taking his entourage and his great army by surprise. During the rest of the day, the Spaniards pursued the remaining military opposition, but the capture of the Inka had thrown the much larger force into disarray.

Peruvian Wealth

Once the Spanish conquerors had captured the Inka, it was time to make use of his authority to reap the rewards of the largest tribute system of ancient America. Pizarro ordered

Atawallpa to assemble a ransom of all the gold in the land. The resulting collection produced 1.5 million pesos of gold and silver jewelry and artwork, the product of hundreds of Andean craftspersons. The Spaniards melted down these objects into crude gold bars to be divided up among themselves; then they put Atawallpa to death. It took Pizarro another year to assemble an attack on Cuzco, the Inka capital. When he succeeded in taking the city, he installed a puppet emperor, Manco Inka, to serve the Spanish interests. However, the cold climate of Cuzco did not appeal to Pizarro who, in 1536, established the Spanish capital at Lima on the temperate coast. His decision violated the precedent set by Cortés to build the new Spanish colonial capital on the ruins of the old Native American capital, the better to control the new subjects. It also bifurcated political power in Peru once again between mountain and coast, as in the days before the Inka.

Upon division of the large cache of booty, the factionalism of the Spaniards burst its bounds. Almagro arrived with his followers only to discover that Pizarro's "men of Cajamarca" had already divided up the gold and *encomiendas* of tribute-paying Native Americans. He was temporarily placated by assuming the leadership of an expedition of conquest to Chile and soon departed with freshly arrived Spanish adventurers and a large number of native auxiliaries and bearers. Manco Inka took advantage of this Spanish diversion to rally his supposed subjects, and they besieged Cuzco with Pizarro's brother and 120 other Spaniards trapped inside. However, more than one hundred thousand Inka loyalists could not dislodge the Spanish defenders, and the returning Almagro, although disappointed at the paucity of gold he found in Chile, helped break the siege. Thereafter, pockets of indigenous resistance remained in the isolated mountains and valleys on the eastern slopes of the cordillera. The last Inka fortress, Vilcabamba, fell in 1572.

The men of Cajamarca had apportioned the Andean villages loyal to the Inka into 100 *encomiendas,* allowing them to collect tribute and demand labor from the natives. Because the *encomiendas* were based on prior political organizations, the first individual allotments of Native Americans in Peru amounted to several thousands of tributaries. The new *encomenderos* enlisted the local ethnic nobility, the *kurakas*, to collect and deliver their tribute and labor. In return, the natives were to receive military protection and religious instruction. The latter promises proved weak, for the quarreling Spaniards were to involve these same tributaries in their own civil wars, and native tribute and labor remained more important to the conquerors than teaching the catechism. Then more Spanish immigrants arrived, each of whom felt entitled to an *encomienda*. Because the indigenous population was beginning to decline at the same time, the size of the original *encomiendas* dwindled, and the *encomenderos* pressed the surviving Native Americans to keep up the former tribute quotas. But as the size of these *encomiendas* got smaller, the number of *encomenderos* actually multiplied. By 1542, an enlarged group of 467 *encomenderos* in Peru was collecting 1.2 million pesos annually in goods and labor services from native tributaries. The private Spanish exaction of tribute after the Conquest was higher and more grasping than that previously conceived by the Inka rulers, who had set up the tribute system mainly to obtain labor services; it had now been converted by the Europeans to deliver goods.

Still more Spaniards were coming to Peru, however, and they had aspirations to acquire their gold and allotments of natives, too. Therefore, additional expeditions of conquest were organized, usually by veterans of Pizarro's band, to satisfy the demands of these troublesome newcomers and to allow the original conquerors to consolidate what they had won. Sebastián de Belalcázar organized a band that extended the conquest to

Quito and eventually into southern Colombia. In each, the conquerors routed the native forces and formed *encomiendas,* but the size of tribute never equaled that of the Inka. Gonzalo Pizarro, Francisco's younger brother, and Francisco de Orellana led an expedition over the cordilleras and down the Amazon River. Pedro de Valdivia led 150 Spaniards and numerous indigenous auxiliaries on the second and definitive conquest of Chile in 1540. Most of these men obtained *encomiendas* of native tributaries, sure enough, but their charges quickly caught European diseases, and a brief boom in panning for gold soon exhausted all the precious metal. The conquerors had to take up farming to supply the Peruvian market. In the meanwhile, the Mapuche of southern Chile checked Spanish advance at the Bío-Bío River. It had been at this point that the previous Inka advance had also stalled. The Mapuche defeated and killed Valdivia himself in 1553 and improved their military capabilities even more thereafter by adopting the horse and Spanish weaponry.

The Crown and the Conquerors

Although royal patent had sanctioned the conquest, the conquerors and settlers themselves had put their own capital and labor into the project. They expected just rewards. The conquistadores had taken for themselves the richest rewards, held tight control over the natives, and ran political affairs according to their own (albeit factious) dictates. Therefore, in order to establish effective royal control over the Indies, the Spanish Crown needed first to tame the conquerors—not a simple task. The Pizarros in Peru, for example, considered that they had a perfect right to oppose the first viceroy sent out by the king. After all, he was bringing the famous New Laws, decreed in Spain to eliminate the *encomienda* system and take control of the Native Americans from the conquistadores. A military force of colonists led by Gonzalo Pizarro confronted the Spanish viceroy in 1546 and killed him in battle.

But the Americas were too rich a prize for the king to abandon to the conquistadores. Their infighting threatened to provoke native unrest and interrupt the flow of commerce and silver to Spain. Besides, more and more Spaniards were emigrating to the Indies, where they found that the powerful *encomenderos* blocked their opportunities to get ahead and monopolized the goods and services of the indigenous population. These newcomers became an important and growing colonial interest group that would help royal authorities overcome the conquerors and diminish their political power. A second royal army arrived in 1548, which defeated and executed Gonzalo Pizarro. The new royal governor, Pedro de la Gasca, consolidated military power in Peru and gained the grudging obedience of the powerful conquerors and *encomenderos*. But royal officials had to suspend the New Laws and permit the *encomienda* to continue a while longer in Peru.

The multiple crises besetting Peru in the 1560s encouraged the expansion of Crown authority. The indigenous population was suffering frightfully from the ravages of epidemic diseases, and the *encomenderos* reacted to their lost income by demanding even more of the surviving tributaries. In the meanwhile, the number of Spanish immigrants expecting access to native labor was growing, and native resistance hardened as a consequence. Rumors spread of a threatened rebellion in support of the last Inka, who was still holding out in the rugged mountains east of Cuzco. At the same time, the unrelated millenarian movement of Taki Unquy was sweeping through the *ayllu* and threatening their cooperation with the *encomenderos* (see Chapter 6). To compound this crisis in Spanish Peru, the first silver boom at Potosí had come abruptly to an end as the richest ores were playing out.

To remedy the Andean crisis, in 1569 King Philip II dispatched a resourceful new viceroy, Francisco de Toledo, to Lima. He would institute far-reaching reforms that, over the next 12 years, reduced the power of the *encomenderos,* resuscitated the silver-mining industry, and extended royal influence over the remaining Indian *ayllu.* First of all, Viceroy Toledo began a program of congregating the dwindling indigenous population into 614 administrative districts. These viceregal decrees forced many native Americans to abandon their ancestral lands to move to new villages, breaking up those *ayllu* based on common lineage and mixing ethnically distinct native peoples. This process of *congregación* (congregation) affected more than a million and a half Andeans. Newly appointed rural magistrates, *corregidores,* were appointed to rule over these settlements. These district officials henceforward collected taxes from the natives and apportioned their labor to Spanish colonists. The viceroy negotiated a gradual end of the *encomienda* system by preventing their inheritance and transference. The discredited *encomenderos* could not prevent the gradual alienation of their right to native tribute. But their families, nonetheless, would remain powerful economic entities throughout the remaining colonial period—and beyond—as they moved to claim land vacated by the relocation and *congregación* of indigenous communities.

ADDITIONAL SPANISH CONQUESTS

Certain areas at the fringe of conquest and Crown interest lacked resources of readily available wealth. Thus, the Europeans settled these fringe areas less intensively and more slowly than they had the great former empires of the Aztec and the Inka. The latter two areas formed the core of Spanish interest in the Indies for the next two centuries. In previous chapters, some of the other fringe areas, which had no great pre-Columbian empires and where the natives lived in decentralized agricultural or hunting groups, have already been discussed. The resistance of these groups tended to be absolute. They had to be laboriously defeated one at a time by the Spaniards, and they had only a limited amount of gold or silver to offer the conquerors. Spaniards who were looking to be supported as great lords did not easily capture the labor and services of these indigenous groups. We have already discussed several of these areas. One by one, the Caribbean islands fell into fringe status once their brief gold booms—and the original inhabitants—began to die out. The northern provinces of New Spain, home of the nomadic Chichimec groups, remained tangential except for those areas where silver mines would be discovered at the end of the sixteenth century. The Indians of the Yucatán and Central America offered little wealth to conquerors, except as temporary sources of slaves. In South America, Chile remained a fringe area compared with the more important colonies of Peru and Bolivia. Indeed, all the rest of South America may also be considered to have been of minimal interest to the Europeans. Areas like Venezuela, Colombia, the Río de la Plata, and Brazil were not so much conquered as settled. Here the patterns differed. In some fringe areas, the settlers nearly eliminated the native Americans through warfare or overwork, while in Paraguay and southern Brazil the settlers practically "lived like the natives," adopting their culture and customs to survive and prosper.

Northern South America

The coast of northern Spanish America, which Columbus explored on this third and last voyage, had been exploited initially by Spaniards as a source of Native American slaves. They were captured and carried off in ships to be sold for work on the new landed estates of Hispaniola and Cuba, which had been depopulated of their own indigenous peoples by disease. Europeans first settled permanently on Margarita and Cubagua, Venezuelan islands that were the source of fabulous pearl fisheries whose intensive exploitation by Spaniards also depopulated the natives. The entrepreneurs then brought in native slaves from one of the first Spanish settlements at Coro. Cubagua and Margarita had a population of 20,000 persons at the height of the pearl boom, although its decline motivated many of these people to move to the coastal settlements, such as the slave trading depots of Coro and Maracaibo. Although certain tribes at first allied with the slavers in order to combat their traditional enemies, the slave raids depopulated the coastal zones and left a legacy of hostility towards the Europeans on the part of the natives of the area. In the meanwhile, the houses that indigenous peoples built on stilts over the shallow waters of Lake Maracaibo gave this land its name, *Venezuela,* or Little Venice.

The earliest Spaniards on the coast of northern South America spread the myth of the existence of a native lord rich in gold called *El Dorado,* the Golden One. Santa Marta was founded in 1526 and Cartagena in 1533 on the Caribbean coast of Colombia as ports, slave trading depots, and jumping-off points for expeditions into the interior. Natives all along the coast pointed out the location of this wealthy lord's city of the same name, El Dorado, high in the northern Andes Mountains of Colombia. No less than three major expeditions competed to discover and conquer this mythical kingdom. Gonzalo Jiménez led the first expedition to penetrate the mountain valleys of Colombia. He left directly from Spain in 1535 with 600 men, whose numbers were soon reduced by hardships and dysentery to 173. The Jiménez expedition had intended to travel overland from Santa Marta to conquer the Inka empire of Peru; this would have been an arduous and fruitless journey because Pizarro had already arrived there. Anyway, closer at hand, Jiménez found evidence of indigenous commerce in luxury goods—including gold, salt, and cotton blankets. His group and its native bearers ascended the highland plains to conquer the Muisca kingdom, which turned out to be a disappointment, especially in comparison to the gold Pizarro and his men had just acquired from the Inka.

No sooner had he subdued the weak and piecemeal resistance of the Muisca than Jiménez learned of the nearly simultaneous arrival of other expeditions in search of El Dorado. Sebastián de Belalcázar and 150 men had approached from Peru and Ecuador through southern Colombia. The second expedition of 160 men came from Venezuela to the east. The king had ceded Venezuela to a group of German bankers, the Welzers, to whom he owed money. The Welzers entrusted their American expedition of exploration and conquest to Nicolás Federmann. The three leaders agreed to have their competing claims arbitrated by the king in Spain, from whom the men of Jiménez received the central environs around Bogotá, which he founded in 1539. Federmann and a successor expedition gained permission to conquer other lands in Venezuela but gave up after 15 years of raiding numerous Native American groups and searching for the elusive El Dorado in the Venezuelan backlands.

Belalcázar, one of Pizarro's lieutenants in the conquest of Peru, lost in a bid to conquer Quito and also failed to take the Muisca kingdom. Instead, he had to be content with the governorship of Popayán province in the mountain valleys of southern Colombia. There he encountered native inhabitants who fled at the sight of the conquerors and needed a bit of coercion to settle permanently in their own villages as *encomienda* laborers belonging to the leading Spanish citizens. The settlers founded numerous small towns in Colombia to be able to control the numerous, independent indigenous groups inhabiting the area. Therefore, the *encomiendas* here numbered fewer natives than in Peru, and the quality of tribute and labor obtained from them diminished even more as they succumbed from diseases. In Colombia, it was impossible for prospective gentlemen to live entirely off of their *encomienda* workers. Instead, these settlers developed their own agricultural and grazing lands, albeit with indigenous labor. The natives also worked for their *encomenderos* by mining for gold. When they died from disease or overwork, their numbers were replaced first by native slaves taken in frontier raids and later by African slaves imported through Cartagena.

The conquerors of Colombia, which the Spaniards now renamed New Granada, settled 24 cities and towns between 1539 and 1576. They elected *cabildos,* town councils, from among the most prominent leaders of conquest. More than two hundred fifty men from the three main expeditions received *encomiendas* of Native Americans. These "first conquerors" became a privileged group and used the tribute and labor of their *encomiendas* to establish mining, agricultural, and transportation interests. However, the *encomiendas* in New Granada were small in comparison to those of Peru, numbering from a dozen to a thousand people each. All the European settlers, whether *encomenderos* or not, felt they were far superior to the Native Americans and the Africans who worked for them and to the mestizos and mulattoes whom they had propagated.

The collapse of the native population more than anything undermined the effectiveness of the *encomienda* system, for few conquerors could sustain the life styles to which they aspired merely on native tribute and labor—especially not when the indigenous population of New Granada, estimated to have been 1.4 million in 1537, declined by half within the first 20 years of conquest. The importation of African slaves for the new gold-mining industry prevented the wholesale enslavement of Native Americans in New Granada. Already in 1550, one conqueror had 50 slaves working in his gold mines. However, the *encomienda* survived in northern South America. It was so inconsequential that Crown officials did not bother to abolish it.

Not until 1547 did the Spaniards make their first serious efforts to settle the temperate and fertile Andean valleys of Venezuela. By this time, the myth of El Dorado had been dispelled, and settlers were attracted to the highlands to set up agricultural and cattle estates, albeit with native labor. They established El Tocuyo and then turned to the vicinity of Caracas. However, indigenous resistance in the area prevented the occupation of Caracas until 1567, when 150 Spaniards and 800 native bearers succeeded in establishing a precarious but permanent settlement. A plague aided the settlers in breaking indigenous resistance soon after the founding of Caracas. Within the span of a few years, the epidemic took the lives of nearly two-thirds of the 30,000 native inhabitants of the valley. Unlike in Colombia, little gold mining was accomplished in Venezuela. The settlers of Venezuela supported their societies of *encomenderos* and native laborers by producing cattle to be driven overland to the mining areas of New Granada. Therefore, few African slaves were imported into Venezuela until later when cacao plantations produced an export commodity for the settlers.

The Río de la Plata

European cartographers first added southern South America to their sailing charts following the 1516 discovery of the estuary of the Río de la Plata by the navigator Juan Díaz de Solís. He and other explorers by then were aware that the continent that they were calling the Indies was not, in fact, the Asia of their commercial dreams; in 1520, Ferdinand Magellan passed along the coast of Argentina and around Cape Horn to Asia on the first circumnavigation of the earth, thus proving without a doubt that Asia was someplace else. These early explorers waded ashore at the estuary of the Paraná River, where they explored and traded with the natives for objects made of silver. They learned that a great civilization to the west, undoubtedly that of the Inka, was the source of this wealth. Hence, the estuary and the entire region came to acquire the optimistic name of the *Río de la Plata,* or River of Silver.

To lay claim to its hoped-for wealth and also to keep the Portuguese from settling the region, the Spanish Crown organized a colonization expedition in 1534. It was one of the

MANUSCRIPT 3.3

The Difficulties of Settling Buenos Aires

The conquest and settlement of the core colonies of Mexico and Peru were accomplished quickly, principally because of the prior political centralization of the Aztec and Inka empires. The Spanish conquerors merely seized the existing political apparatus of tribute and loyalty. However, the Spaniards encountered considerable difficulties in regions dominated by tropical agriculturists and hunter-gatherers. The prior political decentralization of the native clans meant that the Spaniards had to defeat one group at a time and that the defeat of one group had no bearing on its neighbor. This was especially true where there was no known wealth to attract sustained Spanish efforts. The following is testimony about the first failed settlement of Buenos Aires between 1532 and 1541 by a survivor of the expedition, Ulrich Schmidt. The writer was an employee of one of the financial underwriters of the expedition, the house of Welzer, one of the king's favorite bankers.

At this time the Indians came in great power and force, as many as twenty-three thousand men, against us and our town Bonas Aeieres. There were four nations of them, namely, [Quirandis, Charúas, and Timbus]. They all meant to go about to destroy us all. But God Almighty preserved the greater part of us, therefore, praise and thanks be to Him always and everlastingly, for on our side not more than about thirty men, including commanders and ensign, were slain.

And when they first came to our town, Bonas Aeieres, and attacked us, some of them tried to storm the place, others shot fiery arrows at our houses, which, being covered

few expeditions sent out directly from Spain and received financial underwriting from the Welzers, a German bank group favored by the German-born king, Charles V. A Spanish nobleman with no prior experience in the Indies, Pedro de Mendoza, led this expedition of 1,600 men and 16 ships. They established a small settlement called Buenos Aires. Immediately, the ill-prepared settlers grew hungry and fractious as the Querandi and Charrúa peoples refused to provide food and had no gold for the taking. Instead, several bands of natives attacked the settlement, ultimately forcing its inhabitants to abandon Buenos Aires (see Manuscript 3.3). An exploration party sent out from Buenos Aires to find the Inka Empire (which, unbeknownst to them, had already fallen to Pizarro's group) sailed up the Paraná River to the Gran Chaco. On their return, all 170 men were killed by the native Payaguá. The inhabitants of the Río de la Plata were very hostile to Spanish penetration, save for one beleaguered group on the Paraguay River.

After losing a pitched battle against them, the Guaraní of Paraguay accepted the Spanish men of the Mendoza expedition as great warriors in their own struggles with the surrounding bands. The Guaraní assisted the Spaniards in founding Asunción in 1537. Within four years, the 350 surviving Spanish expeditionaries abandoned Buenos Aires completely and moved to Paraguay. There were only four Spanish women resident in Asunción at the time. As if they were native heads of lineage, therefore, Spanish men acquired numbers of Guaraní women who served as wives, concubines, servants, and food suppliers. Spaniards

with straw (only the house of our chief captain, covered with tiles, excepted), were set on fire, and so the whole town was burnt down. Their arrows are made out of cane, and carry fire on their points.

They have also a kind of wood, out of which they also make arrows, which, being lighted and shot off, do not extinguish, but also set fire to all houses made out of straw.

Moreover they burnt down four great ships which were half-a-mile distant from us on the river. The people who were there, and who had no guns, hearing such great tumult of the Indians, fled out of these ships into three others which were not far from these, and did contain cannon. But seeing the four ships burning that were lighted by the Indians, the Christians set themselves on defence and fired at the Indians, who becoming

aware of this, and hearing the firing, soon departed from thence and left the Christians alone. All this happened on St. John's Day, Anno 1535.

All this having thus happened, our people had to return into the ships again, and Petrus Manchossa [Don Pedro de Mendoza], our chief captain, gave the command to Johann Eyollas [Juan de Ayolas] and put him in his place to be our commander and rule us. But when Eyollas mustered the people, he found no more than five hundred and sixty men who were yet alive, out of two thousand five hundred, the others being dead and having been starved for hunger.

SOURCE: *The Conquest of the River Plate (1535–1555)*, trans. Luis L. Domínguez (London: The Hakluyt Society, 1891), 11–12.

yielded to Guaraní marriage customs, rather than vice versa, using polygamy to seal military alliances. Guaraní chieftains were made to offer their daughters to Spaniards in exchange for assistance in battle. Guaraní concubines also worked the fields for the Spanish men. "We find, señor, in this land a very bad custom," one Spaniard wrote to his king, "that it is the women who sow and reap the crop." Their children were mestizos and grew up speaking Guaraní rather than Spanish. The second- and third-generation mestizos became the gentry and leading citizens of the land. They provided the leadership for the numerous military expeditions against neighboring indigenous groups, for the number of native slaves captured in battle helped define wealth and status.

Pedro de Mendoza died on his return voyage to Spain, and the king dispatched Alvar Núñez Cabeza de Vaca to Paraguay as governor, accompanied by more European settlers, all male. Together the Spaniards and Guaraní warriors subdued rival tribes in the Chaco region but, in an attempt to cross the Gran Chaco, Cabeza de Vaca nearly exhausted the manpower at Asunción. The settlers finally learned that the wealth of the Inka had already been claimed by the Pizarro-Almagro group. A land with no gold, Paraguay lost its attractiveness for additional Spanish immigration, and few new arrivals undermined the influence of the original settlers. Dissension broke out among the Spaniards. A coup d'état by the settlers deposed Governor Cabeza de Vaca, whom they returned to Spain in chains; Domingo de Irala, a veteran of the original Mendoza expedition, became his successor. The Guaraní by now had become tired of Spanish demands for workers, women, and foodstuffs. A large number of Guaraní organized a rebellion against the Spaniards in 1545, which the settlers put down with the aid of "loyal" Guaraní who had not rebelled.

In the relative poverty of Paraguay, the settlers enjoyed more political independence from Spain and were free to establish a social system of their own choosing. Irala now divided up the Guaraní into *encomiendas* and distributed them among the Spanish settlers. Because few other Spaniards came to Paraguay, there was little additional demand for natives, and thus the *encomiendas* became permanent. Spaniards passed their *encomiendas* on to their mestizo sons, and other mestizos moved out from Asunción to establish other towns and other *encomiendas* on the frontiers of Paraguay. Aside from food, there was little that the *encomienda* natives offered as tribute. Therefore, the *encomiendas* tended to be small and involved personal service more than tribute, lending the Spaniards and mestizos of Paraguay a reputation for laziness. "Having plenty of all things good to eat and drink," one observer remarked, "they give themselves up to ease and idleness, and don't much trouble themselves with trading at all." This isolated colony, because of its lack of mining wealth, remained relatively free of interference by Crown officials and also of clergymen throughout the remainder of the sixteenth century. Indeed, the libidinous existence of the Europeans and mestizos in Paraguay, most of whom lived in polygamous relationships, scandalized the royal court in Spain.

Here in Paraguay, on the fringe of conquest, the *encomiendas* endured as a feature of a subsistence economy rather than being subsumed by a rising commercial system, as in Mexico and Peru. Decline of the Guaraní population reduced the original size of the *encomiendas.* By 1600, there were only 3,000 natives in the immediate vicinity of Asunción. Settlement of new towns and slave raids by mestizo Paraguayans attempted to replenish the indigenous population and expanded settlement on the frontiers. The mestizos, with their immunities to European diseases, outgrew the purely indigenous population and easily became numerically superior to Spaniards in this outpost settlement. In

Paraguay, mestizo males enjoyed the social status of white Spaniards, although they spoke Guaraní and may have been only one-quarter or one-eighth Spanish.

Nonetheless, the Paraguayans did desire access to European luxury goods to reflect their rank, and they strove to secure a commercial lifeline out of their landlocked settlement. Among the new towns founded by the settler colony of Paraguay were Santa Fe in 1573 and Buenos Aires in 1580. Mestizo men of relatively high social status in Paraguay figured prominently among the 75 founders of the second and permanent establishment of the city of Buenos Aires. These settlements wrested the Paraná River lifeline from Paraguay to Spain as well as to the rest of the Americas, for the fierce Chaco natives would prevent Paraguay's direct trade with Perú, and goods had to be routed through Santa Fe and Tucumán. Thus, the conquest phase in Spanish America ended with the foundation of Buenos Aires, 88 years and 6,000 kilometers from Columbus's original landing in the Bahamas.

SETTLEMENT OF BRAZIL

What about the Portuguese? What about Brazil, today the largest and most populous nation of Latin America? Compared to the spectacular expansion of the Spanish Indies, the Portuguese colony in America began quite modestly. It, too, was settled rather than conquered, just like some of the fringe areas of Spanish America. The Portuguese had been more interested in developing their commercial empire along the west coast of Africa. About the time that Columbus established a settlement on Hispaniola, Portuguese mariners had already rounded Africa's Cape of Good Hope at its southernmost extremity. This exploration had been the result of sponsorship by the Crown of Portugal. Led by Vasco da Gama, who successfully arrived in India in 1498, the Portuguese were concentrating on organizing commerce in the Indian Ocean and the South China Sea, where they eventually established colonies at Goa, Macao, and the Molucca Islands. Portuguese influence in Africa also increased, and this diminutive Iberian nation ultimately would establish large colonies at Angola and Mozambique.

Under the circumstances, Brazil was an afterthought. Pedro Alvares Cabral, the first Portuguese to reach the coast of Brazil, arrived in 1500. His mariners found no gold and silver jewelry. They were singularly unimpressed with the Tupí hamlets they found nestled in the dense forests along the coast. During Cabral's brief visit, four sailors stayed behind and joined the friendly natives. Meanwhile, his expedition continued on to its original mission, which was to sail around South Africa to India and the Orient. There, the Portuguese mariners gained direct access to the spices of Asia, having cut out the Arab and Italian middlemen in this lucrative trade. Brazil remained of secondary interest to the Portuguese during the first half of the sixteenth century. Cabral's visit and subsequent Portuguese explorations of the Brazilian coast justified Portugal's claim to that region of the Americas that juts out most closely to its prized African trade routes. On one of these Portuguese explorations in 1501, the Florentine cartographer Amerigo Vespucci named this entire "New World" for himself. The name on his map stuck, and Columbus's Indies also became known as the Americas.

The Treaty of Tordesillas, which the pope had already mediated for the two Catholic Iberian monarchies in 1494, ceded to Portugal all lands lying east of a line running 370 leagues (1776 kilometers) west of the Cape Verde Islands. Territories to the west of that

An encounter of a Portuguese caravel and indigenous canoes on the coast of Brazil. (Hans Staden, ca. 1550)

line theoretically belonged to Spain. The Spaniards had little reason later to contest the Brazilian coastline, for it held few attractions compared to Mexico and Peru. A Spanish expedition from Quito in 1541, the one led by Gonzalo Pizarro and Francisco de Orellana, crossed the Andes Mountains and explored the entire length of the Amazon River to its mouth on the Atlantic Ocean. The arduous trip proved to the Spaniards that they were better off remaining in the temperate zones, attended by native tributaries and pursuing conventional commercial activities. The vast Amazon Basin, although much of it lay within the territories reserved by treaty for Spain, was to remain empty of European settlement for several centuries. In time, occupation became more important to territorial demarcation than the Treaty of Tordesillas.

Brazil developed slowly. It lacked readily accessible gold, had no silver at all, and did not support an indigenous civilization with an extensive tribute system—factors contributing to the rapid occupation of Andean lands and Mesoamerica. Brazil's first resource for international commerce was a red-colored dyestuff made from the bark of a local tree, the brazilwood, that could be used in European textile shops. A number of *feitorias* were established along the coastline, and Portuguese traders cajoled the Tupí into bringing in the bark. Thus commenced the area's long process of deforestation. Eventually, the Portuguese named their new possession *Brazil* after this dyestuff.

Brazil was the property of the Portuguese king, who followed precedents of European royal patrimonialism. He ceded rights to use his property to loyal (and wealthy) subjects. The king granted licenses to Portuguese merchants, some of them New Christians—Jews forcibly converted to Christianity—to trade in brazilwood. These merchants then paid the king a royalty and shipped the dyestuffs through Lisbon, paying the king's customs taxes, before selling them to merchants in northern Europe. In this manner, the king used his American possession as a source of royal income without having to invest directly in settling the new territories. Nevertheless, this barter exchange with the natives did not promote expansive settlement (and higher royal income) in Brazil, as was the case in the core Spanish dominions.

The settlement of Brazil began in earnest in 1530. A Portuguese expedition of 400 persons established the first colony on the island of São Vicente, in the center south. Royal officials, soldiers, priests, gentlemen, mechanics, laborers, settlers, and a few wives made up the party. Relatively amicable relations developed between the Tupí on the mainland and these settlers. Soon some of the Portuguese men moved out of this tropical island and into the main Tupí village on the plateau of the mainland. This colony became the forerunner of the city of São Paulo. These few Europeans who came to Brazil did not conquer the indigenous peoples, for these groups produced little agricultural surplus and no gold or silver to support a conquest society. Thereafter, the few Portuguese settlers at São Paulo—nearly all of them male—had to adapt to the indigenous ways in order to survive. They integrated themselves into the villages of the indigenous peoples, established families with their women, practiced polygamy, and helped their adopted tribes fight against their enemies. In the numerous Brazilian rivers, native canoes also remained in wide usage, even by Portuguese settlers.

A wholly new mixed-race group arose from the sexual unions of Portuguese men and Indian women. The offspring of these unions became known as *mamelucos,* and, as in Paraguay, they spoke the native language (Tupí in this case) rather than Portuguese. Jesuit priests who arrived later were horrified that the Portuguese settlers had "gone native" and were raising *mameluco* children. As one missionary wrote about the famous Portuguese settler and slave-hunter, João Ramalho of São Paulo, "[He] is well known and well connected by kinship to the Indians. He has many women. He and his sons have relations with sisters and have children by them. . . . They go to war with the Indians and their festivals are those of the Indians and they live naked as the Indians." These Portuguese settlers and their *mameluco* children became involved in the trade in brazilwood, which Portuguese trading posts on the coast exchanged for trinkets, ironware, and weapons. Although the settlers subsisted on native foods, wild game, and especially the flour processed from the manioc root, they also introduced horses, cattle, pigs, and chickens. The new wealth initiated a slow process of social differentiation within this evolving Brazilian society. The Portuguese and their *mameluco* offspring formed the essential link to European trade and began to assume positions of leadership in the Tupí communities. Like Ramalho described above, they became slavers, forcing the natives to provide labor for those European immigrants who came later to work the land.

The Donatary System

Frustrated by the lack of gold and silver in Brazil, the Portuguese monarch soon devised a plan to promote more permanent settlement, again without having to invest directly from royal coffers. In 1533, he divided the coastal region into 14 zones called captaincies. These the king "donated" to wealthy Portuguese "captains," who were then to organize settlement and bear the expense of developing the resources. The 14 *donatarios* were granted extensive powers to distribute land, establish towns, and engage in economic activity and trade. They were to reap financial rewards for their investment as well as gain land for themselves. *Donatarios* could then pass on their captaincies to their eldest sons as inheritances in perpetuity. The king required only the prompt payment of taxes. The captaincy, or donatary, system was another form of private commercial venture—much like the Spanish expeditions of conquest and settlement. Most of these Portuguese captaincies did not succeed. Trade in brazilwood was one of the few economic underpinnings of those few settlements; and soon the arbitrary demands on the coastal indigenous groups, some of whom Portuguese settlers made into slaves, resulted in armed resistance. Only two captaincies prospered.

The Captaincy of Pernambuco, located on Brazil's northeastern "hump," succeeded because of the development of sugarcane as an export crop. The Crown had already been licensing sugar plantations on the island of Madeira off the northwestern coast of Africa and allowing the importation of slaves to work them. Moreover, a brisk trade in Madeira sugar, benefiting the Crown's treasury, had been opened to northern Europe through Amsterdam. The soil and climate of Pernambuco in northeastern Brazil proved ideal for this perennial crop, and Portuguese growers there engaged the natives to cut back the coastal forests and plant sugarcane. As always in these captaincies, only wealthy and influential Portuguese citizens received the *sesmarias,* or grants of the king's land, and in fairly large amounts. King João III even exercised additional patrimonial powers by licensing the *engenhos,* mills with mechanical cane-crushing equipment that were literally called "engines," to the wealthy landowners. In exchange, the monarchy collected fees and assessed taxes on the overseas transport of sugar.

To protect its patrimony, the Portuguese monarchy throughout the fifteenth century developed what were to become the classic policies of mercantilism.[3] Brazil and other colonial possessions of Portugal were to trade directly only with the mother country; foreigners were to be excluded from enjoying the benefits of sugar production and shipping. In other words, only the king and his subjects were to make money from Brazil. But because monarchism with all its protections, licenses, exclusions, and prohibitions was economically inefficient, the system did not work well in practice. Smuggling was rampant. Non-Portuguese traders freely distributed bribes to the very royal officials sent to enforce the mercantilist policies. Even the Crown itself, stingy in investing its own capital, allowed Dutch and English traders with abundant capital and markets to trade in Brazilian sugar.

The presence of Europeans and the development of the cane sugar industry held out dire consequences for the native peoples of Brazil. Diseases had been ravaging the indigenous population along the coast, and at any rate the Tupí's forest culture had not prepared them for the frenetic pace required to tend the fields and crush the cane to extract its sugary juices. Thus, landowners had the indigenous population enslaved to work on the new plantations. Supported by a buoyant European market for sugar, Brazilian planters sent out slave-raiding parties to search for healthy Native Americans deep in the wilderness. A generation of rugged frontiersmen, mostly *mamelucos* of mixed racial heritage, developed to hunt for slaves.

---

[3] Mercantilism is the economic system of the sixteenth through eighteenth centuries in which European nations sought to increase national wealth and power by exporting manufactured goods and importing precious metals in return. Accumulation of gold and silver was considered the measure of national power. Many a nation also sought to prevent trade between its colonies and other European nations in order to preserve markets, bullion, and sources of raw materials for the industries of the mother country.

As the fifteenth and early sixteenth centuries had witnessed Portugal's vigorous expansion into Africa and Asia, so the late sixteenth century was the time for Brazil. But the Portuguese came there not just for trade but for permanent settlement, too. Sugar provided the basis for this development. In the 1560s, Brazil had more than sixty *engenhos* producing 180,000 *arrobas* (2,250 tons) of sugar per year. High prices for sugar at the end of the century boosted Brazilian production even more, until the colony had more than six hundred fifty sugar mills in 1610. Sugar production supported the permanent settlement of Brazil's northeastern coastal region, attracting Portuguese merchants and craftspersons and supporting large and small landholders.

Workers were also needed for the rapidly expanding sugar industry—and in great numbers. Although slaving continued deep into the vast frontier well into the eighteenth century, this labor source did not prove entirely satisfactory: The Native Americans were physically unfit to survive the new diseases and disinclined to bear the work regimen of their masters. The international commercial nexus was to provide a solution. Portugal's numerous *feitorias* along the west coast of Africa, accustomed to exchanging European trinkets for native exotics, had long since added new, more valuable cargoes—the Africans themselves. The first shipments of slaves arrived in Brazil in the 1550s. Within two generations, the Africans had largely (but not completely) replaced Native American slaves and greatly outnumbered Portuguese settlers in the colony. Slavery would leave an enormous impact on Brazilian society, not only in relegating black persons to the lower end of the social scale but also in conditioning the oppressive behavior of the whites.

São Vicente

The other captaincy to succeed in the sixteenth century was São Vicente in the south, the previously mentioned settlement established prior to being designated a captaincy. Sugar plantations on the island of São Vicente never prospered, but Portuguese men found opportunity as landowners in São Paulo, establishing wheat and cattle production. They had children with Tupí women, and their *mameluco* children assumed the production and trade duties of their fathers. As land was abundant, the chief source of wealth that differentiated Portuguese and *mameluco* society came to be slave labor. The land was distributed by local authorities in large *sesmarias* that covered as much as 44 square kilometers each. Not all the land could be cultivated by the owner, least of all by himself. The settlers had developed, along with their Tupí allies, the habit of raiding distant indigenous groups for slaves. It was a source that needed constant replenishment, for the forest dwellers quickly succumbed to overwork and mistreatment as well as to European diseases.

The *mamelucos* of São Paulo became fierce fighters, constantly campaigning farther into the frontier for Native American slaves. The captains of these slave-raiding groups, which became known as *bandeiras* for the banners each group followed, assumed the positions of leadership at São Paulo. Portuguese authorities recognized this leadership, bestowing on these captains even more authority and wealth. The ordinary *bandeirantes* expected to be recompensed with their own slaves and in goods taken on the expedition. In this, they were not unlike the speculative companies of conquistadores that settled Spanish America. Thus, the frontier society of south central Brazil began to develop a socially hierarchical society that would eventually approximate the inequalities of the society developing around the sugar colony of Pernambuco. The landowners were wealthy and powerful, their followers a little less so, and the native slaves were at the bottom. In contrast to Pernambuco and São Vicente, the other captaincies languished as settlements. Eventually, they were settled not from Portugal but from these two expanding bases in the northeast and in the south of Brazil.

The failure of the donatary system prompted the Portuguese Crown to rethink its colonization program in Brazil. Foreign encroachment into South America caused concern that more royal involvement would be needed lest the entire region be lost. Therefore, in 1549 the king appointed the first Portuguese governor, Tomé de Sousa, who set up his capital at Salvador da Bahia. Accompanying the new governor were the first Jesuit missionaries to come to Brazil, who began the process of converting Native Americans to Christianity, gathering them into mission villages, and teaching them European ways. These new converts were to become loyal and productive subjects of the Portuguese Crown. By the end of the sixteenth century, the Jesuits had fanned out to the Amazon Basin to the north and to São Paulo to the south. As shall be seen in subsequent chapters, their missions subsequently came into conflict with the settlers over control of the indigenous population. The Jesuits wanted to keep them isolated on mission lands, whereas the settlers wanted to enslave them for labor on their properties. Brazilwood may have named it, but sugar and slavery made this Luso-American colony a profitable commercial entity.

CONCLUDING REMARKS

Up to that moment, the world had never seen conquest accomplished so quickly over such a huge geographical area. A number of factors explain Portugal and Spain's extraordinary success. First of all, the Iberians represented the technological advancement of the combined cultures of Europe, Asia, and Africa. They had oceangoing sailing vessels and navigational equipment to guide them. Their weapons included gunpowder, crossbows, forged steel swords, and metal armor. Horses gave them maneuverability. Having been separated from these Old World cultures since long before recorded history, the Native Americans shared in none of these technologies. Their warriors fought valiantly on foot and from canoes with obsidian-tipped spears and axes. Only their bows and arrows might blunt a Spanish attack, but not for long. Armies of hundreds of natives, drawn up rank on rank, could be cut to pieces by a mere threescore Spaniards.

Steel, armor, horses, gunpowder, arquebuses, and cannon do not, in themselves, explain European successes in battle. The conquistadores combined business opportunism with the fighting traditions inherited from the Reconquest. And when they arrived at Tenochtitlán and Cajamarca, they also counted on previous experience in native warfare and commercial enterprise in the Caribbean as well. In the final analysis, the fractious Spaniards served the same king and owed allegiance to the same church. Their strategic objectives invariably were the same: to defeat the indigenous political powers, extract wealth from indigenous peoples, and convert them into tributaries and Catholics. Each group of Spanish fighting men formed a self-confident, socially cohesive unit unto itself. No matter how violently they quarreled among themselves before and after—especially over divisions of tribute—they always united when confronting the foe. Diego de Almagro serves as a good example. Despite his hatred toward the Pizarros, he arrived in 1537 from his disappointing campaign in Chile to raise the siege at Cuzco and save Hernando Pizarro, only to fight and lose to the Pizarros later.

By no stretch of the imagination could one even call the Spaniards who conquered the Americas an army. The typical conqueror was a Spanish-born man in his mid-twenties with a lower-middle-class background. He hailed from the province of Andalusía, Castile, or Estremadura and had acquired a rudimentary education and a civilian profession prior to leaving for the Indies. He did not yet have a wife and children and used his own savings to provide the equipment and passage to the Americas. Each of these men expected to share the rewards of conquest—gold and silver, a house full of servants, possession of native slaves to provide food and goods to trade, a prestigious political appointment, and respectability and social status. Although most Spaniards had intended to return to Spain, many conquistadores lived out their days in the Indies. Spain did not engage its impoverished peasants in the Conquest because they lacked the individual means to get themselves to the Indies and to outfit themselves for a military campaign. The commercial aspects of conquest excluded the poorest Spaniards from participating.

Only a few of the conquerors were hidalgos, a contraction of *hijos de algo,* literally "sons of something" and meaning "of noble lineage." This did not prevent a few successful Spaniards from claiming nobility once they struck it rich in the Conquest. Indeed, each participant in an expedition expected to share in the wealth and aspired to be granted an *encomienda* of Native Americans to be able to establish social status and a substantial family lineage. They observed social rankings among themselves, according higher status and leadership roles to those who had more wealth, who invested more in the expedition, who owned horses, who brought along retainers, and who had previous experience fighting indigenous groups. The most prominent conquistadores, therefore, claimed larger *encomiendas* and seats on the town council following the Conquest.

Although the Spaniards came from a fifteenth-century tradition of war against the Moors, their warfare against the Native Americans was much more savage. "For between Christians and Moors there is some well-feeling, and it is in the interests of both sides to spare those they take alive because of their ransoms," said one conquistador. "But in this Indian war there is no such feeling on either side. They give each other the cruelest deaths they can imagine." The Inka siege of Cuzco in 1536 serves as a case in point. Hernando Pizarro had noticed how Inka women were involved in the siege as porters and cooks, so he had all captured women put to death. Moreover, he cut off the right hands of noncombatants to instill fear into the ranks of the Inka forces. Part of the reason for the deep-seated cruelty of the Conquest lay in the nearly insurmountable odds—at least in numbers. When Francisco Pizarro confronted Atawallpa in 1532, he led a force of 65 horsemen and 106 men on foot. This small group overwhelmed the Inka's troops at Cajamarca, which numbered more than five thousand. In the siege of Cuzco four years later, Manco Inka's forces numbered at least one hundred thousand—perhaps more. There were only 180 Spanish defenders, reinforced by several thousand Indian allies.

Previous service in the Indies prepared the conquerors to survive these hardships of exploration and conquest. Both Cortés and Pizarro and their lieutenants had fought in the Caribbean islands or in Central America prior to going to Mexico and Peru. Even so, the odds of survival were not good. Members of expeditionary forces who arrived right off the boat were likely to die of illness or violence. Only about 50 percent of the conquistadores survived to pass on the pride of their exploits and lineage to their children.

Of the 1,930 would-be conquerors in three expeditions in Colombia, probably only 930 survived. The rest succumbed to hardships of the campaign, fighting the natives, or illnesses like malaria or dysentery. More than five hundred Spaniards perished in the 20-year struggle to conquer the indomitable Maya of the Yucatán. In Peru, more Spaniards died fighting each other over the spoils than fighting the Inka, but Europe had a vast pool of replacements for those who died in the Conquest.

Another factor accounting for Spanish success was that Europeans and Africans had long ago developed a resistance to diseases that had periodically ravaged the known world since the times of the Sumerians, Egyptians, and Greeks. However, as previously mentioned, the Native Americans had never known smallpox, typhus, influenza, cholera, or even malaria. In the tropical climates of the Caribbean islands and of the equatorial lowlands, they succumbed quickly to European diseases, disappearing nearly without trace. These diseases also spread like wildfire among the more congested populations of the highland civilizations of the Aztec, the Muisca, and the Inka. Sometimes these pandemics began ravaging Indian populations even before the first European expeditions

---

MANUSCRIPT 3.4

The Sexual Conceits of European Conquerors

The first European descriptions of the indigenous peoples of the Americas often say more about the describer than about the described. Take, for example, these passages from the first explorers among the Carib peoples of the Caribbean and Brazil. Gender differences become more pronounced and misunderstood when women of one culture encounter men of another, which is precisely what happened when European men encountered and interacted with Native American women from the Caribbean through California and south to Tierra del Fuego. The cultural differences caused disgust, fascination, and liberty, more so for the European male than the female Native American. In terms of power, the balance in the relationship tipped toward the European men, and the results of this imbalance will be evident throughout this book. The following passages by a sailor with Columbus and by the explorer Amerigo Vespucci nearly dehumanize the indigenous women, justifying converting them into gifts and objects of sexual satisfaction.

Michele de Cuneo

While I was in the boat I captured a very beautiful Carib woman, whom the said Lord Admiral [Columbus] gave to me, and with whom, having taken her into my cabin, she being naked according to their custom, I conceived desire to take pleasure. I wanted to put my desire into execution but she did not want it and treated me with her finger nails in such a manner that I wished I had never begun. But seeing that, (to tell you the end of it all), I took a rope and thrashed her well, for which she raised such unheard of screams that you would not have believed your ears. Finally we came to an agreement in such manner that I can tell you that she seemed to have been brought up in a school of harlots.

Amerigo Vespucci

They do not practise marriage amongst themselves. Each one takes all the wives he pleases; and when he desires to repudiate them, he does repudiate them without it

sought to engage them in battle. Great as their cities and accomplishments had been, these new diseases greatly undermined the confidence of the Aztec and Inka rulers and reduced their armies and their economic underpinnings.

Miscegenation was also a feature of the first encounters between Europeans and Native Americans during the Conquest period. Both while traveling or conducting military campaigns and once settled, European men freely associated with Native American women and later with African slave women (see Manuscript 3.4). Always and everywhere, white males outnumbered white females among the settlers, so they sought female companionship among the local women. "The women are good looking . . . and more willing to demonstrate their love than what is deemed necessary," reported one Spanish chronicler of the native women of the Colombian highlands, "especially to Spaniards." But, except where no European women followed, few of these men ever acknowledged the result of their unions. In New Granada, among the original white conquistadores, the illegitimacy rate was 95 percent. One leader of Spanish settlers in Chile, Francisco de Aguirre, recognized as his own at least fifty of the children he fathered with

being considered a wrong on his part or a disgrace to the woman; for in this the woman has as much liberty as the man. They are not very jealous, and are libidinous beyond measure, and the women far more than the men; for I refrain out of decency from telling you the trick which they play to satisfy their immoderate lust. . . . They are women of pleasing person, very well proportioned, so that one does not see on their bodies any ill-formed feature or limb. And although they go about utterly naked, they are fleshy women, and that part of their privies which he who has not seen them would think to see is invisible; for they cover all with their thighs, save that part [for] which nature made no provision, and which is modestly speaking, the *mons veneris*. In short they are no more ashamed [of their shameful parts] than we are in displaying the nose and mouth. Only exceptionally will you see a woman with drooping breasts, or with belly shrunken through frequent parturition, or with other wrinkles;

for all look as though they had never given birth. They showed themselves very desirous of copulating with us Christians. . . .

They are so [liberal] in giving that it is the exception when they deny you anything; and, on the other hand, [they are free] in begging, when they show themselves to be your friends. But the greatest token of friendship which they show you is that they give you their wives and daughters; and when a father or a mother brings you the daughter, although she be a virgin, and you sleep with her, they esteem themselves highly honored; and in this way they practise the full extreme of hospitality.

SOURCES: Michele de Cuneo's Letter on the Second Voyage, October 28, 1495, in *Journals and Other Documents in the Life and Voyages of Christopher Columbus*, trans. and ed. S. E. Morison (New York: The Heritage Press, 1963), 212; and Amerigo Vespucci, *Letter to Piero Soderini, Gonfaloniere*, trans. and ed. G. T. Northup (Princeton, N.J.: Princeton University Press, 1916), 7–10; as quoted in Marvin Lunenfeld, ed., *1492, Discovery, Invasion, Encounter: Sources and Interpretations* (Lexington, Mass.: D.C. Heath, 1991), 282–83.

native women. Some mestizo and mulatto children were fortunate if they grew up in their father's household, gaining some economic and social security from this fact; most grew up impoverished in the mother's household and enjoyed little status. The conquerors tended to recognize only their offspring from the younger Spanish women who arrived in succeeding years. Therefore, the Conquest established the basis of many social distinctions that persisted throughout the colonial period in Latin America—even up to the present time. These colonial social relationships will be the subjects of subsequent chapters.

An additional factor accounting for rapid Spanish deployment in the Indies consisted of the disunity among the Native Americans themselves. First of all, the Spaniards provided themselves with intelligence by securing translators and reconnoitering their enemies before engaging them in battle. The natives almost never knew the capabilities of the invaders until it was too late. Everywhere the Spaniards and Portuguese went, they recruited auxiliaries from among the clans and city-states that had been chafing under the tyranny of a neighboring clan or city-state. Working on these divisions, Cortés had enlisted the aide of the Tlaxcalans against the Aztec. Pizarro and his men had benefited from a bitter power struggle between rival claimants to the Inka throne. The agricultural Guaraní of Paraguay became allies of the Spaniards because these powerful new arrivals defended them from the raids of nearby Chaco groups. The Tupí joined the *mamelucos* in enslaving their ancient enemies.

Moreover, the Native Americans had learned to live under domination long before the Europeans arrived. They adapted themselves to the Spaniards as they had been adapting for centuries to the rise of the various ancient empires. The natives' concepts of exchanging tribute and work for protection and patronage enabled Spaniards, in short order, to gain control of whole groups of them and their production. This was especially so in the seats of the great civilizations of Mexico, Guatemala, Colombia, Ecuador, Peru, and Bolivia. Spaniards found less success where indigenous peoples were more dispersed. Hunter-gatherer natives resisted European conquests for longer periods of time, as in the plains and forests of southern South America; the Amazon, Orinoco, and Maracaibo Basins; the semi-arid wilderness of northern Mexico; and what is today the southwestern territory of the United States.

Finally, the European economic infrastructure—the accessibility and size of the European market—contributed mightily to the rapid spread of European control throughout the Indies. It is to the economics and institutionalization of colonialism that this book now turns.

Additional Reading

Andrews, Kenneth R. *The Spanish Caribbean: Trade and Plunder, 1530–1630.* New Haven, Conn.: Yale University Press, 1978.

Avellaneda, José Ignacio. *The Conquerors of the New Kingdom of Granada.* Albuquerque: University of New Mexico Press, 1995.

Bethell, Leslie, ed. *Colonial Spanish America.* Cambridge, Mass.: Cambridge University Press, 1987.

Clendinnen, Inga. *Ambivalent Conquests: Maya and Spaniard in Yucatan, 1517–1570.* Cambridge, England: Cambridge University Press, 1987.

Cook, Noble David. *Born to Die: Disease and New World Conquest (1492–1650).* Cambridge, England: Cambridge University Press, 1998.

Cook, Noble David, and W. George Lovell, eds. *"Secret Judgements of God": Old World Disease in Colonial Spanish America.* Norman: University of Oklahoma Press, 1992.

Hassig, Ross. *Mexico and the Spanish Conquest.* London: Longman, 1994.

Hemming, John. *The Search for El Dorado.* London: Michael Joseph, 1978.

Himmerich y Valencia, Robert. *The Encomenderos of New Spain, 1521–1555.* Austin: University of Texas Press, 1991.

Jones, Grant D. *The Conquest of the Last Maya Kingdom.* Stanford, Calif.: Stanford University Press, 1998.

Kramer, Wendy. *Encomienda Politics in Early Colonial Guatemala, 1524–1544: Dividing the Spoils.* Boulder, Colo.: Westview Press, 1994.

Lang, James. *Portuguese Brazil: The King's Plantation.* New York: Academic Press, 1979.

León-Portilla, Miguel, ed. *Broken Spears: The Aztec Account of the Conquest of Mexico.* Boston: Beacon Press, 1962.

Liss, Peggy K. *Mexico Under Spain, 1521–1556: Society and the Origins of Nationality.* Chicago: University of Chicago Press, 1975.

Lockhart, James. *The Men of Cajamarca: A Social and Biographical Study of the First Conquerors of Peru.* Austin: University of Texas Press, 1972.

Maura, Juan Francisco. *Women in the Conquest of the Americas.* Trans. by John F. Deredita. New York: P. Lang, 1997.

Melville, Elinor G. K. *A Plague of Sheep: Environmental Consequences of the Conquest of Mexico.* New York: Cambridge University Press, 1994.

Morison, Samuel Eliot. *Admiral of the Ocean Sea: A Life of Christopher Columbus.* Boston: Little, Brown, 1942.

———. *The European Discovery of America: The Southern Voyages, 1492–1619.* New York: Oxford University Press, 1974.

Parry, John H. *The Age of Reconnaissance.* New York: Mentor Books, 1974.

———. *Spanish Seaborne Empire.* New York: Knopf, 1966.

Phillips, William D., Jr., and Carla Rahn Phillips. *The Worlds of Christopher Columbus.* Cambridge, England: Cambridge University Press, 1992.

Restall, Matthew. *Maya Conquistador.* Boston: Beacon Press, 1998.

Rouse, Irving. *The Tainos: Rise and Decline of the People Who Greeted Columbus.* New Haven, Conn.: Yale University Press, 1992.

Russell-Wood, A. J. R. *A World on the Move: The Portuguese in Africa, Asia and America, 1415–1808.* Manchester, England: Carcanet, 1992.

Sauer, Carl O. *The Early Spanish Main.* Berkeley: University of California Press, 1969.

Super, John C. *Food, Conquest and Colonization in Sixteenth-Century Spanish America.* Albuquerque: University of New Mexico Press, 1992.

Thomas, Hugh. *The Conquest of Mexico.* London: Hutchinson, 1993.

Varón Gabai, Rafael. *Francisco Pizarro and His Brothers: The Illusion of Power in Sixteenth-Century Peru.* Trans. Javier Flores Espinoza. Norman: University of Oklahoma Press, 1997.

Villamarín, Juan A., and Judith E. Villamarín. *Indian Labor in Mainland Colonial Spanish America.* Newark, N.J.: Delaware, 1975.

Wachtel, Nathan. *The Vision of the Vanquished: The Spanish Conquest of Peru through Indian Eyes, 1530–1570.* Trans. Ben Reynolds and Siân Reynolds. Hassocks, England: The Harvester Press, 1977.

In Spanish and Portuguese

Avellaneda Nayas, José Ignacio. *La expedición de Sebastián de Belalcázar al mar del norte y su llegada al Nuevo Reino de Granada*. Bogotá: Banco de la República, 1992.

Buarque de Holanda, Sérgio. *Visão do paraíso: os motivos edênicos no descobrimento e colonizacão do Brasil*. 4th ed. São Paulo: Companhia Editora Nacional, 1985.

Céspedes del Castillo, Guillermo. *La exploración del Atlántico*. Madrid: MAPFRE, 1991.

Góngora, Mario. *Los grupos de conquistadores en Tierra Firme (1509– 1530)*. Santiago: Universidad de Chile, 1962.

Guillén Guillén, Edmundo. *Versión Inca de la conquista*. Lima: Editorial Milla Batres, 1974.

Roulet, Florencia. *La resistencia de los Guaraní del Paraguay a la conquista española [1537– 1556]*. Posadas: Editorial Universitaria Universidad Nacional de Misiones, 1993.

PART II

PART II

ESTABLISHING THE COLONIAL SOCIAL HERITAGE

For more than three centuries—from the encounter of 1492 until the conclusion of the rebellions for independence in 1826—European powers ruled the Americas. European political domination eventually succumbed to the independence movements of the early nineteenth century, but certain social and economic legacies from the colonial period have endured to the present day. Part II of this book explains how these legacies became entrenched in the formative period of colonial Latin America: the sixteenth and seventeenth centuries.

During the long colonial period, Europeans presided over the forging of a multiracial and multiethnic social order that was characterized by inequality and discrimination. The original inhab-

itants, the Native Americans, composed the initial base of the new colonial social order. The Spanish, Portuguese, French, Dutch, and British came from Europe. These new arrivals then introduced peoples from Africa as slaves.

But Europeans and their progeny in the Americas fully intended to benefit most from the political and economic opportunities within the colonial order. They dominated government at nearly all levels, reserved for themselves the choicest occupations, and encroached on the most fertile and valuable lands. Indians were expected to remain as workers and peasants, retaining some of their own leaders to run their agricultural communities and to organize labor for white employers. The indigenous peoples preserved control of enough land to

sustain themselves, if not to supply the European consumers. Where native labor proved unequal to the task, especially in tropical environments, European overlords introduced African slaves to work the plantations and mines.

Soon after the arrival of the Europeans and Africans, a process of racial miscegenation began to alter the colonial social hierarchy. Middle groups arose from the casual interaction of European males and non-European females. In this patriarchal colonial order, European women served to legitimate the honor and racial purity of elite families; thus, they found themselves privileged, even pampered, within the household but circumscribed in their public roles.

Two variegated mixed-race groups formed as nowhere else in the known world at the time.

Mestizos issued from the unions of European men and native women. Mulattoes issued from the unions of white men and African women. This was not the beginning of a "cosmic race" that would ultimately reduce all American racial differences to narrow variations of skin color. Indeed, miscegenation did not end discrimination based on race and ethnicity. In the colonial social order, most Europeans still retained enormous privileges over everyone else with darker skin. Even mestizos and mulattoes, who identified more with their European heritage, practiced social pretensions over those who looked more Native American and African and who spoke non-European languages.

A certain fluidity as well as ambivalence and conflict marked colonial society. Even though social barriers solidified between the racial groups, a limited amount of mobility did exist. A native who left his village in Mexico or Peru might pass for mestizo if he donned European clothing, spoke Spanish, and worked at a nonpeasant occupation. A light-skinned mulatto in Brazil or Cuba might be accepted into white society if she had enough wealth to afford the trappings of respectability. Spaniards and Portuguese also observed differences among themselves depending on birth, wealth, and family connections. Incessant conflicts and competition existed among members of the same social rank who sought to maximize their limited opportunities for advancement. Upward mobility in such a society always met stiff resistance from the strata above one's station. While the middle groups sought to emulate, as much as practicable, the lifestyles of their social superiors, they profoundly resented them as well.

Violence could also break out along the cleavages of race and status. White domination implied real or potential suppression of subordinate peoples, particularly the Native Americans and the Africans. Slave labor in the Americas encompassed the use of violence in the kidnapping, restraint, and coercion of its victims; therefore, violence prevailed in the resistance of indigenous peoples and slaves and in disputes between master and slave and employer and worker. We know less about family violence engendered by the inherently unequal relationship between fathers, mothers, sons, and daughters, but it also existed.

The largest question seems to be this: If the Europeans established a colonial order in which race and influence determined who enjoyed privileges and who bore most of the burdens, if miscegenation and competition permitted some degree of mobility, and if ambivalence and conflict were found at every level of the social hierarchy, how did the colonial social order survive intact for well over three hundred years?

The colonial state and the Catholic Church played important roles in establishing and maintaining European authority in the colonies. Connections to the official colonial bureaucracy of Spain or Portugal and association with Catholic Christianity did indeed confer power to an individual. However, colonialism was neither politically totalitarian nor theocratic. The colonial state's real source of authority resided more in its ability to mediate conflicts within the inequitable social order than in carrying out the absolute letter of the law. The church ordained the ethnic and racial inequalities in religious doctrine, but it also checked the rapacity and greed of the white settlers. The clergy in the Americas became the chief protectors of the native population. Nonetheless, colonial Latin America remained very much a society of men—and of women—and much less a society of legally or religiously condoned justice. After all, justice was not a distinguishing feature of colonial America.

At base, social position and one's prospects in colonial society were determined by *social power*, a term that may be defined as the ability to dispense privileges, to enjoy status, to mediate disputes, to influence actions of others, and to provide material benefits. Social power resolved how scarce economic benefits were shared. Power existed at all levels of society, but one found greater concentrations of it high on the social scale, as fewer resources of social power existed on the lower end. Men and women exhibited their power by belonging to community and religious organizations, marrying or mating within certain social groups, taking up certain occupations, and making a certain income. Indeed, high status and high income coincided closely, as those with the greatest social power reserved for themselves the best opportunities to make money. Nonetheless, native peoples and slaves did retain certain individual and collective power—of running away or seeking protection among peers—to ameliorate their condition. The weakest in society found power in embracing the political and religious institutions of the powerful. In the final analysis, the dispersal of social power throughout the multiracial and multiethnic hierarchy provided a remarkable cohesion for the volatile amalgam of humanity that was colonial Latin America.

CHAPTER 4

COLONIAL INSTITUTIONS

Although Spain and Portugal became the first European imperial powers in the Americas, Spain acquired the richest prizes in Mesoamerica and the Andean region in terms of surplus wealth, silver and gold deposits, and the size of the indigenous population. Brazil initially offered fewer of these assets. Portugal, therefore, pursued exploration elsewhere, in Africa and the Far East, developing its possession of Brazil almost as an afterthought. There is an economic explanation for the success of the European Conquest, for the first generations of settlers quickly captured existing native wealth and instituted new kinds of agricultural and mining production to integrate the Americas into a worldwide commercial network supporting European conquest and settlement. The export economy did not dictate colonial social life. In fact, the reverse was true—concerns of European social domination determined economic development as the settlers sought to subject the economy to their narrow social interests. They attempted to monopolize the gains from economic activity, as shall be seen in the next chapter, shutting nonwhites out of lucrative trades and subordinating economic activity as much as possible to the maintenance of elite white families. The economy existed for the purpose of perpetuating the power of the individual European settlers who created it in the first place and of bolstering the power of Spain and Portugal, which claimed the Americas.

Other European rivals woke up to the commercial possibilities of American colonies nearly too late. The French attempted settlements in Brazil, the Caribbean, and North America, where they incurred opposition from the Portuguese and Spaniards. The Netherlands and England were also less successful at establishing colonies there. English privateers disrupted Iberian shipping in the Caribbean and Atlantic Ocean but settled for a few less valuable colonies in the Caribbean and on the Atlantic coast of North America. The Netherlands, one of the great commercial powers of the seventeenth century, aggressively converted the wealth and power of its chief port, Amsterdam, into an overseas military adventure that succeeded briefly in snatching northeastern Brazil away from the Portuguese. In the end, Spain and Portugal reigned supreme in the Americas even though they could not dislodge its European rivals from several marginal settlements.

It was left to the Iberian settlers to construct a new social order that would place them and their progeny in permanent control of the native peoples. It was a formidable task, for the original inhabitants continued to outnumber the Europeans in most parts of the Indies well into the seventeenth century. To maintain their narrow perch of privilege in these colonial societies, the settlers had to create durable systems to perpetuate the gains of conquest. They had to maximize their ability to dominate and control peoples of lesser status. For this purpose, they introduced their own European systems of economic exchange, governance, and religious observance.

The political organization of the colonies was expected to serve as a second important adhesive for the fractious, mutually antagonistic social orders. So it did. Loyalty to a benevolent and wise—if distant—monarch united all ethnic, racial, and occupational groups. Although subordinate peoples occasionally rebelled and the powerful hatched conspiracies to resist specific policies and officials, no one seriously contested the rights and prerogatives of Spanish and Portuguese kings. Yet this administrative system, designed to hold the colonial societies together while the royalty of Iberia extracted the economic surplus, was not a totalitarian police state. There existed serious impediments to royal power in the Americas. The monarchies of both Spain and Portugal issued many a decree that was ignored. *"Obedezco pero no cumplo,"* as the famous saying went: "I obey but I do not comply." The colonial state, therefore, found its greatest success as a mediating, reactive power, unifying the disparate peoples of the empire under one crown and one church and then mediating conflicts among the separate social institutions representing those peoples.

As Spaniards and Portuguese conquered Native American peoples, they utilized religion in much the same fashion as had their forebears during the Iberian Reconquest. Catholicism justified conquest and united the new subordinates under European social domination. Individual Spaniards and Portuguese, in purely private enterprises, may have set forth to capture land and labor in the Americas to establish themselves. But they carried their Catholic traditions with them as part of their indispensable cultural heritage and national identities. Catholicism served the ends of imperialism. Still, the colonial social and economic system was fraught with danger and remained extremely volatile. It is unlikely that the European colonialists could have sustained three hundred years of entrenched privilege and exploitation without two great institutions of social control—the church and the state—and without connection to the international economy.

THE ECONOMICS OF DOMINATION

During the period of conquest and settlement, the European colonists actively sought every opportunity to link themselves to world commerce. Why? As indicated previously, Europeans intended to establish a separate, elite lifestyle out of reach of the subordinated peoples. They wanted to live as in Spain or Portugal, with wine, food, clothes, furniture, and jewelry of European rather than indigenous styles. This new colonial elite nourished itself on trade—but now on a scale that dwarfed the tribute and trade that had sustained the ancient American nobility. The new commerce was global in scale and integrated Latin America into an international system. But motivation for its creation was the same: Trade provided the elite goods that sustained the *gente decente* (decent, or upper-class, people) at the apex of society and symbolized their domination over other groups.

Foreign Commerce

The port of Seville in southern Spain served as the first great funnel for the outflow of European goods such as wine, textiles, and ironware as well as the staging area for emigrants to the Indies. Later Cádiz assumed this task. These goods were absolutely essential, for Europeans were determined to recreate in the Americas the lifestyles they had known in their homelands. Settlers paid for these prestige goods with gold and silver that they first acquired from the vanquished Native Americans and then from a formal colonial mining industry. Merchants in southern Spain grew wealthy on the receipt of bullion from their correspondents and commercial agents throughout the Indies. Spanish merchants residing in the colonies made enough to diversify their American investments, placing money into mining, haciendas, plantations, and artisan and textile shops. International and domestic trade formed the basis of their economic clout. Trade even extended from Latin America to Asia. Merchants shipped silver on a few ships heading out from Acapulco that were bound for the Spanish colony in the Philippines. These ships returned with Chinese silks, jades, and ceramics, which were then transshipped to Peru or passed overland to Mexico City.

Towns and cities in Latin America were founded along the major overland trade routes. One commercial network stretched from the wheat lands of central Chile and the cattle ranches of northwestern Argentina through the mining districts of Upper Peru (later Bolivia) to Cuzco and Lima, up the coast to Panama City, across the isthmus to Portobello, and thence to Cuba and Spain. The second great linkage embraced the cattle ranches of northern Mexico and the wheat farms of the Bajío. This Mexican commercial route linked the mines of Zacatecas and Guanajuato through Mexico City to the port of Veracruz, to Havana, and to Spain (see Map 4.1). These were the economic sinews of empire.

The economic infrastructure that the conquerors installed in the Americas—and their integration into the European market—contributed mightily to the consolidation of Spanish and Portuguese control. From the beginning, the export of precious metals incorporated the American colonies into the world economic system. Gold and silver, the universal media of exchange in Europe as well as Africa and Asia, had underwritten the initial spread of Spaniards into the New World. Cortés himself acknowledged as much. He reportedly told a messenger of the Aztec Emperor, Moteuczoma, "I and my companions suffer from a disease of the heart which can be cured only with gold." The conquerors took gold, silver, pearls, and precious stones from the natives. The gold cycle had

Map 4.1 Principal Commercial Routes of the Americas in the Seventeenth Century

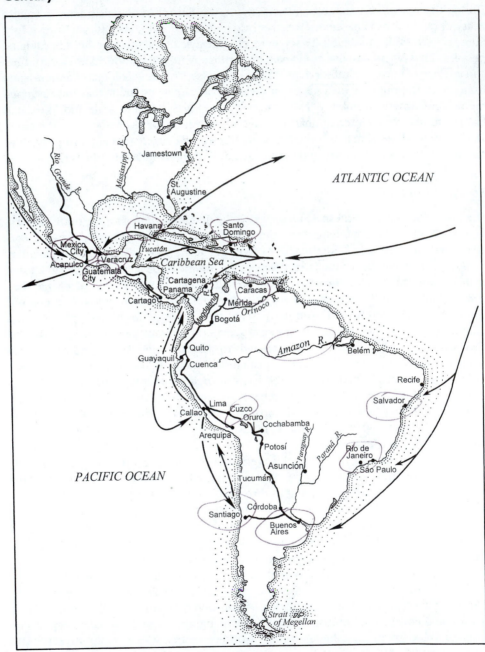

begun in the Caribbean islands during the last eight years of the fifteenth century and continued with the great ransom of gold jewelry for the Inka ruler Atawallpa. Gold was the principal booty that the Spanish conquerors divided among themselves.

As soon as supplies of native ornaments ran out, the Europeans themselves organized the mining of these precious commodities. When the declining indigenous population of Hispaniola and Cuba threatened to retard gold production, Spaniards explored the coastline of Colombia and Venezuela, searching for native slaves to work their placer mines. Later, when the highland peoples proved unable and unwilling to pan for gold in the rivers of the Colombian lowlands, Spaniards brought in African slaves to do it. The search for silver pushed new conquests into the Chichimeca lands of northern Mexico. Enterprising conquerors learned from the Inkas about the fabulous mountain of silver at Potosí in the Altiplano.

Mining became the lifeblood of commerce everywhere in the Spanish Indies. At first, mining depended on native technology, as at the mines of Potosí. Spanish *encomenderos* set natives to work smelting the silver ore in large urns, an ancient method that was soon replaced. Then Spanish miners introduced to Mexico a system of mercury amalgamation, a method for extracting silver by mixing the crushed ore with liquid mercury. It proved to be the biggest technological breakthrough in the colonial industry. Silver production burgeoned at Zacatecas, Guanajuato, and other Mexican mining towns, and mercury amalgamation was introduced to Potosí in 1570. However, mercury was not a local product; Mexico depended on Spain for its supply. A mine at Huancavelica in the Peruvian Andes opened up as the only source of mercury in the Americas, but its production did not meet even Potosí's demand for this resource. Thus, Spanish mercury also had to be imported through Panama, Lima, and Cuzco.

But silver was an important commodity, and Upper Peru and Mexico responded as the world's most prolific producers during the colonial period (see Figure 4.1). By 1600, New Spain had some three hundred seventy refineries that crushed the ore and mixed the mercury on large open patios. Individual mines in colonial Mexico employed large numbers of workers, upwards to one hundred eighty to two hundred each. Potosí itself had 65 refineries. Around these refineries developed communities of workers, their women and families, retailers, and transport services. Nearby to these communities, landowners founded farms to grow foodstuffs and haciendas to raise cattle and mules. In New Spain, the mining industry was especially important for settling the frontier lands of the Chichimec. After all, most mines were located in the near north, far from the more populous heartland of central Mexico.

Potosí served much the same function as the Mexican silver mines, generating secondary economic activity and a free-floating proletariat. The one difference between the two had to do with Potosí's unique geographic location. The mines were situated on the forbidding, windswept Altiplano at 3,000 meters above sea level, where nothing grew nearby. All of the foodstuffs for workers and materials for equipment had to be hauled in from outside the district. Wheat, cattle, hides, and yerba maté for tea came from the Río de la Plata region. Wheat and wine came from Chile and Mendoza. Potatoes and vegetables and corn came from Peru and the agricultural regions of Upper Peru. Woolen and cotton textiles came from Cochabamba and Cuzco. Córdoba specialized in producing mules for the great mule trains that carried supplies into and silver bullion out of Potosí. In the meanwhile, other silver strikes of much less consequence were made in Oruro, Sicasica, and elsewhere in Upper Peru and Peru (see Map 4.1).

Figure 4.1   Registered Silver Production of Mexico and Potosí, 1581–1810

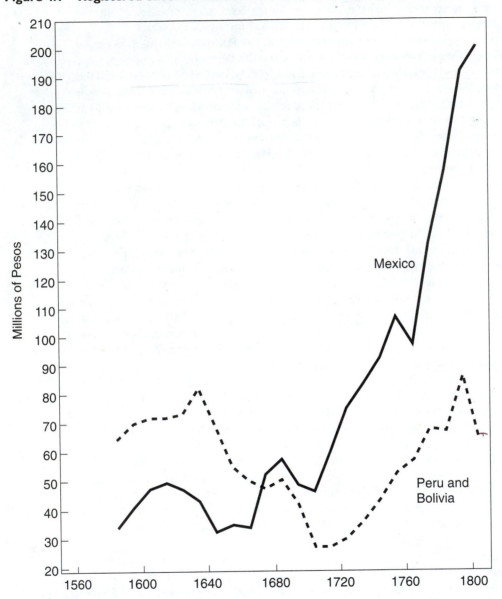

SOURCE: Mark A. Burkholder and Lyman L. Johnson, *Colonial Latin America,* 2d ed. (New York: Oxford University Press), 130.

The mining boom prompted the Spanish entrepreneurs and the colonial state to promote development of a wholly new labor system, partly fashioned after pre-Conquest indigenous institutions as well as elements of slave and free labor. This amalgam of new and old labor arrangements will be presented in the next three chapters. Suffice it to say that the sixteenth-century silver-mining boom helped solidify the European conquest by linking Mesoamerica and South America to European markets.

Domestic Commerce

Certainly, Spanish colonists could neither live on silver alone nor on the expensive imported goods that it purchased. They depended on the rapid expansion of a whole colonial infrastructure of economic support. Native peasants contributed foodstuffs and especially labor for the new Spanish overlords, few of whom desired to live on manioc, corn, and potatoes—the indigenous staples. Initially, they had little tolerance for native drinks such as the Paraguayan tea called yerba maté, *chicha* fermented from masticated corn, pulque made from cactus pulp, or even the chocolate of the cacao bean. Desiring to recreate their European environment as much as possible, Spaniards and Portuguese introduced their own plants; when the natives would not or could not take charge of the production of these foreign commodities, the Europeans themselves organized agricultural production. Spanish land holdings specializing in Old World–style agricultural production occupied the regions serving both the newly established cities and the mining industry.

For items too bulky or perishable to import, the colonists quickly instituted a program of import substitution.. Distance made it prohibitively expensive to import wine into Peru, so European vines were transplanted for a local viticulture industry at Arequipa, Mendoza, and Chile. Grapes and raisins were also made available in this way. Not everyone could afford imported European textiles, so the colonists set up *obrajes* (manufacturing shops) that produced cloth from the wool of sheep imported for that reason. Quito became the center of the colonial textile industry. Its 100 *obrajes* in 1680 employed 10,000 workers, turning out more than six hundred thousand yards of cloth and earning up to 3 million pesos yearly. Ecuadorian cloth sold in Colombia, Peru, and Upper Peru. Thus, the poorer colonists—and the new class of native workers—were clothed. There were few deposits of iron ore in Central and South America, so Spanish master artisans imported raw metal from which they fashioned weapons and a wide variety of ironware. Local craftspersons built all the buildings of the sixteenth century from domestic materials, but the public buildings and elite homes in the heart of their cities were constructed in the architectural styles then prevailing in Europe.

Meat could not be shipped in from Europe, but live animals could. Pigs, goats, and cattle proliferated nearly everywhere and were raised on nearly every farm and hacienda in the Americas. Much livestock escaped and multiplied into wild herds in the unsettled parts of Cuba, northern Mexico, Central America, Chile, and the vast prairies of the Río de la Plata. The proliferation of European cattle was spectacular. In 1620, New Spain had nearly 1.3 million head of cattle—more numerous than the indigenous population—and 8 million sheep and goats. Even the native peoples were affected by the new livestock. They adopted burros and pigs for their own production and had to put up with the horses and cattle of the Iberians trampling on their native crops. The hunter-gatherer peoples of southern South America even quit gathering and took up hunting exclusively, subsisting on the new herds of wild cattle. By the seventeenth century, these plains hunters had taken to riding on horseback.

Cattle and draft animals permitted new territories to be opened up for agriculture and cultivation. The pre-Columbian digging stick, suitable for the softer soils of mountain valleys and rain forests, could do nothing on the tough, root-heavy grasses of the American prairies. Whole grassland regions in North and South America, which had not been developed agriculturally by the ancient peoples, now served as extensive grazing pastures for sheep, horses, and cattle. Oxen-drawn iron-tipped plows began to cut through the thick roots, permitting wheat and other European grains to be sown. European agricultural technology opened up the Mexican Bajío and the Argentine Pampas.

The colonists even found economic opportunity getting into the production of certain native products. On their haciendas, they began the production of cacao, pulque, and cotton in Mesoamerica and of coca in the Andes. The new *encomenderos* and other settlers engaged in intercolonial trade in native products. The tribute they received in cotton cloth and cacao in Guatemala and the Yucatán was sent on to colonial markets in Mexico. At Potosí, the native workers themselves became an important market for Spanish *encomenderos* and merchants. Those who worked as miners purchased dried potatoes and coca leaves that *encomenderos* acquired from their tributaries. As the colonists themselves developed a palate for the native chocolate drink, Spanish landowners responded by acquiring land in Guayaquil and Caracas to devote to cultivation of the cacao tree.

European settlers, of necessity, had to develop a reliable transport system tying one settlement to another over longer distances than those covered by pre-Columbian transporters. In Peru, the Spaniards used the Inka highway system to move trade goods. Native methods—provided by human bearers and llamas—sufficed for the short haul, but the heavier and bulkier commodities required new means. Colonists introduced mules, oxen, and carts, spawning secondary industries in mule and ox-breeding and in cart building. Haciendas in northern Mexico specialized in mules and oxen, while the Argentine settlement of Tucumán became known for the construction of oxcarts using local timbers and cattle hides. In the Río de la Plata, cattle driving became a business and a trade; Santa Fe and Córdoba started out as settlements raising cattle and mules. At the base of the trail leading to the mines at Potosí, the town of Salta specialized as a clearinghouse for the resale of livestock. Furthermore, all along these extensive new lines of communication developed a tertiary industry of roadhouses and remount stations, operated by humble Spaniards, mestizos, and natives, too. In fact, persons of many different racial origins and of middling social status now made their living in the colonial transport industry.

Shipping rounded out the transport system in the rivers and along the coastlines. But it was nearly impossible to import ships directly from Europe to the Pacific coastline, so a shipbuilding industry developed at Guayaquil. There shipwrights constructed European-style sailing vessels from the local hardwoods. Shipping industries also developed on the rivers. The Spanish settlement at Paraguay, too isolated to be connected to intercolonial commerce via native river canoes, developed its own shipbuilding industry to ferry yerba maté to Santa Fe and Buenos Aires for reshipment to other colonial markets. Mule skinning was also an important trade in Colombia and Venezuela, as the Spanish towns of Bogotá and Caracas were located high in the temperate mountain valleys. However, the shipping industry of the relatively shallow Magdalena River, unlike in Paraguay, still relied on boats of native design—poled increasingly by African and mulatto boatmen. Countless thousands of persons served in the water transport industries around Latin America.

A commercial success from the very start, the Indies converted Spain into the wealthiest and most powerful nation on the European continent. Colonial wealth reinforced royal power and absolutism to such a degree that Castile was able to consolidate control over the other Spanish kingdoms and the Hapsburg royal family, which ascended to the Castilian throne in 1521, avoided most checks upon its political powers. Spanish troops occupied parts of Italy and the Netherlands and, between 1580 and 1640, the Spanish Crown occupied the throne of Portugal as well. Colonial trade became a monopoly of the Spanish Crown as well as the exclusive privilege of those merchant houses favored by the Crown. Moreover, the Spanish kings dispensed patronage widely as appointments went only to loyal subjects of Spain. If other Europeans wanted silver and gold, these commodities had to come through Spain. The patronage extended to the arts helped make the sixteenth century the Golden Age of Spain. All of this had been made possible because in 1492 Queen Isabella had taken a chance and sponsored Columbus's voyage. Such colonial success, however, invited competition.

FOREIGN COMPETITORS

The enormous wealth that Spain's and Portugal's American possessions generated for them engendered the envy of several northern European powers that had not been prepared earlier to compete for overseas conquests. But the French, the Dutch, and the English arrived too late. In contrast to Spanish and Portuguese successes, the French expeditions of the sixteenth century failed to established permanent colonies except in uncontested, marginal areas. French incursions, in fact, provoked prior European settlers into defensive expansion. As early as the 1540s, French corsairs sailed the Caribbean, intercepting Spanish gold and silver shipments. They sacked the port of Havana in 1555. French merchants ships also traded illegally with the Spanish and Portuguese colonies. French attempts at settlement in Florida motivated the Spaniards to reply. San Agustín, or St. Augustine, was founded in 1562 to outflank a Florida settlement of Huguenots (French Protestants). Thereupon, Spaniards and their native auxiliaries defeated the French and their native allies—continuing an enduring pattern of involving indigenous military surrogates in European rivalries.

French entry into Brazil proved more serious. The French were the first Europeans to behold the beauty of Guanabara Bay. They established a settlement there in 1550 and were not eliminated by the Portuguese until 15 years later, at which time the latter established their own permanent town at the site, Rio de Janeiro, which was to become one of the great ports of South America and a future capital of Brazil. In the meanwhile, the French made allies among the forest peoples who opposed the Tupí groups friendly with the Portuguese at São Paulo. A confederation of these Native Americans attacked the Portuguese settlement in 1561, but its members were repulsed, hunted down, and virtually wiped out within the next few decades by the Tupí and the *mamelucos*. The French also caused the Portuguese to extend their effective occupation north toward the mouth of the Amazon River. Not until 1616 did the Portuguese secure Maranhão and Belém from several small French trading posts. All that remained for France in South America was a small settlement on the Guiana coast between the Amazon and Orinoco Rivers. As latecomers, the French had to settle for much less than the Spaniards and Portuguese in South America.

Only in North America and the Caribbean did the French gain any success. In the late sixteenth century, French settlers occupied the St. Lawrence Basin in Canada, from which fur traders and missionaries explored the upper Mississippi River and the surrounding area. Far more significant at the time was the French occupation of the western half of the Caribbean island of Hispaniola in which, once the indigenous population had died out, the Spaniards had lost interest. What was to become known as Haiti served at first as a haven for French *boucaniers* (buccaneers) and traders, there being but a narrow distinction between the two. In the mid-seventeenth century, the French succeeded in establishing a sugar colony in this erstwhile pirates haven. It prospered quickly and by the eighteenth century, the French colony of Saint Domingue became the single leading supplier of sugar to Europe. (As shall be seen in Chapter 13, it also spawned the first successful slave rebellion and the first independent republic in Latin America.) France's foothold in Saint Domingue and other Caribbean islands such as Guadeloupe and Martinique involved French shipping in illegal trade throughout the colonial period. They remained in the Americas despite Iberian hostility because Spanish and Portuguese colonists desired the illicit European goods that French *contrabandistas* brought.

The Dutch and English

The Netherlands mounted a second, more earnest challenge in the Americas. The Dutch emerged from their sixteenth-century rebellion against Spanish occupation of their homeland with a renewed sense of national purpose. Its navy and merchant marine came to be among the world's most powerful. The merchants of Amsterdam, where many Iberian Jews had escaped during the Spanish pogroms of the late fifteenth century, were the most aggressive in Europe. Just when the Dutch were ready to take their place among the imperial powers, however, the best American lands had already been occupied by the Spaniards and Portuguese. Therefore, Dutch corsairs, like the French, preyed on Iberian shipping, setting up pirate and contraband trading stations on abandoned Caribbean islands. Peit Heyn captured an entire fleet of Spanish gold and silver carriers off Cuba in 1628.

The master stroke of the Dutch came in Brazil. Taking advantage of a moment of national weakness in 1630, when the Portuguese Crown reverted to the Spanish king, the Dutch invaded Portugal's colony in the Americas, capturing Recife and Salvador. Dutch sugar planters moved uneasily among Portuguese landowners in the prosperous cane-producing provinces of Pernambuco and Bahia. Commercially, the Dutch takeover proved a benefit. Amsterdam became Europe's leading emporium for the import of sugar, prices rose, and Brazilian cane production spread. Dutch shippers brought in plenty of African slaves. Though indebted to Amsterdam merchants, the Portuguese planters were not thrilled to deal with Dutch-speaking administrators, many of whom were Calvinist, to boot. The Portuguese sugar planters raised a rebellion among the popular classes of the Brazilian backlands—though not among the African slaves. Once Portugal's Crown returned to a Portuguese royal family, the rebellion commenced in earnest. In 1654, a mulatto named João Fernandes Vieira led a popular force of *mamelucos* and mulattos to successfully expel the Dutch. Thereafter the merchants, settlers, and ship captains of Holland also had to be content with less conspicuous American possessions. They moved next to the French in the Guianas, took over the Caribbean island of Curaçao, and established an impoverished settlement on the North Atlantic coast called New Amsterdam, which later became New York. Once again, Spanish and Portuguese colonists eager for European goods at modest prices tolerated their presence as auxiliary traders.

In contrast to the French and the Dutch, the English encroachment into the Americas almost seemed minor—at least in the sixteenth and seventeenth centuries. For much of the time, the British Isles were caught up in dynastic and religious conflicts, greatly limiting England's ability to launch a colonial project. An early settlement at Jamestown, Virginia, in 1607 ended in disaster. Its first significant activities farther south, where Iberian interests were really valuable, proved merely piratical. Francis Drake captured bullion shipments in the Caribbean, got around the Strait of Magellan, and raided Spanish settlements along the Pacific Coast as well. But the English never seemed to get much beyond this basic stage of involvement. Like their late-coming predecessors, the French and the Dutch, they also set up pirate and trading stations in the Guianas and in neglected Caribbean islands such as Barbados, Antigua, and Jamaica. Once England had defeated the Spanish Armada off the British Isles in 1588, Spain could do little to keep foreign ships out of American waters. The colonists—particularly those in fringe areas such as Venezuela and the Río de la Plata—benefited from the contraband trade. Britain's part in the dynastic European war over succession to the Spanish Crown in 1713 gained for it the crowning jewel of trade: the exclusive contract to import African slaves into Spanish-American ports. Britain's influence in the Americas would cause greater concern to the Spaniards later in the eighteenth century. By then, the British possessions in the Caribbean and along the North Atlantic coast supplied more powerful bases for colonial operations.

Spain and Portugal regarded colonial wealth and the international competition for it as sufficient excuses to secure administrative control of their American colonies. They could not leave the Americas to the settlers, who would surely lose it to foreign competitors. The imperial powers, therefore, considered themselves justified to intervene in colonial economic and social relationships to preserve order.

THE COLONIAL STATE

Two important European concepts of the sixteenth and seventeenth centuries conditioned the political organization of the Americas: royal patrimonialism and commercial mercantilism. *Patrimonialism* refers to the methods by which the Iberian monarchies sponsored, licensed, and prospered from the conquest and settlement of the Americas. First of all, the royal families were the symbols of the rising nation-states of Spain and Portugal. The kings laid effective claim to all colonial lands and assets in the Americas. However, rarely did the monarchs commit their own scarce resources, which they reserved for their military rivalries with other European nations, to the settlement of the New World. Instead, they gave grants and licenses authorizing their subjects to explore, conquer, or settle the Americas. In return, the monarchies received fees and promises of future tax collections on any profits their subjects were to make in their settlement of the New World.

Control was the chief feature of this patrimonialism. The monarchies sought not to manage the activities of their agents of colonization but to sanction and profit from them. Beginning with Christopher Columbus himself, all the great (and small) expeditionary forces carried the royal seal. Cortés in Mexico, Pizarro in Peru, and the dozens of other Spanish *conquistadores* obtained permission to engage in acts of conquest directly from the king or through his authorized officials. The Portuguese king granted Brazilian captaincies as monopolies to wealthy and influential members of the nobility. The monarch and the captains were to share the wealth and tribute once the ventures became established. In turn, the principle of patrimonialism permeated the mentality of the king's subjects in the Americas. They invoked his name in dividing up the booty and land among

[margin note: Patrimonialism mgt. of colonial admin]

themselves just as they themselves controlled this distribution of wealth to establish control among their followers. Every level of authority, from king to conqueror to follower to new landowner to merchant, attempted to control the wealth and assets created by the European encroachment into the Americas. Therefore, patrimonialism was a system of power that tended to concentrate and monopolize wealth at the higher levels of the society and polity as the time-honored, proven method of controlling people over a long distance.

The second concept underwriting the colonial expansion of Spain and Portugal—as well as that of France, the Netherlands, and England—refers especially to the economic ties between colony and mother country: mercantilism. The speed with which European settlement took place across the difficult geographical terrain and in the sometimes forbidding climatic conditions of the Americas may be explained in economic terms. That is to say, expanding markets existed in Europe for American products such as gold, silver, and sugar. Because each nation-state, in competition with others, depended on its economic assets, the European imperial powers sought to monopolize the wealth of their new colonies. In mercantilism, as developed by Spain, Portugal, and other European states, the colonies existed for the mother country. The colony was to purchase imports only from the mother country and produce exports that the mother country could not; all colonial trade was to flow through ports of the imperial country; and the citizens of other powers were not to benefit directly from colonial trade and production. Spain and Portugal adopted mercantilist policies in the sixteenth and seventeenth centuries for good reasons. Their colonial wealth placed these Iberian nation-states among the major world powers at the time.

But neither patrimonialism nor mercantilism could be practiced exclusively; each had its major limitations. Conquerors, landowners, peasants, and merchants were reluctant to give up all the taxes and fees they owed to the king, and clients sought to withhold tribute owed to conquerors, landowners, and merchants. Native Americans and slaves sought to withhold labor. Prices were artificially high, and contraband trade flourished in the Americas as a natural outcome. Not even the monarchs themselves or their favored merchants had sufficient capital to maintain the exclusive commercial linkages between colonial producers and northern European markets. For this reason, the Spanish and Portuguese kings themselves had to invite the participation of foreign ships and foreign merchants to finance the colonial economies. Moreover, neither patrimonialism nor mercantilism, predicated on relationships of power, were efficient organizers of the flow of economic assets. Productive assets were given to persons of influence and power—and many of these persons proved better at monopolizing these productive assets than making them grow and placing them in circulation. Patrimonialism and mercantilism were powerfully inefficient from an economic standpoint. But as guiding concepts, they performed wonderfully at spreading royal authority over the Americas within a relatively short span of time.

Administrative Organization

Administratively, the colonies formed part of the royal patrimony of the Crowns of Spain and Portugal. The colonies and their economic wealth belonged to the kings, not to the Spanish and Portuguese people. The latter Iberians could emigrate and attempt to exploit colonial resources and subjects, theoretically, as a grant or reward from the monarch. The royal family of Portugal, the House of Avis, ruled until 1580, at which time the Spanish monarch brought Portugal under his royal control. Then the House of Braganca emerged to rule a newly independent Portugal after 1640. In Spain, the Hapsburg royal family ruled the colonies as part of its patrimony until 1700. A 13-year European war then brought about the ascension to the Spanish throne of a branch of the French royal family, the Bourbons, which thereafter provided the kings who held the colonies for Spain into the nineteenth century.

Royal patrimony meant that during the long colonial era, the reigning kings of Spain and Portugal chose the administrators and officials who conducted government and collected taxes. Councils of colonial affairs had been set up as early as the sixteenth century. These councils advised the Spanish and Portuguese monarchies on colonial policy and conducted the day-to-day correspondence with officials resident in the colonies. Separate councils in the royal courts handled matters of colonial trade and taxation. In the Spanish Indies, the viceroys (the Spanish word *virrey* literally means "vice king") were the chief executive officers of two great administrative entities. The Viceroyalty of New Spain, encompassing all of Mexico, the Spanish Caribbean, and Central America, had its capital at Mexico City. The Viceroyalty of Peru took in all of Spanish South America, with its capital at Lima.

Colonial government in Brazil was rather more decentralized, although the same administrative principals applied. The king enjoyed the sole right to benefit from his colony, which he deigned to share with his loyal subjects (especially the more powerful among them) through grants of usufruct. In truth, the Portuguese royal house had fewer assets than its Spanish counterpart to govern Brazil directly, especially in the sixteenth century when the colony's settlement lagged behind that of the bullion-producing Spanish-American dominions. Therefore, in 1532 João III ceded the rights to govern the 12 captaincies of Brazil to the donataries. For this honor and right, these captains were supposed to finance the settlement of the territories themselves. They acted as the king's representatives in parceling out the *sesmaria* land grants. These donataries were to collect the king's taxes and send all export produce on Portuguese vessels back through Lisbon, where the royal customs agents waited. However, as only 2 of the captaincies—at Pernambuco and São Vicente—had any success at all, the king reclaimed the rights of the other 10 captaincies. But even success was no substitute for royal encroachment on colonial governance, for wealth and competition among the settlers motivated the Crown to assume more direct political control. In 1549, the Portuguese king sent his own governor to Bahia. Not until the eighteenth century did a Portuguese viceroy unite the captaincies under one administrative official.

The geographical diversity of the American continent and the ethnic diversity of its inhabitants did not provide much political uniformity within the two Spanish-American viceroyalties. Therefore, the Crowns further broke the administrative apparatus down into more coherent regional centers within the colonies. These regional centers became *audiencias* (audiences). Each *audiencia* was a quasi-judicial, quasi-executive tribunal made up of three to five judges called *oidores* (listeners). *Audiencias* had been established at important cities in the midst of the more heavily populated or commercially important regions such as Lima, Quito, Bogotá, Guatemala City, Mexico City, and Havana (see Map 4.2). Thirty-five outlying territories such as Paraguay, Argentina, Chile, and Venezuela were administered by governors or captains-general. Lesser courts and executive officials governed the local areas, forming the broad base of the formally hierarchical

Map 4.2   Viceroyalties, *Audiencias*, and Donataries of the Seventeenth Century

administrative structure of which the king formed the apex. In addition, the Crown reserved the right to appoint archbishops and bishops of the Catholic Church in the colonies. Therefore, the church maintained a parallel hierarchy of authority from the villages through regional capitals to the viceregal capitals of Mexico City and Lima.

At first, only Spaniards served on these tribunals and in these governorships. Those whites born in the Americas, known as *criollos,* or Creoles, received fewer appointments because Iberian-born whites believed that having been born in the Americas weakened and impaired the Creoles' judgment. But the Hapsburgs needed money and began selling the positions. Wealthy Creoles thus had access to government positions that could last for life if they were willing to pay approximately 9,300 pesos (in contrast, Spaniards had to pay only 6,750 pesos). By the end of the seventeenth century, Creoles had thus acquired more than half of the 76 positions on the *audiencias.* As shall be seen in Chapter 14, Creoles would make the *audiencia* an instrument of American identity and home rule within the Spanish empire.

However, the colonial state was not the all-powerful, streamlined, and efficiently functional machine that its structure might imply it to have been. In the first place, communication between Iberia and the New World was difficult. A voyage by ship between Lisbon and Salvador da Bahia might last several months. A packet of orders from the king and his Council of the Indies, traveling from Madrid via Seville, Havana, and Panama City, might not reach the viceroy in Lima for up to five months. If the king asked for a report, he might not receive a reply for a year or more. Communication within the colonies also was problematic. The viceroy of Peru could communicate more readily with Madrid than with his theoretically subordinate governor in Paraguay.

Rather than permit so distant a colonial power to gain real administrative independence, the Crown purposely encouraged a chaotic welter of checks and balances in the form of administrative overlap. Members of the *audiencias* and archbishops shared some of the executive powers reserved for the viceroy. In turn, viceroys enjoyed religious and judicial responsibilities that permitted them to meddle in the affairs of the church and *audiencias.* Moreover, the king permitted his subjects to correspond directly with him. Each public official, prelate, and town council had the authority to appeal a viceregal order directly to the king himself. Strong viceroys provoked resistance from subordinate officials. Unless they had the support within the royal court, the viceroys and governors found themselves constantly under siege from obdurate associates in the colonies.

The Crowns also established systems of administrative review. Representatives of the royal courts conducted formal investigations of a high official's performance at the end of his term. The king also dispatched special agents called *visitadores* (visitors) to investigate specific abuses and colonial policies. The *visitador* took testimony about an outgoing official's term of duty from local citizens—even from the natives. A public official's future career often depended on mollifying his subordinates and local interests so as to minimize the possibility of their protesting before the *visitador.*

Finally, everyone had the prerogative to complain about their political adversaries directly to the king. But because royal authority lay at such a remove—a message from Quito might take three to nine months to reach Madrid—competing political forces were often motivated to settle disputes among themselves. Colonial history is replete with instances of local rebellions against constituted authority. In 1542, Governor Francisco Pizarro was assassinated in Lima. In 1624, a faction led by the archbishop succeeded in overthrowing the viceroy in Mexico. The first governor of Paraguay succumbed to a coup d'état by the first settlers, who then sent him back to Spain under arrest. Later, in 1721, another royal governor at Asunción was to be deposed by merchants and landowners for his favoritism toward Jesuit missionaries. Spanish authorities could not regain political control over the Paraguayans at Asunción until 1735, then only with the aid of Guaraní troops from the Jesuit missions, about which more anon.

The state of the written law imposed yet another check on colonial authority. There were no legislative bodies, in the modern sense, either in Iberia or in the Indies. The *Cortes,* as the assemblies of nobles in both Spain and Portugal were known, served more as advisories to the king than as true law-making and debating branches of government. In the colonies, the *cabildos*, or city councils, might qualify as true legislative bodies, but they had executive and judicial powers as well. The entire colonial political structure, from the Council of the Indies on down, actually operated under an accumulating body of edicts and strictures. But many laws contradicted other laws. Spain's Council of the Indies drew up a compilation of these laws in 1681, which comprised some four thick volumes. The Hispanic heritage of legalism encouraged the detailed guidance of administrative affairs. It mentioned the exact fines to be levied for a multitude of offenses as well as exactly what services and pay employers should provide for workers under the colonial labor drafts. More often than not, the minutely detailed regulations were impossible to carry out, and colonial officials simply used their judgments or followed expedience. They could be arbitrary, but they were also free to respond to the competing power and prestige of the litigants.

Economic Intervention

Most remarkable was the jurisdiction that the royal authorities had not only over political affairs but also over social relationships and the colonial economy. Although the colonies recognized private property, there developed neither a capitalist free-market economic system nor social relationships based on private contracts between individuals having equal rights before the law. In the first place, Spaniards and Portuguese enjoyed superior prerogatives, both in law and in fact. Native Americans and slaves had fewer. In the second place, the colonies were considered economic assets of the royal families of Spain and Portugal. They were to provide the treasuries with the resources to carry out the king's policies throughout his realm.

The mercantilist doctrine of the age subordinated the economic interests of the colonies to that of the mother countries. Therefore, the king reserved the right to own all land and subsoil properties. He granted rights of possession of land and mines to his favored subjects, for which he expected to receive a tribute or tax. He permitted individual miners to dig for his gold and silver deposits for a royalty of one-fifth of the production; this tax was known as the *quinto real*, the royal fifth. The monarch also required those who possessed land to pay a tithe of 10 percent of their agricultural production to support his church. For the privilege of selling his products, he levied a sales tax, the *alcabala*, on the shopkeepers, who passed it on to their customers and for the privilege of importing and exporting goods through his ports, the king imposed customs duties on the merchants. Naturally, there was a lot of tax evasion.

To maximize tax collections, therefore, the royal authorities heavily regulated the colonial economy. Precious metals especially came under numerous restrictions. Silver could be transferred only over royal highways; it was to be minted nowhere else but in the royal mints of Mexico City, Lima, and Potosí. The official ports of embarkation were to be Callao and Veracruz. Colombian gold was exported only from Cartagena. Trade between the American colonies and Spain's possession of the Philippines was to embark only from the port of Acapulco. The famous Manila Galleons sailed but once a year.

These precious metals could be exchanged for European commodities at trade fairs in Jalapa, Mexico, and Portobelo, Panama. A fleet of ships carrying American bullion and other products was assembled once a year at Havana and sailed together to Spain under navy escort. The only Spanish port for the American colonial trade was to be Seville, which suited the powerful merchant interests of that city. This was the *flota*, or fleet system. The Portuguese also operated a smaller version of the fleet system to protect its sugar shipments from Brazil. All along the way, royal tax collectors regulated the flow of goods as well as the merchants and carriers, who operated under royal licenses.

Other Spanish-American and Iberian ports were not to engage in international commerce. This restriction, of course, was illogical for consumers in Caracas, Buenos Aires, Asunción, and Santiago because it made European goods more costly in these cities. The Spanish Board of Trade, which regulated colonial commerce for the king, had to make exceptions to the *flota* system. They licensed ships to sail directly to the other colonial and Iberian ports. They even sold permits to Portuguese, Dutch, French, and British shippers to carry on the lucrative colonial trade, as Spanish mariners did not have enough vessels for the job.

Consequently, smuggling proliferated right beneath the royal noses. Foreign ship captains colluded with Spanish merchants to haul contraband products along with permitted goods. Silver began to leave illegally from the port of Buenos Aires, and foreign merchants neglected to put in at Seville before passing on to ports in northern Europe. Everywhere smuggling and contraband flourished, with foreigners setting up illegal shipping depots on abandoned Caribbean islands. By the end of the seventeenth century, Amsterdam had actually become a bigger entrepôt for Brazilian sugar than Lisbon. And neither did Portugal's tobacco monopoly work well; as much sweet Brazilian tobacco went legally to Lisbon as illegally to Africa in exchange for slaves. Colonial officials were powerless to stop this underground market; indeed, they even participated in it as a means to increase the flow of trade within their jurisdictions.

Because the commercial system was contrived for tax purposes and because smuggling flourished, bribes became just another cost of doing business in the colonies. Not only did the heavily regulated economy encourage corruption in colonial administration, but also public officials were not paid well. Particularly in the seventeenth century, when royal income slumped because of declines in colonial silver production and in sugar prices, the Crowns of Spain and Portugal raised additional income by selling important colonial posts. Even the collection of taxes was oftentimes farmed out to the highest bidder. Under the circumstances, the holder of public trust expected to earn an income from his position. He used his office to collect fees for his services. He was encouraged to cooperate with the wealthier of the local colonists, granting them licenses and privileges in exchange for favors. However, these commentaries should not condemn all public servants as venal. Viceregal bureaucrats at Lima and Mexico City earned reputations for honesty and service. Career officials serving in the Indian Court of Mexico, for instance, represented the interests of the Native Americans faithfully, despite the high social status of their legal adversaries—the Spanish owners of mines, land, and *obrajes*.

Europeans considered public administration in the Americas to be a legitimate business enterprise, and subjects of the king sought political office to enrich themselves and their families. The *corregidores* became especially enterprising and notorious. In Peru and New Spain, these rural magistrates collected the head tax on natives and retained a portion thereof as expenses. However, the *corregidores* tended to keep so much that Peruvian and Mexican tax revenues in the sixteenth century actually declined more swiftly than did the native population. These district officials also made alliances with the local *hacendados,* owners of haciendas, who paid off the *corregidores* for sending native workers to labor on their estates. These public officials then rented land from the wealthiest Spanish families in their districts and cultivated it with native workers themselves. Whenever they could, the *corregidores* and hacendados suborned or intimidated the *kurakas* to cooperate in their business schemes.

The profitability from public administration confronted every viceroy with keen competition for available colonial positions. "And the hardest work of all is to fill the *corregimientos* and *alcaldías mayores* [rural and urban magistrates], and to search for the right people for offices, and to put up with the conquistadores and their children with all their documents and their demands that they must be saved from starving," said Martín Enríquez, appointed the viceroy of New Spain in 1568. "There are two hundred posts and two thousand people who want them."

Colonial officials straddled the thin line between what they considered legitimate business opportunities and the protection of the native subjects of the Crown. Many a well-intentioned *corregidor*-designate learned all the mechanisms of self-aggrandizement from the official he was to replace. Most Spanish officials returned to Spain before investigations revealed the extent of their business dealings, and everywhere wealth impressed one's peers and seemed to legitimate the methods for acquiring it. Moreover, the Crown was parsimonious. Official pay hardly met average expenditures in the Indies and, in the seventeenth century, the Hapsburg crown increasingly resorted to making money by selling bureaucratic positions. The selling of offices even permitted the wealthiest colonial families to install their own Creole kin in these positions of trust and local political power. In addition, all new appointees posted bonds guaranteeing their good behavior in their positions of trust. Who provided their bond money? The wealthy *hacendados* over whom they were to rule. Combining public administration and private business became a way of life in colonial political circles, and its legacy thrives today.

Social Intervention

There was another reason why the colonial state controlled the economy: to regulate the social order. Royal officials perceived that the plurality of colonial society and the excessive privileges of the few Spaniards might cause a social explosion (see Manuscript 4.1). Times of economic stress and harvest failure were particularly dangerous. First of all, the authorities attempted to ensure a basic subsistence for all individuals regardless of their rank in society. They often took control of basic commodities. The production and marketing of salt, a food preservative, became a monopoly of the Crown so that no elite economic interest might exploit, to the detriment of the public, the salt mines of Zipaquirá, Colombia, or the salt flats of the southern Pampas. Town councils also regulated prices of basic foodstuffs sold locally. They stored grains in case of bad harvests, facilitated the slaughter of cattle for meat, and frequently checked on the supply and prices of bread and tortillas. What they hoped to prevent was a popular riot. The urban rampage that erupted in Mexico City in 1624 might have originated because of political rivalries among the Spanish elite. But the participation of the popular classes threatened the social as well as the political order.

Other critical economic commodities closely monitored by the state included the sale of slaves and mercury. The latter mineral product was the critical ingredient in the process of extracting silver from ore in the Upper Peruvian mining towns of Oruro and

MANUSCRIPT 4.1

One Viceroy's Alarm about the Plurality of Colonial Society

The second viceroy of New Spain, Luis de Velasco, was certainly exaggerating when he worried about the imminent destruction of colonial society. The tone of his letter of 1553 was meant to elicit from his monarch greater authority rather than pit himself against the countervailing power of the audiencia. By the same token, even the elite who benefited most from large numbers of subordinate peoples at their command could not help but experience some paranoia in this ethnically diverse society. Pessimism was the predominant attitude. The viceroy's letter fairly drips with contempt for the character of Spaniards and, most particularly, of the non-European inhabitants. The suggested mass deportations, however, did not take place.

Carrying out the new laws and provisions (curbing the power of the *encomenderos*) that were given me and that have been sent since has put the land in great trouble and necessity, which every day grows greater because their execution came all at once. Among the Spaniards there is great discontent and much poverty, and among the Indians more laxity and ease than their little constancy will suffer. I am afraid that troubles very hard to remedy are going to come from one side or the other, because the country is so full of blacks and mestizos, who greatly outnumber the Spaniards, and all of whom wish to purchase their liberty with the lives of their masters; this bad breed will join anyone who rebels, whether Spaniards to Indians. In order to preserve this land in the service of our Lord and obedience to your majesty, there are some measures I will mention here that are necessary and almost forced upon us if this land is not to be lost. May your majesty order these things to be considered and make what provision you see fit: in advising you what I feel and serving faithfully to death I will do my duty. What I would regret more than death would be that the land should be lost while it was my responsibility. . . .

Next, your majesty should order that part of the Spanish people, mestizos, and blacks be culled out and sent on some conquest, since there are too many in the land; and if this is not to be done, then order the door shut to Spaniards of any kind, so they will not enter New Spain, and deport the mestizos who could be sent in the ships that go back to Spain, because they are very harmful for the Indians; those who remained would take heed, seeing that some of them were being ejected from the country. Your majesty should order that not so many licenses be given to import blacks, because here in New Spain there are more than twenty thousand, and they are increasing greatly; there could come to be so many of them that they would put the land in disorder.

SOURCE: James Lockhart and Enrique Otte, eds. *Letters and People of the Spanish Indies: Sixteenth Century* (Cambridge, England: Cambridge Latin American Studies, 1976), 187–89.

Potosí and in the several mining centers of northern Mexico. Only two areas under Spanish control were known to yield mercury: the mines of Almadén in Spain and Huancavelica in Peru. To make sure that enough mercury was available to the colonial silver mines, upon which so much of the health of the colonial economy and the royal treasury depended, the Crown monopolized its production and marketing. Administrators appointed by the Crown ran the mining operations; merchants bought, sold, and transported the mineral only under license by the state.

Commercial houses also engaged in the sale of slaves in Spanish America and Brazil under exclusive contracts to the Crowns called *asientos.* The problem was that England, France, and Holland had larger merchant fleets than Spain and Portugal. Therefore, the supply of slaves became an object of international diplomacy and even the booty of war. The Spanish Crown had to issue lucrative contracts first to Portuguese merchant houses, then to French merchants, and finally, following its loss in war, to British merchants in 1713. Each *asiento* specified the ports of entry to be used, the numbers of slaves to be involved, and their prices. Slave import contracts excluded commerce in other merchandise—particularly northern European goods. But once again, the connivance of the Crown's own officials in ports like Buenos Aires, La Guaira, Cartagena, Havana, and Veracruz undermined these contract provisions. They often welcomed all ships with Africans to sell. The slave trade probably was the Crown's least effective yet most lucrative monopoly.

Elements of social control also dictated the Crown's manipulation of issues concerning the royal ownership of land. Spanish colonial officials operated under the assumption, backed by years of royal edicts, that Native Americans were to retain enough land to sustain themselves. They were considered a valuable labor source in Mexico, Guatemala, and the Andean regions. Following the Conquest, the terrible decline of the native population everywhere caused concern that this source of labor might be lost to the king's cities and mines; with no labor, there would be little production and lower tax revenues. Therefore, the royal court instructed its colonial officials and clergy in the Indies to preserve land for the indigenous communities. For this reason, the Crown acceded to the natives' desire to preserve their communal agriculture rather than engage in the more commercial market agriculture of the Europeans.

Yet Crown officials also had to be concerned with the supply of land to support the growing nonnative population. Each city council, therefore, was permitted to divide the surrounding lands among its worthiest citizens. Legal possession of land was never absolute in colonial America. If the population became too great, if mulattoes and mestizos suffered from too few opportunities to work the land, or if the wealthiest citizens owned too much of the land, the Crown reserved the right to correct abuses. From time to time, the king's representatives oversaw the redistribution of land. Occupation rather than legal ownership of land often became the cardinal principle. In Arequipa, Peru, for example, the Crown in 1641 forcibly confiscated properties owned by the native communities to provide for the growing population of Spanish immigrants and mestizos. When the seizure was shown to be excessive, some whites had to give parcels back to the natives. Colonial officials accomplished this kind of economic reform to preserve the social order rather than to rearrange it.

Although the state meddled in the social and economic affairs of Latin America, one should not conceive of it as an absolutist political authority that dictated the organization and conduct of society. In the social realm, the state intervened to preserve the social order that had been established and ordained by the conquerors and settlers. Individual Europeans rather than agencies of the state had dictated the settlement of the Indies and Brazil, conditioned on the previous indigenous society and resistance. The expectation of social domination by generations of Spanish and Portuguese immigrants determined how the social hierarchy developed. The state merely acceded to the new social order and sought to prevent competition among the colonists from weakening the colonial enterprise, which, after all, was a valuable tax base for the Iberian Crowns.

In general, the state conserved its considerably circumscribed powers so as to be able to mediate competing interests. It exerted its influence only in specific circumstances. If Mexican natives resisted the loss of their land to a Spaniard, the state's influence could settle the issue. If two merchant clans in Bahia claimed the right to sell slaves at auction, the state's limited power could mediate the dispute. If Paraguayan landowners resented the tax exemptions that permitted Jesuit missionaries to dominate markets for yerba maté, the state's minimal powers could be used to help bring a resolution. Often, the state deliberately compromised disputes. Colonial officials seldom desired to establish clear legal rights or to judge right and wrong. Rather than finding absolute rights in law, they merely wished to mollify the conflicts between individuals and the various social orders, lest those disputes become ruinous to the king's possessions.

The Avis, Braganca, and Hapsburg kings deemed that a strong colonial social order— not necessarily an equitable one—was Iberia's greatest defense in America. Few institutions of government worked as well as religion to unite the diverse peoples of the colonies under royal control. As Spaniards and Portuguese subjugated Native American peoples, they employed religion in much the same fashion that their forebears had in the Reconquest of Iberia. Catholicism justified conquest and brought together the new subordinates under European domination. Individual Spaniards and Portuguese, in purely private enterprises, may have set forth to capture land and labor in the Americas to establish themselves and their families. But they carried their Catholic traditions with them as part of their indispensable cultural heritage and national identities.

THE CHURCH

The clergy in the colonial church were divided into two groups, each with its own hierarchies, supervisors, and channels to king and pope. The so-called secular clergy served in the cities and towns, ministering to parishes of Spanish and Portuguese society. Secular priests also served rural parishes, particularly those representing the population of poor whites, small holders, and persons of color who worked on Iberian enterprises. Slaves in plantations or in urban households fell into this category of parishioners. In the meanwhile, the second category of clergy, the missionaries, inherited the task of ministering to indigenous peoples. Their task was to convert them to Christianity, teach them the catechism and doctrine of the Holy Roman Church, and instruct them in European ways. Both types of clergy, the missionaries and the parish priests, were expected to follow the spiritual leadership of the papacy and the political policies of the Crown in whose empire they practiced. The kings' political supremacy came in the form of a papal charter, the *Patronato Real,* or Royal Patronage. Early in the sixteenth century, as the kings of Spain and Portugal were expending many efforts in the expansion of Christendom, a grateful pope ceded political authority over the church in the Americas to them.

The Most Catholic Majesties of Spain and Portugal promised to uphold the doctrinal authority of the Holy Roman Church and support its clergy in the colonies in return for the clergy's political loyalty to the Crowns. Therefore, the missionaries and secular priests in Brazil followed the imperial policies of the Braganza kings, and the clergy of the Spanish Americas supported those of the Hapsburgs. This web of relationships was not without its internal contradictions.

Missionaries

Efforts to convert the Native Americans followed every conquest of territory in the Americas. One or more friars went on the major expeditions of the sixteenth century. But mass conversions and religious instruction fell to the regular orders of clergy, so called because they belonged to "regulated," almost militaristic organizations of missionaries. The Franciscan order arrived first in the Caribbean islands. Later, after conquering the Aztec capital of Tenochtitlán, Cortés summoned 12 Franciscan friars, symbolic of Christ's 12 apostles, to convert the native subjects. The Franciscans were also the first missionaries on the scene following the conquest of Peru. Other regular orders of monks followed later, such as the Dominicans and the Augustinians. Finding the choicest parishes of Native Americans around the capital cities of Mexico and Lima already taken by the Franciscans, the other missionary orders fanned out into the indigenous towns and groups found in the south and west of Mexico as well as in Ecuador, Colombia, and Bolivia. The conquistadores under Cortés and Pizarro had already destroyed the temples at Cholula (Puebla), Tenochtitlán, and Cuzco, and the Spanish priests supervised the construction of Catholic cathedrals directly over the rubble. In time, these majestic religious buildings inspired awe in the new subjects of the Spanish kings. "The roofs and beams are in many of them all daubed with gold," reported one churchman in the seventeenth century. "Many altars have sundry marble pillars, and others are decorated with brazilwood stays standing one above the other with tabernacles for several saints richly wrought with golden colors. . . . These cause admiration in the common sort of people, and admiration brings on daily adoration in them to those glorious spectacles and images of saints."

The natives accepted the spiritual leadership of the first friars. The conquerors, after all, had destroyed their own priestly class. Still, these friars were certainly not like the conquistadores whom the natives had come to know only too well. Their ascetic lifestyle, vows of poverty and chastity, and example of piousness and rejection of worldliness appealed to and inspired confidence in the indigenous peoples. Moreover, the friars also attempted to protect the natives from the nonnative population as much as possible. Although the newly conquered peoples probably would have preferred to be rid of all the Spaniards, they accepted the friars at least as a lesser burden. But the nomadic groups on the arid and tropical fringes of empire—northern Mexico, Chile, Argentina, and the Brazilian interior—successfully resisted rapid European conquest. These fields of religious conquest became the work of later missionary orders, especially the Society of Jesus, or Jesuits.

Having gained the favor of the Iberian Crowns in the Counter Reformation of seventeenth-century Europe, the Jesuits came to be known for establishing missions and converting Native Americans in colonial areas neglected by the older orders. In the cities, the Society of Jesus set up schools that educated the white elites. They were active in the mining zones and Chichimec lands of northern Mexico. The Jesuits penetrated the rain forests on the eastern slopes of the Andes mountains in Peru and Ecuador. From Caracas and Valencia in Venezuela they crossed the mountains to establish chapels on the *llanos,* or plains. Jesuit missionaries forded the Bío-Bío River in southern Chile to proselytize among the hostile Mapuche. For the Guaraní and other indigenous groups, they established an arc of missions extending from the headwaters of the Paraná River in Brazil across Paraguay and down to the Uruguay River.

Portuguese Jesuits simultaneously pushed inland from the settlements of Recife, Salvador, Rio de Janeiro, and São Paulo to bring the Catholic religion to the Tupí. At São Paulo, this work began in 1553. Father Manuel da Nóbrega and his fellow Jesuits established missions on land donated to them by the Crown. They learned Tupí and other native tongues in order to instruct the natives in the catechism and European crafts and agriculture, including how to weave cloth (see Manuscript 4.2). They also built chapels. In fact, it was the Jesuit mission on the plateau above the coast that first carried the name *São Paulo,* or St. Paul. Although the Jesuits were optimistic about their progress in converting the natives, they were nevertheless dismayed that indigenous pupils who left their missions would revert to the old lifestyles in the forest.

Outside the settlement of São Paulo in southern Brazil, the Jesuits gathered together the Tupí into mission villages known as *aldeias* on land bequeathed to them by Portuguese officials. There the brothers attempted to teach Tupí children the rudiments of the catechism and directed them in a regimented life of work. Once the boys had been taught their lessons each morning, they were dispatched to hunt and fish. At dawn, the girls attended chapel, followed by work at spinning and weaving and making European-style clothes. All the Tupí would be assembled at dusk for religious services once again.

Thus began the Jesuits' mission work, which would eventually spread westward to Bolivia and southward to Paraguay and Uruguay. There on the borders between the Portuguese and Spanish realms, friction developed between colonists and clergy of opposite political loyalties—though all nominally Catholic. By the 1620s, Jesuits loyal to the Spanish Crown had established missions among the Guaraní in the region of Guairá. The Portuguese subjects at São Paulo especially coveted the Guaraní for their reputation as good agricultural workers. The *bandeirante* slave hunters attacked the Guaraní mission and carried off hundreds of natives as slaves. Therefore, the Jesuits decided to move the remaining Guaraní farther south to the region around the Uruguay River. When the slave-hunting expeditions still pursued and attacked the missions, the Jesuits successfully obtained permission from the Spanish Crown to arm the Guaraní. This was a momentous decision, reestablishing the pre-Columbian heritage of military prowess among the otherwise peaceful Guaraní. In 1641, 300 *mameluco* colonists from São Paulo and their 600 Tupí allies attacked the missions, where the *paulistas* met a decisive defeat . This military victory saved the Jesuit missions from further attack, and the *mamelucos* had to redirect their slaving expeditions toward the tribal groups to the west of São Paulo.

To support their work, the regular clergy built their own self-sufficient economic and educational infrastructures throughout the Americas. The missionaries studied and wrote primers for the indigenous languages. In their monastery at Tlatelolco, constructed on the outskirts of Mexico City over the ruins of the Aztec marketplace described in Manuscript 1.3, the Franciscans gathered the sons of the native nobility to teach them a written form of their native Nahuatl. These young scholars returned to their peoples as scribes, maintaining the civil, ecclesiastical, and tribute and tax records for local villages. The Franciscans printed the first Nahuatl catechism in 1539. In Guatemala,

MANUSCRIPT 4.2

Work of the Jesuit Missionaries in São Vicente, Brazil, 1553

Jesuits in São Paulo, among the first priests to minister to the inhabitants of southern Brazil, entered into a world completely different from that which they had known in Europe and, for that reason, one of great challenge to their faith. The enslavement of native peoples by Portuguese settlers, the latter's racial miscegenation with natives leading to a wholly new generation of mamelucos, and the colonial luxury (and laxity) of having devoted servant women placed these first missionaries on the moral edge of the world. Note how Father Manuel da Nóbrega responds to the ambiguities of the colonial situation. He exaggerates his parishioners' adaptation of European religion and culture and emphasizes the work to be done. Father Nóbrega also reaffirms the moral standing of his religious brothers in an environment perceived by Europeans as being sexually licentious.

In this household [Jesuit mission], much has been gained from the bounty of the land, from the sons and daughters of Christians called *mamelucos* (of which there are many), and from slavery. Great fervor goes into the confessions, and many are seen crying, asking for confessions with great pain from not knowing how to confess. All of them know the doctrine better than many of the old Christians of the nation. And many [Indian] slaves who once lived in sin now marry; others separate; many discipline themselves with such great fervor that they amaze the whites.

In this household, there are children who do their exercises well. They learn to read and write and they are advancing well; others learn to sing and play the flute; and others, the most skilled *mamelucos*, learn grammar, taught by a young grammarian from Coimbra who came here as an expatriate. They have

their recitations of "God Our Father" and their ways of praising Him. And much more would be done if there were many priests; but since Pero Correia is the only preacher, more cannot be done. These who are being brought up shall be the true ones due to the great hope that their good principles give us. From Bahia, they will send some priests that they least need there, because they help here greatly and they are linguists and our preachers. They lack neither authority nor age, because Our Lord gives them knowledge and zeal.

When I arrived at this Captaincy, I found Indian women, some free, some enslaved, single and married, who worked as houseservants, brought firewood and water, and took care of children. Although they were well separated from the conversation of the Brothers, nevertheless could be in the same street, and they therefore scandalized those who, from a distance, thought them too intimate. But those of the neighborhood, who knew and saw the truth, were not scandalized. Ever since I arrived, I took charge of the Confraternity of the Infant Jesus, and I had delivered everything necessary for the maintenance and service of this [mission] household. There are two butlers and one purveyor. She is in charge of everyone who serves in this household so that we can remain free from inconvenience and exclusively occupied with spiritual matters, teaching and indoctrinating the children, as well as anyone in the household who wants to learn. Because this land is so spoiled, it is necessary to lay the foundation again.

SOURCE: Father Manuel da Nóbrega to P. Luiz Gonçalves da Câmara, 1553, in S. I. Serafim Leite, *Novas cartas jesuíticas: De Nóbrega a Vieira*. Brasiliana, vol. 194 (São Paulo: Companhia Editôra Nacional, 1940), 45. Trans. Teresa Van Hoy.

where descendants of the Maya had spoken numerous dialects of 13 linguistic sub-groups, the Franciscans and Augustinians learned the native languages in monasteries at Antigua. The same was true for the mendicant orders in the Andean region, whose missionaries mastered the principal languages of Quechua and Aymara; those who worked among the lesser groups in northern and southern South America also learned those indigenous languages. Father Antônio Vieira, the well-known seventeenth-century Jesuit missionary in Brazil, preached among the Tupí in their native tongue.

Many missionary priests had received their training, except for their study of Native American languages, in the colleges and monasteries of Europe. By the seventeenth century, members of the regular orders as well as the secular clergy were receiving their ordination in the Americas. These native-born priests and nuns were exclusively Creoles, Americans born of European parentage. Persons of mixed blood, Americans born of African parentage, and Native Americans were excluded from the priesthood because only whites qualified for this occupation. The schools at which novices studied eventually became the first universities in the Americas—the Royal and Pontifical University of Mexico, San Carlos in Guatemala, San Marcos in Lima, the University of Charcas (in Chuquisaca, Bolivia), and the University of Córdoba. Eventually, these institutions opened up to Creole young men who did not intend to prepare for the priesthood but for careers in law and bureaucracy.

Financial support for these schools and for proselytizing came from a number of sources. The regular orders obtained Crown property (land) and the rights to native labor to support their work. The Jesuits in particular became known as the most savvy of the religious businessmen. Jesuit headquarters in Mexico, Quito, Lima, and Córdoba oversaw a nearly self-contained economic system that included haciendas for wheat, farms for food crops, ranches for cattle and sheep, plantations for sugar and cacao, warehouses for the export of silver and import of wine and slaves, *obrajes* for the manufacture of cotton and woolen cloth, teams of mules for transport, and rental properties in both rural and urban zones. As important economic entities, these religious estates also owned slaves. The Jesuits were the largest slaveholders in fringe areas such as Venezuela, Chile, and Argentina. The missionary orders in Latin America, therefore, were quite well supported.

How receptive were the Native Americans to their conversion? In the indigenous civilizations of Mexico, Central America, and the Andean regions, religious tradition had already been developing syncretically prior to the arrival of the new European overlords. One conquering group imposed its gods on the conquered group. The Inkas and Aztecs even worshipped the gods of vanquished subjects, the better to gain their allegiance. When Spaniards insisted on conversion to Catholicism, therefore, resistance was quite mild. As conquerors, the natives reasoned, the Europeans had a right to this form of homage. However, conversion of the indigenous peoples to Catholicism did not mean that they discarded their ancient religious practices but that they combined the belief systems. Native American receptivity to Christianity will be addressed in the next chapter.

The missionaries succeeded admirably in converting the indigenous population to Catholicism, but they failed at their larger goals: to Europeanize them, to make them less "Indian." In Brazil, many tribes who submitted to Jesuit *aldeias* in the seventeenth century later reconsidered their decision. Some fled westward into the frontier. Several of these groups, like the Chavante and Kaingáng, reconstituted themselves and endured in the rain forests more or less undisturbed until the twentieth century. As regarded those natives who remained under their care, priests complained of the continued usage of traditional language, dress, and customs. Native women in tropical areas continued to enter churches bare breasted. Drunkenness, thievery, and promiscuity were rampant. However, the real issue may not have been one of religion but of labor. Government officials, Iberian settlers, and the clergy clearly wanted to teach their native subordinates to be good workers, a subject that will be taken up again in subsequent chapters.

But the self-interests of the regular clergy militated against their actual commitment to the stated Crown policy of "civilizing" the natives. Representatives of the church often enjoyed excessive privileges and services among their indigenous charges (see Manuscript 4.3). And the natives did contribute their labor to mission estates and to the wealth

MANUSCRIPT 4.3

The Perquisites of the Missionary Priest, 1625

On his journey from Mexico to his new post in Guatemala, the English Friar Thomas Gage of the Dominican Order enjoyed the unpaid services that Native Americans were expected to heap upon missionaries. The abundance of personal service and gifts often conflicted with the missionaries' vows of poverty and humility. Many a priest rationalized it: The natives wanted to show their gratitude for being converted from paganism to the true religion.

Hither when the Prior of [the village of] Comitan had brought me, we were waited for by the vicar or friar of that town with the chief and principal Indians, and most of the canoes. As we ferried over, the little canoes went before us with the choristers of the church singing before us, and with others sounding their waits and trumpets. The friar that lived in this town was called Friar Geronymo de Guevara, little in stature, but great in state, pride and vanity, as he shewed himself in what he had provided for us both of fish and flesh. A brave professor or vower of mendicancy and poverty he was, who in twelve years that he had lived in that town, what by mumming of Masses for the dead and living, what by shearing and fleecing the poor Indi-

ans, what by trading and trafficking with the merchants that used that road, had got six thousand ducats, which he had sent to Spain to the Court of Madrid, to trade with them simoniacally for the bishopric of Chiapa[s], which if he obtained not (yet when I came out of that country the report went that he had obtained it), he would and was well able with a second supply to obtain a better. After two days' feasting with him, he and the Prior of Comitan both joined their power and authority to see me well manned with Indians to the first town of the Cuchumatlanes. A mule was prepared to carry my bedding (which we commonly carried with us in chests of leather called *petacas*), another Indian to carry my *petaquilla* wherein was my chocolate and all implements to make it; and three more Indians to ride before and behind to guide me; but to all these nothing was to be paid (lest a custom of paying should be brought in, for so that doctrined me as a novice in that country) except it were to give them a cup of chocolate if I drank in the way, or when I came to my journey's end.

SOURCE: Thomas Gage. *The English American: A New Survey of the West Indies, 1648* (London: George Routledge, 1928), 171–72.

of the regular orders. In many cases, the missionaries competed with nearby landowners for native workers. After two centuries of presence in some villages, Franciscans and Jesuits were proud to point out that their minions still did not know Spanish. The missionaries had been communicating with them in their native tongues for the whole time. If the natives left their semi-autonomous villages, gave up their traditional garb, and spoke only Spanish, the regular orders would be out of a job because it fell to the secular clergy to minister to the Hispanicized population.

Missionary priests converted African slaves as well, though not as rigorously. They had presided over mass baptisms in the stockades of the slave factories of West Africa, on the slave ships, and in American ports before African slaves were sold at auction. Clergymen even owned slaves themselves, either for personal service or for labor on landed estates operated by their orders. Nonetheless, the teaching of the Catholic sacraments among African slaves—whether in Veracruz, Mexico, during the sixteenth century or Bahia, Brazil, in the seventeenth—was never so scrupulously accomplished as among Native Americans. For the most part, Africans remained under the control of their owners, unlike the natives, who came under the control of missionaries for tutelage.

Three reasons existed for this difference of treatment between the two groups. First, the church and its clergy in colonial America practiced a curious form of racism that was common at that time. Following a heated debate in the 1540s, missionary reformers had convinced the Crown that Native Americans were "human," capable of enough rational thought and contemplative reflection to be able to accept Christianity as the one true religion. On the other hand, the clergy believed that black Africans lacked these minimal human qualities. They had been among the greatest exponents of importing African slaves to replace the indigenous populations decimated by European diseases. Second, it was the secular priests, rather than the missionary orders, that ministered to slaves. The secular church served the interests of the elite, on which it was financially dependent, more than did the self-supporting Franciscans and Jesuits. Third, slaves were property. The lay owners of African slaves exerted a greater degree of control over them in their homes, shops, mines, and plantations than did the employers of "free" natives. Slave owners considered the whip a more effective form of control than religious training. Little wonder that working-class populations with important slave antecedents—Cuba, Haiti, and northeast Brazil are examples—while no less religious, have preserved forms of worship reminiscent of African origins.

The Parish Priests

The secular church was as well financed as some of the regular orders. In recognition of the important role of the church in the Indies, the Portuguese and Spanish Crowns permitted the secular hierarchy to benefit from taxes collected from nonnatives. A tithe of 10 percent of the product of all farms and haciendas and shops were collected by tax farmers or directly by Crown bureaucrats; after commissions were deducted, the proceeds were turned over to the church. As well, the local priests could and did charge parishioners to perform marriages, christenings, burials, and masses. Recurrent morality campaigns to have all cohabitants enter into religious matrimony yielded nice sums to the parish priests carrying out the work, although they never did solve the problems of bigamy and illegitimacy. Finally, the church enjoyed special tax breaks because it was an official institution of the Crown. The clergy did not pay taxes on its properties or on its business profits. Nothing prevented secular priests from also owning businesses, engaging in commerce, and running a farm or two. Appointments to the colonial bureaucracy were also distinct possibilities for the priest who played his political cards astutely.

During the colonial period, the church assumed the tasks of charity as well as education for the civil authorities. The charities were organized within the religious lay brotherhoods, which were known as *cofradías.* These confraternities or sodalities were social organizations among peer groups—towns, neighborhoods, professions, ethnic groups—to sponsor religious festivities and provide burials for members. The Santa Casa da Misericórdia (Holy House of Mercy) was such an institution in Salvador da Bahia, Brazil. Its activities provided for a hospital, a foundling home, criminal aid services, dowries, burials, and a retirement house for unmarried women. The Misericórdia functioned to support white society, as the wealthiest Portuguese landowners and merchants formed its dues-paying membership. Native villages had their own *cofradías,* as did mestizos, mulattoes, and African Americans. They provided their members a measure of social security as well as fraternity.

Indeed, the secular church, under the charge of the bishops and with headquarters in the important Spanish cities, became the biggest banker in the colonies. Church treasuries lent money, secured by rural and urban properties, mainly to white landowners. Accumulating bequests and donations since the sixteenth century, the church by the eighteenth century had become a formidable economic resource; only the wealthy families of import and export merchants could compete with it as accumulators of capital. Merchant wealth was more liquid and sponsored foreign trade and thus was more unstable. In contrast, church wealth was less liquid, as the religious institution accumulated mortgages on rural and urban real estate. As a lender, the church's financial agencies did not pursue its investments with rigor. The interest rate remained at 5 percent, a figure considered below the biblical definition of usury. Often, the church refused to foreclose on a heavily mortgaged property, although it willingly lent additional moneys above and beyond market values. Many a Creole family had rural and urban properties indebted to a lenient and forgiving church lending institution.

Indeed, both the secular church and the missionary orders wielded considerable temporal as well as spiritual power, generating no small degree of envy. Their economic assets bothered many a merchant and landowner who had to compete either with the missionaries for labor and markets or with each other for scarce church finances. An elite family, therefore, profited from having a brother or cousin in the church hierarchy who could throw business its way. Not to have a family member in the church was bad business. In Lima, the Creole elite, particularly the merchant families, dominated the clergy. Half of the viceregal capital's 40 secular priests were sons of merchants, 7 had fathers who were high colonial officials, and only 3 came from the provinces. Likewise, entrepreneurs disliked competing against the tax-free production of missionary farms and *obrajes* (woolen weaving shops). Merchants at the city of Asunción resented paying taxes on the transport of their yerba maté while Jesuit missionaries, without paying the local tax collector, sent bundles of *yerba* leaves down the Paraná River to Santa Fe and Buenos Aires for distribution. However, most conflicts between the clergy and the laity concerned labor. Landowners and miners often thought priests had too much influence in the villages, controlling the allocation of native workers.

Women did not participate in church activities in the same ways as men. Their service did not involve missionary work among indigenous peoples or parish preaching in the cities and towns. Becoming a nun invoked the wider male-imposed principle of sequestration for females. Nunneries were for women who were not chosen for marriage and those who chose not to marry. Wealthy Spanish and Creole families found the nunneries to be convenient and respectable destinations for grown daughters. Families provided generous endowments to the church treasuries to provide yearly stipends for the upkeep of their daughters who took the habit. Nuns continued to enjoy personal service in their cloistered lives, as native and black servants also entered nunneries to serve their mistresses. However, few women of mixed blood and no native or African women, no matter how devoted, were permitted to become nuns.

The nunnery remained an elite institution, but women taking their vows gained a degree of personal independence from fathers and brothers. Battered women (of the *gente decente,* at least) found refuge in the nunnery, though not usually as nuns. Most females gained some freedom from convention in the cloisters. One of America's greatest poets, Sor Juana Inés de la Cruz, took refuge in the solitude of a seventeenth-century Mexican nunnery to compose musings on her gender, her contemplation, and even her sexuality. Eventually, church authorities curbed the poetic indulgences of the famous nun (see Manuscript 4.4). Despite the restrictions, the lives of nuns had not been completely divorced from public service. Women of the habit worked in hospitals, schools, orphanages, and foundling homes established by the church throughout the Indies. In Buenos Aires and other cities, they ran schools for orphaned girls, supported by the proceeds of haciendas operated by the lay brotherhoods.

The Inquisition

The Holy Office of the Inquisition had served as an important instrument in Spain's Reconquest that eventually crossed the ocean to play a much reduced role in colonial life. The reason for the difference has to do with the importance of commerce to the American colonies of Spain and Portugal. In the Reconquest, especially during its last stages of the fifteenth century, the Christian monarchs had imposed religious unity as a method of consolidating political power over the newly reconquered parts of the Iberian peninsula. They established the Inquisition to combat heresy, which was defined as any religious practice or belief contrary to Catholic doctrine. The Holy Office became particularly active after the expulsion of Jews and Muslims who refused conversion to prevent backsliding among the remaining "former heretics" who had converted to Christianity. Both in Spain and Portugal, these New Christians, or *conversos,* were still regarded with suspicion and rarely rose to prominence in politics and landholding. Because numerous professional positions were not open to New Christians, many of them gravitated to commerce and the trades. However, the Portuguese monarchy did not support the inquisitorial authorities as much as the Spaniards. There was no Holy Office established in Lisbon until 1547. The Portuguese Inquisition sent visiting delegations of inspectors to Brazil on only three occasions. Because this maritime country depended on overseas trade, the Portuguese did not choose to monitor too closely the religious beliefs of its merchant class or the moral conduct of its planter class.

New Christians and those who resisted their conversion, known as Judaizers and Moriscos, found their way to Brazil and the Spanish Americas, where they established themselves in the principal ports. This occurred despite the Spanish strictures that emigration to the colonies was permitted only for those who could prove *limpieza de sangre*, or purity of blood, meaning that the applicant had come from a family that had been Christian for several generations. The colonies simply needed the sort of commercial connections that merchant families provided. Therefore, in the 1570s, the king directed that Holy Offices of the Inquisition be established in Mexico City and Lima, followed by a third at the port of Cartagena on the Caribbean Sea. These offices were not too active until Spain and Portugal became united under the Hapsburg crown between

MANUSCRIPT 4.4

On Being a Woman and an Intellectual

Juana Inés de la Cruz entered the nunnery at the age of 18 to gain a haven in which she could continue her passion for learning. Brought up in a town outside of Mexico City, she learned to read at the age of 4 and thereafter practically educated herself by reading her grandfather's books. Arriving at Mexico City at a very young age, she attracted attention for her wide knowledge and ability to debate the learned men of the capital. She carried on an active correspondence with aristocratic women and wives of viceroys, for whom she composed love letters, poems, essays, and plays. However, Sor (Sister) Juana incurred the censure first of her confessor and then a bishop of the church. Their criticisms suggested that women should study the life of Jesus rather than philosophers and poets and that they should not teach but study for the love of learning. In her replies to these criticisms, she defended the pursuit of knowledge by women. But Sor Juana did indeed lay down the pen in the final five years of her life. She died in 1695 at the age of 44.

Women sense that men exceed them, and yet it seems that I place myself on a level with men; some men wish that I did not know so much; others say that I must know more in order to merit such approbation; elderly women do not want other women to know more than they; young women, that others make a good appearance; and both wish that I conform to the rules of their counsel; so that from all sides comes such a singular mar-

tyrdom I deem none other has ever experienced it. . . .

My studies have not been to the harm of any person, having been so extremely private that I have not even had the direction of a teacher, but have learned only from myself and my work, for I am not unaware that to study publicly in schools is not seemly for a woman's honor, because this gives occasion for familiarity with men, and could be sufficient reason for banning public studies, and that if women may not challenge men in studies that pertain to them alone, it is because the republic having no need of such schools for government by magistrates (from which service, for the same reason of honor, women are excluded) has not established them; by private and individual study, who has forbidden that to women? Like men, do they not have a rational soul? Shall they not enjoy the privilege of the enlightenment of letters? Is a woman's soul not as receptive to God's grace and glory as a man's? Why is she not as able to receive as much learning and science, which is the lesser gift? What divine revelation, what regulation of the church, what rule of reason framed for us such a harsh law? . . .

I have this nature; if it is evil, I am the daughter of it; I was born with it and with it shall I die.

SOURCE: *A Woman of Genius: The Intellectual Autobiography of Sor Juana Inés de la Cruz,* trans. Margaret Sayers Peden (Salisbury, Conn.: Lime Rock Press, 1987), 102–4.

1580 and 1640 and Portuguese merchants from Brazil began to encroach on Spanish ports. Certainly not all merchants were New Christians, but Spanish officials and citizens perceived the Portuguese commercial invasion as a Judaizing conspiracy. In addition, the Inquisition moved against Protestants, most of whom were shipwrecked seamen engaged in illegal trade.

The bulk of the *autos-da-fé,* or "acts of faith" in which the accused publicly demonstrated repentance and suffered punishment, occurred around the turn of the seventeenth century. Nonetheless, punishment by death, such as by being burned at the stake or garroted, was rare in the Americas. Less than one hundred victims judged to be incorrigible heretics were condemned to death, though more than two thousand active investigations were undertaken during the colonial period. Most prosecutions resulted in loss of property, imprisonment, flogging, and assignment as oarsmen in naval galleys. It must be said that blasphemy, moral degeneration, homosexuality, bigamy, and other offenses against public morality were the reasons for most such prosecutions. The Inquisition also concerned itself with the circulation of books expressing religious ideas contrary to Catholic doctrine, although those books of the eighteenth-century Enlightenment that challenged political authority did not concern the inquisitors.

However, the Inquisition operated within a legal system of secrecy and prosecutorial immunity, independent of political and ecclesiastical oversight. It accepted unsubstantiated denunciations, incarcerated suspects, and confiscated the accuseds' property without informing them of the charges. Investigations of moral and religious wrongdoing could proceed desultorily over the course of years, during which time the accused remained in custody. The accused had few rights to visitation or to the presentation of evidence, and the Holy Office appointed their defense attorneys. Torture was an accepted technique of interrogation and of searching for truth. The nature of inquisitional procedures involved its personnel in political intrigue and commercial jealousy and did much to set a cultural tone that sacrificed the rights of the accused for the doctrinal purity of colonial society. However, neither in Brazil nor in the Spanish Americas did indigenous peoples become subject to the Inquisition. Political and religious authorities did not consider them to have enough understanding to be able even to maintain doctrinal purity. The Holy Office of the Inquisition served to enforce orthodoxy and moral behavior among the whites and the growing number of mixed-race people without encroaching on family patriarchy or traditional male prerogatives. In its work, the Inquisition seemed to have the support of the colonists—so long as the inquisitors did not perform their duties too strictly or too frequently.

CONCLUDING REMARKS

Settlers and public officials meant for Christianity to bond a fractured and heterogeneous colonial society, giving something in common to the governors and the governed, the privileged and the dispossessed, the rich and the poor. Certainly, the Franciscans, Dominicans, Augustinians, and Jesuits understood something about power over subject peoples. They built churches in villages, directed the natives' work, and tried to keep other Spaniards away. They learned native tongues so that they could preach among indigenous groups. But the friars never once accepted natives into their mendicant orders as priests. They did not consider them as equals. The native faithful might aspire to serve as assistants to the Spanish clergy but could never hope for ordination. And what doctrine did these priests preach to the natives? That they would receive their reward later in heaven. Catholic orthodoxy was a mechanism of social control. Religious instruction prepared Native Americans and the poor to accept their permanently subordinate role in colonial society.

Ultimately, for all its temporal power, the church was very much involved in politics. In those deliberately vague interstices where authority and privilege overlapped, churchmen were found to be political actors. The bishops tested the limits and powers of the highest civic authorities. They sniped at viceroys and governors over appointments and taxes. At the local level, missionaries and parish priests cooperated or competed—both at the same time—with the district's political authorities. They colluded with local officials to intervene in the selection of village leaders or conspired in the allocation of indigenous labor as well. The clergy might also support the demands of their native charges for higher pay or labor exemptions. Understandably, *hacendados* and mine owners sometimes harbored resentments. In Quito, political intrigues and conspiracies were the norm among the officials of the *audiencia* and religious hierarchy. Religious institutions became quite politicized, for the church's authority over Native Americans as well as its disposable income conferred great power on it.

The *Patronato Real,* which granted the Crowns the right to collect taxes for the church and to appoint priests and bishops, merely added additional political relevance to colonial religious affairs. Spanish and Portuguese kings literally owned the property and the wealth that the church acquired in the colonies. If the need arose, the Crowns could claim authority to tax church properties, and they also reserved the theoretical right to banish any priest or religious order deemed too powerful or disloyal, although banishment remained rare. Nonetheless, the church was an integral part of the colonial scheme by which the few Europeans dominated a mass of non-Europeans. As one clergyman in Guatemala observed, European rule depended on "the peace and good harmony between the [rural] priests and their Indian parishioners, upon which depend, as links in a chain, the good of the church and of the state." Without the priests, the result would have been "lamentable anarchy . . . a confused ant-heap, which, lacking its chief conductor, runs in all directions . . . the crazed insects colliding . . . deranged, disturbed, and terrified."

At best, the European institutions that influenced the maturation of colonial society in the sixteenth and seventeenth centuries did not function perfectly. The diverse inhabitants of the colonies—be they Iberian Americans, Native Americans, or African Americans—each appropriated from these institutions the means to negotiate and contest their positions in the social order. Spanish merchants traded with foreign ships despite the restrictive mercantilist laws. Few colonial officials could resist using their offices to engage in business ventures that sometimes contravened the regulatory dictates of their monarch. Even the wealthy elites, those most beholden to European institutions for their positions in society, looked for ways to avoid paying taxes and to suborn public officials with special favors and business opportunities. When possible, the indigenous population avoided and rejected the most draconian of colonial laws while taking advantage of overlapping jurisdictions between executive and judicial branches of government; they sought to exploit the breach between the interests of the clergy and the settlers. Slaves ran away from their masters. Within the flexible limitations that colonial economic, political, and religious institutions placed on everyone, the citizens of the

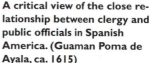

A critical view of the close relationship between clergy and public officials in Spanish America. (Guaman Poma de Ayala, ca. 1615)

Americas contested and negotiated their life prospects according to their varied identities and perspectives. Just how each social group manipulated these institutional arrangements to its own advantage is the subject of the next three chapters.

Additional Reading

Alden, Dauril, ed. *Colonial Roots of Modern Brazil.* Berkeley: University of California Press, 1967.

Alden, Dauril. *The Making of an Enterprise: The Society of Jesus in Portugal, Its Empire, and Beyond, 1540-1750.* Stanford, Calif.: Stanford University Press, 1996.

Andrien, Kenneth J. *Crisis and Decline: The Viceroyalty of Peru in the Seventeenth Century.* Albuquerque: University of New Mexico Press, 1985.

Andrien, Kenneth J., and Rolena Adorno, eds. *Transatlantic Encounters: Europeans and Andeans in the Sixteenth Century.* Berkeley: University of California Press, 1991.

Bakewell, Peter J. *Silver and Entrepreneurship in Seventeenth-Century Potosí: The Life and Times of Antonio López de Quiroga.* Albuquerque: University of New Mexico Press, 1988.

———. *Silver Mining and Society in Colonial Mexico: Zacatecas, 1546– 1700.* Cambridge, Mass.: Cambridge University Press, 1971.

Boxer, C. R. *The Dutch in Brazil, 1624–1654*. Oxford, England: Clarendon Press, 1957.

———. *The Portuguese Seaborne Empire, 1415–1825*. New York: Knopf, 1969.

Burkhart, Louise M. *The Slippery Earth: Nahua-Christian Moral Dialogue in Sixteenth-Century Mexico*. Tucson: University of Arizona Press, 1989.

Cervantes, Francisco. *The Devil in the New World: The Impact of Diabolism in New Spain*. New Haven, Conn.: Yale University Press, 1994.

Cohen, Thomas M. *The Fire of Tongues: António Vieira and the Missionary Church in Brazil and Portugal*. Stanford, Calif.: Stanford University Press, 1998.

Cushner, Nicholas P. *Farm and Factory: The Jesuits and the Development of Agrarian Capitalism in Colonial Quito, 1600–1767*. Albany: State University of New York Press, 1982.

———. *Lords of the Land: Sugar, Wine, and Jesuit Estates of Coastal Peru, 1600–1767*. Albany: State University of New York Press, 1980.

Flusche, Della M. *Two Families in Colonial Chile*. Lewiston, N.Y.: E. Mellen Press, 1989.

Graham, Richard, ed. *Brazil and the World System*. Austin: University of Texas Press, 1991.

Hoberman, Luisa Schell. *Mexico's Merchant Elite, 1590–1660: Silver, State, and Society*. Durham, N.C.: Duke University Press, 1991.

Hoffman, Paul E. *The Spanish Crown and the Defense of the Caribbean, 1535–1585: Precedent, Patrimonialism, and Royal Parsimony*. Baton Rouge: Louisiana State University Press, 1980.

Korth, Eugene H. *Spanish Policy in Colonial Chile: The Struggle for Social Justice, 1535–1700*. Stanford, Calif.: Stanford University Press, 1968.

Lane, Kris E. *Pillaging the Empire: Piracy in the Americas, 1500–1750*. Armonk, N.Y.: M. E. Sharpe, 1998.

Liebman, Seymour B. *The Inquisitors and the Jews in the New World: Summaries of Procesos, 1500–1810*. Coral Gables, Fla.: University of Miami Press, 1974.

MacLachlan, Colin M. *Spain's Empire in the New World: The Role of Ideas in Institutional and Social Change*. Berkeley: University of California Press, 1988.

Marley, David F. *Pirates and Engineers: Dutch and Flemish Adventurers in New Spain (1607–1697)*. Windsor, Ontario: Netherlandic Press, 1992.

Phelan, John Leddy. *The Kingdom of Quito in the Seventeenth Century: Bureaucratic Politics in the Spanish Empire*. Madison: University of Wisconsin Press, 1967.

Poole, Stafford. *Our Lady of Guadalupe: The Origins and Sources of a Mexican National Symbol, 1531–1797*. Tucson: University of Arizona Press, 1995.

Ramirez, Susan E., ed. *Indian-Religious Relations in Colonial Spanish America*. Syracuse, N.Y.: Maxwell School of Citizenship and Public Affairs, Syracuse University, 1989.

Russell-Wood, A. J. R. *Fidalgos and Philanthropists: The Santa Casa da Misericórdia of Bahia, 1550–1755*. Berkeley: University of California Press, 1968.

Schwaller, John Frederick. *Church and Clergy in Sixteenth Century Mexico*. Albuquerque: University of New Mexico Press, 1987.

———. *Origins of Church Wealth in Mexico*. Albuquerque: University of New Mexico Press, 1985.

Schwartz, Stuart B. *Sovereignty and Society in Colonial Brazil: The High Court of Bahia and Its Judges, 1609–1751*. Berkeley: University of California Press, 1973.

Seed, Patricia. *Ceremonies of Possession in Europe's Conquest of the New World, 1492-1640*. Cambridge, England: Cambridge University Press, 1995.

Silverblatt, Irene. *Moon, Sun, and Witches: Gender Ideologies and Class in Inca and Colonial Peru*. Princeton, N.J.: Princeton University Press, 1987.

Soeiro, Susan A. "A Baroque Nunnery: The Economic and Social Role of a Colonial Convent, Santa Clara do Destêrro, Salvador, Bahia, 1677–1800." Ph.D. diss., New York University, 1974.

Turner Bushnell, Amy. *The King's Coffer: Proprietors of the Spanish Florida Treasury, 1565–1702*. Gainesville: University Presses of Florida, 1981.

———. *Situado and Sabana: Spain's Support System for the Presidio and Mission Provinces of Florida*. Athens: University of Georgia Press, 1995.

Uricoechea, Fernando. *The Patrimonial Foundations of the Brazilian Bureaucratic State*. Berkeley: University of California Press, 1980.

Van Oss, Adriaan C. *Catholic Colonialism: A Parish History of Guatemala, 1524–1821*. Cambridge, England: Cambridge University Press, 1986.

Wiznitzer, Arnold. *Jews in Colonial Brazil*. New York: Columbia University Press, 1960.

In Spanish and Portuguese

Bromberg, Rachel Mizrahi. *A inquisição no Brasil: Um capitão-mor judaizante*. São Paulo: Centro de Estudos Judaicos, 1984.

Castillero Calvo, Alfredo. *El casco viejo de Panamá*. Panama City: Ministerio de la Presidencia, 1999.

Ceballos Gómez, Diana Luz. *Hechicería, brujería, e Inquisición en el Nuevo Reino de Granada: Un duelo de imaginarios*. Medellín: Editorial Universidad Nacional, 1994.

Furlong Cardiff, Guillermo. *Misiones y sus pueblos de Guaraníes*. Buenos Aires: Imprenta Balmes, 1962.

Martínez López-Cano, María del Pilar. *El crédito a largo plazo en el siglo XVI. Ciudad de México (1550–1720)*. Mexico City: UNAM, 1995.

Mejía González, Alma Leticia, ed. *Relación de la causa de Juana María, esclava, mulata y hechicera: historia inquisitorial de una mujer novohispana del siglo XVIII*. Mexico City: El Colegio de México, 1996.

de Mello, Evaldo Cabral. *Olinda restaurada: guerra e açucar no Nordeste, 1630–1654*. Rio de Janeiro: Editora Forense Universitária, 1975.

de Mello, José Antonio Gonsalves. *Tempo dos flamengos: Influencia de ocupação holandesa na vida e na cultura do Brasil*. 3d ed. Brasília: Fundação Joaquim Nabuco, Editora Massangana, 1987.

Mott, Luiz Roberto de Barros. *O sexo proibido: Virgens, gays e escravos nas garras da Inquisição*. Campinas, São Paulo: Papirus Editora, 1986.

Moutoukias, Zacarias. *Contrabando y control colonial en el siglo XVII: Buenos Aires, el Atlántico y el espacio peruano*. Buenos Aires: Centro Editor de América Latina, 1988.

O'Gorman, Edmundo. *La invención de América: Investigación acerca de la estructura histórica del Nuevo Mundo y del sentido de su devenir*. Mexico City: Fondo de Cultura Económica, 1984.

Prado Júnior, Caio. *Formação do Brasil contemporânia (Época colonial)*. 20th ed. São Paulo: Editora Brasiliense, 1987.

Sempat Assadourian, Carlos. *El sistema de la economía colonial: El mercado interior. Regiones y espacio económico*. Mexico City: Editorial Nueva Imagen, 1983.

Tarquinio de Sousa, Octavio, and Sérgio Buarque de Holanda. *História do Brasil*. Rio de Janeiro: Livraria José Olympio Editora, 1944.

Vainfas, Ronaldo. *Trópico dos pecados: Moral, sexualidade e Inquisição no Brasil*. Rio de Janeiro: Editora Campus, 1989.

Zavala, Silvio A. *La encomienda indiana*. 2d ed. Mexico City: Porrúa, 1973.

CHAPTER 5

THE IBERIAN-AMERICAN WORLD

Armed with European institutions reinventing economics, governance, and religion, the settlers from the Iberian Peninsula set out to recast American society in their image. These settlers made the city the chief focus of Iberian-American society. Immigrants found security living with fellow Iberians and enjoying European-style amenities—housing, foodstuffs, shopping, clothes, and recreation—in an urban environment.[1] Iberians who had only modest status or fortune back in the home country could use their European knowledge in the Americas to make money and establish a lineage of respect. European immigrants established themselves in leadership positions and "civilized" the natives, a euphemism meaning they taught the natives how to work for them. The wealthiest among them filled their homes with servants. Emigration from the Iberian Peninsula to one of the colonies usually entailed a degree of upward social mobility for the one making the move; the immigrants' command of other persons' labor certainly increased substantially. Moreover, the new European immigrants sought to establish a society very much like the one

---

[1]The term *Iberian* refers to a person born in the Iberian Peninsula, whether Spanish or Portuguese. It also applies in colonial society to a person exhibiting supposedly Iberian attitudes, attributes, and appearance. An *Iberian-American*, as the term is used here, was an inhabitant of colonial Latin America who belonged to social circles dominated by Iberian customs rather than to the world of indigenous and African peoples.

from which they had come and brought with them the principles of family, patriarchy, the subordination of women, and a social order in which one small minority lived a privileged existence supported by the work and service of the great majority.

However, a number of important caveats differentiated American colonial society from the European blueprint. The existence of a large indigenous underclass relegated white society to permanent numerical minority. On the one hand, the privileged newcomers felt insecure in their new environment; on the other hand, the indigenous majority could be made to work for them. Yet the indigenous population had only limited preparation to work in the European sphere, constructing European housing and clothing and producing European foodstuffs, and many Old World diseases threatened to eliminate many native groups as a potential labor force. Iberian settlers, therefore, had to import labor from among the poorest of their fellow Spaniards and Portuguese who had some working knowledge of European wares and crops. Finally, the wealthiest of settlers also saw a need for importing African slaves—to work in the European economic sector, to supervise and instruct indigenous workers, and to produce colonial commodities (such as sugar and cacao) for export markets. Of course, Iberians had had previous experience with social heterogeneity, particularly in the previous centuries in which Islamic and Jewish communities coexisted and communicated with Christian ones. The colonial experience was novel, however, because the combined native and non-European underclass so vastly outnumbered the Christian Iberians.

Furthermore, another great novelty began to create enormous differences among Iberian and colonial American societies. More male immigrants were arriving in the Americas than females, so the new arrivals tended to mingle and mate with women from the subordinate indigenous groups. The first progeny of these unions readily joined the minority Iberian sector of colonial society and tended to identify with their fathers' world. Spaniards and Portuguese who mated with native women produced mestizo and *mameluco* children, respectively. Those who had relations with African women produced mulattoes. On the sugar plantations of northeastern Brazil, for example, white men fathered 20 percent of all children born to native women and 30 percent of those born to Africans. As the formative sixteenth century turned into the mature seventeenth century, these racially mixed groups began to grow in size and lost their privileged status in colonial society. They became separated more from white society and formed a separate society of castes that was subject to some legal as well as societal discrimination. Their illegitimate births now stigmatized racially mixed persons, who were believed to have inherited the supposed worst traits of both races rather than the best. Nonetheless, despite their decline in status, the mixed groups tended to identify with European society while serving as intermediaries and liaisons with subordinate indigenous groups and African slaves. Mixed-blood persons tended to accept some European social conventions while preserving their separate identities and social principles.

Furthermore, the white settler class began to develop social differentiation as time passed and its numbers grew. Very gradually, a distinction was made between those whites born in Spain and Portugal and the whites born in the colonies. Although racially indistinct, the American-born whites tended to lose status. Newly arrived immigrants utilized their European connections to claim superior political positions and especially to dominate the ranks of the merchant class. Soon, the European whites subscribed to vague ideas about the moral and racial purity of European birth and the enervating influence of American birth on one's character and capacities. American whites, even those who achieved and retained great wealth, began to feel the sting of their origin.

Despite the biases of race and birth, colonial society remained an open, fluid social system in which some upward and downward mobility existed. One might rise because of wealth, connections, capacity, education, or behavior. There also existed a second social determinant—based on occupation—distinguishing one type of colonial citizen from another. This occupational or status distinction modified, but did not alter, the multiracial hierarchy, for those who guarded access to the elite professions reserved these economic and political positions for relatives, friends, and others who appeared "respectable." Those with power usually valued persons of European appearance over those with indigenous or African features.

A SOCIETY OF CASTES

To manage the increasing complexity of the colonies, the Europeans in the Americas established a durable social system featuring the creation of urban centers throughout the region, a multiracial hierarchy, a patriarchy that subordinated women to the dictates of family and of males, and the primacy of politically and professionally endowed white groups. By the seventeenth century, there developed in the Spanish-American core settlements of Mexico and Peru, and less so in outlying Spanish settlements, a society of castes. Yet these social categories permitted limited mobility both up and down and countenanced resistance and tensions at all levels.

The organization of society in the Spanish Americas and Portuguese Brazil was not determined by official decree but by social practices in the colonies themselves among European settlers, indigenous peoples, and eventually imported African slaves. At first, the Spanish Crown attempted to divide and govern separately two colonial social entities: the so-called Republic of Spaniards and the Republic of Indians. The two groups were to live separately in the Americas, each subject to Iberian rule. But the interpenetration of these social sectors rendered separation, let alone equality, impossible. The settlers desired servants and laborers, the Native Americans found their numbers reduced owing to epidemics, Africans were imported to provide labor, and the Crowns of Spain and Portugal wanted to collect taxes on colonial enterprise. Therefore, a complex and fluid social order developed to manage the coexistence of three races, European, Native American, and African, an order made even more complicated by the emergence of intermediary racial groups, products of the sexual unions between people of different races. What resulted was a variety of multiracial and multiethnic hierarchies peculiar to time and place but almost universally characterized by privilege and wealth for a few whites and labor obligations and poverty for the mass of nonwhites.

Gente Decente and Gente de Pueblo

Colonial society consisted of two categories of people, each of which contained its own gradations. The self-defined *gente decente* (respectable people) was made up mostly of whites who belonged to the wealthy, educated, and privileged minority of families. Many of these families traced their roots back to the original conquerors and *encomenderos* and reinforced their status through acquisition of land and advantageous marriages into merchant wealth. Others of the *gente decente* could be wealthy merchants, top bureau-crats, ranking military officers, and clerical officials—approximately 4 percent of colo-nial households. In bigger cities, the lower reaches of the *gente decente* were made up of intellectuals, professionals, merchants and businessmen, clerks, militia officers, and lower clergy—perhaps another 15 percent of the urban population. Laws reinforced the discriminatory aspects of the colonial social system. Many statutes permitted only Euro-peans and Creoles (Europeans born in the colonies) to serve in political and ecclesiasti-cal posts. In many cases, the laws served the interests of the Iberian colonists, who de-manded preferential treatment.

Moreover, the importance of the international commercial network reinforced the central role of race and birth. The most prosperous merchants in ports and capital cities were agents, often sons and nephews, of commercial houses in Seville, Cádiz, and Lisbon. These Iberian-born traders had the habit of working and trusting only other Iberians. As government officials extended political benefits mainly to their colleagues, so, too, did merchants provide credit to and make contracts principally with their male kin. These fac-tors reinforced the importance of social status, that is, being accepted as European.

The second basic category of colonial society, like the first, was defined by the priv-ileged Europeans. Persons who worked with their hands formed the so-called *gente de pueblo,* although they did not identify themselves as such. The *gente de pueblo* originally was to consist only of Native Americans and Africans, but the volume of European im-migration into attractive and prosperous colonial areas such as central Mexico and coastal Peru forced many whites of modest family background into this category. Two other groups—mestizos and mulattoes—joined the *gente de pueblo.*

It was the mixing of the races that gave rise to what was called the *sociedad de cas-tas,* or society of castes. The conception of the time held that for a society composed of such racial and ethnic diversity to operate in an orderly fashion, people should have ac-cess to opportunities according to their merit. And race served as the indicator of merit—with Europeans being the most worthy and Native Americans and Africans being the least. Each race was to enjoy the rights and obligations pertaining to its rank in soci-ety. As the progenitors of civilization and Catholicism, the whites were to care for and teach the Native Americans, who could live separately but still needed to supply labor to receive benefits. Africans deserved to live as slaves because, according to the ideology of the time, the stigma of their African births necessitated that Europeans should tutor them on how to work and pray. The natives, at least, were considered to have a childlike ca-pacity for reasoning—and thus were not to be enslaved—but not Africans. And what about that growing sector of society that was neither white, brown, nor black? At first, racially mixed persons were classified according to the relative percentages of their eth-nic backgrounds. Thus, the offspring of a European man and an African woman was known as a *mulato;* a *mulata* and a white male produced a *quaterón* (one-quarter Eu-ropean); a *quaterón* and a white bore an *octerón;* and so forth. These distinctions were important and became codified in the laws that attempted to regulate this society of castes (see Manuscript 5.1).

But as time went on, racial separation actually became less and less of a possibility in the Americas. There were simply too few whites and too much race mixture. European men enjoyed a preponderance of power as well as legal privileges and were disposed to take advantage of their station, particularly over women of inferior social status (that is, darker-skinned females). In the absence of parity between European men and women,

The Multiracial Society of Cartagena, 1735

As a coastal city in the tropics, Cartagena displayed fewer Native American influences than some other parts of Latin America, yet the following description of the racial makeup of the inhabitants is remarkable for its complexity. Apparently, the slightest gradations of skin color meant something in the personal relationships among the various inhabitants of Cartagena. Two youthful Spanish visitors, Jorge Juan and Antonio de Ulloa, also noted how respectable white women stayed at home while women of color were out working at the marketplace. One of their observations conflicts with what we know about the extent of illegitimacy in these multiracial colonial societies. Juan and Ulloa assumed that persons of different races married each other with great regularity. Did this perception result from youthful naïveté or from the fact that Cartagena was the first colonial stop on their itinerary?

The inhabitants [of Cartagena] may be divided into different casts [sic] or tribes, who derive their origin from a coalition of Whites, Negroes, and Indians. Of each of these we shall treat particularly.

The Whites may be divided into two classes, the Europeans, and Creoles, or Whites born in the country. The former are commonly called Chapetones, but are not numerous; most of them either return into Spain after acquiring a competent fortune, or remove up into inland provinces in order to increase it. Those who are settled at Carthagena [sic], carry on the whole trade of that place, and live in opulence; whilst the other inhabitants are indigent, and reduced to have recourse to mean and hard labour for subsistence. The families of the White Creoles compose the landed interest; some of them have large estates, and are highly respected, because their ancestors came into the country invested with honourable posts, bringing their families with them when they settled here. Some of these families, in order to keep up their original dignity, have either married their children to their equals in the country, or sent them as officers on board the galleons; but others have greatly declined. Besides these, there are other Whites, in mean circumstances, who either owe their origin to Indian families, or at least to an intermarriage with them, so that there is some mixture in their blood; but when this is not discoverable by their colour, the conceit of being Whites alleviates the pressure of every other calamity.

Among the other tribes which are derived from an intermarriage of the Whites with the Negroes, the first are the Mulattos. Next to these the Tercerones, produced from a White and a Mulatto, with some approximation to the former, but not so near as to obliterate their origin. After these follow the Quarterones, proceeding from a White and a Terceron. The last are the Quinterones, who owe their origin to a White and Quarteron. This is the last gradation, there being no visible difference between them and the Whites, either in colour or features; nay, they are often fairer than the Spaniards. The children of a White and Quinteron are also called Spaniards, and consider themselves as free from all taint of the Negro race. Every person is so jealous of the order of their tribe or cast [sic], that if, through inadvertence, you call them by a degree lower than what they actually are, they are highly offended, never suffering themselves to be deprived of so valuable a gift of fortune. . . .

These are the most known and common tribes or Castas; there are indeed several others proceeding from their intermarriages; but, being so various, even they themselves cannot easily distinguish them; and these are the only people one sees in the city, the estancias [farms], and villages; for if any Whites, especially women, are met with, it is only accidental; these generally residing in their houses; at least, if they are of any rank or character.

These casts [sic], from the Mulattos, all affect the Spanish dress, but wear very slight stuffs on account of the heat of the climate. These are the mechanics of the city; the Whites, whether Creoles or Chapetones, disdaining such a mean occupation, follow nothing below merchandise. But it being impossible for all to succeed, great numbers not being able to procure sufficient credit, they become poor and miserable from their aversion to those trades they follow in Europe; and, instead of the riches which they flattered themselves with possessing in the Indies, they experience the most complicated wretchedness.

The class of Negroes is not the least numerous, and is divided into two parts; the free and the slaves. These are again subdivided into Creoles and [Bozales], part of which are employed in the cultivation of the haziendas [sic], or estancias. Those in the city are obliged to perform the most laborious services, and pay out of their wages a certain quota to their masters, subsisting themselves on the small remainder. The violence of the heat not permitting them to wear any clothes, their only covering is a small piece of cotton stuff about their waist; the female slaves go in the same manner. Some of these live at the estancias, being married to the slaves who work there; while those in the city sell in the markets all kinds of eatables, and dry fruits, sweetmeats, cakes made of the maize, and cassava, and several other things about the streets.

SOURCE: Jorge Juan and Antonio de Ulloa, *A Voyage to South America* (New York: Alfred A. Knopf, 1964), 158.

white males developed a proclivity to mate or exploit nonwhite females. The result was racial miscegenation. During the three centuries of the colonial period, approximately three hundred thousand Spaniards, mostly but not exclusively men, immigrated to Mexico; roughly two hundred fifty thousand Africans came, unwillingly, as slaves; and a predominantly rural peasant class of 1 million or so natives provided the broad base of colonial Mexican society. Those white males of the *gente decente* who married white females preserved the racial separateness of their families. But the poor whites of the *gente de pueblo* as well as the Africans tended to blend into the mixed-blood society. Within several generations, therefore, the fine racial distinctions among the *gente de pueblo* became as unwieldy and inoperable before the law as they were in practice.

Although they themselves contributed mightily to it, Spaniards did not look kindly on race mixture. They tended to view persons of mixed blood as a criminal element. "Those who are born of such unions are inclined to bad ways," wrote one Peruvian viceroy to his king. "The mestizos and mulattoes are already so numerous, and their ways so wicked, that there is reason to fear, so numerous are they, and so fast are they increasing, that they will cause mischief and agitation in these states." The *gente decente*, being such a minority, always feared a rebellion of the less fortunate and worried that the mestizo and pure-blood native would form an alliance.

Race remained a large factor in one's relative social status, but education, political ability, and wealth did enable a few fortunate light-skinned mulattoes and mestizos to gain admission to the *gente decente.* Predominantly native areas, such as Cuzco in Peru and Oaxaca in Mexico as well as the frontier regions of Chile, Argentina, Venezuela, and northern Mexico, admitted darker-skinned persons into the elite because there were fewer whites in those areas. São Paulo and Paraguay remained regions where mestizos formed the gentry for most of the colonial period, but the darker-skinned elites of the fringe areas behaved just as haughtily as the white elites of Lima and Mexico City. Likewise, the growth of larger European populations in any one locality within the Indies—Guadalajara had a large number of whites, as did Arequipa in Peru—meant that many Europeans there found themselves relegated to the *gente de pueblo.* It did not mean, however, that white workers forged any sort of class identity with the Native American and African-American masses.

Colonial areas with fewer natives, however, did not develop the classic society of castes. African slave imports became more important wherever the indigenous populations declined precipitously, as in Brazil and the Caribbean islands and on the coastlines of Central and South America. These hot, tropical climates attracted few European immigrants, especially after slaving expeditions and the spread of disease had depopulated the indigenous peoples. Eventually, the few settlers began production of tropical and semitropical commodities for European trade—tobacco, cacao, and particularly sugar—and imported substantial numbers of Africans to work these crops. The mix of white bosses with a majority black workforce eventually created a growing intermediary social group of mulattoes. Like the mestizo group in Mexico and Peru, the mulattoes of Brazil gained a higher social status than their slave mothers, spoke Portuguese, wore European styles if they could afford them, and served the economic interests of their white fathers. Light-skinned, well-dressed, and well-spoken mulattoes might gain acceptance in the world of the Portuguese settler (especially when there were few of them). Other mulattoes might serve as artisans, petty merchants, small landholders, and slave overseers, and some even owned a few African slaves themselves. Particularly in the late sixteenth and early seventeenth centuries, the mulatto filled a middle-level social position between the few white officials and landowners and the mass of plantation slaves in Brazil. (For analysis of Brazilian slavery, see Chapter 7.)

Fine distinctions as to skin color, degree of European culture, and family background meant a great deal to one's social position in the maturing colonial society—whether built upon a base of indigenous workers and peasants, such as in the *sociedad de castas* in Mexico and Peru, or on a foundation of African slaves, as in Brazil and the Spanish-American tropics. Yet this social structure did not close off all mobility, and individuals had room to increase or lose social status depending on their wits and social graces. Always, European birth or the perfection of European customs increased one's acceptance at the highest echelons of society, but the fluidity of social categories resulted in tension and insecurity. Nowhere were social distinctions and tensions more obvious than in colonial cities.

The Urban Environment

Iberians were an urban people in the New World. They may have walked through swamps, crossed mosquito-infested forests, traversed arid landscapes, and plunged

Cortés supervising Totonac natives in the construction of Spanish buildings. (Miguel González, 1698)

through snow-covered mountain passes to reach their destinations, but they never liked such rough country. Once the conquest was completed, Europeans settled down in cities. They founded several types of urban environments in the colonial Indies, principally in the sixteenth century, the greatest period of empire and city building. The first type of city was built literally over the ruins of conquered Indian city-states. Repelled by the pagan temples of the native civilizations, the first Spaniards completely destroyed native urban monuments. Native cities like Cholula and Tenochtitlán in Mexico and Quito and Cuzco in the Andes were razed. Spaniards seemed intent on obliterating all vestiges of Native American sovereignty—whether of an architectural or religious nature. No regal order had decreed this; it was the natural inclination of European colonialists intent on intimidating the subordinate non-Europeans. Spanish takeover and rebuilding of these cities symbolized the political and social domination of the indigenous masses.

A second type of city was founded to forge the vital links in the commercial chain to Europe. Santo Domingo and Havana; Veracruz and Acapulco; Portobello and Panama City; Guayaquil and Valparaíso; San Juan, Puerto Rico; Cartagena and La Guaira on the Caribbean coast of South America; Olinda, Salvador, and Rio de Janeiro on the Brazilian coastline; and Buenos Aires and Asunción in the Río de la Plata region—these port cities served as depots connecting the colonies to the European trade routes. Colonists also established cities in the interior to solidify the overland trade routes. In Brazil, São Paulo became an important native slave-trading center. In the Spanish Indies, Guanajuato, Zacatecas, and San Luis Potosí functioned as silver-mining centers well before the close of the sixteenth century, as did Oruro and Potosí in Bolivia. Spaniards and others founded supply points, either for mining or agriculture, at Oaxaca and Guadalajara in Mexico; Santa Fe, Córdoba, and Mendoza in Argentina; Santiago in Chile; Popayán, Medellín, Cali, and Bogotá in Colombia; and Coro, Valencia, Caracas, and Mérida in Venezuela. Moreover, these and many other towns also functioned as social control mechanisms. Set amidst large numbers of indigenous or slave populations, urban centers served to secure labor for European economic entities and to forestall rebellions from below. The towns succeeded in both capacities.

Moreover, the Europeans built each of their cities on the Mediterranean-Iberian model and did not permit much in the way of syncretism, that is, a combination of native and European models. Invariably, each town was founded on a rigid grid pattern, focusing on a spacious central plaza. In cities intended to be capitals, such as Mexico City and Lima and to a lesser extent, Bogotá and Santiago, these central plazas were quite magnificent, serving for both military drilling and commercial exchange. The principal public buildings such as cathedrals and government palaces were arranged around the square. Larger cities would have auxiliary plazas in which religious orders built their chapels and monasteries and artisans also set up shops. The expansion of Mexico City, however, was limited by its location among the lakes of the Valley of Mexico and the attendant problem of periodic flooding. In 1607, colonial authorities began the long process of draining the five lakes that dominated the valley. A German-Spanish engineer named Enrique Martínez (Heinrich Martin) dug a canal and tunnel to divert the waters of Lake Texcoco into the Pánuco River, which carried them on to the Gulf of Mexico.

The most important of the town's Iberian-American founders constructed their personal residences as close to the central square as possible. Their houses were typically Mediterranean in construction. An austere fortress-like wall with iron-grated windows faced directly onto the street or narrow sidewalks; the side walls abutted those of the neighboring house. The family's living quarters focused on an open interior patio, onto which the rooms on three sides of the house opened. The bigger rooms toward the front were reserved for the owner's family. Relatives and white and mixed-blooded employees occupied the middle rooms, whereas native and black servants resided in the small rear rooms. In the larger, more imposing cities, the principal buildings surrounding the main plazas might be constructed of quarried stone. Often the elite family sponsored a shop for the sale of tobaccos, spirits, or European goods in one of the front corner rooms opening out onto the street. The central parts of Mexico City and Cuzco were built from the stones of destroyed Aztec and Inka temples. Most colonists used the familiar adobe brick.

City centers tended to be dominated by the wealthiest Spanish families. The farther one walked from the center, the less Spanish and the more colored the people of the neighborhoods became. The skilled artisans, who made the furniture, baked the bread, worked silver and iron, and stitched the clothing, resided as close to the center of the city as possible, perhaps separated from the plaza itself by the houses of the wealthy elites. Be they whites or persons of mixed races, these artisans used their homes as workplaces and retail shops as well (see Manuscript 5.2). They often housed one or two slaves and native, mestizo, and mulatto free workers right on the premises. Even the independent households of mestizo tradesmen had servants, who might be free natives or slaves. Having servants was a sign of distinction in this status-conscious urban society.

The very outskirts of the cities were reserved for the ramshackle barrios of the most recent native migrants, be they short-term construction workers, retainers of elite families in from the countryside, or muleteers, cartmen, and market women. Chickens, pigs, cows, goats, and dogs roamed freely through these districts. Many modest householders maintained small garden plots. Cities were centers for the acculturation of the natives to the life of the Hispanicized mestizo. In sixteenth-century Oaxaca City, 10 different indigenous groups maintained their separate barrios (neighborhoods) in the city, speaking their own language and wearing their traditional clothes. Gradually, the barrios lost their separate identities as everyone began to speak Spanish exclusively, nonnatives took up residence, and racial mixture obliterated the ethnic diversity.

MANUSCRIPT 5.2

Relations among Members of the *Gente de Pueblo*

Spanish immigrant artisans shared the same occupational status of Native Americans and African Americans. Because they all worked with their hands, they were considered to be part of the gente de pueblo. However, as this tanner made clear in this letter to his wife back in Spain in 1574, he saw very little in common between himself and his assistants. Clearly, his profits, his expertise, and his race set the Spaniard apart.

Milady:

This will be to give you an account of what is happening here and how I am doing up to the day this letter is dated. For about a year now I have been in good health and working at my trade, though I had few Indian helpers. I couldn't find any who were trained, since the other tanners had them, and it was not for me to take them away from them. In this year I must have made 500 pesos profit, and if I said 600 I wouldn't be lying; it's about the same as 500 ducats of Castile. But I no longer have to take off my shoes to work, because now I have eight Indians who work steadily, and a black belonging to my partner who aids me very well, and all I do is give instructions, buy, and sell. That is enough work, and indeed it is not little, though it seems little for me; actually I don't want to work at more than supervision so I won't get some sickness that would be the end of me, because great is my desire to see you again.

SOURCE: James Lockhart and Enrique Otte, eds., *Letters and People of the Spanish Indies: Sixteenth Century* (Cambridge, England: Cambridge University Press, 1976), 121.

During the day, these towns' plazas bustled with market activities. Farmers and farm workers hawked fresh milk and vegetables from the truck gardens surrounding the town, meat and water carts passed through the streets, and servants and slaves washed clothes on flat rocks on the banks of the river. Corrals at the edge of town kept the mules and horses used in travel and haulage to other points in the colony, and a separate suburban corral was set aside for the daily butchering of meat.

The Rural Environment

Europeans imposed more or less this same urban structure throughout the countryside as well, which brings us to consider another production center in colonial America—the rural village. In the more populous regions of the Spanish Indies, Native Americans were brought together, usually under the tutelage of the priests in new rural villages. which were laid out in grids much like the larger cities. They were not encouraged to continue living in their fields (as in ancient times) but had to walk out to them from village residences. Villages were supposed to become a "civilizing" influence, in which idolatrous natives could learn the rudiments of European lifestyles and the Catholic religion. In fact, these rural communities served to control subordinate peoples and provide conduits for labor mobilization and for tribute and tax collection. Some villages retained their ethnic character throughout the colonial period. Their own *caciques* and *kuraka*s provided community leadership, and the village retained sufficient land to provide the basis for subsistence. People in these villages still spoke their native languages. In other rural towns, sometimes nearby to native villages, resided Spaniards or Spanish-speaking farmers and tradesmen. But the Iberians—and their cousins, the *mestizos* and mulattoes—did not reside only in the cities and towns. Some gravitated to the countryside.

The first generation of conquerors did not themselves engage directly in agriculture. Instead, they relied on the natives to produce foodstuffs, which they then requisitioned and distributed to the European population through the *encomienda* system, as the colonists simply permitted the natives to continue in control of their village lands. Gradually, the Spaniards tired of indigenous fare and established farms near their towns to produce wheat and raise livestock. These first Spanish-owned farms employed caretakers, especially recent Iberian immigrants, who worked for an established *encomendero*. Even African slaves worked on these suburban truck farms to produce European crops and livestock. *Encomienda* natives provided labor. However, toward the end of the sixteenth century, the demographic collapse of the indigenous population caused a crisis in colonial agriculture. Peasant production and labor were increasingly unable to supply the growing Spanish population, and colonial authorities also began to take direct control of native laborers away from the *encomenderos*. Therefore, the wealthiest families began to organize their agricultural enterprises on a larger scale. They took ownership of land vacated by the dwindling population of native peasants and set up private rural estates to produce for the commercial market. Thus did the elite families make the transition from control of the indigenous population in the sixteenth century to control of land in the seventeenth century.

Wherever the Europeans themselves had to take charge of agricultural production— whether cattle breeding in northern Mexico and Argentina or cacao and sugar plantations in Venezuela or Brazil—they established a residence on their rural estates. In the Spanish world, these land holdings became known as haciendas and the owners, *hacendados*. In

Brazil, the rural land holdings were called *fazendas;* the owners, *fazendeiros.* If the enterprise turned a large profit, the owner might be able to build an imposing home on his rural estate, as both *hacendados* and *fazendeiros* housed their families there at least part of the year as well as a staff of household servants and perhaps an overseer. Usually, the rural homes of the landowner were simple structures, containing sparse and rudimentary furniture; the hammock at São Paulo was still more ubiquitous than the bedstead. In the wealthiest parts of the colonies, the landowning families commonly resided permanently in the cities, where they marketed the rural production of their nearby truck gardens and their distant estates.

Each *fazenda* and hacienda, like the towns, tended also to become a decentralized institution of social control. The owner congregated his permanent workers or slaves in housing near the big house. Owners did not want their workers living independently out in the fields, although shepherds and cowboys had more freedom living among their herds some distance from the ranch house. The biggest landowner was the social and political authority of the countryside. He enlisted his slaves and workers as a private army, if need be, and extended his will over the smallholders in his district, who were dependent on his access to markets or his line of credit. The *hacendado* and his administrator took it upon themselves to settle disputes among subordinates, and they attempted to govern all aspects of his workers' lives through punishment and reward. Generally, the rural civil authorities conceded judicial prerogatives to the landowner. Many a large hacienda and *fazenda* had its own jail, complete with stocks, iron cuffs, and whipping post—and not just for the slaves. In the countryside, the landowner could live out the seigniorial existence the conquerors had envisioned (see Manuscript 5.3). However, as the next chapters will attest, the landowner's control of the lives of indigenous peoples and even of the slaves met severe limits—not the least of them being the resistance of the native and African workers themselves.

The type of agricultural production and the size of the labor pool determined the number of workers on the rural estate. Sugar plantations in Brazil and cacao plantations in Venezuela required large numbers of gang workers, but few Native Americans survived to form large labor pools there. Therefore, the landowners purchased African slaves who lived on the estates year-round, working under the direction of overseers. On the ranches of southern South America and northern Mexico, the raising of cattle required small increments of labor and the surrounding labor pool was quite scant there as well. Therefore, the mixed-race ranch workers took housing at the estate but labored with little supervision and often moved from one employer to another, bargaining over wages and rations. The areas of central Mexico and the Andean highlands that were still heavily populated by natives presented yet another variation. Here, the production of food crops on Spanish-owned haciendas required few year-round workers but many seasonal itinerants. Therefore, the neighboring native villagers negotiated to provide labor for planting and harvests while a small staff of permanent workers, the peons, supervised them. In this way, the *hacendado* had access to labor when he needed it without having to support these workers during the entire year, while the demand for seasonal labor gave some leverage to native peasants. An ethnic and cultural distinction eventually divided the native language–speaking itinerants and the Spanish-speaking mestizo and mulatto peons. The society of castes also gained some occupational relevance in the countryside.

The smallholder maintained an intermediate social position between the *hacendado or fazendeiro* and the peons or slaves. Racially, he was either a low-status white or a mestizo or mulatto. In the Recôncavo, Bahia's fertile coastal piedmont, free black smallholders grew sugar and even purchased slaves. The farmer might own his own piece of land or rent someone else's. He and members of his family produced vegetables, wheat, or dairy products, usually for local markets. Other small producers more remote from the cities raised mules or oxen for the transportation network and engaged in small-scale cattle and horse raising alongside the large estates. On their parcels, farmers produced wheat for intercolonial trade in the Bajío of Mexico, the central valley of Chile, the sabana of Colombia, the mountain valleys of Mérida and Caracas in Venezuela, and between the coastal plain and the sertão of northeastern Brazil. Farmers worked the soil with their sons or with a reduced staff of slaves or natives, replicating on a small scale the hierarchical social control mechanisms of the hacienda or *fazenda.* On very small plots, families engaged in subsistence farming. Although both were part of the *gente de pueblo* and

MANUSCRIPT 5.3

Potential for Abuse of Social Power, 1648

The colonial social system conferred great privilege on white colonists. When some enhanced these privileges by also wielding great economic power, the potential for abuse became enormous. Those with the least social power suffered. The Dominican missionary Thomas Gage told of one wealthy but uncouth Spanish merchant in Guatemala who owned 300 "lusty" mules and 100 African slaves.

[Juan Palomeque] was so cruel to his black-amoors that if any were untoward, he would torment them almost to death; amongst whom he had one slave called Macaco (for whom I have often interceded, but to little purpose) whom he would often hang up by the arms, and whip him till the blood ran about his back, and then his flesh being torn, mangled, and all in a gore blood, he would for last cure pour boiling grease upon it; he had marked him for a slave with burning irons upon his face, his hands, his arms, his back, his belly, his thighs, his legs, that the poor slave was weary of life, and I think would two or three times have hanged himself, if I had not counselled him to the contrary. He was so sensual and carnal that he would use his own slaves' wives at his pleasure; nay when he met in the city any of that kind handsome and to his liking, if she would not yield to his desire, he would go to her master or mistress, and buy her, offering far more than she was worth, boasting that he would pull down her proud and haughty looks, with one years' [sic] slavery under him. He killed in my time two Indians in the way to the gulf, and with his money came off, as if he had killed but a dog. He would never marry, because his slaves supplied the bed of a wife, and none of his neighbours durst say him nay; whereby he hasted to fill that valley with bastards of all sorts and colours, by whom, when the rich miser dieth, all his wealth and treasure is like to be consumed.

SOURCE: Thomas Gage, *The English American: A New Survey of the West Indies, 1648* (London: George Routledge, 1928), 212–13.

may have been racially mixed, the farmer conducted himself as being a cut above the peon he hired.

FAMILY PATRIARCHY

Members of the *gente decente* agreed on the need to keep the *gente de pueblo* subordinated. Nonetheless, there was intense rivalry among the elite, as evinced by the Peruvian civil war between the original conquerors over the distribution of wealth. After his family and in-laws, the Spaniard gave his loyalty and trust to others born in his province back home. Estremadurans among the newcomers stuck together; so did Castilians and Andalusians. When the dispute for power in newly conquered Peru erupted in 1537, the Pizarro faction purposely recruited allies from among their fellow Estremadurans. Peru's first governor, Francisco Pizarro, depended particularly on Spaniards from his home town of Trujillo. The opposition consisted of men, many of them from Castile, who had followed Almagro on a less successful expedition to Chile. The Pizarrists executed Almagro, whose mestizo son later assassinated Francisco Pizarro. The competition for power was serious business, for winners gained wealth and dominated many subordinate peoples, and the losers got much less of both. Not all cleavages between Iberians were so marked, but constant intrigue and maneuvering did define the rivalry between them.

The resulting cleavages and breaches among the elite could be managed only by the power they all sought to maximize through family and kinship. Family patriarchy[2] implied more than male dominance within the family; it comprised the economic and political maintenance of the family as the ultimate repository of social power. Observing the practice of patriarchy sustained the interests of all members of the family—father and son, mother and daughter, as well as in-laws.

Moreover, another distinction would soon grow to critical dimensions as generations passed: the difference between European-born and American-born whites, or Creoles. Birth initially determined one's possibilities. Immigrant men with connections to merchant families in Cádiz and Lisbon gained enormous advantage over American-born whites. Basque merchants favored dealing with kindred Basques within the colonies rather than with Creoles. Also, Portuguese-born planters enjoyed greater access to merchant capital and political connections than did their Brazilian-born counterparts. Not without reason did the Spanish-born own the best haciendas and mining operations. In the church and government, the higher offices seemed always to go to Europeans and the lower offices invariably went to Creoles. (This distinction would become even more important later, at the end of the eighteenth century.) Therefore, elite families needed to marry off their Creole daughters to successful immigrant men to retain their status and wealth. The family patriarch, himself born in Europe, commonly bequeathed most of the families' assets to a foreign-born son-in-law rather than to his own American-born son. Why? The son-in-law carried the prestige of having been born in Iberia and circulated more easily among his peers in colonial politics. Thus, these families consolidated their prestige and social power over many generations. European renewal was just what the elite family needed to remain part of the *gente decente.*

[2] *Patriarchy* is the principle of the supremacy of the father in the clan or family and the legal dependence of wives and children.

Litter of a Portuguese gentleman in Brazil. (Amedee François Frezier, 1714)

One's best assurance of social status and acceptability was one's family. In an environment in which European males exercised sexual power over non-European females, the cachet of having been born legitimately to a respectable family formed the indispensable foundation of one's prospects in life. A prestigious clan empowered the male offspring and protected the females. Much depended on the purity of white women. No sooner had the conquistadores settled the Indies than they sent back to Iberia for their wives, daughters, and sisters. It became important to maintain the racial purity of one's legitimate offspring. The *gente decente* wished to offer daughters of impeccable lineage to forge commercial and political alliances with other important white families in the colony. Immigrant young men, who showed commercial or political promise by virtue of their education, acumen, or connections back in Iberia, were ever the desirable sons-in-law.

Family economics among the elite, however, teetered precariously on the vagaries of overseas trade and sound financial decision making. Loss of political favor or a business reversal could force an otherwise illustrious family to the brink of financial ruin. Elite survival, therefore, dictated the diversification of the family's economic assets. As much as possible, a European family aspiring to social status needed to manage assets in wholesaling and retailing, to own farms and haciendas, to operate an *obraje,* and to engage in overland hauling. Sons, sons-in-law, and retainers managed these varied operations. Certain high-value activities permitted rather more concentration. A merchant with overseas connections relied more on importing and exporting. The Mexican silver miner and the Brazilian sugar planter devoted themselves almost exclusively to their respective pursuits. But even so, they diversified part of their assets into land, if only to provide some of the goods needed for their business. Oftentimes, the elite family treated land as the only secure investment—and its management provided employment for Creole sons.

Alliances also enhanced a family's economic diversification. A landowner who married his daughter to a merchant connected the family to a source of supplies, markets, and capital. A family member with a political post also offered the advantage of favorable government licenses and contracts. Because the church accumulated land and capital, a son in the church gave the family access to additional economic assets. This was the world from which all nonwhites were purposely excluded. Family lineage and interfamily alliance proved powerful determinants in a society in which social power and status meant a great deal.

As mentioned, Europeans competed incessantly among themselves, somewhat weakening their ability to control the subordinate classes. Despite their shared social attitudes, landowners vied with each other for scarce credit and labor resources. Merchants sought advantage over their competitors in market share and prices. Artisans struggled over access to materials and customers. These Europeans all attempted to control their own competition, before it became ruinous, and to protect their turf from others. They formed exclusive corporations of self-regulation. Ports had their own merchant associations. The larger cities had artisan guilds that regulated prices and quality and determined who became a master (non-Europeans were excluded). These associations then sought favorable treatment—even monopoly status—from colonial political authorities. Landowners sought appointment to town councils so that they could influence the policies of the public granaries and regulate the meat supply. Miners' associations concerned themselves with the distribution of mercury and the supply of labor.

Nevertheless, the competition within these associations could never be contained. The need for spreading a family's assets involved miners and merchants in land and landowners in the church and everyone in politics. Political connections thus became just another variable for the successful business family to manage. And if one did not attend to political matters, a competitor would. For example, when two miners needed labor, the one with political connections had greater capacity to mobilize native workers. An import merchant with superior government connections might avoid paying certain tariffs and fees that burdened his competitor. Everything was connected; everything was subject to politicization. Therefore, members of the *gente decente* protected the economic and political assets of the family as the ultimate repositories of prestige and connections—of social power.

These patterns of family patriarchy replicated each other in cities and towns throughout the Spanish Indies and Brazil. A whole subelite stratum of people found niches as employees and retainers of their more wealthy and connected brethren. They served as overseers on farms and plantations, they ran small retail shops on the credit of wealthier patrons, and they utilized their familiarity with European customs to engage in a wide range of local shop manufacturing. But all Europeans felt a natural superiority to the non-Europeans they met, and Iberian-born artisans did not suffer mestizos and mulattos getting ahead. In towns of lesser importance that were more distant from the capitals, however, persons of mixed racial heritage had opportunities to advance into the ranks of the overseers, artisans, and landowners. The provincial elite in cities like Oaxaca in Mexico, Salta in Argentina, Concepción in Chile, São Paulo in Brazil, Mérida in Venezuela, Cochabamba in Bolivia, and Pasto in Colombia had local elites who were darker in skin color. These second-rank *gente decente* certainly suffered the barbs of polite society when they went to the capital. But back home, the provincial cadres behaved with the same haughty exclusivity as did the big-city elites.

Even the *gente de pueblo* had to keep up appearances. Commoners generally married among their racial and occupation group or with contiguous groups—mestizos with mestizas and so forth. Marriage of members of contiguous groups—a poor white with a mestiza or a mulatto with a free black—was not unknown, but seldom did a Spaniard marry a native or black woman, though informal liaisons were more common. That white women almost never involved themselves in either formal or informal liaisons with nonwhite men says a great deal about gender constructions in the *sociedad de castas*.

Women and Patriarchy

White women proved critical to the maintenance of the social status of elite families. But nowhere in the Spanish Indies or Brazil did the number of white women, whether immigrant or Creole, equal the number of white males. This numerical imbalance, combined with the sexual liberty of European males, motivated elite families to constrict the activities of their respectable womenfolk. The white female of the *gente decente* could pass her life in a pampered, idle, and restricted state. In the home, she was surrounded by servants, over whom she had dictatorial command. But she entered the streets only in the company of men or trusted servants. Shopping, religious observance, and visiting friends were the only regular stops on her itinerary. Daughters of proper families expected to marry whomever the father (and mother) chose. Therefore, women from "good families" usually married older men, sometimes widowers, whose accomplishments and wealth represented an asset to the bride's family. Elite women normally married at age 22 and had up to five or six children, two of whom usually died in infancy. Because many women outlived their older husbands, widows among the *gente decente* could gain a role in the businesses of the family, which they ran as trustees until their daughters married or their sons came of age. Widows managed the hacienda or *obraje* and bought and sold goods—although this was not something mothers ever taught their daughters.

Elite women did have narrow options to pursue. Headstrong young women did elope; others refused to marry or entered a nunnery. In such cases, the woman's family paid the dowry not to the groom but to the church, in the form of a bequest. The church invested the sum and used the interest to support the young woman taking her vows. However, most took their personal servants into the convent with them. (White women of modest means did not otherwise enjoy the option of entering nunneries, and women of color faced impenetrable barriers to becoming nuns.) As described in the previous chapter, Latin America's most illustrious woman during colonial times was the Mexican writer Sor Juana Inés de la Cruz. Disavowing a contracted marriage to an older man, she took her vows and then pursued a life of contemplation and poetry. Even there she could not pursue her intellectual interests in total liberty. Her religious superiors asked her to stop her writing, which she did—but not before contributing to the development of Latin American letters (see Manuscript 4.4). Single women were more common among privileged *gente decente,* who had the income to support them. More Spaniards than natives were unmarried in the cities. But upper-class spinsters seldom lived independently, instead residing with a brother or sister and still having family responsibilities. An unmarried aunt often helped to run the household, bring up the nieces and nephews, and carry out family religious responsibilities. Most elite single women, in fact, did not go into the nunnery.

The existence of foundling homes for white babies born out of wedlock also illustrates that colonial families balanced the sexual irresponsibility of their sons with the need to preserve the honor of their daughters. The elite family hid many an illegitimate birth to avoid having to endure the social embarrassment. Children of color were almost never found in these orphanages sponsored by the exclusive religious confraternities. The Misericórdia, a lay organization to which Brazil's wealthiest planters belonged, ran Bahia's foundling home; the Santa Hermandad, made up of wealthy merchants, operated another in Buenos Aires. So it was in the larger cities of colonial Latin America. The elite

Spanish mistress abusing an Andean household servant. (Guaman Poma de Ayala, ca. 1615)

often operated charities out of its lay religious organizations to preserve the respectability and status of its own families.

Colonial society defined women as much by social status as by gender. White women did not identify with the plight of mulatto washerwomen, Indian servants, mestiza street vendors, or slave women. Among the *gente de pueblo,* the women of color certainly enjoyed more economic freedom. But it was a freedom born of necessity. The mixed-race market woman with several children needed to work. Native and African servant girls needed—or were forced—to work. Native women labored in the fields alongside their husbands and sons during harvests, though men accomplished the tasks requiring strength and women had their own assigned chores. Among the *gente decente,* however, husbands and fathers prevented European women from running the family businesses and did not allow them to work outside the home. Elite women remained in the home, where many gained notorious reputations for their iron-fisted command over household servants. Neither women nor men among the elite were about to give up privilege and respectability to identify with anyone beneath their social status, violating the tenets of family patriarchy. Competition among the *gente decente* made one's social status precarious enough without questioning the social order.

Women of the elite enjoyed protections that women of the *gente de pueblo* did not. There were few legal or customary strictures against physical abuse within the family. A man could beat his wife as a disciplinary measure and punish her for adultery. In Brazil, for instance, a husband who caught his wife *in flagrante delicto* with another man was legally entitled to kill her on the spot. (The prevailing double standard, however, encouraged elite men to commit indiscretions and keep concubines.) However, battered and abused women of the *gente decente* could flee to the protection of their families or repair to a nunnery. They might seek an annulment of their unhappy marriages and, rarely, a divorce. White women seduced by white men who promised marriage could bring suit in court to make them comply. Women of the *gente de pueblo,* of course, could not. Neither legal protections nor family patriarchy availed to empower women of color. Rather, abandonment, beatings, illegitimacy, polygamy, insecurity, and prostitution were common for *mulatas* and mestizas of modest means.

Although marriage between white males and women of color occasionally occurred, especially among the *gente de pueblo,* sexual contact between them happened quite frequently. Mixed-race women, if pretty, often found it expedient for survival to consort with a white male, married or not. Anyway, children of such matches had a better chance in life because their skin would be lighter than their mother's. As well, mestizo and mulatto men, themselves illegitimate and unrecognized by an established family, might be indifferent family men. About a third of the women of color were also heads of households. As a result, rates of illegitimacy in Brazil and the Spanish Indies rose quite high. In Lima, up to 40 percent of the births occurred out of wedlock. At least 40 percent of births among the free population of São Paulo were illegitimate; nearly 70 percent of slave mothers had no formal tie to their children's natural fathers. Only native women who lived in rural villages had higher rates of legitimate birth. The lack of family structure among persons of mixed race in Latin America certainly reduced their ability to advance economically and to be accepted by those with power. It also failed to protect women of the *gente de pueblo* from exploitation in this patriarchal social order.

Nevertheless, women of the *gente de pueblo* exerted remarkable control over their economic lives. Women made up one-third of the workforce in the bigger colonial cities. Native women came to sell fruits, vegetables, flowers, poultry, and fish in the markets. Some urban women of the *gente de pueblo* took in laundry and sewing, while others were food vendors, peddlers, and waitresses. They salted hides, washed and spun cotton cloth, and served as midwives and healers. Single and widowed women of somewhat higher status found employment as apartment building managers. Women of the popular classes were self-employed, caring for children as they cooked food on the street corners or hawked goods in the marketplaces. But three-quarters of working women carried out housekeeping functions in the homes of the *gente decente,* cleaning house, caring for children, and providing meals. Women were barred from many jobs in the clergy, bureaucracy, and military. Although cigarette vending and dressmaking were considered female work, women who did perform the same jobs as men in artisan and retail trades always earned less. Women of the *gente de pueblo* often had few other options. They had to work to support themselves and their children, and few persons in the society of castes obtained jobs above their station in life.

Cities were always skewed toward female numerical dominance, and rural areas were similarly skewed toward male dominance. "Country women come into the cities to serve in the houses . . . and a great number of men leave them to travel through the country as muleteers, or to fix their abode in places with considerable mines," explained one traveler. Village girls (mostly native Americans in Peru and Mexico) came to serve in the households of the wealthy and professional classes. The number of servants in the household indicated fairly well an elite family's social position. But the work was demeaning, and the job placed the vulnerable country girl under the thumb of a tyrannical mistress and abusive master. The hours were long, pay was low, and there was little time off. Few employers respected the native servant girls or appreciated their work. Housegirls who returned to their villages to be married were easily replaced. Although urban centers contained Europeans and the heterogeneous groups serving them, the influence of the cities extended far into the indigenous countryside. Native Americans represented labor to the urbanites, so their demands for workers capitalized on ancient American labor systems as well as the creation of wholly new ones. Labor drafts represented the old; wage labor represented the new. This transition from the old to the new began with the Conquest but would by no means be completed even by the end of the colonial era.

LABOR SYSTEMS

Although royal patent had sanctioned the Conquest, the conquerors and settlers had put their own capital and work into the project. They expected just compensation. The conquistadores had taken for themselves the richest rewards, held tight control over the natives, and ran political affairs according to their own (albeit factious) dictates. Their individual enterprises requisitioned many native workers, extending the influence of Hispanic economic and social institutions into the indigenous communities. In the process of forming new systems of labor, the entrepreneurs had the support of the colonial state.

Spaniards discovered silver at Potosí in 1545. As soon as production began in earnest, there developed a voracious demand for workers. But Potosí, a cold windswept mountain towering over the Altiplano, had not supported a dense indigenous population, and the new mine operators had to import laborers. At first, the class of native personal servants called *yanakona*s came to work on orders of their Spanish masters. This group became the basis for the formation of a free-floating group of wage earners. African slaves transshipped from Panama and Lima also began to serve as permanent mine workers, developing skills to direct the work of others. Drafted native peasants accomplished most of the work, especially the hauling of ore out of the mines, which required no special skills. Spanish *encomenderos* ordered native leaders to send peasant villagers from as far away as 100 and even 500 kilometers. These male workers, who toiled in the mines to pay their tributes, often brought their wives and families. But there were never enough workers once disease began to decimate the indigenous population. To compound this crisis in Spanish Peru, the first silver boom at Potosí had come abruptly to an end as the richest ores were playing out. Therefore, the colonial state stepped in.

Viceroy Toledo claimed royal ownership of the mercury deposits at Huancavelica, and developed this domestic resource to supply the mines at Potosí and Oruro. Henceforward, the miners there had adequate supplies to rework the rich slag heaps deposited by the earlier and less efficient native methods of silver extraction. Mercury became a Crown monopoly, administered completely by royal officials. Amalgamation with mercury also permitted exploitation of the deeper, less rich ores, generating a second and longer life to the mining zones of Upper Peru.

Finally, Viceroy Toledo organized the massive labor draft system, known by its Andean name of *mita*, to provide adequate labor to the mines. This state labor draft utilized the Inka name because it was constructed—though elaborately—on pre-Conquest

Andean precedents. The *mita* obliged every native villager within a certain distance from Potosí to work in the silver mines once every seven years. Approximately fourteen thousand workers annually were to make themselves available under the Andean labor draft. According to Toledo's regulations, their Spanish employers were to pay all *mitayos* (workers) for their labor, provide rations of food, and treat them well. In one of the first minimum wage laws in the Americas, the viceroy decreed that the *mitayo*s be paid 3.5 *reales* per day. (Eight *reales* equaled one peso.) The *kuraka*s gained exemption from the *mita* but were expected to help the *corregidores*, or district officials, organize the village labor drafts. This arrangement did not apply to native peasants in northern Peru and Ecuador because the principal mercury and silver mines lay in southern and Upper Peru.

But the *mita* system worked only in the breach. The indigenous population in Upper Peru and Peru was dwindling at the time owing to the spread of European diseases, raising the demand for workers in other economic enterprises. The *corregidores* conspired with native leaders to divert peasant laborers elsewhere. By 1600, the number of *mitayo*s taking up temporary residence in the workers' barrios of Potosí had dropped to 6,000. Free wage workers, many of them former labor draftees, gradually made up the largest part of the workforce. Fifty thousand Native Americans now lived, more or less permanently, in Potosí. Even women contributed their work to the mine. Besides feeding male workers, women gleaned the ore and engaged in small-scale smelting as well as in urban marketing. Their labor skills were much in demand. Thus developed a force of nonagricultural wage workers from Inka precedents and Spanish imperial necessities.

What Potosí achieved toward forming a modern labor system in South America, a similar mining boom accomplished for northern Mexico. A group of natives led Spaniards to a source of silver ore in the Chichimec region in 1546, and the northern mining boom began immediately. But the nomadic Chichimec of Zacatecas, Nuevo León, and Chihuahua refused to work in the mines; instead, they fled to the mountains, rebelling constantly at the penetration of the European entrepreneurs and their Hispanicized subordinates. The nascent state recognized the importance of mining and established the labor system known as *repartimiento* in New Spain. Once the Native Americans of central Mexico had been removed from the control of the *encomenderos* and their descendants, the state itself assumed an active role in reapportioning their labor to Spanish enterprises—especially mining. In these labor drafts, local Spanish officials requisitioned indigenous peasants for work in the mines for up to several months at a time. Their village chiefs assumed responsibility for choosing the men who undertook this labor. Usually, some village women accompanied the men on the long trek north to the mining zones, for the natives set up temporary households at the mines. Mine owners were to house, feed, and pay the natives for their work and look after their religious welfare.

However, indigenous draft labor accounted for less than a quarter of the workers employed in early Mexican mining. African slaves came to be important permanent workers at the mines. Developing experience and skills, the slaves and mestizos occupied supervisory positions. They were joined by a much larger group of native wage laborers who, not being part of the *repartimiento,* had come individually to work in the mines. In Santa Eulalia, Chihuahua, Indians worked as carpenters' helpers, charcoal makers, or bricklayers but seldom as guards or other jobs with responsibilities. This group of workers, together with their families, were quite mobile. They followed the silver strikes into Guanajuato, Pachuca, Zacatecas, San Luis Potosí, and Chihuahua. These free mine workers formed the nucleus of a new working class at the mines.

A mixture of mestizos, mulattoes, black slaves, and native servants soon formed a kind of privileged, well-paid, highly independent labor aristocracy. Chichimec people captured in battle and imported Africans were enslaved, although the owners complained of their inefficiency. "Bad to have them, but much worse not to have them," went the mine proprietor's lament in the 1560s. Owners valued slaves as a permanent force, unlike the *repartimiento* natives from the central valley, who came and went. However, some migrants from central Mexico who wished to escape communal and tribute obligations stayed on at the mines as unskilled helpers. Some came to earn some cash with which to return to their villages; others stayed.

The scarcity of labor in Mexico's northern provinces created professional mining workers who desired to maintain and jealously protect their dignity and prerogative. They demanded to be treated better than the native peasants, and their demands met with success. Miscegenation proceeded more rapidly and thoroughly among the north Mexican working classes, eroding some of their initial ethnic and racial differences. Nevertheless, those who worked the mercury in the refining patios and the skilled pikemen in the mines maintained their social superiority. The hierarchy of social control operated in the mining industry from the Spanish mine owners and the skilled pikemen to the African slaves and the native ore bearers. Through creation of new labor systems that combined ancient American arrangements with free wage work, the Iberian-Americans expanded their world to take in Africans, mestizos, mulattoes, and eventually Native Americans as well.

CONCLUDING REMARKS

Why were social distinctions so critical to the Spaniards and Portuguese who came to settle in the American colonies? It is only partially correct to conclude that the hierarchy of social status and its corollary, family patriarchy, governed the Iberian world in colonial America because they had strong European precedents. Social hierarchy, family patriarchy, and conspicuous consumption thrived and still persist today for a very good reason: They perfectly suited the colonial need to subordinate a mass of non-European peoples to European necessities. Neither the logic of the export economy nor the colonial state created these interests. It was the white, Iberian settlers of the *gente decente* who maintained and perpetuated the society of castes established by their conquering forebears. Whites did not wish to expend their own labor but to direct the labor of others, and social status mattered because the vast majority of inhabitants in the colonial Americas were not European. Whites in the colonial Americas soon recognized the lesson understood by the indigenous nobility in ancient times—namely, that social exclusivity functions well to command the respect and obedience of the masses. First of all, the elites had to gain wealth, live in great houses, surround themselves with numerous servants and retainers, and maintain connections to local enterprise, external markets, and government officialdom. Wealth and status were inseparable. Ambitious Iberian Americans knew that adoption of the indigenous culture, eating native foods, and marrying non-Europeans would incur only ridicule and exclusion. Therefore, the white elites nurtured their social status through intermarriage with other influential white families and by taking in enterprising European immigrant sons-in-law who connected colonial enterprise with European markets. To operate within the elitist structure of the white gentry, families sought to impose patriarchal principles on their female members. White wives subordinated their independence to the corporate necessities of the male-dominated family, and the daughters exchanged a chaste and dependent existence for status and power over a household of servants. Rather than marry beneath their station, white women accepted (however reluctantly) lives as spinster aunts within the household or as reclusive residents of the nunnery.

Colonialism involved more than dotting the countryside with towns and hamlets on the Iberian pattern. Keeping the nonwhite majority in its subordinate position took active ingenuity—and much compromise. In these, the mixed-race people generally subscribed to the cultural mores of the Iberian-American world. Mestizos and mulattoes maintained distinctions, too, because their lighter skin color and Iberian cultural practices gave them higher status and more opportunities than Native Americans and Africans. They positioned themselves to mediate between those above them and below them in the social hierarchy. The Iberian-American world rested on an economic base of subordinate peoples of African and Native American descent. Therefore, Spaniards and Portuguese settlers had to draw into their orbits the labor of non-European peoples. The institutions they established to accomplish this objective—slavery, personal service, tribute paying, forced labor drafts, and wage work—combined coercion with some forms of incentive, beginning a long process of weaning Native Americans and Africans from their separate existence. In exploiting the labor and surplus of these ethnically distinct peoples, white Iberians had to accept and even adapt themselves to the cultural resistance of these subordinate groups. Not all of the institutions and values that whites established in colonial America gained acceptance among those upon whom they were imposed. Indeed, Native American and African peoples retained their separate identities in defiance of the power of the whites, as we shall see in the next chapters.

Additional Reading

Altman, Ida. *Emigrants and Society: Estremadura and Spanish America in the Sixteenth Century*. Berkeley: University of California Press, 1989.

Bakewell, Peter. *Miners of the Red Mountain: Indian Labor in Potosí*. Albuquerque: University of New Mexico Press, 1984.

Boyer, Richard. *Lives of the Bigamists: Marriage, Family, and Community in Colonial Mexico*. Albuquerque: University of New Mexico Press, 1995.

Chance, John K. *Race and Class in Colonial Oaxaca*. Stanford, Calif.: Stanford University Press, 1978.

Cook, Alexandra Parma, and Noble David Cook. *Good Faith and Truthful Ignorance: A Case of Transatlantic Bigamy*. Durham, N.C.: Duke University Press, 1991.

Davies, Keith A. *Landowners in Colonial Peru*. Austin: University of Texas Press, 1984.

Ferry, Robert J. *The Colonial Elite of Early Caracas: Formation and Crisis, 1567–1767*. Berkeley: University of California Press, 1989.

Franco, Jean. *Plotting Women: Gender and Representation in Mexico*. New York: Columbia University Press, 1988.

Góngora, Mario. *Studies in the Colonial History of Spanish America*. Trans. Richard Southern. Cambridge, England: Cambridge University Press, 1975.

Hoberman, Louisa Schell, and Susan Migden Socolow, eds. *Cities and Society in Colonial Latin America.* Albuquerque: University of New Mexico Press, 1996.

———, eds. *The Countryside in Colonial Latin America.* Albuquerque: University of New Mexico Press, 1996.

Israel, J. I. *Race, Class, and Politics in Colonial Mexico, 1610– 1670.* London: Oxford University Press, 1975.

Johnson, Lyman L., and Sonya Lipsett-Rivera, eds. *The Faces of Honor: Sex, Shame and Violence in Colonial Latin America.* Albuquerque: University of New Mexico Press, 1998.

Keith, Robert B. *Conquest and Agrarian Change: Emergence of the Hacienda System on the Peruvian Coast.* Cambridge, Mass.: Harvard University Press, 1976.

Lavrin, Asunción, ed. *Latin American Women: Historical Perspectives.* Westport, Conn.: Greenwood Press, 1978.

———, ed. *Sexuality and Marriage in Colonial Latin America.* Lincoln: University of Nebraska Press, 1989.

Lockhart, James, and Stuart B. Schwartz. *Early Latin America: A History of Colonial Spanish America and Brazil.* Cambridge, England: Cambridge University Press, 1983.

Lockhart, James M. *Spanish Peru, 1532– 1560: A Colonial Society.* 2d ed. Madison: University of Wisconsin Press, 1994.

MacLachlan, Colin M. *Spain's Empire in the New World: The Role of Ideas in Institutional and Social Change.* Berkeley: University of California Press, 1988.

Martín, Luis. *Daughters of the Conquistadores: Women of the Viceroyalty of Peru.* Albuquerque: University of New Mexico Press, 1983.

Moog, Clodomir Vianna. *Bandeirantes and Pioneers.* Trans. L. L. Barrett. New York: G. Braziller, 1964.

Morse, Richard M. *The Bandeirantes: The Historical Role of the Brazilian Pathfinders.* New York: Knopf, 1965.

———. *From Community to Metropolis: A Biography of São Paulo, Brazil.* Gainesville: University of Florida Press, 1958.

Parry, John H. and Robert G. Keith. *New Iberian World: A Documentary History of the Discovery and Settlement of Latin America to the Early Seventeenth Century.* 5 vols. New York: Times Books, 1984.

Ramírez, Susan E.. *Provincial Patriarchs: Land Tenure and the Economics of Power in Colonial Peru.* Albuquerque: University of New Mexico Press, 1986.

Riley, G. Michael. *Fernando Cortés and the Marquesado in Morelos, 1522– 1547: A Case Study in the Socioeconomic Development of Sixteenth-Century Mexico.* Albuquerque: University of New Mexico Press, 1973.

Seed, Patricia. *To Love, Honor, and Obey in Colonial Mexico: Conflicts Over Marriage Choice, 1574– 1821.* Stanford, Calif.: Stanford University Press, 1988.

Super, John C. *Food, Conquest, and Colonization in Sixteenth-Century Spanish America.* Albuquerque: University of New Mexico Press, 1988.

Swann, Michael. *Tierra Adentro: Settlement and Society in Colonial Durango.* Boulder, Colo.: Westview Press, 1982.

In Spanish and Portuguese

Algranti, Leila Mezan. *Honradas e devotas: Mulheres da colonia: condicion femenina nos conventos a recolhimentos do sudeste do Brasil, 1550– 1822.* Rio de Janeiro: J. Olympia Editora, 1993.

Colmenares, Germán. *Historia económica y social de Colombia, 1537–1719.* Cali, Colombia: Universidad del Valle, 1973.

Dueñas Vargas, Guiomar. *Los hijos del pecado: Ilegitimidad y vida familiar en la Santa Fé de Bogotá colonial.* Bogotá: Editorial Universidad Nacional, 1997.

Faoro, Raymundo. *Os donos de poder: Formação do patronato político brasileiro.* 4th ed. 2 vols. Pôrto Alegre: Editora Globo, 1977.

Glave, Luis Miguel. *Trajinantes: Caminos indígenas en la sociedad colonial, siglos xvi–xvii.* Cuzco: Instituto de Apoyo Agrario, 1989.

Góngora, Mario. *Encomenderos y estancieros: Estudios acerca de la constitución social aristocrática de Chile después de la conquista, 1580–1660.* Santiago: Editorial Universitaria, 1970.

de Melo, Evaldo Cabral. *O nome e o sangue: uma fraude genealógica no Pernambuco.* São Paulo: Companhia das Letras, 1989.

———. *Rubro Veio: O imaginário da restauração pernambucana.* Rio de Janeiro: Editora Nova Fronteira, 1986.

Trelles Aréstegui, Efraín. *Lucas Martínez Vegazo: Funcionamiento de una encomienda peruana inicial.* Lima: Pontifícia Universidad Católica del Perú, 1982.

Wanderley, José Pinho. *História de um engenho do Recôncavo: Matoim, Novo Caboto, Freguesia, 1552–1944.* 2d ed. Rio de Janeiro: Companhia Editora Nacional, 1982.

CHAPTER 6

NATIVE AMERICANS

For the Native American peoples, the colonial epoch of Latin America might have amounted to a cataclysmic dislocation had they not acted to preserve themselves and their cultures. Neither the Iberian settlers nor the colonial officials had wished deliberately to destroy the native peoples—only to transform their lifestyles and beliefs; after all, the settlers intended to live off the labor of the conquered. But millions of natives died of foreign diseases as a direct result of European conquest and settlement. Moreover, those who survived deflected the intentions of their conquerors by effectively negotiating their own labor and resources, resisting the worst features of Iberian rule, and accommodating colonial demands on their own terms as much as possible. Natives even adopted those features of European institutions and technologies that helped preserve their own separate identities. It is a testimony to the indomitable spirit of the Native Americans that their descendants have preserved vestiges of both their cultures and their dignity.

At the time of contact, the indigenous peoples of the Americas did not use the word *indio* and had no concept, no name to distinguish themselves from Europeans. The main expression among the Nahuas of central Mexico became *nican titlaca,* "we people here," as distinct, say, from "those people over there." The Spaniards introduced the term *Indian* to denote anyone belonging to those people whose ancestors had inhabited the Americas before the arrival of the Europeans.

Indigenous peoples in Mexico and Peru were initially to form a separate sector of colonial society, the Republic of Indians, and to supply urban and especially rural labor in the new colonies. But European diseases, to which they had not been exposed prior to 1492, took a terrible toll. A population estimated at one hundred million persons at the time of contact declined to just ten million by 1650. The epidemics were more virulent in tropical regions—the rain forests of Brazil, the Caribbean islands, and the coastal lands of Meso- and South America—than in temperate climates; death tolls rose so high in these areas that the indigenous lowland cultures were all but obliterated. Wherever Native Americans succumbed to the greatest degree, there the European colonists had to import Africans in bondage—with full support of Crown and clergy, as shall be seen in Chapter 7. The population reshuffling that resulted from the Conquest rendered impossible the separate social systems previously envisioned in the Republics of Indians and of Spaniards and instead encouraged a cultural cross-pollination to which the indigenous population both contributed and received.

Native American populations and ethnic cultures, did survive in the temperate highlands despite the terrible consequences of conquest and disease. After much regrouping directed by colonial authorities, indigenous communities reconstituted themselves and continued the task of providing for their own subsistence on community lands that the state allowed them. The colonial regime found it expedient to save the natives as a labor source. Hoping to prevent the colonists from fighting among themselves over how many natives went to whom—as did the Pizarros and Almagro in Peru—the colonial state sought to control access to native labor. After all, the entire colonial system hung in the balance. For these reasons, the state intervened actively in relations between the races and between employers and employees. This right, even obligation, of the state to interfere in social relationships became an abiding legacy of the colonial era.

Besides those tropical Native Americans who died so quickly of imported diseases, other indigenous groups refused to fit well into the new colonial regimes. Those in the most inhospitable regions survived autonomously, and some of them were extremely difficult to conquer. The seminomadic natives of northern Mexico, the Argentine Pampas and Patagonia, the Paraguayan Chaco, and southern Chile proved to be effective military adversaries to Spanish settlement. By the seventeenth century, many had adopted the horse and became formidable cavalry warriors. Likewise, the peoples of the tropical rain forests effectively used blowguns, poison darts, and bows and arrows to defend their autonomy from Portuguese and Spanish expeditions. Iberian economic disinterest permitted some native groups to live in partial isolation for well over three hundred years—in southern South America; the Amazon, Orinoco, and Maracaibo Basins; in the Mayan lowlands of Central America and the Yucatán; and in practically all of North America above the Río Bravo (Rio Grande River). Europeans fashioned core settlements only in Mexico and Peru, where sedentary Native Americans survived diseases in significant numbers and silver mining underwrote the early colonial economy.

Even in the core areas, where the presence and demands of the Europeans were greatest, the native Americans successfully preserved their separate identities and culture. They did so because they selectively adopted European technology and institutions so as to accommodate themselves to their new colonial masters. This accommodation took many forms. The old nobility, much reduced and shorn of political power, acted as the contact between the native peasantry and Spanish demands for tribute and labor. Peasants continued to till the soil much as in ancient times but now became articulated with the new market system that required their itinerant labor. Other indigenous commoners detached themselves from their lineage groups and moved into the Spanish world as artisans, house servants, muleteers, and wage workers. Native Americans formed the basis of an entirely new class that scarcely existed prior to the Conquest—the urban proletariat. To protect themselves, they were not averse to using the court system and institutions established by the Spanish masters. But the Native Americans accomplished these acts of accommodation as a strategy of surviving, of making their way in the new colonial environment, of mitigating the oppression, and of preserving their own traditions and customs. In turn, their own indigenous institutions conditioned the settlement and governance of the Europeans.

DEMOGRAPHIC DECLINE

The Caribbean and Mesoamerica

The extent and accomplishments of pre-Columbian civilizations very much influenced where Europeans would settle and how they would exploit the natural resources of the Americas. The Carib, Aruak, and Taíno of the Antilles Islands had developed the cultivation of root plants such as manioc and fashioned jewelry from gold. They lived in clanlike villages of multifamily dwellings in which relationships between the sexes were loose and among caciques, polygamous. When Columbus's expedition arrived at the island of Hispaniola, the indigenous peoples numbered an estimated one million. First the Spaniards made them provide food and wash for gold in the streams. Those who ran away were seized. When they died of overwork and pestilence, the Spaniards moved to other islands, Cuba, Puerto Rico, and Jamaica, where they began the cycle all over again. Raids for replacement native slaves then took Spaniards to the coasts of Venezuela, Colombia, Panama, and Central America. Within a few years, the indigenous Caribbean peoples and their culture had completely died out—principally because of epidemics. On Hispaniola, all political institutions among the indigenous peoples had collapsed within 10 years of Columbus's landfall; within 25 years, 90 percent of the original population had died (see Table 6.1). The natives of the Caribbean islands suffered catastrophically in their encounter with Europeans.

Other Caribbean territories endured a similar fate of conquest and contagion. The Spaniards' incursion into the tropical peninsula of the Yucatán was particularly arduous because the descendants of the ancient Maya lived in decentralized, fiercely independent political units. The terrain was not conducive to Spanish cavalrymen, many of whom died in ambushes. Native weapons could not kill at a distance but were effective at close range, where the Spaniards countered with crossbows, muskets, and vicious war dogs. But disease accomplished what Spanish arms could not, breaking the will to resist. Yucatán had 800,000 Maya before the first outbreak of smallpox and before Spanish military conquest began in 1517. When the fighting stopped in 1570, in contrast, a mere 150,000 people remained, and the number continued to dwindle thereafter.

Subsequent contact with Europeans—be they conquistadores collecting tribute or Catholic friars saving souls—spread even more diseases among the indigenous population. For the next 100 years, they died in great numbers from influenza, malaria, and other maladies. According to one estimate, the population of central Mexico declined

Table 6.1   Population Decline of the Indians on Hispaniola

Year	Annual Rate of Change (%)	Lowest Estimate	Highest Estimate
1496	−44.20	100,000	3,770,000
1497	−41.50	56,066	2,103,660
1498	−34.39	32,799	1,230,641
1499	−34.70	21,519	807,429
1500	—	14,052	527,251

SOURCE: Samuel M. Wilson, *Hispaniola: Caribbean Chiefdoms in the Age of Columbus* (Tuscaloosa: University of Alabama Press, 1990), 91; as adopted from Shelbourne F. Cook and Woodrow Borah, *Essays in Population History,* vol. 1, *Mexico and the Caribbean* (Berkeley: University of California Press, 1971), 401–5.

Figure 6.1   Maya Population of Guatemala, 1520–1830

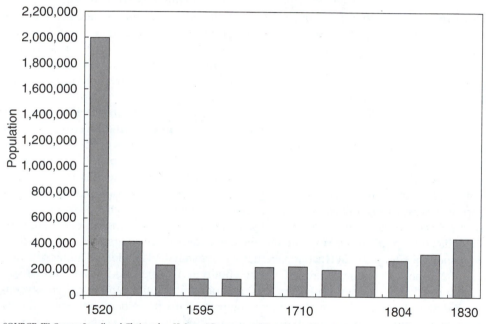

SOURCE: W. George Lovell and Christopher H. Lutz, "Conquest and Population: Maya Demography in Historical Perspective," *Latin American Research Review* 29, no. 2 (1994): 136.

from some twenty-five million Native Americans in 1519, on the eve of conquest, to just over one million in 1650.

Nonetheless, by the mid-seventeenth century, the decline of the indigenous population had halted in both Peru and Mexico, and their numbers rebounded—though never again to reach what they had been at the time of European contact. The population of one cultural group alone, the Maya of Mesoamerica, reached its nadir in 1650 when a mere 120,000 persons survived from the original 2 million. By the end of the colonial era, circa 1826, the number of Maya had grown only to 350,000 (see Figure 6.1).

The Andean Region

Smallpox visited the lands of the Inka even before 1532, when Francisco Pizarro and 126 men seized the Inka emperor at Cajamarca. The pestilence thereafter spread through the highlands as Spaniards traveled the region in search of additional conquests. The natives here also died in vast numbers. Similar epidemics broke out among sedentary natives when Spanish expeditions pushed into northwest Argentina, central Chile, and southern Colombia. On the highland savannah surrounding Bogotá, erstwhile capital of the smaller, more decentralized, Muisca civilization, similar destruction of the indigenous peasantry took place.

The indigenous population of the Andean region declined in a series of epidemics that struck periodically. The measles struck in 1531; typhus, in 1546; influenza, in 1558; smallpox, from 1585 to 1591; and diphtheria, in 1614. In the interim, the original population of 14 million Native Americans in Peru dropped to 800,000 in 1620. The population continued to dwindle until 1650, at which time the indigenous peoples of the Andean region seem to have developed sufficient immunities to European diseases. However, occasional outbreaks of epidemics in the eighteenth and nineteenth centuries still blunted the resurgent growth of the native population. In the epidemic of 1720, for example, a deadly fever swept the Andean region, killing 20,000 in the city of Cuzco and an additional 60,000 in the countryside around the city. The contagion struck down the most impoverished sector of the society, most of which was Native American; in reaction, Crown officials temporarily suspended collections of tribute.

The effect of diseases seemed more pernicious in warm climates, as some tropical native cultures simply disappeared within the span of a generation or two (20 to 40 years). The death rates in temperate climates such as the highlands of Mexico could be as high as 90 percent over the course of three generations. In Ecuador, the long-term death rate among indigenous highland peoples was perhaps 85 percent. However, in the cold, high plains of the Puno and the Altiplano, on opposite banks of Lake Titicaca, European diseases were milder. Here the indigenous population declined by 30 percent over a 30-year period. The ravages of these diseases also skewed the gender balance of the indigenous population. More men than women died; more adults than children died. So among the Chupacho of Huánuco, Peru, there remained 481 children among 882 total in 1562. Among the adults were 256 women but only 145 men. As a result of their survival, some native women broke free of community constraints and, by necessity, entered directly into the labor market, becoming particularly prominent in the households of Spaniards and in marketing in Spanish towns. But they also became vulnerable to abuse, sexual and otherwise (see Manuscript 6.1). Native Americans did not suffer these losses, it should be noted, without fighting back.

The full subjugation of Mexico had not at all been completed by the fall of Tenochtitlán nor by early attempts at Christian evangelization. A millennial movement broke out among the tribes inhabiting the mountains north of Guadalajara. Shamans there began preaching a rejection of Christianity and Spanish domination, reviving indigenous religions and appealing to the Native Americans' autonomous past. These shamans announced the coming of Tlatol, who would reinstitute traditional marriage customs and polygamy. Individual Native Americans could take part in the new age of riches and fine clothes, magic arrows, and crops springing spontaneously from the earth only if they renounced and expelled the Spaniards. In 1541, natives under the influence of this religious revival burned the new chapels and killed the missionaries north of Guadalajara. Two Spanish military expeditions were sent to put down the rebellion but were repulsed. Finally, Viceroy Mendoza outfitted an army of 450 Spanish cavalrymen and thousands of native auxiliaries. They attacked several of the rebels' mountain fortresses and finally used artillery to smash the last of them at Mount Mixton in 1542. The captured Native Americans

MANUSCRIPT 6.1

Abuse of Andean Women, 1625

The conquest of Peru produced contradictory consequences for gender relations among the indigenous peoples. On the one hand, the Conquest liberated females from community and patriarchal restraints because male Native Americans succumbed to European diseases in far higher numbers than women. Therefore, many indigenous women became widowed, and young girls grew up without the protection of fathers and male relatives. As female heads of households, the women had to enter the new marketing structure introduced by Spaniards, working in the households of the new rulers and engaging in trade. But women also became vulnerable. The indigenous chronicler Guaman Poma de Ayala believed that colonialism in Peru was particularly destructive to native women because white men exploited both their labor and their bodies. There were few remedies for such abuses. Even their own menfolk could not protect them, as Poma de Ayala saw it.

In the mines, Indian women are employed as cooks and are made into concubines; under the pretext that they have to work in the kitchen, some daughters of Indian men are kidnapped and forced into service, being raped by the men who run the mines or by their assistants, who even dare to rape married women, and in order to do so, they order their husbands to go work in the mines at night . . . so they can freely commit these atrocities. . . .

In the Indian villages, the *encomenderos,* their sons, brothers, and major-domos rape single women, married women, all women, whom they pervert, converting them into prostitutes. These men as well as their servants, blacks, *mestizos,* and Indians [*yanakonas*] wreck the lives of these women, destroying their possessions, land and goods. . . .

Priests are supposed to educate boys only, but they get girls as well, and the parish priests take advantage of this in order to have concubines at their disposal and consequently dozens of children, augmenting the number of *mestizos.* . . . The priests want money, money, and more money, so they force women to serve them as spinners, weavers, cooks, breadmakers. . . . If they complain . . . and the complaint has been made to the royal inspector, they order the women to his house, where they are forced to work even more. Thus there is no one who takes these women's side. . . .

In the village of Hatun Lucanas, the *corregidor's* lieutenant kept in his kitchen a half-dozen single maidens, as well as a dozen Indian women who were performing mita service, who were forced to work spinning and weaving; and he employed them as bakers and chica brewers; the priest who accompanied him did the same thing. Seeing the impossibility of remedying these abuses, and so as not to be left behind, the mayor kept three Indian women in his service.

SOURCE: Irene Silverblatt, *Moon, Sun, and Witches: Gender Ideologies and Class in Inca and Colonial Peru* (Princeton, N.J.: Princeton University Press, 1987), 135, 139, 142.

were sold into slavery, and their leaders were executed. This final large military operation of the Méxican conquest was called the Mixton War.

As in Mexico, the principal indigenous resistance to the Conquest in Peru came after the Spaniards had established themselves. Despite his early alliance with Francisco Pizarro, the Andean leader Manko Inka grew disenchanted with the Spanish conquerors: "I thought they were kindly beings sent as they claimed by Tecsi Viracocha—that is to say God—but it seems to me that things have turned out to be the opposite from what I believed, for let me tell you brothers, from the proofs they have given me since their arrival in our country, they are the sons not of Viracocha, but of the Devil." Manko Inka subsequently led thousands of Inka in laying siege to the conquistadores at Cuzco in 1536 and 1537. After the Spaniards broke the siege, Inka resistance in the highlands gravitated eastward.

Vilcabamba, a large region located on the rugged eastern slopes of the Andes mountains, became the center of native resistance from 1537 to 1572. Three Inka reigned there among ancient settlements, of which the ruins of one, Macchu Picchu, was not discovered by outsiders until the early twentieth century. Viceroy Toledo finally sent out an expedition to capture the last Inka, Túpac Amaru. He was taken to Cuzco, baptized, and then publicly beheaded in the plaza. The Native Americans of Cuzco still revered the Inka and came at night to worship his severed head, which had been placed on a pike by the Spaniards. Finally, the viceroy had the head removed and buried, but the people remembered their last Inka. (As shall be seen in Chapter 12, a man who claimed to be a direct descendant of Túpac Amaru would lead a great rebellion at the end of the eighteenth century.) Indigenous resistance to Spanish rule in the former Inka domain, for the time being, had come to an end. Thereafter, the Andean peoples resolved to preserve their ancient heritage through selective accommodation to Spanish institutions.

Brazil

The ravages of European epidemics were equally as devastating in Brazil and the vast Amazon Basin, but there the natives survived as a separate people because of their numbers and the buffers of distance and nearly impenetrable forests. The first Spanish expedition from Ecuador down the Amazon River in 1541 reported dense population along the riverbanks. The explorers mentioned that some villages lined the riverbanks continuously for tens of kilometers. However, a century later, when the Portuguese Jesuits arrived to convert the riverine natives, they discovered that the tribes had been so disrupted by slaving and disease that nary a person was found for many days' journey along the Amazon. Fevers afflicted the Tupí of southern Brazil in the mid-sixteenth century. Hundreds of Native Americans succumbed to the plague in 1554, many of them becoming susceptible to the disease after they had been brought into the first Jesuit missions there. "[The plague] struck with such violence that as it appeared it laid them low, unconscious, and within three or four days it carried them to the grave," said one missionary. Smallpox struck later, in 1562, covering many natives with "leprous eruptions" before carrying them away. Some of the Jesuits mistook the ravages of these diseases as God's punishment for the natives' lapse into their old ways. In the meanwhile, the indigenous tribal system and cultures began to break down.

Brazil serves as an example of how some indigenous peoples—albeit unwittingly—became complicit in the spread of European conquest and contagion. Various groups enlisted with the Portuguese to attack and subdue their traditional enemies. The Aruak and Tupí became especially competitive. Indigenous groups adept at agriculture were avidly pursued as slaves—by their native enemies as well as by slavers from the settlement of São Paulo. The various Tupí- and Gê-speaking peoples of western and southern Brazil, therefore, had become prey to the expeditions of the *bandeirantes,* as the São Paulo slave hunters were known, more or less continuously from the mid-sixteenth to the mid-eighteenth centuries.

Once brought back to work in the agricultural settlements expanding westward and southward from São Paulo, the natives lived in virtual slavery. They were not actual slaves, of course, because the Portuguese royal court, like its Spanish counterpart, had decreed that the indigenous peoples were to be considered free citizens. But the settlers exploited a loophole in these decrees stipulating that Native Americans who resisted Christianity could be captured and enslaved. The obligation for the settler then was to clothe, feed, and teach the natives the supposedly superior religion and work ethic of the Europeanized world. Many owners may have performed these obligations with indifference, making such captured natives work under the nomenclature of servants or obliged workers (see Manuscript 6.2). These native servants of Portuguese slavers then joined the frontier expeditions that kidnapped even more indigenous laborers. Owners could even bequeath them in their wills to their heirs, although no appreciable market in the sale and resale of native slaves developed, as would later for the Africans. Slaving expeditions constantly had to replenish the natives who worked on the great estates; captivity greatly reduced the natives' life span due to the hard work, poor treatment, and disease, thus making slaving a self-perpetuating cycle. Although the captive natives had little control of their lives, the colonists were motivated to treat them with care. They did outnumber their masters on these isolated estates, after all, and rebellion and escape remained distinct possibilities. In 1676, approximately seven thousand five hundred *mamelucos* and Europeans lived in the southern Brazilian province of São Vicente along with more than twenty thousand Native Americans. But the social distinction between master and slave remained clear and was expressed in racial terms. The owner, although most likely a *mameluco,* considered himself and his family to be white. The Indian slaves were referred to as *negros da terra,* "native blacks," meaning that the word *negro* denoted "slave" to the Portuguese even before Africans arrived. Native slaves found it difficult to maintain a separate family life, for the women were vulnerable to the sexual advances of the masters. The mixed-race children of these unions, however, were considered to be free *mamelucos* and, as described in the previous chapter, made up the growing free peasantry in southern Brazil. Native Americans who had gained their freedom—either by manumission (release by the owner) or by running away—also joined this emerging and intermediate class of poor peasants.

The natives' experience as slaves on the estates of *paulistas* (as the settlers of São Paulo were known) transformed traditional social and gender relationships. The slave owners preferred women as household servants and concubines: they no longer engaged in agriculture as they had in their native villages, and the men now learned to do fieldwork with their masters' new tools: the hoe, scythe, and ax. Native slaves also learned European crafts and became the cobblers, blacksmiths, weavers, and carpenters of São Paulo. In time, the slave or servant class asserted themselves in the new commercial system to which they had been introduced. They raised crops and livestock and delivered them for sale at local markets, in some cases competing against the commercial

MANUSCRIPT 6.2

Justification for and Reality of Native Slavery in Brazil

Part of the conceit by which Europeans intervened in the lives and cultures of the Native Americans involved the mission—as they saw it—to civilize them and introduce the superior European religion and lifestyles among them. European settlers devised a distinctly self-justifying discourse about their tutorial obligations to care for and teach the indigenous American subjects of Spain and Portugal. The Iberian Crowns became susceptible to this discourse because they depended on tax revenues from labor-starved colonial enterprises; therefore, royal officials in the American colonies often ignored the coercive and illegal nature of colonial labor relations. In Brazil as well in parts of Spanish America among the forest agriculturists and hunting peoples, the colonists enslaved the natives in all but name. São Paulo especially depended on the indigenous slave trade in the sixteenth and seventeenth centuries. Was the tutelage benign and paternalistic or exploitative? The first two of these passages represent landowners' explanations for forced native labor in São Paulo. The final passage comes from the court testimony of a supposedly free Native American woman who was captured and forced violently into slavery.

If [after conquest] we use them in our fields, we do them no injustice for this is as much to support them and their children as to support ours. Far from enslaving them, we render them an unremunerated service by teaching them to till, plant, harvest, and work for their livelihood, something which until the Whites teach them they know not how to do.

I declare that I possess nine native heathens and a child whom I treated always as the freemen they are. Being, by nature incapable of governing themselves, I have administered to them with Christian charity, availing myself of their service in order to feed them and in that same manner my heirs will be able to govern them, not as inherited property, but rather as minors in need of control, lacking for nothing as dictated by law and custom until the king rules otherwise.

I declare that I have some natives of Brazil who by law of His Majesty are free and as such I release them and I beg their pardon for any injury or injustice which I may have done them and for not having paid them for their services as was required and I beg them for the love of God and for the esteem in which I hold them to remain and serve my wife who will pay them for their service in the manner customary in this region. Not one of these of whom I have spoken will be alienated or sold, and I ask His Majesty's courts to uphold, for my peace of mind, this last will and testament.

[Fazendeiro] Bartolomeu Fernandes told her, the witness, "come here, I want you to be my servant," and ordered her to raise her skirt, placing a stick between her legs, and ordered her whipped by his son João Fernandes and by Antonio Fernandes . . . which they did until a quantity of blood ran from her, and Bartolomeu Fernandes de Faria said that he did this so that from then on she would recognize him as her master; and after she, the witness, saw herself cured in this town [of Iguape], the said Bartolomeu Fernandes took her to his farm and dressed her in a Tipoia [a slave dress] and has used her until now as his captive.

SOURCE: John Manuel Monteiro, *Negros da terra: índios e bandeirantes nas origens de São Paulo* (São Paulo: Companhia das Letras, 1994), 139–41; and "From Indian to Slave: Forced Native Labour and Colonial Society in São Paulo During the Seventeenth Century," *Slavery and Abolition* 9, no. 2 (1988): 124. (Translation by Monteira and Teresa Van Hoy.)

interests of their owners. Moreover, slave theft and cattle rustling led to a vibrant black market that the local authorities tended to ignore simply because they could not contain it. The crimes perpetrated by natives reflected the success of their acculturation to new social and economic systems as well as their own ability to forge spaces of independent survival and enterprise.

Despite their slave status, the reduction of their numbers, and the loss of their hunting lands to encroaching settlement, the indigenous peoples contributed much to the frontier society developing in southern Brazil in the sixteenth and seventeenth centuries. Most colonists here, except for those few arriving directly from Portugal, had native blood in their veins. They also spoke Tupí as the lingua franca of the region. As for food, although the settlers raised pigs, horses, and cattle and cultivated rice and wheat, they depended largely on indigenous crops such as manioc and corn. Even their agricultural practices were heavily influenced by indigenous customs. The slash-and-burn method, whereby an area of forest growth would be cut and burned and seeds sown in the fertile ashes, gained popularity. After a few years, the soil was leached of its nutrients and the settler, whether large landowner or poor peasant, moved on to cut and burn a new plot out of the forest. For more than a hundred years of settlement at São Paulo, the basic housing structure remained the straw-covered multifamily lodge of indigenous origin. Native American influence on the evolving society of southern Brazil continued unabated through the mid-eighteenth century when they were displaced as slaves in São Paulo by Africans. All in all, the institutions developed before the Conquest by native civilizations influenced how the Europeans carried out the process of settlement so that the end result was more of a blending of cultural attributes than the wholesale replacement of native culture by that of the Europeans.

Plantation Slavery

In Pernambuco and Bahia in northeastern Brazil, settlers also relied on native labor in developing the important sugar export industry. But they had difficulty in converting the communal, subsistence culture of the Tupí into a rural proletariat. The settlers here had first employed native men to cut brazilwood and deliver it to the coast in exchange for European trinkets and tools. This kind of labor exploitation succeeded, for clearing the forest had always been men's work among the indigenous peoples. Women accomplished the agricultural chores, however, which complicated efforts to use natives in the cultivation of cane. Planters desired male workers in the fields and female labor in the household, but the indigenous peoples had little use for wages or for the market economy. Even the missionary settlements, the *aldeias,* could not convert the natives into day laborers. "Inconstant and changeable," one Jesuit described the natives. "That which they struggle to gain today with great labor and sweat tomorrow they disregard." In addition, the spread of disease was greatly reducing the coastal indigenous population. The local Tupí could no longer produce enough manioc and other foodstuffs for the growing Portuguese settlements. A free peasantry of *mamelucos* moved into farming in order to meet market demand. Therefore, the spread of cane planting beginning in the 1570s required the planters to coerce the labor of the Tupí and other indigenous groups.

The Native Americans resisted. Those enslaved and forcibly set to work on the plantations around the Bay of All Saints at Bahia did not meet the expectations of the planters. They worked indifferently in the cane fields and did not easily master the mechanical skills necessary to operate the crushing and distilling equipment of the *engenhos,* or sugar mills. And neither did the natives seem to take to the catechism taught them by the missionaries and the chaplains on the *fazendas.* In 1567, a millennial movement called Santidade combining Catholicism and native beliefs, much like the Taki Unquy of Peru, swept through the laboring population on the sugar plantations. Santidade led to a series of uprisings in which the slaves killed planters, burned the mills, and ran away to form independent settlements, *quilombos,* in the forests behind the coast. The runaway slaves established their own pseudo-Catholic hierarchy of bishops and priests and propagated the idea of a Tupí resurgence that would eliminate the whites and lead to a tropical paradise in which the natives rested while hoes and bows and arrows working by themselves provided for subsistence. So potent did Santidade become that it and the *quilombos* attracted some of the first runaway African slaves, too. The colonial authorities sent military expeditions against the runaway settlements, and the Jesuit missionaries tirelessly mobilized the Native Americans in the missions against their cohorts in the bush.

The Santidade movement finally disappeared at a time in which the white planters began to make the transition from Native American to African slavery. Although the sugar mills secured replacement slaves from tribes inhabiting the frontier and thus were protected from the influence of Santidade, the natives never turned out to be as productive as the planters expected. Gradually, they brought in the more expensive Africans, who proved more acculturated and satisfactory as slaves. Africans already had the work ethos that the natives refused to adopt and capably learned the skills necessary to run the mills. In the transition period from 1570 to 1620, Africans came to occupy the more skilled positions on the plantation, relegating native slaves to fieldwork, fishing, hunting, and food production. By 1620 indigenous chattel workers had practically disappeared from the expanding sugar plantations of the Brazilian northeast.

Nevertheless, few indigenous peoples of the remote reaches of the Amazon Basin could long avoid the contagions that followed European contact. The Moxo lived in such an inaccessible region of present-day Bolivia that the first European exploratory expeditions did not enter their territory until 1595 and 1617. These short visits sufficed to spread the alien germs. As elsewhere in the tropics, these isolated Native Americans suffered inordinately from the new diseases. The estimated population of three hundred fifty thousand natives began to decline drastically. By the time the Jesuits established the first sustained European presence in 1690, the Moxo population had already declined by 65 percent. Other Brazilian groups, nonetheless, remained in isolated pockets of the backlands and thus survived relatively intact until the twentieth century.

However, nonnative employers viewed the missions in Brazil and elsewhere as representing the monopolization of native laborers by the friars—the more so as the indigenous population declined. Everywhere on the frontiers, be it the Brazilian Sertão and Amazon Basin, the Venezuelan Llanos, the eastern slopes of the Andes Mountains, or Paraguay and southern Brazil, the mestizo and European colonists resented the missionaries. Many considered the natives, whether in the mission or in the forest, as "squalid savages, ferocious and most base, resembling the wild beasts in everything save in human shape." For their part, Jesuits, Mecedarians, and other missionary sects denounced the settlers for enslaving and mistreating the natives.

Unable to compete in the sugar export markets, the local landowners began to produce *cachaça,* a distilled cane brandy that became a favorite drink of the Brazilians. In

1684, acute labor shortages on the cane plantations of Maranhão and Grão Pará drove the settlers to revolt. The colonial government conceded to the settlers' demands, not by freeing up Native American workers from control of the missionaries but by granting more licenses for the importation of African slaves.

In the end, the settlers won. They outnumbered the missionaries, and their vigorous protests eventually forced the colonial state to remove the natives from the clergy's exclusive control. At any rate, the mission settlements had exposed frontier indigenous populations to infections, and their numbers dwindled rapidly in the sixteenth and seventeenth centuries as a result. Shortly after coming into the missions in 1635, the Potiguar tribe of Ceará, near the mouth of the Amazon River, declined from 8,000 to 105. Frontier settlers often killed indigenous Brazilians before the missionaries could intervene. On the banks of the São Francisco River, cattlemen eliminated natives like so many vermin because they were hunting cattle for food. Once again, the indigenous peoples were caught up in and victimized by disputes among Europeans. The frontiers thus became socially homogenized zones—a world inherited by the mixed races who survived by adapting themselves to elements of Native American culture.

Paraguay

In few regions did Native American customs exert a stronger influence on settler society than in Brazil and Paraguay—even though there, too, the natives had to adjust their lifestyles. In the settlements of Paraguay, for example, the few Spaniards melted into the larger population of Guaraní. While retaining their Spanish language and social domination, these European men lived in the extended native households, offering protection and lending prestige to the clans with which they cohabited. They gave in easily to the polygamous customs of the locals, and their mestizo children grew up speaking both Spanish and Guaraní. The consequences of the Conquest may have been most jarring for Guaraní men, because the new rulers converted them from warriors to workers; they fished, hunted for game, cared for the livestock, and even helped the women tend the gardens and fields. As elsewhere, the Guaraní adapted themselves to living with domesticated animals and even grew some wheat. But they themselves provided the commercial linkage between Paraguay and the outside world: They were sent into the forests to harvest the leaves of the *yerba* trees, which, when roasted and crushed, made a fragrant green tea known as yerba maté. Consumers throughout the Río de la Plata region, Chile, and Peru sipped the tea from a *maté* (gourd) through a straw strainer.

The Jesuit missionaries who arrived to establish settlements in eastern Paraguay in the mid-sixteenth century also engaged in stock raising and yerba production. Native Americans were forced into monogamous marriages, taught to wear European clothes, and trained to raise cattle and to tend both native and European crops. In southern Paraguay, the Jesuits also organized their indigenous charges to plant the first cultivated *yerba* trees. As elsewhere, the policy of the Spanish authorities and their religious confederates, if not the lay settlers themselves, was to concentrate the remaining natives into discrete settlements. To the Jesuits, the missions were great experiments in social engineering, imposing cultural change from the top down, but the results of their efforts were far from perfect. More than a few Guaraní men felt the Jesuit lash for having succumbed to their ancient ways of warfare and polygamy.

Agricultural tasks performed by mission natives in Santa Fe, Río de la Plata. (Florian Baucke, 1767)

The exchange was not all one way. Although the Spaniards and Portuguese introduced smallpox, mumps, and measles to the Americas, some scholars speculate that they may also have taken back an American disease to Europe: syphilis. Eventually, the Americas would also contribute manioc, corn, potatoes, tomatoes, chilies, beans, chocolate, and turkey to the diets of Europeans. In turn, Europe contributed pigs, chickens, cows, horses, goats, sheep, donkeys, wheat, and sugarcane. These were the chief elements of what might be called the Columbian Exchange. The natives retained their original diets but gradually added European protein. By the end of the sixteenth century, the consumption of meat became a general practice in Mexico and Ecuador. Only in the southern Andes, where the indigenous peoples already raised llama and alpaca, did European livestock slowly enter their diets. However, sheep eventually thrived and competed with the camelids in the Puno of southern Peru and the Altiplano of Bolivia.

ACCOMMODATION AND ACCULTURATION

The European incursion into the Americas certainly changed the institutions under which the natives of these lands organized and conducted their lives. The Native Americans now had to adapt themselves to excessive demands on their labor and productivity as well as to negotiate an alien world of commerce. Yet they struggled everywhere to preserve their languages, their customs, and a modicum of control over their own destiny. The native nobility may have been reduced and ancient lineages lost, but the peasantry endured to preserve control over their own subsistence, and a class of workers formed to exploit opportunities for advancement in the Spanish world.

Resettlement Policy

The wholesale decimation of indigenous populations created an enormous problem in formulating a rational policy toward those who were to be the workers and peasants. The first conquistadores and their heirs divided up the native groups among themselves, placing them under the private control of the leading colonists in the *encomienda* system. By the mid-sixteenth century, it became evident that the declining number of natives could not sustain the levels of tribute and labor to which the *encomenderos* were accustomed. Crown revenues also were shrinking. Moreover, increasing numbers of Spaniards were coming to the Indies, and they resented the monopoly over the natives enjoyed by descendants of the first arrivals. In the second half of the sixteenth century, the *encomiendas* were allowed to lapse in Peru and New Spain (see Chapter 5). Private tutelage of Native Americans remained a feature of colonial life until the early eighteenth century only in fringe colonies. The indigenous population was more impoverished and Spanish competition for it was less intense in regions such as Colombia, Chile, Argentina, and Venezuela, where the *encomienda* endured.

Simultaneously, Crown officials decided to enlist the aid of the friars to resettle the natives into more compact settlements. The policy was called *reducción,* "reducing" or congregating the natives scattered by disease and rural isolation. Those peasants who still lived dispersed in the countryside were brought into villages, and several villages that had suffered large population losses were consolidated; the resultant resettlement communities were called *reducciones*. In this fashion, the Spanish authorities reconstituted the close-knit family and pre-Columbian clan groupings, the *altepetl* and *ayllu,* that had control over defined districts. The object was to protect the natives and provide for their education in Iberian ways, and the Crown and clergy assumed these functions from individual *encomenderos*. The priests were to tutor the natives in Catholicism and the Spanish language, while Crown officials took over the collection of tribute. Decline of the indigenous population had left a vacuum in the countryside. Because whole fields lay abandoned for lack of people to work them, the second generation of Europeans assumed more responsibility for providing their own foodstuffs and supplies. They took over land vacated by the resettled peasants and imported African slaves to work it. This was especially true in the immediate environs of Spanish towns throughout Mesoamerica and the Andean regions.

Crown officials sometimes gathered Native Americans into *reducciones* without regard for ancestral ties that had always been the basis of the pre-Conquest communities. The *reducción* was not an entirely successful policy, for the natives often abandoned the new settlements and returned to their ancestral lands. As the second viceroy of Peru observed: "The *reducciones* which Don Francisco de Toledo [the first viceroy] established in the Andean provinces are in ruin, because so many Indians have died; some have fled to avoid the *mita de minas* or the personal service to which they are assigned, and others have left to escape the abuses of the *corregidores,* parish priests, and *kurakas,* who are their worst enemies; still other Indians have fled to private estates, where the owners protect them by claiming that they are *yanaconas* [in personal service]. . . . Also, the Indians hide in mountains and isolated pastures, where they can not easily be discovered." However, the natives reconstituted many of their ancient traditions—lineage ties, marriage patterns, village governance, and reciprocal practices and obligations—in the new settlements according to the old ways. Moreover, the native peasants retained their distinctive language and dress to distinguish themselves from other communities and from Hispanicized society.

As for labor, the Crown devised a system of *repartimiento,* or distribution of indigenous workers, to replace the *encomienda.* Local colonial officials and priests were to mediate labor demand and supply. That way, more Spaniards would have access to it, not just the most prominent among them. Officials sent natives from villages to neighboring haciendas and mines for the required temporary work. The *hacendado* and mine owner were to house, feed, and pay a wage to each worker. Making Native Americans pay tribute or taxes in cash was one way the state forced them to leave their subsistence plots to work in *repartimiento* and the *mita* (as the labor drafts were known in Mesoamerica and the Andean region, respectively) for cash wages paid by Spanish employers. However, the villagers retained some control over their own labor. They responded to the labor drafts through the mediation of their local leaders. Thus, *caciques* and *kurakas,* the native town leaders in Mexico and Peru, respectively, acted as the labor contractors, determining how the demands were to be met. To maintain this reservoir of labor, the colonial bureaucrats permitted peasant villages to hold enough land to provide for their own subsistence. The local indigenous nobility often owned private holdings worked by the town's peasants in observation of ancient rights and obligations.

Moreover, the old Andean and Mesoamerican social institutions became the building blocks of European colonialism. The new authorities constructed their Catholic parishes, labor drafts, and tribute systems directly over the *altepetl* and *ayllu.* Survival in altered form of these basic social units also ensured the durability of the native nobility as well. In other words, Native Americans could choose to use their ancient traditions and institutions either to accommodate themselves to European domination or to resist it. But to survive, they did not just reconstitute their ancient traditions but forged new indigenous cultures strongly influenced by European institutions.

The Native Nobility

The native nobility underwent numerous changes as a result of European conquest. In Mexico, the Spanish conquest ended the wars within the nobility that had resulted from political struggles as empires had come and gone. Ritual human sacrifices were also ended. The nobility then stabilized, with fewer entrants than before the Conquest. The classes of warriors and priests were eliminated, and the ruling native nobility was reduced to the level of the village. The high nobility of the Aztec and Inka empires fell into decline, although a number of Native American "princesses" did fuse their noble lineages to the new colonial elite through marriage to some of the first conquistadores. Because Spanish outsiders tended to intervene in the political life of the Native American community, the village *caciques* of the Nahua in the sixteenth to eighteenth centuries did not necessarily have pre-Conquest roots. Many a local native family became wealthy through trade, connection to Spaniards, or adroit collection of lands during the colonial period. But these new dynasties behaved and viewed themselves in very much the same way as did the pre-Conquest local nobility. The nobility of the former Aztec empire, who had developed an extensive and highly developed system of long-distance trade in Mesoamerica, remained in trade after Spanish conquest. But now they were relegated to local and interregional trade, in the latter of which the native traders took second place to

Spaniards. Of course, international trade was firmly in the hands of Europeans who had connections to important merchant houses back in Spain. Native merchant families, however, could gain enough capital to own their own pack animals and lands.

Native American leaders were forbidden their previous symbols of prestige—the feather cloaks or riding on litters—but the most important nobles gained permission to wear European clothes, ride horses, and carry swords. They also received instruction in Spanish, the better to serve as satraps of European power. There developed among these indigenous leaders a familiarity and even a necessity to operate within the Spanish world. They were the first to speak Spanish, to take Spanish names, to dress in European styles, and even to ride on horseback. Their partial Hispanicization permitted the *cacique*s of Mexico and the *kuraka*s of Peru to more effectively represent their communities before the clergy, local officials, and *hacendados*. In Mexico, the noble lineages continued to provide political leadership at the local level. They adopted the Spanish town council, the *cabildo,* but retained their own pre-Hispanic ruling practices. These local authorities kept records in written Nahuatl, as taught to their scribes by the Franciscan priests. Native leaders even adopted the Spanish institution of the *cofradía,* or lay brotherhood, to direct their own observances of Catholic rituals and holidays. Native elders formed the electorate for town officials, much as in pre-Conquest times, except that they now elected local *gobernadores* (governors) and *regidores* (councilors) by their Spanish rather than their ancient Nahuatl titles. The local indigenous leaders exploited the political parallels between their ancient political system and the Spanish model to retain their traditional rulership throughout colonial times.

Despite their service toward a smooth functioning of the colonial social relationships, of which the Spaniards benefited most, these indigenous leaders also incurred resentments. To the Spaniards, the native Americans who spent their lives in personal service to Spanish families or as employees of the clergy, interpreters, artisans, and wage workers in the mines appeared to have left behind the obsequiousness thought proper for lowly natives. In other words, these natives began to act too much like the Spaniards themselves. Spaniards even had a derisive name for them, *indios ladinos,* "Latinized [or Hispanicized] Indians." Most of all, Spaniards held them in contempt for serving as the spokespersons of indigenous demands. They complained and negotiated for their communities—and they were litigious. Very soon, they learned how to use the Spanish court system, tying up *hacendados* and officials in lawsuits lasting many years at a time. They were the ones who brought suit against the corrupt *corregidores* and local landowners (even priests!) who abused native tribute and labor. "Everything is lost in lawsuits with lawyers and litigation officers," the timeless saying went, "such that, at the end, both parties end up without anything except for being very clever at tricks and lies, as is seen every day in the Audiencia [chief tribunal]."

This contemptuous reception of the *indios ladinos* in the Spanish world sometimes caused those labeled by that derogatory term to react quite strongly. Those most familiar with the Hispanic world were precisely the ones leading the rebellion of the Mixton War in Mexico and the nativist movement of Taki Unquy in Peru. It was partly to control this rebellion and litigiousness that the priests railed against the natives' complaints about being abused and exploited. It was clear to Guaman Poma de Ayala, the Andean writer who was a descendant of an Inka prince, how things stood. "[Spaniards] do not want to see Christian *ladino* Indians speaking in Spanish. It frightens them, and they have me thrown out of the village," he wrote in 1613. "All collude in the effort that [we *indios ladinos*] be ignorant asses, to end up by taking all one has, property, wife, and daughter." Guaman Poma himself grew to resent other indigenous leaders who prostrated themselves before the Spaniards, sacrificing the rights of their people in order to be able to "drink at [the Spaniards'] tables." Spanish domination produced just such ambivalence and conflict within the native community.

The colonial justice system did not, however, bestow equal justice upon Spaniards and Native Americans. Usually, white settlers could expect more latitude and consideration from the authorities. Spanish colonists who killed natives in rage or accidentally in the course of corporal punishment for some infraction or another were seldom held accountable—no matter how flagrant the offense. In the Yucatán, a settler killed a local lord in front of the latter's villagers because the Spaniard had ordered carriers from the lord, who did not bring them quickly enough. The deceased's family complained, but the settler had only to compensate the family with two pounds of blue beads. Said one Spanish observer: "[I]t costs more to kill a cow or a horse in Yucatán than to kill an Indian." If Native Americans lacked equal protection before the law, the Spaniard who sought to live off their labor, or take advantage of their property or women, showed little respect for them either.

Village Organization

Basic pre-Columbian social units such as the lineage group, or *ayllu,* of the Andes and the *altepetl* of Mexico survived the Conquest. The indigenous peasants still identified themselves according to the lineage group in which they had been born. In the countryside, the Spaniards organized their institutions of domination and control—such as the *encomienda,* the rural parishes, and the labor drafts—on the existing *altepetl* organization of Nahua society. Eventually the Spanish term came to be *pueblo,* "people," which was accurate, for each *altepetl* imagined itself to be a separate people—separate even from neighboring peasants speaking the same native language. The household structure of the indigenous peasant family continued much as it had in pre-Hispanic days. Parents, grown children, and other relatives and in-laws lived together in a single compound composed of separate one- and two-room buildings facing an inner court and surrounded and connected by a common low stone wall. Completing every household's living space was a small building serving as a saint's house, an adaptation of the pre-Conquest spirit house, a symbolic residence of the family's patron god. Gradually, beginning with the nobility, indigenous individuals began to abandon their names of pre-Conquest origins and adopt the names of saints and Spaniards. In the sixteenth and seventeenth centuries, they combined Spanish first names with native surnames; by the eighteenth century, the full adaptation of Spanish names was completed.

Two agrarian traditions developed alongside each other in the rural areas of the Spanish Indies. Sedentary Native Americans exploited communal lands mainly for subsistence and tribute—much as they had in pre-Conquest times. Mestizo farmers and Spanish *hacendados,* however, worked private holdings mostly oriented toward urban markets. This agrarian duality was most pronounced in areas of dense native population such as central Mexico, Guatemala, Ecuador, Peru, and Bolivia and to a lesser extent in Nicaragua, Colombia, Chile, and northwest Argentina. Nonetheless, Native Americans did gradually adapt themselves to market structures, especially in the Andean region. Individual natives came to own private property and hired wage earners to work them.

Native agrarian communities specialized in certain products—corn, pulque, and cacao in Mexico or freeze-dried potatoes, coca leaves, and *chicha* in Peru. Just as they observed a religion combining old and new rites, so, too, did the natives mix European marketing mechanisms with their older tradition of subsistence agriculture.

The division of land between natives and Europeanized society caused minor friction until the seventeenth century. In general, the natives lost land to Spaniards, but they also had ways of protecting their community resources from total destitution. The conquistadores claimed outright all Inka lands. Then Spaniards and their retainers moved onto land vacated by the villages as epidemics ravaged the countryside. Still, the colonial authorities set aside land for each native village so that the indigenous population might provide its own subsistence and produce a surplus to be paid in taxes. The native lords also held on to excess native lands by renting them out to Spaniards, using the rental fees to pay taxes and tribute. The pandemics in Mesoamerica and the Andes finally drew to a close in the mid-seventeenth century, and indigenous populations began a slow renewal. As the colonial era drew to a close, population growth exerted increasing pressure on the division of landed resources between Native Americans and nonnatives, a phenomenon that will be discussed in later chapters.

It should be fairly obvious by now that where they remained in significant numbers, albeit subordinate to Europeans, Native Americans greatly influenced the shape of the new colonial societies. The fact is that they preserved much of their preferences and characteristics despite the best efforts of their colonial masters. In central Mexico, Guatemala, and the Andean zone, most peasants were never Hispanicized during the long colonial period. They preserved their separate languages, regional customs, and village traditions. Working through power structures ordained by Spanish colonial authorities, natives in Mexico and Peru fought tenaciously to preserve their lands. They used the Spanish court system and the laws protecting them to resist outsiders from encroaching on their subsistence. Their connections with individual Spaniards also worked to protect their independent lifestyles. Native leaders made alliances with powerful Spaniards, favoring a friar or neighboring landowner with their labor and gifts in return for protection. Some natives leased land to powerful Spaniards to keep it out of the clutches of other Spaniards. When laws and patrons failed them, Native Americans resolved not to be intimidated by their lowly social status from taking matters into their own hands. They were known to have forcefully prevented sales of land or to have resorted to mob action to intimidate a local official or priest who attempted to sacrifice their collective interests.

While tribute was not a new feature to the indigenous population, the burden of tax collection probably increased as a result of conquest—particularly in Peru. The Spaniards immediately took possession of the Inka's lands, upon which the villagers had cultivated tribute for the Inka. Now the Spaniards produced their own products on these estates, albeit with native labor. Therefore, the natives were reduced to producing tribute items for the *encomendero* from their own community lands, which had previously been reserved only for subsistence. The Chupacho of Peru complained that they were working seven to eight months a year to pay their tributes to the *encomenderos*. The new tribute demands were overbearing, especially given the reduced number of natives. "And at present they feel more exhausted than ever in the past," reported one investigating official in 1562, "for everybody works, married men and women, youths and girls and children and there is nobody left."

The indigenous communities now owed tribute of goods and labor to the *kuraka* and to the Spanish king. The latter decreed a tax on all Native American male heads of household between 18 and 50 years of age. These *tributarios* were also to provide goods as before, and they owed obligatory *mita* labor to the mines or *obrajes* at least once every seven years. But the Spaniards seldom reciprocated according to Andean tradition. They sent precious little to the *ayllu*. The Chupacho Indians of central Peru complained that they were providing woven textiles and wool to the Spaniards and 18,000 pesos to the king, receiving nothing in return.

The Conquest shifted a heavier tribute burden onto the Native Americans. The early *encomenderos* required tribute in both labor and material goods such as native textiles and foodstuffs. By the seventeenth century, the natives shifted their tribute payments to the state both in labor and in money—the latter of which did not even exist in the pre-Conquest world. "At present [the Indians] pay tribute differently from the way they paid it to the Inca: and now they give more," admitted one Spanish official. *Kuraka*s suffered a loss of prestige among their own peoples as well as with the new overlords, for they had to collect the tribute and also had to pay it themselves—being personally responsible to the *encomendero* and later to the king's tax collectors if their villages' tribute fell below the quota. The Spaniards drained substance from the native sector and did so precisely through the mechanisms of violence and domination.

Economic Exchange

One of the great changes of the Conquest, particularly within the former Inka Empire, was the introduction of the market system. Previously, the economy had been based on redistribution and reciprocity. The *ayllu* contributed its produce to the nobility, the *kuraka*s, and they owed a tribute to the Inka. In turn, both the Inka and the *kuraka*s would redistribute goods back to the *ayllu*. Internal trade and exchange, therefore, was accomplished through this Inka-directed tribute system. The coming of the Spaniards, however, imposed the rule of an external social group with a totally alien economic culture in the form of monetized markets.

The vertical economic system in the Andes regions collapsed soon after Conquest. Under the Inka, the members of an *ayllu* had rights to gather fish along the coast and also cultivate their own supplies of coca on the rainy eastern slopes of the cordillera. This system was now impossible to sustain. The Spaniards divided the natives into geographical *encomiendas* so that communities lost contact and authority over resources. Spanish commerce replaced verticality, and native peasants and workers now acquired traditional commodities, such as dried fish or coca leaves, that they used to obtain through the system of reciprocity and internal exchange as well as new European items through the market system. Money exchange complemented, though never completely replaced, the barter and reciprocity exchanges of the older Andean world.

Not only did Spaniards take over and commercialize certain areas of indigenous production, but they also altered gender categories in doing so. In ancient times, spinning and weaving were the universal activities of native women, both noble and commoner, and thus they produced the cloth that dominated the tribute rolls among the pre-Conquest civilizations and later for the Spanish *encomiendas*. This cottage industry continued throughout the colonial period but was relegated to secondary importance in the seventeenth century, when it was supplanted by the commercial *obrajes*. The Spanish-owned textile shops that produced the cheap woolen cloth for the consumption of the popular classes converted the larger European looms into the property of a class of native men who became skilled weavers. Despite their work on the backstrap looms in their own homes, indigenous women did not work the large looms of the *obrajes,* although they did spin thread there.

But for individuals within the indigenous population of the Andean region, the Conquest also dissolved certain community disciplines. Individual liberation begot insecurity. The new market environment created by Spaniards tolerated and encouraged personal indulgences. Relaxation of ancient restrains increased the natives' exposure to alcoholic beverages and coca leaves that, in ancient times, had symbolic meanings. Previously used in religious ceremonies, these items had been cultivated in small quantities and consumed mainly by priests. With the arrival of the Spaniards, these once spiritual products took on commercial value, were produced and sold by Spanish-owned estates, and were marketed unabashedly among the indigenous population; they became commodities of consumption among commoners, whether peasants or mine workers. *Encomenderos* and Spanish merchants commercialized the usage of coca and strong drink and promoted sales of these items among the commoners despite the opposition of the missionaries. Some of the natives believed that their exposure to these vices was partly responsible for their shortened life spans. "They lived longer because before, they say, they led more orderly lives than they do now," remarked one cleric, "and because there was not such an abundance of things, nor did they have the opportunities which they now have to eat and drink and indulge in other vices, and with all the work they had to do when the Inka reigned, there was not even any wine, which generally shortens life."

Even the manner in which native peasants began to ritualize the use of alcoholic beverages after the Spanish conquest suggests elements of resistance and assertion of independence. Indigenous commoners took advantage of the difficult transition to Spanish rule and markets to acquire liquor and incorporate it into their own religious celebrations. The giving and receiving of alcohol became a ritual whenever men—women's drinking was frowned upon—came together to discuss village business. Workers traditionally demanded liquor from employers after a labor agreement had been reached or produce was delivered. The natives' ritual use of alcohol confirmed the fears and prejudices of the Spanish settlers. "For them there is no tomorrow; they are satisfied with fulfilling their needs for a week and will work no more than is necessary in order to eat and drink that week," said the colonists of the Andean peasants. "They hate work and love idleness, alcohol, drunkenness, and idolatry; while drunk, they commit mortal sins with women. They obey their superiors willingly and therefore it is necessary to rule them, govern them, and make them work—to keep them from idleness and sin."

Indigenous women also felt the conflicting effects of the Conquest. On the one hand, the Spaniards made women a part of the formal labor force, putting them into the textile workshops (though not as weavers) and collecting tribute from them when disease took the male family heads who were supposed to pay. Spaniards also forced many indigenous girls into household service, even to the point of kidnapping them if necessary. On the other hand, the dislocation of conquest presented female Native Americans commercial opportunities they would not otherwise have had. In Mesoamerica and the Andean region, native women ran markets in towns and cities. They operated truck gardens, moved produce, owned property, and bequeathed assets to their heirs. In Mexico, indigenous females operated the manufacture and distribution of pulque, the strong drink of native origin that grew in popularity. The fact that colonial law treated indigenous women as minors to be represented by so-called competent males represented an obstacle, certainly, but not an impenetrable barrier to their involvement in the new commodity and labor markets.

Proletarianization

Commercialization of the economy also introduced Native Americans to the beginning of a process that, even as of the twentieth century, has not been completed—namely, proletarianization, the conversion of the indigenous peasantry into free, wage workers in the market economy. Once the viceroy devised the *mita* labor drafts in 1573, the control of silver production had passed completely out of the hands of native producers and into the hands of Spanish mine operators who owned more capital-intensive refining mills, complete with ore-crushing equipment and patios for mercury amalgamation. The role of the native was to provide labor. In the early seventeenth century, Spanish officials had structured the *mita* obligations to be attractive to the natives. They were to receive one-half wages for each day of travel to the mining job, and they took two weeks off to hire themselves out for the prevailing wages (which were always higher than *mitayo* wages). Moreover, the *mitayo*s could return from the mines with their own ore, which they and their families smelted themselves in their own ovens and sold for profit on the open market.

Early on Monday mornings, the *mitayo*s left the ethnic barrios of Potosí and gathered at the base of the mountain. There they received their assignments to work in the mines and mills of the various Spanish mine operators. Most *mitayo*s worked in the less skilled jobs of hauling ore out of the deep pits, being paid 3.5 reales (less than 0.5 peso) per day plus rations (see Manuscript 6.3). Their womenfolk came to the mines on Wednesday to deliver the only hot meal that they would have all week. The native workers could leave the mines to return to their barrios only on Saturday night.

However, as the mining industry matured and the ore declined in richness, the Spanish mine owners began to abuse *mita* labor. The two-week rests were eliminated, the pits grew deeper and more hazardous, and the white majordomos and native supervisors began to whip the *mitayo*s. Their privilege of carrying home some ore for extra earnings was removed. Finally, the natives began to resist the *mita* as much as they could by taking flight, registering their male children as female, filching the ore for extra earnings, and paying for substitute workers. So effective did the resistance become that the village *kuraka*s began to pay the 7 pesos they owed to the miners for every *mitayo* who failed to show up for his term of duty. The cash payment to the mining sector became like a subsidy from the Andean peasantry to the mining industry. By the end of the seventeenth century, mine owners were accepting one-half of their *mita* quotas in labor and the other half in money. Approximately 76,000 Native Americans were in residence at Potosí in 1611, only one-third of whom were mine workers and one-twelfth of whom were unskilled, itinerant *mitayo*s. The others were free wage earners with some skills who labored in transportation, the urban infrastructure, food preparation, and construction in this mining complex.

Flight came to be one of the most ubiquitous forms of resistance to the worst aspects of native exploitation, and it, too, contributed to proletarianization. Native Americans abandoned their villages to escape epidemic diseases, tax collectors, and most of all, labor drafts. When they left their communities of birth, natives became *forasteros,* "strangers."

Nowhere were *forasteros* more evident than in the Andean region, where most migrants took flight to remain in native society despite having moved out of the *ayllu*. If they moved to Spanish towns or even to another *ayllu* in which they had not been born, they found exemption from *mita* and tribute because they were not *originarios,* or natives. Often a *forastero* married into the new community and brought in earnings to help pay its taxes. Although they were subordinate politically within community affairs, they nonetheless helped the *kuraka*s maintain their authority. They especially fled areas subject to the mining *mita* and often went to Cuzco, which had taken in 11,000 *forastero* migrants by 1690, or nearly two-fifths of the city's indigenous population. These were the

MANUSCRIPT 6.3

Native Mining Labor at Potosí

Viceroy Toledo instituted the famous mining mita in 1573 to ensure enough labor for the Potosí silver mines high in the forbidding Altiplano. The Spaniards designed this labor system from Inka precedents. In this labor draft, Andean peasant communities within several weeks' walk of Potosí were to send male workers to the mines. Each citizen of the peasant community was supposed to provide a year's worth of mining labor once every seven years, for which he was to be paid a minimum salary. In the 1590s, Father José de Acosta described the work of these itinerant and unskilled laborers like that of the carriers (apiri) as arduous and dangerous, factors that made the mita unpopular throughout the Andean highlands. The Spanish mine operators at Potosí actually came to depend more on the free wage labor workers, who outnumbered the mitayos by two to one. But the peasant communities also paid a fine to the mine operators for each mitayo who did not show up, a source of cash subsidy to the mining industry.

They labor in these mines in perpetual darkness, not knowing day from night. And since the sun never penetrates to these places, they are not only always dark but very cold, and the air is very thick and alien to the nature of men; so that those who enter for the first time get as sick as at sea—which happened to me in one of these mines, where I felt a pain at the heart and a churning in the stomach. The [*apiri*] always carry candles to light their way, and they divide their labor in such a way that some work by day and rest by night, and others work by night and rest by day. The ore is generally hard as flint, and they break it up with iron bars. They carry the ore on their backs up ladders made of three cords of twisted rawhide joined by pieces of wood that serve as rungs, so that one man may climb up and another down at the same time. These ladders are twenty meters long, and at the top and bottom of each is a wooden platform where the men may rest, because there are so many ladders to climb. Each man usually carries on his back a load of twenty-five kilograms of silver ore tied in a cloth, knapsack fashion; thus they ascend, three at a time. The one who goes first carries a candle tied to his thumb, . . . thus holding on with both hands, they climb that great distance, often more than 300 meters—a fearful thing, the mere thought of which inspires dread.

SOURCE: Jeffrey Cole, *The Potosí Mita, 1573 – 1700: Compulsory Indian Labor in the Andes* (Stanford, Calif.: Stanford University Press, 1985), 24.

most independent of all, for they were not subject to the direct control of the *hacenda-dos* or the *kurakas*. They were free to engage in services and marketing and to sell their labor full or part time to urban employers. But the demand for labor was high, as evinced by the ability of free workers to enter into contracts as artisans, muleteers, and farm workers and to get advances on their pay. *Forastera* women dominated the urban service sector. The young girls worked in households, and many women engaged in making *chicha*. In fact, the Spanish householders of Quito benefited from a widespread practice of "kidnapping" young indigenous girls from the countryside for household service. Other women sold goods on the markets, and still others engaged themselves as laundresses, wet nurses, and cooks.

Population dislocation and internal migration had a number of long-term effects on Andean rural society. The peasant community of the colonial period came to be based on location rather than common ancestry. This differed from the time of the Inka, when the *ayllu* was an endogamous lineage claiming descent from a common ancestor. Moreover, the introduction of a commercial, money-based economy enhanced the social differentiation present even in Inka times. But now private property, capital accumulation, and access to the means of production became as important as the ancient custom of community reciprocity. Spanish interference in community affairs through tribute and labor drafts reinforced the *kuraka* in his hereditary role as linchpin of relations between the community and the outside world. In the Andean countryside, there was a long transformation from a caste to a class society.

Migrants hired themselves out as wage earners in the mines and cities. The pre-Conquest class of unattached *yanakonas* expanded to 25,000 persons in the mid-seventeenth century. They worked directly for Spanish employers, sometimes for little pay, on haciendas, in the households, and in weaving shops. The advantage of service work for Spaniards was that the native worker thus escaped the head tax and the Potosí labor drafts. Eventually, the *yanakonas* and *forasteros* would become the proletariat of the Andean world—a large and growing class of free wage-earning workers that did not exist before the Conquest.

Native American Catholicism

The indigenous peoples did not abandon their ancient gods or beliefs for Christianity but combined old and new religious elements into many local forms of Native American Catholicism. Mobilized by the clergy to construct the magnificent sixteenth-century cathedrals on the plazas of Mexico City, Puebla, Guatemala, Bogotá, Quito, Lima, and Cuzco, native men and women packed the idols of their ancient gods into the walls behind the altars. The shamans and faith healers of Guatemala still practiced their ancient rites, adding elements of Christian ceremonies. The Guaraní of Paraguay converted their reverence for thunder into reverence for the European concept of God and addressed the Catholic priests just the same as their own shamans. In these ways the indigenous peoples changed Catholicism in order to accept it as their own.

The first Franciscan missionaries in Mexico, however, had desired to silence indigenous voices, impose a European monologue, and replace American cultural diversity with conformity. But they did not accomplish these tasks. In the first place, not enough friars came to spread the new doctrine. Second, the Franciscans and Dominicans found it easier to learn the native languages than to teach the numerous Native Americans the

Guaraní women in European dress on their way to church. (Jean Baptiste Debret, ca. 1820)

Spanish language. Moreover, knowing how to communicate with the natives made the friars important intermediaries between the Iberian and the indigenous communities. Serving as an intermediary signified real power in colonial society, because the natives had become the source of tribute and labor.

In the final analysis, the Native Americans turned Christianity into something of their own. They remained intensely spiritual and religious but retained Catholic dogma rather superficially, as the friars frequently complained. In Mexico, as in other places, the problem lay in communication. Nahuatl did not sufficiently convey European concepts. The friars learned Nahuatl and preached in it, forcing them to adopt Nahuatl words and concepts and thereby leaving the natives to interpret the new religious doctrines according to their own spiritual conceptions and traditions. There are no equivalent words in Nahuatl for *love* and *salvation.* The friars had to express the European terms (and thus concepts of) *good* and *evil* using the Nahuatl words for "order" and "chaos." *Sin* was translated into the native word meaning "damage." Certainly, the friars' usage of the native languages to spread Christianity did not carry the same moral charge as in Spanish.

The Catholic priests not only had to explain the new religion's doctrine to the natives in their languages but also had to resort to using their religious symbolism, which diluted the intended message a great deal. In converting the Tupí of Brazil, the Jesuits adopted the word *Tupan,* the Tupí name for a thunder demon, as an equivalent for "God." But because many of the Native American gods were malevolent, it was not difficult to find a suitable one for "the devil." A spirit who sometimes haunted the Tupí at night, Anhan, was adopted to represent him. Native Americans in Mexico recognized their old gods in the statues of Jesus, the Virgin Mary, John the Baptist, and the numerous saints of Catholic worship. They converted Tlaloc, the Aztec rain god, into St. John and transformed the ancient mother of the gods, Tonantzín, into a Mexican version of the Virgin Mary, the Virgin of Guadalupe. At Cholula, where the old pre-Columbian gods now slumber, the Spaniards built the Sanctuary of Our Lady of the Remedies right over the pedestal of the ancient House of the Devil. Behind this religious sanctuary tower the volcanic peaks of Popocatéptl and Iztaccíhautl, just as in ancient times. In Peru, the Virgin Mary inherited the mantle of the Inka earth goddess Viracocha, whose ancient shrine on the shores of Lake Titicaca, now dedicated to the Virgin of Copacabana, continued to attract indigenous pilgrims from all parts of the Andean region.

Nevertheless, there is reason to suspect that submission to Spanish political authority and to Christianity was quite superficial in Peru. A significant millenarian movement, called Taki Unquy, swept through the indigenous communities there in the 1560s. Taki Unquy was a revival of traditional native culture, transformed and reoriented toward revolt and liberation. Especially in the highlands of southern Peru, native priests spread the word of the resurrection of powerful Inka gods. This revival did not so much preach revolt against the Spaniards as it did rejection of Christianity; believers were called upon to cleanse themselves of Christian beliefs and prepare themselves for the second coming of all the old spirits and gods destroyed by the Conquest. As one Spanish priest understood it, "[T]hey believed that all the *huacas* [native spirits and religious images] of the Kingdom, all those the Christians had destroyed and burned, had come to life once more . . . that they were all preparing in the heavens to do battle against God, to conquer him, and that now they would bring victory. . . . Gold and the Spanish [language] would this time be vanquished and all the Spaniards slain, their cities engulfed and the sea would swell up to drown them and abolish their memory." In other words, the natives themselves did not have to revolt but merely prepare themselves for the new age. They could not wear European clothes, enter Christian churches, or cooperate with Spanish settlers and officials. Panic-stricken, many fled all contact with Spaniards and went into hiding.

Colonial repression of the cult of Taki Unquy was violent, for the leaders of the movement were considered heretics and apostates. Priests and other Spaniards equated the *wak'as* of Taki Unquy with the devil himself. The Spaniards hunted down the priests of Taki Unquy and flogged them, cut off their hair, and sent them into exile. Many Spanish settlers became concerned because the millennial movement coincided with the military conspiracy of the last Inka. Indeed, the Taki Unquy movement finally came to an end with the death of Túpac Amaru in 1572. Despite completion of the campaign against indigenous heresy in Peru, the Spaniards continued to uncover evidence of religious backsliding over the next two centuries. Even the natives themselves admitted to having difficulty separating the practice of Catholicism from the worship of their ancient gods (see Manuscript 6.4). Thereafter, the clergy maintained a constant vigilance against

MANUSCRIPT 6.4

Survival of Ancient Religious Rituals among Andean Peoples

Although the friars enjoyed enormous success in converting and baptizing Native Americans during the sixteenth century, they also realized how superficial the religious devotion of the conquered peoples could be. Often, the natives would combine the rituals and beliefs of the new Catholicism with those of their own pre-Columbian religions. This sort of religious syncretism was tolerated by the clergy, who permitted native artists to depict dark-skinned saints and encouraged the conversion of ancient myths into Christian guise. However, the priests declared war on the so-called idols and amulets of pre-Conquest origin. During such a campaign against heresy in Peru circa 1608, Father Francisco de Avila commissioned native scribes to write manuscripts in Quechua describing such acts of heresy. One of these texts, the Huarochirí Manuscript, demonstrates how the region's Native Americans preserved their ancient traditions and still honored among themselves those indigenous priests who kept alive the old rituals and beliefs. (Indeed, they are practiced even today in Ecuador, Peru, and Bolivia.) Note how the native scribes flatter their patron, Father Avila.

But now let's return to story of Paria Caca [a *wak'a*, or spirit] and to all the things people did during the season of his paschal festival. The story that explains these events is like this.

On the eve of the day when they were to arrive at Paria Caca for worship, people whose kin, whether men or women, had died in the course of that year would wail all night long, saying, "Tomorrow we'll go and see our dead by Paria Caca's side!"

They said regarding their deceased of the year, "Tomorrow is the day when we'll deliver them there."

They offered the dead food and even fed them that night, and spread out the ingredients for their rituals. They said, "Now I deliver them to Paria Caca forever. They will never come back any more!" And they worshiped with the sacrifice of a small llama, or, if they had no llamas, they'd bring coca in large skin bags.

As we know, they'd examine this llama's innards. If the signs were favorable, the *yanca* would prophesy, "Everything is well." If not, he'd say, "It's bad. You've incurred a fault. Your dead relative has angered Paria Caca. Ask forgiveness for this transgression, lest that fault be charged to you as well."

After completing these rituals, the *yancas* carried off the heads and loins of those llamas for themselves, no matter how many thousands there might be, declaring, "This is our fee!"

The *huacsas*, who'd dance on three occasions in any given year, would finish their term on that day. In order to enter a new cycle, when the old dance round was about to come to an end, all the people came to the center in Llacsa Tambo, and the Concha were in the plaza, too, carrying a macaw-wing display or the sort of thing known as *puypu*.

They'd lay these items in the center, on the rock called Llacsa Tambo.

After they deposited these things, they stayed there all night long, in the place where a cross now stands, wondering, "Will I be well this year?"

The next day they went to all the villages, including Macacho hill, Chaucalla, and Quimquilla, and remained there until five days were up.

At the end of the fifth day, all the *huacsas* who'd collected coca in bags would dance.

At daybreak on the same day, in Llacsa Tambo, they used to worship the demon with their llamas or other possessions.

Those who are privy to these customs do the same in all the villages.

Nowadays, it's true, some have forgotten these practices.

But since it is just a few years since they've had Doctor Francisco de Avila, a good counselor and teacher, it may be that in their hearts they don't really believe. If they had another priest they might return to the old ways.

Some people, although they've become Christians, have done so only out of fear. "I'm afraid the priest or somebody else might find out how bad I've been," they think.

Although they say the Rosary, they still carry some pretty *illa* amulet everywhere, although they themselves might not worship these native divinities, they contract some old people to worship in their stead. Lots of people live this way.

SOURCE: *The Huarochirí Manuscript: A Testament of Ancient and Colonial Andean Religion,* translated from the Quechua by Frank Salomon and George L. Urioste (Austin: University of Texas Press, 1991), 73–74.

"idolatry," a certain indication of how the first native converts had combined their older religious observances with Catholic practices.

The role of the church and the clergy in controlling the indigenous population's behavior becomes clear upon reading the catechisms and sermons of the time. Clerics who wrote "The Third Catechism," the chief guide to sermons in the seventeenth century, apparently addressed themselves to the behaviors they most often observed and disapproved. These sermons consistently emphasized the proper moral and political comportment that should be practiced in the local indigenous communities. Especially loathsome to the writers of the "The Third Catechism" were the endless complaints that the natives had been making—and filing—concerning the scandalous conduct of colonists, local officials and even priests. If anything, the sermons stressed, individual natives should inform on their own leaders who did not maintain proper conduct. But as for filing complaints against Spanish political and religious superiors, the catechism clearly stated: "Watch your tongue, brothers and sisters, and you will protect your soul." Natives were to accept the abuses and indignities heaped on them by both the political and the ecclesiastical authorities and to rely on God to punish their offenders in the final judgment.

The European strategy of converting the natives in order to control them worked well—but for the wrong reasons. The natives adopted the Catholic faith with varying degrees of enthusiasm. For the subordinated ones, Catholicism performed both hierarchical and collective functions. It bound the subjects to the Crown and the colonial state, whose laws theoretically protected indigenous peoples from the worst abuses of their social superiors, the Europeans and mestizos. Natives also looked to the clergy for protection from nonnatives. This protection was often more theoretical than real—more symbolic than effective. Priests and nuns themselves required unpaid personal service from their minions and were not above colluding with local Spaniards to exploit native labor. The priests attempted to keep others out of indigenous communities because the presence of outsiders diluted their control over the villagers. Be that as it may, the natives still sought protection in the church. They aggressively pressed clerical officials to preserve their land from outsiders and to reduce labor and tribute demands.

Catholicism also unified the natives within the community by contributing to the solidarity of the conquered. Village elders took charge of the *cofradías,* the religious brotherhoods that organized religious festivals; maintained the village chapel; provided for burials; and assisted the priest in administering the sacraments. All native inhabitants of the village identified with their own patron saint, distinguishing them from the rest of colonial society, even the Spaniards and mestizos who might have lived among them. Native leaders combined religious and civil functions and regained stature among the villagers. *Caciques* and *kurakas* even denounced the occasional backsliding priest who violated excessively the accepted norms of drink, of carnal pleasures, or of exploitation. Hispanicized society denigrated traditional customs and considered their practitioners ripe for victimization. "The bishop and the cleric and the religious and the nun and the viceroy and the judge and the *corregidores, vecinos* [neighbors or citizens, usually white] and soldiers—we all depend on [the natives] and we treat them like slaves," one official informed the king in 1602, "and what is most regrettable is that all the measures that Your Majesty takes on their behalf are subverted and end up causing them harm and further hardship." But the peasants used Catholicism as one of their strategies to accommodate themselves just enough to colonialism to be able to preserve ancient customs and their separate identity as "we people here."

ADAPTATION AND RESISTANCE

Because the indigenous hunters of North America and of southern South America offered no large reservoirs of wealth and labor, they underwent few initial changes to their economic and social lives as a result of European conquest. Transformation in their lifestyles would be more gradual. Yet, in the fullness of a longer contact with Iberian settlers, even these groups would confront disease, trade, and warfare. Just like the counterparts living in the more complex societies of Mesoamerica and the Andean regions, the indigenous peoples of the prairies would respond actively to maintain as many of their traditional values and lifestyles as possible. To accomplish their goal of preserving their autonomy from Europeans, they would eventually adopt those European goods and political institutions that helped them combat outright loss of their own traditions. Frontier groups effectively maintained their independent lifestyles, albeit changed by the presence of Iberians. In fact, successful adaptations of European diet and technology accounts for the initial success that these sturdy hunter-gatherers enjoyed in resisting the loss of their lands.

Chile

The Mapuche (Araucano), a hunter-gatherer people who inhabited the forest and lake regions of the south, had successfully resisted the Inka incursions that had brought the agricultural peoples of central Chile into the pre-Columbian empire. These latter natives submitted to Spanish conquest, paid tribute to the conquerors, and worked in their mining and agricultural enterprises. The presence of gold, which the natives produced by panning the rivers, sponsored the initial settlement of Spaniards in Chile. After 1545, Chile yielded approximately two thousand kilos of gold per year. But the decline of the indigenous population owing to epidemics as well as the exhaustion of the gold-bearing sands contributed to a decline in production. After 1565, only about five hundred kilos of gold were produced each year. Meanwhile, the hunt for gold had pushed Spanish occupation south of the Bío-Bío River, into territory never conquered by the Inka and inhabited by the Mapuche.

It was south of the Bío-Bío that the settlers met the fiercest indigenous resistance. The Mapuche had learned to ride horses, and they had devised an effective cavalry tactic in which a warrior seated behind the rider was free to shoot arrows at the enemy. Other cavalrymen had adopted the use of the long spear, to which they attached tips fashioned from metal captured by the settlers. The spear even became something of a religious relic to the Mapuche. "Here is my master," a warrior would say to his spear before battle. "This master does not make me dig gold, nor fetch him food or wood for his fire, nor guard his flocks, nor sow, nor reap. And since this master leaves my freedom, it is with him that I wish to go." As well, the Mapuche had borrowed other European customs to reinforce their resistance. They took to raising cattle and growing wheat and barley, and they regrouped their scattered clans into larger formations to do battle. But Mapuche resistance depended also on enhancing elements of their traditional religious practices, such as promoting their gods and spirits of war. They may even have adopted cannibalism from other indigenous groups in order to ritualize and fortify their resolve. Finally, in 1598, the Mapuche made their big move. In a savage campaign, they forced the Spanish settlers to evacuate the region south of the Bío-Bío River. And from that time until the nineteenth century, the south of Chile remained their country.

Argentina

The Native Americans of the Pampas were particularly adept at maintaining their independence and autonomy from the Spaniards. The Querandí, who populated the southern shore of the Río de la Plata estuary, besieged and fought to a standstill the remnants of Pedro de Mendoza's expedition at Buenos Aires in 1536. Their hostility forced the Spaniards to abandon the settlement and move up the Paraná River to Asunción. Forty-four years later, the descendants of those Spaniards returned to found Buenos Aires. This time, the Paraguayan expedition headed by Juan de Garay defeated the Querandí, many of whom were given to the victorious conquerors as war slaves and *encomienda* workers. But the prairie natives, especially the men, did not work well for others. A Querandí war party ambushed and slew Garay in 1583. Across the estuary, the Charrúa of Uruguay and southern Brazil also strengthened their autonomy by adapting certain European customs. They began to ride horses shortly after the turn of the seventeenth century. The Charrúa also changed their diet. In addition to their traditional fish and game, they came to subsist on beef from the growing herds of wild cattle. Many of these peoples remained on the prairies separate from the European communities along the riverbanks and, despite trading with the Europeans, continued to raid and make war into the nineteenth century.

These changes—some subtle, others not so subtle—to the lifestyles of indigenous peoples were played out in other southern regions as well. On the broad expanses of the Pampas, the European settlers had introduced horses, sheep, and cattle. Soon the small, seminomadic bands of Native Americans adopted and domesticated these European animals to their own uses. The horse permitted the groups to became even more nomadic, hunting far and wide across the virgin prairies. The men gave up their bows and arrows for the spear and the *bolas,* which were more easily used from horseback. They mounted large hunting expeditions and raiding parties on other indigenous groups as well as on European settlements. Their diets became richer in animal protein, and they converted the hides and leather into housing and daily implements. The women became even more relegated to hand labor, thus freeing the men for hunting; they were subordinated within the roving bands, accomplishing the menial chores around the encampments, preparing the meals, tending to the children, stripping and drying the hides, and making the clothing. The natives periodically raided the settlements along the extended trading route from Potosí down to Buenos Aires. Throughout the entire colonial period, the Spaniards could not establish haciendas on the fertile Pampas beyond a line running 100 kilometers south of Buenos Aires. Behind this frontier, the southern hunters lived off the wild cattle that roamed the plains.

The natives of the Río de la Plata region, like indigenous peoples elsewhere in the Americas, began to use more European goods. To acquire these wares, they developed the economic resources to carry on trade with each other and with settler communities. They began to raise cattle, sheep, and horses. Their women manufactured handicrafts—feather goods, skins, and saddles—from these and other animals of the Pampas. The men raised or raided for cattle to sell in Tucumán and Paraguay or to Araucanian [Mapuche] groups across the southern Andean passes in Chile. Native traders established an extensive system of cattle trails over the southern Andean passes, including corrals and mountain pastures for fattening the cattle for Chilean markets. Indigenous people traded among themselves and with Europeans for Paraguayan tea (yerba maté), tobacco, brandy, arms, metal tools, sugar, and European clothing.

Native society on the southern plains became more differentiated and complex. Fighting men enhanced their status, and the families of great warriors evolved into a kind of lineage of leaders. Group and tribal councils did not give way to authoritarian kings, but great battle leaders and those with oratorial skills consolidated rule over larger and larger conglomerations of indigenous peoples. Successful warriors and families amassed wealth. They possessed many horses, herds of cattle, and numerous personal followers. An important leader could acquire up to seven wives, each of whom linked him in political alliance to other warrior families. Hunting bands stressed capturing women and children, especially from settler communities, who could be used as slave laborers, concubines, and objects for trade.

As commercial exchange intensified at the end of the seventeenth century, so did the tensions between Europeanized settler society and these evolving native societies. Warfare between settlers and natives encouraged the continued militarization of both cultures in the Río de la Plata region. Nonetheless, a coexistence emerged. The settlers remained in their towns, on their lands nearby, and on the great cart trails that linked them to Mendoza in the west, Potosí in the north, and Buenos Aires in the east. South of this arc of settlements remained the world of the southern hunters. Where the two cultures meshed along the frontier line, alternating cycles of trade and warfare occurred.

Paraguay

The indigenous inhabitants of the Chaco of western Paraguay successfully kept the Spaniards at bay as well. In the first place, the Gran Chaco, barren and desolate, held no economic basis for European settlement. Early attempts by the colonists of Asunción to traverse the Chaco to reach Bolivia, the source of silver, ended in vain. The first expeditions, in the 1530s, went awry when attacked by Native Americans. Pizarro's Panamanian-based conquest of Peru in 1538, which led to his men controlling access to much gold and silver, rendered useless any further Spanish excursions from Paraguay. However, the Chaco peoples were soon influenced by the European presence at Asunción. Through trade, they obtained desirable new commodities, textiles, iron weapons and kitchenware, and alcoholic beverages. They adopted pork and beef into their diets; learned to weave cloth from wool, which led to their abandoning skin garments; and increased their consumption of yerba maté. The arrival of the Jesuit missionaries in the seventeenth century certainly upset the shamans and annoyed the chiefs who had more than one wife (an annoyance for which many missionary priests met their martyrdom). But the Chaco hunters also learned to sow the new crops and domesticate the new livestock, which provided a more secure diet.

The horse, however, was the European contribution that, once adopted, changed the lives of the Chaco people most thoroughly. Horses made hunting easier and enabled indigenous groups to burst through their old territorial boundaries. Previously migratory peoples became veritable vagabonds. But the horse enabled the more aggressive hunting groups to incorporate (even enslave) the marginal groups. Jesuit exhortations to the contrary, the Abipón of the southern bank of the Paraguay River took to raiding over long distances. In the mid-seventeenth century, they allied with another tribe to attack the settlers at Santiago del Estero. Intertribal rivalries also intensified, and some smaller hunter cultures, weakened by the ravages of disease, disappeared or were amalgamated into the aggressor groups. For example, the Abipón turned on some of their erstwhile allies, after which these expert horsemen looted the town of Santa Fe in 1751. "The Abipones imitate skillful chess players," said one missionary. "After committing slaughter in the southern colonies of the Spaniards, they retire far northwards, afflict the city of Asunción with murders and rapine, and then hurry back to the south." To a certain degree, the Abipón used the horse to stave off tribal extinction because the diseases that began to ravage them in the seventeenth century had reduced their numbers from 5,000 to 2,000.

On the north side of the Gran Chaco, the largest linguistic group of the region, the Mbayá, also used the horse to consolidate its hegemony over smaller tribes and reinforce its autonomy from the Spaniards and the Portuguese. In 1661 Mbayá horsemen destroyed the missions north of Asunción and attacked settlers' farms, and Asunción itself was threatened. Not until 1744 did the governor of Asunción organize a force that drove out the invaders. Mounted warriors counterattacked and destroyed the settlement of Curuquatí but made peace with the settlers in 1756.

In the meanwhile, other groups of the Mbayá dismounted and allied with the canoe people, the Payaguá, and learned the art of river warfare. They moved north into the region explored by the Portuguese. In 1700, they began ambushing canoe traders and settlers moving into the backlands from São Paulo. Occupying a large territory between two rival European empires, the Mbayá obtained favors from both the Portuguese and the Spaniards. Gifts of food, tools, and weapons were meant to win Mbayá cooperation but did not entirely succeed. This powerful Chaco group killed an estimated four thousand Brazilians during the eighteenth century. The larger Chaco groups remained unconquered by the Europeans, partly by adopting some elements of foreign material culture. However, the Payaguá gave up their independent existence in exchange for the material benefits offered by settler society. In 1741, they moved to Asunción, where they resided in a separate barrio well into the nineteenth century. But the lives of those who remained beyond the frontier also changed in many ways. Warfare intensified, and frontier violence with settlers escalated beyond any possibility of peaceful coexistence. The colonial period proved to be the Indian summer, as it were, of the southern hunters. Their violent resistance was destined to cost them their very cultural and linguistic existence.

Northern Mexico

Although the Nahua of central Mexico had submitted to the Spanish and the Mixton War had pacified their cousins to the west, the hunter-gatherers of the semi-arid region stretching north from the mountains of Zacatecas to the present-day U.S.–Mexican border continued their resistance. War with the Chichimec lasted into the nineteenth century. These numerous peoples were considered to be barbarians, subsisting on fruits and roots and wild game, and their clothes and customs were those of a wandering people (see Manuscript 6.5). This turned out to be a long campaign of annihilation as well

MANUSCRIPT 6.5

Account of the Chichimec

Among those nomadic, hunter-gatherer groups that so stubbornly resisted European encroachment from the plains of Argentina and the jungle lowlands of Venezuela to the plains of North America were the legendary Chichimec. This is the name that the agricultural peoples of Mesoamerica gave to the nonagricultural tribes inhabiting the semi-arid northern plateau stretching from present-day Guanajuato into Texas. These groups spoke many languages, roamed in small bands, and raided and harassed both the settled Nahua and the Spanish settlers who moved into the northern Mexican silver regions. These groups were so formidable because of their political and social decentralization. The Spaniards could not command the submission of these indigenous groups simply by capturing the native king, as they had among the Caribbean, Mesoamerican, and Andean peoples. Governed by councils rather than by powerful chieftains, the Chichimec often fought to the last man, woman, and child. They gained the reputation of being merciless to their enemies. At times equally merciless, Spanish frontiersmen carried on a war with various Chichimec groups for well over two centuries. The last Chichimec war ended in 1748. In the passage below, a Spanish official, Gonzalo de Las Casas, described the Chichimec he had encountered in 1574.

They have marriage, each having his own wife. Marriages are contracted through the mediation of the relatives. Through marriage enemies are often reconciled. Usually, when marrying into another band, the husband adopts the residence of his wife. They also have divorce, although usually it is the wife who repudiates the husband and not the reverse. All the work falls on the women, not only preparation of food but also carrying the children and all the loads on their backs when they move from place to place. The men carry nothing but their bow and arrows for fighting and hunting. The women serve the men like slaves, even giving them tunas [cactus pears] peeled. . . .

They bear their children with great distress, because, having no houses and roaming constantly, they often give birth while traveling. Even with the placenta hanging and dripping blood they walk on as if they were sheep or cows. They wash their infants, or, if there is no water, clean them with herbs. They have nothing to give their children but their own milk, nor do they wrap them in blankets, because they have none. They have no cradles, no houses for shelter, nothing more than a piece of cloth or a rock, and in such harsh conditions they live and rear their children.

Their food consists of fruit and wild roots. They neither sow nor gather any sort of vegetables, nor do they have any cultivated trees. The fruits which they use most are tunas, of many varieties and colors, some of them delicious. They also eat the fruit of another tree called mesquite, a well-known wild tree which bears pods like string beans, which they eat and from which they make bread to keep and eat when the fresh fruit is gone. They have another fruit which we call dates; although the trees which bear them are not date palms they resemble them. Of the roots which they eat, some resemble sweet potatoes or yuca. . . .

The maguey is a great help and support to them, for it is never lacking. They make use of all of it, as do the people of New Spain, except that they do not make clothing from it. They eat the leaves and the root cooked in an earth oven which they call "mizcale," and it is good food, and they also make wine from it. All the roots mentioned above they also cook in the earth oven, since they are inedible raw.

They support themselves mostly on game, which they hunt every day. They shoot hares on the run, and deer and birds and other game, even rats. A few of them also fish. Some fish with arrows; others catch the fish in weirs or basket nets, and some swim and dive for fish. If they happen to kill a deer, the woman must come after it, because the man does not carry loads. The women also have to gather fruit and roots, and clean and cook them, after returning from the hunt. . . .

They go completely naked. The women wear a belt of deer skins, the others go entirely nude. Among themselves they are not ashamed to be naked and do not permit clothing. When they parley with us they show some modesty, and seek the wherewithal, if only rags and herbs to cover their privy parts. They frequently paint themselves, smearing on red ocher and other minerals of black, yellow, and all colors.

SOURCE: As quoted in Harold E. Driver and Wilhelmine Driver, "Ethnography and Acculturation of the Chichimeca-Jonaz of Northeast Mexico," *International Journal of American Linguistics* 29, no. 2, part II (1963): 15 – 18. Translated by Wilhelmine Driver.

as acculturation. Settlers, military garrisons, missionaries, and acculturated Native Americans sent from central Mexico all played a role in pushing back the Chichimec frontier.

The Spaniards might have been content to ignore the Chichimec, but in 1546 an expedition discovered the silver mines of Zacatecas, more than five hundred kilometers north of Mexico City. Additional deposits of silver were discovered farther north in the present states of Durango, Chihuahua, and Nuevo León. Long lines of communication through the deserts and across the mountains were essential to successfully tap this source of wealth, and the royal officials as well as the settlers who managed to establish the mines desired to secure them against disruption. The Chichimec resisted. They besieged Zacatecas in 1561, and in the late sixteenth and early seventeenth centuries, they periodically threatened to cut off the isolated mining towns from Mexico City. The Chichimec became formidable enemies because they adopted the use of horses, became expert cavalrymen, and acquired a taste for cattle, for which they raided the haciendas surrounding the mining zones. Their bows and arrows nearly matched the Spanish arquebuses.

Spaniards adopted several strategies to reduce these needling attacks. Spanish miners and settlers became dedicated to fighting the natives and, indeed, began to hunt them to turn them into slaves for work in the mines. Authorities in Mexico City established small military garrisons, called *presidios,* in the mining zone. Finally came the effort to acculturate the Chichimec. The viceroys began to send out Native Americans from central Mexico who had been adapting themselves to Christianity, European ways, and Spanish political authority for three generations. In 1591, more than one hundred families from the loyal city of Tlaxcala arrived in San Luis Potosí and Saltillo, where they received land and privileges. They and other indigenous settlers were to demonstrate how the natives could benefit from adopting European lifestyles. Finally, the Spaniards sent military expeditions to the extreme northern flank of Chichimec country because the rebels had been trading profitably in stolen cattle with the Pueblo of what is now New Mexico, whom the Spaniards successfully conquered in 1598, at which time they established a settlement at Santa Fe. However, the Apaches and Comanches of the plains and plateaus of the far north preserved their freedom from the European colonists until well into the nineteenth century. Although isolated Chichimec groups held out in the remotest mountains, the mining zones of northern New Spain had been securely established by the mid-seventeenth century.

CONCLUDING REMARKS

How does one account for the fact that, although they outnumbered the Spaniards for the entire colonial period, the Native Americans did not rise up en masse and throw out the colonists? Such a rebellion from below was, of course, an abiding fear among Spaniards. For this reason, they did not tolerate Native Americans in central Mexico and Peru bearing arms or even riding horses. But one might question the effectiveness of outright Spanish oppression, for elite competition weakened the Spanish hegemony considerably. As already mentioned, the natives could and did play powerful Spanish factions against each other in order to preserve some areas of cultural autonomy.

The answer to the Native Americans' inability to unify in resistance lay in the cultural barriers among them. The differences of language, dress, and customs revealed deep-seated, separate identities and mutual rivalries rooted in the pre-Columbian era. Even the Maya of the densely populated highlands of Guatemala lacked cultural unity; when the Spanish arrived, they spoke more than thirty different dialects and were generally unable to understand one another. For these reasons, Europeans always found willing native allies in the business of subjugating other native groups. These pre-Columbian rivalries did not stop after the Conquest; during the long colonial period, villages in central Mexico and Peru haggled with each other over control of land, water resources, and exemptions from tribute and labor drafts. They were more apt to request the assistance of the clergy and administrators against rival indigenous groups than to unite against the Europeans. In this manner, the few Europeans were able to maintain their positions of privilege over the native masses throughout the colonial period.

Nonetheless, the indigenous peoples of the Americas found ways to preserve their own cultural heritage during the formative first two centuries of colonialism. In the first place, the Europeans could not establish themselves as rulers without adopting indigenous crops, strategies of frontier survival, and social institutions. The first Spaniards in Paraguay and the first Portuguese frontiersmen at São Paulo ate the local foods, slept in hammocks, and even merged with established tribal family structures through unions with native women. In Mexico and Peru, Spaniards also built upon existing indigenous social structures much as had the Aztec and Inka before them. The *encomenderos* divided up tribute payers according to the existing structures of the *altepetl* and the *ayllu,* whose indigenous leaders continued to mediate between their groups and the outside authorities. These social units also provided the basis for the European institutions of the Catholic parishes, religious brotherhoods, and labor drafts.

Therefore, where indigenous peoples had already constructed elaborate social institutions to govern dense populations, as in the Andean region and Mesoamerica, and where they survived the carnage of disease, as in the temperate highlands, that is where European colonialism also assumed formal elaboration. More importantly, the natives accepted those elements of European institutions that permitted them to reconstitute their cultures following the Conquest. In the recreation of village life, the local nobility found a new but altered existence, and the peasants combined their old methods of social relations with the new demands for tribute and labor. Their religious practices drew few distinctions between their ancient beliefs and Christian dogma but combined the compatible elements into locally distinctive brands of Native American Catholicism. Indigenous peoples also accepted Iberian material culture—foods, animals, beasts of burden, iron tools, and weaponry—that enriched their diets and fortified their resistance on the frontiers. Considering all the fearful consequences of the Conquest, the indigenous peoples reconstituted themselves and their cultures—albeit in new forms—with remarkable vigor.

But the destruction was worse in some places than in others. Contact with European settlers and diseases wreaked irreversible destruction to indigenous peoples in some tropical and coastal settings. Moreover, the cultures that had developed in the rain forests produced individuals who were ill suited for the most extreme labor demands of colonialism—and thus the Africans were brought in to fill the gap.

Additional Reading

Adorno, Rolena. *Guaman Poma: Writing and Resistance in Colonial Peru.* Austin: University of Texas Press, 1994.

Alchon, Suzanne Austin. *Native Society and Disease in Colonial Ecuador.* Cambridge, England: Cambridge University Press, 1991.

Block, David. *Mission Culture on the Upper Amazon: Native Tradition, Jesuit Enterprise, and Secular Policy in Moxos, 1660–1880.* Lincoln: University of Nebraska Press, 1994.

Burkhart, Louise M. *The Slippery Earth: Nahua-Christian Moral Dialogue in Sixteenth-Century Mexico.* Tucson: University of Arizona Press, 1989.

Calero, Luis F. *Chiefdoms under Siege: Spain's Rule and Native Adaptation in the Southern Colombian Andes, 1535–1700.* Albuquerque: University of New Mexico Press, 1997.

Cervantes, Fernando. *The Devil in the New World: The Impact of Diabolism in New Spain.* New Haven, Conn.: Yale University Press, 1994.

Chance, John K. *Conquest of the Sierra: Spaniards and Indians in Colonial Oaxaca.* Norman: University of Oklahoma Press, 1989.

———. *Race and Class in Colonial Oaxaca.* Stanford, Calif.: Stanford University Press, 1978.

Cline, S. L. *Colonial Culhuacan, 1580–1600.* Albuquerque: University of New Mexico Press, 1986.

Cline, S. L., and Miguel León-Portilla, eds. and trans. *The Testaments of Culhuacan.* Los Angeles: UCLA Latin American Center, 1984.

Collier, George A., Renato I. Rosaldo, and John D. Wirth. *The Inca and Aztec States, 1400–1800: Anthropology and History.* New York: Academic Press, 1982.

Cook, Noble David. *Demographic Collapse: Indian Peru, 1520–1620.* Cambridge, England: Cambridge University Press, 1981.

Espinoza, J. Manuel. *The Pueblo Indian Revolt of 1696 and the Franciscan Missions in New Mexico: Letters of the Missionaries and Related Documents.* Norman: University of Oklahoma Press, 1991.

Gosner, Kevin. *Soldiers of the Virgin: The Moral Economy of a Colonial Maya Rebellion.* Tucson: University of Arizona Press, 1992.

Griffiths, Nicholas. *The Cross and the Serpent: Religious Repression and Resurgence in Colonial Peru.* Norman: University of Oklahoma Press, 1996.

Gruzinski, Serge. *The Conquest of Mexico: The Incorporation of Indian Societies into the Western World, 16th–18th Centuries.* Trans. Eileen Corrigan. Cambridge, England: Polity Press, 1993.

———. *Man-Gods in the Mexican Highlands: Indian Power and Colonial Society, 1520–1800.* Stanford, Calif.: Stanford University Press, 1989.

Haskett, Robert. *Indigenous Rulers: An Ethnohistory of Town Government in Colonial Cuernavaca.* Albuquerque: University of New Mexico Press, 1991.

Hemming, John. *Red Gold: The Conquest of the Brazilian Indians.* Cambridge, Mass.: Harvard University Press, 1978.

Horn, Rebecca. *Postconquest Coyoacán: Nahua-Spanish Relations in Central Mexico, 1519–1650.* Stanford, Calif.: Stanford University Press, 1997.

Hu De-Hart, Evelyn. *Missionaries, Miners and Indians: Spanish Contact with the Yaqui Nation of North Western New Spain, 1533–1820.* Tucson: University of Arizona Press, 1981.

Kellogg, Susan. *Law and the Transformation of Aztec Culture, 1500–1700.* Norman: University of Oklahoma Press, 1995.

Kicza, John E., ed. *The Indian in Latin American History: Resistance, Resilience, and Acculturation.* Wilmington, Del.: Scholarly Resources, 1993.

Knaut, Andrew L. *The Pueblo Revolt of 1680: Conquest and Resistance in Seventeenth-Century New Mexico.* Norman: University of Oklahoma Press, 1995.

Konrad, Herman W. *A Jesuit Hacienda in Colonial Mexico: Santa Lucía, 1576–1767.* Stanford, Calif.: Stanford University Press, 1980.

Lockhart, James. *The Nahuas after the Conquest: A Social and Cultural History of the Indians of Central Mexico, Sixteenth through Eighteenth Centuries.* Stanford, Calif.: Stanford University Press, 1992.

Lovell, W. George. *Conquest and Survival in Colonial Guatemala: A Historical Geography of the Cuchumatán Highlands, 1500–1821.* Kingston, Ontario: McGill-Queen's University Press, 1985.

Mills, Kenneth. *Idolatry and Its Enemies: Colonial Andean Religion and Extirpation, 1640–1750.* Princeton, N.J.: Princeton University Press, 1997.

Newson, Linda A. *The Cost of Conquest: Indian Decline in Honduras under Spanish Rule.* Boulder, Colo.: Westview Press, 1986.

——. *Life and Death in Early Colonial Ecuador.* Norman: University of Oklahoma Press, 1995.

Pagden, Anthony. *The Fall of Natural Man: The American Indian and the Origins of Comparative Ethnology.* Cambridge, England: Cambridge University Press, 1982.

Patch, Robert W. *Maya and Spaniard in Yucatán, 1648–1812.* Stanford, Calif.: Stanford University Press, 1993.

Powell, Philip Wayne. *Soldiers, Indians and Silver: North America's First Frontier War.* Tempe: Arizona State University Press, 1975.

Ramirez, Susan E. *The World Upside Down: Cross-Cultural Contact and Conflict in Sixteenth-Century Peru.* Stanford, Calif.: Stanford University Press, 1996.

Restall, Matthew. *The Maya World: Yucatec Culture and Society, 1550–1850.* Stanford, Calif.: Stanford University Press, 1997.

Salles-Reese, Veronica. *From Viracocha to the Virgin of Copacabana: Representation of the Sacred at Lake Titicaca.* Austin: University of Texas Press, 1996.

Schroeder, Susan. *Chimalpahin and the Kingdoms of Chalco.* Tucson: University of Arizona Press, 1991.

Schroeder, Susan, Stephanie Wood, and Robert Haskett, eds. *Indian Women of Early Mexico.* Norman: University of Oklahoma Press, 1997.

Silverblatt, Irene. *Moon, Sun, and Witches: Gender Ideologies and Class in Inca and Colonial Peru.* Princeton, N.J.: Princeton University Press, 1987.

Spalding, Karen. *Huarochirí: An Andean Society under Inca and Spanish Rule.* Stanford, Calif.: Stanford University Press, 1984.

Stern, Steve J. *Peru's Indian Peoples and the Challenge of Spanish Conquest: Huamanga to 1640.* Madison: University of Wisconsin Press, 1982.

Taylor, William B. *Landlord and Peasant in Colonial Oaxaca.* Stanford, Calif.: Stanford University Press, 1972.

Wightman, Ann M. *Indigenous Migration and Social Change: The Forasteros of Cuzco, 1570–1720.* Durham, N.C.: Duke University Press, 1990.

In Spanish

Carbonell de Masy, Rafael. *Estrategias de desarrollo rural en los pueblos guaraníes (1609–1767).* Barcelona: Antoni Bosch, 1992.

Carmagnani, Marcello. *El regreso de los dioses: El proceso de reconstitución de la identidad étnica en Oaxaca, siglos xvii y xviii.* México City: Fondo de Cultura Económica, 1988.

García Martínez, Bernardo. *Los pueblos de la Sierra: El poder y el espacio entre los indios del norte de Puebla hasta 1700.* México City: El Colegio de México, 1987.

Jara, Alvaro. *Guerra y sociedad en Chile: La transformación de la guerra de Arauco y la esclavitud de los indios.* Santiago: Editorial Universitaria, 1971.

León Solís, Leonardo. *Maloqueros y conchavadores en Araucanía y las Pampas, 1700-1800.* Temuco, Chile: Ediciones Universidad de la Frontera, 1990.

Monteiro, John Manuel. *Negros da terra: índios e bandeirantes nas origens de São Paulo.* São Paulo: Companhia das Letras, 1994.

Río, Ignacio del. *Conquista y aculturación en la California jesuítica, 1697–1768.* Mexico City: Universidad Nacional Autónoma de México, 1984.

Sánchez Albornoz, Nicolás. *Indios y tributos en el Alto Perú.* Lima: Instituto de Estudios Peruanos, 1980.

Szeminski, Jan. *Un kuraca, un díos y una historia.* Buenos Aires: Facultad de Filosofía y Letras, Universidad de Buenos Aires, 1987.

Vainfas, Ronaldo. *A heresia dos índios: Catolicismo e rebeldia no Brasil colonial.* São Paulo: Companhia das Letras, 1995.

CHAPTER 7

AFRICAN AMERICANS

Within a few years of the voyage of Columbus, the Spanish Crown made the fateful decision to permit the importation of Africans as slaves into the Americas. "[Do not] give permission to come there Moors, nor Jews, nor heretics, nor persons newly converted to our faith," decreed the Catholic rulers, Ferdinand and Isabella, "except if they are Negro slaves." Thus began history's greatest forced migration of human beings. The Iberian nations that colonized the Americas first entered the slave trade in the early sixteenth century; the last of the Spanish colonies, Cuba and Puerto Rico, did not abandon the institution of slavery itself until 1866. From the sixteenth century, Brazil depended on slave labor more than any other area in the Americas outside of the U.S. South. In 1850, Brazil became the last nation to outlaw the slave trade and not until 1888 did it emancipate its slaves—the last American nation to do so. Although both Spaniards and Portuguese settlers had enslaved indigenous peoples, slavery in the Americas came to be identified more with Africans.

Ten to 13 million Africans arrived in the Americas during the 350 years of the trans-Atlantic slave trade. However, at least two and a half million other Africans may have died en route. Indeed, some scholars estimate that up to 50 percent of Africans taken for slavery may have perished before arriving at their intended destinations. Many succumbed in Africa to the violence of capture and initial incarceration. The poor conditions aboard

Table 7.1   African Slave Imports and Iberian Immigration to Spanish America and Brazil

	SPANISH AMERICA		BRAZIL	
	Immigration	*Slave Imports*	*Immigration*	*Slave Imports*
Sixteenth century	243,000	75,000	30,000*	50,000
Seventeenth century	450,000	292,500	100,000*	560,000
Eighteenth century to 1810	N/A	578,600	400,000	1,891,400

* These figure represent the approximate number of resident whites (whether native born or immigrants).

SOURCES: Nicolás Sánchez-Albornoz, "The Population of Colonial Spanish America," and Maria Luiza Marcílio, "The Population of Colonial Brazil," both in *Cambridge History of Latin America* (Cambridge, England: Cambridge University Press, 1984), 3–36, 37–65; Magnus Mörner with Harold Sims, *Adventurers and Proletarians: The Story of Migrants in Latin America* (Pittsburgh: University of Pittsburgh, 1985), 8–9; Philip Curtin, *The Atlantic Slave Trade: A Census* (Madison: University of Wisconsin Press, 1969), 116, 119, 216; Lyle N. McAlister, *Spain and Portugal in the New World, 1492-1700* (Minneapolis: University of Minnesota Press, 1984), 342; and Celso Furtado, *The Economic Growth of Brazil: A Survey from Colonial to Modern Times* (Berkeley: University of California Press, 1965), 911.

the slave ships took additional victims. Moreover, the newly arrived slave had to undergo a period of "seasoning," the brutal introduction to work discipline in the Americas. Thereafter, the rigorous work regimen and poor nutrition considerably shortened the life span of those Africans who survived the journey. The number of Africans slaves who landed in the Spanish-American and Brazilian colonies surpassed the number of European immigrants who freely went there to seek new lives. In Brazil, perhaps as many as five Africans entered the colony for each white Portuguese immigrant (see Table 7.1). True, the Africans' immunities from Old World diseases prevented them from sharing the frightful demographic losses of the Native Americans. Yet their own suffering was equally significant—and premature death was ever present.

Blacks imported to the New World endured multiple indignities and even lacked many of the legal protections of the natives. They were slaves, after all—considered to be property rather than a part of humanity. The voyage from Africa to select locations within the Americas had been involuntary, degrading, and dangerous. Their owners feared them. So slave traders and buyers purposely diluted their cultural unity—separating Africans of common regional, linguistic, cultural, and religious backgrounds. Typically, recently arrived slaves could not even communicate with each other, for shipments consisted of African peoples of diverse origins. Slavery meant that Africans had no legal status and fewer remedies to ameliorate their conditions. Having sole and nearly unlimited authority over their slaves, owners could abuse their property as they saw fit, with no accountability. African females (males, too) fell prey to sexual depravities; family life was difficult. They did not own land, and few were permitted to practice a trade. Only through the cracks of the slave system could the slaves gain access to independent subsistence in the Americas.

When the occasion presented itself, some Africans found amelioration of their suffering by joining the system that oppressed them. They became supervisors for their owners; a few purchased their freedom. Finally, Africans contributed their blood to a uniquely American caste—the mulattoes. Born of a white male and a black female (seldom the reverse), the mulattoes identified with Europeans in dress, manners, and language and developed a culture containing elements of their African heritage but without identifying with newly arrived Africans. As was the case with mestizos, these crosses between black and white did not find wholehearted acceptance in the European world, and their fathers seldom acknowledged their paternity. But in the Portuguese and Spanish Americas, mulattoes did not confront the opposition of a large white working class. They summoned enough social status to gain acceptance as small farmers and lower-ranking artisans. Most mulattoes were born free and joined the social system that condoned slavery. A few themselves owned slaves.

Yet despite all the disadvantages, African slaves contributed to shaping their new environment. In plantations, farms, and mines across the hemisphere, Africans resurrected their traditions and created new ones. They reconstituted families and religion. They revived their songs and dances, melding together hundreds of tribal influences and the language of their masters into distinctive cultural forms. The resilience and determination of these slaves explains the survival today of African music and religion in places like Cuba, Brazil, coastal Peru, and Panama. But the ownership of slaves also affected the attitudes and behaviors of the white colonial elite in ways that are perceptible today. Slavery corrupted the heritage of both the African and the European.

THE MIDDLE PASSAGE

Europe had known the African slave trade long before the voyage of Columbus. Portuguese mariners who navigated the African coasts introduced African peoples to Europe. Those Europeans who settled the Atlantic islands of Madeira, Cape Verde, and the Canaries introduced slaves there, too. When the Portuguese colonized the island of São Tomé, off the West Coast of Africa, they introduced slave labor to the production of sugar. So firm was Portugal's control of Africa's West Coast in the sixteenth century that Spain had to use Portuguese merchants to supply the slaves for its New World colonies. Portugal had certain advantages in the African slave trade that benefited its traders: They already had trading factories along the coast, and the profits of their lucrative Native American trade provided the credit to sell slaves to cash-short American colonists. So prominent in the slave trade were sixteenth-century Portuguese merchants that they counted themselves among the wealthiest residents of Spanish cities such as Lima and Buenos Aires. Some might make 20 to 30 percent on their investments in a good year. The only way the Crown could control them was through the Holy Office of the Inquisition, because the merchants had the civilian officials in their pay. In fact, 12 prominent Portuguese slave traders in South America were burned at the stake in 1635. Rather than being charged with fraud in the slave trade, the Inquisition accused these men of being crypto Jews—which most denied.

The Spanish Crown established a slave-importing monopoly, called the *asiento*, which it issued first to Portuguese traders. Throughout the sixteenth century, the *asiento* permitted Portuguese ships to enter Spanish-American ports such as Veracruz, Portobello, and Cartagena to sell Africans. Brazil also became an important emporium for the reexport of slaves to the Río de la Plata. In the seventeenth century, the Dutch and French merchant houses occasionally held some of the *asiento* contracts, displacing the Portuguese. British traders dominated the slave trade in the eighteenth century. By then, the British possessions in the Caribbean, especially Jamaica, emerged as important slave

African slaves grinding cane at a sugar mill on Hispaniola. (Teodoro de Bry, 17th century)

trading entrepôts. The *asiento* was the long-term contract between the Spanish Crown and an individual or company for what was in fact only a semimonopoly of the sale of licenses to import slaves into the Spanish Americas. These permits became part of the king's foreign policy, as the wholesale licenses went to important bankers and trading companies in Portugal, Flanders, France, and England.

The Crowns of Spain and Portugal regulated the slave trade for their own financial benefit. Only the king's staunchest supporters in the mother country and the colonies received the coveted licenses to buy and sell slaves within the Americas, usually after paying a handsome fee. At the ports, Crown officials collected duties on the importation of African slaves. Finally, royal officials collected sales taxes on each slave sold at auction or in individual transfer thereafter. Tax evasion was rampant and also a great source of graft for colonial authorities seeking to gain financially from their political positions. As the Spanish-American colonies matured, the number of slaves imported for the mines, cities, and plantations also grew. Five hundred Africans per year were entering the Spanish Americas by 1550. By the end of the sixteenth century, that number had risen to 810 per year. The figure for slave imports rose sharply to approximately two thousand eight hundred eighty Africans per year by 1640.

African Origins

That African languages and ethnic identities did not survive intact should not be surprising, given the conspiratorial efforts of Europeans to undermine those very elements. First of all, the origins of the Africans who were brought to the Americas were varied. In the sixteenth and seventeenth centuries, slave traders of many nationalities (French, Dutch, and British as well as Spanish and Portuguese) established trading posts and fortresses along the West Coast of Africa. European traders gathered cargoes of slaves from the Gold Coast, directly below the Sahara Desert, from the Congo and Angola. Other traders less frequently picked up human cargoes on the East Coast of Africa at Mozambique. They dealt with tribal chieftains, who brought them prisoners taken from rival tribes in battles and raids. European trinkets, hardware, fabrics, and guns formed the medium of exchange. From the New World, tobacco, sugar, manioc flour, and rum also entered into the bargain.

The demand for slaves encouraged warfare and mutual raiding among the tribes of West Africa. The Bioho of Guinea carried on a thriving business with the Portuguese by raiding the villages of their neighbors. Heavily armed groups of Portuguese hawkers traveled to the interior of Africa, bartering imported trinkets with the tribes and marching long lines of chained captives to the trading factories on the coasts. Along the Guinea coast, the principal barter items were textiles (some of which the Portuguese imported from India), wine, garlic, beads, gunpowder, and iron. On the coast, the captors held victims in stockades, where they ate poorly, endured the first lessons in "work discipline," and boarded wooden sailing ships in lots of 100 to 400 persons. Many of those entering the slave trade died before they ever embarked from their homelands.

As the king required the slaves to be given the benefit of religious instruction, the slavers assembled the human cargoes at a chapel prior to embarkation. Portuguese priests delivered sermons on the superiority of Christianity and then passed among non-Portuguese-speaking slaves to assign them Christian names and distribute their first communion to them. "Look, you people are now children of God," the priests would pronounce. "You are going to the lands of the Spaniards where you will learn the things of the Holy Faith. Think no more of the lands you are leaving, and don't eat dogs, rats, or horses. Now go with a good will."

The clergy felt little moral repugnance for their role in promoting and participating in the slave trade. Padre Bartolomé de las Casas, who gained fame for his attacks on the enslavement of Native Americans, petitioned the court to send African slaves to the Americas, and his order, the Dominicans, supported the appeals. After all, the colonial clergy seemed to subscribe to the widespread belief that the Bible justified enslaving Africans. The Franciscan Juan de Torquemada wrote in the seventeenth century that blacks descended from Ham, the son of Noah, who had incurred a divine curse. It was therefore permissible to keep Africans in bondage and to teach them to work "for their own good." Although individual priests independently exposed the abuse of slaves, almost none spoke out against the institution of slavery for Africans. Church coffers provided credit for the purchase of slaves, African bondsmen worked on the landed estates of Jesuits and other religious orders, and individual clerics kept slaves as servants and cooks.

The slave trade shifted southward along the West Coast of Africa as European imperialism matured. A high proportion of the first Africans in the slave trade came from West Africa, in what is today Senegal and Gambia, especially during the breakup of the Jolof empire in the mid-sixteenth century. The successor states engaged in protracted warfare, and the competing African powers found economic backing by selling prisoners of war to Portuguese traders on the coast. Although persons from approximately sixteen major cultural groups were enslaved in this early trade, the Wolof especially yielded large numbers. In the seventeenth century, the focus of the African slave trade shifted southward to the Congo and Angola. Relations between the Portuguese and the African kingdom of Kongo were deteriorating. African political authority declined, and the Portuguese made

Map 7.1   African Sources of the American Slave Trade

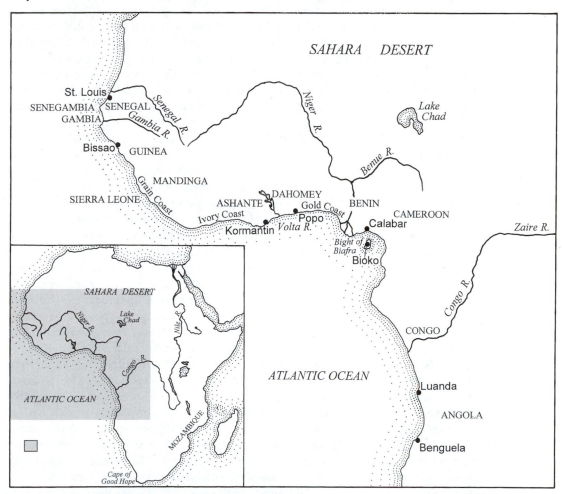

military incursions inland to consolidate direct control of the territory of Angola inland from Luanda. These Portuguese conquests contributed more slaves from the Bakongo, Tyo, and Ambundu cultural groups. At this time the sugar island of São Thomé also became an important center for slave reexport (see Map 7.1). These changes on the supply side showed up in the Americas even in the distant and remote Charcas (today Bolivia). The Wolof predominated among slaves imported into the Charcas early in the sixteenth century. Then Africans from the Bight of Biafra began to show up, and finally, by 1600, Angolans entered the area as slaves.

The Voyage

The sea voyage to the Americas could not have been more unpleasant and degrading for the Africans. The captives endured the trip on a meager diet and chained in tight quarters. In most cargoes, male slaves always outnumbered females by a ratio of two to one, because the need for field workers and the attrition through death of field hands were always greater. Women certainly worked in the fields but were bound for households and urban settings with greater frequency. "Men were piled in the bottom of the hold, chained for fear that they would rise up and kill all the whites aboard," reported a priest on a slave ship bound to Brazil. "If they tried to sleep, they fell on top of one another. There were bilges for natural needs, but since many were afraid of losing their place they relieved themselves wherever they happened to be, especially the men who were cruelly cramped. The heat and stench became unbearable." In all, the death rates among slaves on the trip from Africa averaged about 20 percent of the cargoes but reached as high as 50 percent on particularly bad voyages.

The infamous Middle Passage (referring to the mid-Atlantic shipping route between Africa and the Americas) might last from one to several months. Generally, sailing ships picked up the southeast trade winds at the equator on the West African coast. Halfway out into the Atlantic Ocean, the ships headed northward across the equatorial calms to catch the northeast trade winds that would carry them into the Caribbean. A prolonged crossing of the doldrums in midvoyage meant shortages of food and water. Disease spread at even greater speed in the slave holds during these times of calm. Scurvy and dysentery ravaged the human cargoes packed tightly in the holds of the ships. Even among the best and most efficient slave vessels, the spread of disease on the trip often took the life of 1 in 10 or even 1 in 5 of the involuntary passengers. Those who survived still suffered wounds, bruises, abscesses, scurvy, dysentery, and yaws. Less commonly, virulent bouts of typhus, measles, smallpox, yellow fever, or malaria broke out in the slave holds. Shipwrecks spelled certain doom to the shackled Africans. Only 30 survived of the 900 blacks on board a slave ship from Angola that hit a sand bank in 1599 and sank within sight of Cartagena. Once in port, the human cargoes were unloaded, fattened for market, and sold at auction or in lots. The symbols of their new condition—chains, leg irons, cuffs, collars, stocks, and whips—confronted the Africans in all the slave markets of the Americas.. In Olinda, sister city to Recife in the state of Pernambuco, a pillory stood in the center of the slave market; there new arrivals could witness the whippings of slaves accused of breaches of discipline. Others were branded. Merchants at the ports then found buyers locally or in the interior. In this manner, Africans were introduced to the Americas through Havana, Veracruz, Cartagena, La Guaira, Recife, Olinda, Rio de Janeiro, and Buenos Aires.

Cartegena became the chief entrepôt for the slave trade to Spanish South America. Approximately one thousand five hundred to two thousand slaves were arriving each year between 1580 and 1640. Its officials were particularly venal, as the placing of a few good bribes enabled merchants to import two to five times more Africans than their licenses would permit. But slaves did not stay in Cartegena, for most of them then boarded ships bound for Portobello, walked through the Panamanian rain forests, and entered slave markets on the West Coast of South America. The slave trade to Guayaquil, Trujillo, Callao, and Valparaíso was not insignificant; between 1555 and 1615, approximately two thousand Africans made the long journey across the Isthmus of Panama and down the coast all the way to Chile. This final leg of the slave's journey presented many dangers, and 1 in 10 Africans might succumb on these final treks and voyages.

All along the route from the African coast to the plantations and cities of the New World, the slaves' European masters worked assiduously to dilute their cultural heritage.

Africans from the same religious background (be it Islam or one of the animistic and spirit cults), from identical language groups, and from similar regional and tribal groups were separated. So were family members. Two reasons account for the intentional deculturation of the new slaves. The first was fear. European traders and planters, always few in number compared to their more numerous cargoes, did not want slave rebellions. It was thought that Africans from similar backgrounds could more easily conspire against their new owners. Second, the Africans were expected to become tractable workers. They needed to be prepared to follow instructions in Spanish and Portuguese and accept the sacraments of Catholicism as well as understand its religious teachings of obedience. But despite their power and intentions, the Europeans never succeeded in completely acculturating the Africans.

SLAVERY IN THE SPANISH AMERICAS

The major reason why the Europeans brought Africans involuntarily to the Americas has to do with the Native Americans. Where the indigenous population of the colonies suffered radical depopulation from the ravages of diseases and lacked the work skills required by their new overlords, there the Europeans saw fit to import slaves. The cycle began in the Spanish Caribbean shortly after Columbus's voyages. When the Carib and Aruak died out, the first Africans came to the Caribbean area in the early sixteenth century as gold miners and farmers. "Here the chief urgency is Negroes," reported a Spanish official in Cuba. "We pray license for each citizen to bring four Negroes and Negresses free of all duty." From the Caribbean launching pad, Africans accompanied Spaniards on all the great expeditions that rapidly covered the vast New World. Africans helped the Spaniards conquer the Aztec and Inka empires. The slave Esteban was one of the first four nonnatives, survivors of the Florida expedition of 1528, who traveled (by foot, no less) through what would later be Texas and the southwestern United States to Mexico. Blacks marched into Chile in 1535 and again in 1537, subdued the Muisca of the Colombian Sabana in 1537, marched into Chile yet once again and floated down the Amazon River in 1542, explored the trans-Mississippi West with Coronado in 1543 and opened up the silver mines of Upper Peru (now Bolivia) in 1545 and of northern Mexico in 1550. Practically everywhere Spaniards traveled in the Indies, Africans went along as auxiliaries.

Mexico

In the colony of New Spain, African slaves made up for the lack of Spanish settlers by directing the work of the indigenous masses and replacing natives who were dying in great numbers. They worked on the first haciendas established to produce European foods like sugar, wheat, beef, and mutton. In Mexico's new sugar estates of Veracruz and present-day Morelos, Africans worked the cane fields as gang laborers. At night, they were locked up in slave houses, and when recalcitrant, they were chained and whipped. Other pursuits accorded them more freedom. On wheat farms near Mexico City and on cattle ranches near Tehuantepec, Africans oversaw native workers and circulated relatively independently. Second-generation slaves (that is, those born in the Americas who could speak Spanish) could be found in the artisan trades, making European goods, and supervising work in *obrajes* and silver mines. In the cities, many white women owned a slave or two who could be hired out to do odd jobs that provided income for the owner. "I am very poor," stated one Spanish woman, "and I have no other means of sustenance except that which the Negro earns."

So important was this African contingent in Mexico's early development that, at the beginning of the seventeenth century, they easily outnumbered Spaniards. Probably half of all the slave trade for the Americas prior to 1620 (or nearly one hundred fifty thousand Africans) landed in Mexico. "All this black labor is necessary for the maintenance of human life," admitted one settler, "since neither the Spaniards who come from Castile nor those born here, when they incline to this sort of work, which is very improbable under present circumstances, are sufficient for the tenth part . . . of what is required." So prevalent did the African and the mulatto population become in the capital of Mexico City that they greatly outnumbered the whites. In 1612, 15,000 Spaniards had to share the city with 50,000 blacks and mulattoes and another 80,000 Native Americans. According to public officials, blacks were "more feared than the Indians." Colonial authorities attempted to prevent the sale of the strong drink pulque among the slaves—but to no avail. White society also resented the fact that slaves adopted the Catholic institution of the religious brotherhood, the *cofradía,* with so much enthusiasm, for their religious processions appeared to be displays of defiance, African-style dancing and singing, and racial pride.

After the mid-seventeenth century, the slave trade to New Spain tapered off as the indigenous population recovered from its losses due to epidemic disease. Despite sharing a lowly status in early colonial Mexico, the Africans and Native Americans seldom made common cause against the Europeans. The slaves ran away, formed *palenques* (fugitive slave villages), and organized conspiracies and rebellions, but they neither counted on nor received aid from indigenous groups. To the Native Americans, the blacks were just as alien as the whites. African runaways who had to turn to brigandage to survive often preyed on native villages, carrying off the women as the men stood by helplessly. Slaves who supervised native laborers on Veracruz sugar plantations could be as abusive as the white owners were to them.

At the end of the seventeenth century, slavery in Mexico began to lose its early importance. Many second-generation slaves easily ran away or otherwise gained freedom. Compared to native labor, slave imports became expensive, and only the wealthy households and prosperous urban artisans could afford to purchase a slave. Moreover, the slave population did not reproduce itself in captivity. The males outnumbered females by a three-to-one ratio, and overwork and poor health contributed to a low birth rate. After 1650, the Mexican slave population slowly declined, and the *castas,* or mixed race of mestizos and mulattoes, grew more prominent. When owners allowed them to do so, many slaves took up conjugal relationships with Native Americans and free persons of color. Racial mixture gained impetus as the second and third generation of Mexican-born blacks intermarried with mulattoes, mestizos, and natives. Children of such unions nearly always were considered free rather than slave.

Spanish South America

The first Africans formed important constituencies in the cores of the colonial world, where they served as intermediaries between European owners and indigenous workers.

Table 7.2 Estimated Racial Composition of the Population of Lima, 1636

Category	Men	Women	Total
Blacks	6,544	7,076	13,620
Spaniards	5,109	5,649	10,758
Native Americans	812	614	1,426
Mulattoes	276	585	861
Mestizos	142	235	377
Chinese	22	—	22
Total	12,905	14,159	27,064

SOURCE: Frederick P. Bowser, *The African Slave in Colonial Peru, 1524-1650* (Stanford, Calif.: Stanford University Press, 1974), 341.

The African contributions to the conquest and settlement of Peru cannot be discounted. In 1535, nearly as many blacks as whites—400 African slaves and 600 Spaniards—departed from Panama City for settlement in Peru. Africans were present in each and every group of conquistadores. Some won freedom by distinguishing themselves in battle, and a fortunate few in Chile and other places actually received *encomiendas* of native tributaries. Blacks assisted the Spaniards in putting down the great rebellion of Manko Inka in 1536. Africans were as foreign in Peru as the Spaniards in the period of conquest—and they, too, terrorized native villagers and had their own staffs of native servants. Spaniards particularly wanted workers to support them in the new settlements on coastal Peru—and the natives were not the answer. Between 1525 and 1571, the native population of Peru declined from 6 million to 1.5 million. The death toll was particularly high on the coast, where 9 of every 10 natives died. On the Peruvian coast, Africans worked on farms, in artisan shops, as household servants, as cattle and mule drivers, and finally as gang laborers in the sugar haciendas. Slaves lived in close proximity to Spaniards in their cities and on their farms. That is, they lived in and about the coastal cities of Guayaquil, Trujillo, and Lima and even in Santiago, Chile. Fewer Africans lived in the Andean highlands, where the native population was denser. But Africans might be found in the farms and shops around Quito and Cuzco as well as in the mining community of Potosí. Everywhere, Africans either worked directly or supervised Native Americans.

Until the mid-seventeenth century, the size of the African population in Peru nearly equaled that of the Spaniards, and half the residents of both groups resided in Lima (see Table 7.2). Perhaps another ten thousand blacks resided in other parts of the country. The ownership of slaves became a certain sign of social status, encouraging all self-respecting Spanish families to acquire as many as possible. Households of wealthy residents might have up to twenty blacks and about the same number of Native Americans in domestic service. Fine ladies had uniformed slaves to carry them about the streets in handsome sedan chairs and liveried black coachmen in the richly appointed carriages. Africans served as cooks, laundresses, maids, wet nurses, handymen, and gardeners in Spanish homes. Slave ownership was widespread, as artisans and petty tradesmen might also have one or two slaves in the house and at the shop. Slaves also figured prominently

Table 7.3   Estimated Racial Composition of the Population of Chile, 1540–1620

Year	Spaniards	Native Americans	Mestizos	Blacks/ Mulattoes	Total
1540	154	1,000,000	—	10	1,000,164
1570	7,000	550,000	10,000	10,000	624,000
1590	9,000	540,000	17,000	20,000	582,000
1620	15,000	480,000	40,000	22,500	557,000

SOURCE: William F. Sater, "The Black Experience in Chile," in *Slavery and Race Relations in Latin America*, ed. Robert Brent Toplin (Westport, Conn.: Greewood Press, 1974), 39.

among workers on the coastal truck farms, at the sugar plantations of Trujillo, and in the vineyards of the Moquegua Valley and Arequipa. They were also extensively employed in the transportation system—on the ox and mule carts and on the mule trains from Potosí and Cuzco. Usually, there was one worker or slave for every 5 to 10 mules, and up to ten blacks might work the largest packs of 100 animals. Africans also served as seamen and fishermen on the West Coast of South America.

Such a sizable population of slaves caused concern among the very whites who imported them in large numbers. As the population of slaves, free blacks, and mulattoes expanded, racial prejudices grew among both the white and the native populations. "They are rebellious, liars, thieves, pickpockets, highwaymen, gamblers, drunks," wrote one white of the Afro-Peruvians. "They are liars and nincompoops, they mouth the words and have the rosary in their hands, but they are hypocrites; they think only of stealing, they neither listen nor pay attention to sermons and preachings; whippings and beatings matter not to them." Slaves were branded to differentiate them from the larger numbers of mulattoes and free blacks. Moreover, as free persons, blacks encountered discrimination on the job markets. American-born blacks made only half the wages of white mariners and held positions of less responsibility but did more physical work.

The first slaves in Chile fought against the natives with their conquistador owners. Then both the indigenous peoples and the newly imported slaves were set to work panning for gold. They also worked as tanners, cowboys, shepherds, and domestic servants. At least one-quarter of the slaves in Chile became skilled artisans: shoemakers, blacksmiths, tailors, saddlemakers, and carpenters. Santiago's black population approached two thousand in 1630 (see Table 7.3). A majority of the town criers throughout the seventeenth century were also black. The Jesuit Order came to be the biggest owner of slaves in Chile, controlling nearly two thousand slaves on its many and far-flung agricultural enterprises.

In Santiago, the whites lived in constant fear of the blacks joining up with the Native Americans to plot lawlessness. Spanish law favored natives over Africans; fugitive natives could not be legally mutilated or executed in punishment, but such was not the case for fugitive black slaves. They could be publicly lashed, branded, and dismembered as a lesson to others. Nevertheless, some few legal protections did exist for blacks. In Santiago, the court removed a black servant girl from the owner's control because both her master and mistress began beating her—the first for not yielding immediately to his sexual advances, the second for having succumbed. On the other hand, a male slave was executed for killing his mistress despite the fact that she had overworked him, whipped him until his back was a festering open sore, and poured hot oil and chili sauce on his genitals. Blacks often lived lives of violence.

In the seventeenth century Buenos Aires also became an important entrepôt of the slave trade, most of it contraband. In just one year, more than a dozen ships docked there laden with 4,000 blacks. Half were sold in the cities of Argentina, and the others were marched and carried on oxcarts to Potosí and Chile. The journey took several months, the passage through the Andean passes between Mendoza and Santiago de Chile being particularly treacherous. This internal trade in slaves increased in the eighteenth century. The South Sea Company of England held the *asiento* at Buenos Aires in the beginning of the eighteenth century, introducing several thousand slaves. Half were shipped across the Pampas and Andes to Chile.

Resistance and Accommodation

In much of the Spanish Americas, the Africans found room for maneuver and resistance. Black slaves ran away from the tobacco and sugar plantations of Veracruz. They established *palenques* high in the Sierra Oriental of Mexico and maintained themselves as highwaymen, cattle thieves, and petty traders. These runaway slaves then fomented rebellions among their brethren still in captivity, as in the slave uprisings of 1725, 1735, 1741, and 1749 in the region of Córdoba and Orizaba. When Spanish slave-catching expeditions failed, colonial authorities had to accept some of these communities as legal colonial townships. In this manner did the descendants of runaway slaves gain recognition as free villagers by civil authorities. Native-born black slaves learned Spanish, observed local traditions, and increased their ability to resist the limitations of slavery. They malingered, worked slowly, and ran away, a strategy that led some white administrators to consider American-born African workers as "being lazy, secretive, crafty, escapists, thieves, robbers, drunkards, and lacking in humility."

In Cuba, for instance, second- and third-generation slaves commonly adopted Hispanic names, eagerly discarding names like Bangolo and Congolo that emphasized their African origins. Moreover, slaves born in Cuba served in armed expeditions that recaptured other slaves who had run away into the forests and mountains. Many Afro-Cubans wished to be accepted on a par with Spaniards. But to Spaniards, when third-generation slaves began wearing shoes and silver ornaments, their imitation of Spanish dress smacked of unwelcome arrogance. "Their audacity and impudence has led them to do in the [city of] Santiago de Cuba what they had never dared before," reported one Spaniard, "that is to wear hats and cloaks." Although Spaniards had imported African slaves, they did not always like the result.

One thing is certain: Africans felt no kinship—no common identity—with the subordinate Native Americans. Blacks in the Spanish Indies looked down on the natives and gained notoriety for invading peasant villages, stealing from their inhabitants, and violating the women. Even though slaves, as property, had fewer legal protections than Native Americans, only the *bozales,* recently arrived slaves of African birth who lacked knowledge of their owners' language and customs, shared their lowly social status. Second-generation blacks born in the Americas, who often served as intermediaries between

European masters and native workers, enjoyed a socioeconomic status higher than that of the indigenous peasants.

Slavery in the Americas was widespread. Discounting, for a moment, the enslavement of Native Americans in southern Chile, Amazonia, and other frontier areas, a remarkable number of colonials owned black slaves. Elite households in cities as disparate as Guadalajara, Guayaquil, and Buenos Aires made it a mark of status to have African men and women as servants. Artisans owned slaves, and so did small farmers. Widows and spinsters of modest means even used slaves as a form of social security: They sent their slaves into the marketplace as peddlers, sellers of sweetmeats, and prostitutes. The slaves then brought home to their mistresses the revenues earned in such trades. African slaves and black servants lived with their employers, most of whom were white. It was not uncommon for high-born young women to enter the nunneries accompanied by maids, the latter of whom did not serve God so much as their mistresses. In the countryside, slaves lived singly or in small groups on small farms, on haciendas, and in mines.

Most slaves in the Spanish Americas had very intimate relationships with owners, because such a large cross section of free men and women in the Americans owned at least one slave. Conditions probably varied considerably. Some masters and mistresses, no doubt, treated their slaves with affection and concern. But slaves were considered to be inferior, even subhuman. The general view held that they were born to work and that discipline was good for them. Despite the laws, there existed few remedies for abuse aside from the slave running away. Few rebellions threatened the privilege of the slave owners, notwithstanding their constant fear. Punishment might account for slave obedience, on the one hand, for whipping, mutilation, and torture surely awaited the recalcitrant slave. But on the other hand, their multi-ethnicity and status variations prevented Africans from achieving the solidarity necessary for collective action. Their condition produced a hierarchy of status and slender privilege among them. Household slaves clung to their tenuous positions vis-à-vis the field laborers, and slaves born in the Americas or who knew Spanish enjoyed the small privileges of supervising the work of others. Overt disobedience to the owner threatened these small but tangible benefits. Moreover, slaves worked ceaselessly for eventual freedom.

Manumission, an act by which the owner freed the slave, served as a safety valve for slaves whose every waking minute could not be monitored by supervisors, a fact that was more common outside the tropical plantation settings. Therefore, slaves in Mexico and Peru and Chile had one less reason to rebel or run away, for their jobs as artisans and vendors gave them opportunities to buy their freedom. Manumission occurred rarely but certainly more frequently in urban than in rural settings, because slaves found opportunities to keep some of the money they might earn on the street. Black women shared the main squares of cities across the Americas with native women vendors. "Mulattoes, blacks, Indians, and mestizos [sit beneath] the awnings to protect themselves from the sun," said one observer. "The Indian women place everything they sell on the ground on blankets and mats, and the mulatto and black women their goods on wooden tables." Manumission posed no threat to the institution of slavery, for the owner accepted the payment to purchase a replacement. Not every slave actually purchased his or her freedom, but enough held out hope, so much so that it disciplined them to their lives of servitude. Truth be told, most Africans in the Americas died as slaves.

Yet there were discrete regions of colonial Latin America where classic plantation slave systems contributed both to large numbers of slaves, to poor work and living conditions, and paradoxically, to greater opportunities for African cultural expression. In Mexico, slave gangs worked the sugar and wheat haciendas of Veracruz province. In Colombia, gangs of 20 and more Africans labored in the gold-washing enterprises in the tropical lowlands of the Cauca and Magdalena River valleys. In Ecuador and Venezuela, they toiled on cacao plantations. (Part III will present more information on slavery in these locales.) But the greatest slave society of the seventeenth century developed in the sugar economies of northeastern Brazil.

SLAVERY IN BRAZIL

Where the proportion of slaves to the general population was high, mortality among slaves was especially severe. The plantation slave economy of northeastern Brazil serves as a case in point. Portugal's settlements in the Americas turned to sugar—and to predominantly male African gang labor—for its economic livelihood. There slaves became an expendable item of investment, as owners calculated that the work of each slave returned the investment within three or four years only. Therefore, treating one's slave harshly did not violate the planter's balance sheet because it was less expensive for masters to buy another slave than to spend money to take care of those they had. The slaves' working conditions deteriorated, and their mortality soared. Thus, Brazil had high rates of slave imports and low rates of reproduction in its slave population. At any one time, those born in Africa constituted more than two-thirds of the slave population, while those born into Brazilian slavery made up less than one-third. The slave trade at the prosperous sugar ports of Pernambuco and Bahia always replenished the plantation society's demand for chattel labor.

But, in the long run, the reliance on slavery distorted values in peculiar ways. The fact that Africans and Native Americans performed labor as slaves diminished not only the status of Africans and natives but also the value placed on manual labor itself. To work hard became identified with Africans and slavery, so free men and women who worked hard risked losing social standing. Moreover, skin color also determined one's chances in life. White skin marked one as a person of command and leisure, and dark skin meant that one was destined for a life of brutish work. Those of mixed racial backgrounds could only hope to order themselves in the multiracial society according to the texture of their skin, with the light-skinned mulatto or *mestiço* accorded a higher—though not the highest—status. Slavery also skewed the distribution of income. The few owners of sugar mills commanded large incomes upon which depended a whole hierarchy of retainers—such as church and government officials, tenant farmers, smallholders, artisans and free laborers, and supervisors. The mass of workers, the plantation slaves, earned nothing but meager rations of food, clothing, and housing. Moreover, slave ownership spread widely through the middle and upper levels of society so that churchmen, public officials, artisans, widows, and small farmers all owned slaves. The missionary orders ran their own sugar plantations with gangs of African chattel laborers. Finally, the prominence of slavery may have prevented technological innovation in northeastern Brazil. Family connections and social status predominated over entrepreneurial enterprise, and skilled labor

Fazenda overseer punishing a slave. (Jean Baptist Debret, ca. 1820)

never received commensurate recompense. Sugar and slavery made Pernambuco and Bahia prosperous in the colonial period, but over the long term they impoverished the economy and population.

Plantations

Slavery and sugar dominated Brazil's northeast. At least one-third of the captaincy's population was enslaved, and in the fertile Recôncavo coastal plain, where cane growing predominated, slaves comprised as much as 70 percent of the inhabitants. Because their diets were so meager and their work conditions so arduous, the slave population did not reproduce itself; therefore, most slaves were African in origin. The biggest *fazendas* had slave populations numbering in the hundreds, although slaves also toiled in smaller land holdings and in cities and towns. The average sugar plantation employed between 60 to 80 slaves. The sexual balance was highly skewed; males constituted two-thirds of all slaves, whereas women made up only a quarter or less of the field workers, though their numbers in household jobs neared parity with those of males. Female slaves worked in domestic occupations as wet nurses, nannies, cooks, servants, lace makers, and seamstresses.

The cane-cutting slaves, as previously mentioned, formed the broad base of plantation slavery. White administrators considered force to be the indispensable element of work and discipline. Overseeing up to fifty slaves, the slave drivers habitually used verbal and physical abuse to prevent malingering and rebellion. "Whoever wants to profit from his Black," says a seventeenth-century planter's refrain, "must maintain them, make them work well, and beat them even better; without this there will be no service or gain." Back in the slave huts, owners and supervisors could exercise sexual and sadistic freedoms over slaves; the owners' wives, in fits of jealousy, devised punishments and mutilations for female slaves. Free society in the sugar regions of northeastern Brazil became inured to the abuse and indignities suffered by Africans (see Manuscript 7.1).

Sometimes, conditions for slaves between plantations owned by lay persons and those run by the clergy differed only in degree. In any case, individual slaves had little recourse to protest their ill treatment among ecclesiastical or judicial authorities. Though laws existed that aimed to protect slaves from harsh abuse, the judiciary always treated the aristocratic planters with leniency.

Usually, conditions were difficult for the most recently arrived African-born slave, called the _boçal_ in Portuguese. The new slave had just suffered the dehumanizing indignities of capture, sale, a cramped voyage across rough seas, resale, and a period of conditioning to the new environment. The _boçal_ was put to work with other Africans of different cultures and languages. A white overseer or a second-generation Brazilian-born slave, neither of whom appreciated the cultural and linguistic richness of their subjects, directed the _boçal's_ work, often harshly. The large field crews that cut and bound the cane consisted predominantly of _boçales_. It was widely believed that African field workers did not perform well unless driven by the whip.

MANUSCRIPT 7.1

Immorality Fostered by Owners among Slaves

Occasionally, slavery revolted the moral sense of priests sent to minister to the peoples of Brazil. In this essay written in 1700, the Italian Jesuit Jorge Benci comments on the moral outrages—concubinage and prostitution—that both masters and mistresses promoted among their slaves. Note that Benci does not condemn slavery in this selection but merely objects to the behavior of some slave owners, blaming them for forcing their slaves into lives of immorality.

From this we may surmise the main reason for the scandalous life which slave men and women normally lead in Brazil. But how can it be otherwise, if in masters and mistresses they do not see Christian models, but rather outrageous behavior suitable for pagans? . . . However often the master may teach them that God wants them to remain chaste, how should they be persuaded to lead an honest and pure life when they see the master himself keeping a concubine in his own house. . . .

That there should be masters who give no thought to the great harm they do to their slave girls, dividing up among them the provisioning of the house, and imposing a share upon each one! To one the flour or bread for the table; to another the meat or fish for the plate; this one must pay the rent on the houses; that one must provide the oil for the lamps; and each must contribute that which she is responsible for. And that this should happen among Christians! That there should be so little fear of God, that no thought is given to the consequences of these tributes which are so unworthy of a Catholic! Tell me, masters, or tell me, mistresses (and it is mainly to the latter that I speak); where should your slave girls go to satisfy these payments? Do they perhaps have some income from which to acquire that which you order them to pay? Certainly not. Thus, where should it come from, except from sin and the wanton use of their bodies? And in supporting yourselves with this tainted money and from these sins, what are you yourself but a living, walking sin?

SOURCE: _Children of God's Fire: A Documentary History of Black Slavery in Brazil_, ed. Robert Edgar Conrad (Princeton, N.J.: Princeton University Press, 1983), 176–78.

In contrast, the black slave born in the Americas, known in Brazil as a *crioulo,* spoke Portuguese, had a higher status, and aspired to work with more privileges and freedom. Males in cities learned carpentry, masonry, baking, or iron work. In the countryside, they might help run the owner's small farm or enjoy relative independence as muleteers, shepherds, and herdsmen. Because they spoke Portuguese and remembered little of their African heritage, *crioulos* were entrusted with supervising natives and new slaves in the *fazendas* and mines. Second-generation slaves might even bear arms, if their masters fought against the natives, and earn enough personal funds to purchase their own freedom. Mulattoes and *crioulos* worked in skilled positions at the *engenhos,* the crude cane-crushing and sugar-making factories found on the larger plantations. They had grown up in Brazil speaking Portuguese and were more acculturated than the recently arrived African to the practices of the dominant society. Although the hours were long during the harvest season, these slaves in the *engenhos* did not suffer the whip as in the fields. They were privileged workers and received extra rations and opportunities to earn extra cash. The mulatto and *crioulo* slaves supervised the work of others. Therefore, slave society created a hierarchy of status and privilege even among its chattel workers.

Not all of the plantation societies developing at Bahia and Pernambuco consisted of just the masters and the slaves. Between these polar opposites of status and privilege existed a hierarchy of whites and free people of color, whose numbers grew during the seventeenth century. The plantation system nurtured a growing class of free workers. Many persons benefited from the prosperity brought about by plantation slavery— attorneys and notary publics in the cities, skilled artisans in the cities (nearly all of whom were white), white and mulatto persons of skill who signed on as overseers, and master mechanics and carpenters at the *engenhos.* Those persons possessing modest skills in felling trees, making fences, digging trenches, and fishing and hunting (for game and runaway slaves) received itinerant work on plantations. Others in this group of free (and mostly black and mulatto) category also took up farming on small properties on the outskirts of the plantations to provide foodstuffs for local markets. The existence of this group of poorly paid yet free workers served as an essential prop supporting the system of slavery, for "good" slaves worked hard, behaved well for the master, and saved money to buy their freedom and join the class of free colored persons. Slave purchase of manumission occurred often enough to function as a disciplinary check on rebellion.

The independent cane farmers, or *lavradores,* came to be the most important subordinate social group within the plantation system. Of course, the center of sugar production was the *engenho,* located on the owner's own plantation and supplied by the plantation's own fields—but not exclusively. The average *engenho* also received cane grown and harvested on adjacent, smaller land holdings operated by cane farmers. The *lavradores* themselves may have been renters or sharecroppers on land belonging to the big planter, but they could also be owners themselves of medium-sized estates. As debtors, they often borrowed operating cash from the mill owners, sugar merchants in the ports of Salvador and Recife, and church financial institutions. The Benedictine friars and the lay confraternities of northeastern Brazil provided much credit for the operation of the plantation economy. In the seventeenth century, most of the four hundred or so *lavradores* of Bahia were white and Portuguese-born merchants, militia officers, and government officials. Catholic priests also counted among those who conducted farming operations as a primary or secondary occupation. Of course, they owned slaves, too, in groups of 2 to 40,

Table 7.4 Distribution of Income in the Plantation Slave Society of Bahia, 1666

Occupation	Payment (in reís*)
Mill owner	36,500
Cane farmer	5,160
General overseer	2,750
Goldsmith	1,300
Blacksmith	710
Carpenter	685
Mason	550
Subsistence farmer	525
Tailor	490
Fisherman	438

* The real (pl. reís) was the basic monetary unit of the Portuguese empire, then a copper coin. One thousand réis equalled a milreís or about two and one-half gold coins.

SOURCE: Adapted from estimations provided in Stuart B. Schwartz, *Sugar Plantations in the Formation of Brazilian Society: Bahia, 1550–1835* (Cambridge, England: Cambridge University Press, 1985), 333.

depending on the size of the cane farm. As a group, the *lavradores* sustained the institution of slavery and supported the exclusivity of the planter class that they longed to join. Once again, the rise of the cane farmer to the status of a mill owner remained a remote possibility, given the difficulty of obtaining the credit and assistance of Portuguese-born governors and merchants as well as the power of elite planter families.

In terms of distribution of wealth, clearly the *fazendeiros* who owned the mill equipment captured the preponderant share of income in the plantation society based on slavery. The average mill owner earned 7 times the income of a cane farmer and 30 times the yearly remuneration of the most prosperous artisan (see Table 7.4). There was also a strong correlation among race, social status, and income. Portuguese-born whites made up the wealthiest citizens, whites occupied most of the intermediate positions, and free colored persons ranked near the bottom of the socioeconomic spectrum. Among the slaves, the Brazilian-born mulattoes and *crioulos* enjoyed higher status than the more numerous Africans.

The planter class retained its hegemony in society by employing a number of strategies already discussed in Chapter 4 that maximized profit, took in new wealth, found advantageous marriages (especially for its female progeny), and closed off opportunities to outsiders. Family strategies centered on the women. The *fazendeiros* arranged marriages of their daughters to other planter families or to wealthy immigrant merchants and Crown officials who might support elite business enterprises. The nunnery served as the refuge for unmarriageable or recalcitrant young girls. Elite women lived with great privilege and much attention from slave servants but little opportunity to circulate outside the household. Nothing threatened to dishonor the planter family like rumors of unfaithful wives and headstrong daughters. On the other hand, as elite women generally married

Family life in the slave quarters of Brazil. (Johann Moritz Rugendas, ca. 1830)

older men, many widows came into control of *engenhos* and directed the fortunes of the planter families. However, they, too, had to subscribe to the values of their class or risk losing land and status. Although inheritance laws and economic fluctuations motivated the frequent sale of *engenhos,* a small group of elite families still retained control of the biggest plantations from the late sixteenth century into the nineteenth.

Slave Agency

The information presented in the preceding section is not to imply that slaves in Brazil and other plantation societies could not and did not influence their own lives. That they did. Naturally, they faced the enormous power of their owner, who might not be economically or morally motivated to care for them. Owners provided slaves with poor housing and little time off to provide their own food in small gardens surrounding the slave quarters. Only the household slaves dressed well, and some field slaves went entirely naked, although most had a crude dress or pair of cotton trousers. A scanty diet and fetid housing conditions, frequent overwork, and occasional punishments undermined the health of slaves. Generally, owners calculated that a newly purchased African slave would work for little more than 10 years before death. The slave could expect no official or religious protection from a cruel and ruthless owner. Nevertheless, the chattel laborers undertook individual and collective actions to ameliorate their burdens.

Despite the fact that few owners permitted marriages or promoted family life among slaves, the latter chose to live together in family groups. Slave households had men, women, extended relatives, and a few children. Slave sales, of course, threatened these makeshift households. But slaves had been known to refuse work or threaten suicide unless reunited with a partner sold off the plantation, and the owners sometimes acceded so as not to lose their investment. To survive, slaves also adopted institutions that were essentially European in origin though parallel to their African heritage. Formal godparenting was one of them. When they bore children, slave women frequently utilized itinerant priests to baptize them, at which time ritual godparents were appointed. Black children usually had black godparents, but a slave mother of a mulatto child might enlist a free colored person or even a *lavrador* as godparent. Slave owners seldom acted as godparents to their own slaves, though the birth of a mulatto might imply the master's own complicity. The practice of godparenting widened the number of adults responsible for the protection of the children and engaged secondary parties to possibly intervene with masters in the interests of preserving the nuclear slave family.

Although they adopted the culture of their owners, Africans preserved enough of their own traditions to give a unique flavor to life and leisure in northeastern Brazil. Slaves hardly ever received a visit on the plantations from the priests, except maybe on the feast days of the patron saint of the locality—at which time marriages, baptism, and confessions occurred, one after the other. Slaves learned religion from other slaves. For the master, the slave's Christianization meant humility, obedience, and deference. Africans learned the ritual usage of religious vocabulary in greeting the owner: "Your blessing, my master," to which the owner would graciously reply: "God bless you, amen." These traditional formulas are still in use between humble folk and their wealthy employers in northeastern Brazil. Slaves thus melded elements of ritual Catholicism with their music and dance, encouraged by the absence of Catholic evangelism (missionaries worked among Native Americans, not slaves) to continue to observe their own religious beliefs. The famous rhythms and music of Bahia and Pernambuco attest even today to the influence there of African motifs.

In spite of the danger, the slaves could exert pressure on the masters. Their constant complaints about poor food rations forced owners to allow them more land on which to plant gardens. Then slaves also employed the typical weapons of the weak. They worked slowly, they malingered, they "accidentally" broke tools, and they refused to start the harvest season without a round of rum. Occasionally, there were enough conspiracies and rebellions to keep the owners and supervisors on guard. But the most common form of resistance was to take flight.

In Brazil, as throughout the American plantation societies, runaway slaves escaped to the thinly settled hinterlands. There they established their own communities, called *quilombos,* where they set up African-style polities and observed their own religions, which by this time were hybridized systems of ritual and belief taken from Catholicism and various African cultures. Raiding parties harassed nearby native communities, held up mule trains and travelers on the country roads, or freed slaves from their places of bondage. In Brazil, *quilombos* were sought out by Portuguese frontiersmen and their mulatto mercenaries. One seventeenth-century *quilombo* in the backlands of Pernambuco, at Palmares, had gathered together a population of 30,000 Africans in several integrated communities, complete with its own farmers, artisans, and warriors (see Manuscript 7.2). Palmares did not fall until 1695 after several armed excursions underwritten by the wealthy and concerned planters of Recife finally destroyed it completely. Slave flight posed no more threat to slave society than did the destruction of Palmares end the establishment of settlements by runaway slaves. As long as slavery continued, as it did until 1888 in Brazil, those in bondage continued to exercise the option of running away into the frontier to set up *quilombos.*

MANUSCRIPT 7.2

Account of the *Quilombo* of Palmares, 1677

Palmares was a large community of runaway slaves that flourished in the modern state of Pernambuco in northeastern Brazil. The inhabitants of this self-contained, self-governed refuge numbered in the thousands and organized agricultural subsistence and military defenses to withstand both Dutch and Portuguese efforts to destroy it over the span of five or six decades. Other, smaller maroon settlements dotted the vast map of Brazil from the forests of the interior, where the blacks shared and competed for land with the indigenous population, to the outskirts of the major cities along the coast. Naturally, the planters and other settlers desired to locate and destroy such settlements, for the existence of the quilombos *encouraged slaves to run away from their owners. Moreover, the inhabitants of such African communities often raided nearby estates, robbing from the slave owners and even freeing their comrades. Mixed-race soldiers of the backlands made a living fighting both the natives and the runaway slaves. In the following description of Palmares, the author is one of these soldiers, a* capitão-mor. *He has every reason to describe the strength of this community even while discrediting its leaders and followers, because he was unsuccessful in defeating Palmares. Nevertheless, it is quite clear that the former slaves created an eclectic culture of both African and European influences but that African heritage predominated. This* quilombo *did not fall until 1695, after having a continuous existence of more than ninety years.*

[T]he king who is called *Ganga-Zumba*, which means Great Lord, . . . is recognized as such both by those born in Palmares and by those who join them from outside; he has a palatial residence, *casas* for members of his family, and is assisted by guards and officials who have, by custom, *casas* which approach those of royalty. He is treated with all respect due a Monarch and all the honours due a Lord. Those who are in his presence kneel on the ground and strike palm leaves with their hands as sign of appreciation of His excellence. They address him as Majesty and obey him with reverence. He lives in the royal enclave, called *Macoco*, a name which was begotten from the death of an animal on the site. This is the capital of Palmares; it is fortified with parapets full of caltrops, a big danger even when detected. The enclave itself consists of some 1,500 *casas*. There are keepers of law (and) their office is duplicated elsewhere. And although these barbarians have all but forgotten their subjugation, they have not completely lost allegiance to the Church. There is a *capela*, to which they flock whenever time allows, and *imagens* to which they direct their worship. . . . One of the most crafty, whom they venerate as *paroco*, baptizes and marries them. Baptismals are, however, not identical with the form determined by the Church and the marriage is singularly close to laws of nature. . . . The king has three (women), a *mulata* and two *crioulas*. The first has given him many sons, the other two none. All the foregoing applies to the *cidade principal* of Palmares and it is the king who rules it directly; other *cidades* are in the charge of potentates and major chiefs who govern in his name. The second *cidade* in importance is called *Subupuira* and is ruled by king's brother (Gana) *Zona*. . . . It has 800 *casas* and occupies a site one square league in size, right along the river Cachingi. It is here that Negroes are trained to fight our assaults (and weapons are forged there).

SOURCE: From R. K. Kent, "Palmares: An African State in Brazil," in *Maroon Societies: Rebel Slave Communities in the Americas*, 2d ed., ed. Richard Price (Baltimore: The Johns Hopkins University Press, 1979), 179–80.

CONCLUDING REMARKS

What prevented the Native American and African masses, who vastly outnumbered all others, from rising up and throwing out the whites and people of mixed race? Their own ethnic and cultural diversity. Of course, the European overlords deliberately structured the social order to foster such disunity among their subject peoples. Indigenous leaders, some of whom continued to trace their lineage back to the pre-Columbian nobility, enjoyed more privileges than the commoners, who worked the lands of their leaders. Members of one native village rivaled those of another in disputes over land and work obligations, while differences of language and customs also engendered mutual hostility among different indigenous communities that suffered more or less equally from discrimination. Among slaves, differences in language, custom, and religion marked those coming from separate regions of Africa. Moreover, slaves born in America had higher social and economic positions than did slaves born in Africa. Most of all, the Africans and Native Americans were antagonistic toward each other. These differences and divisions allowed the few Europeans to retain their hegemony over the multiracial colonial hierarchy.

What made colonial society so durable, even as it became increasingly complex, was the fact that the middle groups became sturdy supporters of the social distinctions and legal discriminations. Mulattoes and mestizos did not identify with the condition of their half-brothers and -sisters of darker complexion. Fearing any decline of status, they took pains to distinguish themselves from Native Americans and Africans. As a middle group, the mestizos and mulattoes were more urbanized and more skilled. They supervised the work of natives and Africans. Some became hunters of runaway slaves. If they could, racially-mixed persons took advantage of their supposed inferiors in commercial transactions, much as mestizo and mulatto men strove to take advantage of non-European women. The irony is this: The more complex the racial mixture of America became, the more entrenched and stable became the social system that preserved privilege and status.

Part II shows how social power determined the relationships among different members of the exceedingly heterogeneous peoples of colonial Latin America. Each individual's power established what status he or she would occupy in society and what kind of access that person would have to economic wealth and political influence. This was at once a rigid and a fluid society. Colonial subjects had opportunities to advance themselves within well-defined limits. They also might fall backwards in status.

Social power consisted of a large number of factors that one used to maximize rank and status. Family provided the basic ingredient of one's social power, making important the accident of birth and inherited privilege. Thereafter, race and skin color were essential to social power. The lighter the skin color, generally the higher the social ranking. Native Americans and African Americans began life at the bottom of the social ladder, and mestizos and mulattoes began more toward the middle. As a consequence, the social climber in colonial America sought to marry a lighter-skinned person from a respectable family. Wealth also contributed to social power. To be rich enabled one to forego some of the other ingredients of social power and still be recognized as someone important. But there was a catch. A person did not often have the opportunity to become wealthy in the first place unless he or she already possessed some of the other prized attributes. Whites had more opportunities to make money than did anyone else; Iberian-born whites had the most.

Culture and behavior also enhanced one's social power. If the colonial subject dressed like a European, spoke Spanish or Portuguese, and had an occupational skill, he or she might advance. Thus, some Native American persons might be accepted as mestizo, and second-generation *crioulo* slaves enjoyed positions superior to those of African-born slaves. In similar fashion, gender conferred possibilities and limitations on a person. Women normally found themselves subordinated to men in business and family life. But combined with other factors, family and ethnicity, for example, a woman could be subordinated at a high rank. A woman of the *gente decente* had considerable power over women (and men, too) beneath her social rank, even though her economic possibilities could be quite restricted compared with her brothers'. To be subordinated on a lower social scale conferred on the woman economic freedom. But paradoxically, a low-status woman was also exposed to the abuse of her social superiors (especially males).

Finally, voluntary associations and office-holding augmented one's power. Among the *gente decente,* one aspired to political and religious office and to joining the most prestigious *cofradías.* For the *gente de pueblo,* belonging to a collective of some kind— a peasant village or a *cofradía*—helped one gain protection and identity. Workers might choose a powerful patron to achieve these same goals. Indian and mestizo peons worked for *hacendados,* reaping thereby a measure of security and status. Control of one's subsistence was also important. Artisans and agricultural smallholders maintained a middling status because they produced a modest, independent income. Persons of this middle rank aspired to controlling the labor of at least a few natives and blacks. All in all, social power was itself a fluid commodity. It could be enhanced or diminished during a person's lifetime, and it resulted in intense competition for control over economic resources between and among all social groups. In fact, competition could be so keen at times that conflict and violence often resulted in the normal course of pursuing power.

For much of the early colonial period—the sixteenth and seventeenth centuries— two colonial institutions effectively held this competition within reasonable bounds. Both the state and the Catholic Church functioned to control the subordinate classes and to prevent the colonists' abuse of subject peoples from becoming destructive and ruinous. Their success in these twin endeavors were impressive. Native Americans and, to a lesser extent, African Americans became united with their social superiors by converting to Catholicism. Moreover, colonists accepted the role of the state as a mediator in their domestic relationships to each other and to the subordinate classes. Safely far away, the state did not become so intrusive as to be a threat to the social elites, and everyone accepted the role of the state in curbing the excesses of unbridled competition for the sources of power. Therefore, despite its often bewildering pluralism and complexity, the colonial social system based upon inequality and power hung together. Nay, it even flourished.

However, colonial Latin America's last century—the eighteenth—was to be a time of change and impending crisis. The social order became destabilized as the native population began to grow. A new working-class culture began the process of resisting extant social norms. In addition, economic growth and the intensification of international competition unbalanced the relationships of power within the elites themselves. These conditions of change challenged the traditional roles of the state and church in mediating social conflicts within the colonies. It is to these growing pressures that this book now turns.

Additional Reading

Aimes, Hubert H. S. *A History of Slavery in Cuba, 1511– 1868.* New York: Octagon Books, 1967.

Bowser, Frederick. *The African Slave in Colonial Peru, 1524– 1650.* Stanford, Calif.: Stanford University Press, 1974.

Carroll, Patrick J. *Blacks in Colonial Veracruz: Race, Ethnicity, and Regional Development.* Austin: University of Texas Press, 1991.

Conrad, Robert Edgar. *World of Sorrow. The African Slave Trade to Brazil.* Baton Rouge: Louisiana State University Press, 1986.

Curtin, Philip. *The Atlantic Slave Trade: A Census.* Madison: University of Wisconsin Press, 1969.

Díaz, María Elena. "Constituting Identity: Socio-Cultural Changes in a Black Colonial Village (El Cobre, Cuba, 1670–1800)." Ph.D. diss., University of Texas at Austin, 1992.

Flory, Rae Jean Dell. "Bahian Society in the Mid-Colonial Period: The Sugar Planters, Tobacco Growers, Merchants, and Artisans of Salvador and the Recôncavo, 1680–1725." Ph.D. diss., University of Texas at Austin, 1978.

Flusche, Della, and Eugene H. Korth. *Forgotten Females: Women of African and Indian Descent in Colonial Chile,* 1535–1800. Detroit, Mich.: B. Ethridge, 1983.

Freyre, Gilberto. *The Masters and the Slaves [Casa-Grande e Senzala]: A Study in the Development of Brazilian Civilization.* 2d ed. Trans. Samuel Putnam. New York: Knopf, 1966.

Klein, Herbert S. *The Middle Passage: Comparative Studies in the Atlantic Slave Trade.* Princeton, N.J.: Princeton University Press, 1978.

Margolis, Maxine L. *The Moving Frontier: Social and Economic Change in a Southern Brazilian Community.* Gainesville: University of Florida Press, 1973.

Mattoso, Katia M. De Queirós. *To Be a Slave in Brazil, 1550– 1888.* Trans. Arthur Goldhammer. New Brunswick, N.J.: Rutgers University Press, 1979.

Palmer, Colin. *Slaves of the White God: Blacks in Mexico, 1570– 1650.* Cambridge, Mass.: Harvard University Press, 1976.

Russell-Wood, A. J. R. *The Black Man in Slavery and Freedom in Colonial Brazil.* New York: St. Martin's Press, 1982.

Schwartz, Stuart B. *Sugar Plantations in the Formation of Brazilian Society: Bahia, 1550– 1835.* Cambridge, England: Cambridge University Press, 1985.

Solow, Barbara L. ed. *Slavery and the Rise of the Atlantic System.* Cambridge, England: Cambridge University Press, 1991.

Toplin, Robert Brent, ed. *Slavery and Race Relations in Latin America.* Westport, Conn.: Greenwood Press, 1974.

In Spanish and Portuguese

Aguirre Beltrán, Gonzalo. *El negro esclavo en Nueva España: La formación colonial, la medicina popular, y otros ensayos.* Mexico City: Fondo de Cultura Económica, 1994.

Brito Figueroa, Federico. *El problema tierra y esclavos en la historia de Venezuela.* Caracas: Ediciones de la Biblioteca, 1985.

Deíve, Carlos Esteban. *La esclavitud del negro en Santo Domingo.* 2 vols. Santo Domingo: Museo del Hombre Dominicano, 1980.

———. *Los guerrilleros negros esclavos fugitivos y cimarrones en Santo Domingo.* Santo Domingo: Fundación Cultural Dominicana, 1989.

Díaz Soler, Luis M. *Historia de la esclavitud negra en Puerto Rico*. San Juan: Editorial Universitaria, Universidad de Puerto Rico, 1974.

Duharte Jiménez, Rafael. *El negro en la sociedad colonial*. Santiago de Cuba: Editorial Oriente, 1988.

Forender, Jacob. *O escravismo colonial*. 2d ed. São Paulo: Atica, 1978.

Freitas, Décio. *Palmares: a guerra dos escravos*. 5th ed. Porto Alegre: Mercado Abrierto, 1984.

Moura, Clóvis. *Rebeliões da senzala: Quilombos, insurreições, guerrilhas*. 2d ed. Rio de Janeiro: Conquista, 1972.

Palacios Preciado, Jorge. *La trata de negros por Cartagena de Indias*. Tunja: Universidad Pedagógica de Colombia, 1973.

Romero, Fernando. *Safari africano y compraventa de esclavos para el Perú (1412–1818)*. Lima: Instituto de Estudios Peruanos, 1994.

Scheuss de Studer, Elena Fanny. *La trata de negros en el Río de la Plata durante el siglo xviii*. Buenos Aires: Libros de Hispanoamérica, 1984.

PART III

PART III

ECONOMIC FLORESCENCE AND SOCIAL CHANGE IN THE EIGHTEENTH CENTURY

*I*n the eighteenth century, the booming colonial economies exacerbated many contradictory tendencies that both enriched and complicated the lives of the common folk. It also enriched and challenged the colonial powers of Spain and Portugal—and Britain and France. Economic influences very much intertwined the destinies of the peasants and workers with the fate of the imperial order. The increased trade of the eighteenth century contributed to expanding traditional exports—especially silver, gold, and sugar. New colonial products from ranches and plantations such as hides, tobacco, cacao, cotton, and even coffee also began to figure in international commerce. In turn, export production stimulated the settlement of new territories at the fringes of the old colonial centers. Commercialized agriculture spread into areas heretofore considered wastelands. This economic revival generated a heightened demand for free workers, who utilized the opportunity to push up wages, to exercise choice, and to enhance horizontal mobility. In the meanwhile, European merchants and entrepreneurs increased their profits, landowners maximized their wealth, and mestizos and mulattoes found enlarged opportunities in petty trade and supervision. The colonial state collected larger and larger revenues and also attempted to expand its regulatory powers over the economy.

Was everything tranquil? Not exactly. The rapid economic changes widened the profound cleavages and inequalities in colonial Latin American society. In the rush to exploit the frontiers, the elite Creoles and Europeans used their social

and political connections to capture the more fertile lands. They converted their wealth into dispossessing the indigenous inhabitants of the land, buying more slaves, and hiring more workers. In older, densely settled areas, resurgent population growth and the increasing power of the elite-owned haciendas increased the pressure on native agricultural communities. Iberian-born merchants and artisans practically excluded their Creole competitors from international commerce. If anything, growth led to a deterioration of labor conditions for African slaves in the plantation economies of Brazil, Cuba, and Saint-Domingue (Haiti).

Everywhere the populace chafed under the exaction of the king's proliferating tax collectors. The colonial state reformed and expanded its bureaucracy and control of commerce. It established new political jurisdictions and appointed additional public officials to staff them, with a view to gaining control over the expanding colonies. But the power of the imperial state was illusory. Its modest successes in taxation and regulation tended to expose its corrupt and heavy-handed practices, alienating the colonial citizens it governed. Colonial officials could not contain the rising social conflicts and, in fact, appeared to provoke them. The stability of the economic and social system proved increasing fragile. Why? Because the countervailing tendencies of economic growth and popular discontent in eighteenth-century Latin America actually undermined the colonial state's ability to mediate the social and political turmoil. And turmoil increasingly engulfed the Atlantic world throughout most of the century.

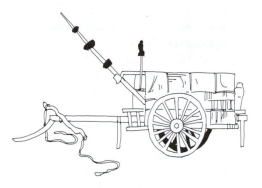

CHAPTER 8

ECONOMIC AND SOCIAL CHANGE
IN SPANISH NORTH AMERICA

Both markets and productive capacity in colonial Latin America expanded at unprecedented rates during the eighteenth century. The industrial revolution had commenced in England, spread slowly to northern Europe, and promoted increased rates of commerce throughout the world.[1] At the same time, industrial capitalism spread far and wide its message of individual entrepreneurial initiative, private property, and minimal government interference. These factors, combined with simultaneous population growth in Great Britain and northern Europe, created new, expansive markets for Latin America's raw materials and food products. Colonial trade now passed nearly in its entirety through Spain to the manufacturing countries of northern Europe, sometimes completely bypassing the Spanish middlemen.

Historians of Latin America debate the long-term impact of the economic growth of the late eighteenth century. Few doubt that all economic indicators pointed to increased levels of production, distribution, and creation of wealth. But do these statistics indicate

---

[1] The term *industrial revolution* refers to the economic and social changes that mark the transition from an agrarian and commercial society to a modern industrial society relying on complex machinery rather than tools. In the eighteenth century, the industrial revolution began in the British textile industry, creating the factory system of large-scale machine production and forming a class of industrial wage workers.

that the Latin American economies were actually developing? That is to say, were they preparing for self-sustained growth? Were entrepreneurs rewarded for taking risks and adding to the economy? Was production becoming more efficient? Did workers learn new skills? Did they share in the growth by earning higher incomes and consuming more goods and services?

One school of historians doubts that eighteenth-century growth amounted to sustained development and emphasizes instead the dependent nature of Latin American colonial economies. Not only did the imperial powers discourage manufacturing in the colonies, but commerce with northern Europe also promoted export production at the expense of local markets. Some scholars even contend that expanded foreign trade promoted the transfer of wealth to Europe, actually impoverishing the colonies. Labor coercion also resulted directly from the penetration of capitalism, they say. The process of industrial development in northern Europe, therefore, had as its inevitable corollaries the spread of slavery and the impoverishment of the Americas.

In response to this dependency school, as it were, other scholars point out that colonial Latin Americans lacked the technology and market infrastructure to autonomously modernize production and distribution. Without the expansion of external trade, the colonial subjects of Spain and Portugal could neither have sustained the growth of the colonial population nor prepared themselves to benefit from the economic forces unleashed by the transformation in European manufacturing. And neither was labor coercion present everywhere in the Americas, because labor relations depended on local—not international—circumstances.

In Spanish North America, the economic growth of the eighteenth century intensified many changes initiated by the Conquest. Mexico benefited from sending its silver bullion to Europe, which needed American precious metals to finance growing international commerce. The growth in external trade stimulated domestic demand for local goods and services, and internal markets also began to grow. Colonial populations expanded during the eighteenth century, frontier land was settled, internal commerce proliferated, and agricultural production grew. This century of economic florescence also affected the far-flung dependencies of the Spanish empire in North America. The Spanish-speaking population spread north into what is now California and Texas. Cuba became an exporter of sugar, and the economies of southern Mexico and Central America expanded by exporting dyestuffs. But many effects of growth were contradictory. Some workers came to the selected work sites under pressure, and others came only for higher wages. Settlement of the frontier also tended to erode the culture and domain of indigenous peoples.

The answer to the question of whether this expansion amounted to development per se depends on how one measures the distribution of its benefits. No doubt, market relations benefited certain sectors of colonial society more than others. The expansion of trade allowed white entrepreneurs and immigrant artisans to expand their incomes and growth potential but placed great pressure on workers, hacienda peons, and the indigenous peasantry. Neither can there be much doubt that colonial social relations presented many obstacles to economic modernization in terms of poor distribution of income, coercive labor systems, the reluctance of peasants to enter the market, and government corruption and controls. For every unit of new wealth produced in the eighteenth century, an intense struggle developed over how to share it.

PRODUCTION FOR EXPORT

The power of Europe's industrial revolution eventually reached the vast tracts of colonial America. Initiating the first breakthroughs in eighteenth-century manufacturing, British textile factories began to harness new machines to water power and later to steam-driven engines. The technological improvements spread to other industries. Factory production expanded, simultaneously lowering prices of industrial goods. The industrial revolution—and a simultaneous growth in Europe's population—also stimulated the demand for raw materials. Thus began the so-called grocery trades across the Atlantic Ocean. Fish, animal skins, lumber, tobacco, and cotton came from the North American colonies of England and France. These latter countries and the Netherlands imported sugar from their heretofore relatively neglected Caribbean possessions. Hides, dye stuffs, and cacao from Central and South America entered Atlantic commerce. Venezuelan exports of cacao proliferated, while Brazil continued to contribute its sugar. From the Río de la Plata, Europe commenced buying hides, dried meat, and animal fats. But the burgeoning Atlantic commerce involved more than just these groceries.

Mining

Europe's industrial revolution stimulated Latin America's traditional exports of bullion and precious gems as well. Mining production had declined in the second half of the seventeenth century for a number of reasons. The richest ores had been used up, the technology of mercury amalgamation had not changed, and supplies of mercury in Europe had become scare and expensive. To stimulate renewed productivity of the colonial mines, Spanish officials responded to the demands of European industrial capitalism by undertaking a number of administrative reforms. They reduced the royalty tax from one-fifth (the old *quinto real*) to one-tenth of production, which guaranteed the mine operators a higher yield on their investments. Royal officials also took measures to increase production and reduce the price of mercury, the essential ingredient for separating silver from the crushed ore. Toward the end of the century, the Crown encouraged technological innovation in the industry by sponsoring expeditions of mining engineers from Spain and Germany. The old mining technology of patio amalgamation persisted, although the Spanish Crown sponsored the widespread use of gunpowder for blasting deeper pits. Increased production of Spanish American mines—and greater revenues for the colonial state—remained ever the goal.

The great Valenciana mine of Guanajuato, New Spain's leading mining center, was the marvel of the late eighteenth century. One of its three vertical shafts descended 550 meters into the earth, from which mine workers dug out horizontal galleries to follow the veins of ore. Blasting with gunpowder was commonplace, and a system of animal-driven hoists raised most of the ore out of the ground. More than three thousand men worked underground, and the Valenciana's refineries processed nearly all of its ore production. It sold the rest to independent smelters. The Valenciana alone produced almost 70 percent of Guanajuato's total silver production. At the time, Guanajuato was the largest silver district in Mexico, providing more than 60 percent of the silver from all of Spain's colonies.

Miners responded to the new demand and to the government's encouragement. From its seventeenth-century bastions of Taxco, Pachuca, Guanajuato, and Zacatecas,

Map 8.1   New Spain

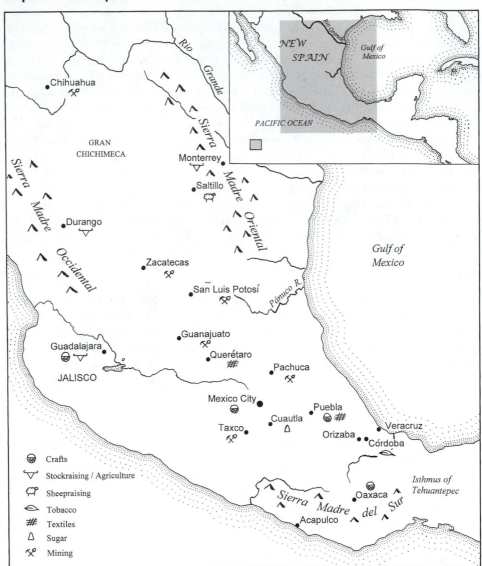

the mining frontier of New Spain expanded north and west (see Map 8.1). Entrepreneurs and workers formed new mining settlements in Chihuahua and Sonora. For its part, the colonial state provided security for the mining frontier by enlisting the Jesuit and Franciscan missionaries to establish missions out beyond the northernmost mining centers. The mission settlements would form a buffer zone to protect the mines from attack by hostile Native Americans and prevent encroachment by foreign powers. By 1700, the Franciscans had established several missions along the Río Grande, and by 1725 they were in San Antonio. Eusebio Francisco Kino led his fellow Jesuits into

Mexican muleskinners on the outskirts of Guanajuato. (F. Lehnert, ca. 1840)

Sonora and Arizona, a northwestern push that the Franciscans led by Junípero Serra would extend into California. Spaniards founded a settlement at the bay of San Francisco in 1776.

Within this expanding frontier, new silver discoveries reversed Mexico's century-long decline in production. In 1700, New Spain produced only about twenty-five million pesos of silver. That production rose nearly to sixty-five million pesos in 1750 and to ninety-one million in 1775. At its height, the Mexican mining industry turned out approximately one hundred twenty-two million pesos in 1805.

Mining expansion stimulated secondary economic activity in northern Mexico. Mule trains connected the remote mines to the commercial towns of the north, and oxcarts (large, two-wheeled Spanish wagons) carried freight between these towns and Mexico City. The Bajío, a region bordering the cities of Guadalajara, Zacatecas, and Guanajuato, opened up to extensive agriculture. During the course of the eighteenth century, farmers and hacendados converted the Bajío from a land ruled by the Chichimec to a cattle- and mule-breeding ground and finally to a zone of mixed agriculture. Large haciendas staffed by scores of peons shared production with ranchero (smallholder) families. Even some smaller subsistence producers found room in the Bajío. Commonly, large landowners converted former cattle ranches to cash crops in the Bajío and the nearby state of Jalisco by renting out parcels to sharecropping families. This conversion process picked up pace toward the latter quarter of the eighteenth century. Cattle herds moved to the more arid pastures of the northern provinces. The bustling population of the north, primarily Creoles and mestizos, forged a free wage labor force. Commercial agriculture of Creole hacendados and mestizo rancheros and peons predominated, for indigenous peasant villages had not been a feature in the north even in the days of the Aztec. North Mexican society, therefore, differed substantially from the Spanish hacienda–native village complex of central and southern Mexico.

In the meanwhile, eighteenth-century frontier expansion provoked conflict with the seminomadic natives of North America. What had transpired among the Chichimec of the near north in the late sixteenth and seventeenth centuries—warfare, virtual genocide, and dispersion—now visited the Mayo and Yaqui in Sonora. Creole and mestizo frontiersmen plowed the fertile valleys and ran cattle on their hunting grounds. Mounted soldiers equipped with steel-tipped spears and muskets took the field against those natives who resisted the invasion. In the central plateau of northern New Spain, the Comanche and Apache found their winter hunting grounds much reduced. North Mexican cattlemen became what their North American counterparts would become a century later—alert and adept fighters of the nomadic natives. Much of the northern New Spain mining frontier remained in a state of low-level conflict between the Hispanic settlers and the indigenous hunter-gatherers.

Spaniards and Creoles

In all cases, the numerous mining booms of Latin America produced a new generation of wealth, which was absorbed and distributed according to colonial patterns. In most cases, Spanish-born gentlemen enjoyed the advantages of economic and political clout. They were in the socially advantageous positions to mobilize the capital needed to finance and revive the older mines. In New Spain, most of the fabled silver barons of the eighteenth century were Spaniards. They used their wealth to establish finely appointed residences in the heart of Mexico City, the viceregal capital. They adorned their social prominence with membership in the *cofradías,* contributed to the correct charities, and filled many political offices, some purely honorary and others offering real influence. Elevation to the nobility rounded out the mining magnate's social credentials. The Spanish-born Count of Regla owned the Real del Monte silver mines at Pachuca and was reputedly the wealthiest man in New Spain. He served on the capital's city council *(cabildo),* giving him access to markets for products from his many haciendas, and belonged to the board of the Hospital de Dios (Hospital of God). The count's retinues and employees numbered in the hundreds, and his urban and rural properties were numerous. The small group of wealthy, titled silver barons of Mexico, like the Count of Regla, counted themselves among the true grandees of colonial Latin America.

Occasionally, a Mexican-born white gained entry into the highest social echelon of colonial society. A fortunate silver strike on some remote mountaintop could enable an intrepid Creole entrepreneur also to buy one or more haciendas, partly to support his mining operations but also to confer prestige on his family. Great wealth afforded the native-born white the right to enter the rarefied society of high government and church officials, mining barons, and export merchants, most of whom were Spaniards. The few Creole miners who succeeded were especially avid pursuers of the costly titles of nobility. Nonetheless, they often felt the barb of social discrimination as well as business disadvantages when Spanish-born officials and merchants gave out contracts and loans. New wealth never quite erased the disdain that Spaniards held toward the Creole parvenu.

After the miners, Spanish merchants formed a second tier at the apex of the multiracial hierarchy established by Spanish conquistadores two centuries before. A small group of successful wholesalers engaging in overseas commerce had the capital necessary to rejuvenate the mines. They provided the financing for labor, mercury, gunpowder, oxcarts, mules, and supplies. These Spaniards still retained a great advantage over the Mexican-born whites, for the leading import-export merchants of Mexico City were related to the great merchant families of Seville, Cádiz, and other Spanish ports. Their advantage consisted of these commercial connections, which were inseparable from their family ties back in Spain. The merchant houses in the Spanish ports negotiated with British, French, and Dutch traders who offered the latest manufactured textiles—or wines and perfumes—and obtained the necessary permits from the royal court to transport them to the American colonies. These great merchant houses used their correspondents in the Americas to distribute colonial products throughout Spain and Europe.

To solidify their connections in the Indies, these commercial families would dispatch a son or nephew to New Spain and Guatemala. There the young Spaniard entered into a kind of apprenticeship with trusted relatives or kinsman until he had enough capital and knowledge to establish his own merchant house. For marriage partners, Spaniards who by their thirties had gained independence and wealth in their own right chose brides from among the native-born teenage daughters of established Spanish merchants. Depending on their rank, Spanish-born officials and clergy shared the high status of the wealthiest merchants.

Being a native-born Creole woman *(criolla)* carried no real onus for daughters of Spanish merchants as long as the fathers could arrange a marriage with an eligible and successful Spaniard. Wives usually did not have much economic influence unless they could bring to the marriage a dowry of haciendas, urban property, or cash. The married woman usually retained control of her own dowry, even though she most often combined her assets with her husband's. Was there love in the marriage for the young elite woman? Sometimes. She could, after all, refuse to marry the Spaniard. But such a decision relegated her to marrying a less-advantaged native white man, to spinsterhood, or to living in the nunnery. The proper marriage brought additional commercial benefits to her family, a factor that weighed powerfully on conscientious daughters. Father and son-in-law expected benefits from each other. The younger, because he was a Spaniard and "family," could expect the financing necessary to branch out into mining, where a fortune might be made, and land, where wealth could be preserved. Secondary investment in country stores, urban retail shops, or a string of packmules also proved wise. The vagaries of international trade in the days of pirates, international wars, and ship disasters required such diversification. After all, merchants wanted to ensure their fortunes—and social status—from the uncertainties of eighteenth-century commerce.

In New Spain, the Mexican-born son of a successful Spaniard did not enjoy the same advantages as the immigrant merchant. After receiving a private, Catholic education, the Creole son learned his Spanish father's secondary businesses. He directed the mule trains, managed the hacienda, operated the retail shop, or collected the rent from lessees of urban properties. Eventually, some of these assets became his inheritance. Mexican sons could aspire to a low-level job in the church or a modest sinecure in the bureaucracy. Neither occupation really prevented the Creole from also owning property or running a business. In most cases, however, the assets and connections of Mexican sons did not suffice to generate the amount of wealth to which their Spanish-born brothers-in-law might aspire. Only by superb luck (a mining strike) or extraordinary skill could the Creole rise to the ranks of the wealthy nobility. Those native whites of less exalted birth had their life prospects determined in large measure by their father's accomplishments. If he had married a white woman and been moderately successful in operating an hacienda or provincial shop, the son might aspire to respectability. However, business failure presented a great social setback to the Creole.

Table 8.1   Estimated Population of New Spain, 1814

Racial Group	Number	Percent
Spanish-born whites	15,000	0.2
Creole whites	1,093,000	17.8
Mestizos/mulattoes	1,338,000	22.0
Native Americans	3,676,000	60.0

SOURCE: Timothy E. Anna, *The Fall of the Royal Government in Mexico City* (Lincoln: University of Nebraska Press, 1978), 6.

The vast majority of Creoles who were sons of other Creoles—not of Spaniards—had even fewer advantages. The Creole grandson might be accepted at a low level of the elite in the viceregal capital of Mexico City, or at a higher level in important provincial towns like Querétaro or Guatemala City, as long as he had the wealth and lineage to be accepted. An overwhelming majority of second- and third-generation Creoles had to settle for positions secondary to the Spaniards. Insofar as economic success marked one's social status, wealth tended to make one more acceptable at the high reaches of the elite. (Occasionally, darker-skinned men might overcome the lack of European lineage with wealth. But in most cases, mestizos and mulattoes lacked the opportunities and connections of Creoles to acquire even modest wealth.)

Yet Spaniards had more advantages than native-born Creoles. As the eighteenth century drew to a close, however, the lower levels of the *gente decente* were filled by the far more numerous Creoles. Demographically, the Creole was more predominant in Iberian society of the Americas at the end of the century. For every Spaniard in New Spain, there were at least five hundred Creoles, depending on location (see Table 8.1). Creoles especially predominated in the provincial towns and cities of New Spain. Understandably, they increasingly developed ambivalent feelings about the few Spaniards who seemed to monopolize the social and political opportunities so necessary to create economic wealth.

DOMESTIC MARKETS

Economic growth in New Spain had another, related dimension also contributing to resentment: poor distribution of income. The wealthy tended to use their social power to capture the greatest increment of growing income. Take the viceregal capital of Mexico City. At the end of the eighteenth century, Mexico City had a population of 168,000 persons. It was the largest of the American cities, including New York and Philadelphia. Nothing in the New World equaled the splendor of Mexico City. It had seven causeways across Lake Texcoco, connecting the island to its hinterland in Mexico's central valley. More than one hundred churches and chapels, numerous convents and monasteries, 12 hospitals, several secondary schools, a great university, a botanical garden, and extensive markets graced this majestic capital. Its immense central plaza, fronted by the governmental palaces and the cathedral, inspired awe. Here resided the richest families in all the Americas.

Urban Society

The fine distinctions that the *gente decente,* the well-born people of Spanish descent, observed among themselves might be measured by the numbers of servants per elite households. Miners, merchants, top bureaucrats, ranking ecclesiastical and military officers, and the titled nobility comprised the 4 percent of households each having three servants or more. A second tier (18 percent of the population) of intellectuals, professionals, merchants and businessmen, clerks, militia officers, and lower clergy had only one servant each.

But the viceregal capital also displayed great squalor. Its canals, dating from Aztec times, were filled with refuse and human waste, which also spilled into the surrounding lakes. Beggars and the homeless filled the broad streets. The workers and their families resided in ramshackle huts and lean-tos on the outskirts of the prestigious downtown neighborhoods. These persons, overwhelmingly native and mestizo, suffered most from the fearsome epidemics that periodically struck the congested city. Epidemics occurred in 1736, 1761, 1772, 1779, 1797, and 1813. Nearly half the population had been lost in the first epidemic. Furthermore, less than 2 percent of the population owned any urban property. The colonial government and the various orders of the church possessed almost half of the land and buildings of Mexico City. Most persons rented their places of residence. At the end of the eighteenth century, 41 truly wealthy citizens owned an average of 11 buildings each; another 370 wealthy proprietors owned an average of 2 properties each. According to Bishop Manuel Abad y Queipo, Mexican society seemed to be divided into two groups: those who had nothing and those who had everything. The statement, though exaggerated, does capture the inequitable character of income distribution.

The wealthiest Spanish families resided at the city's center, and the farther one walked from the impressive Plaza de Armas, the less Spanish and more colored the people of the neighborhoods became, until at the outskirts of Mexico City, one found the ramshackle barrios of the most recent native migrants. Spanish-born males headed the families of the elite and the mid-level professional classes. But in Mexico City, half the population was Iberian and many Spanish immigrants and Creoles also worked as artisans and skilled laborers. But Native Americans formed the most destitute and miserable of the city's population. It was a rare marriage indeed that joined a Spanish man and a native woman, and a match between a white woman and a native man was rarer still.

More women than men lived in the cities of New Spain, and more men than women inhabited the countryside. "Country women come into the cities to serve in the houses," explained Baron Alexander von Humboldt, "and a great number of men leave them to travel through the country as muleteers, or to fix their abode in places with considerable mines." Village girls (mostly natives) migrated to serve in the households of the wealthy and professional classes. They may have been only 16 to 22 years of age, but the work was demeaning. The hours were long, pay was low, and there was precious little time off. Few employers respected the servant girls or appreciated their work. They were easily replaced when they returned to the village to be married.

Four of every 25 women of Mexico City never married. Women of the privileged, white classes could afford spinsterhood, although upper-class spinsters seldom lived independently, still having family responsibilities, helping to run the household, bringing up the nieces and nephews, and carrying out family religious responsibilities. Most elite single women, in fact, did not go into the nunnery. But even among married women of the *gente de pueblo,* there was much independence—even economic power. Many women outlived their husbands and carried on with the trades and households. Others were abandoned and stayed to bring up the children, dominating the open-air markets and sidewalk vending of the capital. An 1811 census of Mexico City indicated that women headed one-third of the urban households.

The story of poverty did not differ substantially in the countryside. Basically, from 1789 to 1810, the droughts and crop failures that punctuated population recovery and the economic boom spread uncertainty and resentment among New Spain's rural population. The long decline of the indigenous population had halted in the previous century—although periodic epidemics raged even thereafter (see Document 8.1). By 1650, the birth rate among Native Americans in Mexico finally surpassed the death rate for the first time since the Conquest. But 90 percent of the natives of central Mexico

MANUSCRIPT 8.1

The Social and Economic Cost of Pestilence

Since the mid-seventeenth century, the indigenous populations of highland Mexico and Guatemala had been slowly recovering from their precipitous decline that had commenced with the Conquest. The colonial economy benefited from this long-term recovery because native peasants in many parts of the Viceroyalty of New Spain remained the primary producers of foodstuffs and an important source for labor in commercial agriculture, construction, and mines. But population recovery suffered numerous setbacks. Besides the occasional drought that stressed the peasant population, pestilence broke out periodically to afflict those colonial residents least able to resist. Their poverty and lack of sanitary conditions often made the peasants vulnerable to the continued ravages of disease, although not on the scale of the sixteenth century. Here a Ladino (nonnative) resident of Guatemala's Cuchumatán Highlands describes the effects of the typhus epidemic of 1805.

For four years now in the towns of Soloma there has been great distress due to the mortality caused by the typhus epidemic which kills the Indians without relief or remedy, leaving them only in dire hardship. Through fear of death, we [the Ladino residents] fled with our families to the solitude of the mountains and the rocky wastes of Chemal, suffering there from the extremity of the climate, leaving our houses and possessions abandoned in Soloma. But God having seen fit to end this terrible affliction, we have returned once again to our homes. We find that the majority of the Indians of Santa Eulalia have perished and are lying unburied all over the place, their decaying corpses eaten by the animals which stalk the countryside. Because of this and the fact that countless sheep also perished, neglected in their pens, the pestilence raged even more. What grieves us most, however, as it would any

still lived in villages whose lands had been consolidated during the seventeenth century to accommodate their dwindling numbers. Consequently, population pressure on native lands became severe in the late eighteenth century. While the number of indigenous peasants increased, the landholdings of the indigenous communities did not, leading inevitably to conflict. Peasant villagers began to dispute the control of land and water among themselves as well as with white-owned haciendas. In Jalisco, where half the population was indigenous, expansion of the numbers of peasant villagers reduced the ratio of land to residents. In 1750 the pueblo of Tizapán el Bajo had a population of 1,000 souls. But by 1819, its population had grown to 1,700, even though Tizapán's landed resources remained the same. Consequently, many residents found they had to find wage work outside the community to survive. Free Native Americans replaced slaves on the haciendas, and the African slave trade in Mexico declined drastically as a result. But the growing number of peons seeking hacienda work did not reduce their bargaining power, for economic growth simultaneously increased the demand for labor. Labor shortages on haciendas in northern and western Mexico continued to be chronic.

pious heart, is to see the great number of orphaned children crying for the laps of their parents, asking for bread without having anyone to receive it from; to behold many widows and widowers mourning the loss of their consorts; and to watch old people lament the death of their offspring. After so much hard work, these unfortunate Indians have been reduced to a life of misery. Having returned to their town [the Indians who survived] are without homes to live in, without resources to pay their expenses and tribute, and without corn to feed themselves and their families. If no measures are taken to assist these wretched people, they will without doubt starve to death, because they did not plant corn in the places where they sought refuge and so have nothing to live on, both for this year and for next, since it is now too late to plant their fields. It is a common thing in this parish to encounter Indians from Santa Eulalia, old and young alike, walking from town to town, from house to house, begging and searching for corn or charity. Others seek loans, leaving as security one of their children, for they have nothing else to offer. Señor Alcalde Mayor, because I witness these setbacks from such close quarters, for the sake of God and a sign of His mercy, inform the President that help should be extended to the towns of this parish; at the very least, the people of Santa Eulalia and San Miguel Acatán could be exempted from paying tribute for the years during which they have suffered great misfortune.

SOURCE: Marcos Santiago to the Alcalde Mayor, May 5, 1806, Archivo General de Centroamérica, Guatemala City, A3.16, leg. 249, exp. 5036, folio 2, as quoted in W. George Lovell, *Conquest and Survival in Colonial Guatemala: A Historical Geography of the Cuchumatán Highlands, 1500–1821* (Kingston, Ontario: McGill-Queen's University Press), 169.

Manufacturing

As markets expanded because of international trade, so did the domestic industries given over to satisfying internal demand. Domestic textile production flourished on several levels. In the countryside far from commercial centers, Native American women and mestizas often spent part of the day with narrow hand looms strapped around their waists. They then sewed the colorful woolen and cotton strips together to form ponchos and blankets. Closer to provincial and capital cities, local merchants invested in *obrajes* specializing in the production of woolen and cotton cloth. At their highest level of organization, these *obrajes* might gather together up to two hundred men and women who cleaned the raw wool and cotton; carded, spun, and wove them at stationary broadlooms; and finished and dyed the product into bolts of cloth. However, workers accomplished these processes by hand, in contrast to the use of mechanical looms in the English industrial revolution. The *obrajes* of Latin America did not represent technological innovation in textile production.

Wherever large concentrations of population existed that were somewhat removed from direct international trade, there one found the *obraje.* Its primitive technology prevented the colonial textile plant from competing directly with industrial textiles from Europe. *Obrajes* were located in the highlands away from the great ports and were protected by high freight charges. Mexico City, Puebla, and Querétaro became centers of *obraje* production in Mexico. In these places, Spanish and Creole merchants provided the credit needed to collect the various stages of hand production into one central shop. Creole managers kept the accounts, and mestizo and mulatto foremen supervised the work. Women also entered the *obraje* workforce. They cooked meals for the workers, many of whom had quarters at the shop, and also assisted in the washing and spinning of wool. The most skilled workers at the *obrajes,* the professional weavers, could be a difficult lot. Their work determined the rate of production of the whole shop, and they dominated the staff of weaver assistants. Because good weavers were not easily replaced, the manager and foremen were unable to exhort them to work more quickly. Most often, supervisors had to use incentives rather than punishments to motivate the skilled weavers, who were mestizos. The *obraje* foremen reserved their physical and verbal abuse for the poorly paid unskilled workers, mainly Native Americans.

Profits for these *obrajes,* pressed as they were by European competition, were never large. The popular classes could not afford to pay high prices for coarse woolens, and owners were therefore motivated to keep wage rates down, especially for the unskilled natives, who consequently attempted to avoid work in the *obrajes.* Because the *obrajes* clothed the masses, however, the local authorities cooperated with the owners. Officials drafted peasant villagers to work the *obrajes* and also sent convict labor to the owners, who consequently had to build jails on the property and hire guards. If the incessant complaints of the owners are to be believed, convict and forced labor did not prove to be efficient, but the *obrajes* might not have survived economically without this form of government subsidy.

The vast working population of the colonies, the *gente de pueblo,* were the ultimate consumers of this domestically produced cloth. Only the less numerous but wealthier elite could afford the industrially manufactured, imported European cloth. Consequently, both markets expanded together as the colonial economies generated income for both the elite and the wage earners. Obviously, clothing further identified and separated the various ranks in society. A member of the *gente de pueblo,* even though he or she may have been light skinned, needed merely to appear in *obraje*-made cloth in order to be recognized as a worker. Both workers and elite may have increased their material possessions during the eighteenth century, but the distinctions of social status remained.

Other economic activities became increasingly important in the eighteenth century. The popular alcoholic drink of pre-Conquest origins, pulque, gave rise to a complex of taverns in towns and hamlets catering especially to men of the *gente de pueblo.* These taverns were called *pulquerías.* Workers gathered here to exchange stories and jokes, discuss job opportunities, and enjoy leisure time. The viceregal authorities in Mexico City became disturbed at the laziness and drunkenness that the *pulquerías* supposedly produced, but they felt constrained from doing anything about it. Members of the popular classes demanded the freedom to drink with peers, and many Creole businesses profited from selling pulque. Not ones to overlook a source of revenue, royal bureaucrats and town councilors alike choose to levy taxes on the otherwise objectionable popular liquor.

The preparation of tobacco also developed into a thriving business in the eighteenth century. Thousands of small shopkeepers, street vendors, and rural peddlers were engaged in rolling and selling cigarettes and cigars. Neither powerful planters nor elite merchants dominated the tobacco industry. Here was another occupation in which women of the *gente de pueblo* found much opportunity. By the hundreds, they either owned or operated these family businesses, for they accomplished their tobacconist chores while caring for children and cooking for family members. Tobacco came from both *hacendados* and numerous small producers. This democratic crop was especially suited to family farmers with modest holdings. Colonial authorities spotted another source of revenue and, in 1765, made all branches of the tobacco trade a royal monopoly. Gradually, the viceregal state in Mexico City consolidated the industry. Farmers legally planted tobacco only under royal license in Orizaba and Córdoba. By 1790, six state-run tobacco factories turned out cigarettes, cigars, and snuff, to be sold only at government-licensed stores throughout New Spain. Twenty thousand persons became employed in the tobacco monopoly. Second only to the silver mines in generating tax revenues, this monopoly industry provided approximately one-fifth of the viceroyalty's revenues. Nonetheless, government authorities never succeeded in eliminating the contraband trade in tobacco products.

Most remarkably, the economic expansion of the eighteenth century spread to the fringes of Spanish settlement in North America, areas either neglected beforehand or lying beyond the frontier. Northern New Spain expanded its mining and cattle operations, as already mentioned. In addition, the Atlantic trade boom redounded to the commercial advantage of the non-silver-producing peripheries of Spanish North America. Spain's Caribbean possessions of Cuba, Santo Domingo, and Puerto Rico entered Atlantic commerce by developing exports of sugar. Central America developed exports in indigo, a blue dyestuff, and New Spain's southern province of Oaxaca expanded on the production and export of the red dyestuff, cochineal. Both products were used in European textile factories. In each of these cases of growth on the fringes, however, existing colonial elites and immigrant Spanish merchants reaped the material benefits, while the state jealously claimed regulatory and taxing authority.

Cochineal

The economic history of Oaxaca serves as a case study of the confusion between political and commercial functions. It also illustrates how growth increased social tensions in the province. In the sixteenth and seventeenth centuries, much of the province had belonged to the Marquisado (a private fiefdom) of the family of conqueror Hernán Cortés. His successors attempted to prevent other Spaniards from entering, and few did. Oaxaca did not attract much European settlement because it did not contain great deposits of silver like the provinces of northern Mexico. Therefore, Cortés's real heirs were the Native Americans who continued to make up the vast majority of the population there. The other heirs were the missionary orders. Dominicans, Franciscans, Augustinians, and Jesuits established the major monasteries, churches, and supporting haciendas in the first two centuries following conquest, and at least five important nunneries were built in the provincial capital, Antequera de Oaxaca. The religious orders also attempted to prevent the entry of Spaniards, Creoles, and mestizos into native communities.

Protecting the natives became the primary responsibility of the local Spanish magistrates, the *corregidores* and *alcaldes*. But the low salaries of these royal officials merely encouraged them to abuse their power to collect tribute from natives and distribute their labor. Spanish officials often performed these functions for their own profit. To this end, the local officials established financial connections with the great merchants—also Spanish born—of Mexico City. Having received advances from merchants in the viceregal capital, the magistrates reciprocated by acting as their local agents. The *corregidores* and *alcaldes* sold commercial goods to the natives, often forcing them to purchase faulty and inferior products at inflated prices. They also used native labor, through the *repartimiento* labor draft, to collect Oaxacan goods, cotton and woolen textiles and vanilla, for redistribution. The natives did resist these abuses. They rebelled in 1660, rising up and killing the *alcalde* of Tehuantepec and burning down the royal warehouse. The revolt spread to 20 other towns before the bishop of Oaxaca intervened to pacify the province. Nevertheless, the abusive commercial system persisted because the international market for Oaxacan products grew enormously in the eighteenth century.

The most important of these local products for export was cochineal. The textile factories of England and the Low Countries became voracious consumers of this scarlet dye. Approximately one-half of the native population of the province was involved part time in the cultivation and collection of cochineal. Production consisted of growing cactus and maguey plants on the haciendas and peasant lands of the region. The cochineal insect proliferated on these cacti. Several times during the year, indigenous laborers collected the bugs, dried them, and crushed the residue into a reddish powder. Native villagers cultivated their own stands of cactus as well as those on the haciendas. They sold the cochineal to the same local officials who had integrated them into the monetary market by forcing them to buy goods sent down from Mexico City. The cochineal trade attained its peak between 1769 and 1778, when annual production surpassed 1 million pounds. Revenues amounted to 4 million pesos per year, approximately one-third the value of Mexico's silver production. In Spain, cochineal was the fourth most important trade product, most of it re-exported through the port of Cádiz to northern Europe (see Table 8.2).

Although exploited, the indigenous peasants of Oaxaca managed to retain possession of their peasant lands, but prosperity and population growth did exacerbate the

Table 8.2   Spanish-American Trade at the Port of Cádiz, 1786

Ranking	Spanish-American Product	Value in Pesos
1	Coined silver pesos	238,687,185
2	Indigo of Guatemala	49,840,000
3	Royal Tobacco Monopoly	46,418,880
4	Cochineal	30,057,754
5	Coined gold pesos	24,981,145
6	Venezuela cacao	22,253,940
7	Hides from Buenos Aires	16,420,544
8	Peruvian quinine	12,375,904
9	White sugar	10,615,131
10	Cacao of Guayaquil	9,870,169
11	Indigo of Caracas	4,825,890
12	Palo (timber) from Campeche	4,711,992
13	Unclarified (crude) sugar	4,707,717
14	Copper	3,065,344
15	Unseeded cotton	2,601,354
16	Brazilwood	1,953,420
17	Gold disc coined pesos	1,671,835
18	Tabasco pepper	1,460,870
19	Purge of Jalapa	1,220,544
20	Cedar wood	1,210,080
21	Crafted silver	1,146,210
	Total value of all trade	501,001,664

SOURCE: Brian R. Hamnett, *Politics and Trade in Southern Mexico, 1750–1821* (Cambridge, England: Cambridge University Press, 1971), 174.

cleavages among them. Oaxaca's population ended its steep decline in the mid-seventeenth century and thereafter rose from nearly seventy thousand in 1740 to one hundred ten thousand in the 1790s. Native Americans formed the vast majority of this province's population, especially in the rural districts. Only the provincial capital of Antequera de Oaxaca contained a majority of nonnatives—but even there, the mestizo neighborhoods had indigenous origins. Sixteenth-century Antequera de Oaxaca had contained 10 distinctive barrios surrounding the Spanish city center, and residents of each barrio spoke their own language and wore ethnic clothes. By the eighteenth century, however, these barrios had lost their separate identity. Spanish slowly replaced the native dialects, nonnatives took up residence, and racial mixture reduced the ethnic distinctions.

In the rural districts, the story was different. Here the indigenous peoples retained control over their own cultural life. They also possessed much of the arable land, competing only with the few haciendas belonging to the religious orders and nonnatives. However, the natives did not form one monolithic group. Their rural communities were divided among three principal ethnic groups, the Nahuatl-speaking Aztecs, the Zapotec, and the Mixtec. Each group had its own customs, dress, language, and native-Catholic religious observances. The ancient noble families of the native leaders retained their primacy within these communities. The *caciques* owned private estates and represented the natives in dealings with the clergy and with the Spanish magistrates. In a way, they mediated the commercial and political demands between the natives and nonnatives. The *caciques* acted as labor bosses in the *repartimiento*. They collected tribute and allocated the sale of European goods within their communities. To an extent, these native elites participated in the system of exploitation—but in such a way as to preserve the integrity of their communities. The power of these native lords, despite their gradual absorption into the racial and ethnic community of nonnatives, persisted through the eighteenth century. Their status was not so much under pressure from Spaniards as it was from the native commoners, who increasingly contested the control and authority of the *caciques* as population pressure rose in the eighteenth century.

Although committed to community-based agriculture, many native commoners had adapted to certain advantageous European techniques. The indigenous population in these areas clung to subsistence agriculture based on village production of corn, beans, and chilies, but they also adopted European sources of protein such as chickens, pigs, and goats. Many native peasants also abandoned the traditional digging stick and plowed European style, with yokes of oxen. Their productivity, along with their growing numbers, caused peasants to encroach upon the adjacent haciendas and each other's village lands. Contemporary observers remarked on how aggressive peasants had become in contesting land and water rights. They defended their community lands through force and tenacity but also through the Spanish legal system. So adept did the natives become in litigation that the viceroy feared for the continuation of social and economic order in Oaxaca. "There is a shortage of agricultural labor; residents of the countryside are growing accustomed to the laziness and vices of the cities," he wrote. Other Native Americans began to purchase private holdings and became a separate class of smallholders; in time, they would begin to lose the ethnic identities reinforced by village living, becoming culturally if not racially mestizo. Economic prosperity based on exports certainly brought about neither the demise nor the destitution of the *gente de pueblo* in Oaxaca. The same conclusion obtains for Central America.

CENTRAL AMERICA

On the fringes, commercial expansion often did not mean that white elites prospered to such an extent that they eliminated opportunities for local merchant families. Much less did it signify that mestizo and mulatto smallholders, native peasants, and modest carters and muleskinners were crushed under a juggernaut of commercial capitalism. In many ways, the indigo boom of eighteenth-century Central America, then a political dependency of the Viceroyalty of New Spain, provided for the expansion of the *gente de pueblo*. Opportunity actually spread widely among all social groups, and the *hacendados* paid dearly for scarce labor. At the same time, however, the economic growth of Central America did not transform the multi-ethnic colonial social order any more than it had in Mexico.

The southern provinces of New Spain stretched from the Isthmus of Tehuantepec to the Isthmus of Panama. It also responded to the first stirrings of the industrial revolution, whose textile factories expanded to meet the demand for dyestuffs to color and decorate

Map 8.2   Central America and the Caribbean Islands in 1790

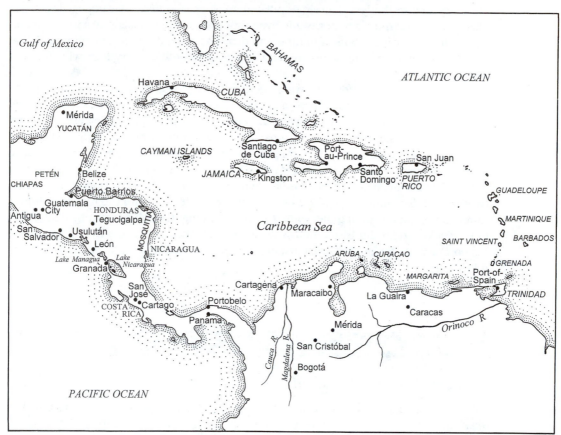

the cotton cloth they manufactured. At the time, only natural dyestuffs were available. As previously mentioned, the peasant producers and commercial agents of Oaxaca benefited. Central Americans also participated in these expanding opportunities to trade in dyestuffs. The indigo bush, whose branches and leaves yield a blue coloring, grew wild on the western slopes of the Sierras in Chiapas and El Salvador (see Map 8.2). It could also be cultivated on the humid plains along the Pacific Coast. After rudimentary processing in boiling vats, indigo moved via mule trains up to the provincial capital of Guatemala City and thence down the eastern slopes to Puerto Barrios on the Caribbean Sea (see Manuscript 8.2). Taxation of this trade yielded the colonial state more than 1 million pesos yearly by the 1770s. In the ports of Spain, the value of indigo cargoes were overshadowed only by silver and gold bullion shipped from Veracruz, Cartagena, and Buenos Aires. Other products, Venezuelan cacao, tobacco from Cuba and Paraguay, and hides from the Río de la Plata, ranked a distant third. Furthermore, an unknown quantity of Central American indigo found its way as contraband into the holds of British and French ships.

All in all, Central America's population rose from 797,214 persons in 1778 to 1,287,491 in 1825. Indigenous agriculturists still remained the largest portion of the population in the highland provinces of Chiapas and Guatemala. Native Americans also predominated in the less densely populated areas of Honduras, Nicaragua, and Costa Rica. Spaniards formed a minority and lived especially in Guatemala City and, to a lesser extent, in the smaller towns of Central America. The population of the region included a substantial number of African slaves and, in the eighteenth century, a growing number of mulattoes.

A separate cultural identity was emerging in the region, eventually to become known as *Ladino,* a term identifying all persons of mixed Native American, African, and Iberian blood. Ladinos dressed more in the European fashion, spoke Spanish nearly exclusively, and considered themselves separate from and superior to the natives. However, natives who left their highland communities, spoke Spanish, and dressed in European clothes became part of this Ladino group. In Usulután, one indigo district of El Salvador, the mixed-race inhabitants formed more than 85 percent of the population. The 76 resident Spaniards composed only 1.2 percent of the population, and the rest were Native Americans. Opinion among the *gente decente* regarding the Ladino was not at all generous. "Blacks and mulattoes and Indians [living outside their communities]," reported one *hacendado,* "are inclined to evil, most of them thieves, and with many other vices harmful to [society]."

MANUSCRIPT 8.2

Transport and Marketing in Guatemala

Mesoamerica's unique geography of steep mountains, highland valleys, and tropical lowlands compounded problems for transportation. It meant that few products—only those of high value and low volume—could be transported profitably over long distances. Exports consisted principally of silver, gold, and dyestuffs such as indigo and cochineal. Imports were fine cloth, wine, slaves, and mercury for the mining industry. Therefore, each region of New Spain that was connected to international commerce engendered its own regional market for domestically produced, cheap, bulky products such as foodstuffs, coarse woolens, and artisan products. The following vignettes describe both the transportation problems and the ubiquitous local markets.

Besides the distance from the ports [to Guatemala City] must be added the roughness of the roads, which are such that it causes terror even among those who travel through them every day. On the route to the Gulf [of Honduras], used for the transportation of indigo to Cádiz, there is a particular mountain the description of which cannot be heard without a sense of terror. This is the cause for the high freight rates, which do not increase according to distance but according to the road's roughness, to the danger for the muleskinner of losing his mules, and to the short day's journeys multiplying [the journey's] duration and its expenses. The roads linking the provinces differ little [from the road between Guatemala City and the Caribbean coast].

SOURCE: "El Consulado de Guatemala evacúa el informe. . . ," (1798) as quoted in José Antonio Fernández Molina, "Coloring the World in Blue: The Indigo Boom and the Central American Market, 1750–1810" (Ph.D. diss., University of Texas at Austin, 1992), 130.

Mulattoes as well as mestizos numbered among the new group of Ladinos that expanded during the eighteenth century. Mulattoes came to specialize as part-time soldiers during the eighteenth century. British corsairs had attacked the West Coast of Central America in the late seventeenth century, and officials in Guatemala City responded by organizing the local population into militias. Not enough Spaniards willingly joined, and the officials distrusted placing arms in the hands of natives. The least objectionable solution was to allow mulattoes and free blacks to become defenders of the realm. Mulattoes used militia service throughout the century to reinforce their separate identity and expand their privileges. The grant of a separate legal status, with the military *fuero,* or special legal privileges for soldiers, linked this expanding popular class to the colonial state. Chapter 14 will show that the formation of colonial militia forces provided mulattoes elsewhere with similar opportunities and privileges in the eighteenth century.

The indigo boom was made to order for the Ladinos who formed the upper ranks of the *gente de pueblo.* They easily descended into unclaimed frontier lands, establishing smallholdings and hunting for the wild indigo bushes across the slopes and forests. El Salvador especially became the land of opportunity for Ladinos. They settled and controlled at least one-third of the land there, leaving another third to the indigenous agricultural communities and the rest to haciendas. In fact, the haciendas could not easily displace the independent producers, because smallholding Ladinos produced the highest quality of indigo. Moreover, the *hacendados* were confronted with labor scarcity. Colonial authorities did not permit the big landowners to use native workers in the indigo industry because the peasants were to grow foodstuffs and provide raw materials for the towns. Therefore, only Ladinos could be hired as peons. But Ladinos had so many other opportunities, such as working for themselves, that white *hacendados* had to provide generous cash advances to attract employees. Many Ladino workers thought nothing of running away and defaulting on their wage advances. Moreover, the military *fuero* protected those militiamen who absconded with cash advances or who simply refused to work for *hacendados.*

The towns and provincial capitals of Central America grew as a result of the indigo boom of the eighteenth century. Guatemala's capital had been moved to a new site in 1773 and renamed Guatemala City following the destruction of the old capital in a series of earthquakes. The new provincial capital's population multiplied from nearly six thousand inhabitants in 1774 to twenty-four thousand in 1800, a definitive boon to the urban construction industry. The capital city's population consisted overwhelmingly of craftspersons. Weavers, dryers, tailors, leather workers, cigar rollers, and ironmongers of the provincial capital elaborated cotton and woolen thread, leather products, tobacco, and iron into final consumer goods. Guatemala City even took on the social ills associated with colonial urban development—unemployment and beggars. Other cities of the realm were much the same, although the market towns of Cartago in Costa Rica and Granada and León in Nicaragua lacked the Iberian-born merchant class of Guatemala City. Creole and Ladino shopkeepers and artisans filled the bill as the local *gente decente* of these smaller towns.

The indigo prosperity of Central America stimulated local markets in foodstuffs, coarse woolen cloths, iron products of local manufacture, and internal transportation. Market fairs were held in several towns in Guatemala and El Salvador at the beginning and end of the harvest seasons so that peasant and *hacendado* producers of indigo could lay in supplies. Many of these trading fairs coincided with local religious celebrations. Pilgrimages became excuses for making a little money and gathering some material goods. Farms and haciendas located on the Pacific side of Nicaragua shipped foodstuffs to local markets in oxcarts operated by Ladinos and Native Americans. As a major source for municipal budgets, city officials at León taxed each oxcart entering the city. Peddlers connected the outlying districts to the local markets. Indeed, Nicaragua became the corridor for indigo sold illegally and directly to the British shippers based at Jamaica, some of whom had settled on the Atlantic coast of Nicaragua. Nicaraguan cattle were also an important commodity in local trade. The whole economic system of Central America came to depend upon external markets. The same can be said for the Spanish Caribbean.

THE SPANISH CARIBBEAN

Sugar's Difference

Although they were among the first lands discovered and settled by Spaniards, Santo Domingo, Puerto Rico, and Cuba lost prominence before the sixteenth century was out. They became mere commercial way stations in Spain's far more lucrative trade with the silver-producing colonies of New Spain and Peru. Besides, the Spanish Caribbean was difficult to defend. Its ports and settlements proved vulnerable to attack by the buccaneers of Spain's enemies, England and the Netherlands. Spanish settlers introduced sugarcane to the islands of Hispaniola, Jamaica (lost to the British in 1655), Cuba, and Puerto Rico in the sixteenth century. African slaves arrived to tend the fields and small mills. But Brazil's rapid expansion as the premier sugar producer for Europe forestalled further development in the Caribbean. New Spain and Peru proved to be no market for Caribbean sugar, for each viceroyalty had its own domestic cane production.

Therefore, the Spanish Caribbean settled into its role as commercial intermediary for the silver fleets, for which the Crown invested in fortifying the ports of San Juan, Santo Domingo, and Havana. The latter port dominated the island of Cuba to such a degree that in 1774 just under half of the island's 171,620 inhabitants lived and worked there. In the hinterlands of these port cities, free people of color spread out onto the sparsely settled lands as cattlemen, subsistence farmers, and tobacco growers. Rural life in Cuba took on an egalitarian flavor very much unlike the more densely settled and prosperous Spanish territories of the mainland. However, all this rural egalitarianism began to change because of events abroad.

In the mid-seventeenth century, the Dutch converted Amsterdam into Europe's leading entrepôt for sugar. Once eliminated from Brazil in 1654, the Dutch West Indian Company introduced capital into the sugar industries of the Caribbean. Barbados and Guadeloupe began cultivation of sugarcane first, and the dawn of the eighteenth century witnessed the heyday of plantation slavery in the Caribbean islands. In 1715, English traders gained the lucrative *asiento* slave-trading license from the Spanish Crown, with exclusive rights to import slaves into Spanish-American ports. Together, the English, Dutch, and French linked Caribbean sugar production to markets in Europe and labor supplies in Africa. French planters introduced slaves to the western end of Hispaniola, making Saint-Domingue one of the foremost sugar producers in the Americas. Probably half of the 10 to 13 million Africans who survived the Middle Passage ended up in the

Table 8.3   Racial Composition of Cuba and Puerto Rico, 1812–1817

	Puerto Rico (1812)	*Cuba (1817)*
African slaves	17,536 (9.6%)	199,145 (36.0%)
Free blacks	15,883 (8.7%)	
		114,058 (20.6%)
Free mulattoes	63,983 (35.0%)	
Whites	85,662 (46.7%)	239,830 (43.4%)
Total	183,064	553,033

SOURCES: Jorge Dominguez, *Insurrection or Loyalty: The Breakdown of the Spanish American Empire* (Cambridge, Mass.: Harvard University Press, 1980), 30; and Luis M. Díaz Soler, *Historia de la esclavitud negra en Puerto Rico* (San Juan: Editorial Universitaria, 1974), 117.

Caribbean islands. In contrast, Spanish planters still lagged behind. Until 1750 or so, most peasant producers in Cuba, Santo Domingo, and Puerto Rico served as suppliers for the plantation islands belonging to the British and French. They furnished foodstuffs, timber, and draft animals. Puerto Rico's leading crops in the early 1700s were coffee and tobacco produced by smallholders, not large landowners. Spanish planters in the Caribbean did not begin sugar cultivation seriously until the mid-eighteenth century, eventually importing some five hundred eighty thousand slaves, or 10 percent of the market.

Spanish Caribbean sugar production awaited the exhaustion of some of its British and Dutch competitors. Sugarcane rapidly depleted the nutrients in the fertile but fragile soils of the smaller islands. Deforestation also contributed to soil erosion there. When Barbados and Guadeloupe declined as exporters, Cuba and Puerto Rico took up much of the slack. British and Dutch planters profited in reselling slaves from their own deteriorating plantations to Spanish planters in San Juan and Havana. British Jamaica lost its preeminence in sugar production by the 1780s, and Dutch Surinam commenced a slow decline as a sugar exporter at about the same time. Sugar production in the French possession of Saint-Domingue (later Haiti) succumbed to a slave rebellion in the 1790s (see Chapter 13), and many of the French planters who escaped merely began anew in Cuba. Selling slaves from declining Caribbean islands to the rising Spanish colonies became a brisk business. Cuba received a large boost when, in the British-French-Spanish conflicts of the 1760s, the British navy captured Havana. The brief occupation swept away Spanish regulations inhibiting direct commerce to northern Europe. British merchants became even more accustomed to selling slaves to—and buying sugar from—Spanish merchants, who dissolved their nationalistic pride in an orgy of profit. English merchants introduced 10,700 *bozales,* African-born slaves, to Cuba in just five months. In the treaty ending the war, Spain gave up Florida to the British but regained Havana. Before the sugar revolution, Spanish officials had been talking about inviting in white Canary Island immigrants in order to "improve the quality" (that is, whiten the population) of the racially mixed society of Cuba. The proposal was quickly abandoned, and slave imports added even more to the racial diversity of the island (see Table 8.3).

Slave Society

In subsequent expansion, the merchants and planters of Cuba constantly surpassed Crown limits on slave imports. Many illegal shipments arrived at Havana while local officials, for extra fees, looked the other way as planters satisfied their desperate demand for chattel labor. "The annual loss [of slaves] by death has been eight or ten, at least, out of eighty," reported one planter. "[A]nd unless cargoes of slaves come to the island, its produce must diminish as a necessary consequence." Early on, male slaves outnumbered females by a ratio of three to one. But as the slave population matured, female slaves took their places alongside the men in the fields and in the cane-crushing plants. The old mills added the latest technologies. Mule-driven cane presses replaced the oxen-driven models, and water-powered machinery was also introduced (see Manuscript 8.3). Consequently, the island's slave population rose from 44,300 in 1774 to 186,000 in the 1820s. Some third-generation Afro-Cubans, who had considered themselves free, were kidnapped and sold into slavery. Tobacco and stockraising became relegated to secondary rural activities in the Spanish islands, and a rigidly demarcated multiracial plantation so-

MANUSCRIPT 8.3

The Cuban Sugar Plantation

The Cuban sugar boom had already commenced when Baron Alexander von Humboldt arrived at Havana in 1801 on his grand tour of Spanish America. He took time to survey one plantation, known by the Spanish word for "mill," ingenio, on the plain of Guines outside Havana. His description amounts to a business profile of the Cuban industry in its infancy. The reader should note that at this early date, all processing and refining of sugar occurred right on the same premises where the sugarcane was cultivated. It had to be crushed and processed within hours of being cut because otherwise it would lose all of its fructose content. Slow-moving oxcarts, the principal transportation within the plantation, prevented the cane from being transported rapidly. Therefore, every large plantation had its own ingenio, which processed its own cane as well as that of smallholders in the vicinity. Moreover, each ingenio produced a number of different products: several grades of white and brown sugars, molasses, and rum. Plantation owners, mostly Spaniards, owed much of their wealth and political influence to their command over this emergent economic unit on the island.

A large sugar plantation producing from 2,000 to 2,500 boxes, generally has fifty *caballerías* of land (about 1,600 acres), one-half of which is planted in cane, and the other is appointed for alimentary plants and pastures, which latter are called *potreros*. The value of the land naturally varies accordingly to its quality, and vicinity to the ports of Havana, Matanzas, or Mariel. In a radius of twenty-five leagues around Havana, the value of each *caballería* may be estimated at two or three thousand dollars.

That a plantation may produce 2,000 boxes of sugar, it must have three hundred negroes. An adult male slave, who is acclimated, is worth 450 or 500 dollars, and an unacclimated, newly imported African, 370 to 400 dollars. A negro costs from 45 to 50 dollars a year in food, clothing, and medicine, consequently, including the interest on capital, and throwing off the holidays, the cost of labor is

ciety replaced the more racially mixed egalitarian one. Cuba's trade with Spain at the end of the century equaled that of New Spain, and its capital and port of Havana, with 70,000 residents, had become the second largest city in the Americas. In the meanwhile, Spain lost the island of Trinidad, off Venezuela, to the British in 1797. Trinidad had remained underpopulated and out of the main commercial streams for two centuries. The Spanish Crown made up for the loss by collecting export duties on sugar and sales taxes on slaves in its remaining—and booming—Caribbean possessions. The expansion of sugar and slavocracy saved Cuba, Santo Domingo, and Puerto Rico for Spain.

Similar to the economic expansion of other fringe areas of New Spain, the rising plantation export economies of the Caribbean did contribute to the social opportunities of the *gente de pueblo.* Poor whites and free persons of color moved into shopkeeping, artisanry, and smallholding to supply the growing domestic market. But those who benefited most were Spaniards of the *gente decente.* Crown officials who happened to be in place in the 1770s easily obtained licenses to import slaves. They acquired public land on favorable terms, and Spaniards used their political connections to gain advantages in domestic commerce and markets. The families of the future Cuban oligarchy traced their

a little more than twenty-five cents a day. The slaves are supplied with jerked beef from Buenos Aires and Caracas, and salt fish, when meat is dear; with vegetables, such as plantains , pumpkins, sweet potatoes, and corn. In the year 1804, jerked beef was worth 5 to 6 cents a pound in Guines, and in 1825, its cost is from 7 to 8 cents.

On a sugar plantation such as we are describing, producing 2,000 or 2,500 boxes of sugar, there are required, 1st, three cylinder mills, worked by oxen or water-power; 2nd, eighteen kettles, according to the old Spanish method, which, having a very slow fire, burns much wood; and according to the French method, introduced in 1801, by Bailli, from St. Domingo, under the auspices of Don Nicolás Calvo, three clarifiers, three large kettles, and two boiling trains (each having three boilers), in all, twelve pieces. It is generally said that seventy-five pounds of purged sugar yields one keg (seven gallons) of molasses; and that this, with the refuse sugar, covers the expenses of the plantation; but this can be

true only where large quantities of rum are made. Two thousand boxes of sugar give 15,000 kegs of molasses, which will make 500 pipes of rum, worth $25 each. . . .

The profit of a plantation, established some time since, consists in, 1st, the fact that, twenty years since, the cost of making a plantation was much less than now; for, a *caballería* of good land cost then only $1,200 or $1,600, instead of $2,000 or $2,5000, as now; and an adult negro $300, instead of $450 to $500; and, 2nd, the variable returns—the prices of sugar having been at times very low, and at others very high. The prices of sugar have varied so much, during a period of ten years, that the return on the capital invested has varied from five to fifteen percent .

SOURCE: Alexander von Humboldt, *The Island of Cuba,* trans. J. S. Thrasher (New York: Derby and Jackson, 1801, 1856), 258–62, as quoted in *Slaves, Sugar, & Colonial Society: Travel Accounts of Cuba, 1801–1899,* Louis A. Pérez Jr., ed. (Wilmington, Del.: Scholarly Resources, 1992), 41–42. Accents added.

ancestry to these late eighteenth-century officials, many of whom had acquired enough wealth to purchase titles of nobility.

African slaves benefited least from the expansion of the export economies of the Caribbean sugar islands. Slaves had few rights before Spanish law, which considered them to be property, after all, rather than free workers. Their work lasted 14 to 16 hours per day during harvest time, and the overseer's lash—rather than wages—served as their chief motivation. Nevertheless, slaves maintained distinctions among themselves. Household and urban slaves received more privileges and freedoms, although they worked under the close supervision of the mistress and were vulnerable to abuse by the master. Native-born slaves who spoke Spanish also were accorded the opportunity to develop work skills and the freedom to circulate, either in the towns or on the plantations. These privileged slaves could even earn money on the street and save toward purchasing their freedom.

All the while, the slaves in Cuba fought against their servile status. They established two traditions. The first consisted of petty resistance, working slowly for the master, exerting energy when the overseer was present but resting and visiting among themselves when he was elsewhere. Slavery was inefficient, but free wage earners would not devote themselves to difficult work in the cane on near-starvation wages so that the planters could grow wealthy. The second tradition of resistance involved escape. As in Brazil and other Caribbean plantation societies, African slaves ran away to the forests and mountains. There they established *palenques* from which they raided lowland plantations. Public officials periodically mounted slave-hunting parties to reduce these maroon settlements, deemed inimical to social discipline in the plantation society of Cuba.

Two other social groups formed in the plantation societies of the Spanish Caribbean. The free nonwhite residents having origins in pre–sugar industry settlement now grew with the influx of mulatto children born to African women and European masters and overseers. These free persons of color filled the middle levels of society, serving as artisans, townspeople, free wage earners, smallholding agriculturists, slave drivers, and slave hunters. Although part African, they did not identify with slaves but with the Spanish elite, whose language and dress they aspired to imitate. The free nonwhites amounted to about 15 percent of the population in Cuba. By law, they were restricted to certain occupations and prevented from participating in the lucrative trades reserved for whites. However, they could enlist in the militias. Colonial officials raised the number of mixed-race companies from 1 to 16 in 1800. They defended the coastline from pirate attack and also mobilized to put down slave revolts, hunt runaway slaves, and destroy the *palenques*.

Colonial societies conferred most advantages upon Europeans. The actual number of planters was quite small in Puerto Rico and Santo Domingo, but they made the most money. The families of many of the 29 Cuban nobles in 1810—individuals paid dearly for these titles of nobility—had originally settled there at least a century before. Merchants, public officials, military officers, and immigrant Spanish artisans and shopkeepers rounded out the group. Whites comprised about 44 percent of Cuba's population and 51 percent of Puerto Rico's. New wealth reinvigorated the older families. As long as sugar sustained these plantation slave societies, as it did in the Spanish Caribbean throughout the last half of the eighteenth century, skin color and cultural origins determined the person's status and opportunities. Correspondingly, the larger the slave population, the more pronounced were the social inequities. More than 40 percent of Cuba's inhabitants in 1820 were slaves. The prosperity of eighteenth-century sugar economies accentuated distinctions within the social hierarchy of the Spanish Caribbean.

CONCLUDING REMARKS

Colonial society attempted to manage growth, redirect its impact, and mold its consequences to sustain rather than rearrange existing social relationships. True, *hacendados* and smallholders exerted individual initiative in cultivating and collecting the products for export. Private entrepreneurs produced silver, cochineal, and indigo for foreign markets and wheat and livestock for internal markets. Urban craftspeople manufactured durable goods for sale, and independent muleteers and oxcarters hauled freight from producer to consumer. Everyone conducted their exchanges in monetary units, the silver peso, or its equivalent in paper drafts. Workers hired on at the haciendas at a certain wage, even if they accepted food and dry goods as payment. Market mechanisms operated in this eighteenth-century economic boom—but only to a certain extent.

The colonial state as well as social conventions intervened in the economy in a manner that interrupted those private economic exchanges and went beyond the mere collection of taxes. Colonial authorities regulated private economic relations between their colonial subjects. Ships from Peru landing at Puerto Limón on the Pacific coast had to send their manifests for official approval in Guatemala City before off-loading their cargoes. Governors restricted Native Americans from working in certain industries, such as indigo, and forced them to work in others, as cochineal and the *obrajes*. In the meantime, the natives had to pay tribute to and perform unpaid labor for the state. Spanish merchants lent money to *hacendados,* miners, and transporters. Defaulting debtors who were also militiamen or priests, however, used their military and religious *fueros* to prevent the merchants from foreclosing on their properties. Although the merchants were granted the right to form *consulados* (guilds) of merchants with royal charter, the colonial authorities hesitated to give them too many legal prerogatives.

Moreover, the Spanish-born merchants and Creole landowners found it difficult to accumulate capital through savings. Their elite social status dictated that they fulfill the cultural obligation of consuming conspicuously. They spent money lavishly on retinues of retainers and imported luxury goods, and ate European foods rather than cheaper "Indian" fare. Elite families also had to invest in economically unproductive religious ceremonies. They spent money on bequests to the church, which funded convents, monasteries, and masses for departed family members. The church in New Spain accumulated capital; as a bank, however, it was woefully useless. Religious institutions invested in urban consumption and real estate but seldom put enough money in haciendas to finance solid advances in technology and productivity. Social status remained more important to colonial Spanish North America than did class relations. If this were not so, then Cuban sugarcane would have been grown by free wage workers. But it was not. Planters and merchants confronting labor scarcity subscribed to older traditions of expedience by importing slaves from Africa. Despite the economic stimulus, the colonial elite chose to preserve the familiar social relationships established at Conquest—or at least that was the intention.

In the eighteenth century, however, economic growth compounded the task of maintaining the integrity of Spain's colonial empire. For instance, the ideal colonial worker was supposed to be disciplined and subservient, yet rapid economic expansion stimulated the development of a vibrant and rambunctious class of free workers. Colonial social institutions could not contain the spirited resistance of free workers to the accepted norms of income distribution and social discipline, as shall be seen in the next chapter.

Additional Reading

Almaraz, Félix D. *The San Antonio Missions and Their System of Land Tenure*. Austin: University of Texas Press, 1989.

Arrom, Silvia Marina. *The Women of Mexico City, 1790–1857*. Stanford, Calif.: Stanford University Press, 1985.

Bannon, John Francis. *The Spanish Borderlands Frontier, 1513–1821*. New York: Holt, Rinehart and Winston, 1970.

Bergad, Laird W. *The Cuban Slave Market, 1790–1880*. Cambridge, England: Cambridge University Press, 1995.

Brading, David A. *Miners and Merchants in Bourbon Mexico, 1763–1810*. Cambridge, England: Cambridge University Press, 1971.

Fernández Molina, José Antonio. "Coloring the World in Blue: The Indigo Boom and the Central American Market, 1750–1810." Ph.D. diss., University of Texas at Austin, 1992.

Fisher, J. R. *Commercial Relations Between Spain and Spanish America in the Era of Free Trade, 1778–1796*. Liverpool, England: Centre for Latin American Studies, 1985.

Garner, Richard, and Spiro E. Stefanu. *Economic Growth and Change in Bourbon Mexico*. Gainesville: University of Florida Press, 1993.

Hamnett, Brian R. *Politics and Trade in Southern Mexico, 1750–1821*. Cambridge, England: Cambridge University Press, 1971.

Hinojosa, Gilberto Miguel. *A Borderlands Town in Transition: Laredo, 1755–1870*. College Station: Texas A&M University Press, 1983.

Jackson, Robert H., and Edward Castillo. *Indians, Franciscans, and Spanish Colonization: The Impact of the Mission System on California Indians*. Albuquerque: University of New Mexico Press, 1995.

Jacobsen, Nils, and Hans-Jürgen Puhle, eds. *The Economies of Mexico and Peru during the Late Colonial Period, 1760–1810*. Berlin: Colloquium Verlag, 1986.

Knight, Franklin W. *The Caribbean: The Genesis of a Fragmented Nationalism*. 2d ed. New York: Oxford University Press, 1990.

Ladd, Doris M. *The Mexican Nobility at Independence, 1780–1826*. Austin: University of Texas Press, 1976.

Lindley, Richard Barry. *Haciendas and Economic Development: Guadalajara, Mexico at Independence*. Austin: University of Texas Press, 1983.

Moreno Fraginals, Manuel. *The Sugar Mill: The Socio-Economic Complex of Sugar in Cuba, 1760–1860*. Trans. Cedric Belfrage. New York: Monthly Review Press, 1976.

Nunn, Charles F. *Foreign Immigrants in Early Bourbon Mexico, 1700–1760*. Cambridge, England: Cambridge University Press, 1979.

Salvucci, Richard J. *Textiles and Capitalism in Mexico: An Economic History of the Obrajes, 1539–1840*. Princeton, N.J.: Princeton University Press, 1987.

de la Teja, Jesús F. *San Antonio de Béxar: A Community on New Spain's Northern Frontier.* Albuquerque: University of New Mexico Press, 1995.

Weber, David J. ed., *New Spain's Far Northern Frontier: Essays on Spain in the American West, 1540–1821.* Albuquerque: University of New Mexico Press, 1979 .

Weber, David J. *The Spanish Frontier in North America.* New Haven, Conn.: Yale University Press, 1992.

Wortman, Miles L. *Government and Society in Central America, 1680–1840.* New York: Columbia University Press, 1982.

In Spanish

Florescano, Enrique. *Precios del maíz y crisis agrícolas en México, 1708–1810.* Mexico City: Ediciones Era, 1969.

Fonseca Corrales, Elizabeth. *Costa Rica colonial: La tierra y el hombre.* 2d ed. San José: Editorial Universidad Centroamericana, 1984.

Ortiz, Fernando. *Contrapunteo cubano del tabaco y el azúcar.* Barcelona: Editorial Ariel, 1973.

Pastor, Rodolfo. *Campesinos y reformas: La mixteca, 1700–1856.* Mexico City: Colegio de México, 1987.

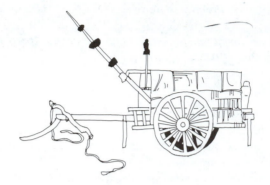

CHAPTER 9

THE WORKING PEOPLE OF MEXICO

Europe's control of the American colonies never appeared stronger than in the eighteenth century. Portugal's Braganças and the new royal dynasty in Spain, the Bourbons, were reforming colonial administration. New territories were settled, new mining areas were exploited, defenses were strengthened, trade flourished, and revenues burgeoned. The view from below contrasted sharply, and slave and native rebellions grew in frequency and intensity as a result. This saga of change and conflict at the end of the eighteenth century began with the gradual formation of a new and separate—albeit fractured—working-class culture in colonial Latin America that developed to resist exploitation. As peasants left their own land to make the transition to working as hacienda peons, full-time miners, or urban laborers, they were forming a new class,[1] and from the peasant world they took with them tactics of survival that they used to their advantage in the new workplaces. The basic questions are the following: How active and successful were peasants and workers

---

[1]The working class is a term referring to a whole social sector defined by its relationship to the means of production, especially in an industrialized society. The working class consists of proletarians, or free workers who engage in wage labor on properties owned by others, the capitalists or the bourgeoisie. Mexico and other Latin American nations would not become industrial until the twentieth century, even though a small class of proletarians without other means of subsistence besides working for wages did begin to form during the colonial period. The full process of working-class formation, however, would not be completed until much later.

in creating their own world? Were they capable of ameliorating the conditions of their low status?

This chapter explores the making of this working class in colonial Mexico, a case worth investigation because the historiography is exceptionally rich and Mexico remained the most valuable jewel in the imperial crown of Spain. Of course, as described in other chapters, workers throughout the Americas were creating their own lives in much the same manner. But colonial New Spain nurtured a particularly vibrant working class because of its abiding native and peasant traditions and its expansive preindustrial economy. Therefore, this analysis begins with the origins of the working class in the peasant villages and then follows those individuals who moved out into Mexico's preindustrial work places—the haciendas, the mines, the *obrajes,* and the artisan shops. The Mexican working class never began or concluded its own making at any definitive period of time. It was constantly in the process of becoming.

Throughout the three centuries of colonial rule, Mexican workers developed two strategies to gain dignity—solidarity and mobility. They did so to maximize their survival in a society in which economic and social power was so unevenly distributed. They maintained a commitment to solidarity that combined the native peasant's loyalty to the village, the slave's preservation of the heritage of Africa, the mestizo and mulatto's identification as citizens with rights, and the poor white's stigma of having to earn a living through manual labor. In other words, those who worked as wage earners on the properties of others began to develop a shared sense of class identity and interests. This class identification coalesced at times when the demands of owners intensified. It allowed workers to overcome their differences and deal collectively with the bosses.

To gain protection, peasants and urban workers also relied on the very social hierarchy that subordinated them. Each workplace—the hacienda, the shop, the mine— formed its own decentralized hierarchy. Workers gained in social welfare insofar as they attached themselves to the hierarchies that provided them income, shelter, and food. Some individuals found opportunity and income by relying on the paternalism of a landowner. Others moved from the *obrajes* to the mines, demanding subsistence and protection from each. In essence, they left one hierarchically organized workplace for another. Thus, Mexican as well as other Latin American workers used mobility to survive and to escape exploitation. But they found dignity in association—in solidarity. Generally, the individual worker sagaciously combined strategies of solidarity and mobility without contradiction.

However, disadvantages did exist (they lived in a colonial society, after all), forcing workers to make choices. The hierarchy of work that provided income and security also engendered a degree of exploitation among workers themselves in the form of petty bossism, or *caciquismo.* The *cacique* might be a village chief, a labor contractor, or leader of a work gang. Workers tolerated the tyranny of the petty boss because he protected his clients from greater exploitation at higher levels—such as by overseers or owners. Workers also had to negotiate with a colonial state often aligned with employers. After all, Spanish-born bureaucrats were socially close to those Spanish and Creole landowners, mine owners, and shopkeepers. The state took an active role in coercing various individuals to work for these enterprises. But workers also learned to manipulate the state, to secure the assistance of Crown officials in protecting their most basic rights of subsistence, and to alleviate the worst abuses. And to keep the social peace, the state responded.

PEASANTS TO PEONS

Mexico's working-class culture has its origins among the Native American peasants; it subsequently spread to mestizo peons and then to miners and urban workers. In spite of the colonial epidemics, natives still outnumbered nonnatives by a wide margin. The indigenous population rebounded in the seventeenth and eighteenth centuries, growing by 44 percent between 1750 and 1800. By 1810, more than 60 percent of Mexico's colonial population consisted of native peasants. In the central valley surrounding the viceregal capital of Mexico City, the indigenous population was even more dominant. Of the valley's more than one million inhabitants, 8 percent were white, 10 percent were mestizo, 5 percent were mulatto, and 77 percent were Native American, even though the nonnative population was growing at a faster rate. In central Mexico toward the end of the eighteenth century, 90 percent of natives still lived in their villages. But the rebound of indigenous population placed pressure on the land, for the villagers were unable to expand their landholdings at the expense of the haciendas. In the eighteenth century, land disputes grew faster than the population. This factor pushed some peasants out of their villages to seek work in the commercial economy.

Peasant Resistance

The labor of the subordinate groups was commanded by a social hierarchy of Spanish and Creole employers, white overseers, mestizo foremen, and native leaders. These superiors always dealt with subordinates with the mindset of command and the expectation of subservience. Anything less was considered a weakness. Equanimity in dealing with one's social inferiors invited disrespect and advantage taking. Therefore, each relationship between members of different castes involved the higher-ranking individual's domination over the person of lower rank.

Nevertheless, the expectations of subservience were seldom reciprocated by subordinates. They responded instead with an obsequiousness that cloaked their resistance, an attitude that might be called "submissive disobedience." They feigned a lack of understanding, they equivocated, they avoided contact, they worked slowly for the master, they procrastinated, they malingered, they drank on the employer's time, and they took his tools. These were the evasive and protective behaviors of the socially less powerful. But they acted subserviently only just enough to avoid their superior's retribution. Creoles did it to Spaniards, mestizos and mulattoes did it to Creoles, blacks did it to mestizos, and natives did it to all the above. This caste-based behavior also became translated into occupational relationships. Peons acted evasively to hacienda administrators; administrators, to owners; unskilled workers, to the skilled; subjects, to officials; taxpayers, to tax collectors; villagers, to caciques; apprentices, to masters; and everyone, to the king. Control of land and subsistence remained the indigenous peasants' foremost refuge from exploitation. Because they had retained enough of their lands, the Native Americans of Mexico survived the Conquest, the frightful population losses, Spanish acquisitiveness, and the state's labor demands. They preferred to live in semi-autonomous villages, tending to communal lands they themselves governed. Despite adopting their own version of the conquerors' religion as their own and allowing the new priests in their communities, native peasants did not much care to have other Spaniards around. Thus they maintained their solidarity for three centuries and more. How? Peasants actively used and took part in Spanish courts, Catholic brotherhoods, ritualized drinking, and local fiestas to consolidate their village solidarity. And they rebelled. Whenever Spaniards raised new taxes, threatened to take communal lands, or attempted unacceptable forms of exploitation, the natives showered them with stones and insults. Native women especially stood out at the forefront of such protests, shaming the authorities all the more. Officialdom tolerated a certain degree of interpersonal violence and resistance from below as long as the rebelliousness was short-lived and did not threaten a general uprising. The peasants thereby successfully kept their losses of land to a minimum. South of Mexico City in Oaxaca, where natives still made up 90 percent of the population at the end of the colonial period, they retained fully two-thirds of the land—a remarkable achievement for those at the bottom of the colonial hierarchy.

Such resilient village solidarity was achieved often at the cost of enduring the tyranny of petty bosses. The *caciques* were critical leaders in the struggle to preserve village lands, negotiating with *hacendados* and with religious and government officials. *Caciques* often owned their own properties and worked them with the unpaid labor of villagers. But in addition to its exploitative features, this petty bossism also offered protection. These local leaders served as the chief brokers among community residents and outside *hacendados* and Spanish officials. They offered some relief from the abuses of mestizos and Spaniards. Because being a *cacique* offered access to economic assets, competition for these posts became quite fierce, giving Spanish officials and parish priests the opportunity to manipulate local elections and commit fraud. "The Indian villages are governed by magistrates of the copper-coloured race," Alexander von Humboldt observed at the end of the colonial period, "and an Indian alcalde [mayor] exercises his power with so much the greater severity, because he is sure of being supported by the priest or the Spanish subdelegado. Oppression produces everywhere the same effects, it everywhere corrupts the morals."

Nonetheless, the *caciques* also formed an essential bridge between the peasant village and the outside world. In central Mexico, where most Native Americans still lived in their communities well past the eighteenth century, their own leaders often acted as labor brokers. They received cash payments from nearby *hacendados* and organized the native work gangs that toiled seasonally on the great estates; population pressure on finite communal lands required the peasants to earn income from other sources to be able to continue their separate village existence. The community notables also served as spokesmen before the church and state. In seeking the aid of these powerful institutions, the *caciques* were instrumental in protecting the separate status of the native population.

Peonage

Although peasants clung tenaciously to their villages—to solidarity—more and more young natives drifted into the commercial world. They became peons, sharecroppers, and squatters, often exchanging their native *cacique* for the white *hacendado.* These peasants-cum-peons sought the kind of security and dignity in commercial agriculture that communal agriculture was increasingly incapable of providing. This ongoing transition from peasant to peon implied an ethnic and cultural change as well. Peons were more likely to speak Spanish and wear European clothes. Their children would have little or no connection to communal life, and racial miscegenation proceeded more rapidly in the Hispanicized world than in the village. Indigenous workers experienced this kind of transformation as they migrated out of central Mexico to take up jobs as peons in the agricultural boom in the Bajío. The process of change from peasant to peon actually began shortly after the Conquest, but it speeded up during the eighteenth century, and it would continue into the twentieth.

Though leaving behind their indigenous languages and village customs, the peons nonetheless preserved the peasants' strategy of solidarity. The haciendas of colonial Mexico contained elements of communal self-sufficiency. At Guadalajara, some of these haciendas housed resident populations of 200 laborers and family members. These estates served as surrogates for peasant villages. Workers produced cattle, corn, wheat, and vegetables for the consumption of the hacienda's employees. Leather and even some hand-loomed cloth were also produced for the peons' clothing and equipment. Rural workers, therefore, identified with the white owner, helping in territorial disputes against peons from neighboring estates. In reciprocation, they expected the owner to care for them. He (or she, because women also owned haciendas) was supposed to spring them from jail. He or she was to provide a chapel and priest for their religious observances, liquor for their fiestas, and rations and commercial goods for their material needs. The *hacendado* was to take care of them in times of crisis.

Furthermore, these hacienda resources substituted for the peasant villages in guaranteeing subsistence. Landowners confronted periodic market depressions by turning the hacienda land over to peons, who could then fend for themselves as tenant farmers. During droughts, estate owners allocated stored grains to peons, deducting the cost from future wages. The Mexican drought of 1785 was particularly severe, and landowners in the far north fed their cattle to their peons. Even peasant villagers of central Mexico who had provided itinerant labor to nearby haciendas depended on these same commercial estates to sell them stored grains—albeit at inflated prices. The connection to a large hacienda offered a kind of subsistence insurance to villagers and peons.

Despite the solidarity implied in joining the hierarchy of work in the Hispanicized world, the hacienda exploited labor. It converted the work of the peons into a profit for the owner. Moreover, discrimination and unequal sharing was built into its decentralized hierarchy. Hacienda owners and administrators were white. The mestizo, who usually had more specialized skills, tended to look down on the less-skilled native peon. Every sort of nonnative desired to live a dignified life supported by the labor of others. Therefore, each labor relationship between unequal members of colonial society implied exploitation. How did peons cope? They protected themselves mainly through use of individual mobility—so much so that they created a labor shortage.

The labor shortages in Mexico cannot be explained merely as a product of the scant population. If that were the entire cause, why could Spanish *hacendados* not find enough laborers even in more densely populated Oaxaca? Most Native Americans neither wanted nor needed to work exclusively for Spaniards, preferring to remain in the villages and pursue their own autonomous means of subsistence. Because of labor shortages, peons willing to hire themselves out had choices. They could move from job to job. They could work for wages or work on their own account as tenants. In labor-scarce northern Mexico, landowners often allowed squatters to take up nearly independent residence on their land so that they could provide seasonal help during planting and harvest times.

The native refusal to work for Spaniards provoked the coerced labor measures that were devised early in the colonial period. In other words, coercion was used to make the natives work in an imperfect labor market (made imperfect, of course, by the actions of the natives). This was why the colonial state created the *repartimiento* labor draft of the sixteenth and seventeenth centuries. But by the eighteenth century, resistance had rendered the *repartimiento* nearly extinct. Residents of entire native towns openly defied local authorities by refusing to serve in the *repartimientos.* Natives in the highlands of Veracruz pushed up wages because they were reluctant to tend the tobacco fields. The planters complained of having to pay for three gangs of itinerant peons just to get one. The remaining nonmonetary labor arrangements between native villages and outside entities also began to break down. For example, villagers who owed traditionally unpaid labor to the Franciscan monastery near Guadalajara refused to show up for work. When they did, they worked with *mala gana* ("bad desire," or unwillingly) and demanded to be paid. Apparently, the Indians had too many other wage opportunities to be bothered with providing unpaid labor for the monks any longer.

The peons' well-developed strategies of resistance, such as working slowly, sometimes provoked draconian reprisals from landowners. Local officials sent gangs of labor recruiters to round up "vagrants" for hacienda work. During the sugar harvests in Morelos, overseers made examples of slow workers by flogging them in front of their peers. Each estate maintained a primitive jail complete with chains, collars, and handcuffs. Consequently, the surrounding hills became filled with many runaway sugar workers who made new lives for themselves as bandits. The labor scarcity of colonial Mexico was due, in part, to the workers' desire to escape unrelieved exploitation.

The landowners' use of debt in securing labor may not have been disadvantageous to the workers. In fact, the cash advances that extended the workers' work obligation, which has been called "debt peonage," actually demonstrated the weakness of the landowners. Peons and seasonal workers could often demand cash advances before they would work for a labor-hungry proprietor. Most debts remained quite small, and peons easily abandoned the hacienda to which they were indebted and moved on. In other instances, the debts could be greater. On the sugar estates of Morelos, the most skilled were able to extract the largest advances and also exercised the most personal independence. The shepherds of Nuevo León and Coahuila in northern Mexico had little hesitation in leaving one employer to work for another. When eighteenth-century Spaniards wanted to institute debt peonage and gave resident workers hefty cash advances to tie them to the haciendas, many workers simply ran away with the money.

Even on the large haciendas that dominated the semi-arid lands stretching from Querétaro north to Chihuahua, the owners could not easily dominate the workers. Here peons took advantage of the limited labor supply to bargain for higher wages and larger rations. Few of their cash advances were ever repaid. On the Sánchez Navarro estates in Coahuila, absenteeism among the 1,500 resident peons was chronic. Peons did not show up for work about 20 percent of the time. These malingerers lived right on the estate. The administrator could not fire the laggards, for then he would find himself without any peons at all. Landowners in central Mexico also had to tolerate the irregular work habits of itinerants from the nearby villages. A peon might come for two days' work at planting and harvesting, leave before the job was done, and then return for a few days the following week. The majordomos learned to tolerate such work habits or do without labor altogether.

These worker actions explain the conditions of labor scarcity that beset Mexican landowners throughout the colonial period. Peasants left their villages only when they needed cash to pay their head tax or when forced by the state labor drafts; they used government and clerical protection to keep to themselves. Toward the end of the eighteenth century when the peasant villagers had to work more and more on neighboring haciendas while peon wage labor and sharecropping expanded, the decentralized institutions of social domination, the haciendas, still proved insufficient to close off alternative behavior to those at the bottom of the hierarchy. Peons voted with their feet. They moved from job to job, remaining in one position as long as they—not the employer—pleased. Despite their lowly positions in the colonial order, Mexican peasants and peons were not helpless victims. They strove to shape their own environment and their own lives. The strategies they used—solidarity and mobility—were also adopted by mining and urban workers. The latter, after all, were only once removed from their country cousins—and sometimes less.

MINING WORKERS

When they work for wages on someone else's property, workers surrender themselves to what is known as *proletarianization.* That is, those colonial Mexicans who entered the textile shops, mines, or artisan shops were selling not their produce but their labor power. In classic proletarianization, wages become the workers' principal means of subsistence; they give up all others, such as working on their own plots of land. Furthermore, this process presumably gives the employers greater control over the lives of workers, permitting them more opportunity to exploit their labor. However, Mexico's preindustrial workers never completely gave up alternative means of making a living and therefore never submitted completely to proletarianization or to the bosses' control. Acting always to preserve independence and choice, they submitted to employment, as much as possible, on their own terms. They moved on when conditions were unbearable or when opportunities elsewhere were better. Mexican workers resisted permanent proletarianization with a resounding degree of success. Their actions even made labor coercion increasingly less operable.

Mobility and Independence

Colonial mining subjected workers to a more intensive experience of proletarianization because of its size and importance. It was particularly harsh work. Living conditions in the mining camps were spartan, and mine operators behaved arrogantly toward workers. The largest Mexican mines employed from 180 to 200 employees each, and most mines were located far from the populous heartland of central Mexico. The nomadic Chichimec of the north refused to work in the mines. Indeed, they fled to the mountains, rebelling against the penetration of the Europeans and sedentary native peoples. At first, in the sixteenth century, labor markets were anything but perfect. A scarcity of settled natives there motivated owners to combine *repartimiento* labor drafts, free wage workers, and African slaves in the mines. When captured, the rebellious Chichimec were also forced into slavery, although the owners complained of their inefficiency. "Bad to have them, but much worse not to have them," went the mine proprietor's lament in the 1560s. A survey of the northern Mexican mining industry in 1590 counted approximately nine thousand workers. Two-thirds were indigenous wage workers; nearly one-quarter were *repartimiento* natives; and the rest (14 percent) were black and native slaves. African slaves and mestizos held the more skilled positions; natives were seldom found among the guards or others with responsibilities. Instead, they worked as helpers for black or mestizo carpenters, charcoal makers, or bricklayers.

After this early experimentation with drafted native labor, Spanish mine operators came to rely increasingly on free wage laborers. A mixture of mestizos, mulattoes, black slaves, and native servants *(naboríos)* soon formed a kind of privileged, well-paid, highly independent, and skilled labor group. Slaves were valued as a permanent force, unlike the Native American migrants from the central valley, who came and went freely. Some natives came to earn some cash with which to return to their villages; others stayed. By the end of the eighteenth century, free wage workers predominated. Slavery survived, but the use of *repartimiento* labor had declined drastically. This, however, did not automatically mean upward mobility for Native Americans. The Spaniard performing carpenter's work at the mine might earn 70 pesos for two months' work while his native assistant might earn just 15 pesos. The opportunity to get ahead was denied to natives.

The scarcity of workers in Mexico's northern provinces nurtured professional mining workers who were jealous of their dignity and prerogative. Together with their peers, they demanded to be treated better than the native peons, and they succeeded. Mexican mining workers enjoyed higher wages than agricultural workers and shared in a percentage of production. Because mine owners were always short of operating capital and could not pay their workers entirely in cash, they developed the *partido,* a system by which they shared portions of the mined ore with workers in addition to giving them a cash wage. With the *partido,* workers avoided complete dependence on the wage. They sold their *partido* ores to small refiners in town, supporting an informal economy outside the employers' control. Earning a *partido* also meant that the worker did not have to work at 12-hour shifts seven days a week, as owners desired. Employees were able to sign up for only three or four shifts per week and still make a decent living.

Being so much in demand also conferred many other advantages to the mine workers. Owners had to offer large advances equivalent to several months' wages—just to attract workers. Free housing and rations of meat and corn were also used to attract workers, the skilled worker being much sought after. In the meantime, they also earned extra income in pilfering the owners' tools, blasting powder, candles, sacks, rope, and leather buckets. It was quite common for mine owners to poach each other's workers as well. Mine owners whose shafts had momentarily run out of silver ore found themselves at great disadvantage. Their labor force would leave for other mines, where the *partido* shares were richer. Labor scarcity in the mining districts was as much a function of miners' mobility as of the scant population.

Mine workers operated within a working-class hierarchy in which divisions based on skill gradually replaced those of ethnicity. Miscegenation and Hispanicization proceeded rapidly and thoroughly among these preindustrial workers. By the end of the eighteenth century, more mestizos worked in mining than Native Americans and blacks. Those skilled men who mixed ore and mercury in the refining patios and the underground pikemen *(barreteros)* rose to the top of the workers' hierarchy. They directed the work of the less skilled, preventing greater exploitation on the part of mine overseers. Workers did not lightly accept their lost income and protested the loss of the ore shares whenever the owner had to cut back. The skilled *barreteros* led the resistance of all workers whenever mine operators threatened the employees' welfare. In these cases, hierarchy among workers promoted collective protection.

On the other hand, miners were also a mobile lot. They packed up and headed to the latest silver strike—and the richest *partido* ores—at will. After the first silver discoveries of 1550, the mine operators of Zacatecas found themselves attempting to outbid each other for workers. Finally, they established a maximum wage for the district—which they then honored only in the breach. Nothing worked except wage and benefit hikes. Workers in distant mines even commanded advances of 6 to 15 times their monthly pay. Still, they often left anyway. An experienced worker could always find another job. In the seventeenth century, the Zacatecas labor shortage did not seem to respond at all to the decline of the indigenous population. Rather, the availability of labor depended on the richness of a mine's veins of silver. Workers presented themselves wherever wages were highest and the share ores were the richest.

Therefore, employers simply had to make do with an independent and mobile mining labor force. Mobility and high turnover expressed the cultural preference of the workers. They easily moved back and forth between mines in the same and in different localities. Even more importantly, mine workers also found temporary employment in

MANUSCRIPT 9.1

Petition of the Pikemen of the Real del Monte Mines, 1766

The skilled underground workers at the Real del Monte mines had a strong sense of their customary rights and also felt responsible for the welfare of the less-skilled peons who toiled with them. In this protest addressed to the viceroy, delivered in person by a delegation of workers, they couched their grievances in terms of justice under religious precepts and royal laws. They wished the viceroy to know that their defiance of the owner did not extend to church and king, both of which commanded their loyalty. But in the protesters' view, the owner had changed the work rules in a manner that violated workers' ancient rights. They appealed to the viceroy to countermand those changes.

The old custom observed between the owners of that mining *Real* [royal property] and the workers, principally the pikemen, was to designate a daily quota or task, more or less large depending on the difficulty or ease of the ground which was being worked, a quota that would be given to the owner for his profit, and to the workers his daily cash wage. Once the quota was filled, the pikeman would continue his work, and everything he could pry out and take out would be divided equally between him and the company.

Little by little, don Pedro Romero [the Count of Regla] has been changing this custom. First, he introduced the innovation that if the pikemen and other workers who were permitted partido took out a number of bags that were better than the quota, half of the one would be exchanged for half of the other. Once this exchange was made, the partido, composed of those two halves, would be divided. This change was hard to take, indeed, since it altered the deep-rooted, firmly established custom of that mining camp. But in the end we all suffered it, as all miserable people do, for fear of this powerful man and believing that the evil would end there.

artisan shops, textile factories, and agriculture—and then they moved on again. One remedy for the owner was to hire a work gang *(cuadrilla)* of between 6 and 85 natives to work in the mine shafts and on the patios when mercury was mixed with the ore. Thus, the burden of providing labor on a daily basis was shifted from employer to labor boss. Each day, different men made up the *cuadrilla.* In return, the power of the labor contractor grew as another hierarchy developed among the workers. He was like a village *cacique,* assembling and directing the work of itinerant harvesters.

Mexican mine workers developed such strong traditions of resistance that in 1767 they launched one of the first known labor strikes in the Americas. In the process, they defeated a nobleman who was the richest man in Mexico. The Count of Regla wanted to proletarianize the workers in his famous Real del Monte silver mine at Pachuca. He decided to eliminate the source of their independence, the *partido*. He also desired to make his workers more efficient and docile. Press gangs were dispatched into the workers' villages to round up men who took days off at home or in the *pulquería* taverns. The townspeople showered these press gangs with rocks, and the skilled pikemen, the *barreteros,* led the others in a walkout. Local priests and lawyers helped them draw up protests to deliver to the viceroy (see Manuscript 9.1). New Spain's highest royal official might have been expected to support the mine owner, who was

---

But we were deceived. . . . [The administrators] are not issuing the candles, blasting powder, and proper tools needed to complete the task they set for us. This obliges us to work twice as much, and the costs eat up all our wages, so that we find ourselves without anything to take home.

En fine, sir, if the mines are profitable, God intends all who participate to benefit. After the owner, it is especially for his instruments, however he obtains them. We workers who are the instruments have come to profit the least, for drained in so many ways of what is rightfully ours, we benefit nothing.

This injury, sir, is the injury of an entire people, more than 1200 men. We who have been driven out by these tyrannies have taken to the road to represent them before the authority of Your Excellency, for we fear that in Pachuca the royal officials' respect for the almighty owner will close the doors of the tribunals to us. . . .

Let [the owner] be compelled to pay the peons, manual laborers, and other laborers the four reales that are customary, and not take one away, which is what has been done. That is also just. When there is no other test possible, custom should command because it is a precept in all natural, divine, and secular systems of law that there should be a just proportion between labor and profit. For this reason, those who weigh justice are repeatedly entrusted with that maxim. . . .

We beseech Your Excellency to provide and order as we petition, as a matter of justice.

We swear in the name of God on the holy cross, etc.

SOURCE: "Miners of the Veta Vizcaína to the Viceroy, Pachuca, Friday, 1 August 1766," trans. Doris M. Ladd, in Doris M. Ladd, *The Making of a Strike: Mexican Silver Workers' Struggles in Real del Monte, 1766–1775* (Lincoln: University of Nebraska Press, 1988), 133–38.

Table 9.1   Employment of Women and Men over the Age of 15 in Mexico City by Race and Marital Status, 1811

Category	Females (%)	Males (%)
Spanish	12.5	63.0
Mestizo/mulatto/black	38.3	84.7
Native American	45.7	88.5
Single	34.2	75.4
Married	17.9	87.0
Widowed	31.8	68.2

SOURCE: Silvia Marina Arrom, *The Women of Mexico City, 1790–1857* (Stanford, Calif.: Stanford University Press, 1985), 159.

the colony's richest citizen, if the treasury had not been losing tax revenues because of the prolonged strike. Instead of taking the side of the Count of Regla, the viceroy sided with the workers. He reinstated the share ores and denounced the press gangs. Collective action and solidarity on the part of Pachuca mine workers made Mexico's most powerful employer back down. They set standards of solidarity that few urban workers were able to imitate.

URBAN WORKERS

Like their mining brethren, urban workers also developed a rather distinct hierarchy, based originally on race and ethnicity and later on occupation. Race and ethnicity never ceased to matter, however, as Native Americans and blacks seldom had the opportunities that were open to others. In Mexico City, persons of darker skin, whether male or female, married or single, were more likely to be employed as workers than the whites (see Table 9.1). However, the urban setting permitted employers to maintain tighter social controls than on the mining frontiers. The decentralized shop environment of urban work often reduced the urban laborers' independence while increasing employers' ability to impose labor discipline. But especially in larger factorylike workplaces, wage earners still bargained successfully to control their own lives. Mexico City, the greatest city in the Western Hemisphere, offers an appropriate example of the manner in which the colonial urban workplace operated.

Mexico City Workers

Having grown from 112,500 residents in 1772 to 169,000 in 1810, Mexico City was the largest and most developed domestic market in the Americas. The wealthiest consumers lived here, and viceregal spending in the capital enhanced the demand for domestically crafted products. The masters of numerous craft occupations controlled most urban services and consumer goods. Roughly one-third to one-half of working males in Mexico

**Cigarette vendors in Mexico.
(Miguel Cabrera, 1763)**

City participated in artisan crafts. They were blacksmiths, carpenters, silk weavers, furniture makers, stonecutters, dressmakers, tailors, sword makers, and bakers. The worth of the finished product determined the social respectability of the craftsman. Silversmiths ranked ahead of shoemakers, who looked down on the butchers. And in their small shops, artisans owned slaves and bossed around Native Americans.

Did the colonial city develop a sense of egalitarianism among various members of the working class? It did not. Each craft was similar to the hacienda in its labor hierarchy. All 27 of Mexico City's bakeries in 1753 were owned and operated by Spaniards. Each had either a Creole or Spanish-born administrator. Although bakery workers did not work together in large numbers—11 was the average—they were for the most part natives, mestizos, and mulattoes. About half of these lived on the premises of the bakeries with their families. After all, the Spanish immigrant baker aspired (in vain) to be accepted among the *gente decente* rather than to identify with the majority *gente de pueblo,* who were dark skinned and ate homemade tortillas. Even the domestic servants in the large households of the wealthy Spanish miners and merchants were organized hierarchically. With as much authority as if they themselves were conquerors, Spanish majordomos and

Table 9.2   Distribution of Mexican Tobacco Workers by Gender, 1809

Location of Workers	FEMALES		MALES	
	Number	Percent	Number	Percent
Mexico City	3,883	71	1,554	29
Guadalupe	492	59	348	41
Guadalajara	1,136	98	24	2
Puebla	744	61	484	39
Querétaro	2,574	69	1,132	31
Oaxaca	586	96	24	4
Orizaba	140	42	195	58
Totals	9,555	72	3,761	28

SOURCE: Susan Deans-Smith, *Bureaucrats, Planters, and Workers: The Making of the Tobacco Monopoly in Bourbon Mexico* (Austin: University of Texas Press, 1992), 212.

housekeepers ordered about the mestizo and native washerwomen, maids, and houseboys. Democracy among workers? This multiracial colonial environment did not promote such a thing.

The crafts such as metalworking and cabinetmaking also engendered a corporatist social organization in which the stability and security of the European masters governed the day. Craftsmen joined guilds that attempted to regulate all those working within the craft. Each guild had its own *cofradía,* a religious lay brotherhood, which provided for the spiritual and material welfare of its members and organized the craft's religious processions and fiestas. Colonial guild regulations reserved the positions of master for Spanish-born craftsmen, kept natives as perpetual apprentices (for Spaniards, apprenticeships lasted just four years), and prevented blacks and mulattoes from having their own retail shops. The master craftsmen controlled entrance and advancement examinations, promotions, and even prices. Essentially, the Spanish-born and Creole artisans wanted to preserve their own status in the crafts by controlling the labor market of the unskilled workers.

Yet their control was imperfect. Growth of these urban industries permitted some natives, mestizos, and mulattoes to run their own shops—in violation of guild regulations. Even the colonial society's tendency toward rigid social order had to yield to the breakneck growth of the urban marketplace. Still, Europeans and Creoles retained control of the most valuable trades.

Besides the master artisans, perhaps the most privileged workers in the colony were the nearly fifteen thousand employees of the Royal Tobacco Monopoly. Colonial authorities consolidated the tobacco industry under state management in 1765 as a tax measure. Most persons who had previously manufactured and sold cigarettes and cigars out of their homes were given employment by the monopoly. Urban workers of the Royal Tobacco Monopoly had several advantages over other members of the nascent Mexican working class. Most were white; they enjoyed job security and were employed by the state rather than private employers; and the Mexico City employees worked within marching distance of the viceregal palace. That most workers also were women did not seem to undermine their relative privileges (see Table 9.2).

Despite the fact that the cigarette and cigar rollers labored in overcrowded, closely supervised, factorylike conditions, they were still able to determine much of their own working lives. They came and left work or stayed home from work without suffering consequences; few were dismissed except in extreme circumstances. Moreover, long-term workers had opportunities to move into supervisory positions—though female supervisors made less money and supervised only other women in segregated work rooms. The rollers also had the right to prepare the rolling papers at home, providing them the opportunity to exchange the imported papers for cheaper ones, keeping the difference as extra income. State administrators attempted to remove this privilege in 1794. It nearly provoked a strike; in protest, four male workers led a march of more than one thousand Mexico City tobacco workers on the viceregal palace. The viceroy gave in immediately and reinstated the paper privilege. Once again, in the interests of public tranquility, the political authorities yielded to workers' solidarity.

Textile Workers

There was considerably less advancement for the textile workers who toiled in the *obrajes* of Puebla and Querétaro. Employing from as few as a handful to upwards of two hundred workers, the *obrajes* produced the woolen cloth consumed by the popular classes. The poor working conditions in these preindustrial factories embarrassed even colonial officials. Low wages, coercion, and fraudulent labor contracts were commonplace among *obraje* operators. African slaves at first supplemented Native American workers, although by the early seventeenth century many *obrajes* seemed to rely exclusively on slave labor. In the late eighteenth century, when fewer slaves were available, *obrajes* had to compete for available urban and rural labor. Many natives found themselves working in the weaving shop via a system of subterfuge and force. Despite its bad reputation, the textile shop attracted workers with quick cash if not good pay. In the *obrajes,* as Humboldt observed, "Free men, Indians and people of colour, are confounded with condemned criminals." The imperfection of the labor market accounted for this odd labor system. Because wage incentives did not attract enough workers, the textile owners got government assistance. Officials "sold" convicted criminals to *obraje* owners, who did not like the expense of guarding and locking up these inefficient workers. But they had few other choices. There never seemed to be enough workers willing to work for the low wages that the owners were willing to pay.

But once again, race determined one's status in the *obraje.* Spaniards and Creoles owned the plants, while local Creoles and mestizos formed the staff. Native American wage earners, who often lived at the shop on one-year contracts, did the work. They passed through the skills from combing and carding the wool to spinning and weaving. Only men were the weavers, the most skilled employees; women served as cooks in the larger shops. But *obraje* workers were not helpless either. They ran away without fulfilling their contracts and sold their skills to competing *obrajes* for higher pay.

Neither did workers make the *obrajes* their only profession. Weavers in Zacatecas also worked in the mines and smelting works. In Querétaro, about a third of the residents of the nearby native villages moved from their fields to small textile shops *(trapiches),* then to larger *obrajes,* and back again to their fields. Toward the end of the colonial period, when free wage labor predominated, a textile operator complained about his workers: "[S]ome days more show up, and some days less." When owners wanted increased production to take advantage of strong markets, the workers extracted higher advances. Worker slowdowns and outright sabotage drove owners to retaliate. But force was becoming increasingly ineffective. Locally mobile employees, who had other means of subsistence and who knew how to complain to colonial authorities, came to predominate in the *obraje* workforce.

Ultimately, the free workers gained a measure of independence within the textile shops. At the end of the colonial period, the viceroys decreed an end to slavery in the *obrajes*. Factory owners were immediately confronted with the workers' demands, which included taking an extra day off on "Saint Monday." Sometimes they even turned Tuesdays and Wednesdays into extra "holy" days of rest. Competing employers began to lend money to workers so that they could pay off their advances to the *obrajes* and leave to work elsewhere. Laborers often filched some of the factory's wool, selling it in back-alley stores or weaving ponchos and blankets at home. Clearly, Mexican preindustrial workers knew how to exploit the weaknesses of their employers. Through solidarity and mobility, they achieved a measure of dignity in the workplace. Moreover, the workers learned how to manipulate the levers of colonial political power.

WORKERS AND THE STATE

In colonial society, the state empowered itself to regulate the relationships among the social castes and between labor and employers. The socially active state in Latin America was a creation not of industrialization but of the preindustrial age. Why? The state sought, above all, to preserve the fragile and explosive structure of the multi-ethnic society. In so doing, it assumed a perspective independent of its most powerful clients, the *gente decente,* because it served a larger interest. On the one hand, the Crown intervened in Mexico to prevent the extinction of the indigenous population, which had occurred in the earlier Spanish settlements on the Caribbean islands of Cuba and Hispaniola. On the other hand, the colonial state sought to prevent rebellion from below, a massive upheaval from the less privileged of society. Such an uprising might destroy the narrow elite and end the Crown's claim to taxation on commerce and mining.

In theory, the king's bureaucracy prevented Iberians and Creoles from taking full advantage of their social positions to grossly exploit the *gente de pueblo.* It sought to prevent selfish elites from provoking resentment among the masses. Therefore, the state did not solely represent the wealthiest class of landowners, mine operators, and merchants in New Spain, whether Iberian or American born. The colonial state served to preserve the entire social structure—and inevitably itself. It was perfectly willing to act against the class interests of the *hacendados* or the textile and mining operators, taking the side of peasants and workers when necessary. It set limits on the amount of capital with which the *hacendado* could entrap the peons by getting them in debt. Given the frequency of debtor's flight, however, these regulations might also have protected the landowner.

Legal Framework

In the interests of social stability, the state combined political and economic powers. The Crown had legal authority over everything in the Indies, which colonial law considered as the king's property. The land, the mines, and other natural resources belonged to the king, who leased or gave them to private entrepreneurs in exchange for royalties and taxes. Moreover, the Crown assumed the responsibility for the welfare of its indigenous subjects. The colonial state retained authority to name those who benefited from the labor of the king's native subjects under the *repartimiento* labor drafts, and the royal court constantly felt obliged to ban known abuses. It outlawed the unpaid travel, flogging, poor housing, low wages, and long hours of work to which Spanish employers subjected Native Americans. In part, the authorities feared that the natives would be provoked to leave areas where they were subjected to harsh treatment and would abandon their agricultural pursuits. Most of all, especially during the epidemics, the viceregal authorities sought to prohibit the employment of natives underground in the mines. "It has resulted in the death of many of them," proclaimed one viceregal edict in 1716.

Still, the Spanish bureaucracy was limited in its ability—or even in its desire, considering that many officials made extra income from apportioning indigenous labor—to enforce these detailed regulations, in part because it was quite small. In 1811, there were only 600 viceregal officials in Mexico City. It may be wrong to interpret officialdom's frequent complicity in subverting these labor regulations as evidence that the workers' mobility and solidarity were circumscribed. Such a view ignores the evidence that the workers themselves resisted successfully. However, the workers had a juridical justification for their resistance, and they believed that they had the Crown's tacit support for their grievances. Skilled workers in the mines and tobacco factories and even peasants and peons were aware of their legal rights and based formal protests to employers and public authorities on them.

As mentioned previously, the Crown assumed the responsibility of caring for its weakest citizens, the Native Americans and the "impoverished" workers. Natives could communicate to the viceregal government to seek redress from the abuses of landowners, employers, priests, other natives, and public officials. Crown officials had the authority to take up the grievances of workers, too. Spain's colonial legislation concerning labor filled numerous legal tomes. Government at the municipal level, moreover, had the day-to-day responsibility for governing the artisan guilds. It fined members for infractions of the regulations and could revoke a guild's charter if necessary. In turn, the guilds attempted to influence city government by placing members of the crafts on the *cabildos*. The colonial state also undertook to prevent abuses peculiar to bakeries and to the weaving and spinning shops and prevented owners from locking native workers into debt servitude. Yet municipal governments, recognizing the difficulty that bakers encountered in securing free wage workers, often condemned criminals to serve their prison terms working in bakeries and *obrajes*. After all, the wage-earning workers needed these industries' products. Local municipalities also regulated the prices of basic foodstuffs so as not to provoke rebellion and food riots among hungry urban proletarians.

Conversely, the state also felt obliged to comply with its second objective—social control. It assumed the mission of controlling the working class, and public officials had to deal with resistance. Native Americans sometimes resisted working for others, would not go to the obligatory labor drafts, and did not show up for hacienda work. So the authorities permitted the mines to operate prisons for recalcitrant workers and ordered the punishment of *caciques* who encouraged such resistance. Fifty lashes or six months' hard labor in the mines were not uncommon penalties for these preindustrial labor leaders. It was obvious that individual workers had the habit of moving from one job to the next and of fleeing after having received large pay advances, so colonial authorities asked local authorities to apprehend these criminals and ordered employers not to give out large advances. They often accused employers of provoking these kinds of resistance by abusing their workers.

Government edicts simultaneously prohibited abuses of natives and granted permission to punish them. In essence, the state sought to mediate and arbitrate these countervailing activities. The state's social mission was to protect the working class and to control workers at the same time (see Manuscript 9.2). It was this very confusion of purpose that peasants and workers learned to exploit in pursuit of their own rights.

MANUSCRIPT 9.2

State Intervention into the Relationship between Workers and Employers

The colonial government took upon itself the task of protecting the Native Americans and other workers from being abused by employers, most of whom were Spaniards or Creoles. Part of the justification for such state interference in the relationship between labor and capital had to do with its recognition of the unequal rights enjoyed by the two entities. Therefore, state officials felt justified in attempting to balance and assuage the injustice. Second, the colonial government wished to preserve a valuable labor resource for the king, who received tax revenues based on the work of his colonial subjects. Therefore, public officials were motivated to prevent overwork and dangerous work conditions. Finally, the state was interested in social control, and selfish and shortsighted employers—and local officials—might provoke popular resistance and rebellion. Other interests of the state ran counter to these sentiments of protecting labor. Public officials believed that the natives were lazy and needed to be taught how to work. The state also stood in need of tax revenues, which employers could pay only if they obtained labor. The following edict by the high Crown official, José de Gálvez, in 1769 illustrates the dual interests of the state: to protect laborers on the one hand and to make them work on the other. Here Gálvez is establishing a kind of minimum wage as well as attempting to force Native Americans and castas into the workplace.

But the reader should bear in mind that neither workers nor employers were inclined to follow state decrees unless it suited them.

In order to make sure that workers needed for the cultivation of lands and the grazing of cattle are not lacking, through agreement with the mine owners and hacienda owners, I have resolved upon a measure that will benefit the poor and promote the public welfare, namely to set a quota upon salaries and rations of goods that will prevail in the future in the provinces of this jurisdiction [New Spain], for workers, wage earners, and servants, of the following classifications:

1. The leaders, captains, and heads of mining labors; majordomos of haciendas and ranches, whether for agriculture or for grazing; mule-train shippers; and the overseers of other kinds of occupation equivalent to these, are to receive from their masters the wages and rations that they may negotiate with them in accordance with the skill and circumstances of each one, with the indispensable requirement that wages must be paid in reales or in silver.

2. Workers in mines and others laboring at equivalent tasks should receive at least seven pesos per month in money, and each week they should receive two almudes [9.25

Humble though they may have been, Mexican workers developed definite strategies in dealing with the state. First of all, they called on colonial authorities to uphold the considerable number of laws protecting the poor and downtrodden of society. They found their defense in citing religious precepts and legal codes, as in the cases of the miners of the Real del Monte and the cigarette rollers of the tobacco factory. Native Americans had access to the Indian Court, to which *caciques* appealed when the labor drafts were too burdensome or local officials carried them out abusively. Moreover, groups of aggrieved peasants and workers went straight to the top. They wrote

---

litres] of maize and one-half arroba [507 kilograms] of dried meat, whether they be married or single, and with no innovation for the present in the arrangement commonly granted to mine workers by the owners of mines.

3. The same salary and rations are to be paid to the principal cowboys, farm hands, muleteers, horse guards, and others of similar work in other tasks and occupations, except that carriers are to receive six pesos with the same ration.

4. Subordinate shepherds and cowboys who are aides in mule trains or have other equivalent work are to receive the same weekly ration and are to receive as salary five pesos per month in reales, or in silver if reales are lacking. But if they are Indians under the age of eighteen they are to receive only four pesos in money, with the same rations.

5. In accordance with the laws, I prohibit vagabonds in these provinces and order that everyone is to have a precise job or office, under penalty of one month in jail for the first offense, whether he be Spaniard or Indian or person of reason; and a fine of twenty pesos against anyone who protects him under pretext of refuge and fails to report him to the judge, so that he may be punished and set to work. And with any repetition of the offense,

the vagabonds will be assigned to the public or royal works, with rations but without wage for two months.

6. Servants have a natural freedom to leave one master in order to make arrangements with another, but this freedom is used by some with such impudence and to such excess that the matter requires some effective correction; there is also the opposite extreme, wherein servants are forced to work for masters who do not treat them well or do not pay them the wages agreed upon. To remedy both abuses, I declare and order that the worker who is in debt to his master cannot leave him without first fulfilling the terms of the contract, and no other employer may accept him without having assurance that this is the case, in the form of a written statement by the former employer. And no master may advance the wages of his workers or servants more than the amount of two months' wages; nor may he stand in the way of those who have paid up their debt and who want to look for better employment, at least so long as they are not repartimiento workers.

SOURCE: Charles Gibson, ed., *The Spanish Tradition in America* (Columbia: University of South Carolina Press, 1968), 231–33, as translated by Gibson from *Legislación del trabajo en los siglos XVI, XVII, y XVIII* (Mexico City: Fundo de Cultura Económica, 1938), 156–57.

the viceroy, the top royal official in New Spain, and sent delegations to deal personally with him.

In spite of the employers' wealth and power and in spite of the hostility of local officials, peasants and workers could and did take direct action. They blamed their occasional violent outbursts, walkouts, and protest marches on the owners' refusal to honor tradition and law. In all cases, neither the natives in the villages nor the urban workers were revolutionaries. They sought neither to bring down the colonial regime nor to attack the property rights of employers. Peasants and workers did not even dispute their lowly positions in society. Mostly, they struggled to dignify their hard work and to force employers to give them just compensation. When their own mobility and solidarity could not secure that dignity, they turned to the colonial state.

CONCLUDING REMARKS

In the eighteenth century, the superstructure of Mexico's colonial society rested solidly on a multiracial, preindustrial, and agrarian base. To a large degree, race and ethnicity determined who was the employer and who was the employee. The *gente decente,* made up of Spaniards and Creoles, formed the ownership class. Consisting of a heterogeneous mass of poor whites and of non-European peoples, the *gente de pueblo* performed the labor, although the highest ranks of the laboring class also tended to be small property owners and artisans. The workers' race and ethnicity often determined their social status and possibilities for upward mobility. Their labor was demanded—but seldom accorded dignity—by European elites. A Spaniard, if impoverished, might fall back into the category of worker, but seldom did a dark-skinned person rise to join the economic and social elite. Therefore, in colonial Mexico, peasants and workers formed a class apart, divided unto itself by race, ethnicity, and skill levels.

But those at the bottom of the social hierarchy were not helpless. Mexican peasants, peons, and workers adapted themselves to strategies of solidarity and mobility that resisted and deflected social domination. Workers kept on the move to prevent employers from taking advantage of them, to escape abuses, and to pursue more advantageous job opportunities. In the process, individual mobility contributed to the labor shortages that benefited all workers. On the other hand, individual workers might employ a strategy of solidarity, uniting under the leadership of those having more skills and prestige, to defend their customary rights and privileges. When all these strategies failed, the workers appealed to the state for mediation. At least, this had been the case among workers in haciendas, mines, textile factories, artisan shops, and tobacco factories. Many more Mexican workers have yet to be studied, such as those who toiled in the transport trades (such as muleskinning and oxcarting) and the informal market of buying and selling.

Colonial officials had their own interests in preserving the fragile and potentially explosive social structure. Therefore, they tried to prevent the worst abuses of the colonial elites while maintaining control of the masses. Because of its small size and its limited powers, the state could not always manage the serious social cleavages created by demographic and economic change during the eighteenth century. This was true in Mexico as well as in South America, which is examined in the next chapter.

Additional Reading

Altman, Ida B., and James Lockhart, eds. *Provinces of Early Mexico: Variants of Spanish American Regional Evolution*. Los Angeles: UCLA Latin American Center Publications, 1976.

Arnold, Linda Jo. *Bureaucracy and Bureaucrats in Mexico City, 1742–1835*. Tucson: University of Arizona Press, 1988.

Barrett, Ward. *The Sugar Hacienda of the Marqueses del Valle*. Minneapolis: University of Minnesota Press, 1970.

Borah, Woodrow. *Justice by Insurance: The General Indian Court of Colonial Mexico and the Legal Aides of the Half-Real*. Berkeley: University of California Press, 1983.

Brading, D. A. *Haciendas and Ranchos in the Mexican Bajío, León, 1700–1860*. Cambridge, England: Cambridge University Press, 1978.

Deans-Smith, Susan. *Bureaucrats, Planters, and Workers: The Making of the Tobacco Monopoly in Bourbon Mexico, 1740–1810*. Austin: University of Texas Press, 1992.

Gutiérrez Brockington, Lolita. *The Leverage of Labor: Managing the Cortés Haciendas in Tehuantepec, 1588–1688*. Durham, N.C.: Duke University Press, 1989.

Harris, Charles H. *A Mexican Family Empire: The Latifundio of the Sánchez Navarro, 1765–1867*. Austin: University of Texas Press, 1975.

Kicza, John. *Colonial Entrepreneurs: Families and Business in Bourbon Mexico City*. Albuquerque: University of New Mexico Press, 1983.

Ladd, Doris M. *The Making of a Strike: Mexican Silver Workers' Struggles in Real del Monte, 1766–1775*. Lincoln: University of Nebraska Press, 1988.

Lipsett-Rivera, Sonya. *To Defend Our Water with the Blood of Our Veins: The Struggle for Resources in Colonial Puebla*. Albuquerque: University of New Mexico Press, 1999.

Martin, Cheryl English. *Governance and Society in Colonial Mexico: Chihuahua in the Eighteenth Century*. Stanford, Calif.: Stanford University Press, 1996.

———. *Rural Society in Colonial Morelos*. Albuquerque: University of New Mexico Press, 1985.

Radding, Cynthia. *Wandering Peoples: Colonialism, Ethnic Spaces, and Ecological Frontiers in Northwestern Mexico, 1700–1850*. Durham, N.C.: Duke University Press, 1997.

Semo, Enrique. *History of Capitalism in Mexico: Its Origins, 1521–1963*. Trans. Lidia Lozano. Austin: University of Texas Press, 1993.

Stern, Steve. *The Secret History of Gender: Women, Men, and Power in Late Colonial Mexico*. Chapel Hill: University of North Carolina Press, 1995.

Taylor, William B. *Drinking, Homicide and Rebellion in Colonial Mexican Villages*. Stanford, Calif.: Stanford University Press, 1979.

———. *Landlord and Peasant in Colonial Oaxaca*. Stanford, Calif.: Stanford University Press, 1972.

Tutino, John. "Creole Mexico: Spanish Elites, Haciendas, and Indian Towns, 1750–1810." Ph.D. diss., University of Texas at Austin, 1976.

———. *From Insurrection to Revolution in Mexico: Social Bases of Agrarian Violence, 1750–1940*. Princeton, N.J.: Princeton University Press, 1986.

Van Young, Eric. *Hacienda and Market in Eighteenth-Century Mexico: The Rural Economy of the Guadalajara Region, 1675–1820*. Berkeley: University of California Press, 1981.

Viqueira Alban, Juan Pedro. *Propriety and Permissiveness in Bourbon Mexico*. Trans. Sonya Lipsett-Rivera and Sergio Rivera Ayala. Wilmington, Del.: Scholarly Resources, 1999.

In Spanish

Artís Espriu, Gloria, et al. *Trabajo y sociedad en la historia de México: siglos XVI-XVIII*. Tlalpan: CIESAS, 1992.

Castro Gutiérrez, Felipe. *La extinción de la artesanía gremial*. Mexico City: Universidad Nacional Autónoma de México, 1986.

Florescano, Enrique, et al., eds. *La clase obrera en la historia de México, de la colonia al imperio*. Mexico City: Siglo Veintiuno, 1980.

Frost, Elsa Cecilia, Michael C. Meyer, and Josefina Zoraida Vázquez, eds. *El trabajo y los trabajadores en la historia de México.* Mexico City and Tucson: El Colegio de México and University of Arizona Press, 1979.

Pérez Toledo, Sonia. *Los hijos del trabajo: los artesanos de la ciudad de México, 1780–1853*. Mexico City: El Colegio de México, 1996.

del Río, Ignacio. *Conquista y aculturación en la California jesuítica, 1697–1768*. Mexico City: Universidad Nacional Autónoma de México, 1984.

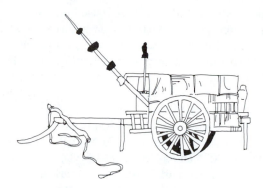

CHAPTER 10

THE EMERGENCE OF SPANISH SOUTH AMERICA

The economic growth of the eighteenth century had contrary effects on Spanish South America similar to those seen in New Spain. The colonial core of Peru and Mexico attracted more European settlers early on than did regions such as Venezuela, Chile, and Argentina, which had weaker economic links to the Iberian metropolis. In the eighteenth century, however, these fringes of empire in both northern and southern South America came into such prominence that each individually began to challenge the economic hegemony of Peru. These areas began to develop their own direct economic connections to European markets, and their populations became more fluid compared with the rigid social structure of Peru. This is not to say that market forces overrode the traditional social order in Spanish South America. On the contrary, dynamic new colonial societies emerged on the South American continent in the eighteenth century. They were economically rambunctious yet socially structured in the familiar hierarchical patterns of the core areas. But as the fringe areas grew through economic integration with Europe, these societies were falling away from Spain as well as from each other.

The economic florescence contributed to the self-assurance of Spanish South Americans. Silver mining revived in the core areas of Peru and Bolivia, enriching the royal coffers with tax revenues and financing European commercial expansion. Yet the eighteenth-century economic boom also stimulated some rather nontraditional exports as well. Cacao flourished in Venezuela. Settlers raised mules and hunted cattle in Uruguay and Argentina, contesting the Native Americans for the lush grasslands of the Pampas. In Chile, farmers of the central valley harvested wheat, which enriched the merchants at Santiago and Valparaíso who traded with Peru. Based on its position as gateway to the hardwood forests of the Ecuadorian lowlands, Guayaquil gained stature as a shipbuilding city. Gold mining expanded in the lowlands of western Colombia; Medellín became its important highland entrepôt, while the gold rush reinforced the importance of the slave trade at Cartagena. Even domestic demand and production burgeoned. In the highlands, Quito became an important center for the textile industry, as did Cochabamba in the Charcas, or Upper Peru (today Bolivia).

As in New Spain, the economic activity in South America pushed back the frontiers. Creole, mestizo, and immigrant smallholders moved into the fertile highland valleys north of Bogotá and in the Andean regions south of Lake Maracaibo. Paraguay expanded its export of yerba maté to other markets in South America, and cattle raising and farming flourished in the mission region along the Uruguay River and in the zone east of Asunción. Interior Argentinean cities such as Mendoza, Córdoba, Tucumán, and Salta prospered from shipments of mules, cattle, and wheat to the mining regions of Peru and Bolivia. Buenos Aires became a major port, and in its hinterland landowners commenced breeding cattle.

The expansion of trade stretched the older administrative apparatus of the colonial state, particularly in the new areas of commerce. New viceroyalties were created in the northern Andes (Ecuador, Colombia, and Venezuela) and in the vast Río de la Plata region. The Spanish Crown, after all, had not forsaken its prerogative of collecting taxes on the growing economic activity. It therefore reinforced and augmented its bureaucracy in the new regions, which annoyed the independent residents. Most of all, rapid economic growth exacerbated old social antagonisms. The delicate equilibrium between the state and Spanish employers over the use of scarce native labor often led to the breakdown of authority and outright rebellion. For their part, the natives who were made to suffer increased labor as well as higher taxes grew restive. As their populations rebounded from a century and a half of epidemics, Native Americans in Paraguay, Bolivia, Peru, and Colombia attempted—by rebellion if necessary—to loosen the pressures imposed upon them. Native-settler violence intensified on the frontiers as well. As settlers descended from the mountain valleys into the tropical and temperate forests and uncharted prairies and deserts, the nomadic natives offered effective resistance. Frontiers on the Pampas, in the forests of southern Chile, in the Chaco, and in the Orinoco River Basin became areas of conflict between settlers and indigenous groups.

The colonial state certainly remained involved in this vigorous expansion. Not only did it have an interest in taxing the new industries of South America's expansion, but it also sought to mediate the clash between the simultaneous frontier movements of Spanish America and Portuguese Brazil. The Río de la Plata region took on strategic value as the new transport route for the Upper Peruvian silver exports, and the colonial state paid increasing political and military attention to its defenses in the southern tip of the continent. It is no exaggeration to point out that the eighteenth century in South America was a time of international tension as well as internal rebellion. The more economically prosperous the Spanish colonies became, the more insecure became Spain's control of their political and social affairs.

CHANGE IN THE CORE REGION

The late seventeenth century had not been particularly kind to the old Andean core of colonial South America. Peru was declining economically. The great silver mines of Potosí in Upper Peru had begun to play out, as the richest ores had already been extracted. With the decline of commerce in silver, domestic demand also fell for hacienda produce and for local textile and artisan wares. Import-export merchants in Lima were falling on hard times, as were the white shopkeepers in the provincial cities. Perhaps the Native Americans were the only large group that did not complain of the economic downturn. Clinging to their peasant communities, they busied themselves with traditional subsistence agriculture. The peasantry welcomed the relief from constant demands for their labor by white silver miners, hacienda owners, and public officials. Besides, the pandemics had run themselves out as the new generations of natives finally developed immunities to European diseases. The indigenous population once again began to grow. The turnaround in Peru waited until the 1720s, fully three-quarters of a century after the halt in Mexico's indigenous population decline.

These conditions of economic lethargy continued into the first quarter of the eighteenth century, after which Peru's economy followed suit with its northern counterpart and began to respond to rising international demand—but slowly. First came the revival and expansion of its mining industry. Increased domestic and international trade followed in due course, as did the demand for domestically produced products. Merchandising, crafts, and hacienda production revived. But with this revival came a renewed need for labor from the majority of the population—the indigenous peasantry. The state attempted to tighten its collections of taxes, and white miners and landowners made increasing demands on natives in the mines and on the haciendas. As we will see later, the eighteenth century became a time of serious rebellion in Peru.

Mining Revival

Mining was key to the slow economic revival of Peru. When silver production reached a nadir in 1737, the Spanish Crown reduced the mining royalty from 20 percent of production (*el quinto real*) to just 10 percent (*el diezmo*). This lower tax remained intact until the end of the colonial period, although many mine owners and silver smugglers avoided paying taxes whenever possible.

Since the late sixteenth century, the production of silver had also depended on mercury, and Spanish authorities acted to enlarge the supplies of this important commodity. As a Crown monopoly, mercury for silver amalgamation came from three sources. The Spanish mercury mine at Almadén supplied New Spain. Huancavelica in Peru supplied only a portion of the mercury needed for the silver mines of South America, and a third mercury mine in Slovenia, on the Adriatic Sea, periodically made up for shortfalls. Consequently, imports of mercury were essential to mining in the Americas. The Crown owned the mercury mine of Huancavelica, although it had been operated by a private contractor. In the 1780s, however, the colonial state took over direct management of the operation. It had, after all, always been determining its price and distribution. But the results of the colonial government's direct managerial takeover were disastrous. Domestic production of mercury at Huancavelica declined, necessitating increases in the import of expensive foreign mercury. Other policies favorable to private miners were

Figure 10.1   Registered Silver Production in Peru, 1771–1824

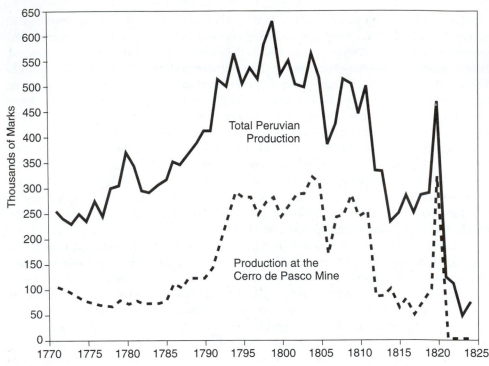

SOURCE: J. R. Fisher, *Silver Mines and Silver Miners in Colonial Peru, 1776–1824* (Liverpool, England: Centre for Latin American Studies, University of Liverpool, 1977), 109.

also undertaken by the state to stimulate silver production in the last quarter of the eighteenth century. However, these may have amounted to a misallocation of resources, because Peruvian silver mining remained only marginally profitable. Public assistance took over when merchants refused to lend investment money to miners, who had high rates of default. Government's assistance and subsidies might well have had greater impact in neglected areas such as textile manufacture and agriculture.

Nonetheless, the Crown's subsidies and favoritism flowed into the mining industry, and Peru's silver production responded. Despite the transfer of Potosí and other mining centers of Charcas to the new Viceroyalty of the Río de la Plata in 1776, silver production in Peru doubled in the 15 years afterwards. It reached a maximum production of 637,000 marks in 1799 (see Figure 10.1). (The mark was the standard unit of weight equaling eight ounces of gold or silver.)

The revival of mining gave a new economic impulse to the Andean region of South America. Potosí's fabulous mountain of silver had yielded diminished returns throughout the seventeenth century as mercury grew scarce and as the indigenous population suffered further epidemics, and as native resistance to the *mita* forced up labor costs. But government favoritism and new silver markets in the eighteenth century stimulated a remarkable expansion of production there that featured the dispersal—rather than the concentration—of production throughout the Andean region. New mines were opened up in highland communities other than just Potosí. Oruro and Chuquisaca became important mining centers in Alto Peru (Bolivia). In Peru, several smaller mines were established from the Puno in the southern Peruvian highlands northward into Ecuador. In the mountains east of Lima, a new silver mine opened up at Cerro de Pasco, at times employing as many as 2,000 workers. Even in Colombia, successful efforts to find new sources of gold and silver produced rising production in these precious metals. Emeralds also became an important extractive industry. Farther south, in Chile, entrepreneurs opened new silver and copper mines, which will be discussed in detail later in this chapter.

Moreover, South America's internal consumption of silver also increased along with sales of consumer items. The now-growing numbers of Native Americans and mestizos became more accustomed to the money-based economy. Even members of peasant communities were not entirely self-sufficient. The royal government required every male head of household in an indigenous community to pay a yearly head tax; therefore, the natives were compelled to hire themselves out for cash wages at nearby mines or haciendas or comply with the forced-labor drafts. Moreover, residents of even the most remote rural districts desired certain basic consumer goods. Even in the territories of the southern Pampas and Patagonia, indigenous hunters traded ostrich feathers and woven leather goods for tobacco, yerba maté, brandy, cloth, and ponchos—goods of the Europeanized world. Rustic ranchers from Venezuela's Llanos region sold cattle for those same consumer items and for cash, both of which the mulatto and mestizo ranch hands demanded as payment for their labor. The cash economy spread throughout South America, even as silver and trade linked the Americas to Europe and Asia.

Silver exports underwrote the Peruvian economy. Jesuit haciendas along the coast and in the highlands began to expand their marketing of Peruvian wine and sugar into Chile and the Río de la Plata. And neither was the market at Potosí entirely lost to Andean producers. Hacendados and smallholders at Cuzco and in the Puno region continued to send foodstuffs and woolen goods to this mining community. Nevertheless, the new and newly resuscitated mines of Peru, except the Cerro de Pasco mine, were small affairs. Most had fewer than 500 employees. The mining camps joined the cities as major markets for internal commerce in agricultural products. And Peru remained South America's dominant market for European goods. Its trade with Spain's chief port of Cádiz outweighed those of Venezuela and the Río de la Plata combined.

However, the economic revival did not benefit all regions of the core colony of Peru. The region of Cuzco and the Puno may have suffered the consequences of the transfer of the Charcas to the Viceroyalty of the Río de la Plata in 1776. Agriculture and livestock production declined in the southern Andean region. So did cloth production in this colony's *obrajes*. These shop producers had been pushed out of the Charcas market by aggressive trade from Tucumán and Salta south of the Altiplano. In the late eighteenth century, the economic center of gravity in Peru shifted toward the new mines of the Sierras farther north and especially to the coastal plantations near Trujillo. Lima's import merchants sent most of their textiles and goods to the northern mining zones. The Potosí silver mines and the peasant and mining populations of Upper Peru fell away from Lima's commercial orbit.

Draft Labor

Perhaps in compensation, merchants and colonial officials redoubled their efforts to force native villagers of Peru into the money economy. Native peasants had to pay head taxes, were forced to purchase goods from district magistrates, and were obliged to respond to labor drafts. Nonetheless, the existence of a large population in the Andean valleys always placed limits on the extent to which Lima's merchants could commercially penetrate the region. The Andean peasant, who subsisted on the land, did not need to engage in the market system as much as merchants and landowners might have preferred. Moreover, the Andean peasant communities seemed more entrenched than Mexico's. Whereas the mines of northern Mexico were surrounded by a fluid frontier society of mestizo wage laborers and commercial hacienda suppliers, Peru's mines remained awash in a sea of relatively rigid and unresponsive peasant communities. The economic integration between capitalist mines and subsistence peasants remained less articulated in Peru because peasants had other things to do with their time than to hire themselves out to the mines, and most of their agricultural produce was consumed internally rather than sold to mining communities. This added to the cost of doing business in Peru, retarding commercial possibilities. Labor and supplies remained inelastic in the Andes.

A number of other important differences distinguished the Andean economy from that of New Spain in the eighteenth century. Many of these differences had to do with geography, whereas others had their roots in the contrasting distributions of the ethnic population. First, the Europeans of colonial Peruvian society resided on or close to the coastal plain. Spaniards and Creoles remained in the cities of Lima, Trujillo, and Arequipa. If they were found in the mountains at all, they resided in Cuzco or perhaps Ayacucho. The more Hispanicized coastal zones depended on a variegated working class. Although some natives retained land, most of the farms and truck gardens were given over to the slaves, mestizos, free persons of color, and poor whites. Wheat, vegetables, grapes, and sugar were cultivated along the coast. Consequently, the Native Americans of the Andean region had the mountain valleys of Peru's interior to themselves. Only a few white officials passed through their districts, although a separate class of mestizos (or *cholos,* as they are known in the Andean world) came to own some land and live in small towns as petty tradesmen and shopkeepers. The composition of the population in Peru contrasted greatly with that of Mexico, where the Spanish world had formed its center directly over the pre-Columbian native realms of the central valley.

In Mexico, white *hacendados* and mestizo smallholders had been responsible for the raising of livestock. In Peru, indigenous peasants undertook this work. In the absence of large numbers of whites and mestizos in the cordillera, natives owned and herded sheep and pigs. Peasant communities in the southern Andes, near Cuzco, owned nearly two-thirds of the sheep in their districts. The breeding of sheep and pigs was undertaken eagerly by Andean peasants, who already had a long tradition of herding alpacas and llamas. Peasant villagers commonly raised a variety of livestock in addition to producing potatoes, corn, and in the humid eastern slopes of the Andes Mountains, coca. *Kuraka*s maintained separate estates in their own names. There they bred cattle and horses for small and dispersed regional markets. A smattering of Spanish and church-owned haciendas produced the remaining third, with native labor. For the most part, these estates were much smaller than the huge cattle and sheep ranches then existing in northern New Spain.

Since the late sixteenth century, draft labor had been a critical element of mining's success, especially in the Charcas. The mines at Potosí were located in the high and barren Altiplano; few natives lived in the area. Therefore, the Crown had assigned peasant communities in the Andean valleys from as far away as Cuzco and Tarija to provide itinerant workers for this critical industry. Under the *mita*, the village dispatched a certain number of able-bodied men to Potosí or Huancavelica for six or more months at a time. The women also went along to help set up households at the mines and perform menial jobs around the mills. Men performed all jobs underground. Working in the mining industry was not an assignment that natives readily leapt at, because it disrupted community and family life and because Potosí and the mines could be unhealthy. Although the surface of the Altiplano (which means "high plain") might be freezing, the work environment 600 feet underground reached intolerably high temperatures. After blasting rock with gunpowder became commonplace, dust floated everlastingly in the tunnels. It was not uncommon for fatigued *mitayo*s to fall down the treacherous mine shafts.

However, the mines required skilled workers, and gradually a wage labor force developed in the mining districts. Individual *mitayo*s stayed on at the mines, attracted by higher wages for free workers, and slaves also formed a more permanent workforce. In time, draft workers only accounted for a third of the 12,000 workers needed at Potosí. By the late eighteenth century, the wage labor force had grown at Potosí and at the Peruvian mining districts, including the mercury center of Huancavelica. Three-quarters of the nearly 6,000 workers at Potosí were salaried, free workers. The *mita* now only provided approximately 1,500 workers, thousands less than had been the case a century and a half before. The reason was clear: While silver production in Peru and the Charcas rebounded in the eighteenth century, Potosí itself (which had yielded about half of all the silver in the Spanish Empire in 1600) did not recover its former glory. In the meanwhile, the new economic dynamism was migrating elsewhere in South America.

NORTHERN SOUTH AMERICA

Ecuador and Colombia

Alone among South American cities during the eighteenth century, Quito could not seem to recover from its isolation and loss of markets. The increased European trade undercut its lively textile industry, and development of Peruvian and Upper Peruvian *obrajes* undersold Ecuadorian coarse woolens in those markets. Thus, Quito lost its status as South America's leading textile center, and cloth production declined by 50 to 75 percent. Even the efficiently run Jesuit *obrajes* had difficulty selling their goods. The population of this important administrative center—an *audiencia* was located in Quito—declined from approximately twenty-five thousand inhabitants in 1780 to 13,400 in 1825. Its labor force migrated to other regions, especially to Cuenca and the port of Guayaquil. Those who remained worked as resident laborers on the 346 haciendas of the province, producing wheat, wool, vegetables, and livestock for local markets. A small but closely knit group of elite families, making up just 1 percent of Quito's population, owned 34 percent of the land, most of which was mortgaged heavily to the financial institutions of the church. The remaining Native Americans of the highlands worked in towns or cultivated communal lands and small freeholds (see Table 10.1). In the capital city, many Andeans worked as servants and artisans or cultivated small suburban plots of land.

Colonial officials responded to the economic decline of Quito not by granting tax relief but, in fact, by raising tax rates so that the royal revenues would not fall off. Tax enforcement also increased, as native and mestizo cultivators now had to pay on their land

Table 10.1   Estimated Racial Composition of the Population of Ecuador, by Province, ca. 1780

	Quito	*Cuenca*	*Guayaquil*
Whites	76,747 (26.9%)	33,316 (30.7%)	5,037 (15.8%)
Mestizos/Mulattoes	7,006 (2.5%)	5,587 (5.1%)	15,961 (30.3%)
Native Americans	199,073 (69.8%)	69,160 (63.7%)	10,011 (48.3%)
Slaves	2,302 (0.8%)	566 (0.5%)	2,068 (6.2%)
Totals*	285,128	108,629	33,007

* The total population of Ecuador amounted to 438,724 persons.

SOURCE: Kenneth J. Andrien, *The Kingdom of Quito, 1690–1830: The State and Regional Development* (Cambridge, England: Cambridge University Press, 1995), 36.

as well as on their produce when delivered at the gates of the city. Spanish and Creole owners of *obrajes* had to pay for licenses to manufacture and sell the famous blue cloth of Ecuador. Native Americans rebelled in several communities throughout the highlands, although their resistance was piecemeal, easily settled, and inconsequential. The most serious resistance came in 1765, when royal officials took control of liquor taxes in Quito. The city's artisans, butchers, peddlers, small farmers, and shop owners gathered before the hated customs building, which they then destroyed. Rioters soon took over the city, overthrew the *audiencia,* and established a popular government that ruled the city for one year. Iberian-born Spaniards went into hiding and took refuge in churches and convents. Most members of the Creole elite remained neutral, especially after false rumors spread that natives from the countryside were about to enter the rebellion. The arrival of loyal troops in 1766 finally restored the *audiencia,* and the tax system was thoroughly overhauled within 10 years. However, the Quito rebellion did not reduce the burden of taxes, which were eventually restored and increased even as the province's economy continued to stagnate. Another rebellion took place in 1777. The indigenous people of Otavalo, north of Quito, rose up to protest taxation and resist a new census, for they knew that Spanish officials were preparing the foundation for more efficient tribute collections. Unpopular priests and officials were beaten up, one Spaniard was killed, and the properties of whites were sacked over the course of a month. A militia force battled a rebel force of 2,000 men, killed 40 natives, and executed 3 ringleaders.

The two other provinces that made up colonial Ecuador were better placed to take advantage of expanding foreign trade. Cuenca profited from exports to Europe of *cascarilla,* a tree bark rich in quinine for medicines, and *obrajes* there were better placed to capture the remaining trade with Peru from Quito. Unlike Quito to the north, most of the indigenous peoples of Cuenca, upwards of 60 percent of the entire population, remained in their traditional settlements, not on Spanish estates. However, high tribute taxes of 6 to 9 pesos per annum forced them out of their subsistence plots for parts of the year to earn cash on haciendas or in the textile industry. Forced labor also pried them away from their peasant villages.

The province of Guayaquil expanded the production of cacao beans, as European consumers began to buy increasing amounts of chocolate from South America (see Map 10.1). Newly established plantations on the coast of Ecuador created a labor shortage

Map 10.1   Northern South America in 1790

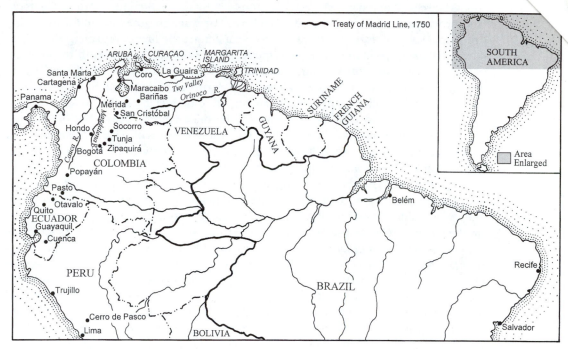

that was eased by the importation of African slaves and by migration from the highlands. Five families alone dominated the cacao production; they owned 40 percent of the cacao trees in the region and became the most powerful among the small group of planters who were the leading citizens of Guayaquil.

The 300 mestizos and mulattoes who worked in the shipyards formed the highest-paid and most-skilled sector of Ecuadorian workers. These carpenters and caulkers organized a guild in 1777 that was headed by a Spanish master artisan. The Spanish navy commissioned its Pacific fleet at the Guayaquil shipyards, but most of the orders for new ships and for refitting old ones came from merchants at Lima and Panama. Expansion of the cacao exports also stimulated the construction of ships. Most of the materials came from the surrounding areas; the hardwoods grew in the numerous tropical valleys along the coast, textile manufacturers at Cuenca produced the cotton sails, tar came from the oil pools south of the port, and the skin of a locally grown coconut served as caulking material.

Colombian Gold

North of Ecuador lay the vast territory known in colonial times as New Granada and today as Colombia. Located just above the equator, the hot, humid lowlands of Colombia did not attract many European settlers except at the port of Cartagena on the Caribbean coast. A majority of Spanish immigrants instead found their way up the Magdalena and Cauca Rivers and into the temperate highlands. The heaviest concentration of the pre-Conquest indigenous population had also resided in these temperate lands, although disease had much reduced their numbers by the eighteenth century. The highland province of Antioquia, whose capital was Popayán, became known for the entrepreneurial spirit of its residents. They had been among the first to organize placer gold mining in the tropical river valleys of the region. In the late seventeenth through the eighteenth centuries, these enterprising miners revived the industry and spread gold mining west into the sparsely inhabited Chocó province. Production and export of Colombian gold reached unprecedented levels. In Antioquia itself, free persons of color opened up many new gold-washing sites for the mine entrepreneurs, but burgeoning production and profits paved the way for increasing imports of slaves. The number of slaves made to work in the gold washings of Antioquia grew from an estimated nine hundred in 1759 to as many as thirteen thousand in 1778.

The export of gold from New Granada contributed to immigration, settlement, and the expansion of slavery in the remotest parts of northern South America. Highland agriculture developed as well as the beginning of a textile industry; strong domestic demands produced by the gold industry partially counterbalanced the difficult transportation problems of mountainous Colombia, where it remained faster to sail to Spain than to travel overland from Cartagena to Bogotá. However, the benefit of commerce in Colombian gold did not always accrue to Spanish royal coffers. Contraband had rooted itself firmly in the soil of New Granada, and perhaps as much as a third of gold production did not pass through the royal mints at Popayán and Bogotá. Foreign ships exchanged slaves and merchandise for gold in the numerous inlets along the Caribbean coast. In fact, smuggling came to be considered normal in Colombia, so much so that officials of the royal customs houses at the port of Cartagena were among the most prominent smugglers of all.

Lowland gold mining was the job assigned to Africans. Some seventeen thousand blacks resided in the three principal mining provinces of Antioquia, Popayán, and the Chocó. The lowland natives had succumbed to European diseases and to work in the gold placer mines. In the Chocó of the 1770s, less than five thousand five hundred natives remained of a population that had been more than ten times larger a century before. But only about half the lowland miners were slaves. Free-born blacks and mulattoes moved into the occupation, attracted by high wages but also by need, as commodity prices in the lowland also remained high. The state finally reduced the *quinto* tax on gold to 10 percent in 1778, stimulating higher exploitation. The tributaries between the Cauca and Magdalena Rivers in Antioquia had been the center of Colombia's earliest gold regions. But by the eighteenth century, their production had been surpassed by Popayán to the south and especially by the Chocó to the west. In the latter province, troops of blacks panned and sluiced extensively in the river gravel on the mountain slopes facing the Pacific Ocean. Everywhere the story was the same. The arrival of the gold miners brought enslavement to the indigenous population, which declined and finally was replaced by a mixed population of enslaved Africans and free blacks.

The gold mines of the Colombian Chocó region, located inland from the Pacific coastline, attracted Spanish settlement in 1690. From then until the end of the colonial period, the mines of the Chocó yielded more than 75 million silver pesos worth of gold. Well over 90 percent of the gold production came from the labor of African slaves and free black workers. The indigenous population had quickly succumbed to diseases and overwork by the Spanish taskmasters. In 1782, persons of color dominated the population of the Chocó. There were only 359 Spaniards, as most owners and gold merchants preferred living in the temperate Colombian highlands of Antioquia. The remaining population included 7,088 slaves, 3,899 free persons of color, and 6,552 Native Americans.

Bogotá, site of the *audiencia* since 1548, remained primarily an administrative and commercial center. The city also had a substantial clerical population of some eight hundred priests, nuns, and monks, who serviced 30 churches and eight monastic houses. It became the capital of the new Viceroyalty of New Granada in 1739. The wealthiest residents of Bogotá, some of whom traced their lineage to the conquistadores, owned large haciendas on the broad highland savanna that stretches out below the city; there they raised livestock and cultivated commercial crops. However, the countryside appeared abandoned to many visitors, provoking some comment about the poor distribution of land. "[T]he limitless extent of many haciendas causes a great vacuum in the population of these territories," noted one observer in 1790, ". . . turning wheat lands into pastures, and depriving the Kingdom of a great number of people who could find their livelihood on lands which now feed animals." Smallholders dominated the adjacent highlands of Tunja and contributed to the great Comunero Rebellion of 1781 (see Chapter 11).

Venezuelan Cacao

Cacao production commenced in Venezuela during the seventeenth century when collapse of the lowland indigenous population of Central America undermined the cacao industry there. The *encomenderos* of Caracas directed their remaining native workers along the Caribbean coastline to plant the trees and deliver the cacao beans. From then on, Venezuelans took over the Mexican market by shipping the product directly from La Guaira to Veracruz in exchange for European goods. Toward the end of the century, the indigenous population declined to the point that the former *encomenderos* now had to acquire the land and go into production themselves, importing African slaves as laborers. Nevertheless, even by 1700, the trade languished because of the small size of the Mexican market. Few Spanish-bound vessels deemed it worthwhile to come directly to the Venezuelan port at La Guaira. The eastern ports of Venezuela developed a lively contraband trade with non-Spanish privateers, whereas other sections of Venezuela nurtured their own trade linkages to adjacent colonial territories. The Andean communities of Mérida and San Cristóbal traded with New Granada (Colombia) both overland and through the port of Maracaibo. The cattle and tobacco of Bariñas went to Colombia rather than overland to Caracas. At the end of the seventeenth century, Venezuela's domestic economy was hardly dynamic. It provided the crops and cattle needed to feed some half million settlers as well as the Native Americans of the frontier missions that the Jesuits and Franciscans had formed in the Llanos, the plains, as the vast basin of the Orinoco River system was called.

At the beginning of the eighteenth century, an extraordinary thing occurred. The Dutch introduced chocolate to Europe through the port of Amsterdam, where it was combined with the milk of the Netherlands and another colonial product, sugar. The consumption of chocolate suddenly burgeoned. Rather than allow the Dutch to enjoy the benefits of this new European cacao trade from their Caribbean islands of Curaçao and Aruba, the Spanish royal court attempted to obtain tax revenues from Venezuela. It awarded a monopoly contract to a group of Basque merchants, who thereafter held the exclusive right to all Venezuelan trade, which they were to expand and on which they were to pay proper taxes. They made their headquarters at Caracas. The Caracas Company, as it was called, could purchase African slaves from British traders for expanding the cacao plantations and export cacao directly to most ports in Spain. Along with the exclusive right to import European goods through La Guaira and Maracaibo, the Caracas Company was also supposed to provide naval patrols to eliminate pirates and illegal trade from the Venezuelan coasts.

The cacao industry boomed in the first half of the eighteenth century. Plantation production skyrocketed as merchants and Creole landowners set newly arrived slaves to planting new groves of cacao trees. Port facilities were developed, roads were improved, and a centralizing bureaucracy developed at Caracas. British traders who held the *asiento* contract brought record numbers of Africans to the port of La Guaira. Plantation production spread from the Caribbean coast to the Tuy Valley east of Caracas. The old elite families purchased large plantations in the Tuy Valley, and numerous Canary Island immigrants (the *canarios,* as they were called) established smaller cacao farms. More than five million cacao trees were planted in the Tuy Valley. Unlike sugar, cacao production did not stimulate the development of a draconian labor system. There was neither a high-anxiety harvest season nor any intense primary refining as in the *ingenio* mills of the sugar industry. Laxity characterized cacao growing. *Canario* administrators of the absentee *hacendados* living in Caracas were free to engage in their own businesses on the side, and even the slaves had opportunities to sell beans on the black market.

However, the Caracas Company's monopoly profits, garnered from buying cacao production cheaply and selling European goods dearly, generated its share of local resentments. Planters did not like having to sell their produce to one agency; Venezuelan-born merchants did not enjoy losing their independent trade in cacao to the Basque merchants of the Caracas Company; and slaves became disenchanted that they had to underwrite the prosperity with their unpaid labor. A rebellion broke out against the Caracas Company in 1745, and the Basque governor fled Caracas before a mob of *canario* farmers led by Juan Francisco de León. "Long live the king," the rebels shouted, "and death to the Basques." The *hacendado* elite favored the popular revolt, then distanced themselves when the king dispatched Spanish troops to catch and execute de León. Ultimately, the Crown curtailed the privileges of the Caracas Company until the monopoly became extinguished in 1789.

Venezuela—especially the environs of Caracas—continued to expand as a cacao-exporting plantation society into the nineteenth century. Exports of cacao nearly doubled between 1775 and 1810, while agricultural diversification in the area of Caracas added new exports, such as tobacco, sugarcane, indigo, and coffee. Contraband expanded along with official commerce, in part because of the vigorous black market. "[T]he abandoned state in which many hacendados keep their slaves," explained one Spanish official, ". . . keeps them in great poverty and extreme need, from which they redeem themselves with the property of their masters and others who do not watch them carefully." Slaves then sold purloined cacao beans to itinerant peddlers. The city and its surrounding valleys eventually contained more than four hundred thousand people, one-half of the population of the vast captaincy of Venezuela. Slaves formed 15 percent of the inhabitants, and persons of color comprised fully three-quarters of all Venezuelans (see Table 10.2). The economic boom tended to spawn a very progressive local Creole elite. Some Creoles were in trade, although they took a second position in exporting and importing to the Spaniards and Canary Islanders who had commercial ties in the metropolis.

Table 10.2   Population Growth and Race in the Caracas Region of Venezuela, 1785–1800

Race	1785	% of Total	1800	% of Total
Whites	79,232	24	108,920	26
Castes*	147,564	44	197,740	46
Native Americans	53,154	16	56,083	13
Slaves	53,055	16	64,462	15
Total	333,005	100	427,205	100

* Castes (*castas*) include mulattoes, mestizos, and free blacks.

SOURCE: P. Michael McKinley, *Pre-Revolutionary Caracas: Politics, Economy, and Society, 1777–1811* (Cambridge, England: Cambridge University Press, 1985), 4.

Native-born whites dominated land ownership. They served as cacao planters, farmers, and coffee producers. Several crossed the Andes range into the Llanos to establish cattle ranches, called *hatos*. Most of the high administrative and ecclesiastical positions were reserved for the European-born, who comprised less than one-tenth of the white population at the end of the eighteenth century. Perhaps the political and commercial monopoly enjoyed by Europeans drove the Creoles to became obsessed with status symbols. The wealthiest Creole landowners spent fortunes to secure titles to the nobility, which denoted racial purity. Less wealthy Creoles sought military titles, the officer assignments in the new militias that the Crown organized in the late colonial period. They also held the petty bureaucratic positions as local justices, agents in charge of dealing with Native Americans, and tax collectors.

The Africans imported as slaves formed an important part of the workforce of the cacao plantations. But by no means did they replace the free colored workers. In fact, the majority of the cacao workers were wage earners, not chattel labor. Imported slaves were found on plantations but also resided in urban areas as well. In 1796, 8,000 slaves lived in the city of Caracas, where they served as household servants. Free labor already took precedence over slavery, as the late-eighteenth-century economic boom began just as slave imports started to diminish. The reason for the discrepancy had to do with land ownership. Compared to the sugar plantations of Brazil and the Caribbean islands, the Venezuela cacao plantation was quite small. Most haciendas had fewer than five thousand cacao trees, and planters were not wealthy enough to afford large gangs of slave laborers. The prominent Creole family of the future crusader for independence, Simón Bolívar, had only 14 slaves on its plantation.

In the ranches and farms, persons of color, be they mulattoes, mestizos, or free blacks, worked as wage-earning peons. Free persons of color (the *castas*) formed a mobile force of rural workers who were used to moving about and alternating between wage work, squatting on unused land, and perhaps thievery. Local authorities discriminated against them, preventing their upward social mobility, and also feared them. To force the *castas* into permanent employment for the Creole landowners, it was proposed that Venezuelans of color carry identification papers attesting to their satisfactory employment. But enforcement of such a code was impossible so long as Venezuela had vast open spaces. Nonetheless, landowners feared this restless class of free persons of color and resented their lack of control over them. One prelate estimated that one-third of the Caracas population were those "who live without exercising an occupation capable of providing their daily substance, whilst the public beggars gather . . . 1,200 [strong] in front of the bishop's place every Saturday."

However, many Venezuelans of color as well as poor whites took up positions in the ranks of the militias or on frontier smallholdings. But to preserve discrimination in the general society, the companies of whites and persons of color were segregated. It was assumed that mulattoes who served as soldiers were "men of infamous and twisted lineage, uneducated and easily moved to commit the more horrendous of excesses." Most officers were Creoles. Although the few wealthy mulattoes might gain acceptance to society, most persons of color felt more comfortable in their own world. Numerous mulattoes, Native Americans, and runaway slaves formed their own communities at isolated frontier outposts throughout Venezuela. This spatial outlet considerably reduced the danger of popular revolts. There was only one rebellion, undertaken by 250 slaves in Coro in 1795. A few score whites were killed, but the reaction was overwhelming. One hundred seventy slaves and free persons of color were executed for their role in the rebellion. The reaction proved the sensitivity of the outnumbered whites in this multiracial society. These racial hatreds boiled over in the crisis of 1810, when Venezuela became the cradle of the independence movement (see Chapter 15).

THE SOUTHERN CONE

Paraguay

On the east side of the Andean mountains, only Paraguay had developed a distinctive colonial civilization in the sixteenth century—distinctive because of its adoption of indigenous culture. This had occurred principally owing to the presence of the Guaraní, who had supported the Spanish city of Asunción, labored on the garden plots, tended to the cattle herds, and entered the forests to harvest the *yerba* tea leaves. From this Paraguayan base, settlers (most of them first- and second-generation mestizos) had descended the Paraná River to establish permanent Spanish settlements at Santa Fe and Buenos Aires at the end of the sixteenth century. Nonetheless, its isolated location 1,600 kilometers upriver from the Atlantic shipping lanes and another 1,900 kilometers across desolate plains and formidable mountain peaks from the silver mines of Potosí kept Asunción in a state of economic lethargy throughout the seventeenth century. Few Spanish immigrants entered the region. The mestizos (who nevertheless called themselves *españoles*) established a familiar social hierarchy with the wealthier landowners and merchants at the apex and the indigenous laborers at the bottom. That these mestizo elites spoke the Guaraní language did not exempt native workers from suffering their demands for labor and concubines. In the absence of Spanish women, sexual license became quite ingrained in this isolated setting. As an early friar said, a Spaniard is considered poor who has only five or six concubines, "most having fifteen, twenty, thirty, and forty."

But what they had nurtured at Asunción was a tradition of political autonomy that, come the eighteenth century, the Crown could no longer ignore. In the first place, the Paraguayan settlers were responsible for their own defense from the surrounding hostile Native Americans. The Charrúa and Abipón inhabited the Chaco and Entre Ríos, and they soon became expert horsemen. The war canoes of the Payaguá infested the Paraguay River north of Asunción. Therefore, each male Paraguayan was also a militiaman, who could be summoned to defend the territory or to mount a punitive expedition against indigenous raiders. However, the Paraguayans never could subdue the warriors of the Gran Chaco during the colonial period.

The local mestizo gentry were accustomed to a great deal of local autonomy. Any Spanish governor or religious prelate who judged them too harshly for their treatment of the natives or for their liberties with women was hounded unceremoniously from office. The very first royal governor, Cabeza de Vaca, had been dispatched in chains back to Spain by his colonial subjects because he disputed their control of the Guaraní. Indeed, the *encomienda* survived there into the eighteenth century, having long since been abolished in Mexico and Peru where the colonial state had taken over indigenous labor and tribute. Not so in Paraguay. Here the mestizo elite jealously preserved its domination over the Indians with little interference from the colonial state—reason enough that the Jesuits came to be resented in Paraguay.

Having arrived at the end of the sixteenth century, the missionaries of the Society of Jesus accepted the supposedly heroic mission of bringing so-called civilization to the indigenous peoples of the region. But the citizens of Asunción did not wish them to take charge of the Guaraní villages close to that city. The Jesuits went into the wilderness regions up the Paraguay and Uruguay Rivers in territories that today form parts of Brazil. In the course of the seventeenth and eighteenth centuries, they brought the Guaraní into mission villages and taught them the rudiments of Western civilization and religion. Not a few missionaries became martyred for their efforts. For the most part, however, the indigenous forest peoples adapted to the new regime. They built villages and churches, cultivated manioc and corn, and learned to breed cattle, horses, and pigs. They also took to learning the catechism in their own language, which they embraced fervently, and to practicing marital monogamy, which apparently some did not. From the natives' standpoint, however, the bargain was not entirely negative. The Jesuits neither reduced them to slavery nor converted the women into concubines. Moreover, the missionaries introduced the Indians to crops and farm animals, such as chickens and cattle, that enriched their diets. Tax rates on the mission Guaraní remained low, and the Jesuits offered protection from their native enemies, from the Paraguayans, and from the *paulistas*.

Fierce raids by Brazilian slave hunters from São Paulo forced many Jesuits to abandon their missions during the seventeenth century. In 1676, the *paulistas* overran the yerba maté production center of Mbaracaú, located 195 kilometers northeast of Asunción. The refugees then established Villa Rica nearby to become the new center of *yerba* collection in the nearby forests. Brazilian raiders also motivated the Jesuits to undertake the military organization of the mission natives. The *paulista* threat to the area of the upper Uruguay River was deflected just before the mid-seventeenth century. Spanish authorities permitted the Jesuits to arm and train the mission natives for their own defense. In 1641, the battle was engaged. At Mbororé, the Jesuit-led native militias routed the *paulistas* and their Tupí allies. Thereafter, the Guaraní safely reoccupied some of their old lands east of the Uruguay River. The main settlements lay south of Asunción between the Paraná and Uruguay Rivers. But the Jesuits established seven missions in the present-day Brazilian states of Santa Catarina and Rio Grande do Sul, raising numerous cattle herds on the prairies. Now the missionaries had turned the mission natives into as formidable a military force as that of the Paraguayans themselves, mainly to protect Spanish interests in the Río de la Plata from the Portuguese in Brazil. However, arming the missions did not sit well with secular residents at Asunción, and neither did the demographic resurgence of the Guaraní. The native population at the missions reached a nadir at the beginning of the eighteenth century. In 1710, approximately 100,000 Native Americans inhabited 30 Jesuit missions, rising to 130,000 by midcentury. In the meantime, the natives serving the Paraguayans at Asunción numbered only 12,000.

Paraguay's chief export was yerba maté, but the crop never gained a European market. Even so, Latin American consumption of yerba maté grew enough to sponsor the slow transition from *rescate,* the gathering of *yerba* leaves from trees growing naturally in the forests, to the planting of *yerba* trees in plantationlike estates. The Jesuit missionaries helped integrate Paraguay into the economies of the rest of colonial Latin America. Besides gathering together the frontier Guaraní and other indigenous groups into mission settlements, the Jesuits oversaw the planting of *yerba* trees. By the end of the seventeenth century, the friars' business practices annoyed many a secular merchant living in Asunción. The Jesuits enjoyed the typical religious exemptions from most colonial taxes and also controlled much of the available native labor. In addition, the Jesuit missionaries enjoyed commercial linkages with other Jesuit institutions—haciendas, chapels, schools, and urban headquarters called *colleges*—which facilitated their intracolonial trade. Finance capital arrived from the colleges, along with European and American-produced textiles, ironware, and wine. The missions exported *yerba* and some handicrafts directly to other Jesuit institutions in the Río de la Plata (today Uruguay and Argentina), Chile, Upper and Lower Peru, and Ecuador. There the Jesuit commodities would enter the secular markets. At the beginning of the eighteenth century, the Jesuits already had great advantages over their secular competitors at Asunción.

Therefore, as the domestic South American markets advanced on the strength of export and population growth, so did the export commerce of Paraguay. The Spanish Jesuits extended their missions in a wide arc from what is now Minas Gerais, Brazil, through Paraguay down the Paraná River into the Banda Oriental (the East Bank, or today Uruguay). Its large haciendas on the eastern side of the Uruguay River specialized in cattle and mules, which were sold on the hoof and driven via Salta to the mining camps of Upper Peru. (The Gran Chaco, flooded part of the year and arid for the rest, was conceded to its original indigenous inhabitants and did not serve as a direct trade route between Paraguay and Bolivia. Even the *yerba* sold at Potosí traveled in a roundabout way from Asunción through Santa Fe and Salta. Lima's supply of Paraguayan tea was transshipped from Chile.) Jesuit haciendas along the opposite bank of the Paraná River specialized in producing hides for international trade at Buenos Aires and in wheat and other foodstuffs for the growing Hispanicized population of the region. The Jesuit estates brought in Guaraní workers from Paraguay and bought African slaves at Buenos Aires to staff these estates. By virtue of entrepreneurial talent and generous tax breaks, the Society of Jesus became one of the most successful colonial economic institutions of the eighteenth century.

But as the economy of the Río de la Plata region became more complex, the Jesuits' empire made more enemies. Penurious colonial officials at Asunción envied their exemptions from taxes, small merchants disliked their commercial advantages, and modest ranchers resented their control of indigenous workers. Local political opposition grew. In 1721, a revolt broke out at Asunción against the Spanish governor who was perceived as being a partisan of the Jesuits. The governor was executed, and his place was taken by

Map 10.2 Southern South America in 1790

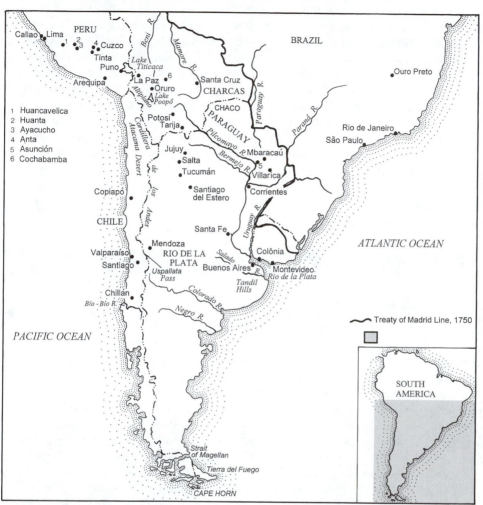

1 Huancavelica
2 Huanta
3 Ayacucho
4 Anta
5 Asunción
6 Cochabamba

Paraguayan-born citizens. Indeed, on this occasion, the poorest elements among the mestizo farmers seemed to participate in politics with such relish that even the local elite had second thoughts. Not until 15 years later, in 1735, did Crown officials reestablish authority in Asunción. The so-called Revolt of the Comuneros, or townspeople, refers to the modest mestizo ranchers, farmers, and merchants who rose up against the Spanish governor. The Comuneros were not the Guaraní. The natives' loyalties remained with the Jesuits—their paternalistic benefactors. Armed Guaraní from the missions helped reestablish Spanish authority at Asunción, no doubt adding to the humiliation of the Paraguayan mestizos. Subsequently, mission natives helped build fortifications at Montevideo and Buenos Aires, and the Guaraní militias fought in 1742 to drive the Portuguese out of Colônia do Sacramento, a port the latter had established on the estuary of the Río de la Plata.

Despite Guaraní loyalty to the Crown, the 30,000 Native Americans who inhabited the seven mission towns east of the Uruguay River became angry when their own Jesuit superiors had to order them to retreat back to Paraguay. Spain and Portugal had signed the Treaty of Madrid in 1750, which recognized Portugal's claim to Rio Grande do Sul and Santa Catarina in exchange for its renunciation of all designs on Uruguay. The Guaraní protested their loyalty to the Catholic Church and to the Spanish king but rebelled against their own priests. Indian *caciques* ordered the wagons burned and shot arrows at Spaniards who attempted to move them from the towns. The Guaraní turned their religion against those very Spanish authorities who had forced it upon them in the first place, claiming that God had given them the land and refusing to believe that their beloved Christian king would make them abandon their churches to the godless Brazilians. "If the Portuguese want our towns and our lands," they told their priests, "then they will pay for them with their blood" (see Manuscript 10.1). The Guaraní rebellion lasted from 1754 to 1756.

MANUSCRIPT 10.1

Response of the Guaraní to the Loss of Village Lands

In 1750, the Treaty of Madrid fixed the boundaries between the Spanish and Portuguese possessions in South America. The royal authorities of both Spain and Portugal generally observed the rights of possession, which meant that colonial subjects of both Iberian monarchies were to remain on those lands they already occupied. But the exact geographic locations of many frontier settlements in the vast hinterlands of what is now Brazil were only dimly known in Iberia. In other cases, the Crowns traded New World territories. The treaty stipulated that Portugal gave up all claim to present-day Uruguay in exchange for the territories east of the Uruguay River (in the present-day states of Santa Catarina and Rio Grande do Sul) in which Spanish Jesuits had established seven missions for the Guaraní. The natives were loath to give up the villages they had built, the lands on which they ran cattle, and the cemeteries in which their parents and grandparents were buried. They rebelled when their Jesuit priests ordered them back to Paraguay. Here is their protest to their Jesuit superior. Note the religious devotion and their reference to service and loyalty to the king.

Under no circumstances do we want the Portuguese on our lands, not even Spaniards, not even those who came to fix the limits on our lands because we will get incredibly angry with them. They should know what we will do with them because we never get tired of fighting. . . . God himself has given us this land; our Holy King who loves us so much and for the love we have for him, and because we are the children of the Holy Mother Church, he is among us for our defense, and we are at his disposal so he could care for us: it is not good for us to hear for no reason the bad [the Portuguese] have caused or how they offend the customs or belongings of our holy church [in earlier *paulista* raids on the missions] no matter how much the missionaries tell them that they are Christians like the Spaniards and that our kingdom is Portuguese; Holy Father Superior, you have come to fulfill the will of our Holy King or you are here for the love of our Holy King, because of this we want you to know that we will not leave these, our poor lands, which God himself has given us, for any reason whatsoever.

This second major disturbance in this region was not quelled until the Spanish and Portuguese mounted a joint military expedition against the Guaraní rebels. Even so, Spain subsequently repudiated the treaty because the Portuguese had not completely abandoned Colônia. Some Guaraní returned to their old missions in the 1760s, although the days of glory were over. But the royal courts of both Spain and Portugal resented the Jesuits who, after all, had been granted much temporal power in the colonies for the very purpose of controlling the indigenous population; the earlier Paraguayan Revolt of the Comuneros as well as the Guaraní revolt seemed to indicate that the Jesuits were not the solution but the cause of disruption in South America.

The jealousy of the colonists, combined with the Crown's resentment of Jesuit political machinations, reached a critical mass in the 1760s. First the Portuguese and then the Spanish Crown ordered the Jesuits to be banished from the realm. (For more on the expulsion of the Jesuits, see Chapter 14.) Carrying out the order was a delicate matter. Special emissaries of the king of Spain, accompanied by cavalry units, conveyed the

The Portuguese have no need for these lands for we are in charge of them for God, and those in his place, and our Holy King, fulfilling his holy words, and his holy will we have gone to Paraguay to humiliate [the Comunero rebels of 1721], and subjected and made them obey the King, who made the peace. Also for the reverence we have for our Holy King, there should be a house for the priests, we went to Montevideo to build a fort. Not only did we do this for the reverence of our King, but we also built in our poor land a very large and lovely house of God with a tall and beautiful bell tower where there is a great view. All this we have done for the reverence we have for our Holy King who stands in place of God, and the Holy Spirit who shines a great deal, also we have built a very good house for the priests; and even better than what they had before, all for reverence towards God and our Holy King. We have also made our poor houses into good ones and with lovely arcades and covered walkways made of stone, making everyone understand by these actions that we are the vassals of our Holy King, whose holy will has always been fulfilled, without failure. Oh Holy King you should have been in Buenos Ayres when we were building that fort! We would have thrown ourselves on the ground before your holy feet, to kiss them, to show the great reverence we have for you, and because we know that you love us a great deal, Holy King. We do not want to leave this land. The seven towns cannot hear the word *Portuguese*. After all the hard work we have done, we should enjoy it; it is not good for the Portuguese to enjoy it: this is our poor land which is something the Portuguese do not need. Maybe they are looking for the road to Hell; that is the place where they should go. We, your poor vassals have always prayed for forgiveness, therefore. Holy King, may your compassion always continue with us.

SOURCE: "Carta de indios de San Juan Bautista," [circa 1752], Archivo de Simancas, Spain, Estado 7426, as quoted in Barbara A. Ganson, "Better Not Take My Manioc: Guarani Religion, Society, and Politics in the Jesuit Missions of Paraguay, 1500–1800," Ph.D. diss. (University of Texas at Austin, 1994).

secret edict to Asunción in 1767. They arrested the Jesuit priests—sometimes in the dead of night—and quickly packed them into riverboats carrying them to Buenos Aires for embarkation to their exile in Italy. Few localities learned about the royal orders until the Jesuits were gone. The authorities confiscated the missions and haciendas and distributed them to other missionary orders or to the merchant brotherhoods.

Nonetheless, Paraguay survived the Jesuits quite easily. The economy and its principal export, yerba maté, continued its expansion based on the concomitant growth of the Río de la Plata. Private entrepreneurs assumed the cultivation and harvesting of the *yerba* leaves and established commercial links with merchants at the expanding port of Buenos Aires. Now versed in Hispanic customs, the Guaraní took up work as peons for Paraguayan agriculturists. Many also settled as squatters on the abundant land south and east of Paraguay. Colonial authorities now taxed all commerce flowing down river from Asunción and used the proceeds to finance military patrols to prevent Portuguese incursions. The reasons for Paraguay's continued prosperity after the expulsion of the Jesuits lay elsewhere, in Argentina.

Argentina

As the eighteenth century progressed, the economic boom made more and more of an impact on the city of Buenos Aires. Spain's southernmost American port, located on the estuary of the Río de la Plata, Buenos Aires had been but a frontier outpost for its first century of existence. Hostile natives behind the city prevented the spread of cattle haciendas and wheat farms in its hinterlands; these were found instead in the cities of the interior, such as Córdoba and Mendoza, which provided foodstuffs for the mining regions of Upper Peru. Meanwhile, the port of Buenos Aires grew through trade in contraband. Throughout the seventeenth century, first Portuguese, then French, and finally Dutch vessels sneaked into the estuary of the Río de la Plata to trade African slaves and European textiles for Potosí silver, which was quite illegal. The Crown had decreed that the silver be exported through Lima, but logic dictated that bullion come down to Salta on muleback and to Buenos Aires on oxcarts. Portugal sponsored the founding of a settlement across the estuary at Colônia do Sacramento just to circumvent Spain's declared monopoly on the silver trade. For the first third of the eighteenth century, the British possessed the Spanish *asiento* to post commercial agents at Buenos Aires for the purpose of importing African slaves. Although they had no legal authority to deal in European merchandise or in Potosí silver, the English merchants did so, with the full knowledge of the Spanish authorities and grateful consumers of the region.

The city of Buenos Aires grew. In 1720, nearly nine thousand people lived in the city, and the population multiplied to twenty-two thousand in 1770 and to more than forty-two thousand by 1810, growth that caused a change in cattle husbandry of the surrounding countryside. Rather than raising cattle, the people of Buenos Aires had simply supplied themselves through hunting expeditions among the wild cattle of the Pampas. The tongues, considered a delicacy, were used for the local meat supply, and the hides supplied the modest export trade. The rest of the tough, lean carcasses were left on the Pampas as carrion. Slowly, settlers populated the environs of the city, domesticating cattle to provide dried hides for international commerce. Hides and dried meat for export also arrived by riverboat from cattlemen on the Banda Oriental, Corrientes, and Santa Fe.

In recognition of its rising commercial importance—accomplished against the Crown's policies—Buenos Aires was made capital of the newly created Spanish Viceroyalty of the Río de la Plata in 1776. The tactic worked. The establishment of the new viceroyalty reinforced Spanish occupation of colonial Uruguay and kept the southern part of the continent from Portuguese incursion. As an integral part of its ambitious reforms (of which more is discussed in Chapter 14), Spain and Spanish merchants began to claim control of commerce at Buenos Aires. Contraband did not end but legal, Spanish-controlled commercial exchange burgeoned at the port. Agents of the great trading houses of Cádiz, Seville, and other Spanish ports arrived at Buenos Aires to establish merchant families. With their connections to the metropolitan economic and political powers, the merchants collected silver from Upper Peru for export. They imported mercury, tobaccos, and African slaves. Hardware and textiles came from northern Europe, as always, but now through the warehouses of Spain and in greater volume. Likewise, these wholesale merchants collected and warehoused the major exports of the port: silver, hides, dried meat, and exotic commodities like nutria pelts and ostrich feathers for Europe's fashionable salons.

The great merchant families paralleled the characteristics of their peers at Mexico City and Lima. Young Spanish men, emigrating especially from the Basque provinces of northern Spain, vied for success as apprentices. Once successful, they then married the native-born daughters of older Spanish merchants. They invested in retail shops and transport facilities, established their relatives and kinsmen in the cities of the interior, joined the correct lay brotherhoods, gave to the church, and competed for political honors and offices. Their Creole sons were destined for the church, the shop, the bureaucracy, or the military. Their daughters who had dowries were reared to marry other Spanish merchants, and those without dowries expected to marry into families of upstanding Creoles, go to the nunneries, or enter spinsterhood. In all respects, the merchants of Buenos Aires comported themselves with the same haughtiness and commercial behavior as those in Mexico City and Lima. However, the *porteño* merchants, meaning those of the port of Buenos Aires, did not invest in haciendas. Profits in the long-distance trade in silver, mercury, slaves, and merchandise were just too plentiful here, and land was so available and cheap as to offer few returns on investment—at least not yet.

Below this group of Spanish commercial moguls existed a vast network of warehousemen and retailers. Approximately 600 retailers of cloths and imported goods operated in Buenos Aires, as did 700 taverns and general stores selling wines, spirits, candles, salt, bread, kindling and other consumer items. These retailers—and the street peddlers who competed with them—were often beholden to rich merchants from whom they received goods on credit. Spanish immigrants swelled the ranks of artisans who especially served the luxury market with silver items, fashionable clothes, and European-style furniture. Mulatto freemen and African slaves owned by Spanish-born master artisans worked in trades such as baking, masonry, carpentry, tailoring, and shoemaking. A numerous body of free laborers such as tanners, lime burners, and sellers of kindling wood also hawked their trades in this port city. Porters were particularly visible, running around the streets unloading merchandise from horse-drawn carts.

Increased legal commerce and relaxed trade restrictions did not resolve all the market conditions giving rise to smuggling. Clandestine commerce continued on a smaller scale because Bourbon reforms neither eliminated high customs duties, ended certain monopolies, nor permitted unrestricted foreign shipping in the Río de la Plata. Smuggling was still a welcome vice among otherwise respectable colonial merchants. By participating in contraband now and again, they realized greater profits on their investments. *Porteños* often dealt directly with foreign ships in the estuary and brought goods ashore to their warehouses under the cover of darkness. Contraband was never surreptitious enough to escape the notice of viceregal authorities. Indeed, without their compliance, smuggling could not have reached such heights. Those very functionaries charged with suppressing contraband—customs officials, coast guard officers, and the viceroys themselves—profited from condoning it.

Owing to its population growth, administrative importance, and commercial wealth, Buenos Aires soon became the largest and most important domestic market in the entire region. Ponchos and cheap native textiles from Tucumán and Santiago del Estero found their biggest markets in the port city, where they were sent via oxcart in bundles of 50 ponchos each. In the highlands, Cochabamba's weaving workshops flourished in the late eighteenth century by dispatching their famous cotton cloths to markets in Salta, Córdoba, and even faraway Buenos Aires. Raw cotton, in turn, came from fields in Tucumán and even Peru. Córdoba's leather industries supplied Buenos Aires and other provinces with chamois and suede. Paraguay also found greater markets in Buenos Aires for its hemp, fruits, vegetables, raw cotton, and native textiles.

The transport trades, benefiting directly from the commercial development of the port, flourished throughout the Río de la Plata. Legal trade between Buenos Aires and Potosí expanded significantly, although Lima served as an alternate outlet for Upper Peru. In 1800, Potosí received 600,000 pesos worth of goods from Buenos Aires and approximately half that amount from Peru. This commerce redounded to the prosperity of trade centers between the two poles of the La Plata economy. Already, in the early 1770s, caravans of 20 carts or more regularly arrived in Buenos Aires with dried fruits, wines, brandies, flour, dried peaches, and passengers from provinces like Mendoza and San Juan. Chilean trade, formerly conducted through Lima, now flowed by way of Buenos Aires, overland to Mendoza, and through the cordillera to Santiago de Chile. Tucumán and other trading towns participated in the export market of Buenos Aires as teamsters transported silver and vicuña wool from Jujuy to Buenos Aires for export overseas. Increased river trade in hides and domestic products gave rise to considerable boat building not only in Buenos Aires but also in those river towns closer to the forests—such as Corrientes and Asunción. The volume of such commerce in the interior of Argentina probably grew 20 times over during the latter half of the eighteenth century.

The Banda Oriental, or East Bank (today the nation of Uruguay), also emerged as an exceptionally productive supplier to Buenos Aires. In the latter quarter of the eighteenth century, smallholders and largeholders alike sent hides, dried meat, and wheat to Buenos Aires. The first cattle-slaughtering plants were located on the Banda Oriental. These plants, called *saladeros,* produced salted meat and hides through factorylike production for export. This was the first step in eliminating the time-consuming and labor-intensive process of slaughtering cattle from the hacienda itself. But the age of intensive specialization in the cattle industry was yet to come. As trade rose in the estuary of the Río de la Plata, Montevideo (founded in 1726) became a complementary port of call for foreign ships, especially for local produce and trade with southern Brazil. Many merchant houses at Buenos Aires also maintained branch offices and warehouses at Montevideo. The port of Colônia do Sacramento, taken back from the Portuguese in 1776, served local

Method of slaughtering cattle in the Río de la Plata. (Anonymous artist, 1791)

shipping that carried to Buenos Aires the ranch products from the Banda Oriental and the Uruguay River.

On the Pampas south of the port of Buenos Aires, colonial ranching remained a relatively modest endeavor fit for Creoles who had some commercial connections in the city and for many small farmers of immigrant or racially mixed backgrounds. These ranchers domesticated the cattle herds that, when slaughtered right on the ranch, provided the hides for export. Some cattle were sold on the hoof to supply the city with meat. These landowners also produced wheat, which they delivered to Buenos Aires in hide bags via oxcarts. The bigger ranch families tended to intermarry among themselves and act as bourgeois imitators of their wealthier Spanish cousins. But they were a rustic lot, and the ranchers and their sons accomplished the branding and butchering alongside the hired gauchos (rural workers, cowboys), while the women churned butter or tended the orchards and gardens. Close to the city, small farmers harvested vegetables from truck gardens and produced milk and cheese from small herds of dairy animals.

In domesticating their herds, ranchers of the Pampas depended on two traditional Hispanic practices: the *rodeo* and the brand. Town councils granted both land and brands to prospective ranchers among their citizens. (In the nineteenth century these cattle ranches became known as *estancias* but were still known by the generic name of *haciendas* during the colonial period.) On the hacienda, the rancher's men gathered the cattle into designated pastures called *rodeos* to accustom them to domestication. An hacienda might consist of several *rodeos* within its perimeters, each tended by one or two cowhands whose principal task was to ride the limits of their areas to keep the herds together. As yet, there were no fences on the Pampas. If several head of the *hacendado*'s cattle strayed, he could reclaim them when all cattlemen in the vicinity rounded up their herds at branding time. Labor now became an important consideration, for the cattle owners needed cowhands to watch their herds all year long. Itinerant gauchos—Guaraní, free blacks and mulattoes, and mestizos—came to Buenos Aires from the interior provinces. The work of these hired men consisted of rounding up strays, branding and slaughtering, breaking and training the horses, and maintaining the corrals. They were adept at lassoing, horsemanship, and use of the knife and the *bolas,* the native weapon used to bring down game and cattle. Together, the *hacendados* and the itinerant cowboys produced the sun-cured cattle hides that increasingly entered foreign trade.

Most agricultural and cattle production was located north of the Salado River; south of the river reigned the indigenous peoples. The former hunter-gatherers of the Pampas had adopted the horse into their culture, and they began to subsist nearly exclusively on hunting the wild cattle and horses that proliferated on the grasslands. Occasionally, they helped themselves to the domesticated herds of the Spanish haciendas to the north. To secure the frontier, the colonial authorities established forts along the Salado River, mounted patrols into the frontier, and attempted to keep the natives from raiding the haciendas by giving them horses, cattle, and other goods.

Although they had not yet been subdued by European settlers, the autonomous native groups that inhabited the prairies and hills of the southern Pampas and Patagonia nonetheless did undergo momentous changes. They themselves transformed their lifestyles, adopting some of the settlers' material goods so as to resist the pressures of the expanding European towns. For example, by the beginning of the eighteenth century, the natives had already developed a brisk trade among themselves in European cattle and horses. They also began to congregate in larger and more complex groups, dividing themselves among wealthy chieftains and poor followers. Male hunter-warriors gained higher status, whereas women and the elderly correspondingly lost status.

The final stage of this transformation of indigenous society—whose purpose, after all, was to preserve its autonomy in the presence of European settlements—concerned warfare. Powerful hereditary chieftains emerged in the eighteenth century to lead bands of mounted warriors in raids on Spanish settlements for booty and captives. Two leaders, Cacapol and his son, Cangapol, emerged to lead the group called the Tehuelches. This group roamed along the Negro and Colorado Rivers in northern Patagonia, ranging up to the Tandil Hills on the southern Pampas. These two chieftains united many other tribes in the great uprising of 1740. More than one thousand mounted warriors swept north to raid for cattle, horses, and human captives (see Manuscript 10.2). The raid came in response to the expansion of the Hispanic population onto the frontier south of Córdoba and Buenos Aires.

Spaniards, Creoles, and gauchos alike had noticed the political changes occurring among the indigenous groups , a process they called "the Araucanization of the Pampas." The Araucanians were the Mapuche peoples of southern Chile, whose resistance prevented the Spanish population there from spreading south below the Bío-Bío River. The indigenous groups in Chile and Patagonia had been trading among each other across the southern Andean passes for at least two centuries. Now the Araucanian peoples began to mingle and intermarry with indigenous groups of Patagonia and the Pampas. Araucanian social practices and rituals also were adopted on the Argentine prairies, as were the warrior societies and tighter political alliances. More and more Native Americans in southern Argentina even began to speak the Mapuche language.

A tense standoff reigned between the indigenous peoples and the Hispanicized residents of the Río de la Plata when the viceregal government, established at Buenos Aires in 1776, founded a line of forts along the frontier. These forts performed several functions. As a line of defense, they prevented native warriors from raiding in the territory being settled by Spanish landowners and cattlemen. The forts also became centers of trade between the indigenous and Hispanic cultures. Viceregal officials even instituted an effective policy of supplying the indigenous groups with cattle and horses. Nevertheless, this process of the Araucanization of

MANUSCRIPT 10.2

The Great Native Uprising on the Pampas, 1740

The peace between the various hunting tribes of the Pampas and Patagonia broke down in 1740 because of the zealous and precipitate action of a Spanish constable, the Maestro del Campo described below. This officer led a troop of soldiers into Native American territory in pursuit of a raiding party that, according to the authorities, had engaged in theft and robbery. However, the troops could not locate the culprits and instead took retribution on a number of innocent and peaceful indigenous groups, on one occasion attacking a sleeping village and putting women and children to the sword. The various groups inhabiting the Pampas at the time reacted by resolving their own mutual hostilities and uniting to attack the encroaching Spanish settlements. The correspondent was an Englishman who had joined the Jesuit Order at Buenos Aires to work among the southern hunters.

This cruel conduct of the Maestr[o] del Campo so exasperated all the Indian nations of Puelches and Moluches, that they all took arms against the Spaniards; who found themselves attacked at once, from the frontiers of Cordova and Santa Fe, down the whole length of the River of Plate, on a frontier of a hundred leagues [323 miles or 557 kilometers]; and in such a manner, that it was impossible to defend themselves: for the Indians, in small flying parties, falling on many villages or farms at the same time, and generally by moon-light, it was impossible to tell the number of their parties; so that while the Spaniards pursued them in great numbers on one part, they left all the rest unguarded.

Cacapol, who, with his Tehuelhets [sic], as yet had lived in friendship with the Spaniards, was highly irritated at the attempt made on his son, the slaughter of his friends the Huilliches, the murder of his best-beloved kinsman and other relations, and the unworthy manner in which their dead bodies had been treated; and though he was at that time near seventy years of age, he took the field at the head of a thousand men (some say four thousand) consisting of Tehuelhets, Huilliches, and Pehuenches, and fell upon the District of the Magdalen, about four leagues distant from Buenos-Ayres, and divided his troops with so much judgement, that he scoured and dispeopled, in one day and a night, above twelve leagues of the most populous and plentiful country in these parts. They killed many Spaniards, and took a great number of women and children captives, with above twenty thousand head of cattle, besides horses, &c. In this expedition the Indians lost only one Tehuelhet, who, straggling from the rest in hopes of plunder, fell into the hands of the Spaniards. Cangapol, the son of Cacapol, was pursued and overtaken; but the Spaniards had not the courage to attack him, though at that time double in number, both they and their horses being quite tired with their expeditious march of forty leagues, without taking any refreshment.

SOURCE: Thomas Falkner, *A Description of Patagonia and the Adjoining Parts of South America* (Chicago: Armann & Armann, 1935), 106–7.

the Pampas would intensify at the beginning of the nineteenth century, again in response to important events in the Hispanicized world in Chile and Argentina. Even more warlike and powerful chieftains would follow in the footsteps of Cacapol, continuing the heritage of resisting the encroachment of European settlement.

Chile

While Peru revived its economic fortunes by producing yet more silver for the European market, the colony of Chile became economically more diversified. Nearly three-quarters of its trade in the eighteenth century was with other American colonies. It produced wheat and copper, both of which were exported to Lima. Annual wheat exports to Peru amounted to some ten million kilograms at the end of the eighteenth century. In the colonial period, Chilean copper was fashioned into tools, weapons, and eating utensils. Chileans were shipping more than nine hundred thousand kilograms of copper to foreign markets in the 1790s, mostly to Peru and Spain. Buenos Aires also imported Chilean copper on ships passing around Cape Horn. In return, Chileans purchased Peruvian sugar and yerba maté from the Río de la Plata. Increasingly, Chilean imports of European goods came from Buenos Aires or around Cape Horn rather than from across the Isthmus of Panama through Peru. Slaves for household service traveled overland from Buenos Aires and through the Andean passes. Unlike New Spain, Colombia, Peru, and Bolivia, Chile had few remaining deposits of gold and silver. Its principal export to Spain consisted of copper, for which there was only a modest demand in Europe.

Little of the trade at the colony's chief port, Valparaíso, came directly from Europe. Chile obtained many of its European exports, such as slaves and textiles, in transshipments from Lima and Buenos Aires. Of necessity, the immigrant Spanish merchants of Valparaíso and Santiago became quite diversified. They engaged in both long-distance trade with Spain while maintaining important contacts with other Spaniards in Peru and the Río de la Plata. Their increasing importance within the empire gained these merchants their own *consulado,* or merchants' guild, in 1795, which meant that their commercial disputes and affairs no longer came under the jurisdiction of Lima's powerful merchant guild.

The Chilean economy remained rooted in agricultural production for export markets. Creoles settled in haciendas in the central valleys stretching north and south from Santiago and within view of the towering Andes Mountains. These large landed units became veritable communities. Professional administrators ran the largest of them, while some of their wealthy owners resided in the capital, where they arranged with merchants for the sale and export of wheat and other products. In most cases, however, the owners themselves lived at their estates. They directed the work of a core of service tenants called *inquilinos.* Often mestizos and mulattoes, the *inquilinos* inhabited shacks throughout the estate. The wives and children maintained garden plots for subsistence and shared in the work of the men. When it came time to sow or to harvest the wheat, the *inquilinos* hired and supervised the work of temporary workers, usually smallholders living nearby or landless itinerants. Specie was in short supply in Chile, as in other parts of the Americas, due to the excessive exports of gold and silver to Spain; consequently, few landowners paid their *inquilinos* and peons entirely in money. Instead, the workers received food rations and goods that the owner acquired from the merchants in Santiago. Resident *inquilinos* also got a house and access to the owner's land, for which they had to work in the owner's fields. As the position conferred a degree of privilege and security, the *inquilinos* tended to identify with their landowners and shared their dim view of the itinerant workers. Production of such estates remained diversified. Besides wheat, the peons tended grapevines, fruit trees, and a few milk cows. A Chilean hacienda usually made its owner a profit of 5 to 7 percent per annum, depending on market and weather conditions. But the export market occasionally distorted domestic provisions to such an extent that the town councils often felt obliged to intervene in the market. At the mining center of Copiapó and towns in the central valleys, the *cabildos* frequently regulated the producers to secure sufficient supplies of foodstuffs for the local population. They issued edicts against big *hacendados* for hoarding wheat and driving up prices.

By no means were nonelite rural residents deprived of resources. Land was plentiful and labor was dear. Therefore, land was constantly being subdivided. Family farmers of modest social background had opportunities to possess or rent land. Small truck gardens providing fresh vegetables surrounded the towns, especially Santiago and Valparaíso. At Chillán, south of Santiago, in 1744, farms rather than haciendas predominated in the countryside. At the fringes of the central valleys, especially toward the south, extensive haciendas enclosed the scrublands and specialized in cattle grazing or sheep raising. Mixed-race Chilean cowboys, called *huasos,* developed Spanish husbandry and horsemanship to domesticate cattle for urban and foreign markets. The dried meat, hides, wool, and tallow from these cattle estates found markets in Santiago and Valparaíso, and dried hides were sent to Lima.

Native American labor became scarcer and scarcer in the eighteenth century as the working class became racially mixed and Hispanic in culture. Sedentary indigenous villagers gradually converted themselves into smallholders or gave up their lands to expanding haciendas. The natives of the central valleys gradually lost their ethnic identities and melded into the rural underclass. The lack of village focus among the rural population of Chile accounts for the fact that the church and Catholicism in general exerted less influence on Chile's rural population than elsewhere, such as Ecuador, Guatemala, and Mexico. Clerics were always in short supply in rural areas, but particularly so in southern South America. Chile did not have communities whose indigenous residents nurtured the local *cofradía* as a sign of the towns' religious (and ethnic) identity. Discriminated against because of their skin color and legally barred from holding office and serving as priests, mixed-race Chileans worked the mines and haciendas or took up vagabondage and criminal lives. Cattle rustling remained a major problem throughout the colonial period, justifying the extrajudicial authority enjoyed by many cattle *hacendados.* Powerful landowners maintained their own jails, ordered suspects to be flogged or executed, and supported laws restricting free movement through the countryside.

Always, the elite considered the rural underclass to be corrupt and thieving, in need of severe disciplinary measures to be made productive. For their part, the rural workers struggled to maintain their independence and to hire out their labor only on their own terms. Mining offered additional work opportunities for those willing to migrate to the remote settlements. The copper miners of Copiapó, Chile, jealously guarded their leisure time. They worked from sunup to sundown and lived on jerked beef and bread so that they could spend their earnings and what ore they took from the mine in the *pulperías,* establishments that served as taverns and stores catering to workers. Sundays and holidays were particularly important. The 52 *pulperías* of Copiapó in 1781 served as social centers where miners, out of the view of employers and public authorities, could gamble, dance, and meet women.

Table 10.3   Growth and Racial Composition of the Population of Chile, 1770–1813

Year	Whites	Native Americans	Mestizos	Blacks/Mulattoes	Total
1777	124,292	18,798	16,609	22,815	182,514
	(68.1%)	(10.3%)	(9.1%)	(12.5%)	
1813	281,287	36,739	34,061	30,617	382,704
	(73.5%)	(9.6%)	(8.9%)	(8.0%)	

SOURCE: William F. Sater, "The Black Experience in Chile," in Robert Brent Toplin, ed., *Slavery and Race Relations in Latin America* (Westport, Conn.: Greenwood Press, 1974), 39.

The merchants of Santiago invested their commercial profits in urban and rural real estate but not to the degree that they financed Chilean copper mining. The deposits of copper in the more remote foothills of the cordillera had been known since pre-Columbian times. Independent and underfinanced miners had been working the richest lodes since the Spaniards settled in Chile. Increasing trade with other American colonies promoted merchant financiers to advance money to miners in return for the product or part ownership of the mines. Additional economic activities included shipping and transport. If a wealthy merchant family owned rural haciendas, they were assets to be rented out to Creoles or immigrant Spaniards. Some merchants purchased ships made in the shipyards of Guayaquil, which they used to carry their produce to and from the Pacific ports of South America. Oxcarts and mule trains carried goods within Chile. Colonial authorities completed construction of the cart road between Santiago and Chile's chief port of Valparaíso in 1797, greatly facilitating exports.

In the countryside and cities, marketing was accomplished through warehouses and the ubiquitous *tiendas,* small shops operated by a retailer who usually had a silent partner in the import and export business at Santiago. Peninsulars, or immigrants born in the Iberian peninsula, formed the majority of Santiago's tight-knit merchant elite, most being Basques from northern Spain or Castilians from central Spain. Among the less wealthy group of merchants, perhaps with fewer international connections, native-born Chileans (but still of European descent) competed with foreigners in the bustling domestic commerce. Smuggling flourished among all the merchants but especially among the Chileans. French and British ships put into many inlets along the vast coastline of Chile during most of the eighteenth century, with German and U.S. merchants arriving at the beginning of the nineteenth. Domestic commerce grew to provision a growing population. By 1810, the Chileans numbered about five hundred eighty-three thousand, nearly twice the population of a half-century before. The capital of Santiago boasted 30,000 inhabitants. It had its own mint (Casa Moneda) and the new University of San Felipe (see Table 10.3).

Beyond the central valleys, where most of the Europeanized population lived in the eighteenth century, Chile was sparsely settled. The forbidding Andes Mountains to the east separated this long, narrow country from Mendoza and Potosí. The Uspallata Pass between Santiago and Mendoza connected these regions, but passage could be made safely only for three or four summer months. Between Peru and Chile lay the vast Atacama Desert, so coastal shipping logically united these two colonies more than did overland transportation.

Southern Chile retained its distinctive frontier character. The seminomadic Mapuche enjoyed virtual sovereignty in the forest and lake regions south of the Bío-Bío River. Hispanicized settlers from north of the river continued to make occasional slave-raiding forays into their territory, and Mapuche war parties raided frontier settlements and haciendas in response. Although the frontier forts were centers of exchange between Hispanic and indigenous groups, they often came under attack. Several were destroyed and abandoned in the Native American uprising of 1723. Thereafter, Mapuche raiding parties often descended on the haciendas of the south, rustling cattle by the hundreds for their own consumption.

CONCLUDING REMARKS

By now, it is obvious that the fringes of settlement in North and South America did not create colonial societies fundamentally more egalitarian than in the older cores. Even here on the frontiers, new elites emerged that combined the older considerations of rank and privilege to seize a disproportionate share of wealth and opportunity. Perhaps frontier societies permitted social mobility for those who moved into it, particularly from Europe, but it also brought disruption of indigenous culture and African slavery. The leaders of settlement carried with them the familiar institutions and methods of social control. They sought to establish in areas of new settlement similar privileges of land ownership and entrepreneurial activity and the same political and religious endorsement for indigenous and African labor that the conquerors had created two centuries before in Mexico and Peru. What distinguished the areas of eighteenth-century settlement from those of the sixteenth century was the minor role played by the indigenous masses. Native Americans in Venezuela and Colombia did not survive in large numbers as in central Mexico or the Peruvian highlands. Therefore, racial miscegenation, ethnic acculturation, and private ownership of land spread more widely in fringe societies, rendering them commercially fluid. But they were not egalitarian.

Rapid development of the fringes of empire presented Spain with problems of imperial proportions. First of all, the Crown had to expand the mechanisms of control, creating new administrative centers in these areas and sending more royal bureaucrats and clergy to oversee its interests. How Spain managed this new task—and its financial underwriting—is examined in Chapter 14. Second, the expanding fringes caused friction with other imperial powers. Spain had to contest with England and France for continued control of North America and the Caribbean and had to consider the presence of the Portuguese in South America; all of these other countries had expanding American interests. European imperial ambitions and clashes had widespread repercussions on non-European populations, as the African slave trade grew rapidly and the labor demands on indigenous peoples intensified. Witness how the political competition between the Portuguese and Spanish officials in the Paraná River basin of South America pulled the Guaraní and other forest agriculturists into the struggle. Finally, the extension of settlement into virgin territory, a cardinal feature of eighteenth-century economic florescence, placed pressure on autonomous indigenous societies beyond the frontier. The Apache and Comanche of northern Mexico, the forest dwellers of Venezuela and Brazil, and the Mapuche and Tehuelche to the south had to rearrange their own political and social practices to cope with demographic decline and the potential loss of territory.

Finally, economic growth everywhere in the Spanish colonies exacerbated exploitative relationships among the different strata of colonial society. Commercial prosperity exposed the corruption of public officials and the privilege of landowners. Growth tested relationships between employers and employees as bargaining for labor intensified. Economic expansion also exposed the social practices favoring whites over nonwhites in the division of income and opportunity. Not all the conflict would come between the separate castes in society. Economic expansion also challenged relationships within social groups as wealthy families formed political factions to undermine their elite competitors for wealth and influence. Spaniards attempted to claim a greater share of growth than Creoles. By the same token, commercial pressure and population growth among the indigenous population of Peru and Mexico tended to set one peasant village against another in disputes over land.

Perhaps few incidences in the eighteenth century demonstrate more starkly how economic and political pressures unbalanced the colonial equilibrium than the several great rebellions that shocked the colonial order in the latter quarter of the eighteenth century. They are the subjects of the next two chapters.

Additional Reading

Andrien, Kenneth J. *The Kingdom of Quito, 1690–1830: The State and Regional Development.* Cambridge, England: Cambridge University Press, 1995.

Barbier, Jacques A., and Allan J. Kuethe, eds. *The North American Role in the Spanish Imperial Economy, 1760–1819.* Manchester, England: Manchester University Press, 1984.

Bauer, Arnold. *Chilean Rural Society from the Spanish Conquest to 1930.* Cambridge, England: Cambridge University Press, 1975.

Brown, Jonathan C. *A Socioeconomic History of Argentina, 1776–1860.* Cambridge, England: Cambridge University Press, 1979.

Clayton, Lawrence A. *Caulkers and Carpenters in a New World: The Shipyards of Colonial Guayaquil.* Athens: Ohio University Press, 1980.

Fisher, J. R. *Silver, Mines and Silver Miners in Colonial Peru, 1776–1824.* Liverpool, England: Centre for Latin American Studies, University of Liverpool, 1977.

Ganson, Barbara A. "Better Not Take My Manioc: Guarani Religion, Society, and Politics in the Jesuit Missions of Paraguay, 1500–1800." Ph.D. diss., University of Texas at Austin, 1994.

Johnson, Lyman L., and Enrique Tandeter. *Essays on the Price History of Eighteenth Century Latin America.* Albuquerque: University of New Mexico Press, 1990.

Kinsbruner, Jay. *Chile: A Historical Interpretation.* New York: Harper & Row, 1973.

Lamar, Martha. "The Merchants of Chile, 1795–1823: Family and Business in the Transition from Colony to Nation." Ph.D. diss., University of Texas at Austin, 1993.

Larson, Brooke. *Colonialism and Agrarian Transformation in Bolivia: Cochabamba, 1550–1900.* Princeton, N.J.: Princeton University Press, 1985.

Larson, Brooke, et al., eds. *Ethnicity, Markets, and Migration in the Andes: The Crossroads of History and Anthropology.* Durham, N.C.: Duke University Press, 1995.

Liss, Peggy K. *Atlantic Empires: The Network of Trade and Revolution, 1713–1826.* Baltimore, Md.: Johns Hopkins University Press, 1982.

Lombardi, John V. *People and Places in Colonial Venezuela*. Bloomington: Indiana University Press, 1996.

Loveman, Brian. *Chile: The Legacy of Hispanic Capitalism*. 2d ed. New York: Oxford University Press, 1988.

McKinley, P. Michael. *Pre-Revolutionary Caracas: Politics, Economy, and Society, 1777–1811*. Cambridge, England: Cambridge University Press, 1985.

Minchom, Martin. *The People of Quito, 1690–1810: Change and Unrest in the Underclass*. Boulder, Colo.: Westview Press, 1994.

Palmer, Colin. *Human Cargoes: The British Slave Trade to Spanish America, 1700–1739*. Urbana: University of Illinois Press, 1981.

Piñero, Eugenio. *The Town of San Felipe and Colonial Cacao Economies*. Philadelphia: American Philosophical Society, 1994.

Sharp, William Frederick. *Slavery on the Spanish Frontier: The Colombia Chocó, 1680–1810*. Norman: University of Oklahoma Press, 1976.

Socolow, Susan Migden. *The Merchants of Buenos Aires, 1778–1810: Family and Commerce*. Cambridge, England: Cambridge University Press, 1978.

Tandeter, Enrique. *Coercion and Market: Silver Mining in Colonial Potosí, 1692–1826*. Albuquerque: University of New Mexico Press, 1993.

Twinan, Ann. *Miners, Merchants and Farmers in Colonial Colombia*. Austin: University of Texas Press, 1983.

Tyrer, Robson Brines. "Demographic and Economic History of the Audiencia of Quito: Indian Population and the Textile Industry, 1600–1800." Ph.D. diss., University of California at Berkeley, 1976.

West, Robert C. *Colonial Placer Mining in Colombia*. Baton Rouge: Louisiana State University Press, 1952.

Zulawski, Ann. *They Eat from Their Labor: Work and Social Change in Colonial Bolivia*. Pittsburgh: University of Pittsburgh Press, 1995.

In Spanish

Aizpurua, Ramón. *Curazao y la costa de Caracas: Introducción al estudio del contrabando de la provincia de Venezuela en tiempos de la Compañía Guipuzcoana, 1730–1780*. Caracas: Academia Nacional de la Historia, 1993.

Borde, Jean, and Mario Góngora. *Evolución de la propiedad rural en el valle de Puangue*. 2 vols. Santiago: Editorial Universitaria, 1956.

Brito Figueroa, Federico. *La estructura económica de Venezuela colonial*. 2d ed. Caracas: Universidad Central de Venezuela, 1983.

Cooney, Jerry W. *Economía y sociedad en la intendencia del Paraguay*. Asunción: Centro Paraguayo de Estudios Sociológicos, 1990.

Florescano, Enrique, ed. *Haciendas, latifundios y plantaciones en América Latina*. Mexico City: Siglo Ventiuno, 1975.

Garaveglia, Juan Carlos. *Economía, sociedad y regiones*. Buenos Aires: Ediciones de la Flor, 1987.

Moreno Yáñez, Segundo E. *Sublevaciones indígenas en la Audiencia de Quito: Desde comienzos del siglo XVIII hasta finales de la colonia*. Quito: Ediciones de la Universidad Católica, 1985.

Saguier, Eduardo. *Mercado inmobiliario y estructura social: El Rió de la Plata en el siglo XVIII.* Buenos Aires: Centro Editor de América Latina, 1993.

Suárez, Margarita. *Comercio y fraude en el Perú: Las estrategias mercantiles de un banquero.* Lima: IEP-BCR, 1995.

Villalobos R., Sergio. *El comercio y la crisis colonial: Un mito de la independencia.* Santiago: Universidad de Chile, 1968.

CHAPTER 11

REBELLION IN THE ANDES

1780

As illustrated in the previous chapters, the economic expansion of the Americas in the eighteenth century did not occur without causing severe strain on the delicately balanced social system. Increased wealth unleashed a frenzy of rapaciousness among colonial elites. Privileged Spaniards and Creoles sought to maximize their profits at the expense of less privileged groups. Throughout the Indies, merchants colluded with local officials to purchase native commodities at low prices and to sell shoddy goods to peasant villagers—by force, if necessary—and local officials also used their public offices to profit from native labor. The scramble for competitive advantage also widened the cleavages among the elites. The breach became especially severe between Creole landowners and merchants and tax-collecting Spanish officials, whose authority was being reinforced by certain administrative reforms.

In the Andean regions of South America, the divisions fostered by economic growth led to three great rebellions in 1780. One uprising occurred in the highlands of Peru surrounding Cuzco, which provoked a second in the Altiplano of Bolivia outside of La Paz. The third rebellion took place farther north in the Colombian highland towns near Bogotá. They were mainly rebellions of the countryside, as few urban folk supported revolt. There were no uprisings in cities such as Bogotá, Quito, Lima, Cuzco, Arequipa, La Paz, and Cochabamba. Nonetheless, these three rebellions represented serious challenges to colonial authorities because they occurred in some of the most populous rural areas of South America. In addition, the rebellions momentarily united all rural social groups against the Spanish representatives of the Crown.

Despite the differences of motives and objectives between the three rebellions, several conclusions clearly emerge. The leaders of these rebellions did not intend to bring about the independence of the colonies from Spain. Everywhere, the rebels cheered for Carlos III, the Spanish monarch. With the possible exception of the Bolivia rebellion, these were not race wars of the Native American masses against the outnumbered Europeans; many whites assumed leadership positions in the revolts. Instead, the rebels struggled principally against excessive taxation, unfair labor drafts, and corrupt officials. They sought to increase local autonomy. The rebels' credo was *¡Viva Carlos III y muere mal gobierno!* (Long live Carlos III and death to bad government!). The rebels claimed that the Spanish king was being poorly served in the colonies by incompetent and corrupt officials. Their defiance to these colonial officials, therefore, showed no disloyalty to the king. As the rebels believed, their rebellion represented a form of direct communication with the distant monarch.

Here resides the paradox of the 1780 rebellions. Residents of the Andes Mountains were contesting various inequitable aspects of the colonial order while, at the same time, upholding the authority of the very institution—the Spanish Crown—that sanctioned colonialism. Or was their professed loyalty to the King a mere ploy?

Equally paradoxical is the fact that the rebellions aligned native peasants with non-native colonists, despite the obvious antagonisms between both groups. Alliances between colonial elites and masses were fraught with danger. The elites often advanced political demands, requesting local autonomy and fewer taxes. But these leaders were playing a dangerous game: If the masses became involved, they might press for social reforms harmful to elite interests. Demands for the elimination of forced indigenous labor, freedom for slaves, or the expulsion of whites certainly alarmed local elites, and this is precisely what happened in each rebellion. Elite leaders launched the rebellions with limited political aims, but the participation of the masses eventually added more popular demands. As the rebellions threatened to become radical, the local gentry turned more conservative. The same elites who had started the rebellions then accepted some temporary concessions and cooperated to return Spanish officials to their positions of power. In this manner, the three Andean rebellions exposed all the internal contradictions of the colonial social order.

THE CAUSES OF REBELLION

The roots of Peru's rebellion grew deep in the fertile soil of colonial social inequities, but the immediate cause was political. Many South Americans rose up in dramatic fashion in 1780 to protest the so-called Bourbon Reforms. These administrative and fiscal reforms were initiated first in Spain and later in the Indies by the new royal family, the Bourbons, who came to rule in Madrid following the War of the Spanish Succession of 1703. Related to Louis XIV of France, the Bourbon monarchs adopted many French administrative reforms. They intended to tighten control of the kingdom and colonies by ending administrative loopholes and expected the colonists to provide more troops and fortifications for their own defenses. Trade was liberalized, and the colonial authorities actually encouraged greater economic activities. The sale of colonial political offices ended, curbing many official abuses but also curtailing the opportunities of wealthy colonial elites to participate in governing the Indies. The Bourbons dismissed incompetent officials and dispatched more fiscal agents to the ports and capitals of the Indies. The upshot of these reforms: The Crown collected old taxes more effectively and even added new ones. However, the reforms did not end corruption among local officials. (For more on the imperial reforms, see Chapter 14.)

Corruption

The Bourbon reforms opened old wounds. Social unrest, especially in Peru, preceded and accompanied many of these reforms, which merely exacerbated long-term inequities in Andean society already exposed by the economic expansion. Despite growth of the free labor market in colonial Peru, the economic resurgence did not eliminate draft labor, the infamous *mita*. Theoretically, every adult Native American male owed 6 to 12 months of work in the silver and mercury mines on a rotating basis every seventh year. But the natives of many highland provinces were exempted, so the remaining natives greatly resisted what remained of the *mita* obligations. *Mitayos* now entered into service with increasing frequency—once every four years rather than every seven years as in the sixteenth century. Most natives still owed additional labor to the *obrajes* of the highlands. Women especially toiled in these primitive textile manufactories, owned by whites and producing poor-quality fabric that many peasant villagers were forced to buy.

Because there was little escape, Andean peasants hated the forced distribution of goods above all. After 1756, Spanish *corregidores* (district officials) had the legal duty to force Native Americans into the free labor force. To do this, they had to pry them away from their subsistence plots. The old way of doing this had been to charge them tribute in the form of a head tax, payable in cash, which required peasants to leave their villages to earn wages in white-owned *obrajes,* mines, and haciendas. The indigenous leaders, the *kurakas,* took charge of collecting the tax and often arranged outside labor opportunities for the members of their respective communities. But many Peruvian peasants subverted the system. They earned their tribute payments by renting village lands to outsiders and by growing cash crops such as grains, coca, and potatoes. Native resistance resulted in a labor shortage for white-owned enterprises. So in 1756, a new colonial law empowered the *corregidores* to force peasants to purchase the domestic woolen production of *obrajes,* pushing Andeans even more firmly into the cash economy and into wage labor. The natives again resisted. They were paying high prices for inferior goods, many of which were substitutes for items already produced in their villages. Besides, many *corregidores* used the laws to line their own pockets. For these reasons, residents of the highlands began to identify the Spanish district officials, who were short-term autocratic intruders, as the cause of higher taxes and increased labor demands.

Even the older authorities in the highlands grew to distrust the new power of the *corregidores.* The local *kurakas* resented the Spanish district officials, because each of them had to collect the tribute and provide peasant villagers for the *mita*. Although these native leaders enjoyed many personal privileges—owning land and using their Indian subjects as peons—they realized that carrying out unpopular laws threatened their legitimacy among those they ruled. And the *corregidores* were raising the ire not only of the Native Americans but also of the Creole and mestizo shopkeepers in the Andes who had to collect the unpopular sales tax, the *alcabala,* from their customers and pass the proceeds on to these Spanish officials. Muleteers also had to purchase their mules through the *corregidores.* In order to pay for them, the muleteers provided the district officials with free freight services. Peruvian *hacendados,* most of whom were native-born whites, also disliked having to pay taxes on their production. Even priests resented the local Spanish officials, with whom they disputed the control of indigenous labor and surplus production. Peruvian-born white priests charged fees for ministering to Native American parishioners; many also owned highland haciendas on which natives labored. Although natives resisted the worst abuses of the white priests, the Spanish-born district officials were the more formidable adversaries. Their presence reduced the authority of the clergy in the highlands. In short, the growing power of Spanish officials, especially the *corregidores,* reduced the traditional prerogatives of indigenous leaders and local white elites.

Resistance

The Spaniards of the eighteenth century were well aware of the reverence held by Native Americans toward their own heritage. At the festival of the Virgin Mary, the natives in most towns of the kingdom paraded through the streets in their ancient costumes and reenacted the execution of the Inka Atawallpa. "The Indians have not forgotten him [Atawallpa]; the love they bore their native kings makes them still sigh for those times," reported one observer in 1711. "[T]he Spaniards are not safe at this time and the prudent shut themselves up in their houses."

Such resentments raised the tempo of violence within Peru throughout the eighteenth century. Between 1720 and 1790, more than one hundred separate instances of rebellion broke out against colonial authorities. Native Andeans became involved in all these rebellions, although most often they were led by mestizos and whites. A simple assault on the new customs house at Huanta in 1720 set the tone. Numerous riots took place between 1726 and 1737, a period in which the Spanish viceroy was particularly determined to increase Crown revenues. Then in 1742, an ominous indigenous rebellion broke out in the Peruvian rain forests on the eastern slopes of the Andes. This region of new settlement had for decades been attracting native migrants from the central highlands. Many of these *serranos* (literally, residents of the sierras, or mountains) had taken flight from tribute, which by law every male adult native was obliged to pay in his home village. Native men who left their ancestral villages owed smaller tributes, whereas those who went deep into the rain forests avoided payment altogether. These were the very persons who flocked to the banner of Juan Santos Atahualpa, the self-proclaimed descendant of the Inka Atawallpa. His guerrilla forces drove most Spaniards and Creoles from the eastern slopes, from which they were then excluded for 10 years.

Atahualpa's 1742 revolt transformed the Andes into an armed camp and polarized the population. He even had many followers among the peasants who remained in their highland villages. "The biggest enemy is the internal one in the highland Province, secretly favoring the Rebel," worried one royal official. "If we do not take other measures and precautions, we will be the target of further blows, with danger to the entire Kingdom." Spanish authorities reacted in two ways. On the one hand, they gave in to some of the popular resentments, exempting one province entirely from the *mita* labor draft for the Huancavelica mercury mine. On the other hand, they increased repression elsewhere. Exploiting ethnic rivalries, Spanish officials extended patronage to cooperative

Table 11.1   Peru's Colonial Population
According to the Census of 1795

Racial Group	Number	Percent of Total
Whites	140,890	12.6
Mestizos	244,313	21.9
Free Blacks	41,004	3.7
Native Americans	648,615	58.2
Slaves	40,385	3.6
	1,115,209	100.00

SOURCE: Scarlett O'Phelan Godoy, *Rebellions and Revolts in Eighteenth Century Peru and Upper Peru* (Cologne, Germany: Böhlau Verlag, 1985), 47.

*kuraka*s and broke up conspiracies among others. Many indigenous leaders in the more densely populated highlands supported Crown officials because they, too, felt threatened by the grassroots support for Atahualpa. Military presence in the highlands also increased. Even after the revolt was crushed, five companies of militia forces continued to garrison the central sierras. Local Peruvian troops recruited on the coast were stationed at several forts and continued patrolling the eastern slopes. Thereafter, the unrest in the highlands involved mere riots and angry confrontations between irate taxpayers and tax collectors. Often native *mitayo*s attacked and burned textile factories, mining camps, and other isolated locations of forced labor.

Repression

Ostensibly, the Crown encouraged the creation of colonial militias to protect the colonies from foreign aggressors. But the Peruvian militias began increasingly to reinforce internal security. The first two regiments of colonial militia were organized at Lima and Cuzco in 1742, the year of Juan Santos Atahualpa's uprising. By 1760, more than four thousand one hundred fifty militiamen formed 76 companies, which were segregated by race. Spaniards and Creoles served as officers, although Spaniards received the highest promotions. Creoles and mestizos served in their own units as militiamen. But Native Americans, mulattoes, and blacks made up most of the units, as these groups perceived military service as an opportunity for personal advancement. Most militiamen were recruited on the coast; as Hispanicized, Spanish-speaking people, they did not identify at all with the Quechua-speaking natives of the highlands. As one Spanish *corregidor* commented, the militiamen were "held in respect and terror by Indian, Negroes, and other libertines whose obedience had formerly been difficult to command." Although they themselves were members of the less privileged groups, the militiamen carried out the viceroy's orders.

Keeping the lid on Peru's explosive social situation cost a great deal of money. The militias were expensive. Therefore, Spanish officials raised the *alcabala* sales tax from 2 to 6 percent. At various times, proposals went forward to apply the tributary tax to mestizos, mulattoes, and *zambos* (persons of African and Native American ancestry). Such proposals unnerved these groups, which were a minority in Peru—but a growing one (see Table 11.1).

Rising commercial activity also contributed to social unrest because it increased the exploitation of the peasantry. In the 1750s, many isolated local rebellions were directed not at public officials but at grasping priests, who overcharged natives for religious services, and even at those *kuraka*s who increased their own labor demands on the peasants. These and other local rebellions occurred mostly in the rural highlands where peasant villagers were involved in filling the labor drafts for the mines and textile factories. Fewer disturbances took place on the coastal plantations, which produced export crops such as sugar, cotton, and rice through the labor of mainly free workers and African slaves. No *mitayo*s served these coastal enterprises. Likewise, peasants in the northern highlands of Peru and Ecuador did not protest excessively. All the important mines were located in the central and southern Peruvian highlands, and natives in the north were not subject to the mining *mita* at all. Moreover, the larger cities did not support these frequent tax rebellions; after all, urban elites profited by the expenditure of tax revenues and prospered from the economic florescence. Unlike rural peasants, urban workers were exempt from forced labor. Even though the struggle over autonomy and peasant labor caused this unrest, taxation provided the spark.

Serious troubles began in 1770, when the Crown assumed direct responsibility for collecting taxes. Previously, local citizens had collected taxes in exchange for a percentage of the total and then passed the proceeds on to the Crown. These "tax farmers" had been susceptible to bribery by numerous local interests. But now new Spanish officials, the intendants, assumed the collection of taxes, and they increased the efficiency, incommoding local interests. Mestizo middlemen in the highlands, such as the muleteers and shopkeepers, found it more difficult to evade taxation. In Cuzco, the silversmiths—representing a trade reserved for whites only—led a conspiracy of landowners, textile producers, and *kuraka*s. The Creoles and mestizos of the highlands especially suffered from the Crown's campaign against tax evasion. These multiple resentments soon boiled over.

THE TÚPAC AMARU REBELLION

The first rebellion began with a seemingly small instance of defiance. One morning in November 1780, the native lord of Tinta jailed the Spanish *corregidor* of the town and had him stand trial for crimes of corruption and abuse of power. The town council found the Spanish *corregidor* guilty of malfeasance and had him executed, an incident that presented colonial officials with several special problems. First, the natives of Tinta had no authority over Spanish officials, so their act amounted to mutiny. But this *corregidor* was particularly unpopular even among his Spanish peers. He had just been excommunicated by the bishop of Cuzco, with whom he had been feuding. Ridding the highlands of this unpopular Spaniard struck a responsive cord with many local elite residents. Second, rather than being a mob action of short duration, this act of defiance proceeded in an orderly fashion under the direction of a community leader who was one of the most respected members of highland society.

Leadership

Tinta lay 50 miles west of Cuzco on the important Royal Road to Lima, over which most of the colony's silver passed. Its *kuraka* was a mestizo nobleman named José Gabriel

Condorcanqui Noguera Túpac Amaru. He was more than just the chieftain of the native town of Tinta; he was also heir to the Spanish noble title of the Marquis of Oropeza and had the blood of Inka rulers flowing through his veins as well. Moreover, he was an important highland businessman. Túpac Amaru owned several hundred mules engaged in overland transport, and his family and business associates counted among the most prominent members of the highland elite, made up of both Creoles and other *kuraka*s.

Why did this particular man risk so much by overseeing the execution of a *corregidor?* The Spanish official probably infringed intolerably on the traditional authority of the Creole landowners and the *kuraka*s. Such intrusive Spanish officials, particularly those intent on closing tax loopholes and carrying out the labor drafts, could be particularly disruptive to vested rural interests accustomed to long years of isolation and independence. Furthermore, the execution of the unpopular Spanish official by an individual of such status as Túpac Amaru lent a hint of legitimacy to direct action in other highland communities. Other *corregidores* and Spanish officials soon fled the rural towns. Most especially, Túpac Amaru appealed to indigenous peasants. He claimed direct descent from the last Inka ruler, who had been executed by the Spaniards in 1572. To the Quechua-speaking peasants of the Cuzco region, he was known as Túpac Amaru II.

Furthermore, this was no frontier rebellion, as was Atahualpa's four decades earlier. Túpac Amaru immediately recruited a devoted band of 6,000 men. He marched north, attacking *obrajes* and freeing native workers being held there. His followers defeated the militia forces commanded by other *corregidores*. Túpac Amaru's movement spread through the densely populated Andean provinces stretching from Lake Titicaca down to Huarochirí, just 30 miles from the viceregal capital of Lima. Practically all the productive silver mines lay within this zone of rebellion, the rural heartland of the Viceroyalty of Peru. Those highland districts that owed heavy labor obligations to the mines and *obrajes* subscribed to the movement, as did those provinces where Túpac Amaru had influential *kuraka* relatives and important commercial connections. The hierarchy of each community was important during his campaign: Those with more Spanish residents and *hacendados* tended to remain loyal to colonial authorities, but smaller indigenous villages containing fewer Spanish residents and correspondingly more labor obligations responded to the rebellion with alacrity.

The leadership of the Túpac Amaru rebellion rested firmly on the social structure of Peru's central highlands. The combatants respected the clergy and the churches and welcomed the support of some priests. Its leaders neither called for the natives to be disobedient nor renounced the king. The hierarchical nature of rebel organization followed the colonial pattern. Creoles, mestizos, and *kuraka*s held the highest posts, those of captain and commandant. Those few indigenous commoners who came into the command of troops because of their battlefield bravery received immediate promotion to the social rank of *kuraka* by Túpac Amaru himself. Moreover, Spaniards and Creoles took up rearguard assignments in supply, recordkeeping, maintenance of arms, and treasury so as not to come into personal danger.. The rebels established their own government in the zones they controlled, even to the extent of collecting the king's tribute and taxes, which they applied to the rebel cause. Above all, family remained important. Nearly all of Túpac Amaru's closest advisers were members of his extended family. His wife, Micaela Bastidas, practically served as his chief of staff (see Manuscript 11.1). His half brother, Diego Túpac Amaru, became head of the movement after the royalists captured Túpac Amaru and Micaela Bastidas.

MANUSCRIPT 11.1

Letter from Micaela Bastidas to Túpac Amaru

Micaela Bastidas, the wife of José Gabriel Condorcanqui, or Túpac Amaru II, was of equal social status to her husband in the Andean highlands; she was also descended from Spanish conquistadores and Inka nobility. She, too, had grown up used to high social position, and her family had also contributed to the prominent class of kurakas and businessmen of the highlands. Not without precedent, therefore, she quite naturally became one of the important advisers to her husband as he led the greatest rebellion challenging Spanish authority in Peru since the sixteenth century. As the following letter attests, she did not desist from giving full and frank advice to Túpac Amaru or from leading troops herself. Here Micaela Bastidas chides the rebel leader for failing to seize Cuzco.

I have warned you again and again not to dally in those villages, where there is nothing to do—but you continue to saunter, ignoring the fact that the soldiers are running short of food. They are receiving their pay, but the money will not last forever. Then they will all depart, leaving us to pay with our lives, because you must have learned by this time that they came only for reasons of self-interest, and to get all they could out of us. They are already beginning to desert. . . . Thus we will lose all the people that I have gotten together for the descent on Cuzco, and the forces at Cuzco will unite with the soldiers from Lima, who have been on the march for many days.

I must tell you this, though it pains me. If you want to ruin us, continue to sleep and commit such follies as that of passing alone through the streets of Yauri, and even climbing to the church tower—actions certainly out of place at this time, and that only dishonor you and gain you disrespect.

I believed that you were occupied day and night with arranging these affairs, instead of showing an unconcern that robs me of my life. I am already a shadow of myself and beside myself with anxiety, and so I beg you to get on with this business.

You made me a promise, but henceforth I shall not heed your promises, for you did not keep your word. . . .

I gave you plenty of warnings to march immediately on Cuzco, but you took them all lightly, giving the Spaniards time to prepare as they have done, placing cannon on Picchu Mountain, and devising other measures so dangerous that you are no longer in a position to attack them. . . .

In fine, God must want me to suffer my sins. Your wife.

After I had finished this letter, a messenger arrived with the definite news that the enemy from Paruro is in Acos; I am going forward to attack them, even if it costs me my life.

SOURCE: Micaela Bastidas to José Gabriel Condorcanqui Noguera Túpac Amaru, December 6, 1780, in *Martires y Heroínas*, ed. Francisco A. Loáyza (Lima: D. Miranda, 1945), 48–51, as translated by Benjamin Keen, in Benjamin Keen, ed., *Readings in Latin-American Civilization: 1492 to the Present* (Boston: Houghton Mifflin, 1955), 75.

To prevent social tensions from bubbling over and to save whites from becoming the targets of rebel forces, rebel leaders took great care to maintain discipline within their movement. The foot soldiers and cannon fodder of the Túpac Amaru rebellion remained the indigenous peasants. Mulattoes and free blacks were accepted into the movement but in subordinate positions, with most serving as cooks for the troops. Black slaves were not welcomed in the movement, and those Africans captured from the haciendas of royalists were made to serve as personal servants to rebel leaders. Mestizos from the central highlands of Peru also joined the rebellion in large numbers. They had worried that the Bourbon Reforms would eventually convert them into tribute-paying subjects like the native commoners. Mestizo artisans and traders took intermediate positions of command over indigenous combatants. And neither did the rebel leadership condone attacks on property. True, rebels did torch some customs houses, but they confiscated the haciendas and mines only of those whites and *kuraka*s who opposed them, operating these assets to supply the movement. Aside from the abolition of certain taxes and *mita* obligations, there was little in Túpac Amaru's program that deliberately appealed to the oppressed Native Americans or to the African slaves. He did nothing to threaten the interests of the highland elites, of which he himself was one.

His interest in preserving the local social hierarchy explains why Túpac Amaru did everything in the name of his king, Carlos III. He stated that he wished to rid Peru of the corrupt Spanish officials and rule the kingdom for the monarch's loyal subjects—whites and natives alike. Túpac Amaru did not view these goals as antithetical.

Decline

In the end, however, the Túpac Amaru rebellion deteriorated into a struggle between indigenous leaders. Highland districts remained loyal to colonial authorities or went over to the rebellion according to interethnic rivalries of long standing among the Quechua-speaking peoples of Peru. These rivalries even predated the Conquest. According to its commander, the royalist expedition to quell the uprising in the Puno area succeeded because of "effort, courage, fierceness and loyalty demonstrated by the Lupaca Indians in combat, which was the result of ancient rivalry between them and the Indians from Callao." In another engagement, "the auxiliary Indians from Chincheros and Anta attacked the rebels like a pack of wolves." Many *kuraka*s who had successfully bargained for exemptions from the *mita* resisted the rebels, and those whose native followers had no exemptions joined the movement of *amaristas,* as supporters of Túpac Amaru were known. Also, personal relationships among highland elites counted for a great deal. Although Túpac Amaru's extensive relatives throughout the central highlands and his many associates in the mule transport business responded to his call, his business competitors often assisted the royalists.

Túpac Amaru's failure to unite all the indigenous leaders under his banner explains why he ultimately failed. In 1781, his troops surrounded the city of Cuzco, capital of the last Inkas and a city whose capture would have provided the movement even greater legitimacy. But Túpac Amaru failed to attack the city in a timely fashion. His procrastination permitted the royalist forces, assisted by loyal indigenous troops, to reinforce the city and defeat the rebel army. Túpac Amaru and Micaela Bastidas were captured and brought to Cuzco. He stood trial in May 1781 and was drawn and quartered on the city plaza from which, three centuries before, his Inka ancestors had reigned; his wife and a son were executed with him. But this was not the end of the rebellion.

As unrest persisted, the rebel movement survived the death of Túpac Amaru to become less elitist and more egalitarian. Without its prestigious leader, the movement had to pander increasingly to popular concerns to recruit and retain peasant troops. Racial antagonism inevitably motivated the indigenous followers. Proclaimed one native attacker of the mining town of Oruro, "The time [has] come for all the Spaniards and mestizos to die." Many who had once been *mitayo*s remembered suffering at the hands of white and mestizo mining supervisors. Diego Túpac Amaru, who had inherited command from his half brother, decreed the abolition of slavery at the end of 1781. This represented an attempt to attract Africans and Peruvian blacks, even though they were still not accorded much mobility within the rebel cause. The Quechua masses in Peru also took advantage of the death of Túpac Amaru II. They refused to pay their tribute not only to Spanish officials but even now to the rebel tax collectors. Pockets of *amarista* resistance thus continued for another year in the central highlands of Peru. In the meanwhile, the challenge to colonial authority posed by Túpac Amaru had provoked a more radical, bottom-up movement in the neighboring rural provinces of Alto Peru (Bolivia).

THE TÚPAC CATARI REBELLION

No sooner had Túpac Amaru's rebellion spread to the indigenous peoples of the Bolivian Altiplano on the eastern side of Lake Titicaca than it generated a more radical popular program. The Aymara-speaking peasants of the Altiplano were also led by a prestigious *kuraka,* Tomás Apasa, who assumed the name of his noble ancestor, Túpac Catari. The Túpac Catari rebellion also relied for leadership on the family and personal network of its leader. But there the similarities ended. In the Altiplano, Native Americans were predominantly of the Aymara culture. Having been incorporated into the Inka empire only a few decades before the Conquest, they retained language and belief systems distinct from those of the Quechua peoples. Therefore, Túpac Amaru's Quechua movement and the Túpac Catari's Aymara cooperated uneasily with one another. Leaders of one movement distrusted the other; indeed, they could not communicate with each other except through interpreters. Moreover, fewer whites and mestizos lived in the forbidding, windswept high plains of the Altiplano. The peasant communities of the Altiplano had survived without as much competition from haciendas and towns. Consequently, native councils figured more predominantly in the leadership of the Túpac Catari rebellion; Spaniards were absent entirely. Creoles and mestizos also appeared in fewer numbers, functioning mainly as clerks because of their skill at reading and writing. Indigenous officers commanded indigenous troops on the Altiplano, a fact that also explains the lack of skill in using modern weaponry among the *cataristas,* as the Bolivian followers of Túpac Catari were called. Colonial authorities had never allowed Native Americans to own guns. Túpac Catari had few firearms among his troops. Only one unit of mestizos, blacks, and mulattoes, led by a mestizo commander, had modern weapons.

The program of the Altiplano rebellion also suggested an agenda more consistent with indigenous and peasant concerns: an end to native tribute, termination of the *mita* labor draft, and expulsion of Spaniards. The Aymara peoples still suffered *mita* drafts for the mines at Potosí. In fact, many *mitayo*s at Potosí asked Túpac Catari "to accept them in his ranks so they could carry the revolt to the mines." In this rebellion, Spaniards and even Creoles became targets. "The principal objective of the [Túpac Catari] uprising was to get rid of all white people," one indigenous leader later admitted, "because the native Spaniards had allied themselves with the Europeans, who the King had ordered should be expelled." Rebel natives said they believed that the "infallible" Spanish sovereign they

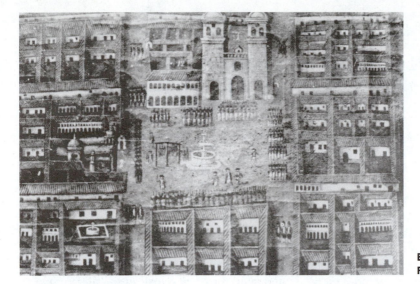

Execution of *cataristas* in La
Paz, 1781. (Florentino Olivares)

revered from a distance did not approve of the "traitorous" Spanish officials who represented him in the Andes. Once again, the rebels fought in the name of Carlos III.

Túpac Catari was caught and executed in January 1781, four months before Túpac Amaru. Others took over leadership of both the Peruvian Quechua rebellion and the Bolivian Aymara movement, the latter of which had a more decentralized command structure. The conflicts continued with varied intensity for two more years. As this less intensive but lengthier phase of the rebellions dragged on into 1783, internal rebel divisions began to take their toll. Spanish authorities deliberately dealt leniently with white and mestizo captives while torturing and executing most captured indigenous leaders. In this manner, Creoles began to abandon the Túpac Amaru cause. More and more, the rebellions were cast as a "dangerous" native affair, and the radical Bolivian *cataristas* discredited the more conservative Peruvian *amarista* movement among nonnative highlanders. The royalists succeeded in arousing fears of a race war in the Andes, especially following a number of massacres of whites by the Bolivian rebels. At any rate, the whites, mestizos, and mulattoes on the Peruvian coast had always seen the Andean rebellions principally as indigenous threats. After 1780, many Creoles on the coast enrolled in militia units in order to help suppress these "Indian" rebellions.

In fact, the Bolivian Aymaras were hostile to Peruvian Quechua hegemony, and officers of the *cataristas* and *amaristas* were not above betraying each other to the Spanish authorities. In the important siege of La Paz, the Peruvian rebel forces commanded by whites and indigenous nobles encamped above the city. The native-led Bolivians of Túpac Catari set up their camps below the city. Each group suspected the other, and together they could not seize La Paz before militia units arrived from Buenos Aires and Lima to relieve its defenders (see Manuscript 11.2). Finally, rising rates of desertions from their forces caused the two rebel camps to abandon the siege. Now that their prestigious leaders were dead, the rebellions of Túpac Amaru and Túpac Catari clearly were losing momentum. The years of 1782 and 1783 consisted mainly of defensive and uncoordinated efforts by both rebel groups to resist being captured by the colonial militias and their

MANUSCRIPT 11.2

The Proclamation of Julián Puma Catari to the People of La Paz

When the rebellious indigenous forces surrounded the Spanish city of La Paz in Bolivia, their commander issued a threat to the defending residents. Puma Catari took over leadership of the cataristas after the death of Túpac Catari, and he meant to punish the whites who had oppressed his people—be they bad Creoles, Spanish immigrants, or corrupt public officials. In this document he seems to demand that three Spanish "thieves" be turned over to the rebel forces, who would then spare the city. Aside from its malevolence, one other characteristic of the proclamation stands out. Puma Catari has inverted the hierarchy of status and cloaks his rebellion against the Spaniards by referring to their own political and religious doctrine. Note how he refers to himself as the viceroy and appeals to the Christian God, indicating that the indigenous peoples had adopted elements of Spanish institutions to defend their own interests.

And in this manner, you Christians who act badly, tomorrow you will see that with God's grace, I already have a way to advance [my soldiers], and in that manner there is no other remedy; even if you would be able to do more, it would not be enough to resist us even for three hours; with God's grace, my soldiers say they will end it without a doubt and in that manner there is no other remedy that those with arms would have. . . . And you should know that they will come back by land and dust and let us see which one of us will have help from God and which ones will be men with courage and this will be decided at the top. It is convenient for me, don Julian Puma Catari, to demand that you *criollos* bring me the three thieves well tied down, and in turning over those thieves, you will be forgiven; all of you *criollos* and [the *corregidores* and customs officers sheltered in La Paz] and more enthusiastic *chapetones* [newly arrived immigrants from Europe], with that also they will remain completely forgiven and will be loved and dear to my heart and soul; they will remain firm children and have neither pain nor caution, and all my Indians will not come in if they bring me those *chapetones* thieves; and if not [my soldiers] will bring together all the *criollos* to take their lives; likewise all the thieves and *chapetones* will remain under three oaths and under the witnessing of most Holy Sacrament of the Altar and his Most Holy Mother, Queen of Mercies. And I have it send and signed like this, and keep in mind this is my warning from now on. If this is disdained and the opposite executed, everything will turn into ashes, without doubt in eight days; in the meantime I expect to close this point today, April 7, 1781. I, Viceroy Puma Catari, who hopes to receive from God all the venerations and reverences of the High King. Amen.

SOURCE: María Eugenia del Valle de Siles, *Historia de la rebelión de Túpac Catari, 1781–1782* (La Paz: Editorial Don Bosco, 1990), 10–11. Translation by Soraya Margarita González Rodríguez.

loyal native allies. In the end, the increasing radicalization of the movements frightened Creole and mestizo sympathizers in the Peruvian and Bolivian highlands. By that time, a third rebellion in the Andes had begun and ended on less violent, more conciliatory terms. At the height of this separate revolt far to the north in Colombia, its leaders proclaimed their allegiance to both Carlos III and Túpac Amaru II. Again, they intended no irony.

Table 11.2   Population of Comunero Towns, 1779–81

	SOCORRO		SAN GIL	
	Number	*Percent of Total*	*Number*	*Percent of Total*
Whites	17,738	52.6	4,511	26.8
Mestizos/Free Blacks	14,944	44.3	10,699	63.5
Native Americans	537	1.6	1,141	6.8
Slaves	491	1.5	489	2.9
	33,710	100	16,840	100

SOURCE: John Leddy Phelan, *The People and the King: The Comunero Revolution in Colombia, 1781* (Madison: University of Wisconsin Press, 1978), 42.

THE COMUNERO REVOLT

Society in the Colombian highlands contrasted starkly with that of Peru and Bolivia—though social pretensions and the political regime did not. Created in 1739, the Viceroyalty of New Granada took in Ecuador, Colombia, and Venezuela, which had previously been parts of the old Peruvian viceroyalty, and Bogotá became the viceregal capital. As in Peru, Spanish authorities in New Granada were engaged in tightening their control over the local economy and society. Expanding royal economic monopolies and collecting taxes were essential parts of the administrative reforms. As in Peru and Bolivia, however, these efforts bred resentments among the prosperous Creoles and mestizos and among the oppressed Native Americans.

Social Organization

Colombia was not Peru. That is to say, the subordinated indigenous groups formed a minority in highland society and a dwindling one at that. In the two principal highland provinces of Santa Fe and Tunja, location of the pre-Columbian Muisca culture, the natives numbered just 68,881 in 1778—a mere 5 percent of the population. In most indigenous villages, nonnatives outnumbered the native residents. In the growing nonnative towns of the Colombian highlands, whites and mestizos predominated. Socorro and Tunja, two towns that would play important roles in the Comunero Revolt, are cases in point. Whites formed 68 percent of Socorro's 12,700 inhabitants, and mestizos made up the majority of Tunja's residents (see Table 11.2).

Despite the higher percentage of European and mixed-race peoples in its highland towns, Colombia still shared with Peru the same principles of a racially based social hierarchy. Relatively well-to-do Spaniards and Creoles formed the apex of colonial society. Whites retained the larger haciendas, lived in houses closer to the center of town, and had natives and slaves as servants. They held positions of town counselors, *alcaldes,* and notaries. The town notables also engaged in domestic commerce, retailing, and farming.

Such a man was José Francisco Berbeo, future leader of the revolt. Berbeo owned a house on Socorro's main plaza, two farms, a few slaves, and a personal library of 20 books. Even by Colombian standards, he was just modestly well off. One brother was a rural policeman and another, a priest. His wife, who came from a prominent family, had brought a large dowry to the marriage. Much of his capital gain, apparently, was dissipated by a common rural affliction: Berbeo loved to gamble. But he also had military qualifications reserved only for whites. He had been an officer on several military campaigns against the natives of eastern Colombia, and his business interests took him to Bogotá, where he acquired contacts with influential Creoles. Moreover, Berbeo looked good on horseback. Not as wealthy as Lima's merchants, Caracas's cacao planters, or Mexican silver miners, Colombian notables still subscribed to the same social values. They looked down on those who worked with their hands.

Due to their comparatively greater numbers, however, many Spanish immigrants and Creoles did indeed have to work with their hands. Most shopkeepers, butchers, artisans, and smallholders were white. They lived less-than-genteel lives of toil, like many of the mestizos and free blacks who also found niches as small farmers and tradesmen. Mestizos and free blacks worked alongside poor whites in the artisan shops. Mestizo housewives also wove cotton cloth and made their own clothes, just like the poor white women. Most whites and persons of mixed race were illiterate or only semiliterate. These rural townspeople of the Colombian highlands gained a reputation for their fierce independence. "In general they are uncouth, uncivilized, haughty, restless, and quarrelsome," said a visiting priest, "much given to fighting with machetes and sticks." Sometimes only social pretensions, again based on race, differentiated the Creole from the mestizo. "Any white person, although he rides his horse barefoot, imagines himself to be of the nobility of the country," observed the famous German traveler, Alexander von Humboldt. Only whites might aspire to rising above their station at birth, although social mobility was not a cardinal feature of town life in the eighteenth century.

Numerically in the minority, the descendants of the ancient Muisca nevertheless clung to their dwindling communities. Each head of an indigenous household owed the king a tribute of 4 pesos per year. The indigenous patriarch worked his land within the community, mainly for his family's subsistence. The women helped out in the fields and had the principal responsibility for cooking, rearing the children, and taking care of the house. To pay the tribute, natives engaged in the wider economy. Women took jobs in a nearby *obrajes,* which produced the traditional *ruana,* a woolen poncho worn by plebeians of both indigenous and nonindigenous origins, and men hired themselves out to tobacco and sugarcane farmers. The Colombian natives had been mingling so much with wider society that, unlike the Peruvian Quechuas and the Bolivian Aymara, nearly all of the native men spoke Spanish. But increasingly the indigenous villagers rented their excess lands out to mestizo and Creole farmers. Indeed, nonnatives in the Colombian highlands began to believe that the natives had too much land. Although they resented indigenous control of certain lands, Creoles and mestizos could do little but complain about it. Why? Because the king of Spain owned the lands, called *resguardos,* that the natives tilled and on which their villages were built. Although the nonnatives coveted the native lands, they could neither seize them nor buy them.

However, the Crown finally responded to Creole complaints and, in 1780, consolidated the native *resguardos.* Royal officials at Bogotá reduced the number of *resguardos* from 60 villages to just 27. This meant that the natives were forced to move from 33 villages of their ancestors and relocate, while colonial officials sold the formerly indigenous lands. Congregating the natives into larger communities also facilitated tribute collection. Rather than blaming the covetousness of their white and mestizo neighbors for the loss of their lands, the natives were ready to hold the colonial officials accountable.

They resented the sudden reforms by which the authorities had divested them of some of their ancestral lands.

Taxes

Resentments over tax collections united all Colombian highlanders, Creoles, mestizos, and Native Americans alike. Crown officials raised prices for its monopoly products, salt, tobacco, and the domestic liquor called *aguardiente,* a rum made from sugar. Especially prominent among the changes was an increase on the sales tax paid by all social classes. Unfortunately for the Spanish tax collectors, the announcement from Bogotá of new tax levies arrived at the highland towns at the same time as news of Túpac Amaru's rebellion. Colombian townspeople mistakenly believed the Peruvian rebels had taken Cuzco and Lima, which inspired them to do the same.

In March 1781, antitax riots broke out in a number of Colombian towns. Women and poor Creoles and mestizos predominated among the protesters. They put the shops of the state's rum and tobacco sellers to the torch and sacked the monopoly's supplies of salt. Besides denouncing Spanish tax collectors, the crowds also stated their opposition to the high fees exacted by churchmen for the sacraments. These first rioters did not harm the priests or denounce the king—both the church and Crown being sacrosanct to members of the *gente de pueblo.* But the town notables, who also resented higher taxes, worried that the plebeians might get out of control and start attacking property. Therefore, after a month of rioting, they began to organize the leadership of the revolt. They selected the military veteran José Francisco Berbeo of Socorro as their leader. The rebels also gave themselves the name *comuneros* to symbolize their status as citizens of the king's community, or *común.* Berbeo quickly assembled a fighting force of 20,000 men. Volunteers came from neighboring villages in the provinces of Santander and Santa Fe.

The Native Americans also joined in, expressly hoping for reduced tributes and a return of their *resguardo* lands. Indigenous Colombians were especially inspired by the Peruvian leader, Túpac Amaru II, and they appointed as their leader a similar mestizo descendant from the last Muisca kings. That man was Ambrosio Pisco, a *cacique,* landowner, and merchant who had a personal interest in maintaining the existing social order. Therefore, the Creole leadership of the Comuneros accepted Pisco into their midst, even though they had cause to dispute the return of native lands. Together, Berbeo and Pisco prevented the Comunero Revolt from becoming radicalized. The Comuneros destroyed little property, aside from a few shops belonging to the state monopolies.

In the Colombian revolt, there were only two instances in which the protagonists attempted social reforms. Both of these movements took place outside of the populous highlands of Santander and Santa Fe, which formed the heart of the Comunero movement. They were mere sideshows. On the hot plains of the Llanos in eastern Colombia, where they still formed a majority, Native Americans took advantage of the turmoil in the viceroyalty to attack the outnumbered whites. The Dominicans and Franciscan priests were run out of this frontier territory, and white families were besieged in their homes. Because the men were out working the cattle on the plains, native women assumed leadership of the rioters. "One sees and hears nothing but crimes," said a clergymen who wished to disparage the uprising in the Llanos, "proof of which is the childishness which had led them to appoint women captains whose principal activity is to mistreat white women." The second instance concerned the slave conspiracy in Antioquia, which demanded the freedom of all slaves in Colombia. Apparently, the only military conflict of the uprising, the seizure of the river port of Hondo by a column of Berbeo's forces, raised some expectations among slaves. As a mere tactical measure to gain a few more recruits, the expedition's commander emancipated the slaves at one gold mine. But the highest Creole leaders of the Comuneros were not out to start a social revolution. What they desired instead was greater political autonomy and fewer taxes. This conservatism—and the subordinate role of the Native Americans in the movement—explains how quickly a negotiated settlement brought the Comunero Revolt to an end.

Negotiation

Berbeo's army of 20,000 men advanced on Bogotá and stopped nearby at the indigenous town of Zipaquirá. Because colonial militias were stationed at Cartagena and other locations on the coast, the viceregal capital lay defenseless. The viceroy and other Spanish officials fled from Bogotá. Fearing pillage, Bogotá's Spanish and Creole citizens elected the archbishop, Antonio Caballero y Góngora, to exercise royal authority. The archbishop ventured forth to deal with the rebel leaders at Zipaquirá. In reality, few of the Comunero leaders wanted to sack Bogotá, a city of 18,000 persons. They merely wished to exact some concessions from viceregal authorities, leaving the region's social hierarchy and the king's authority very much intact.

Archbishop Caballero y Góngora gave them what they wanted. He promised a reduction in the prices of monopoly goods such as salt, tobacco, and *aguardiente*. The archbishop reduced the sales taxes and the tribute that natives and free blacks were obliged to pay the Crown. Other taxes were given up completely, such as the one on playing cards. The archbishop even agreed to lower the fees that priests charged to parishioners for the sacraments. The seventh clause of the agreement concerned the grievances of the natives: Not only were they to get their old lands back, but the Crown would also give direct ownership of those lands to the natives "to dispose and to sell as they see fit." This satisfied the Creoles, who desired to be able to buy land from the natives rather than rent it. Creoles, mestizos, free blacks, and Native Americans all considered that they had achieved some concessions. Only the African slaves got nothing.

Of all the Colombian groups, the free blacks and the African slaves had not become very much involved in the Comunero Revolt. Living principally in the tropical lowlands along the Magdalena and Cauca Rivers and on the seacoasts, African Colombians had little in common with the highlanders. White gold miners of Antioquia still ran slaves through the tropical rain forests of the Chocó, panning and mining for gold. Slaves were more apt to resist by running away than by joining a rebellion of the Creoles (some of whom owned slaves). Anyway, free blacks who lived in the Chocó and Cartagena had not been asked to join, and neither did they have the opportunity. Bogotá seemed very far away, as indeed it was, given the primitive transportation of river canoes and mule trains at the time.

The Capitulations of Zipaquirá, as the agreement between Berbeo and Archbishop Caballero y Góngora is known, answered to no new precedents but instead to time-honored Iberian political traditions. The rebels neither invoked John Locke's "rights of the governed" nor referred to the ideas of Thomas Jefferson. They simply subscribed to the rights and interests of the *comuneros,* loyal citizens of the king. None of the leaders denied the right of the Crown to collect taxes from them. They desired to use their disobedience to royal officials as a way to request from the king a just reduction of the tax burden and wished to remind the Crown that, despite the Bourbon Reforms, there remained a place in the colonies for old-fashioned local autonomy. The native-born Creoles claimed equal right to Spaniards in holding public offices (see Manuscript 11.3).

MANUSCRIPT 11.3

The Capitulation of Zipaquirá

The Comunero uprising might be likened to a middle-class tax revolt. It produced a conservative leadership, no demands at all for social reforms, and an overriding penchant for conciliation with colonial authorities. The Comuneros did not engage in large pitched battles and inflicted and suffered few casualties. When their volunteer forces drew up to the viceregal capital of Bogotá, the leaders did not so much desire to sack the city as to negotiate a settlement of their grievances. Therefore, the ultimate document representing this negotiation attempted to minimize their own internal social differences, to present a united front to the authorities, and to settle merely for the promise of lower taxes. The resulting document, signed by Juan Francisco Berbeo for the Comuneros and Archbishop Caballero y Góngora for the colonial government, covered up the growing breach between imperial administrators and the governed in Colombia.

Article 16: His Majesty keeps the income from the *alcabala* [sales tax], sales tax, *aguardiente* [sugar brandy], tribute, salt, mail, stamped paper, and other such sources that we have not troubled ourselves to mention; and we propose that, in order for His Majesty to avoid burdensome administrative costs, we will pay two percent annually of the value of our commercial property whether it be stores, slaves, livestock, merchandise, and all types of business except houses, their furnishings, and tools of the trades; and all of the poor people including whites, Indians, free blacks and mulattos shall pay one peso per person annually. Such a regulation would bet-

ter serve His Majesty's interests and would relieve the inhabitants of the administrators, and customs officials in the aforementioned branches of this agreement including in the proposal also the stamped paper. The latter will be taken with the customs leaden seal of the year at one-fourth of the paper money. Let also the income which is produced serve in part respectively to the city council which seals it, entrusting to the principal mayor the collection of the sums from all that which is important in the sworn accounts of the hacendados, the import-export houses, and traders, and the pesos of each of the whites, Indians, and healthy free blacks and mulattos able to pay the tax from their daily effort and work. And if someone hides any part of his income which had been certified, let him pay it double. And said mayor has to render accounts with the payments without giving any discounts and he must personally select all the collection agents. This collection should commence the week of Easter and be completed by the first week of November. The interval is ample enough to prevent anyone's falling behind, the amount is placed safely in the hands of the royal officials, with whom they will maintain good relations, treating them the same as they have been treated, and notwithstanding the fact that there is an Ordinary Judge overseeing this matter, they alone bear responsibility for the tax collection.

SOURCE: Juan Friede, ed., *Rebelión comunera de 1781: Documentos,* (Bogotá: Instituto Colombiano de Cultura, 1981), 1:97–98. Translation by Teresa Van Hoy with the assistance of Soraya Margarita González Rodríguez.

When the capitulations seemed to give in to the Colombian rebels, the latter dispersed and returned home. Like their comrades in the Peruvian Andes, they shouted once again, "Long live the king and death to bad government." But the Colombian Comuneros were not the Peruvian *amaristas* and even less the Bolivian *cataristas.*

The Comunero Revolt spilled over into the highlands of Venezuela, where the small farmers, artisans, petty traders, and laborers engaged in their own armed insurrection. They, too, complained of higher taxes, the imposition of monopolies, and the arrogance of Spanish officials. "Rich and poor, noble and commoner, all complain," said the Venezuelan Comuneros. But not all of the complainers rebelled. The wealthy plantation owners and merchants of Caracas and Maracaibo, near the coast, actually assisted the Crown officials in settling the rebellion for fear that it might disrupt production and trade. In these slave-holding areas, where up to 60 percent of the population consisted of African slaves and free persons of color, the elite did not want to encourage resistance. Therefore, the Venezuelan rebellion remained isolated in the highland provinces, among poor whites and mestizos and where slavery was not an important institution of labor. When peace was concluded in Bogotá, the Venezuelan rebels returned quietly to their farms.

CONCLUDING REMARKS

The Peruvian and Bolivian rebels certainly had less cause to shout the king's praises, for his officers returned to the Andes with vengeance. The authorities singled out mestizo and especially Native American rebel leaders for harsh treatment; those who were not executed received public whippings. The punishment meted out to the followers of Túpac Catari was particularly severe. In contrast, those Creoles who served as Túpac Amaru's closest advisers got off leniently. Some were stripped of their property and exiled to other parts of the Indies; most received royal pardons. The punishment reflected the objectives of the counterinsurgency policies of colonial officials. They attempted to separate Creoles and mestizos from the natives, characterizing the latter as dangerous revolutionaries. The viceregal authorities wished to convince the whites and mestizos that the rebellions in the Andes had been a strictly indigenous and anti-European affair. And it worked! But, truth be told, the natives suffered far more casualties in battle than any other social group: The rebellions in Peru and Bolivia took the lives of 100,000 people, most of them native Andeans.

In contrast, the death toll and repression in Colombia was mild. Only one Comunero military leader was executed, and his head was displayed in town plazas throughout the highlands. After all, José Antonio Galán was a plebeian, and he was also the military commander who had attempted to free some slaves. However, most of the Colombian Creole leaders received pardons—and a few even became royal officials in time. Berbeo returned to Socorro to act as its *corregidor,* though he soon lost this position. He suffered no other punishment and died quietly in his bed in 1795. King Carlos III expressed his gratitude to Archbishop Caballero y Góngora by appointing him as the permanent viceroy of New Granada. Caballero y Góngora reestablished Crown authority with the help of ultramontane priests of the Capuchin order. They filled parish posts throughout the viceroyalty, zealously upholding the monarch's infallibility. However, unlike the Peruvian Creoles, the Colombian native-born elites had learned no lessons about the dangers of revolution from below. They later became early proponents of the independence movement in 1810, driving the Capuchins out of Colombia without ceremony. In contrast, Peruvian elites would become indifferent supporters of independence from Spain.

These Andean revolts, in the short term, did succeed in lessening the colonial burdens in Peru as well as in Colombia. As already explained, the Capitulations of Zipaquirá that ended the brief but intense Comunero Revolt offered tax reductions for all Colombians except the slaves. During the course of fighting, the viceroy at Lima also saw fit to reduce the taxes and eliminate the forced sale of goods. Generous tax deductions and elimination of the *mita* labor draft for their communities sufficed to win over wavering *kuraka*s to the royalist camp. After the rebellion, the use of draft labor for mines was not as rigorous or as severe as previously. The Crown also eliminated the office of the *corregidores* only in Peru, where the Spanish district chiefs were so hated by Creole and Native American alike.

However, no sooner did the rebellions wind down than two trends reappeared in the Andes. Royal authorities continued the Bourbon Reforms, especially the replacement of local officeholders with Spaniards and, insofar as fiscally possible, the maintenance of the colonial militias—and not merely for defense of the ports against pirates. Units of militias were now brought up to the viceregal capital of Bogotá, and the troops at Cuzco were reinforced. Also, the Crown tightened the tax loopholes and intensified the collection of tax revenues. The second trend, which also resumed following the rebellions, pertained to the expansion of the colonial economies. Silver production grew in Peru under government stimulation, and agricultural production on haciendas and smallholdings responded to the increases in domestic trade and commerce. Demands for indigenous labor did not decline, and neither did the need for expensive colonial militias.

In other words, the cause for the estrangement of the colonies from the mother country—namely, colonial economic prosperity—did not halt its long-term effect, which was to place pressure on the rigid social structure. The king could not honor his concessions to the taxpayers and natives of the Andes. The Spanish monarch, who did not desire to lose his valuable colonial assets, could not afford to give in to the colonists' demands for greater political autonomy. This was a serious predicament. The so-called Bourbon Reforms were disruptive to be sure. But it was precisely to manage colonial social upheaval and movements for local autonomy that the Crowns of both Spain and Portugal had instituted a long-term program of colonial administrative reforms in the first place. Those reforms had to and did proceed, as shall be seen in Chapter 14. It is fair to say that the Iberian colonial authorities in the Americas learned nothing from the great Andean rebellions, yet they did not forget them either.

Another kind of popular explosion worried both royal officials and colonial elites in the Americas, namely a revolt on the part of slaves. The eighteenth century was a time of record slave imports to Brazil and to the Caribbean islands, thus enhancing the danger of African resistance. The next two chapters shall analyze how the Portuguese in Brazil managed the growth of slavery without a major slave revolt while the French in Haiti did not.

Additional Reading

Campbell, Leon G. *The Military and Society in Colonial Peru, 1750–1810*. Philadelphia: The American Philosophical Society, 1978.

Cornblit, Oscar. *Power and Violence in the Colonial City: Oruro from the Mining Renaissance to the Rebellion of Tupac Amaru (1740–1782)*. Trans. Elizabeth Ladd Glick. Cambridge, England: Cambridge University Press, 1995.

Fisher, J. R., Allan J. Kuethe, and Anthony McFarlane. *Reform and Insurrection in Bourbon New Granada and Peru*. Baton Rouge: Louisiana State University Press, 1990.

Fisher, Lillian Estelle. *The Last Inca Revolt, 1780–1783*. Norman: University of Oklahoma Press, 1966.

Kuethe, Allan J. *Military Reform and Society in New Granada, 1773–1808*. Gainesville: University of Florida Press, 1978.

Jacobsen, Nils, and Hans-Jürgen Puhle, eds. *The Economies of Mexico and Peru During the Late Colonial Period, 1760–1810*. Berlin: Colloquim Verlag, 1986.

O'Phelan Godoy, Scarlett. *Rebellions and Revolts in Eighteenth Century Peru and Upper Peru*. Cologne, Germany: Böhlau Verlag, 1985.

Phelan, John Leddy. *The People and the King: The Comunero Revolution in Colombia, 1781*. Madison: University of Wisconsin Press, 1978.

Stern, Steve J., ed. *Resistance, Rebellion and Consciousness in the Andean Peasant World, 18th to 20th Centuries*. Madison: University of Wisconsin Press, 1987.

In Spanish

Arciniegas, Germán. *Los comuneros*. Caracas: Biblioteca Ayacucho, 1992.

Galindo, Alberto Flores. *La ciudad sumergida: aristocracia y plebe en Lima, 1760–1830*. 2d ed. Lima: Editorial Horizonte, 1991.

González, Margarita. *El resguardo en el Nuevo Reino de Granada*. 3d ed. Bogotá: El Ancora, 1992.

Mörner, Magnus. *Perfil de la sociedad rural del Cuzco a fines de la colonia*. Lima: Universidad del Pacífico, 1977.

O'Phelan Godoy, Scarlett. *La gran rebelión en los Andes: De Túpac Amaru a Túpac Catari*. Cuzco: Centro de Estudios Regionales Andinos "Bartolomé de las Casas," 1995.

Sánchez, Ana. *Amancebados, hechiceros, y rebeldes: Chancay, siglo XVII*. Cuzco: Centro de Estudios Regionales, 1991.

del Valle de Siles, María Eugenia. *Historia de la rebelión de Túpac Catari, 1781–1782*. La Paz: Editorial Don Bosco, 1990.

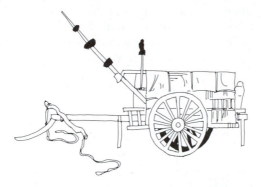

CHAPTER 12

BRAZIL'S AGE OF GOLD

Just before the dawn of the eighteenth century, an expedition of *bandeirantes,* back-woodsmen from São Paulo, stumbled upon natives of the Catagua people wearing gold ornaments in their lips. Unlike the peoples of Native American cultures elsewhere, al-most no indigenous Brazilians had fashioned jewelry from precious metals. This lack of gold and their political decentralization had spared the natives of Brazil's vast hinterlands from being overrun immediately by the Europeans, as had the Aztec and Inkas—until that moment. The Catagua led the *paulistas* to the sources of the nuggets in the streams of the forested highlands northwest of Rio de Janeiro. Finally, after nearly two centuries of colonial existence, Brazil was to have its first gold rush, and the indigenous peoples of the Brazilian interior would lose even more of their refuge.

The impact of this gold bonanza on Brazilian colonial society was very similar to how mining booms had affected various parts of the Spanish Americas from the first moments of contact through the eighteenth century. Gold motivated settlers to push back the fron-tiers in a frenetic search for new sources of the precious metal. It created a bawdy, out-law ambiance in which violence ended disputes and moral excess was common. Initially, the new frontier society provided avenues of upward social mobility not found else-where in the colony. The mining boom stimulated agriculture and cattle raising and pro-moted internal as well as external commerce. Just as in the Spanish Americas, Brazil's mining boom strengthened the political autocracy of the mother country's royal family even as it destabilized Portugal's economy. This particular gold boom, however, differed in one important respect: Slavery was more prominent in Brazil's age of gold than it had been in most Spanish-American mining areas, save Colombia's Chocó region. Colonial elites considered work to be beneath their social status, and the natives were not used to such heavy labor. The widespread employment of chattel labor in mining enterprises highlights the pernicious nature of Brazil's otherwise brilliant economic expansion of the eighteenth century. Slavery and social discrimination prevented the benefits of growth from being shared widely, a situation that limited the colony's capacity to sustain its market expansion without the aid of international markets.

FRONTIER SOCIETY

The Brazilian gold boom appeared chaotic and violent, even though the mining entrepreneurs succeeded because they relied on the traditional colonial institutions of family, hierarchy, and slavery. *Paulistas* swept in from their base at São Paulo, and smallholders, many of them free blacks and mulattoes, abandoned their farms and families on the coast at Bahia and Rio de Janeiro to migrate to the gold zones. When Portugal received word of the discovery, many young peasant men, especially from the impoverished northern province of Minho, borrowed and scraped together money for the passage to Brazil. By 1710, Portuguese immigrants outnumbered *paulistas* in the vicinities of the mines. The frontier's urban architecture, baroque churches, and religious practices had more in common with Portugal itself than with the old plantation areas of the Brazilian northeast. The immigrant influence during the formative period was just that strong. Males and bachelors vastly outnumbered females among the newcomers. These prospectors fanned out in all directions from the new mining town aptly named Vila Rica do Ouro Preto, "Rich Village of Black Gold," or simply Ouro Preto.

Conflicts arose over the claims in the uncharted frontier, and in the absence of any judicial authority, competitors settled them with weapons. Mining towns gained a reputation for lawlessness and the bawdy behavior of their mainly male inhabitants, and the *paulistas* and Portuguese immigrants settled their disputes by force. The *paulistas,* most of whom were *mamelucos* (of mixed Native American and European ancestry) and spoke Tupí, called the greenhorn Portuguese *Emboabas,* a derogatory native term. Competition and hostility arose between the two groups almost immediately. The *paulistas* acted as if they owned the mines and treated the *Emboabas* with ill-disguised disdain. Moreover, the first *paulista* miners mainly had indigenous slaves working for them, whereas the Portuguese brought African slaves. In the bellicose mining towns, the *paulista* captains paraded through the streets, barefoot, dressed in cotton drawers, with sword in hand, bandoleer across the chest, pistols in the belt, and carbines under the arm, shouting, "Kill the *Emboabas.*" They would be followed by native slaves and *mamelucos,* armed to the teeth and playing drums and trumpets.

Nevertheless, the demographic trend of continued immigration favored the Portuguese, who soon outnumbered the *paulistas.* When a mob of immigrants lynched two *paulistas* in 1707, low-level hostilities broke out. Members of each side laid ambushes for the other in the countryside. One pitched battle, in which the *Emboabas* massacred a small band of *paulistas* at São João d'El Rei, occurred before the civil authorities

A gold washing in Minas Gerais. (Johann Moritz Rugendas, ca. 1830)

succeeded in restoring a modicum of order. The *paulistas* lost this so-called War of the Emboabas. Just as in similar civil conflicts in the Spanish Americas, the state claimed the ultimate victory, for the Portuguese-born governors of São Paulo intervened to establish civil authority in the mining towns. In the process, they obtained grudging and outward obedience from both factions. Soon a new captaincy was created out of the backlands and named, again quite aptly, Minas Gerais, "General Mines."

Slavery in Mining

It was said that the workings of the farms of Brazil depended on blacks and more blacks. The same applied to the gold mines of Minas Gerais. Why? The white colonists by now had a long history in Brazil of responding to labor shortages by importing more African slaves. Although the Portuguese outnumbered the *paulistas*, slaves and other persons of color (free blacks and mulattoes) vastly outnumbered all others. Minas Gerais had 300,000 inhabitants by 1775, which amounted to 20 percent of the Brazil's population, and half of them were slaves. Many of the new miners brought in their slaves from the coast, and those who found gold purchased other slaves from planters at Bahia and from the docks as well. Because those Africans originating from the Gold Coast were considered to have aptitudes for mining, the Brazilian slave trade gave a temporary reprieve to other peoples in West Africa. For the first time, Brazil's African heritage seemed to solidify in the eighteenth century. The Brazilian gold miners' demand for slaves from the Gold Coast brought a large number of Yoruba-speaking Africans to the sugar plantations as well as the interior. The distinctive influences of Yoruba culture, music, religion, and language have survived to this day throughout Brazil.

Slaves worked in gangs of 2 to 40, panning for gold in the rivers and operating the sluices of the bigger mining operations. Said a Portuguese colonist in 1730: "It is not the style for the white people of these parts, or of any other of our colonies, to do more than command their slaves to work and tell them what to do." It is little wonder, consequently, that the slave's working life lasted only from 7 to 12 years (see Manuscript 12.1). But even

MANUSCRIPT 12.1

The Violence of Brazilian Slavery

Violence and abuse that Brazilian owners brought upon their slaves caused surprisingly little comment from colonists and authorities during the colonial period. Every now and again, someone took note and felt ashamed. Father Manoel Ribeiro Rocha's testimony of 1758 is remarkable not for the details of the cruelty but for its justification by owners. Custom rather than law governed the manner in which owners and overseers treated the slaves, and owners seldom had to answer for their acts. Slavery as an institution rested on a foundation of coercion rather than consent, and the owners practiced violence on the slaves as an everyday form of social control.

At Brazil's plantations, mills, and mines there are men who even today are so inhuman that their first act toward their slaves when they first appear before them after their purchase, is to have them severely whipped, with no cause other than their desire to do so, and they even boast of this as if to say that only they were born with the right to dominate slaves, and as if to make themselves feared and respected. And if their Confessor or another intelligent person objects and tries to raise some doubts in their minds, they reply that such a precautionary measure is reasonable to prevent the slaves under their control from behaving badly, so that from the outset they will conduct themselves correctly. They also add that once the slaves are theirs, the rule that each person can do with his own property what he likes, in conformity with his own understanding, goes into effect. . . .

Similarly, when punishing with the whip, it is not proper afterward to incise the skin, or to prick the buttocks of the slaves, ordering such bleeding on the pretext of releasing the bruised blood which could become abscessed. It is true that the people who commit these acts are to be found at our plantations, mills, and mines, and that they are not men, but wolves and bears. This madness, this fierceness, this rage and brutality has descended from the human level to the beastly. . . .

The same level of cruelty, or even worse, occurs when, after whipping, they cauterize the bruises with drops of melted sealing-wax, and there are other similar torments which each of these monsters of arrogance (this is the source of all their excess) conceives and carries out against these miserable slaves.

SOURCE: Robert Edgar Conrad, ed., *Children of God's Fire: A Documentary History of Black Slavery in Brazil* (Princeton, N.J.: Princeton University Press, 1983), 294–95.

though the regime was harsh and overwork and undernourishment were rampant, some slaves were able to accumulate sufficient gold to buy their freedom. They had ample opportunity to steal gold from the works, for the owners could never hire enough overseers. Other slaves ran away, forming settlements called *quilombos* farther out on the frontier; they took up banditry to survive and, like the indigenous warriors, wreaked havoc on caravans of settlers and gold shipments. *Paulista* frontiersmen gained renewed importance as bush captains. They formed bands of mulattoes, free blacks, and natives to hunt down the runaway slaves and destroy their *quilombos.*

Additional gold discoveries were made deeper in the backlands by the intrepid frontiersmen. In territory that would become the states of Mato Grosso and Goiás, gold began to be produced in the mid-1720s. Once again, the gold rush caught the imagination of coastal farmers and freedmen and of Portuguese youth. They poured into these regions, trekking from Rio de Janeiro via the difficult portages between the flooded headwaters of the Paraná River and paddling canoes up the São Francisco River from Salvador and Recife. Once again, African slaves made the journey as well, sometimes armed to fight the indigenous peoples. But the gold seekers encountered an entirely traditional situation in Mato Grosso and Goiás. The native population had not been reduced, despite *paulista* expeditions deep into the backlands, and they proved to be formidable defenders of their territories.

Indeed, the gold rush had opened up the frontier to settlement so rapidly that it overran numerous wilderness areas that remained the domain of the indigenous peoples. The most important of these native territories lay within the low mountain range in eastern Minas Gerais. Indigenous groups of several cultures and dialects, many of them Gê speakers, made up the inhabitants of this region. The Portuguese lumped these groups together and called them the Botocudo. For more than a century, the Botocudo's control of eastern Minas Gerais forced gold traders and royal authorities to send gold shipments via the longer northern and southern land route, which eventually became the Caminho Novo. This long interior trade route passed between Rio de Janeiro and Bahia. The Botocudo's presence prevented contraband trade eastward from Ouro Preto to the port of Vitória in Espírito Santo. To be able to control and tax the commerce in gold and diamonds, products already having created a large black market in the backlands, colonial authorities did not authorize military expeditions into or settlement of Botocudo territories until the gold rush had waned in the late eighteenth century. It would not be until 1808 that the state launched a final campaign to exterminate the "heathens and savages" who blocked settlement and development of the land.

Farther out on the frontier, two other indigenous groups stood in opposition to Portuguese settlement. The Paiaguá (Payaguá in Spanish) had lived in splendid isolation in the dense forests of Mato Grosso until the gold strikes. Caravans of gold prospectors then fanned out in canoes from the town of Cuiabá. Paiaguá warriors, who were expert canoeists, ambushed these voyagers, disrupting the transport of gold and supplies and killing the miners. The settlers finally sent several expeditions against the Paiaguá villages, and rival indigenous peoples were enlisted to help annihilate this riverine people. The second group, the Guiacurú, were nomadic horsemen of the uplands of Mato Grosso who specialized in lightning raids on miners and settlers. They were responsible for taking the lives of 4,000 *paulistas* and Portuguese during the eighteenth century. But the settlers had persuaded the Guiacurú to help subdue other indigenous groups before they, too, succumbed to waves of immigrants at the end of the century. By the time that

Guiacurú people in search of new pastures. (Jean Baptiste Debret, ca. 1820)

the gold rush had ended, native resistance to other kinds of exploitation of their territory, such as cattle raising and farming, had moved farther west and northward to the Amazon Basin.

Women and Mobility

Women—especially white women—were not found in great numbers in the frontier society of Minas Gerais and Mato Grosso. The migratory flows had consisted almost exclusively of males. Few Portuguese women penetrated into the frontier wilderness, and neither did white women come overland from the cities of Recife, Salvador, and Rio de Janeiro. At first, the only women in the mining zones were enslaved Native Americans and Africans and free blacks and mulattoes who served as prostitutes—at least, this was the view of the first clergymen to tour the mining zones.

The absence of white women engendered a frontier society quite different from that of coastal Brazil. Marriage in the mining zone was a novelty among most social groups, even the whites, and concubinage and bastardy was even more common than on the coast. Therefore, the races quickly blended on the frontier to an extent unknown in the older sugar-producing regions. Color still mattered, and those with lighter skin received opportunities in excess of their individual abilities. Persons with light skin or free blacks with enormous talents could expect some mobility in this fluid social milieu. But not everyone approved of this racial mixture in Minas Gerais. "Mulattos being unstable and rebellious are pernicious in all Brazil," observed one royal official in 1720. "In Minas they are far worse because they are rich, and experience shows us that wealth in these people leads them to commit grave errors, chief among them being disobedience to the laws." The remark displays the white prejudice that greeted any degree of independent behavior on the part of free persons of color.

Thus, Brazil's frontier movement of the eighteenth century meant that although the number of slaves had increased and spread dramatically throughout the colony, a rural population of free and mostly racially mixed people had been created. People of color worked as laborers and tenant farmers on the land of others. They engaged in subsistence agriculture, made a living from illicit mining, oversaw the work of slaves, drove mule teams and cattle herds, and avoided the law and press gangs. In the early days, men and women of color had moved from the coast to the frontier in order to gain the possibility of improving their social status. Even for slaves, the possibility for independent action and the purchase of freedom may have been greater on the frontier than on the plantations of coastal Brazil.

Within a generation or two, more women appeared in the population of the interior, and mulattoes predominated among these. Mulatto women figured prominently in the retail trade of the mining towns, running taverns, stores, shops, and food stalls. They turned to farming along with the men when gold production went into decline beginning in 1760. Apparently, they had entrée at all levels of society. A woman of color named Xica da Silva, who had been born a slave, gained fame for her beauty. Upon her emancipation, she became the influential mistress of the wealthiest Portuguese-born miner in Minas Gerais—mistress, not wife, for such a legal union did not meet public approval among the frontier's new elite.

Social maturation on the frontier eventually closed out many of these early opportunities for social mobility. Toward the close of the century, society at Ouro Preto took on the rigidity and pretensions of the familiar plantation social order of the coast. Gold miners established important families that intermarried among themselves and with Portuguese officials and immigrant merchants. They cultivated the standard refinements, supporting the church, joining the correct lay brotherhoods, and sending their male children to local church schools and to Coimbra University in Portugal. The original gold seekers had failed to establish in the hinterland anything approaching an egalitarian society, but such had not been their intent. Fact is, success came to those who relied on family networks, commercial ties to the coast, entrée to political authority, and ownership of slaves. These entrepreneurs were mainly Portuguese and colonial-born elites. In the end, discrimination operated in Minas Gerais every bit as much as in Salvador da Bahia and Rio de Janeiro.

Frontier Politics

Initially, the royal court in Lisbon had been quite unprepared and ambivalent about the gold rush because its colonial authorities could not control it. Not wanting to harm the sugar economy, Crown officials at first sought to slow down the gold boom. In 1711, when French corsairs attacked Rio de Janeiro authorities feared an invasion of its gold fields. Therefore, they sought to regulate gold mining. They issued edicts that no free blacks and mulattoes, the farmers and smallholders of the coastal regions, were permitted in the mining zones. These strictures remained unenforceable. Then the Crown worried that Portugal itself might become dangerously depopulated of its most vigorous peasants and workers, but its restrictions on emigration to Brazil met evasion everywhere. An estimated fifteen hundred people were leaving for Brazil each year. Nothing could staunch settlement on the mining frontiers.

Public authorities in the colony confronted yet another problem in the gold fields—what they considered to be social instability. The colonial state did not have enough officials who could handle the claim disputes and control the violence. In time, the colonial governors established administrative districts at principal mining towns such as Ouro Preto and eventually detached whole frontier regions from the ill-defined captaincy of São Paulo to create the districts of Minas Gerais, Mato Grosso, and Goiás. These administrative actions brought about the desired effects. In the mining town of Jacobina, west of Salvador da Bahia, the establishment of a town government in 1721 effectively reduced deaths by gunshot, which had been amounting to 50 per year. Magistrates arrived to adjudicate competing claims and to give out concessions. Many officials, however, were accused of being corrupt, of having their own mining interests, and of favoring the most powerful miners. The priests who arrived in the early days engaged in the frantic search for gold like any other miner. and their moral laxity became legendary (see Manuscript 12.2). To bring order to the countryside, companies of Native Americans, *mamelucos,* free blacks, and mulattoes were organized under white officers. Gradually these militias took over from the *paulista* bush captains the task of fighting indigenous peoples and hunting runaway slaves. In so doing, the authorities had to concede that they would never be able to enforce many of their edicts. For example, the law forbidding free blacks and mulattoes from bearing arms was widely ignored. Persons of color— even some slaves—simply had more room for mobility in the mining zone than in the plantation society of the coast.

MANUSCRIPT 12.2

The Damages Caused by Mining

Religious and civil authorities recognized immediately that the chaotic social freedoms of the frontier mining districts threatened their notions of an orderly and obedient colonial society. This certainly was the view of the Italian-born cleric André João Antonil, who wrote of his Brazilian experiences in 1711. Note his concern for the scandalous laxity of his fellow priests, the violence of the miners, and the immorality of people of color. It is equally interesting that Antonil voiced the opinion shared by many of the planters on the coast. With self-evident interests, they considered that the gold rush in Minas Gerais, Goiás, and Mato Grosso harmed the traditional agricultural economy—as if a punishment from God.

There is no thing so good that it cannot also cause great harm through the fault of those who do not use it well. Even in our sacred places, great sacrileges are committed. How amazing, then, that gold, being such a beautiful and precious metal, so useful for human commerce, and so well-suited for use in vases and temple ornaments for the divine cult, should serve also as a constant instrument for the insatiable greed of men and cause so much damage. The fame of Brazil's abundant mines enticed men from all castes and places, some men of property and others drifters. For those of property, who took out a great quantity of gold from the pits, it caused them to be proud and arrogant, to travel always accompanied by guards, to remain ready at any moment to perpetrate violence, and to undertake without any fear of justice great and sensational acts of vengeance. Gold enticed them to risk recklessly and to spend extraordinary quantities on extravagances without sharing their wealth, buying (for example) a black trumpet player for one thousand cruzados and a mulatta of ill repute at double the

Crown officials concerned themselves most with the collection of taxes from the mining economy. Insofar as customs officials were able to charge duties on imports and exports at the ports, the new commercial activity spurred by the mining boom raised Crown revenues substantially. The royal court also benefited from its long-held monopolies on slaves, salt, wine, and olive oil. But the fact remained: Much contraband gold found its way to Africa, London, and Amsterdam without anyone paying the Crown so much as a réis, the basic coin of the realm. Royal treasury officials were placed at posts along the trails and in the towns, levying sales taxes on the movement of goods and charging fees for retail and wholesale licenses. Although landowners were supposed to pay a tithe on their production equal to one-tenth of its value, this tax was the most generally avoided of all.

The biggest windfall to the Crown came in the collection of the Royal Fifth. As in the Spanish Americas, the Crown technically owned the land and its resources. Those who held a concession to mine the king's precious metals were to pay a royalty of 20 percent, or one-fifth, of the value of gold production. In the expansive and underpopulated frontier districts, miners easily evaded this tax. They complained that the costs of slaves and supplies had climbed so high that the addition of taxation to their burden often drove them to bankruptcy. Moreover, gold did not require the same sort of elaborate factorylike processing that sugar and silver did. Slaves did not extract gold from mining shafts but

price in order to engage with her in continuous and scandalous sins. The drifters who went to the mines to take gold not out of the streams but out of the shafts in which they gather, perpetrating crimes which go unpunished, because in the mines human justice still does not have a court nor even the fear of the garrison which exists in other places, and only now may some remedy be possible because the governor and ministers are going there. Even the bishops and prelates strongly regret not having undertaken censures in order to eliminate from their dioceses and convents several clerics and monks who scandalously run around there, or who are apostates or fugitives. Furthermore, the departure to the mines of the best of everything which can be desired caused a great increase in the prices of all which is sold, so that sugar mill owners and cane growers find themselves enormously indebted, and due to the lack of

blacks, they can produce neither sugar nor tobacco, which they used to do easily in times past, and which were the true mines of Brazil and Portugal. And the worst is that most of the gold which is extracted from the mines turns to dust or to coins for foreign kingdoms and only a small portion remains in Portugal and in the cities of Brazil, save that which is spent in gold chains, earrings, and other jewels with which mulattas and black women of ill repute are seen loaded, much more so than the ladies. There is no prudent person who does not acknowledge that God permitted so much gold to be discovered in the mines in order to punish Brazil with it, just as He is punishing at the same time with a plethora of wars, the Europeans with their iron.

SOURCE: André João Antonil, *Cultura e opulência do Brasil* (São Paulo: Edições Melhoramentos, 1976), 194-95. Translation by Teresa Van Hoy.

"washed out" gold mainly from the placer works along the waterways; the process required no ore grinding and little mercury amalgamation (see Manuscript 12.3). The king's officials attempted to collect the Royal Fifth directly from production by visiting the mobile placer operations. Finally, they settled on collecting the royalty at the authorized royal foundries, the only legal places where gold could be measured, graded, and melted into

MANUSCRIPT 12.3

African Slaves in Mining

As in Brazil's sugar and tobacco industries and subsequently on the cotton and coffee plantations, the entrepreneurs of frontier gold mining found the indigenous slaves incapable of undertaking the arduous labor they desired from them. The enslavement and importation of larger numbers of African slaves solved their problem. During the eighteenth century, slave traders brought nearly three million slaves to Brazil. A majority of them came in chains from the entrepôts of Salvador da Bahia and Rio de Janeiro to work the gold and diamond mines of Minas Gerais. The slaves of the mining zone also led harsh lives of heavy labor, just as on the sugar plantations. It was said that the average slave lasted from 7 to 12 years in the gold washings before succumbing to an early death due to overwork and malnourishment. A British visitor described their work at a gold operation in 1807.

Suppose a loose gravel-like stratum of rounded quartzose pebbles and adventitious matter, incumbent on granite, and covered by earthy matter of variable thickness. Where water of sufficiently high level can be commanded, the ground is cut in steps, each twenty or thirty feet wide, two or three broad, and about one deep. Near the bottom a trench is cut to the depth of two or three feet. On each step stand six or eight Negroes, who, as the water flows gently from above, keep the earth continually in motion; with shovels, until the whole is reduced to liquid mud and washed below. The particles of gold contained in this earth descend to the trench, where, by reason of their specific gravity, they quickly precipitate. Workmen are continually employed at the trench to remove the stones, and clear away the surface, which operation is much assisted by the current of water which falls into it. After five days' washing, the precipitation in the trench is carried to some convenient stream, to undergo a second clearance. For this purpose wooden bowls are provided, of a funnel shape, about two feet wide at the mouth, and five or six inches deep, called Gamellas. Each workman standing in the stream, takes into his bowl five or six pounds weight of sediment, which generally consists of heavy matter, such as oxide of iron, pyrites, ferruginous quartz, &c. of a dark carbonaceous hue. They admit certain quantities of water into the bowl, which they move about so dexterously, that the precious metal, separating from the inferior and lighter substances, settles to the bottom and sides of the vessel. They then rinse their bowls in a larger vessel of clean water, leaving the gold in it and begin again. The washing of each bowlful occupies from five to eight or nine minutes; the gold produced is extremely variable in quantity and in the size of its particles, some of which are so minute, that they float, while others are found as large as peas, and not infrequently much larger. This operation is superintended by overseers, as the result is of considerable importance.

SOURCE: John Mawe. *Travels in the Interior of Brazil, Particularly in the Gold and Diamond Districts of that Country* (London: Longman, Hurst, Rees, Orme, and Brown, 1812), 78–79.

coins and bullion. The royal foundries used only authorized plates and designs, yet once again miners and merchants dodged the tax and counterfeited the designs. Contraband trade in Brazilian gold remained widespread within the colony as well as abroad.

In the 1720s, someone discovered diamonds, which *paulista* bush captains had always mistaken for worthless quartz or crystals, in the stream beds at Serro do Frio. The authorities had even less control of diamond mining. No one processed diamonds in Brazil but exported them in their natural state to Europe, where they were eventually cut in the diamond shops of Amsterdam. The king's tax collectors could assess the larger operators, whose gangs of slaves washed for diamonds much as they did for gold. But many small operations went unnoticed, and diamonds entered the diverse avenues of contraband from Minas Gerais to Rio de Janeiro to Amsterdam. Persons who practiced illicit diamond mining came to be called *garimpeiros,* the name by which independent Brazilian miners are known to this day. Even the slaves entered this illicit commercial system, becoming adept at hiding diamonds between their toes or by swallowing them. "Ten whites are not enough to watch one Negro," said an eyewitness of this form of slave resistance. "For this reason, the Negroes give very few large diamonds to their masters [but] sell them in the taverns to whites who buy them secretly. The Negroes only give the small diamonds to their owners." Approximately nine thousand African slaves worked in the diamond districts in 1740. To end the rampant smuggling, the Crown made a monopoly of diamond production in 1771, but it worked only in the breach.

Suffice it to say, nonetheless, the Portuguese royal house of Bragança profited immensely from Brazil's gold and diamond booms of the eighteenth century. Political life in the mother country itself was enormously influenced. As in Spain, the mining revenues reinforced the autocracy of the Crown. The Portuguese kings consolidated their domestic political power during the course of the eighteenth century. They never once had to call upon or compromise with the Portuguese nobles to raise revenues because the royal patrimony that was the colony of Brazil provided all the revenues that they needed. Eventually, the Portuguese kings would also use this increasing wealth, as did their Spanish royal cousins, to increase control over colonial political and social life. Brazilian gold enabled the Portuguese monarch, Dom João V, to emulate the despotism and absolutism of the French Sun King, Louis XIV. Imports of gold into Portugal undermined local crafts and agriculture, as the inflated Brazilian coins easily purchased imported manufactured goods from England and the Low Countries. Ironically, while the colonial economies expanded, mercantilism as practiced by both Spain and Portugal led to the impoverishment rather than development of the Iberian imperialists.

Mining in Brazil also increased the communication and conflicts between colonial neighbors. The gold strikes in Mato Grosso, which lay within the watersheds of the Paraná and the Amazon Rivers, placed the Portuguese subjects in direct contact with Spanish missions. Spanish-American Jesuits had established missions among the indigenous Chiquito and Moxo peoples well within their territorial rights according to the 1494 Treaty of Tordesillas, which divided Spanish and Portuguese possessions in South America. But the gold seekers had little understanding or interest in the Tordesillas line, and both the Spanish and Portuguese Crowns became concerned. The Spaniards wanted to prevent an attack on their mines at Potosí, and the Portuguese desired to protect their new gold-mining provinces.

One of those isolated gold districts lay to the west in Cuiabá. It took six months by caravan to travel from São Paulo along the complicated monsoon river route. But by

1740, the district contained nearly six thousand Portuguese subjects, most of whom were well armed to fight natives. While the two colonial powers pondered a solution as to whom Cuiabá actually belonged, these gold miners made the decision for them. Brazilian explorers opened a second supply route to Mato Grosso down the Madeira River into the Amazon and thence to Belém. Paddling upriver, troops and supplies could reach Mato Grosso in nine months, and the return trip for gold took three months. With no hope of supporting Spanish subjects in the region, in 1750 the Crown of Spain conceded the vast tropical basins to Portugal. The Treaty of Madrid ensured that the major part of the future populations of the great watersheds of the Paraná and Amazon Rivers would speak Portuguese rather than Spanish. This very treaty provoked rebellion among the mission Guaraní, as was discussed in Chapter 10.

GOLD'S ECONOMIC AND SOCIAL IMPACT

Brazil's mining cycle reached its zenith just after the mid-eighteenth century, when it was producing approximately thirty-five thousand pounds of gold per year. By then, the economic effects of the gold boom had developed fully. Migrants settled new towns deep in the hinterlands. High food prices stimulated farming and ranching in the frontier zones adjacent to the mines, where large operators as well as smallholders had access to land. But the frontier settlement disrupted the native inhabitants. Remnants of indigenous tribes that had escaped the slave expeditions from São Paulo and the epidemic diseases brought by the Europeans still clung to their ancient lifestyles in the rain forests of the vast Amazon basin. Even after what was by that time two centuries of frontier slaving, some isolated native groups still had not come into contact with Europeans. Other indigenous groups, such as the Botocudo mentioned previously, formed pockets of resistance, causing widespread violence and warfare. Moreover, the Sertão, or "wasteland," which lay to the west of Minas Gerais and Bahia, had become a refuge for runaway African-born slaves who escaped captivity after having been brought into the gold-mining areas and established *quilombos* on the frontier. Both indigenous peoples and runaway slaves had armed themselves to resist the encroachment of Luso-Brazilian society and caused fear among would-be settlers. Therefore, the Portuguese authorities sanctioned armed expeditions sponsored by leading citizens who sought to tame the backlands.

Frontier Expansion

These frontier expeditions, not unlike their *bandeira* forerunners, amounted to business enterprises of conquest and settlement that attracted the participation of free settlers as future gold miners and landowners. The expeditions might take several years to complete. The leader was always a wealthy, Portuguese- or Brazilian-born white entrepreneur with previous frontier service who collected sponsorship for the expedition from his business partners and whose substantial family could readily obtain the necessary licenses and other exclusive rights from royal authorities. The leader, who styled himself the *mestre de campo,* "master of the countryside," brought along his free-born retainers who might be mulattoes and *mamelucos.* He and his subordinates also brought their slaves, who bore arms, though to fight runaway slaves, native warriors, and troops of pack animals. The participants of these expeditions, though rustic and uneducated,

Map 12.1   Frontier Expansion in Eighteenth-Century Brazil

always observed the proper etiquette and ritual of "civilizing" the frontier. The musician slaves of the *mestre de campo* played sacred music at dawn and dusk, a chaplain accompanied the expedition to lead masses and prayer, and at sunset each day, the members of the expedition recited the rosary. To entertain comrades around the campfires, they made up poems extolling the virtues of European-style civilization and of their leader. The musicians struck up a fanfare praising God before the party forded a mighty river.

The expeditions hunted for new gold outcroppings as well as the *quilombos* set up by runaway slaves. They killed and captured any maroons they could find, but most often their advance caused their opponents simply to abandon these settlements and flee deeper into the vast frontier. Then the expeditionaries would occupy the *quilombo* itself, which was always strategically located on the terrain and fortified with trenches and palisades. They dedicated a chapel, occupied the habitations, and cultivated the fields of manioc cleared and planted by the runaways. For this reason, many a Brazilian town today can trace its origin directly back to a *quilombo* (see Map 12.1). Once he secured a permanent settlement, the *mestre de campo* then petitioned royal officials for generous land grants for himself and his free retainers. Usually, the leader obtained 100 or more square kilometers of frontier land, and his followers received lesser amounts. This division of the rewards of conquest paralleled the strategies adopted among the Spanish conquistadores of the sixteenth century.

In the Sertão of Bahia and Pernambuco, lying to the north of the mining region, cattlemen settled the semi-arid uplands and produced meat and hides to provision the miners. The slave and free *vaqueiros* (cattlehands) of the Sertão worked for powerful cattle barons, who were called *os poderosos da sertão,* "the powerful masters of the Sertão," for their economic and political clout. Ranchers in Bahia and Pernambuco sold cattle herds of 400 to 500 head for the drives to Minas Gerais. But the spread of cattle into the Sertão did not occur without native resistance. The Piauí revolted in 1712 against the cattlemen in the border districts of Maranhão and Ceará. Mandú Ladino, who had once been trained by Jesuit missionaries, led the revolt. His forces defeated two detachments of soldiers and destroyed nearly one hundred cattle ranches, a quarter of those then established in the area. In 1716, however, the settlers and Jesuits had recruited mission natives who were loyal to the Brazilian state and helped put down the Piauí rebellion and kill Mandú Ladino. Expansion of frontier cattle raising in Brazil was reminiscent of the situation in northern Mexico, even to the deleterious effect it had on the original inhabitants of the area.

In similar fashion, settlers moved south into Rio Grande do Sul even as far as the bank of the Río de la Plata estuary to produce cattle as well. There, however, the *gauchos* independently bred half-wild herds of cattle and horses on the vast prairies not yet claimed by landowners. The southern Brazilians also raised mules, which they sold at annual trade fairs in Sorocaba, west of São Paulo. At the end of the century, Rio Grande's citizenry exceeded 18,000. Whites formed the majority, but slaves still made up nearly 30 percent of the population of Rio Grande do Sul. The late-developing cattle ranches were called *estancias,* sharing these names and much more with the cattle culture of the Banda Oriental (Uruguay) and Argentina.

Renaissance on the Coast

In the meantime, the eighteenth-century gold boom complicated and complemented the sugar economy of the Brazilian coast. At first, the impact proved negative. Prices for slaves and foodstuffs everywhere on the coast rose and squeezed the profit margins of the coastal planters, the *fazendeiros.* But the trade in gold bolstered the colony's economy during the prolonged sugar depression from 1720 and 1760, the period in which new Caribbean sugar production depressed international prices. Tobacco exports, too, had fallen on hard times, due partly to the number of smallholders who abandoned agriculture near the coast.

The older plantation societies of Bahia and Pernambuco underwent additional subtle changes as a result of the gold boom. The relative decline of the sugar industry vis-à-vis the mining districts transformed the relationship between the planters and their cane growers, the *lavradores.* Those *lavradores* were sharecroppers and small farmers, whites mostly but also some mulattoes. As sharecroppers, they owned their own slaves, worked on the land of the *fazendeiros,* and processed their cane at the planter's mill, the *engenho.* In the bargain, the sharecropping *lavradores* received one-third of the profit.

Commercial life on the Rua Direita in Rio de Janeiro. (John Luccock, ca. 1810)

Small farmers had capital to buy their own slaves but processed their cane at the *engenho* of the large planter, making the smallholder dependent on the *fazendeiro*. A big planter might have 10 to 30 *lavradores* on his estate while, at the same time, his overseers and slaves cultivated cane in his own fields. But the mill owner's expenses remained low insofar as the sharecroppers assumed for him the cost and the management of planting his fields. The planter's advantage came in owning the land and the mill. Most *lavradores* aspired to be *fazendeiros,* although the rise occurred rarely and planters treated the sharecroppers with imperiousness. Nonetheless, most *lavradores* shared the planters' attitudes toward the slaves and free colored population. These traditional relationships changed, beginning in the sugar depression of the last quarter of the seventeenth century and continuing during the gold boom of the next century.

The continued crisis of the sugar industry in the early eighteenth century aided the planters in consolidating their social predominance over the *lavradores*. Low sugar prices permitted the planters to reduce the sharecroppers' portion to one-fifth of the harvest or less. Under these conditions, few *lavradores* could afford to buy slaves when the mining boom sharply raised the prices of chattel labor. Many sharecroppers abandoned Bahia and Pernambuco altogether, taking their slaves to the gold fields. When sugar prices rose at the end of the eighteenth century, therefore, plantation mill owners reaped a majority of the financial benefits and shared neither the production nor the profits with a middling class of smallholders and renters. At that time the planters themselves produced most of the cane that their *engenhos* crushed, and they became an even more exclusive but less dynamic oligarchy. By 1800, Salvador da Bahia regained its commercial importance. Its 50,000 inhabitants made this sugar port one of the most populous cities of the Americas. The return of commercial prosperity did not equalize economic opportunity or produce a more egalitarian social order in Bahia. It accomplished precisely the reverse, an increasingly stratified and rigidly hierarchical society in the older plantation areas.

Colonial ports were flourishing by exporting gold and importing slaves, mercury, and merchandise. Operators of riverboats and muleteers integrated the frontier mining

Figure 12.1   Registered Gold Production in Eighteenth-Century Brazil, in Thousands of Kilograms

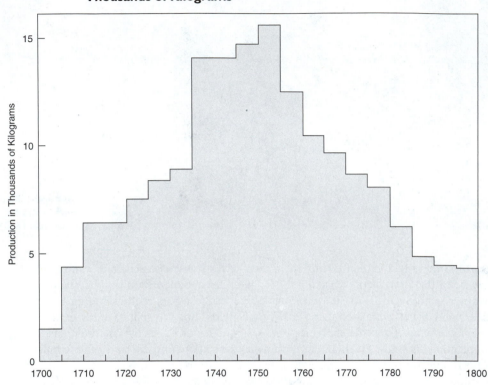

SOURCE: Virgílio Noya Pinto, *O ouro brasileiro e o comércio anglo-português* (São Paulo: Companhia Editora Nacional, 1979), 115.

outposts to the coast. Rio de Janeiro rose to importance because of the mining development to the west, becoming the principal port of call for ships bringing slaves and supplies for the mines and for the export of gold and diamonds. Rio's urban growth was spectacular in the eighteenth century, spawning additional economic pursuits in the south of Brazil. Landowners began planting coffee trees outside Rio de Janeiro, manioc and other crops for domestic consumption, and bags of rice and indigo (the blue dyestuff) crowded casks of sugar on the wharves of Guanabara Bay. Rio soon had a population second only to Salvador, which it supplanted as capital of the colony in 1770. The economic locus was definitively moving southwards away from the Brazilian northeast.

When gold production began to taper off, shortly after midcentury, the Brazilian economy went into depression (see Figure 12.1). Many a merchant faced bankruptcy. Gold miners drifted into subsistence agriculture, and the Portuguese royal exchequer fell on hard times. Because the king's tax farmers in his most important colony owed him several years' accounts, Portugal could no longer pay for its imbalance of trade with Great Britain. The severe earthquake and fire that destroyed Lisbon in 1755 compounded the financial problems of the mother country. Despite government reforms (about which,

Table 12.1   Population Growth in Eighteenth-Century Brazil

	CA. 1776		CA. 1800	
	Number	*Percent of Total*	*Number*	*Percent of Total*
Amazonia (Rio Negro, Pará, Piauí, Maranhão)	139,521	8.9	210,581	10.1
Northeast (Ceará, Rio Grande do Norte, Paraíba, Pernambuco, Bahia)	666,249	42.6	893,565	43.2
South Central (Minas Gerais, Rio de Janeiro, São Paulo)	652,422	41.7	815,337	30.3
South (Santa Catarina, Rio Grande do Sul)	30,309	1.9	62,283	3.0
Far Interior (Goiás, Mato Grosso)	76,480	4.9	79,766	3.8
Total	1,564,981		2,061,532	

SOURCES: James Lockhart and Stuart B. Schwartz, *Early Latin America: A History of Colonial Spanish America and Brazil* (Cambridge, England: Cambridge University Press, 1983), 399; Dauril Alden, "Late Colonial Brazil, 1750–1808," in Leslie Bethell, ed. *Colonial Brazil* (Cambridge, England: Cambridge University Press, 1987), 286–87; and Dauril Alden, "The Population of Brazil in the Late Eighteenth Century: A Preliminary Survey," *Hispanic American Historical Review* 43, no. 2 (1963): 173–205.

more in Chapter 14), the economy sputtered until it was revived on the strength of international markets.

A surge in demand by industrial countries stimulated a renaissance in Brazil's coastal agriculture. Growth of international markets encouraged increased output of rice and tobacco, and wheat production commenced in Rio Grande do Sul. The planting of coffee trees spread from the Amazon region to Rio de Janeiro and São Paulo, where this crop's preeminence awaited the nineteenth century. Cotton production expanded in Maranhão to supply British and French textile factories, a development that accentuated this captaincy's slavocracy. Nearly half of Maranhão's population of 79,000 in 1800 were slaves, and another 15 percent were free blacks and mulattoes. "White cotton turned the Maranhão black," went the saying (see Table 12.1).

In colonial Brazil, farmers cultivated tobacco on modest-sized farms along the coastal plain from Maranhão to Rio de Janeiro. The Recôncavo of Bahia, Brazil's premier sugarcane area, also became the site of the colony's second most important export crop. Small growers—low-status whites, mulattoes, and free blacks—used family labor and only a few slaves in the intensive cultivation of tobacco. Both the gold boom and the agricultural renaissance increased the demand for African slaves and widened the West African market for Brazilian tobacco. Slave traders customarily bartered rolls of tobacco for captive

Africans. Partly with the use of additional chattel labor, tobacco production increased. By the second half of the eighteenth century, Brazilian growers began to cultivate Virginian and Cuban varieties that could be sold in Europe as well. So valuable a commodity naturally interested the colonial state. Tobacco had become a Crown monopoly in the seventeenth century, and during the export's growth of the next century, colonial officials tightened their control over distribution and marketing, although a brisk contraband trade in Brazilian tobacco still flourished.

Farther north, at the mouth of the Amazon River, agricultural expansion promoted the transition of the surviving indigenous peoples from hunters, fishermen, and tropical agriculturists to wage laborers. Jesuit missionaries had first taken charge of "civilizing" the natives, teaching them work skills. The missionaries were influential in preventing the natives from being enslaved in Amazonia. As the number of settlers in the region grew, so did their demands for labor. The industries of the Amazon—collecting cacao and other forest products, fishing, cattle raising, rice growing, canoe paddling, cotton spinning, and wood cutting—had to rely on native labor. Therefore, colonial officials increasingly intervened, prying the natives from the clutches of the missionaries and allotting them to private entrepreneurs, relocating whole families in the process. Individual employers sometimes forced natives into employment. Colonial officials also conscripted them to garrison the frontier fortifications and to construct public buildings and roads. The high death rates from epidemics, however, constantly reduced this labor pool, requiring missionaries and employers to go farther into the rain forests for new sources of Native Americans. Despite continuous recruitment, the number of adult male natives available for labor never exceeded four to six thousand throughout the entire eighteenth century. By the end of the century, those natives who survived the ravages of disease joined with the mixed-race descendants who formed the free labor pool in cities such as Belém and Macapá.

Native Americans resisted proletarianization in the Amazon region. White settlers were not always enlightened employers, and the state itself could be equally demanding. The natives took flight from their assigned jobs, frequently after receiving an advance in pay. Pressed into service on a government expedition upriver to Mato Grosso in 1780, for instance, 300 indigenous workers died or deserted; many simply stayed on the frontier when the expedition returned to Belém. African slaves provided a partial solution to the lack of servile labor for the settlers of Amazonia, but slaves ran away to establish *quilombos* and engage in rural banditry. Nearby French Cayenne became a special haven for fleeing slaves, and Portuguese authorities even considered that the French authorities there encouraged the flight. To a certain extent, indigenous and slave resistance prevented the Amazon region from developing a secure and prosperous economic base.

Finally, international sugar prices rebounded when the Caribbean island of Saint-Domingue (Haiti) suffered a slave revolt in 1791. Imports of slaves increased with the new agricultural boom. More than one and a half million Africans arrived at Brazil between 1750 and 1805. Once again, they hailed from diverse areas such as the Bight of Benin and Angola, adulterating somewhat the cultural dominance in Brazil of the Yoruba from the Gold Coast. Did this economic resurgence benefit royal coffers? Yes, it did, but contraband also proliferated, tying Brazil tightly to its ultimate trading partners of England and France while bypassing the Portuguese middleman. The prevalence of this contraband heralded a trend—direct trade between Brazil and northern Europe—that would come fully to fruition in the next century.

COASTAL SOCIETY AT SÃO PAULO

The gold rush and frontier development of the eighteenth century helped shift the economic locus of colonial Brazil from the northern sugar zone to the emerging commercial metropolises of São Paulo and Rio de Janeiro in the south central area of the country. Despite the violence and competition, the Brazilian frontier had not developed outside the bounds of traditional patterns. Individual adventurers of social status and connection with important coastal elites and economic interests usually led the frontier expeditions. They organized serious and hierarchically structured business enterprises. The elite of the established towns near the coast financed the gold expeditions in much the same fashion that they had outfitted other frontier enterprises for nearly two centuries. Town leaders furnished the capital and materials for gold mining, contributing Native Americans and, increasingly, African slaves. They recruited free workers and peasants for the expedition, too, and obtained the necessary grants and permissions from royal authorities. These entrepreneurs expected to gain the major share of the profits. In this manner, the elite increased its wealth and further entrenched itself in the rigid class system. Once again, the family formed the important unit of expansion, for the sons of elite families usually led the expeditions and used them to strike out on their own, spreading the wealth and privilege of the elite onto the frontier.

Slaves and Masters

Back in the more settled communities along the coast, the gold rush tended to develop and embellish the social order. The first important consequence was the replacement of Native Americans by African slaves. The profits from trade to the gold-mining areas enabled the slave-holding planters to act on their preferences for Africans over indigenous workers because the former had immunities to European diseases and could be made to work harder. Moreover, the law recognized African bondage and not that of the natives and facilitated the marketing of black slaves. In addition, the offspring of Africans frequently remained in slavery. Males naturally outnumbered females among the newly arrived African slaves, but miscegenation proceeded in time, and a sizable population of Brazilian-born blacks (with a more nearly equal male-female ratio) and mulattoes arose. By the last quarter of the eighteenth century, free blacks and mulattoes born in Brazil began to move into the ranks of the poor peasantry and the artisans and workers of the cities. Although the enslavement of indigenous peoples continued on the far frontiers, Native Americans practically disappeared from the coastal regions of south central Brazil—though not without contributing their blood and culture to many a peasant and local patriarch.

Nevertheless, slavery remained a very hard regime for Rio de Janeiro and São Paulo's growing population of blacks (see Table 12.2). Except on large plantations, forming a family of any permanence among slaves was difficult. Formal marriage between slaves was not the norm, although bondspersons did occasionally marry or cohabit with free persons. But for survival and mutual support, slaves struggled to form nuclear families where possible, although matrifocal families remained most common. When the slave owner died, the heirs separated the slave parents from the children and sold them individually. Corporal punishments for the men and unwanted sexual advances toward the women remained features of slave life on the plantations. Poor diet, unsanitary housing,

Table 12.2   Estimated Growth of the Slave Population of Rio de Janeiro, 1799–1828/29

Year	Total Population	SLAVE POPULATION	
		Number	Percent
1799	43,376	14,986	34.6
1808	54,255	—	—
1821	79,321	36,182	45.6
1828/29	150,000	50,000	33.3

SOURCE: Mary C. Karasch, *Slave Life in Rio de Janeiro, 1808-1850* (Princeton, N.J.: Princeton University Press, 1987), 61.

inadequate clothing, and overwork carried many a slave to an early grave. Few protections existed from arbitrary or violent treatment on the part of owners and overseers.

Nevertheless, as much as possible, the slaves of the late eighteenth century did act to influence their life choices. As ever, the slaves fixed their eyes on freedom. They knew that manumission for long and obsequious service was a distinct possibility, and many saved to purchase their freedom eventually. The owner could use the proceeds of such a sale to purchase a new slave, but manumission remained a cruel promise many owners held out in order to control their slaves, who usually had to wait until their owners died before being freed. For a woman, one of the benefits of being mistress to the owner or owner's son concerned the favors and possibilities of freedom she expected for the children of such liaisons and for herself. Certain slaves who had the owners' trust to move about did earn extra income, which they saved to buy their freedom. Ex-slaves usually moved into the class of poor peasants or urban workers. Running away was also a possibility, especially closer to the frontier, where slaves could disappear in the forests and live a meager life of basic subsistence. But woe to the runaway slaves who got caught! Branding, collar and leg irons, and brutal whippings could be their lot. Yet as long as fresh slaves could be imported, as they were in record numbers at the end of the eighteenth century, owners tolerated a certain amount of latitude. And the possibility of freedom—perniciously dangled in front of them—encouraged slaves to submit to their lives of bondage and to behave to gain the favor of their owners, yet the truth was that most Africans in Brazil died as slaves and not as free men and women.

The wealth from increased commerce enriched the elites of São Paulo and Rio de Janeiro and allowed them to adopt more elements of European lifestyles. Planters got into cash crops and produced cane for sugar exports and, at the end of the century, a new product, coffee. Now the *paulista* planters and *carioca* (as residents of Rio de Janeiro are known) merchants could furnish their homes with furniture, sleep in beds instead of hammocks, and dress in the latest European fashions. The wealthiest families now had two homes, one in the city and another on their country estates. Population growth, the more intensive cultivation of the land, and multiple inheritances tended to reduce the size of the land holdings. But the great planter families still measured their wealth in terms of how many slaves they owned. Differentiation among planters became pronounced; a group of small planters developed among those having 10 slaves or less, while another narrow and powerful group of planters might own several hundred African slaves each. The wealthiest planters tended also to dominate local politics.

In Rio de Janeiro and São Paulo, a curious family strategy developed to consolidate wealth and power among the elite. The patriarchs were able to maintain the lands pretty much intact by sending their sons, who could be otherwise impatient to gain their inheritance, off on expeditions to the gold fields and the frontier. There the sons could establish their own patriarchies. The dowry of land and money now became an important instrument to bring a son-in-law into the family who would be groomed to take over the family estate and business. Young elite women exercised little control over marriage partners because the patriarch selected for them older men, usually in their thirties, who had established useful commercial and political ties. These new sons-in-law usually came from more modest families and might even be Portuguese immigrants, which tended to whiten elite Southerners who had historically been *mamelucos*. The patriarch could control the grateful son-in-law, who waited patiently for the patriarch to die before gaining control of the estate. These family bases of enterprise had parallels in Mexico, Peru, and other American colonies.

The Free Poor

While the elite families consolidated their wealth and power in the eighteenth century, the poor peasantry in the coastal provinces also underwent change. Like the elite, they, too, began to speak Portuguese rather than Tupí as in the old days. Free blacks and mulattoes merged with and gradually replaced the *mamelucos* within the class of poor farmers. Now title to the land on which one lived became important. The peasants had always lived independently, producing their subsistence on land owned by the elite, and as long as land was plentiful, the planters did not mind. But in the late eighteenth century, growth of the population and commerce made land more valuable. Some poor families began to lose the land on which they had always worked and were converted into retainers of the planter class. Others moved off the land and into the cities or else drifted out to the frontier. In the cities, these former peasants became petty tradespersons, with the women taking up weaving, doing others' laundry, and working in elite households. Beggars and the homeless seemed to proliferate in the cities of Rio de Janeiro and São Paulo. Those peasants who moved out to the frontier began the process all over again; they took up residence as squatters on the abundant land of the frontier, slashing and burning the forests to live as independent but poor subsistence farmers and perpetuating patterns established generations before on the coast.

Peasants pursued two strategies to survive: seeking favor of the powerful and exchanging assistance with their own kind. For generations, small farmers and squatters had sought the patronage of the powerful landowners. They asked the local patriarchs to serve as godparents to their children and requested their intervention with the local authorities. Many were beholden to the large landowners for allowing them a bit of land to till independently. In return, they lent these owners their labor, supported them politically, and served on their frontier expeditions. Among peasants, there also developed much camaraderie and cooperation. At harvest or clearing time, they reciprocated in helping each other with the heavy chores. "He who wishes to establish his farm or clearing in the woods calls all his neighbors for a certain day in which, after eating a lot and drinking more, they take up their axes and billhooks, more animated by the spirits than by the love of work," reported one observer, but not without condescension. "This becomes the only time when they work." The peasants did not extend this spirit of cooperation to slaves, however. Despite being a step or two removed from slavery themselves, Brazilian peasants and free workers of color regarded slaves with contempt. The greatest violence in these communities—homicides, fights, robberies—occurred not between vengeful slaves and their masters but between free peasants and slaves. The free worker of color seldom missed the opportunity to insult and jeer at slaves, whom they saw as lesser beings.

The cities of the coast now assumed more importance as political and economic centers. But the urbanization of the Brazilian coastal regions did not benefit family nucleation among the new urban poor. As elsewhere in Latin America, more women lived in town than men, who might be off on an expedition to the frontier. Whereas nuclear families with a father and mother and numerous children predominated among peasants in the countryside, the Brazilian city fostered matrifocal families. Urban poor families were small, and nearly half the households in São Paulo were headed by women. Many of these poor women had two or three children from as many men, who might come and go from the house. Poor women became important to the functioning of urban life as seamstresses, street vendors, laundresses, artisans, and servants. Through hard work and grit, the low-status whites and people of color who made up Brazil's free peasant and urban working population coped with the social pretensions of the wealthy and carved out a meager share of the economic expansion.

CONCLUDING REMARKS

This extraordinarily robust expansion of the colonial economy concealed numerous weaknesses. Although it was true that the gold boom made Brazil's population twice as large as the mother country's, much of the colonial population remained outside the market system—or only marginally connected to it—in the eighteenth century. Slaves were estimated to make up some 45 percent of the colony's total population, and the owners severely constricted consumption. Even though the wages of slaves hired out to others increased by 150 percent in the second half of the eighteenth century, the benefit accrued to the owners. Also, most of the free people of color living in rural areas remained imperfectly integrated into the market or lived independently at subsistence levels. The social organization of Brazil, as in the rest of Latin America, tended to concentrate income among the privileged but narrow and white elite. They spent their money on conspicuous consumption of foreign merchandise and bought more slaves for their estates. Therefore, much of the income produced by the robust economy leaked abroad for purchases from Africa and Europe.

In Brazil, the gold and diamond rushes did not contribute to the democratization of society. In fact, the reverse was true. The elite captured the largest increments of economic expansion, and class distinctions became even more pronounced. The gold rush enhanced the encroachment of Europeanized society into the hinterlands, destroying the indigenous peoples and taking over their hunting grounds in its wake. As a group, women were not able to raise their status in the more prosperous society. Single women of color who headed their own families—and this number was growing—gained some independence, but they formed the most marginal part of the free poor. Elite women, though pampered and secure, did not seem to have gained control of their lives and even less of their choices for husbands. The poor peasantry became infused with more African heritage and moved horizontally—to work on the planters' estates, to take up urban occupations, or to move out to the frontier as subsistence producers—but certainly not upwards on the social scale. The elite became more distant. Portuguese immigration tended to whiten the elite and generate a middling class of officeholders, small planters, and business families. African slaves arrived in record numbers, which the elite used to reinforce a class structure that reserved wealth and privilege for itself, relative poverty for free people of color, and bondage and dependence for most Africans. Only in the interior and on the fringes of internal commerce did the *mamelucos* continue to form an important part of the rural poor. Racial and class lines elsewhere in colonial Brazil became more rigid.

However, the importance of plantations, gold mines, and exports of primary products masks the vibrancy of Brazilians of lower social rank in forcing concessions and a minimum distribution of income from the elites. Frontier development provided a measure of social advancement to the free poor of the coast who willingly followed the bush captains into the interior. They aspired to own land and slaves. Although they suffered cultural dislocation, individual Native Americans could also join frontier society as specialists in river transportation and as food producers. Slaves regularly stole gold and diamonds they had mined and sold them on the flourishing black market. Freedom on the frontier may have been difficult to purchase, but some Africans successfully fled deep into the forests and established independent yet tenuous lives in the *quilombos*. Resistance and independent activity of this kind impressed on the elites that their economic and social status depended more on importing and exploiting new servile labor than on perfectly controlling all individuals of low social status. In fact, the difficulty of social control perhaps saved the Brazilian elite from its greatest fear—a successful revolt of their slaves. To imagine the worst, Brazilian and Spanish-American slave owners only had to contemplate what happened in Haiti in 1791.

Additional Reading

Alden, Dauril, ed. *Colonial Roots of Modern Brazil.* Berkeley: University of California Press, 1973.

Bethell, Leslie, ed. *Colonial Brazil.* Cambridge, England: Cambridge University Press, 1987.

Boxer, C. R. *The Golden Age of Brazil, 1695–1750: Growing Pains of a Colonial Society.* Berkeley: University of California Press, 1969.

Hemming, John. *Amazon Frontier: The Defeat of the Brazilian Indians.* London: Macmillan, 1987.

Karash, Mary C. *Slave Life in Rio de Janeiro, 1808–1850.* Princeton, N.J.: Princeton University Press, 1987.

Kuznesof, Elizabeth A. *Household Economy and Urban Development: São Paulo, 1765 to 1836.* Boulder, Colo.: Westview Press, 1986.

Metcalf, Alida C. *Family and Frontier in Colonial Brazil: Santana de Parnaíba, 1580–1822.* Berkeley: University of California Press, 1992.

Miller, Joseph C. *Way of Death: Merchant Capitalism and the Angolan Slave Trade, 1730–1830.* Madison: University of Wisconsin Press, 1998.

Prado Junior, Caio. *The Colonial Background of Modern Brazil.* Trans. Suzette Macedo. Berkeley: University of California Press, 1967.

Schwartz, Stuart B. *Slaves, Peasants, and Rebels: Reconsidering Brazilian Slavery.* Urbana: University of Illinois Press, 1992.

Sweet, David G. "A Rich Realm of Nature Destroyed: The Middle Amazon Valley, 1640–1750." Ph.D. diss., University of Wisconsin, 1974.

In Portuguese

Cardoso, Fernando Henrique. *Capitalismo e escravidão no Brasil meridional: O negro na sociedade escravócrata do Rio Grande do Sul.* São Paulo: Difusão Européia do Livro, 1962.

Carrato, José Ferreira. *Igreja, iluminismo e escolas mineiras colonais.* São Paulo: Companhia Editora Nacional, 1968.

Carreira, Antônio. *As companhias pombalinas de Grão-Pará e Maranhão e Pernambuco e Paraîba.* 2d ed. Lisbon: Editorial Presença, 1983.

de Carvalho Franco, Maria Silvia. *Homens livres na ordem escravócrata.* 3d ed. São Paulo: KAIROS, 1983.

Maestri Filho, Mário José. *O escravo no Rio Grande do Sul: A charqueada e a génese do escravismo gaúcho.* Pôrto Alegre: Escola Superior de Teologia São Lourenço, 1984.

Shorer Petrone, Maria Thereza. *A lavoura canaveira em São Paulo: Expansão e declínio (1765–1851).* São Paulo: Difusão Européia do Livro, 1968.

Simonsen, Roberto Cochrane. *História econômica do Brasil, 1500–1820.* 7th ed. São Paulo: Companhia Editora Nacional, 1977.

Souza, Laura de Mello E. *Desclassificados do ouro; A pobreza mineira no século XVIII.* Rio de Janeiro: Edições Graal, 1982.

———. *O diabo e a Terra de Santa Cruz: feiticaria e religiosidade popular no Brasil colonial.* São Paulo: Companhia das Letras, 1986.

Vidal Luna, Francisco. *Minas Gerais: Escravos e senhores: Análise da estrutura populacional e econômica de alguns centros mineratórios, 1718–1804.* São Paulo: Instituto de Pesquisas Econômicas, 1981.

CHAPTER 13

THE HAITIAN SOCIAL REVOLUTION

Slavery had expanded appreciably throughout the Americas as the economic boom enlarged the demand for labor and colonists reverted to traditional means to meet that demand, whether by hunting native slaves or importing African slaves. Brazil alone brought in nearly 2 million Africans as slaves in the eighteenth century, and the plantation and mining economies of the Spanish Americas imported 300,000 just in the half-century leading up to 1810. The presence of so many slaves—and their black and mulatto progeny—caused anxiety among the privileged whites. Cuba at the time was developing a society in which slaves comprised more than 40 percent and free nonwhites comprised another 20 percent of the total population. Runaways, small revolts, and even the whisper of conspiracy among the slaves met with harsh retribution. If the American colonists feared the consequences of a race war, they had only to look at the case of Saint-Domingue (today Haiti).

The French sugar-producing colony in the Caribbean entered its colonial golden age in the fourth quarter of the eighteenth century. Producing 130 million pounds of sugar annually in the late 1780s, Saint-Domingue came to be France's leading trading partner. But none of this growth would have been possible without exceptionally huge imports of slaves. More than thirty thousand Africans a year were arriving at this French possession during the 1780s. By 1787, slaves comprised 90 percent of the colony's population.

The great slave revolt of Saint-Domingue demonstrated the vulnerability of a colonial export economy based exclusively on coerced labor. The French Revolution shocked this Caribbean plantation society. As would become typical of all subsequent revolutions in Latin America, the disunited elites of Saint-Domingue fell to quarreling over politics, in this case French revolutionary doctrine. In 1791, thousands of slaves revolted, seizing the plantations, putting the owners and slave drivers to the sword, and burning the sugar mills. There followed 13 long years of fighting, in which all the social groups formed confusing alliances with and engaged in conflicts against each other. At the end, Haiti's plantations lay in ruins, and the former slaves drifted into the hills to settle on subsistence plots. The contagion of slave uprisings even threatened to spread to the American mainland.

If the great Andean insurrections had not sufficiently sobered the numerically vulnerable whites, the slave revolt on Saint-Domingue demonstrated the vulnerability of European possessions—including those of the British. The French colony experienced the first social revolution of the Americas—a rebellion from below that completely overturned the social order. The former slaves destroyed the plantation society and the export economy and triumphantly converted themselves from bonded laborers to independent subsistence producers.

PLANTATION SOCIETY

Saint-Domingue covered the western third of Hispaniola, the Caribbean island originally settled by Columbus in 1492 and whose indigenous population all but died out within three decades. Thereafter, the colony settled into a long period of a sparsely populated neglect, as Spanish conquistadores and settlers went to Mexico and Peru. Most Spaniards, their African slaves, and the free inhabitants of color lived on the eastern side of the island, near the port of Santo Domingo. In the seventeenth century, however, French *boucaniers* (buccaneers) did not conquer so much as settle the remote western section. Buccaneers were men who lived by pillage, contraband, and the hunting of wild herds of cattle and swine. Louis XIV forced Spain to recognize the French claim to Saint-Domingue in 1697, and infusions of a few French women and numerous African slaves soon turned some of the descendants of the buccaneers into respectable slave-owning family men. Then soil exhaustion in the older British sugar colonies, Jamaica and Barbados, as well as in the French sugar islands of Martinique and Guadeloupe brought a sugar boom to Saint-Domingue.

The French possession entered its colonial golden age in the fourth quarter of the eighteenth century. Saint-Domingue boasted 655 sugar plantations, 1,962 coffee properties, and 398 cotton and indigo farms. Producing 130 million pounds of sugar annually in the late 1780s, Saint-Domingue was providing fully one-third of France's foreign commerce. But none of this growth would have been possible without exceptional imports of labor. Some planters from Martinique and Guadeloupe had brought their own slaves, but the majority of workers came from the West Coast of Africa—especially Angola and the Congo. Demand for labor consistently outstripped its supply as the sugar economy boomed from 1750 onwards. Prices for individual slaves rose. French merchants at Le Havre and in the colonial ports of Le Cap François and Port-au-Prince prospered, as did the masters of British and colonial North American slave ships, who traded quite openly in this French possession. Nearly thirty thousand Africans a year were arriving legally (and thousands more illegally, thus avoiding taxation) during the 1780s. As many as one in four Africans, chained between the narrow decks and stuffed into dank holds of slave ships, died during the horrific Middle Passage between the West Coast of Africa and the Caribbean sugar colony.

Once ashore, they found little relief from misery. Contemporary observers estimated that one-fifth to one-half of the Africans sold to Haitian plantations died during the ritual "seasoning period," their introduction to field and gang labor. They planted and harvested with the simplest of hand tools, a digging pole, a hoe, and a machete. Beginning at 5:30 A.M., the slave was expected to work as long as the sun was up. Breaks for field hands included only a half-hour's breakfast and an hour's lunch. The harvest was worst, for ripened sugarcane had to be cut immediately to keep it from losing its sugar content on the stalk, and then it had to be crushed in the mechanical presses of the mill almost instantly after that. Slaves were made to work nearly around the clock during the sugar harvest.

Slave Life

French colonists did not busy themselves with moral reservations, for they seldom viewed the Africans as other than beasts of burden, work animals, divinely ordained to serve the superior European race. Male slaves vastly outnumbered females. African women worked predominantly in the rural and urban households of their masters while the men remained in the fields, a separation that rendered the slave family a rarity. Small wonder that the slave population at Saint-Domingue—and other Caribbean colonies for that matter—did not reproduce itself. The final product of this equation: Planters and merchants concluded that it was cheaper to replace slaves, despite the high prices, than to care for them.

What kind of work ethic did slavery instill? A poor one for both owner and slave. Whites and even free mulattoes had so many slaves as personal servants that they neither cooked nor cleaned for themselves. They did not so much as carry their own children or packages through the streets. And neither were there any incentives or rewards for the slaves' hard work, so they learned to respond only to the *arceau,* a short-handled whip used by the slave drivers. "There are negroes who must absolutely be beaten before they can be put in motion," said a visitor to the island. The traveler could not help but note that the slave's resistant attitude toward work was "marvelously seconded by the inactivity and sloth of their masters . . . [who] find the plan of beating more practicable than that of instructing!"

Africans in Saint-Domingue and other Caribbean sugar colonies (whether Spanish, French, English, or Dutch) did not enjoy even the minimal protections that Native Americans in colonial New Spain and Peru had come to expect—and demand. Natives were difficult to replace as laborers in the highlands. Peasant villagers often had independent control over part of their own subsistence, and they even assumed responsibility for their own religious rituals and observations. Not so for the African slaves in Saint-Domingue. They seldom had access to their own means of subsistence, living instead off refuse fish, salted meat, and the paltry gleanings of the cane fields. Slaves were fortunate if they had access to small garden plots for their own use. Even so, owners often worked them so hard they had little time to grow their own produce. Their French masters had no interest in utilizing the Catholic religion as a device for social control—the rights of property ownership sufficed to discipline the Africans. And anyway, what did it profit the master or the sparse clergy to waste time and effort in converting to Catholicism those who were not considered people? Elites in Saint-Domingue thought that slaves did not live long enough to learn—or were incapable of understanding—the catechism. Priests in Saint-Domingue, therefore, settled for populating their parish houses with mulatto children. Likewise, there was little to motivate the French colonial authorities to undertake the paternalistic protections of chattel labor. Slaves were a renewable resource.

Of course, the French Code Noir (Black Code) of 1685 stipulated that slave masters were to treat their slaves benignly, raise them in the Catholic faith, place no restrictions on their purchase of emancipation, and keep slave families intact. The Code Noir even permitted slaves to bring suit against their masters in colonial courts. But the laws were rarely observed. In 1788, when a tribunal heard the complaints of 14 slaves that their master had brutally tortured 2 slave women for allegedly having contributed to his field hands suffering from food poisoning, a mob of enraged white planters attacked the judges. They accused judicial authorities of inciting the slaves to riot. The defending planter won acquittal.

As an additional strategy to control the large slave population, the French owners necessarily had to develop an internal social hierarchy. Trustworthy and capable slaves and those who were more acculturated to the French language and customs gained higher status among their peers. They received promotion to less-demeaning jobs—as coachmen, household servants, artisans, or watchmen—than those performed by Africans just off the boat. They dressed and ate better, even taking charge of supervising the work of lower-ranking slaves. Slave supervisors found themselves in an ambivalent position, looking up to the whites for reward and authority and looking down on the slaves they supervised. Those few born into slavery in Saint-Domingue and having no memory of their African homeland often found themselves in these positions of privilege. These slave supervisors earned the respect of their fellow slaves. But they were also responsible to the owner for disciplining and punishing those under their supervision, even though the whites would never accept their black stewards as equals. Slave managers who failed to carry out their master's policies toward their fellow slaves could find themselves demoted back to the fields and working under the lash. Although necessary to labor control, the slave supervisors could be the source of conspiracy against the masters. These privileged but frustrated slaves might lead their peers in running away and, in 1791, would come into leadership positions among the rebels.

Although African slaves in Saint-Domingue had few outlets for solidarity and resistance, they were not without identity or notions of dignity. Under the circumstances, it is remarkable that the slaves preserved a separate cultural unity and identity, hybrid though it may have been. As elsewhere, moreover, there was little ethnic unity among the slaves. The Africans had come from several different cultures, the Mandingo, Senegalese, Ibo, and Arada. Slaves born in Saint-Domingue had little in common with the Africans, and the slaves born in the other Caribbean islands had less in common with either group. Europeans spoke French, as did the mulattoes who desired to participate in the world of the whites. A few mulatto slaves who, according to skin color rather than civil status, had higher social standing than many free blacks, worked for their masters as small farmers and tradesmen. Nevertheless, a separate language taken from African and French derivations—called Creole—developed among the slaves. Africans also clung tenaciously to their dancing and musical instruments. Favorite dances came to be the Chica, danced to the accompaniment of drums, calabashes, and a four-string African violin called the *banza.*

African religious practices and beliefs became the ultimate refuge. Slaves widely observed the rituals of Voodoo, an animistic religion that featured an array of gods and goddesses, none of whom pretended to exert moral authority. Instead, the African deities intervened in the lives of mortals in arbitrary ways, bringing either ill or good fortune. In other words, if a slave had an accident or had a good crop of vegetables in his garden, these were the acts of the spirits. The peevish gods demanded attention in the form of ritualistic ceremonies and dancing. They were known to possess their worshippers who engaged in frenzied dance and devotion. Voodoo terrified and repulsed the Europeans, who mistook the African religion for black magic or devil worship (see Manuscript 13.1). Yet their heritage gave the Africans a dignity and identity that their low civil status and harsh labor conditions in Saint-Domingue did not. They cultivated these activities on work breaks, Sundays off, and local market days. The more the white oppressors disapproved of their music, dancing, and religion, the more determined the slaves became to cultivate them as symbols of their separate worth.

African slaves in late-eighteenth-century Saint-Domingue required all the cultural identity they could muster. The greatest problem of the slave was that nothing inhibited the cruelest treatment of overseers and owners. Many slave drivers practiced the most barbarous punishments imaginable for the slightest infractions: burning genitalia, dousing with boiling syrup, roasting over hot fires, live burials, excessive whipping, and the pouring of salt and lemon juice on wounds. These methods were utilized particularly for interrogating slaves about some suspected wrongdoing. Neither the civil nor religious authorities desired to stand between masters and their slaves. The owner could drive his slaves to death, satiate his sexual desires with the slave women, brand the men with hot irons for the slightest infractions, and tether them like animals and place iron leg cuffs on them if he so desired. Overseers exercised their unchecked dominion over the slaves as well. If work supervisors beat the men just for pleasure and defiled the women, they knew they would never be held accountable. On the other hand, some masters treated their slaves paternally, caring for the sick and nurturing an avuncular regard for the women and children. Yet in the end, the slaves were property. They had no control over the conduct of the owner.

Africans in Saint-Domingue, as elsewhere in the American slavocracies, did resist their treatment. On occasion, they rebelled against their overseers, assassinating supervisors and burning plantation houses. Three hundred slaves revolted and were suppressed on the north coast in 1700, and the slave François Macandal was burned at the stake in 1758 for having plotted another slave rebellion. Slaves were also known to take their own lives rather than endure the hardships as well as to intentionally deprive the master of his property. Slave women underwent primitive abortions so as not to bring up their children in slavery. It was said that trusted house servants developed the arts of administering poison to exact revenge on the families of slave owners.

Flight served as a common form of resistance. Individuals and groups escaped from the slave quarters and the fields. Deep in the rain forests of the rugged mountains, which the slaves called Haiti, they established settlements of runaway slaves. These maroons, as they were called, carried on trade, grew crops, raised families, and avoided the slave catchers. In the mountains, they developed skills of combat and provided a disruptive source of inspiration and communication to the slave houses back on the plantations.

MANUSCRIPT 13.1

The Religious and Cultural Refuge of Voodoo

Voodoo, or Vaudoux, the Arada people's worship of animistic deities and spirits, contributed a common cultural identity to blacks of several different origins in Saint-Domingue (later Haiti). The following document, written by Moreau de Saint-Méry, who had made his home in Le Cap François (now Cap Haïtien), describes some of the rituals as practiced among slaves and other people of color in the 1780s. Note the Frenchman's revulsion and fear of the cult, which were subsequently borne out by the leadership of Voodoo priests in the very first uprising of slaves following the political upheavals between whites and mulattoes. Although nominally Christian, the slaves practiced African religious rites, such as Voodoo, that they brought with them on the Middle Passage, the arduous voyage on the slave ships from Africa to the Americas. Preservation and observation of their ancient customs, albeit in hybrid form, preserved the separate identity of Africans and nurtured their desire for personal freedom from bondage.

The meeting for the true disciples of Voodoo, or at least the ones which have lost least of their primitive purity, is always secret. It is held in the dark of night and in a place closed and sheltered from all profane eyes.

Once at the rendezvous, each initiate puts on a pair of sandals and places around his body a more or less considerable number of red handkerchiefs or of handkerchiefs in which that color dominates. The Voodoo King has more beautiful handkerchiefs and a larger quantity of them; also he has something which is all red and which encircles his brow—his diadem. A cord, generally blue, helps to set off his flashy dignity. The Queen, clad in simple luxury, shows also her preference for the color red, most often in her ornamental cord or her waistband.

The King and Queen take their places at one end of the room. Nearby is a species of altar on which is a chest containing the snake, where every member can see it through the bars.

When they have ascertained that no one has entered the precincts out of curiosity, the ceremony is started. It begins with the worship of the adder, through protestations of loyalty to its cult and being submissive to its orders. Led by the King and Queen, each renews his oath of secrecy, which is the foundation of the whole thing. Then follow all the rites which anyone in his delirium can imagine, anything that is most horrible, to render the ceremony more impressive emotionally.

When the votaries of Voodoo are thus ready to receive what the King and Queen affect to share with them, the royal pair adopt the loving tone of a sensible mother and father. They boast of the good fortune which is the endowment of everyone who is devoted to the Voodoo god. They exhort their adherents to have confidence in him and give him proof of it, while taking his counsels as to the proper course in various circumstances.

Then the crowd scatters and each person, according to his need and according to his seniority as a member, goes to plead with the Voodoo. Most slaves ask for the ability to direct the thoughts of their masters. But this is not enough. One begs for money. Another seeks the gift of pleasing a girl who will pay no attention to him. This one wishes to call back an unfaithful mistress, that one asks to be made well or to have a longer life. After them, an old woman wants to implore God to stop the scorn of someone whose happy youth she would capture. A young girl asks for everlasting love—or repeats the wishes that hatred dictates to her as a preferred rival. It is not passion which proffers a wish, and crime itself cannot always disguise who the interested parties are.

For each of these invocations he receives, the Voodoo King meditates. The Spirit acts in him. Suddenly he takes the chest containing the adder, places it on the ground, and makes the Voodoo Queen stand on it. Once the sacred refuge is under her feet, [she] is possessed by God. She shakes, her whole body is convulsed, and the oracle speaks through her mouth. Sometimes she flatters and promises happiness, sometimes she thunders and utters reproaches. In keeping with her desires, her own interests, or her whims, she speaks as if she is the law and there is no appeal. She says whatever she likes, in the name of the adder, to that assembly of imbeciles, who never raise the slightest doubt over the most monstrous absurdity. They know nothing else but to obey her or the adder's despotic fiat.

This is the moment when one takes up his tribute, which each has tried to render especially worthy of him. It is put in a covered hat, so that no one may be made to blush by some other's jealous curiosity. The King and Queen promise to make them pleasing to him. It is by the profit from these offerings that the expenses of the meetings are covered, and that help is procured, both for those present and for those absent who have some need, or from whom the society expects some thing for its glory and its renown.

After that comes the dance of the Voodoo. . . . [T]he King puts his hand or his foot on the adder's cage and soon is possessed. He then transmits this mood to the Queen, who in turn passes it on to those in the circle. Each makes movements, in which the upper part of the body, the head and shoulders, seem to be dislocated. The Queen above all is the prey to the most violent agitations. From time to time she goes up to the Voodoo snake to seek some new magic and shakes the chest and the little bells with which it is adorned, making them ring out in a very climax of folly. But the delirium keeps rising. It is augmented still more by the use of intoxicating drinks, which in their frenzied state the participants do not spare and which help to sustain them. Faintings and raptures take over some of them and a sort of fury some of the others, but for all there is a nervous trembling which they cannot master. They spin around ceaselessly. And there are some in this species of bacchanal who tear their clothing and even bite their flesh. Others who are only deprived of their senses and have fallen in their tracks are taken, even while dancing, into the darkness of a neighboring room, where a disgusting prostitution exercises a most hideous empire. Finally, weariness brings an end to these afflicting scenes. This is not before a decision has been announced as to the time of the next meeting.

SOURCE: Médéric-Louis-Elie Moreau de Saint-Méry, *A Civilization That Perished: The Last Years of White Colonial Rule in Haiti,* trans. and ed. Ivor D. Spencer (1798; reprint, Lanham, Md.: University Press of America, 1985), 3–5.

Historians estimate that as many as one of five slaves successfully ran away. But the consequences of being caught were fearsome. Runaway slaves were beaten, branded, and mutilated. Therefore, the most common form of resistance of all was for slaves to develop a slow, deliberate pace of work, even malingering, while maintaining an outward show of exaggerated deference to the whites. They worked when the overseer was looking and stopped when he was not.

The Elites

Africans and native-born slaves outnumbered all others in Saint-Domingue by a wide margin. The original inhabitants, the Aruak, who knew the land as Ayti, had long ago succumbed to European diseases. By 1787, slaves amounted to 408,000 souls, and the *gens de couleur,* or mulattoes, numbered 20,000. The French and other European whites comprised some 24,000 people. As one might imagine, the control of such a mass of slaves by so narrow a group of privileged souls required an extraordinary concert of opinion. In fact, subjugating the slaves was the only policy shared by the 10 percent of the population that was not African.

Otherwise, dissension, competition, conflict, and differential privileges afflicted the idle elite. The *grands blancs,* the European-born Frenchmen, flaunted their superior privileges and wealth at every opportunity. They ridiculed the whites born in Saint-Domingue, even those few who were wealthy planters. They declined to gaze upon or to address the mulattoes. Such arrogance had economic and political underpinnings. French-born males monopolized most of the political positions within colonial government, and French merchants dominated the lucrative houses of trade because they had the connections back in Le Havre and in the slave factories along the coast of West Africa. Wealthy French politicians and merchants also bought the largest sugar plantations, worked by the largest slave gangs, and surrounded themselves with black servants. As one resident observed, "[T]he dignity of a rich man consisted in having four times as many domestics as he needed." Native-born whites, the *petites blancs,* had to settle for scraps of power and privilege, serving the French as local traders and merchants or lowly bureaucratic clerks. They felt the tinge of prejudice from the haughty French-born Europeans.

Like their Creole half brothers and sisters, free mulattoes enjoyed considerable social privilege. Many owned slaves and engaged in agricultural and commercial pursuits on a lesser scale, but they did not have political rights. Free people of color did not enjoy French citizenship, and neither could they hold any public office, however insignificant. Most professional occupations were closed to mulattoes. They served instead in auxiliary positions, permitting them to defend the multiracial hierarchy without hope of rising to the status of the whites. Mulatto men served in the constabulary and policed the cities. Dressed in military uniforms, they pursued runaway slaves, attempted to suppress the practice of Voodoo, and attacked the maroons in the mountains. "These coloreds," said one observer, "imitate the style of the whites and try to wipe out all memory of their original state." By 1789, the *gens de couleur* also made up 104 companies of militia, which supplemented some two thousand French troops. No matter how much they imitated the French manners of the whites or how much capital they might amass or how many slaves they might own, African features condemned mulattoes to an inferior civil status in Saint-Domingue.

The multiracial hierarchy also rendered impossible gender relationships based on equality between men and women. There were few stable relationships between mulatto men and women, for the latter often preferred to get ahead by establishing extramarital liaisons with white men. Most nights, one could see mulatto women promenading through the streets, dressed for their trysts and accompanied by one or more of their own slaves. French and Creole men perfected an exact science of calculating the ratio of European and African ancestry in the women. Sixteen different categories comprised the range of possible mixtures. French women, prized as wives for the purpose of establishing families and respectable social standing, lived idle lives. They were attended by black cooks, housekeepers, nannies, gardeners, and coachmen. Not as pampered, free mulatto women had greater freedom to move about but also served as targets of sexual conquest by white males. Black women were pursued by mulatto males. To make a franc, the white widow sent her winsome slave girls onto the streets at night. Sexual perversion and exploitation reigned in this society, so much so that stable family lives were impossible to maintain at the lower reaches of the social scale. By the same token, rigid family structure and absolute male authority obtained at the peak of the multiracial hierarchy, among the whites.

The *grands blancs,* the *petites blancs,* and the *gens de couleur* all observed the strict pretensions of their rank—for the practice of equality among these narrow elites would risk having to grant equality to the slaves. No non-African wanted that. But the fragile unity of these elite groups, shot through with tensions and fissures, was vulnerable to external shock.

REVOLT OF THE SLAVES

The French Revolution provided the shock for the elite in Saint-Domingue. As would become typical of all subsequent revolutions in Latin America, the disunited elites fell to quarreling, and this breach then allowed the aggrieved lower classes to erupt. Within days of the fall of the Bastille in Paris to the mobs in 1789, the French National Assembly met to adopt the Declaration of the Rights of Man and Citizen. The measure was intended to reduce the powers of the nobility and the royal family. The colonial delegation from Saint-Domingue understood immediately the danger of the declaration. That "men are born and remain free and equal in rights" was not a sentiment that served the social interests of elites in a slavocracy—although slavery itself was not outlawed. In Saint-Domingue, the *gens de couleur* immediately demanded equality to the whites. However, worried about the breakdown of order, the Creoles rebelled against the local French bureaucracy that seemed to be taking the side of the mulattoes. The *grands blancs* saw their safety in supporting the French state, even though it was then in the hands of Liberals. The ideas of the French Revolution soon began to filter down. The house slaves in the city overheard their masters talking of the Rights of Man and of French citizenship. These concepts were then communicated to their brothers and sisters on the plantations. If the competitive Europeans, Creoles, and mulattoes fell to fighting one another, the slaves surely would join the fray. The *gens de couleur* broke ranks first.

In 1790, the authorities discovered a mulatto conspiracy to rebel against colonial authorities who had hesitated to give them French citizenship. The leaders were publicly tortured and executed. Then the Creoles became alarmed about the French Assembly's 1791 enfranchisement of the mulattoes and resisted the arrival of government troops dispatched from France. Revolutionary turmoil thoroughly divided the French, Creoles, and mulattoes. In August, the inevitable occurred. Thousands of slaves revolted in the north under the leadership of a Voodoo priest. They seized the plantations, put the owners and slave drivers to death, and burned the milling equipment. Forty thousand slaves descended on Le Cap François and laid siege to 10,000 whites. In the south and west, free mulattoes rebelled and attacked the city of Port-au-Prince, but they stopped momentarily to help the whites suppress slave rebellions in the region.

There followed 10 long years of fighting and confusion in which all the social groups found themselves in alliance with or conflict against the others. Rebellious ex-slaves roamed the backlands, while the whites and their reinforcements from France held the larger cities on the coast. Nevertheless, Le Cap François was sacked in 1793 and Port-au-Prince, on several occasions. The warfare destroyed the power of the white planters, for black troops in particular seldom failed to burn cane fields and destroy sugar mills—the productive symbols of their servitude. Those who escaped the wrath of the mulattoes and blacks emigrated to the other Caribbean islands. Rivalries between rebel chieftains thereafter set the former slaves to fighting each other.

Eventually, a coterie of able black military leaders began to consolidate military power. François-Dominique Toussaint, or as he was known later in life, Toussaint-Louverture, became the acknowledged leader of the insurgents in the north. He had been born into slavery in Saint-Domingue and grew up with knowledge of the French language and the Catholic religion. Toussaint's master had freed him, and he subsequently remained on the plantation as a slave steward, invaluable in running the estate because he had learned to read and write in French. As the supreme military leader of the black, ex-slave faction among the rebels, he was supported by able lieutenants, Jean-Jacques Dessalines, Moyse, and Henri Christophe. These leaders had come from the privileged group of slave supervisors, except for Dessalines, who had been a field hand. Meanwhile, governments in France, which were going through their own revolutionary turmoil, responded with abrupt policy changes that alienated everyone in the colony.

The revolution also incurred foreign intervention, which was to be another prominent feature of revolution in the Americas. Although the newly independent United States chose to trade with the insurgents (although it did not condone slave rebellions), the British and the Spanish sought to prevent the contagion from reaching their Caribbean colonies, sending troops to intervene either on the side of the white landowners or on the side of the various rebel factions. Toussaint's greatest military achievements came in defeating the British troops. Yet the Spanish side of Hispaniola threatened the Haitian Revolution, for Spanish expeditions periodically crossed into Haiti to capture newly freed slaves and return them to the brisk Caribbean slave trade. At one point, Toussaint felt compelled to invade the neighboring Spanish colony of Santo Domingo, which he held from 1801 to 1804. In all cases, European troops suffered more from yellow fever and malaria than from the blows of the insurgents. Britain and Spain withdrew, and the forces of the ex-slave Toussaint and the mulattoes under General André Rigaud then commenced a savage civil war. Suspected conspirators suffered summary execution, as did troops captured in battle. Five hundred *gens de couleur* were slaughtered after Toussaint took one coastal town. By 1800, the mulatto resistance was crushed.

At no point did the insurgents under Toussaint press for political independence. Instead, they gained a French promise not to resurrect slavery. Toussaint desired appointment as governor of the French colony. Where his forces controlled the countryside, he attempted to reestablish the plantation system (see Manuscript 13.2). His generals became the new owners. However, the ex-slaves, now free laborers, proved no more willing to cut cane for black generals than they had been for white overseers. Instead of slavery, they were to work under stringent three-year contracts that required them to obtain the planters' permission to leave the estates. Toussaint invited back some of the white planters, rented out other plantations to newcomers, but forbade the use of the whip. He believed in social control and even promoted monogamous marriages. Vagabonds and criminals were assigned to work gangs or military service. There was no breakup of the large estates, and the former slaves did not become the new class of smallholders. Nearly two-thirds of the land in Saint-Domingue reverted to state control. In effect, it meant that Toussaint and his lieutenants became exceedingly wealthy. He even attempted—unsuccessfully—to suppress the cult of Voodoo. The black leader

MANUSCRIPT 13.2

Toussaint Decrees the Reestablishment of the Plantation System

In the first chaotic and destructive years of the revolution, Saint-Domingue would become subject to outside intervention from former slave owners in exile and from French, British, and Spanish armies. The black general Toussaint-Louverture gradually established military control over the French- and Creole-speaking side of the island and attempted to use his army to consolidate control of the colony. His remedy consisted of reestablishing the plantation export economy—even though the former slaves had successfully and finally destroyed the old plantation labor system. Unable to return his followers to slavery, in this decree of 1800 he sought instead to militarize society and to raise the welfare of the state above that of the former slaves. Thus began Toussaint's estrangement from his followers, who preferred lives of independence, subsistence farming, and free wage labor. Note Toussaint's own acknowledgment of the predilections and desires of the black majority.

Whereas, since the revolution, labourers of both sexes, then too young to be employed in the field, refuse to go to it now under pretext of freedom, spend their time in wandering about, and give a bad example to the other cultivators; while, on the other hand, the generals, officers, subalterns, and soldiers, are in a state of constant activity to maintain the sacred rights of the people. . . .

I do most peremptorily order as follows:

Art. 1. All overseers, drivers, and field-negroes are bound to observe, with exactness, submission, and obedience, their duty in the same manner as soldiers.

Art. 2. All overseers, drivers, and field-labourers, who will not perform with assiduity the duties required of them, shall be arrested and punished as severely as soldiers deviating from their duty. After which punishment, if the offender be an overseer, he shall be enlisted in one of the regiments of the army in St. Domingo. If a driver, he shall be without ever being permitted to act as a driver again. And, if a common-labourer, he shall be punished with the same severity as a private soldier, according to his guilt.

Art. 3. All field-labourers, men and women, now in a state of idleness, living in towns, villages, and on other plantations than those to which they belong, with an intention to evade work, even those of both sexes who have not been employed in field labour since the revolution, are required to return immediately to their respective plantations, if, in the course of eight days from the promulgation of this present regulation, they shall not produce sufficient proof to the commanding officers in the place of their residence of their having some useful occupations or means of livelihood; but it is to be understood that being a servant is not to be considered a useful occupation; in consequence whereof, those amongst the laborers who have quitted their plantations in order to hire themselves, shall return thereto, under the personal responsibility of those with whom they live in that capacity. By the term "an [sic] useful occupation" is meant, what enables a man to pay a contribution to the State.

Art. 4. This measure, indispensable to the public welfare, positively prescribes to all those of either sex that are not labourers to produce the proofs of their having an occupation or profession sufficient to gain their livelihood, and that they can afford to pay a contribution to the Republic. Otherwise, and in default thereof, all those who shall be found in contravention hereto, shall be instantly arrested, and if they are found guilty they shall be drafted into one of the regiments of the army, if not, they shall be sent to the field and compelled to work. This measure, which is to be strictly enforced, will put a stop to the idle habit of wandering about, since it will oblige everyone to be usefully employed.

SOURCE: From *Supplement to the Royal Gazette* (Jamaica), 22, no. 47 (November 15 – 22, 1800); 9 – 10, as reproduced in George F. Tyson Jr., ed., *Toussaint Louverture* (Englewood Cliffs, N.J.: Prentice-Hall, 1973), 53 – 54.

himself took on increasingly Frenchified habits, such as practicing the Catholic faith and keeping three white mistresses.

In 1802, a new French invasion force of 12,000 men came to put an end to black power in Saint-Domingue. Napoleon Bonaparte had consolidated political control in France and decided to resurrect the French colonies in the Caribbean and Louisiana. Toussaint, Christophe, and Dessalines submitted to the French forces and even helped suppress other Haitian chieftains, such as Moyse, who had promised land to the blacks and warned of the reestablishment of slavery. Toussaint himself then went into retirement on his numerous estates. But the French seized him and sent him back to France in chains, where he died in a French prison in 1803.

The martyr's death inspired many insurgents to take up arms against the French once again. The ex-slaves carried on with resistance and guerrilla insurrections until their leaders came to resist, too. At first, Jean-Jacques Dessalines collaborated with the French authorities to brutally suppress the rebels until the former became weakened by malaria and yellow fever. As one soldier said, "This is the graveyard of the French; here one dies

General Dessalines hanging white captives following the French slaughter of Haitians, 1803. (Marcus Rainsford, 1805)

off like flies." Casualties were high on both sides, because none of the combatants took prisoners of war. They usually slashed to pieces all the captured troops with machetes. Finally, Dessalines rallied his troops to join the insurgents and assumed command of all the anti-French forces.

They now fought for independence of their country, no longer to be known as Saint-Domingue but rather as Haiti. Independence was the only guarantee that slavery would be ended once and for all. French atrocities—in one instance, the use of killer dogs imported from Cuba—against both the mulattoes and blacks provoked a final insurgent onslaught. The plantations were destroyed yet again, and hundreds of whites met the same fate as had thousands of people of color. When the defeated French troops finally evacuated, Dessalines and his generals met on January 1, 1804, to proclaim Haiti the second independent republic in the Americas. The first, which had gained its independence in a very different revolution, had been the United States.

Within nine months, Dessalines consolidated his power. He slaughtered hundreds of whites who did not have the good sense to leave Haiti and crowned himself Emperor Jacques I. Without a white upper class, the surviving mulattoes constituted a socioeconomic elite, although they had to share power thereafter with black generals. The assassination of Dessalines in 1806 threw the politically autocratic young nation into turmoil once

Map 13.1   Slave Rebellions in the Caribbean, 1791–1823

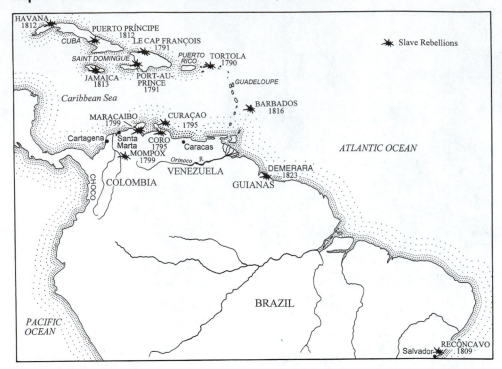

again. But now, no foreign nation bothered to reestablish control of the former colony. Its plantations lay in ruins, the workers divided the plantation cane fields into subsistence plots, sugar production declined, and meager coffee exports did not provide enough revenues to attract other European colonizers. Saint-Domingue had produced the only slave revolt that had succeeded in overturning the institution of slavery, destroying the ruling class, and gaining political autonomy for the those formerly held in bondage, but its aftermath was domestic chaos and economic decline. However, the African slaves of Saint-Domingue had fought to destroy the plantations that enslaved them and to establish their own independence in subsistence agriculture. To the extent that they had succeeded in these two goals, they considered their revolution to have been a remarkable triumph.

EPILOGUE

The repercussions of the Haitian slave revolt reverberated everywhere in Latin America, sending shudders through the ranks of the privileged but most particularly terrifying those in slaveholding areas. Each of the regions had, of course, experienced its own slave revolts. Most of these were isolated affairs in which the slaves rose up and killed the overseer or the master and his family before running off. But the very idea of a coordinated, generalized rebellion of slaves raised fears in Cuba, Puerto Rico, Venezuela, and Brazil (see Map 13.1). In fact, the economic booms of the late eighteenth century and the record numbers of slaves being imported into these plantation societies had raised the number of such rebellions. And after the Haitian Revolution had begun, slaves elsewhere now had a precedent to emulate.

Venezuela was particularly vulnerable to such resistance from the slaves. Some Haitian slave owners and mulattoes—even former slaves—had taken refuge in Venezuela, spreading word of the revolt. The Venezuelan slaveholders were particularly concerned about the spread of the ideas of the French Revolution, such as "liberty" and "fraternity." The province of Caracas alone had more than one hundred thousand slaves at the time. However, Coro became the scene of rebellion. Two free blacks, José Caridad González and José Leonardo Chirino, led the 300 blacks and *pardos* (people of color or mulattoes) of this sugar-producing region in an uprising in 1795. They proclaimed freedom for the slaves, an end to the sales tax, and the establishment of a republic under the laws of France; they then seized haciendas, put the owners to death, and invaded the city of Coro. But the response was swift and savage. Roving bands of whites hunted down blacks, killing them without trial. The rebellion did not spread, but Haiti would yet engender further trouble. In 1799, a Haitian expedition arrived to assist a small rebellion of blacks in the western Venezuelan city of Maracaibo. There more than two hundred *pardos* from the local militia had set out to kill whites, create yet another republic, and establish a system of liberty and equality. It, too, was quashed, but the frequency of these rebellions from below reminded the whites in Latin America that their privileges might be in danger.

The restiveness of the slaves spread, or more precisely, was duplicated in Colombia as well. In the slave regions of the gold-bearing Chocó on the Pacific Coast and in Cartagena and Santa Marta on the Caribbean coast, slave rebellion was endemic from 1750 to 1790. Runaway slaves established armed communities, the famous *palenques,* that spread terror among the colonists and fomented additional trouble among the slave houses. In 1799, the slaves rose to take control of the plantation on which they had been working at Mompox. They vowed that "they were ready to die rather than serve any white or submit to any white in that hacienda . . . and their machetes are always at the ready." Though the Mompox slave rebellion was repressed ruthlessly, the plantation owners and even free people of color feared the prospects of widespread unrest among the slave population.

The stakes also were higher in Brazil, where record imports of slaves in the second half of the eighteenth century had infused the society with large numbers of ethnic Africans. The planters there had always feared the collaboration of free people of color and slaves, but this never happened either prior to or during the eighteenth century. In fact, the presence of a large number of free blacks and mulattoes in Brazil had engendered among them a separate social interest that sought to repress rather than join slave restiveness. Free-born Brazilians of color did not at all identify with their African origins and cultures. Prior to the late eighteenth century, slave runaways had been more prominent than rebellions. But the sugar industry revived in northeast Brazil when the Haitian revolution destroyed competing French sugar plantations in the Caribbean. Brazilian planters expanded cane production, imported more Africans, reduced acreage in food crops, intensified the labor demands on slaves, and increased the brutal disciplinary measures. Sex ratios again became skewed in the black population, as young males predominated among the growing number of African-born workers. Some plantation zones of northeastern Brazil now contained more Africans than non-Africans in the population. The growing wealth of the planter class came at the expense of expanding the misery and desperation among the slaves.

African ethnicity appeared the crucial ingredient to the beginning of organized slave resistance in Brazil. In 1789, the entire body of slaves at the Engenho Santana in Bahia rose up and took flight. As a condition of their return, the Santana fugitives proposed to negotiate with the owner, demanding a change of overseers, more opportunities to market their own produce, and Saturdays and Sundays off to cultivate their own plots. "We shall be able to play, relax and sing any time we want without your hindrance," they demanded. The owner of the Engenho Santana pretended to accept these conditions but then arrested and sold off the leaders of his rebellious slaves. Nonetheless, resistance activities such as slave flight increased throughout the plantation districts, to which the colonial government responded with military expeditions. Runaways from the *quilombos* attacked plantations and stole property. In 1807, authorities uncovered a number of conspiracies by African slaves to rise up and even to poison the drinking water in Bahia. Two conspirators were executed and 11 others were flogged. The population of fugitive slaves continued to grow, heightening the fears of the white population, which responded by outlawing the dances and social gatherings of both free blacks and slaves. At Christmas 1808, 600 ethnic Africans rose up and attacked one of the outlying towns in the southern Recôncavo. A military expedition captured only 95 of the rebels, the rest having fled into the backlands. The slave war of Bahia continued into the next decade, as plantation revolts, formation of *quilombos,* and slave conspiracies kept the planters fearful and the authorities vigilant.

Slave revolts also broke out in Cuba, whose slave population had tripled to more than two hundred thousand slaves during its late-eighteenth-century sugar boom. On one of the newly opened plantations in the center of the island, a group of slaves rose up in January 1812 and succeeded in killing five whites before they were subdued. Several slaves escaped into the mountains, but the authorities executed 10 rebels and sent 63 prisoners to the penal colony at Saint Augustine, Florida. Several months later, a second uprising took place outside of Havana. The militia quickly restored order, but the fearful white residents insisted on a thorough search for slave and free black troublemakers.

The backlash proved more virulent than the original threat because the mere rumor of slave rebellion reminded Cuban whites of the Haitian Revolution. Militia troops rounded up refugees from Haiti, and port officials scrutinized incoming ships in order to prevent "French" ideas from spreading sedition in Cuba. In searching for conspiracies and Haitian influences, white plantation owners and public officials rejected the notion that the institution of slavery itself might incite rebellion. They apprehended several free artisans of color and searched their homes and workshops. When they found drawings of Haitian generals like Toussaint-Louverture as well as copies of the new Spanish slave code, which ostensibly proffered slaves some basic protections, officials announced they had suppressed the Aponte conspiracy, named for its alleged leader. Indeed, the free black artist José Antonio Aponte and his friends admitted to admiring the Haitian revolutionaries; they were executed.

The second largest slave rebellion in the Americas (after that of Haiti) took place in the British possession of Guyana. At the time, the colony had a population of 2,500 whites, 2,500 free blacks, and 77,000 slaves. At least 10,000 of those slaves rose up on some sixty sugar plantations along the coast near the mouth of the Demerara River. By the time that the British-owned slaves revolted, they had already developed an intelligence network that informed them of the European reformist movement clamoring for an end to the slave trade. They knew of the "glorious" Haitian revolution and seized upon the division of opinion between British plantation owners and the reformist clergy sent to Guyana to spread Christianity. The rebel slaves actually protected white owners and their families from harm, although some whites ended up in the leg irons and stocks intended for Africans. Slaves repeatedly demanded their rights, that is, the freedom they thought the English king had declared for them. Nonetheless, official retribution was brutal. As white-led colonial militias took back the plantations, they butchered the rebels, decapitated the leaders, and displayed their heads on pikes. One Anglican missionary was tried and executed for his role in the rebellion.

CONCLUDING REMARKS

Fear of slave resistance was a matter of great concern and raised questions among the colonists about whether the imperial political order had lost its ability to control the subordinate classes. Those few whites with wealth and power felt threatened by the demand of the nonwhite majority for rights. In other words, the rebelliousness among the slaves and Native Americans in the eighteenth century served as one of the wedges breaking up the consensus of opinion between Iberian- and American-born whites. The colonial elite responded in fear every time Crown officials back in Europe even debated colonial policy on slavery and indigenous labor. It had been precisely to control the colonial masses and also to put the colonial elites in their place that the imperial powers, Spain and Portugal, had undertaken extensive administrative reforms. The brutality with which the white minority reacted to even a rumor of slave resistance highlights how colonialism militated against the development of civility. The most privileged became the most violent.

Additional Reading

Bell, Madison Smartt. *All Souls Rising.* New York: Pantheon Books, 1985.

Blackburn, Robin. *The Overthrow of Colonial Slavery, 1776–1848.* London: Verso, 1988.

da Costa, Emilia Viotti. *Crowns of Glory, Tears of Blood: The Demerara Slave Rebellion of 1823.* New York: Oxford University Press, 1994.

Fick, Carolyn E. *The Making of Haiti: The Saint Domingue Revolution from Below.* Knoxville: University of Tennessee Press, 1990.

Fouchard, Jean. *The Haitian Maroons: Liberty or Death.* Trans. A. Faulkner Watt. New York: Edward W. Blyden Press, 1981.

Gaspar, David Barry, and David Patrick Geggus, eds. *A Turbulent Time: The French Revolution and the Greater Caribbean.* Bloomington: Indiana University Press, 1997.

Geggus, David Patrick. *Slavery, War, and Revolution: The British Occupation of Saint Domingue, 1793–1798.* Oxford, England: Clarendon Press, 1982.

Genovese, Eugene. *From Rebellion to Revolution: Afro-American Slave Revolts in the Modern World.* Baton Rouge: Louisiana State University Press, 1979.

James, C. L. R. *The Black Jacobins: Toussaint L'Ouverture and the San Domingo Revolution.* 2d ed. New York: Vantage Books, 1963.

Ott, Thomas O. *The Haitian Revolution, 1798–1804.* Knoxville: University of Tennessee Press, 1973.

Ros, Martin. *Night of Fire: The Black Napoleon and the Battle for Haiti.* Trans. Karin Ford-Treep. New York: Sarpedon, 1994.

Stein, Robert L. *The French Slave Trade in the Eighteenth Century: An Old Regime Business.* Madison: University of Wisconsin Press, 1979.

————. *Léger Félicité Sonthonax: The Lost Sentinel of the Republic.* Rutherford, N.J.: Fairleigh Dickinson University Press, 1985.

Stinchcombe, Arthur L. *Sugar Island Slavery in the Age of Enlightenment: The Political Economy of the Caribbean World.* Princeton, N.J.: Princeton University Press, 1995.

In French and Spanish

Brito Figueroa, Federico. *Las insurreciones de los esclavos negros en la sociedad colonial venezolana.* Caracas: Editorial Contaclaro, 1961.

Brutus, Edner. *Revolution dans Saint-Domingue.* 2 vols. Paris: Editions du Pantheon, 1973.

Cordero Michel, Emilio. *La revolución haitiana y Santo Domingo.* Santo Domingo: Editorial Nacional, 1968.

Cordova-Bello, Eleazar. *La independencia de Haiti y su influencia en Hispanoamérica.* Caracas: Instituto Panamericano de Geografía e Historia, 1967.

Di Tella, Torcuato S. *La rebelión de esclavos de Haiti.* Buenos Aires: IDES, 1984.

Duharte Jiménez, Rafael. *Rebeldía esclava en el Caribe.* Xalapa, Veracruz, Mexico: Comisión Estatal Conmemorativa, 1992.

Laurent-Ropa, Denis. *Haiti, une colonie francaise, 1625–1802.* Paris: L'Harmattan, 1993.

Pluchon, Pierre. *Toussaint Louverture, de l'esclavage au pouvoir.* Paris: Ecole, 1979.

PART IV

PART IV

THE AGE OF REFORM AND INDEPENDENCE

By the beginning of the eighteenth century, colonial administrators and settler elites had become aware that growth of the economies and societies of the American colonies was accentuating the contradictions inherent in colonialism. The Hapsburg and Bragança kings had governed the colonies in a loose and inefficient political system that promoted patronage, unclear lines of authority, corruption, tax evasion, and flouting of the law but also allowed for considerable administrative laxity and independence among those who were governed. However, a new royal family, the Bourbon cousins of Louis XIV of France, assumed the throne of Spain in 1701. Under Bourbon rule, Spain began a long process of tightening imperial control of its American colonies. New viceroyalties were created, additional political offices were established, and loopholes were closed off to Creole office seekers. Most of all, the colonial state refurbished the system for collecting taxes. The House of Bragança in Portugal undertook similar administrative reforms.

These changes came none too soon, for the dangers they were designed to combat grew appreciably in the eighteenth century. In the first place, Spain and Portugal had been declining economically and militarily in Europe, and the commercial and industrial revolutions were benefiting their national enemies, Britain, the Netherlands, and France. These northern European countries became increasingly aggressive in trading throughout colonial Latin America and in encroaching militarily in the hemisphere, so much so that the outbreak of

hostilities in Europe had its military repercussions in the colonies. Therefore, the rising tax collections, creation of colonial militias, and economic reforms of the Bourbons and Bragança were designed to defend the realm.

A second, but not less significant, reason to strengthen imperial controls had to do with social unrest. The economic boom and increased taxation opened old wounds of those classes of persons intended to do the work in the colonies, namely Native Americans and Africans. As the economy expanded in the eighteenth century, so did the demand for labor. Institutions of labor coercion such as slavery and the mita found new life, increasing the pressure on African slaves and indigenous peasants. Moreover, a robust new class of rural and urban proletarians was forming that

challenged the old control mechanisms intended to keep subordinate peoples in their places. Higher taxation and military recruitment exacerbated the burden of the natives and free persons of color, to whom the employers and shopkeepers passed on the higher taxes. Resentments among the popular classes increased to the point of explosion, as evinced by the great Andean rebellions and numerous slave revolts of the period.

The Creoles and mestizos also grew restive, challenging European officials over rising taxes and what seemed an assault on local autonomy. Even the growing economy conspired against royal authorities. Local production and consumption, particularly of agricultural productions, grew, and colonial Latin America became more tightly integrated with northern Europe. Contraband trade continued apace, and even Iberia's commercial revival merely reinforced its status as a way station in the trade between its colonies and France and England. Such a contradictory situation made Spain and Portugal's colonies vulnerable to disruption of monumental proportions. Extended wars in Europe, coming at a time of social upheaval in the Americas, wreaked economic havoc at the end of the eighteenth century. This combination of affairs called Iberia's political suzerainty into question and, in the second decade of the nineteenth century, led to open rebellion in many important colonies.

The conflicts took on the character of civil wars, pitting some colonial subjects fighting to preserve European political control against other colonials seeking independence from Iberia. Because the rebellions took on an increasingly social content, mobilizing much of the mixed-race working classes, the Creole political leadership eventually had to compromise. By 1826, most of the Spanish Americas had won independence because the Creole leaders acted to assuage the restive lower orders with token reforms while preserving as many of the whites' privileges as possible. Colonial elites in the plantation slave societies of Brazil and Cuba, however, preferred not to dabble in political experiments. They feared provoking a second great slave revolt in the Americas. The old political order may have faltered in Latin America, but vestiges of the colonial social order remained—even if in a somewhat altered state.

CHAPTER 14

THE FAILURE TO AVERT THE COLONIAL CRISIS

By the eighteenth century, several conclusions were becoming painfully clear to the imperial powers of Iberia. Policymakers in both Spain and Portugal realized that the colonies had become more developed economically than the mother countries themselves. It is estimated that in 1800, Spain had a population of ten and a half million while its American possessions had a population of fourteen and a half million. Portugal was even more underdeveloped. It had few goods to trade with its colonies, only olive oil and wine; moreover, despite its far-flung empire stretching from Brazil through Angola and Mozambique in Africa to Goa, Macao, and the Moluccas in Asia, Portugal was militarily vulnerable. This small imperial country depended on its alliance with Great Britain and the British navy to guarantee its existence.

The Iberian imperial powers also knew that mercantilism was becoming increasingly ineffective in view of the widespread tax evasion and contraband trade in its American colonies. In the meantime, trade was increasing between the Indies and Europe, to be sure, but Spain and Portugal were not benefiting. The commercial revolution of northern Europe and the industrial revolution of England stimulated commerce to Latin America as the century progressed. This meant that Portugal and Spain were providing fewer and fewer items of export and receiving less of the colonial produce. Official American trade did pass through the ports of Cádiz and Lisbon, yet now most of this commerce passed directly on to Portsmouth, London, and other ports of the North Atlantic. Contraband trade, which was increasing, passed directly to northern Europe and neither contributed to Iberian economies nor benefited royal coffers. Moreover, two centuries of social development in the Americas had sustained a vibrant—if inequitable—society in the colonies that grew increasingly more independent and restive.

Internationally, Spain and Portugal felt increasingly vulnerable. The time had long passed when Spanish armies inspired respect and fear in Europe. Spain and Portugal's early lead in overseas colonization had ended as France and Britain, in the eighteenth century, were expanding their colonial dominions in Asia, Africa, and the Americas. Increasingly, Iberia's rich American colonies seemed threatened. Control over the colonial subjects appeared less complete and, to Spain and Portugal, the frequent acts of rebellion and social unrest seemed to invite outside intervention. What if their own colonists were foolishly to renounce their allegiance to Spain and Portugal? Something had to be done to save the colonial empire.

The Iberian powers decided to strengthen their empires through a series of administrative and economic reforms. In Spanish America, these became known as the Bourbon Reforms, after Spain's new royal family, which had gained the crown in 1701 during a dynastic struggle known as the War of the Spanish Succession. Louis XIV of France ultimately settled that conflict by installing a member of his royal household on the Spanish throne. In Portugal, the reforms became associated with the Marquês de Pombal, chief adviser to the Bragança royal family from 1750 to 1777. However, one should consider the entire eighteenth century as having been a time of gradual and piecemeal imperial reform. All ministers of the royal family and most of their colonial officials became imbued with new visions of power and were cognizant of the need to strengthen Iberian suzerainty in the Indies.

The basic long-term objectives of these reforms can be summarized under several headings. First of all, the Bourbons and Braganças sought to strengthen the administration of their colonial possessions. Then they sought to recapture control over trade and commerce. Part of these economic and administrative reforms involved rationalizing the collection of taxes and closing tax loopholes. Moreover, the Crowns desired that their American subjects participate more in the defense of the empire through territorial expansion into the frontiers and also by serving in colonial militias. Finally, the reforms struck at the autonomy of colonial society. Plans were devised to curb the power of local elites and manage more effectively the volatile social resentments that might ruin the entire colonial enterprise. Because so many Iberian soldiers and officials were dispatched to reinforce royal authority, the Bourbon and Pombaline Reforms have been termed "the Reconquest of the Americas."

Taking these reforms as a whole, one cannot escape the conclusion that they succeeded so well in the Americas that they ultimately undermined, rather than strengthened, Iberian imperialism. The Pombaline and Bourbon Reforms gave focus to resentments at all levels of society. They provided the spark for several rebellions, as we have seen. But most of all, they fastened the colonies so securely to their mother countries that the Americas became unwittingly involved in several European wars that eventually provoked what the reforms were intended to avoid: social unrest, rebellion, and movements for political independence and social change.

IMPERIAL REFORM

The new imperial administrative policies were intended to alter the relations between the major power groups in the colonies, and in this they did succeed. The goal was to enhance state power vis-à-vis the church, give Europeans additional leverage over the colonial elite, and restructure governance of the Indies in a way that increased tax collections. Their success could naught but alienate the local elites, who attempted to resist many reform measures handed down from Spain and Portugal. We shall consider these new policies according to their category, but the actual process of reform proceeded chronologically, in piecemeal fashion, and not a little contradictorily.

The Bourbon Reforms

In terms of colonial administration, the changes were far-reaching. The imperial system under the Hapsburg monarchy was a loose, permissive structure that tied together sectors of the colony through loyalty to the Crown and religion. The Bourbon monarchs breathed new life into colonial administration and scrapped the old setup that divided all Spanish America between the viceroyalties of New Spain and Peru. Many new administrative entities were carved out, particularly in South America (see Map 14.1). The Viceroyalty of New Granada, with its capital at Bogotá, was established in 1739, with authority over Ecuador and Venezuela as well as Colombia. Venezuela and Chile became separate captaincies-general. Peru lost more territory and influence in 1776, when Spaniards founded a third viceroyalty in South America with its capital at Buenos Aires. This administrative change seemed to confirm the logic of contraband, for Buenos Aires got all the hinterland with which it had been trading—illegally for the most part—for more than a century. Thus, Argentina, Uruguay, Paraguay, and Upper Peru (Bolivia) all became part of the Viceroyalty of the Río de la Plata, a momentous administrative change that removed the silver mines of Potosí and Oruro from the control of Lima.

Additional changes were made in the *audiencias,* the judicial tribunals of Spanish America. Their number was expanded, and their judges were Europeanized. Through purchase of office, many Creoles with connections to economically and politically powerful local families had obtained positions on the *audiencias.* Often wealthy Creoles purchased their posts through the Hapsburg habit of filling the royal treasury through sales of public offices. They formed the majority of members of *audiencias* in Mexico City, Lima, and Santiago de Chile. Of the 93 *oidores* throughout the Spanish Americas in 1750, 51 were Creole. The Spanish official José de Gálvez became an outspoken enemy of Creole privilege in the Americas, and he was instrumental in ending the practice of the sale of *audiencia* offices. Now the judges were appointed, mostly from Spain, and paid well enough, it was thought, to avoid establishing economic ties with Creole landowners. When new *audiencias* were established at Caracas, Buenos Aires, and Cuzco, Gálvez selected only two Creoles among the 34 appointments of judges to the expanded posts in 1785. By the end of the eighteenth century, Creoles held less than one-quarter of the posts on these important tribunals, and most of them had to leave their places of birth to accept posts in other colonies.

Following the Andean rebellions, the Bourbons finally got around to getting rid of the corrupt *corregidores,* although official corruption itself remained. These district officials

Map 14.1   Colonial Administrative Reforms, ca. 1790

Spanish Audiencias

were replaced with intendants whose authority extended into the rural village through subordinates called subdelegates. To prevent the temptation toward corruption, the new public officials received higher salaries. Moreover, the forced draft system that public officials had so often abused, the *repartimiento,* was also scheduled for elimination, giving Native Americans the right to trade and work independently. A 1747 law stipulated that the natives were to pay all tribute in cash, attempting to get all of them into the money economy. This reform, once again, merely acknowledged what was already becoming a fact. The labor system of the colonies was shifting toward free wage labor, and forced labor drafts were no longer particularly effective or necessary, as explained in Chapter 11.

The Bourbons tried to end *repartimiento* everywhere, but white colonists resisted. Local officials still depended on the *repartimiento* to finance themselves in the interior, and indigo farmers of Salvador relied upon these labor drafts as did Honduran mine operators. In addition, although Native Americans attracted by high wages were entering labor markets, not all employers in Central America wished to pay what the free workers demanded. Some still lamented the "good old days." Rather than acknowledging their own ineptitude, the bosses blamed the lack of productivity on the scarcity of workers in this new labor system dominated by a free-floating population of mixed-race persons. "I understand that many [Ladinos] go begging in the haciendas and *trapiches,* many hide in the mountains. Others go to the [land of the] Lacandones." said the governor of Honduras, who wanted nonnative workers to give their labor to the mines of his province. "It is impossible to know how many people live in the haciendas. . . . Today they are here and tomorrow, elsewhere."[1] Though labor drafts were becoming a thing of the past, they remained in the minds of the native-born elite as a solution to the shortage of workers.

Defense of the empire remained a prime concern of the Iberian powers, and they intended both to bolster colonial military forces as well as to shift the expense for defense onto the colonies. Starting in 1760, new militias were created all over the Indies, manned and paid for by the Americans themselves (see Table 14.1). Ostensibly, the Crown encouraged the creation of colonial militias to protect the colonies from foreign aggressors. But the military forces in Peru began to be used increasingly for internal security. Following the Andean rebellions, more and more militia units were moved to the interior provinces.

Military service was not altogether attractive, especially for the lower-ranking personnel. Therefore, to enlarge the military forces, the *fuero militar* was extended to mulattoes and mestizos throughout the Indies, meaning that the privilege of immunity from civil courts, which had been reserved only for Spanish soldiers, was now extended to their colonial counterparts, even those of mixed race. Ordinary citizens who brought suit against members of the militias now had to do so in military courts. The Creole elites were not pleased, for they resented the *castas* having received identical privileges to theirs. As well, Creole militia officers, who often joined the officer corps for the titles and privileges of military duty, could not rise to the top military ranks; Spaniards reserved the ranks of colonel and general only for themselves. The military reforms of the Bourbons thus appeared to be yet another incident in a long succession of attacks on Creole privilege. Later on, when the empire came into crisis, these Creole officers would take matters into their own hands.

---

[1]*Trapiches* were small shops, especially for the making of textiles, and the "[land of the] Lacandones" probably refers to the highlands of Chiapas.

Table 14.1   **Estimated Number of Troops Stationed in Spanish America, 1771 and 1799**

Location	1771	1799
Cuba	4,851	
Puerto Rico	2,884	
Buenos Aires	4,628	
New Spain		9,971
Peru		1,985
Chile		1,249
Cartagena		2,759

SOURCE: D. A. Brading, "Bourbon Spain and its American Empire," in Leslie Bethell, ed., *Colonial Spanish America* (Cambridge, England: Cambridge University Press, 1987), 123.

Free Trade

Commercial relations simply had to change because Spain's mindless trade sanctions could not accommodate the economic expansion of the eighteenth century. The fleet system was in a shambles, so the trade ministry loosened its grip in the 1740s and allowed single ships to trade in the Americas. The more flexible shipping arrangements, an end to many trade restrictions, and lower tariffs in Latin America permitted Spain to respond to British commercial pressure. Many of these trade reforms, like many other changes, were instituted during the long reign of Carlos III (1859–88). He appointed an especially energetic minister, José de Gálvez, who had long experience in Mexico, Peru, and New Granada (Colombia) before returning to take charge of the king's administration of the colonies.

What the Spanish reformers called "free trade" finally arrived in 1778 following their abolition of the Cádiz port monopoly. Henceforward, merchants and shippers could use 10 ports in Spain and trade directly with Buenos Aires, Valparaíso, Callao, Guayaquil, Cartagena, La Guaira, Veracruz, and Havana, all the major ports in Spanish America. At long last, the official requirement that all trade in Chile and the Río de la Plata had to pass through Lima—which had not been observed for at least a century—came to an end. Taxes on silver production were also reduced from 20 percent to 10 percent, and other tax rates went down—though tax loopholes were closed. Spanish authorities finally ended the monopoly in slave trading, the old *asiento,* which had been deemed as promoting contraband trade, and permitted the import of slaves on licensed ships. In freeing up the slave trade, the Crown was responding to demands from Cuban planters, who said they had not been able to import enough slaves to take advantage of new markets for sugar in the latter quarter of the eighteenth century.

The economic results of the so-called free trade reforms were dramatic. Spanish commerce with its American colonies rose 300 percent. The increase of trade was primarily the result of expanding external demand and only secondarily attributable to the economic reforms. In the eighteenth century, the booming economies and rising populations of Europe increased the market for colonial commodities such as chocolate and sugar. Expanding international commerce also enlarged the demand for those indispensable media of exchange, Mexican and Peruvian silver and Brazilian and Colombian gold. Therefore, the economies of colonial Latin America expanded on primary exports, with only secondary development of the manufacturing sector. Anyway, the trade reforms responded to commercial realities rather than actually stimulating economic exchange; they represented Spain's belated attempt to regain administrative control of its colonial commerce. The actual imperial economic benefit was rather minimal, as the Iberian Peninsula became even more of a clearinghouse for the trade of products manufactured in northern Europe. Most of the ships carrying this expanded colonial trade, too, were non-Spanish. Merchants and shipowners ignored even the remaining restrictions and continued contraband trading.

However, we should not assume that European imports undermined secondary production in Latin America. Changes in trade certainly caused some readjustment to textile manufacturing in the colonies in the late eighteenth century. Expanded imports of European textiles produced wild fluctuations in Mexican textile production at Puebla and in Ecuadorian production at Quito. But the American industry regrouped. New *obrajes* opened up in Cuzco and Cochabamba, Bolivia. Querétaro, situated closer to the sources of Mexican wool, became a leading textile producer, and Puebla also experienced a resurgence from 1790 to 1805, when war cut off the sources of European imports. Quito itself recovered in the 1780s to provide cloth for markets in New Granada, to whose viceroyalty Ecuador now belonged. The late eighteenth century was the heyday of domestic textile manufacturing in the infamous *obrajes* of Mexico, Peru, and Bolivia.

The Pombaline Reforms

In the case of Portugal, the imperial reforms were named for the Marquês de Pombal, chief minister to José I (1750–77), even though several ministers who followed Pombal also engaged in the process. The Pombaline Reforms tightened up the administration of Brazil and the empire, strengthened the defenses within the colonies, sought to increase commerce and tax collections, and fomented improvements in agriculture and manufacturing. Most of all, the state removed many restrictions on the slave trade within the empire, facilitating the supply of chattel labor to meet the prodigious Brazilian demand in the eighteenth century.

Administratively, Brazil also underwent changes. All of Brazil became a single viceroyalty in 1774, bringing under its control the northern region formed by Pará and Maranhão, which had been governed separately up to that point. Rio de Janeiro became the capital from which the viceroy ruled over the separate captaincies-general established at Santa Catarina and Rio Grande do Sul. However, the governors of the eight other captaincies-general reported directly to Portugal. Crown judges having administrative as well as judicial responsibilities gained in power at the expense of the elected town councils. No intendancy system had been installed in Brazil, as in Spanish America. Even so, the reforms rationalized tax collections, which rose considerably.

In Portuguese America, the liberalized trade reforms, of which freeing up the slave trade was one, conformed more closely to mercantilist tenets of the past. The *frota* (fleet) system between Portugal, Salvador da Bahia, and Rio de Janeiro came to an end in 1766, and the monopoly companies that had been licensed to trade at Maranhão and Pernambuco were terminated in 1778. Some state monopolies were also abolished. The repeated prohibitions on colonial textile production clearly indicated that mercantilism governed the economic thought of the Marquês de Pombal and his successors, even though Portugal itself was not a manufacturing center. The liberalization of trade actually had little immediate impact on the Brazilian economy, which entered a period of slump in the third quarter of the eighteenth century. The gold rush had pretty much played out by this time, and the rapid expansion of Haitian sugar production captured many of Bahia's markets in Europe. However, the liberalized shipping reforms of the 1770s did permit economic recovery later when Bahia revived, following the collapse of the sugar industry on Saint-Domingue (Haiti), and São Paulo began exporting coffee and other agricultural products. After sugar, the cotton of Maranhão and Ceará was Brazil's second most prosperous export.

The value of colonial commerce doubled in the last decade of the eighteenth century, redounding to the benefit of the royal treasury. However, Brazil accounted for 80 percent of Portugal's colonial trade, and a majority of its sugar and cotton simply passed through Lisbon on its way to London and Amsterdam. The Portuguese metropolis had a population of 3.5 million, which was nearly the population of its American colony. "So heavy a branch," remarked a British visitor to Lisbon, "cannot long remain upon so rotten a trunk." This very fear motivated both the Braganças and the Bourbons to enhance the defenses of their American colonies.

The Portugese empire also undertook to refurbish its military presence in the colonies. To defend Brazil from Spanish encroachment, Portugal had always sent troops composed of delinquents and vagrants from home as well as enlisting similar elements in the colonies. Consequently, its colonial defenses suffered from high rates of desertion and low levels of esprit de corps. A series of embarrassing defeats in the 1760s exposed the military weaknesses of Portugal's colonial enterprises in the Americas. Not only did Spanish troops from Buenos Aires seize Colônia do Sacramento in 1762, but they briefly invaded southern Brazil in the very next year. Renewed efforts and financial backing went into expanding the *milicias* at the level of the captaincies. Thus, the more prosperous and populous provinces supported the larger *milicia* units, usually recruited from among the free men of color but commanded by white officers. Theoretically, these regional troop units were to cooperate with each other in case of an attack anywhere in Brazil. Military duty was not always a welcome alternative to other endeavors for poor men of color. In southern Brazil, where Portuguese officials were organizing *milicias* for service guarding the ports, fighting the natives, and conducting military campaigns against the Spanish in Uruguay, the peasants often preferred to leave their plots and get themselves lost on the frontiers. They also resisted forced labor drafts for repairing the road from São Paulo to the thriving port of Santos. Nonetheless, in Salvador da Bahia and Rio de Janiero, military service attracted free men of color as an opportunity to advance their social status.

Taxation

Bourbon and Pombaline reforms concerning defense and many other matters depended on enlarging the tax base and increasing imperial revenue. Tobacco, spirits, gunpowder, salt, and other items were converted to royal monopolies, their manufacture and distribution run by government-appointed administrators—an old practice seemingly at odds with the trade reforms. The small producers and free workers of these products either be-

Officers of the colored militia units in Brazil. (Carlos Julião, ca. 1815)

came incorporated into the royal reorganization of the industry or faced elimination. The profits from the sale of tobacco and spirits, sold only in monopoly stores, went directly into the royal coffers. With monopoly control of these popular articles of consumption, the state merely had to raise prices to make more revenues from sales. New Spain supported the most elaborate monopoly on tobacco, in which it employed a workforce of 17,000 people and produced yearly profits of nearly four million pesos for the Crown.

Not only did the list of taxable items expand, but the collection of taxes was also rationalized. Previously, tax farmers had assumed the responsibility for the tax collections, and these individuals could be local Creole merchants who received tax payments from shopkeepers and producers in exchange for a percentage of total collections. Such a decentralized system contributed to a great deal of evasion and preferential treatment, so an important element of the Bourbon Reforms concerned centralizing the collection of taxes.

A new group of professional bureaucrats connected to the intendancy system assumed the burden of collecting taxes from the tax farmers. Again, Spaniards gained because the bureaucrats were Spaniards, whereas many of the old tax farmers had been Creole merchants. Moreover, each new tax official had his own detachment of guards. The Bourbon offensive against merchants and landowners culminated in the 1780s, when the establishment of the intendancies finally permitted the king's ministers to

Figure 14.1   Revenues Collected in the Royal Treasury of México, 1751–1810*

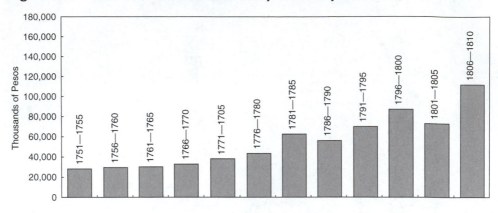

Figure 14.2   Revenues Collected in the Royal Treasury of Perú, 1751–1810*

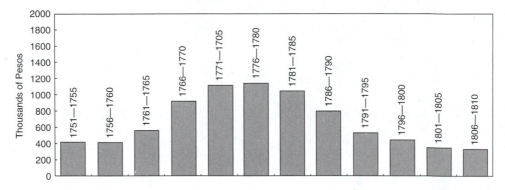

base the fiscal system on trade and production rather than the native head tax. Eight intendants were assigned to the principal cities of the Viceroyalty of the Río de la Plata in 1782; another 8 were assigned in Peru in 1784, followed by 12 in New Spain. Cuba received 3 intendancies; Chile, 2; and Caracas, 1. The intendancy district became an administrative unit of considerable importance. In Guatemala, intendancies were established in each interior province, some of which would later become independent nations—El Salvador, Chiapas, Nicaragua, and Honduras.

New Spain remained the jewel in the imperial crown. Its yearly tax collections yielded revenues upwards of twenty million pesos in the 1780s (see Figure 14.1). Crown collections of sales taxes increased dramatically in Peru. By the 1790s, the intendants were collecting upwards of five million pesos per year, reflecting the regional economic expansion as well as increases in silver production. However, the wine and sugar industries were not as healthy as the rest of the economy, and Peruvian landowners lost domestic markets to producers in Mendoza and Tucumán. Peru's loss of the Potosí mining complex to the Viceroyalty of the Río de la Plata, the disruption of the Túpac Amaru rebellion, and eco-

* John J. Tepaske, "General Tendencies and Secular Trends in the Economies of Mexico and Peru, 1750–1810: The View from the Cajas of Mexico and Lima," in Nils Jacobsen and Hans-Jürgen Puhle, eds., *The Economies of Mexico and Peru During the Late Colonial Period, 1760–1810*. (Berlin: Colloquim Verlag, 1986), 336-37.

Table 14.2   Major Sources of Royal Revenues from Guatemala

	Native Tribute	*Alcabala*	*All Other*	*Total*
1694–98	172,518	16,881	46,709	236,108
1744–48	202,968	18,500	32,392	252,860
1764–68	140,139	98,989	99,792	338,920

NOTE: Annual averages for three quinquennia from 1694 to 1768.

SOURCE: Miles L. Wortman, *Government and Society in Central America, 1680–1840* (New York: Columbia University Press, 1982), 146.

nomic decline all contributed to a fall in revenue collections (see Figure 14.2). In Guatemala, an additional feature of tax collections became clear: The burden of revenues was shifted from the natives to the whites. Receipts from indigenous tribute actually decreased while the revenues from Creole-dominated commerce were going up (see Table 14.2). To Creoles, the shift in the tax burden was perceived as one more example of how they had become the targets of the Bourbon Reforms.

Tax policy also served the function of stimulating the economy. Because the Crown wished to reverse the seventeenth century's slow decline of silver production in Mexico and Peru, it had invested money in the supply of mercury and gunpowder for colonial mining so that the reduction in cost of these essential supplies would encourage production. Mining equipment became exempt from sales taxes. Finally, royal authorities also considered changes to the old *quinto real,* by which the king had collected 20 percent of mining production for the mine operators in exchange for their privilege of exploiting the king's silver and gold deposits. Mining taxes were reduced from 20 percent to 10 percent of production. Again, the tax reductions served to promote production, yet the new tax collectors simultaneously closed tax loopholes and reduced the tax evasion that had always been a feature of mining in the Americas.

A brief review of the tax reforms in one jurisdiction, that of Ecuador, will demonstrate what pernicious effects the Bourbon Reforms could have on the colonies. In 1765, a new governor arrived, ostensibly to reform the old, decentralized, patrimonial fiscal bureaucracy in the colony. A prominent feature of the old policy had been to have colonial merchants act as "tax farmers," collecting taxes for the Crown. Other than ending tax farming for the sales tax *(alcabala)* and establishing a royal monopoly on *aguardiente,* however, Governor José García de León y Pizarro did not correct the flaws of the old system. Instead, he turned it to his own personal advantage. Tax collections continued to be made at three locations, the capital of Quito, the port of Guayaquil, and the highland city of Cuenca. He expanded the number of tax collection offices and appointed his relatives, friends, and political supporters to the important fiscal positions. The results were dramatic. Tax revenues increased two- and three-fold in the next decades, and García de León and his successors were able to remit to Spain increasing amounts of currency (see Figure 14.3).

However, the consequences on all Ecuadorian social classes were dire. The natives were now paying twice what they had contributed before García de León had arrived. The Europeans and *castas* (mestizos and mulattoes) paid even more, their tax burdens increasing by 500 percent. Moreover, Ecuador was depleted of larger and larger amounts of investment capital, for nearly half of everything collected by the royal treasury officers

Figure 14.3   Revenues Collected in the Royal Treasury of Ecuador, 1750–1803

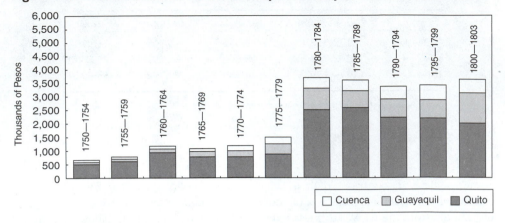

was sent to the Crown in Spain. Rather than reflecting the growth of Ecuador, the increased tax collections actually tended to depress the economy, and Ecuadorians could not help but resent them.

But no matter how much tax income it took in, colonial governments could not afford to send 40 percent of their revenues to Spain and also support their increasing defense and bureaucratic obligations. Budget deficits began to grow. In New Spain, the debt grew from 3 million pesos in the 1770s to more than 31 million in 1810. The viceregal governments borrowed heavily from the funds of the church and *consulados* (merchant guilds). Still, many frontier garrisons did not receive their pay because the colonial governments could not raise sufficient funds. By 1810, the state in colonial Spanish America was approaching the point of financial collapse.

Church-State Relations

As the civil authority expanded, the Crown also sought to exercise its patronage over the church by reducing the clergy's temporal power in the colonies. The Jesuits became the first victims of this policy. Not only had they caused resentment among some local elites with their success at controlling indigenous labor and at commerce on their wealthy mission estates, but they also had become implicated in Iberian politics. The Jesuits were perceived as more loyal to the pope in Rome than to the king under whose patronage the religious order had grown wealthy. Two years before the Jesuits were expelled, a government economic planner imbued with ideas influenced by the Enlightenment proposed that idle lands controlled by the church would be better developed if in private hands. Finally, officials of the Crown exploited the rumor that the Jesuits had inspired the popular Esquilache riot of 1766, which attacked royal absolutism in Spain. In 1767, the Crown expelled the Jesuits from the colonies and Spain.

True enough, local merchant groups might have applauded the humbling of the powerful Jesuit "state within a state." But certainly not all Creole families liked the decision because, by the eighteenth century, most of the Jesuits had in fact been born in the

Americas and were from influential Creole families. Of the 680 Jesuits who were exiled from Mexico, 450 were themselves native-born whites. Fifty-eight percent of the 160 Jesuits in Chile were native born. Even though only 2 of the 20 friars of the Jesuit Order in Guatemala had been born there, they nevertheless had close contact with Creole society as educators of the elite. Most Creoles owed their education to Jesuit colleges located in nearly every colony. From their exile in Rome and Germany, these learned but homesick brothers wrote of their experiences in the Americas, nurturing an American identity separate from that of Spain.

The reorganization of the militias paid off handsomely for royal officials when the Crown made the decision to banish the Jesuits from the Spanish empire. Every public official charged with the expulsion order believed that the removal of the Jesuits might provoke rebellion by the natives and slaves under their control. Therefore, the Viceroy of Peru dispatched a force of 700 militiamen to arrest the sleeping Jesuit brothers at night and confiscate their buildings and landholdings quickly and efficiently. In Paraguay, the Jesuits were particularly powerful. Their missions there contained more than ninety-six thousand Guaraní, who maintained their own armed militias. Nevertheless, the exile of the Jesuits came off without great violence.

Their agricultural estates, schools, and other properties, many of them large and containing hundreds of African slaves and indigenous workers, became a resource for local officials to rent out to members of the gentry. Some estates were well maintained, and others were not. In São Paulo, after the Portuguese expelled the Jesuit Order in 1759, these estates began a long decline toward ruin. The buildings were allowed to deteriorate, the crops and tools were looted, and those slaves who did not flee were sold. *Fazendas* that once produced corn, beans, wheat, peanuts, cotton, manioc, honey, wine, cane brandy, and rice—all of which had gone to support the Jesuit college in the city of São Paulo—gradually went to ruin. However, one of the largest Jesuit estates in Uruguay, that called the Estancias de las Vacas, was taken over by the lay brotherhood of the wealthy Spanish merchants at Buenos Aires. The Hermandad de Santa Caridad sent out professional administrators and extra workers to the estate. The cattle herds proliferated. Cattle hides were sold for export, and wheat and dried meat were brought in to Buenos Aires to support the orphanage and girls' school that the brotherhood also managed. Meanwhile, the king's officials collected the rent.

The church still retained the Jesuit lands in many places. The Franciscans acquired 23,000 head of cattle in Chiapas and a big sugar hacienda in Guatemala. Although in decline, the Franciscans remained the most numerous missionary order, as 177 Franciscans still ministered in Guatemala as late as 1810. The secular clergy had became more numerous than the regular clergy, but the 276 parish priests were poorly trained and not particularly wealthy, although many were from Creole families and had their own farms and businesses. The great mission system of Paraguay deteriorated greatly after the Jesuits departed. However, their tutelage of the Guaraní had prepared these natives to articulate with the rising market system of the Río de la Plata. Guaraní migrants contributed their free wage labor to the expansion of cattle raising in Uruguay and Buenos Aires.

Next came the reduction of the rights and privileges of the secular clergy, the thousands of parish priests throughout the towns and villages of the Americas. They had always enjoyed a special *fuero,* or immunity, from the civil courts. Therefore, all their business and personal dealings were protected from interference from civil authorities, and disputes against the secular clergy had to be adjudicated in religious courts only. For many humble clergymen, the *fuero* was virtually their only material asset. Its elimination by the Bourbon Reforms disgruntled many a parish priest, so much so that they would later became important leaders of rebellion, particularly in Mexico.

The state's attack on church power also served as an offensive on indigenous village autonomy. Decline of the missionary orders in Mexico, Guatemala, Ecuador, and Peru removed their protection of peasant villages, and the state then initiated a crusade against the treasuries of the *cofradías,* or sodalities of Native American communities. These represented the savings funds of the indigenous organizations that financed local religious rites and fiestas. Some of these sodalities could be quite prosperous, such as those belonging to villages that held indigo lands in El Salvador; nonnative landowners and businessmen often turned to them as a source of credit. In flexing its authority over the church and all religious institutions, the state began to tax and withdraw money from the savings funds of indigenous *cofradías.* Although the old Hapsburgs had recognized and protected the free native villages and tried to bar nonnatives from the *pueblos,* the Bourbons envisioned an agricultural wage-earning class and a free peasantry of smallholders. Native Americans were to be equal to white colonists. The final result was a political assault on the concept of the Two Republics—one for Europeans and one for native Americans—and the removal of natives from special protections under the Crown.

The Bourbon Reforms included attempts at social engineering and considered the role of women in the modernization process, urging their education to prepare them to be responsible mothers and thrifty housewives. "Enlightened" Bourbon administrators believed that even poor women could be profitably instructed in habits of order, economy, and work. An order of nuns opened up boarding schools in Mexico City in 1753, one for the elite and another for native girls. The nuns taught the girls basic reading and math skills as well as embroidery and household skills. Other wealthy girls received private tutoring at home. But because the school for native girls had room for only 100 pupils, it hardly served the education needs of the masses. In its attack on church privilege, Bourbon legislation even penetrated the terrain of the family—particularly the elite family. Members of the nobility, military, and bureaucracy after 1728 needed to obtain government permission to marry, and interracial marriages also required official approval after 1805. But such approval was rarely withheld.

In the minds of Bourbon and Bragança administrators, few realms remained outside the scope of their reforms. The colonial state fully intended to secularize and modernize its administration of the colonies with an eye toward strengthening the Crown's authority in the empire at the expense of the church and the local elite. Moreover, the Iberian monarchs acted under the assumption that the colonies deserved to contribute more to their own defense as well as to the mother country. Political authority even encroached into areas of education and social engineering, though with little real impact. Such experimentation, however, was certain to satisfy few residents of the colonies; in particular, the colonial elites began to perceive that they were the intended victims of the Bourbon and Pombaline Reforms.

THE ENLIGHTENMENT AND THE CREOLES

Spain and Portugal participated in the general European intellectual ferment of the eighteenth century. The Enlightenment in France and Great Britain questioned authority and promoted rational thought and experimentation. In Spain and Portugal, the kings' ministers adopted only the latter ideas, as questioning authority might lead to the loss of their positions or worse. In the Iberian brand of the Enlightenment, they discovered methods not of promoting industrial revolution but of strengthening agricultural exports and old-fashioned mercantilism. The Iberian Crowns also entertained those Enlightenment notions that promoted secular over religious power, the better to control the powerful institution of the church. However, the concepts of "popular sovereignty," "the social contract," and "consent of the governed," as developed by the French philosopher Jean-Jacques Rousseau, did not resonate among the imperial ministers, again for obvious reasons.

Political Ideas

However, those ideas spurned by the imperial ministers did make their way to Latin America. The books of Locke, Newton, Descartes, Voltaire, and Rousseau were illegally imported through colonial ports. Literate members of the elite, of the bureaucracy, and of the clergy became familiar with the new philosophy. Elite education proliferated in the early eighteenth century with the establishment of numerous universities in the major cities of the Americas. The older schools in Mexico City, Lima, and Córdoba were joined by the University of Chuquisaca (Bolivia) in 1725 and the University of San Felipe in Santiago, Chile, in 1758. Mainly, these universities taught law and religious philosophy, the better to prepare elite youth for careers in the lower levels of the bureaucracy and the church. The elite responded to these educational opportunities with alacrity. The University of San Carlos in Guatemala graduated more men with legal degrees from 1775 to 1799 than it had during the previous 50 years. Moreover, these universities disseminated the ideas of the Enlightenment without an imperial filter. But truth be told, the ideas came late to Latin America—in the 1790s. They did not inspire the Andean revolts and had less to do with the Haitian revolution than the political turmoil in France and the social resentments in what was then Saint-Domingue.

The youth of the elite immediately familiarized themselves with Enlightenment ideas when they did finally arrive. The Venezuelan Francisco de Miranda read the new philosophies as a young military officer training in Spain. Simón Bolívar, son of a wealthy Venezuelan planter, became a lifelong devotee to the political thought of Hobbes and Locke and to the social ideas of Montesquieu and Rousseau. The ideas of the Enlightenment inspired the 1797 political conspiracy in La Guaira, Venezuela. Manuel Gual and José María España recruited *pardos* and poor whites, appealing to them to support a republic in which slavery and native tribute would be ended. The conspiracy came to nothing, although it did scare the local officials. In the emerging region of the Río de la Plata, the merchant's son Manuel Belgrano read the new books from his study in Buenos Aires. Mariano Moreno, graduate of the University of Chuquisaca and a young Creole bureaucrat, edited an edition of Rousseau's *Social Contract* "for the instruction of young Americans." Other young scholars translated these works. In 1793, Antonio Nariño of Bogotá printed a translation of the French Declaration of the Rights of Man. His temerity resulted in the confiscation of his press and forced Nariño into exile. In Quito, a mestizo lawyer named Francisco Javier Espejo used the ideas of the Enlightenment to write and publish his criticism of Spanish rule and economic mismanagement. For his troubles, Espejo received a jail term in 1795.

Except for a few social idealists, the French Revolution did not gain many admirers either among the royal ministers of Iberia or among colonial elites. If anything, the regicide, the attacks on property, and the flight of the nobility caused revulsion among the upper class of Latin America. The American Revolution, in fact, appealed much more to the youth of the conservative, privileged Creole class. Creoles circulated and admired the Spanish translations of the works of Paine, Jefferson, and Washington, partly because the latter two were themselves American-born planters and owners of slaves. Moreover, the American Revolution had proceeded with a minimum of social chaos and upheaval so as to represent a more attractive example for those few who might have sought an alternative to continued rule by Spain and Portugal. Some Latin Americans, such as Miranda, actually visited the young North American republic. It was not lost on them that American independence had been consolidated in a way that preserved existing property rights and social relationships.

Brazilian Thought

If anything, the intellectual ferment of the age may have been more intensive in Brazil. Its easy communication with Portugal and Europe drew the sons of Brazil's wealthiest families to study at the University of Coimbra in Lisbon; others went to universities in France and Great Britain. They gained a taste for European books, which found their way to Brazil despite the best efforts of the Board of Censorship. Consequently, the voices of the Brazilian elites raised a chorus of criticism of the remaining vestiges of Portuguese monopoly practices, of the rigorous tax collections, and even of royal absolutism. These educated and enlightened critics spoke out for freer trade and more political participation for Brazilian whites.

Some of the very same impediments to a full intellectual rebellion based on the Enlightenment also applied to Brazil. The powerful native-born elite families retained close personal connections with Portuguese officials and immigrants. Their political and commercial positions made them ideal business partners—and sons-in-law—to the important planter families. The slave trade remained very much a Portuguese commercial enterprise, and the Brazilian planters were terribly dependent on this source of labor. Moreover, no matter how many political positions the Portuguese monopolized, they could at least be counted on to reinforce the social privileges of all the whites. The Brazilian whites, outnumbered three to one by nonwhites, did not wish to encourage social reforms that could get out of hand. The existence of more than one million slaves in Brazil always reminded the planters—and others, too—of what might happen to them if the slaves rose up as they had in Haiti. That Brazil experienced no rebellions like those of Túpac Amaru and the Comuneros should not be surprising.

However, as in Spanish America, the Pombaline Reforms did heighten the tensions among those annoyed at higher taxes and growing political arrogance of Portugal. The new Portuguese officials could be every bit as corrupt as the Spaniards. In Minas Gerais, a notable group of businessmen, landowners, and lower-ranking officials—nearly all of them Brazilian-born and educated abroad—formed a conspiracy in the 1780s. Its original intent had been to pressure the imperial authorities to lower taxes and reduce corruption, but several young intellectuals had admired the American Revolution and even suggested independence for the state of Minas Gerais. Ultimately, the conspiracy was exposed before anything happened. Several leaders were exiled, and Joaquim José de Silva

Xavier, better known as Tiradentes, the Toothpuller, paid the supreme penalty. He was hanged.

A final conspiracy in the Portuguese colony portended more danger for the Brazilian social structure. This time the conspirators were more radical, represented the free colored sector of the population, and admired the French rather than the American Revolution. In the 1790s, the Bahian sugar economy was booming once again. Slave imports increased as a consequence, and the social order was becoming ever more unequal. A third of the population consisted of African slaves. Moreover, the free persons of color were so numerous in the Bahian capital of Salvador that the whites were outnumbered by a ratio of five to one. It was a serious matter, therefore, when the conspirators proposed political independence from Portugal, democracy, republican government, virtual free trade, and an end to slavery and all other forms of racial discrimination. The elites reacted harshly when they learned of the conspiracy, for they wanted nothing that threatened a Haitian-style revolt. The police rounded up several dozen conspirators of the so-called Tailors' Revolt. Four of the leaders were hanged, drawn, and quartered, while the authorities banished six others to Africa.

Nationality

Perhaps an intellectual sentiment of greater power than the ideas of either the Enlightenment or the American Revolution were those concerning simple identity. More Creoles began to identify themselves as American as opposed to European. The Bourbon Reforms increased the tax burden on the colonials without ending the corruption of the Spanish-born officials, which only heightened American nationalism. After all, the demographic trend favored the Americans even among the elite. Creoles formed the overwhelming majority of the more than 1 million whites in Mexico; only 14,000 of them were *peninsulares,* whites born in the Iberian Peninsula. Even so, more Spaniards were immigrating to the American colonies in the eighteenth century than ever before, taking up lucrative posts in the import-export houses and moving into professional and artisan positions. They were especially filling the bureaucratic positions now being denied to the Americans. Creoles increasingly felt the sharp barbs of Spanish arrogance. Even Humboldt noticed that "[t]he lowest, least educated and uncultivated European believes himself superior to the white born in the New World." (See Manuscript 14.1.)

In Venezuela some antagonism developed between the Creole landowners and the powerful Spaniards. The youth of the local elite, who might indeed have a few drops of African or Native American blood, could not aspire to lucrative and powerful positions in commerce or the bureaucracy. Those positions were going to Spaniards who seemed to have no superior knowledge or skills. Moreover, the Basques, Catalans, and Canary Islanders then arriving in Caracas soon came into ownership of the warehouses, stores, shops, and taverns. They certainly gained control over foreign commerce but also much of the domestic trade as well. *Peninsulares* were taking over the important posts even in the local *cabildos,* favored in this endeavor by royal policy. Moreover, the landowners who owned slaves were beginning to feel that the royal authorities were too indulgent toward people of color. The Creoles in Venezuela unsuccessfully petitioned that the *pardo* militias be disbanded because these military units might possibly give the mulattoes an instrument of revolution. Creole protests over the new Spanish slave code were even more vociferous. In 1789, Spain issued a new law that regulated

MANUSCRIPT 14.1

Differences between Spanish-born and Mexican-born Whites

Baron von Humboldt was a keen observer of Spanish America in the first decade of the nineteenth century. As an official guest of the Spanish king, Humboldt traveled throughout the Viceroyalties of New Spain and New Granada between 1803 and 1807. Although he was engaged mainly in scientific and geographical observations for the Crown, Humboldt also turned his gaze to the organization of colonial society in the Indies. Often, the outsider is capable of noticing those mores and practices that are so commonplace to the native born that they pass without notice. Humboldt thus observed the widening breach within the colonial elite between the Europeans and the Creoles that had been caused, in large measure, by the Bourbon Reforms. He advised "wise administration," but his advice was not heeded.

Amongst the inhabitants of pure origin the whites would occupy the second place [to Indians], considering them only in the relation of number. They are divided into whites born in Europe, and descendants of Europeans born in the Spanish colonies of America. . . . The former bear the name of *Chapetones* or *Gachupines,* and the second that of *Criollos.* . . . The Spanish laws allow the same rights to all whites; but those who have the execution of the laws endeavour to destroy an equality which shocks the European pride. The government, suspicious of the Creoles, bestows the great places exclusively on the natives of Old Spain. For some years back they have disposed at Madrid even the most trifling employments in the administration of the customs and the tobacco revenue. At an epoch when every thing tended to a uniform relaxation in the springs of the state, the system of venality made an alarming progress. For the most part it was by no means a suspicious and distrustful policy, it was pecuniary interest alone which bestowed all employments on Europeans. The result has been a jealousy and perpetual hatred between the Chapetons and the Creoles. The most miserable European, without education, and without intellectual cultivation, thinks himself superior to the whites born in the new continent. He knows that, protected by his countrymen, and favoured by chances common enough in a country where fortunes are as rapidly acquired as they are lost, he may one day reach places to which the access is almost interdicted to the natives, even to those of them distinguished for their talents, knowledge, and moral qualities. The natives [whites] prefer the denomination of Americans to that of Creoles. . . . we frequently hear proudly declared, "I am not a *Spaniard,* I am an *American!"* words which betray the workings of a long resentment. In the eye of law every white Creole is a Spaniard; but the abuse of the laws, the false measures of the colonial government, the example of the United States of America, and the influence of the opinions of the age, have relaxed the ties which formerly united more closely the Spanish Creoles to the European Spaniards. A wise administration may re-establish harmony, calm their passions and resentments, and yet preserve for a long time the union among the members of one and the same great family scattered over Europe and America, from the Patagonian coast to the north of California.

SOURCES: Alexander von Humboldt, *Political Essay on the Kingdom of New Spain,* 4 vols., trans. John Black (London: Longmans, 1811; reprint, New York: AMS Press, 1966), 4: 204–6.

the relationship between master and slave, seeking to protect the slave and improve the conditions under which they worked. Slaveholders in Venezuela resisted. They claimed that slaves were vice ridden and lazy and that the economy would deteriorate without forcing them to work. Under the circumstances, the Creoles stored up grievances against Spaniards and lost confidence in the royal government.

While the Bourbon Reforms and the ideas of the Enlightenment certainly increased social tensions in the Indies, they did not suffice in and of themselves to begin the independence movements. The very social class most affected by the Bourbon Reforms, the Creoles, was in fact the most conservative. Even though they suffered the indignities of taxes and loss of jobs to Spaniards and may have lost some control over the nonwhite workers, the Creoles remained privileged—and frightened. They feared a massive social upheaval and knew full well that the imperial systems of Spain and Portugal protected their remaining social privileges and wealth, which were not insubstantial. The Bourbon and Pombaline Reforms served only as the dry tinder of insurrection. The actual spark that would set off the conflagration came from elsewhere.

CRISIS OF THE COLONIAL ORDER

The spark came from war in Europe. Being the possessions of major European powers meant that the American colonies would become a venue of military activity and, most particularly, a victim of the costs of warfare. Even though its gold and silver had financed Spain's armies and Portugal's fleets in the sixteenth and seventeenth centuries, Latin America had not otherwise been too discomforted by European warfare. True, pirates sacked a few coastal settlements, and privateers captured several ships. But the colonials had also traded with some of these very same interlopers in the old days. The eighteenth century was to be different. Particularly in the last decade of the eighteenth and the first of the nineteenth century, European warfare would disrupt commerce in the Americas, expose Spanish corruption, reveal imperial weaknesses left unresolved by the Bourbon and Pombaline Reforms, and permit a resurgence of Creole power.

The first wars of the eighteenth century began increasingly to involve the Americas in Europe's disagreements—and Great Britain seemed to benefit most in the long process. The War of the Spanish Succession from 1700 to 1713, by which France's Louis XIV was able to place a Bourbon on the throne of Spain, resulted in a compromise in which British merchants gained the coveted *asiento,* the royal monopoly to legally import slaves into the American colonies. British merchants consequently established import offices in Buenos Aires, La Guaira, Portobelo, Havana, and Veracruz. To the delight of the colonials, they also used these slave-trading privileges to import illegal textiles and other British goods. Colônia da Sacramento, a center for contraband across the Río de la Plata estuary, went to England's ally, Portugal. Spain got the Family Compact, a mutual defense pact with the Bourbon Crown of France.

Then came the so-called War of Jenkins's Ear (1739–48), the conflict that was said to have been caused by the loss of a British mariner's ear to a Spaniard's knife. The British sacking of Portobelo, Panama's Atlantic Coast port, provided the coup de grâce to Spain's fleet system, although the British gave up the slave *asiento* and the Portuguese allies gave back Colônia da Sacramento in the treaty ending this war. In this and the subsequent Seven Years' War (1756–63), the Europeans involved the indigenous peoples of the

Americas in their disagreements. The struggle in North America became known as the French and Indian War, while the Spaniards mobilized the Guaraní militias from the Jesuit missions to defend Buenos Aires. However, Spain suffered the British capture of the ports of Manila and Havana. The British merchant fleet, in the meanwhile, flooded Havana's wharves with manufactured goods at cut-rate prices and bought up all the cane sugar available. The Spaniards were embarrassed, but the Cubans took advantage of the period of open trade to expand sugar production on the island and to import more slaves. The British took Florida from the Spaniards, and Portugal took back Colonia da Sacramento but gave French Louisiana to Spain and returned the two captured ports.

The Family Compact gained a bit of revenge during the American Revolution (1779–83). French and Spanish troops helped the colonials gain independence from Great Britain, despite the irony that both allied powers still retained their own colonial empires. Spain got Florida back and recaptured Colonia de Sacramento, changing the name from Portuguese back to Spanish in the process. For years, British merchants from Jamaica had been trading in dyewoods and hardwoods of the Yucatán Peninsula and the Mosquito Coast of Nicaragua, aided and abetted by Central American officials and merchants who appreciated the cheaper sources of European imports than those obtained by the Spanish merchants of Guatemala City. In the Treaty of Paris in 1783, the British obtained rights to establish logging camps in Belize in return for recognizing Spanish sovereignty. These wars, however deadly for those who fought them, would seem like games between imperial powers compared to what was about to occur.

Revolution in France

The French Revolution of 1789 altered the parrying nature of previous European warfare. Spain retained a tenuous partnership with the more powerful revolutionary France, while Great Britain's navy remained the guarantor of Portugal's independence. Therefore, whenever France and Great Britain engaged in hostilities, which they did frequently after the French Revolution, Portugal and particularly Spain would be drawn in to the fray. At first, these conflicts were not too costly to Portugal, but they were to Spain, for the latter's empire lay across oceans now commanded by hostile British fleets. Spain first joined the war against Republican France between 1793 and 1795 only to be defeated by French armies. Thereafter, Spain became allied with France again, risking the hostility of France's bitterest enemy, Great Britain. In the wars lasting from 1797 to 1802 and from 1805 to 1808, British ships blockaded Spanish ports, cutting off its commerce with the Indies just at the moment that colonial commerce was reaching its highest levels in 300 years. Spain lost Trinidad to England and Louisiana to Napoleon, who sold it to the United States.

In these times of war against England, the Spanish merchants in the Americas were particularly on the defensive. Their advantage had always laid in their monopoly of ties to the powerful merchant houses of Cádiz, Sevilla, Bilbao, and Barcelona in Spain. The imports of Spanish mercury, for example, dropped off; consequently, silver production declined, and tax collections slumped. Spain was forced to permit either friendly or neutral shipping into its colonial ports. Vessels of the United States and Hamburg began to appear frequently and had few reservations about trading with Creole merchants, who were eager to deal in contraband goods. Between 1788 and 1809, 257 U.S. merchantmen passed through the Strait of Magellan and stopped along the coasts of Peru and Chile.

Spaniards with port connections in Iberia now lost their advantages and had to share control of colonial trade with Creoles. The native-born merchants of Latin America got a taste for an authentic free trade and requested that commerce be extended to non-Spanish vessels even during peacetime. They were turned down.

The wartime conditions seemed to dampen Spain's economic enlightenment and revive its commercial obscurantism. In 1800 and again in 1801, the king decreed a prohibition against the establishment of manufacturing plants in the colonies, his reasoning being that the disruptions to trade caused by war would serve as a boon to *obraje* manufacturing in Latin America. "Each of the wars which we have had with the English nation," said one Spanish official in 1811, "has been a cause of increase in the manufactures of New Spain." In the interludes between the wars, the Crown again forbade the colonial ports to trade with foreign ships. All commerce had to be in ships proceeding from Spain and licensed by the Crown's customs agents. But no one paid attention. The merchants—both Creoles and Spaniards—at all colonial ports had grown accustomed to the lower prices that direct foreign shipping brought, and the old Spanish trade monopoly could not be reimposed.

Impact in the Colonies

The wars of the French Revolution exposed the empire's true weaknesses, the most glaring of which was Spain's utter dependence on its colonies' financial resources. Taxes were raised in 1796 and again in 1804. Donations were demanded of the wealthy families in Mexico and Peru, sometimes in excess of one hundred thousand pesos. Spanish officials made additional demands on the corporate funds of the merchant guilds, the municipalities, and even the Native American sodalities.

But in looking far and wide for money, Spanish ministers chose to loot the wealthiest single institution in the Indies: the church. For three centuries, the various church funds had been amassing capital in the colonies. Wealthy Creole families had bequeathed property and money to the church when they desired a nunnery for a daughter, a parish for a son, or a mass for a deceased loved one. It leased most of its land and buildings. The various church treasury offices lent the accumulated liquid capital to the owners of land and urban real estate, taking mortgages at the rate of 5 percent per annum. In all the Indies, the church was not only the largest banker, responsible for nearly two-thirds of all investments, but a most gracious one as well. It did not like to foreclose on its debtors and always allowed mortgage payments to fall into arrears, banking practices that endeared the church to Creole property owners. These massive mortgage holdings became the target of a desperate Spanish wartime treasury.

In 1804, the Crown ordered the church to call in its loans and send the proceeds to Spain. Bishop Manuel Abad y Queipo, who estimated the total value of church capital to be in excess of forty-four million pesos in Mexico alone, went in person to plead with the Spanish monarch, Carlos IV, to countermand the order. He was rebuffed by Manuel Godoy, the king's chief minister. Thereafter, many a wealthy *hacendado* and many a small proprietor alike suffered when their loans were called in. They were forced to sell out cheaply to pay for the Crown's perfidy. In the next few years, more than ten million pesos were removed from the colonial economy in this *consolidación,* or consolidation, of church wealth. To add insult to injury, corrupt Spanish officials deducted personal fortunes from these tax funds before remitting them to Spain. The viceroy of Mexico himself took a 500,000-peso commission for his work in collecting the mortgage funds. Before the *consolidación* was finally ended in 1808, nearly all the colonies—but most particularly the wealthiest, New Spain—suffered this form of imperial decapitalization. Colonial blood ran hot over this affair.

A second weakness of the empire became manifest in the Río de la Plata: Spain's colonial defenses were worthless, and her military officers were incompetent. In 1806, British troops at war with Spain and France boarded a fleet in South Africa and invaded Buenos Aires. The invasion was unauthorized, a lark of the commander, General William Beresford. No sooner had British troops disembarked at Buenos Aires than the viceroy, his highest-ranking Spanish commanders, and the wealthiest Iberian merchants fled unceremoniously from the viceregal capital. Creole militia officers commanding mestizo and *pardo* soldiers, however, remained and fought. Rallied by a French-born officer, Santiago Liniers, they expelled the British troops, who retreated from Buenos Aires to seize Montevideo across the river. Pressured by the militias, the *audiencia* of Buenos Aires then deposed the king's appointed viceroy and elected Liniers to replace him. In the meanwhile, some of the Spanish merchants returned to trade surreptitiously with British ships at Montevideo, rousing the resentment of the Creoles and *castas* who were laying siege to the British troops in the city.

These invading forces received reinforcements from England and launched a second attack on the viceregal capital of Buenos Aires. Apparently, the British political and military leaders mistakenly believed that the colonials had desired to exchange the corrupt and weak Spanish imperial masters for more economically powerful British imperialists, but they did not. Once again the colonial militias at Buenos Aires expelled the foreign invaders. After a useless venture of two years in the Río de la Plata, the British forces then abandoned Montevideo, too. The Spaniards came back to Buenos Aires after it was all over, but the Creoles never allowed them to regain their old autocratic powers. The militias backed the *cabildo,* which was dominated by Creole members. The Spaniards who had collected the *consolidación* funds from the church in Bolivia attempted to send it to Spain, but the Creole-backed political authorities sequestered the revenues for use in Buenos Aires instead. Spain's wartime incompetence and greed were trying the patience of the Creoles.

Yet this conservative colonial elite would not move, as became evident in Venezuela. An early conspiracy to start a rebellion for independence came to naught. General Francisco de Miranda, a Venezuelan officer in the Spanish army, organized a small expedition to free his homeland in 1806. He had visited England and the United States beforehand, gaining ideas for Venezuelan independence, and he shared his elite countrymen's aversion to social chaos. "God forbid that the other countries suffer the same fate as Saint-Domingue, scene of carnage and crimes, committed on the pretext of establishing liberty," he wrote; "better that they should remain another century under the barbarous and senseless oppression of Spain." But on its way to Venezuela, his expedition stopped off at Haiti. Rumors spread that General Miranda was now commanding Haitian troops, who would stir up the blacks and *pardos* of Venezuela. Therefore, the Creoles did not support his landing, and his independence movement died stillborn. Something spectacular was still needed to overcome the natural conservatism of the colonial elites. That something occurred in 1807 and 1808, when Napoleon's armies invaded the Iberian Peninsula.

Napoleon in Iberia

In November 1807, French troops sought to seal off Europe from their English enemies by striking at England's ally, Portugal. The ministers of the Portuguese monarchs, Queen Maria I and the Prince Regent João, had anticipated the French invasion. They bundled the royal family, together with the entire royal entourage and all the government archives, onto several merchant vessels and sailed away to Brazil under the protection of a British naval escort. The Portuguese royal family received a warm welcome from their colonial subjects in Salvador da Bahia and then again in Rio de Janeiro. Soon Prince Regent João declared Brazil a kingdom with equal status to the former mother country of Portugal and began to rule the far-flung Portuguese empire from Brazil. He converted Rio de Janeiro from a viceregal to an imperial capital. The trade of Portugal's British allies enjoyed preferential status in Brazil. Imports of English manufactured goods and the exports of Brazilian cotton, sugar, and coffee prospered. However, the Portuguese sovereign skillfully resisted British demands that the slave trade be ended. With their old privileges intact and prosperity abounding, Brazilian elites had little reason not to accept their new political status with pride.

Politics were not so tranquil in the Spanish Americas, especially after Napoleon turned on his incompetent Spanish ally and imprisoned the entire Bourbon royal family. French troops overran much of the peninsula and installed Napoleon's brother as King Joseph of Spain. The only resistance was to come—in time and ferociously—from Spanish commoners who carried out a bitter and bloody guerrilla war against French forces. (They were supported by [the] British fleet [stationed at Gibraltar since] 1704 and, eventually, by a British expeditionary army.) The once powerful Spain was a mere shadow of its former self; it had been reduced to occupation by foreign troops, and its once autocratic and omnipotent kings were in captivity. Imperial Spain had become rotten and weakened by the manner in which, over the course of three centuries, it had mismanaged the riches of its empire. The corruption and depravity of Spanish officials in the Indies had come home to roost, undermining the imperial base beyond remedy. The one country that rose to support Spain in its rebellion against occupation by its former ally, France, was its long-time enemy, Great Britain. Warfare created endless ironies.

BREAKDOWN OF ELITE CONSENSUS

Conservatism of Slave Societies

The elites of Brazil were in no mood to question Portuguese colonial authority for a number of reasons. First of all, the Pombaline Reforms had not been as harsh to the Brazilian families of wealth as had the Bourbon Reforms in Spanish America. Second, the Brazilian economy remained ever more dependent on imports of slave labor in the late eighteenth century, and the Portuguese colonies in Africa provided much of this need. Third, the Brazilians of wealth and influence knew full well that even the slightest challenge to Portuguese political authority might encourage the aggrieved, subordinate, nonwhite classes to press for social reforms. Fourth, sugar exports and slave imports had revived in Brazil since the Haitian Revolution had eliminated that former Caribbean competitor.

This is where Brazil can be compared to Cuba and Puerto Rico, two Spanish colonies where slavery was paramount and the export sector was expanding. All colonial elites in Latin America were conservative by nature because they were outnumbered and enjoyed privileges quite disproportionate to their actual contributions to society. But the elites in slavocracies were the most reactionary of all: They feared a slave revolt that, if the Haitian formula were followed, would certainly mean ruin and death to the slave-owning class.

These attitudes permeated the middling sectors of Brazilian society, too, a phenomenon that rendered social conservatism immune to change. Small proprietors, artisans, and free workers—whether white or nonwhite—all treated Africans with contempt and feared the slaves' potential for revolt. Therefore, more people than just the elites tolerated political corruption and social inequality because so many benefited disproportionately from the unpaid labor of African slaves. Together, they marginalized the slaves, the poorest free people of color, and the isolated poor peasants.

Moreover, the European wars did not affect Brazil as much as Spanish America. The latter depended on silver mining as the great motor of its economic well-being, and the British blockades of Spain had periodically cut off supplies of the mercury needed to efficiently separate the silver from the ore. When silver production dropped off, so did the sales of agricultural supplies and livestock to the mining sector, which hurt the big *hacendados* and the small proprietors alike. The European wars and the French invasion of Spain, consequently, affected Mexico, Peru, and the Río de la Plata. Venezuela encountered economic problems, too, insofar as a significant part of its cacao production had always been destined for Mexico, which could afford less chocolate after 1793.

Brazil as well as Cuba and Puerto Rico were not at all dependent on mining, but they did depend on fairly unrestricted trade. Portugal's military alliance with Great Britain had meant that trade from Brazil to this expanding industrial market would remain open despite Continental warfare—whether Portugal acted as an intermediary or not. If anything, the capture of Portugal even solidified the Brazil–Great Britain commercial connection. Cuba and Puerto Rico, like Brazil, were plantation economies whose principal markets depended on open commerce rather than on supplies of mercury. Cuban and Puerto Rican landowners were not discomforted too much by British blockades of Iberia because Spain had never been their principal market; rather, it had always been the intermediary. As long as neutral shippers, like the Yankees and the Germans, put into Havana and San Juan, then the sugar planters and tobacco farmers could prosper.

The differential political outcomes of the reforms also influenced the subsequent independence movements. Generally speaking, one can conclude that the Bourbon Reforms created more political grievances than did the Pombaline Reforms. Both attempted to reassert Iberian political authority and to increase imperial revenues at the expense of local interests. The Bourbon Reforms had been more rigorous and successful in these objectives, and the attacks upon Creole officeholders and on church prerogatives were very effective at creating resentments among the elites. It was not lost on the colonialists that the imperial reforms did nothing to curb the rapacious corruption and arrogance either of Spanish or of Portuguese officials. But at least the Portuguese had been less efficient, which could be counted as a blessing in Brazil. Therefore, Brazilians welcomed the Portuguese monarchy when Napoleon had sent it packing.

Elite Unrest in Spanish America

In the Spanish-American mainland, the story could not have been more different. The capture of the Spanish king actually began the process of "the breakdown of elite consensus" in the colonies. This term refers to the breach of the political agreement among the *gente decente,* in this case, the Spanish-born and native-born whites in the Americas, who had maintained their social hegemony over the mass of nonwhites for 300 years. It was a fairly rapid deterioration that rent asunder, for once and for all, those ties of family, mutual economic benefit, and allegiance to the king that had bound together the Spaniards and their Creole cousins.

The issue was political. Now that Joseph Bonaparte claimed the Crown of Spain, did the colonials owe the same loyalty to him as to the Bourbons who, after all, had originally been French? But King Joseph I was a commoner! Did sovereignty over the empire then reside in a rump assembly of Spaniards who resisted the French? The problem was that there were two Spanish assemblies, each claiming precedence over the other. Did sovereignty reside in those incompetent and grasping viceroys who, like the one at Buenos Aires in 1806, had fled at the first sign of danger? Did sovereignty now reside in the *cabildos,* the town councils whose elite native-born members had always claimed more loyalty to the king than to his viceroy? All these questions became hopelessly complicated when Princess Carlota, the sister of King Ferdinand VII, escaped capture by the French and claimed the regency for her imprisoned brother. Princess Carlota might have provided some political solution except that she had married the Portuguese Prince Regent João, who was in Rio de Janeiro. Was Spanish America to be ruled from Brazil?

The Spaniards themselves grappled with these very questions and attempted to resolve the question in Iberia itself. They established a junta at Sevilla that called for all parts of the realm, colonies included, to elect delegates to a congress, called the Cortes, which would govern Spain and the empire until the king was restored to power. This would mark the first time that the colonials had been invited to participate in any European political processes at all, and some Spanish-American notables took the opportunity very seriously indeed. A restricted group of voters, principally men of learning and property, elected delegates who represented the major cities and towns of Spanish America. But this exercise in sovereignty provoked a rift between the Spaniards and the Creoles; electoral results favored the latter, who were in a vast majority among the *gente decente.* For the Spanish merchants, already reeling from the cutoff of trade through Spain, and for Spanish officials, this election represented an enormous decline in authority in the colonies. The capture of the king had damaged them incalculably, but they were not, of course, dissuaded from attempting to regain some of their losses.

One might even say that the Spanish-American revolts began with this essential breakdown of elite consensus between Spaniards and Creoles. Despite American membership, the subsequent Spanish juntas and meetings of the Cortes between 1809 and 1814 provided no solution to the political questions. In the first place, the Spanish members consistently denied the colonials equal representation, for disenfranchised slaves and Native Americans, which formed a majority of the Spanish-American population, were counted against colonial representation. The Cortes also attempted to impose social reforms that gave pause to the American Creoles—such as the abolition of native tribute and the extension of enfranchisement to free people of color. Moreover, the Spanish majority also blocked all colonial proposals for free trade. Therefore, because they gained little satisfaction attempting to participate in Spanish political solutions, the Creoles increasingly sought to exert their interests at the local levels back home.

Everywhere in Spanish America, political unrest arose between 1808 and 1810 in the forms of coups and countercoups, viceroys against either Spaniards or Creoles, *audiencias* against *cabildos,* the latter against intendants, and one region against another. The real contest was between Spaniards and the most outspoken Creoles. Unrest took varying forms. In Mexico, the Spaniards soon hatched a reactionary conspiracy to bring down their own viceroy because he appeared to favor the Creoles on the question of home rule. The Creole-dominated city council of Mexico City, which was holding up the transfer to Spain of the funds consolidated from the church, had become too influential for some Spaniards. After the successful coup, they rounded up the Creoles who belonged to the *cabildo* and flung them into prison. These reactionaries even organized their own Spanish militias, made up of clerks from the Spanish merchant houses, to reinforce their control. In Buenos Aires, an influential merchant led a similarly reactionary conspiracy against the French-born Viceroy Liniers. The Spanish governor of Montevideo also separated his city from Liniers's authority because the latter was thought to be a tool of the French "impostor," King Joseph I. Even though Liniers had the backing of the local Creole-led militias, he was replaced by a viceroy appointed by the junta in Spain. By 1810, nonetheless, the *cabildo* of Buenos Aires emerged as the most powerful local political entity, precisely because it had the backing of the militias—and the Creoles dominated the town council.

In Venezuela, Peru, and Chile, the Spanish authorities survived Creole-led conspiracies and remained in tenuous control—at least for a while. A delegation of important Creole landowners in Caracas presented a petition to form a local junta to govern the captaincy-general until Ferdinand regained his throne. The Spanish captain-general took umbrage, rallied the *pardo* militia units to his side, and threw the petitioners in jail for a few days. In Peru, the Spanish viceroy secured enough support from the Creole class, which vividly recalled the great Túpac Amaru revolt. He then helped Spanish officials defeat Creole militants in La Paz. A Creole junta in Quito deposed the Spanish governor and claimed political jurisdiction over Cuenca and Guayaquil, both of whose Creoles refused to throw off their own Spanish officials just to be governed in dictatorial fashion by fellow Creoles from Quito. The viceroy of New Granada, in the meanwhile, was diverted by his own political crisis quashing rebellious Creoles in the capital, Bogotá. The diversion prompted the viceroy of Peru to intervene in the southern province of the viceroyalty of New Granada, and a counterrevolutionary force was sent to put down the Ecuadorian junta, which collapsed from internal bickering just as the Peruvian forces approached Quito. A momentary compromise was reached between Spaniards and Creoles only in Chile, where a junta was established in which moderate Creoles held four of its seven seats in 1810. They provided for a kind of home rule that had no legitimacy in law or precedent and would soon succumb because not even the Creoles were united behind one political plan.

CONCLUDING REMARKS

This sort of pushing and tugging between Spaniards and Creoles could not go on interminably. Similar kinds of local struggles between the two groups played themselves out, over and over again, throughout the Spanish Americas, but even in the short term it caused such a breakdown of social authority that inevitably another force took control of events: the majority population. The popular classes, after all, harbored grievances of considerably more gravity than either the Spaniards or the Creoles, both of whom had been too self-absorbed to understand this. Thus, after three centuries of colonial rule, a breakdown of elite consensus led to insurrection. The question was: Would the outcome of this revolt be a radical social revolution on the model of Haiti or a moderate political revolution like that of the United States?

Additional Reading

Alden, Dauril. *Royal Government in Colonial Brazil: With Special Reference to the Administration of the Marquis of Lavradio, Viceroy, 1769–1779*. Berkeley: University of California Press, 1968.

Andrien, Kenneth J. *The Kingdom of Quito, 1690–1830: The State and Regional Development*. Cambridge, England: Cambridge University Press, 1995.

Andrien, Kenneth J., and Lyman L. Johnson, eds. *The Political Economy of Spanish America in the Age of Revolution, 1750–1850*. Albuquerque: University of New Mexico Press, 1994.

Barbier, Jacques A. *Reform and Politics in Bourbon Chile, 1755–1796*. Ottawa, Canada: University of Ottawa Press, 1980.

Brading, D. A. *Church and State in Bourbon Mexico: The Diocese of Michoacán, 1749–1810*. Cambridge, England: Cambridge University Press, 1994.

———. *The First America: The Spanish Monarchy, Creole Patriots, and the Liberal State, 1492–1867*. Cambridge, England: Cambridge University Press, 1991.

Brown, Kendall W. *Bourbons and Brandy: Imperial Reform in Eighteenth-Century Arequipa*. Albuquerque: University of New Mexico Press, 1986.

Brown, Kendall W., and D. S. Chandler. *From Impotence to Authority: The Spanish Crown and the American Audiencias, 1687–1808*. Columbia: University of Missouri Press, 1977.

Burkholder, Mark A. *Politics of a Colonial Career: José Baquíjano and the Audiencia of Lima*. Albuquerque: University of New Mexico Press, 1980.

Chandler, D. S. *Social Assistance and Bureaucratic Politics: The Montepíos of Colonial Mexico, 1767–1821*. Albuquerque: University of New Mexico Press, 1991.

Farriss, Nancy. *Crown and Clergy in Colonial Mexico, 1759–1821: The Crisis of Ecclesiastical Privilege*. London: Athlone Press, 1968.

Fisher, J. R. *Government and Society in Colonial Peru: The Intendant System, 1784–1814*. London: Athlone Press, 1970.

Kuethe, Allan J. *Cuba, 1753–1815: Crown, Military, and Society*. Knoxville: University of Tennessee Press, 1986.

Lynch, John. *Spanish Colonial Administration, 1782–1810: The Intendant System in the Viceroyalty of the Río de la Plata*. 2d ed. Westport, Conn.: Greenwood Press, 1969.

Maxwell, Kenneth R. *Conflicts and Conspiracies: Brazil and Portugal, 1750–1808*. Cambridge, England: Cambridge University Press, 1974.

———. *Pombal: Paradox of the Enlightenment*. Cambridge, England: Cambridge University Press, 1995.

McFarlane, Anthony. *Colombia before Independence: Economy, Society, and Politics under Bourbon Rule*. Cambridge, England: Cambridge University Press, 1993.

Spalding, Karen, ed. *Essays in the Political, Economic, and Social History of Colonial Latin America*. Newark: University of Delaware Press, 1982.

Taylor, William. *Magistrates of the Sacred: Priests and Parishioners in Eighteenth-Century Mexico*. Stanford, Calif.: Stanford University Press, 1996.

TePaske, John, and Herbert S. Klein. *The Royal Treasuries of the Spanish Empire in America*. 4 vols. Durham, N.C.: Duke University Press, 1982.

Washburn, Douglas Alan. "The Bourbon Reforms: A Social and Economic History of the Audiencia of Quito, 1760–1810." Ph.D. diss., University of Texas at Austin, 1984.

Weber, David J., and Jane M. Rausch, eds. *Where Cultures Meet: Frontiers in Latin American History*. Wilmington, Del.: Scholarly Resources, 1994.

In Spanish and Portuguese

Castro Gutiérrez, Felipe. *Nueva ley y nuevo rey: Reformas borbónicas y rebelión popular en Nueva España*. Zamora, Michoacán, Mexico: Colegio de Michoacán, 1996.

Halperín Donghi, Tulio. *Reforma y disolución de los imperios ibéricos, 1750–1850*. Madrid: Alianza Editorial, 1985.

Novais, Fernando A. *Portugal e Brasil na crise do antigo sistema colonial (1777–1808)*. São Paulo: Editôra Hucitec, 1979.

Rodríguez Garza, Francisco Javier, and Lucino Gutiérrez Herrera, eds. *Ilustración española, reformas borbónicas y liberalismo temprano en México*. Mexico City: Universidad Autónoma Metropolitana, 1992.

CHAPTER 15

CIVIL WAR AND INDEPENDENCE

Historical instances of what we today call "revolution" have come in many varieties. This book has already mentioned the industrial revolution, a dramatic transformation in the way that men and women manufactured consumer goods in factory settings by substituting inanimate for human or animal power and by applying mechanical technology to production. The industrial revolution began in England in the eighteenth century and gradually spread to Continental Europe and to the United States. It became a powerful agent in changing the way people lived and worked, but economic forces tend to provoke gradual rather than abrupt change in the human condition.

Political and social revolutions are different. In both of these, the use of violence tends to bring about sudden transformation. Political revolutions usually change the leadership of government and introduce reforms to the political system without fundamentally interrupting the underlying structure of society. Some examples of these limited political revolutions have already been presented here, such as the coup d'état in which the Spanish reactionaries in Mexico City deposed a Creole-backed viceroy in 1808. But some political revolutions are more far-reaching than a mere coup d'état. The achievement of independence for the United States in 1782 and for Brazil in 1822 introduced fundamental changes in both countries that represented a new direction in their political development. However, even political revolutions of this more pervasive kind leave social structure virtually intact, despite constitutions that set out new rights of citizenship and mandate the reform of social conditions deemed to be unjust by those coming to power. And any violence associated with political revolutions is usually limited to a narrow group of competing politicians.

Although rarer than political revolution, social revolution produces great change. Both may share the elements of violence and transformation, but social revolution involves all social classes, not just the political leadership, and eventually leads to rapid shifts in the structure of society as well as in the political regime. A social revolution mobilizes the masses and places arms in their hands, leading to consequences far more chaotic and destructive than those associated with mere political revolutions. The newfound power of the armed masses to determine the outcome of mainly political disputes among the elites allows the popular classes to contribute their own agenda to the fight. They might seek legal equality with elites, an end to social restrictions, or even a redistribution of income and property. Although the masses may not achieve all of their goals and although some powerful leader may eventually emerge to restore familiar elements of the old order, social revolution seldom permits a complete restoration of the status quo ante.

What was about to happen to many colonies of the vast Spanish Americas in 1810 amounted to social revolution. The breakdown of consensus among the political elites would lead to a mobilization of the masses; the resulting violence would be widespread and destructive; social reforms like the end of native tribute and the African slave trade would be enacted; and eventually a new group of autocratic leaders would attempt to restore order, often with little immediate effect. Yet within a decade and a half, nearly all the Iberian colonies in the Americas would achieve a costly political independence.

REBELLION OF THE MEXICAN MASSES

The Hidalgo Revolt

Two years of reactionary rule from 1808 to 1810 had unnerved the Creoles of New Spain. A group of young militia officers, whose careers were thought to be stifled by Spanish monopoly of the higher military ranks, were planning a rebellion in the Bajío region north and west of the viceregal capital. They recruited an older Creole parish priest, Father Miguel Hidalgo y Costilla, the curate of the relatively undistinguished town of Dolores. Father Hidalgo had reason to participate in sedition. He was, after all, not a Spaniard but the native-born son of a Spanish hacienda administrator. His brilliant student career in the seminaries of Valladolid (today Morelia), though interrupted when his Jesuit teachers were expelled in 1767, resulted eventually in his appointment as rector. But he ran afoul of his clerical superiors, all Spaniards, who suspected that he was reading and discussing the outlawed books of the French Enlightenment and consorting openly with women in Valladolid. He avoided being defrocked but had to endure the demeaning appointment as curate of this small town in the Bajío. In Dolores, Father Hidalgo had thrown himself into ministering to his flock, earning a reputation as a priest devoted to economic reforms in his parish and to intellectual discussions with other Creoles.

Father Hidalgo's parishioners responded enthusiastically when their respected parish priest set them to fashioning homemade weapons. Most of the residents of the Bajío were small proprietors and tenant farmers and mestizo or Hispanicized native workers on the surrounding haciendas. Few native peasants actually remained in this region of commercial farms, whose former prosperity had been based on providing crops, mules, and livestock to the mining camps. The offspring of the Otomí-, Tarascan-, and Nahuatl-speaking indigenous peoples worked as dependent peons on lands owned by others. Their direct overseers were mestizos and mulattoes who worked for the Creole and Spanish owners. The Bajío developed as a commercial agricultural zone and had grown wealthy and diversified by providing the mining zones farther north with wheat and other products.

However, the once prosperous Bajío region was now destitute. Commercial growth in the eighteenth century had permitted large landowners to consolidate control of the land. They eliminated most of the subsistence and small producers, converting them into peons, which was tolerable as long as the commercial prosperity of the region continued. It did not. The European wars had interrupted world trade, ravaging the mining industry, and the droughts of 1785 and 1808 produced sharp famines in succeeding years. The cost of living soared for the rural workers. Corn prices rose from 16 reales per *fanega* (roughly 115 liters) in 1790 to 21 reales in 1809 and then to 36 reales in 1811. (The specter of famine recalled the epochs before the Aztec, when central Mexican empires had risen and fallen according to the droughts and famines, as described in Chapter 1.) The economic conditions in the Bajío provided a perilously unstable fuse for popular rebellion.

Thus, it was a humble people that the Creole conspirators, Father Hidalgo among them, sought to enlist in their struggle against the Spaniards. With other Creoles sitting on the fence, this ambitious group had little other hope than to enlist the popular classes in effecting a successful campaign for liberty and independence from the exploitative Spaniards in Mexico. But someone betrayed the conspiracy to the authorities. Hidalgo acted fast and, on September 16, 1810, he rang the church bells in Dolores. In the Grito de Dolores (Cry of Dolores), Father Hidalgo summoned his parishioners to rebellion with shouts of "Death to bad government," "Death to the *gachupines* (a derisive term for "Spaniard" in late colonial Latin America)," and "Viva Ferdinand VII." They marched off to seize the neighboring towns following the banner of the Virgen de Guadalupe, potent symbol of the Mexicans' devotion to a religious patroness identified not only with Mexico but also its pre-Spanish origins. As the followers of Father Hidalgo reached the mining city of Guanajuato, they had grown to a poorly armed but enthusiastic horde of 25,000 people. Except for the leaders, who were all white, only 100 other Creoles had joined the rebellion.

Then came the event that was to define the rebellion for many a cautious Mexican Creole—the sack of Guanajuato. The Spanish intendant gathered together all the wealthy Spanish residents, some Creoles as well, and their liquid assets into the fortresslike public granary in the city. In a savage attack, Hidalgo's horde surrounded and stormed the granary. The commoners who followed Hidalgo then killed every man, woman, and child who had taken refuge there—500 in all. The slaughter of so many Spaniards shocked the elites of Mexico to the point that they easily dismissed the 2,000 insurgents who also died in the attack. One young Creole witness to the sack of Guanajuato later expressed the fear of the whites toward the insurgency of the common people, whom he called *"indios,"* "people of the countryside," and the "plebeians of Guanajuato." Lucas Alamán explained why these people became revolutionary: "When the dominant vice in the mass of the population is the propensity for robbery," he wrote, "a revolution can easily find partisans."

Hidalgo's forces picked up even more humble supporters as he led them west to seize Valladolid in the province of Michoacán, where Hidalgo had been a seminarian. Like the pre-Colombian armies of old, the troops of Father Hidalgo formed a community on the move. Women and children joined the campaign, accomplishing essential transport and mess duties for the troops. In the meantime, a group of coconspirators had taken Guadalajara. Everywhere that these rebels went, they left a wake of destruction and pillage. Father Hidalgo gave in to popular desire for vengeance, looking the other way as his troops executed Spanish captives in cold blood. He also realized that to keep his forces together, he had to allow them to pillage. They seized Spanish property for redistribution.

The program of Hidalgo stands as testimony to just how beholden this Creole leader became to his followers. He soon revealed his real political pretensions, announcing that his movement was for liberty and Mexican independence. Hidalgo dropped all references expressing loyalty to the Spanish king incarcerated in France; instead, Spaniards were to be banished from Mexico, and their property was to be confiscated. To gain the commitment of his lowly followers to his political aspirations, however, he and his commanders had to create a program that addressed their social concerns. Hidalgo abolished native tribute, outlawed slavery, and ordered that land taken from the indigenous villages be returned. However, the contradictions of his movement became evident when his force, now numbering 80,000 people, approached Mexico City in November 1810.

The Spaniards, after all, had not been idle as Hidalgo consolidated his military control in the west; they were busy exploiting the symptoms of three centuries of colonial social divisions. To retain the loyalty of the many indigenous peasant communities that still dominated the rural landscape of the Valley of Mexico, the viceroy [himself] decreed an end to native tribute. The specter of race war, in the meanwhile, sufficed to gain Creole support for the defense of the capital from Hidalgo's troops. Spanish propagandists portrayed the rebels as "Indians," which technically was incorrect (in more than one sense, of course) but still had the effect of rousing the racist fears of the Creole population; the latter ignored the fact that the rebellion killed more Spaniards than native-born whites and that nonwhites suffered the overwhelming majority of casualties. In the meanwhile, loyal militia troops had been brought into Mexico City from the northern mining zones. Considerably better trained and equipped than Hidalgo's combatants, these outnumbered troops inflicted 2,000 casualties on Hidalgo's forces in the first military encounter outside Mexico City. Then Hidalgo pulled back, and nearly forty thousand volunteers immediately deserted his army. Nonetheless, Hidalgo refused to pursue what was still his military advantage. He waited three days for the peasants of the Valley of Mexico to rally to his banner. They did not. Three centuries had taught the indigenous peoples that the Creole landowners were less preferable than Spaniards. The colonial state and its "Indian" court at least had protected their villages from the harshest exploitation, which had come principally from Creole employers. Even though Hidalgo issued a decree abolishing native tribute, the peasants in the Valley of Mexico still decided to remain neutral in the military contest for the viceregal capital. What could they expect from independence if it meant Creole political domination?

As women of the popular classes were assisting their menfolk in Hidalgo's forces, so did the elite women of Mexico City organize to resist. Spanish women in the capital formed the Patriotas Marianas when Hidalgo's "rabble" surrounded the city. They took charge of rallying the defenders to the Virgen de Remedios, patroness of the Royal Army, and sewed her image onto the banners of the troops to counter the insurgents' use of the Virgen de Guadalupe. The Marianas mobilized 2,500 women to support the forces defending the viceregal capital.

Waiting in vain for the natives of the Valley of Mexico to arise, Hidalgo's movement began to collapse, slowly at first and then with alarming rapidity. He withdrew from Mexico City, regrouped in Guadalajara, suffered a stunning defeat at a village north of the capital, retreated northward as his last troops deserted him, and was captured in Coahuila. His captors transported him to Chihuahua. There Father Hidalgo was tried and, together with three other rebel leaders, executed by firing squad. In July 1811, their severed heads were taken to the granary at Guanajuato and displayed on pikes for the next 10 years. Yet rebellion was not snuffed out.

The Morelos Rebellion

Leadership now passed to a number of different Creole and mestizo *caudillos,* popular military leaders, who operated against the Spaniards and their many allies among the Creoles. Ignacio Rayón, Guadalupe Victoria, Vicente Guerrero, and the Bravo brothers provided insurrectionary leadership over the next decade. More immediately, however, José María Morelos picked up the fallen banner of Father Hidalgo. Morelos was the son of a mestizo carpenter from the western province of Michoacán. Although his swarthy complexion was sure to limit his prospects, Morelos enrolled in the same seminary that had trained the older Hidalgo. As a native-born parish priest, Morelos was stuck in a poor parish in rural Michoacán when the Hidalgo revolt broke out. He rushed to meet Father Hidalgo prior to the advance on Mexico City and agreed to organize the revolt in western Mexico. Hidalgo had ordered him to take the port of Acapulco. Following his mentor's execution, Morelos took it upon himself to maintain the political and social struggle.

Father Morelos proved a more effective military commander than his predecessor. Preferring to operate with a guerrilla force numbering no more than 2,000 to 3,000 experienced troops, he ranged widely west and south of Mexico City. Morelos received support from the indigenous peasants and small proprietors in the provinces that formed a wide arc from Michoacán south into the state that now bears his name and east to Puebla. However, Morelos preferred that his partisans remain on the land, providing support for his guerrilla troops, as they moved quickly in small columns to engage or flee from the militias fighting for the Spaniards. His mobile force escaped a three-month siege at Cuautla and survived to capture Oaxaca from the loyalists in 1812.

Thousands of women mobilized in wars of independence on both the insurgent and royalist sides. For the insurgents, women carried messages across the lines, smuggled goods and ammunition, and fraternized with enemy troops—many of whom were mestizos—to get them to end their war on the insurgents, urging them to desert with promises of a plot of land. Most of all, they accompanied the combatants, preparing food and nursing them. Creole wives became famous for their sympathies for the insurgents and for sowing dissension in the households of their husbands, the Spanish officers. The most famous case is that of Doña Leona Vicario, who defied her wealthy family by defending the insurgents and by smuggling money and arms to them. Doña Leona was imprisoned in 1813, and her property in Mexico City was confiscated. She escaped to join the forces of Morelos, marrying one of his chief lieutenants, Andrés Quintana Roo, and remained a rebel until independence was finally gained.

In Mexico as subsequently in the rest of Latin America, federalism become the political program of the insurgents, although they remained divided on social reforms. Morelos assembled a congress at Chilpancingo in 1813 to formalize the rebels' plans for reform. The Creole political leaders who attended the congress found it easy to ratify a Declaration of Mexican Independence. Their vision for an independent Mexico included a powerful congress, a federalist political structure, and a weak national executive, all of which Morelos thought would be entirely unworkable. With less enthusiasm, however, the congressmen passed constitutional provisions outlawing slavery and ending native tribute. In truth, slavery had all but passed into irrelevance, not the least because many of the remaining slaves had joined the rebel movement in the mountains of Veracruz. Also, few natives had been paying tribute since the first days of the Hidalgo revolt. But the Creole delegates drew the line at eliminating legal distinctions among the various races and castes that made up Mexican society.

Morelos himself had insisted that all Mexicans—be they native, white, mestizo, or mulatto—should be considered equal before the law and be able to rise to all public offices (see Manuscript 15.1). Although he often hinted about the need to equalize the distribution of property and to institute a graduated system of taxation, he did not actually draw up a plan to attack the inequality of wealth that reinforced racial and ethnic inequalities. Replicating the programmatic weakness of other rebels before and since, Morelos had to acknowledge the importance of the Creoles. "The whites are the principal representatives of the kingdom, and they were the first to take up arms in defense of the Indians and other castes, allying with them," he said; "therefore the whites ought to be the object of our gratitude and not of the hatred which some people are stirring up against them." As a man of his time and place, Morelos misplaced his loyalty and his own best interests in survival. He could not sustain his mainly nonwhite troops in the field against enormous odds, granting them the social reforms they demanded, while at the same time attempting to assure native-born whites of his conservative social intentions. Few Creoles rallied to his cause, and quite a few found advantage in joining the fight against the *caudillo.*

Father Morelos's direct downfall can be attributed to the Spanish military onslaught and to the fact that he perhaps wasted his military strength by complying with Hidalgo's

MANUSCRIPT 15.1

Popular Reforms Advocated by Morelos, 1815

The leaders of the popular rebellions during the Wars of Independence, such as Hidalgo and Morelos, had to become spokesmen for the concerns of their followers. Therefore, the basic institutions by which the elite had reinforced their social status throughout the three previous centuries thus came under review by the insurrectionaries who fought the Spanish forces. In Mexico, the popular demands included the abolition of slavery; the end to legal restrictions on persons of mixed race, or castas; free elections of village leaders; and the suspension of personal service. Morelos needed to respond to the causes

of the popular classes because he depended on volunteers to fight for independence. In response to these demands, José María Morelos penned the following decree.

America must distance itself from Slavery and everything associated with it; therefore, I order the Provincial Intendants and other magistrates to oversee that all those remaining enslaved shall be set free and all the Indians who constitute Towns and Nations should have their free Elections presided over by the Parish Priest and the Territorial Judge

original order, which was to take Acapulco. This sleepy port once had been the terminus of the famous Manila galleons but had long ago lost most of its commercial value. Nevertheless, Morelos spent several precious months besieging this port on the sweltering Pacific Coast while loyalist forces destroyed his village bases in the higher, temperate valleys of Michoacán. In the meanwhile, the Creole lawmakers who made up the Congress of Chilpancingo began to bicker among themselves. They even removed Morelos from his command for a time until loyalist forces put the congress itself on the run in 1815. Then the congressmen returned Morelos to his military command. He protected the escape of many of these patriot politicians, but militia forces under Spanish command captured Morelos. The priest-cum–guerrilla commander was tried for treason and heresy, found guilty, and executed by firing squad in December 1815.

The Unrest Persists

Land did not seem to have been an issue in the Hidalgo and Morelos revolts, and they certainly did not become class wars. The Creole leadership held very general political notions and did not at all espouse any ideological commitments that would motivate indigenous peasants to revolt en masse. The fact that peasants and peons in some areas joined the revolt while others did not suggests that issues of village identity and autonomy remained key factors. Villagers could be xenophobic and reactionary in the face of the outside encroachment that some of the Bourbon Reforms might have provoked without becoming revolutionaries. One native town, Tonalá in Jalisco, had had a long history of insolence toward Spanish officials, yet it failed to rise up in support of either Hidalgo or Morelos. Apparently, this village was secure in its autonomy, because few nonnatives lived among them and it had always prospered on its fine crafts. Still, other villages reacted to the higher taxes and unscrupulous gouging imposed by royal authorities in Mexico City and

who will not repress any person, even if the ineptitude of the elected person can be demonstrated with proof to the superior body in charge of approving the Election: thereby preventing the Nations and Judges from Enslaving the Indians from the villages with personal services which they owe only to the Nation and sovereignty and not to any individual; it will be sufficient to render service only to the sheriff, the subdelegate, and Judge, and only for one year and this service should alternate between the Villages and the Haciendas which employ at least 12 servants without distinctions of caste which shall remain abolished. And in order that everything is punctually and well executed, I order the Intendants to circulate the Necessary Copies to anyone who requests them for their instruction and compliance.

SOURCE: Decreto de José María Morelos, Chilpancingo, October 5, 1813, in Manuel Arellano Z ., ed. *Morelos documentos*, 2 vols. (Morelia: Gobierno del Estado de Michoacán, 1965), 2:58. Translated by Teresa Van Hoy with the assistance of Pablo Atilio Piccato Rodríguez.

Guadalajara. Rebellion and revolutionary unrest thus persisted in certain locales of the provinces to the north, west, and south of the capital.

The Mexican countryside remained fairly rebellious following the defeat of Morelos. In the provinces west of Mexico City, bandit gangs had always operated, carrying out robberies and preying on rich and poor alike. They divided up the booty according to who planned the robbery and who carried firearms. Those with the most experience or the longest prison records—or Creole ancestry—generally assumed leadership of the gangs. The rise of insecurity in the countryside during the Hidalgo and Morelos revolts only proliferated the operations of these bandits.

Nevertheless, in 1817, following the execution of Morelos, the loyalist cause appeared to have triumphed in New Spain even if the economy lay prostrate. Mexican silver production dropped precipitously after the Grito de Dolores. From a high of 122 million pesos per year, the mines were reduced to producing less than 50 million pesos between 1810 and 1814. In just five years, the revolution for independence had set back the Mexican silver industry by three-quarters of a century. The mining industry collapsed during the independence movement not because of violence and depredations but because it had long since become a drag on the economy. Wages had failed to keep up with inflation, and agricultural markets were nearing a grave crisis. Yet the colonial state continued to promote and subsidize the silver mines. In other words, the ill-conceived colonial economic policies were also contributing to the breakdown of Mexico's economy.

Therefore, the defeat of Morelos proved illusory to the Spanish loyalists in Mexico. Society was growing weary of civil war, of an economy destroyed in the fighting, and of unrepentant Spaniards. The Creoles were frightened and confused, and the popular classes had neither forgotten Hidalgo and Morelos nor forgiven those who executed them.

Native Revolt in Peru

During the revolutionary period, the Creole class of Peru suffered some of the same handicaps as its counterparts in Mexico. Creoles outnumbered the Spaniards by a wide ratio, it was true, but they in turn were outnumbered by the natives three to one. White Peruvians had not forgotten the rebellion of Túpac Amaru just 30 years previously. Despite some early experimentation at challenging Spanish political authority in Lima and elsewhere, the Creoles succumbed to their characteristic conservatism and fear of social change. As obnoxious as Spanish rule was to the local elite, at least the *gachupines* could be relied upon to keep the indigenous masses in line. Therefore, the Spaniards utilized their relatively secure bastion at Lima to send counterrevolutionary expeditions to Chile, Upper Peru, and Quito, as shall be seen anon. Creole support and participation in these expeditions served to prevent racial strife, which often attended revolution, from reaching Peru. Once again, the social constitution of a colony determined the nature of its revolutionary experience during this critical time.

In all of Peru during the entire 16-year period of the independence wars, there was only one real Creole conspiracy of significance, which took place in Cuzco in 1814. The conspiracy also stood out for the Creoles' having enlisted the subordinate classes—in itself, not an unusual occurrence in this era. But in this case, the subordinates, who were native Andeans, took control of the rebellion from the Creole leadership and threatened to make it an indigenous movement on the order of the original Túpac Amaru rebellion. The Cuzco rebellion of 1814 did not lack irony: it was led by a *kuraka* who had opposed Túpac Amaru in 1780 and who had faithfully served the Spanish counterrevolution, too.

Mateo Pumacahua was already 70 years old in 1814 and had amassed an impressive record of service to his king. In 1780, he had led his people, the Chincheros, against Túpac Amaru although—or perhaps because—he, too, was descended from the Inka nobility of old. Spanish officials rewarded Pumacahua and his people with honors and properties for their loyalty. After 1811, additional Spanish requests for assistance came to the elderly *kuraka*. He personally led his people into Upper Peru to sack the rebellious city of La Paz, and his troops helped subdue the restless natives of Cochabamba and Oruro. The Spaniards promoted Pumacahua to the rank of brigadier general. He also received appointment as president of the *audiencia* of Cuzco in 1814, an absolutely rare instance of a Native American reaching such a high office in the Spanish government. Did this mean that indigenous Andeans would gain their equality through cooperation with Spaniards? Not in Pumacahua's case. The Spanish viceroy soon countermanded his promotion to the highest tribunal of Cuzco. The *audiencia* was already embroiled in a power struggle with the Creoles of Cuzco, and the authorities did not want a native-born person—whether indigenous or not—presiding over this important institution. Pumacahua was crestfallen that the Spaniards at long last would question his loyalty or that of his people.

In the meantime, the Creoles on the *cabildo* seized the incident as a way to increase their own power vis-à-vis the Spaniards of Cuzco. They imprisoned all the Spanish authorities in the city and sent for Pumacahua. The elderly native leader joined the Creoles, who even conferred military command on the venerable *kuraka* while they retained political command at a safe distance from battle. What they most desired, of course, was to enlist the indigenous masses to the Creoles' political project of wresting power from the Spaniards. Peruvian Creoles also desired to end the counterrevolutionary military campaigns, for which they were paying taxes. Their program did not encompass any changes to the social order in the Andean region.

Nevertheless, the natives and mestizos of the highlands rallied to the banners of the Pumacahua insurrection. Expeditions against Puno succeeded without bloodshed, but the native and mestizo troops became uncontrollable in La Paz. They sacked the city, slaughtered the garrison, and hunted down the Europeans. Pumacahua led the expedition from Cuzco to Ayacucho, which his native troops overwhelmed without too much trouble. When a Spanish army approached the city, executing indigenous captives in the process, Pumacahua put the captured Spanish intendant to death in reprisal. By now, it was evident that those Creoles who had enlisted the natives to fight had lost their taste for rebellion. Several wealthy Creole families of the highlands began to doubt the wisdom of unleashing the indigenous masses and might have been relieved when a disciplined Spanish unit in Upper Peru recaptured La Paz and Puno. The Creoles who had encouraged Pumacahua now abandoned him. Defeated in battle in March 1815, Pumacahua was taken by the Spaniards to his home town and executed there in front of his own people. Thereafter, for the next five years, the Creoles never again challenged the Spanish rulers. Peru remained staunchly royalist.

THE REVOLUTION IN THE RÍO DE LA PLATA

The Río de la Plata was the one region where the independence movement took hold early and endured only to devolve into chaos and dissolution. Creole insurrectionary leaders could not maintain unity among themselves and, unable to overcome their racism, lost the initiative to the popular rebellion from below. The rural gauchos and the urban blacks and *pardos* took matters into their own hands. Colonial social controls lost their old power (they had always been imperfect, anyway). The popular classes gained a measure of revenge for past discrimination by engaging in attacks on property and direct appropriation (which the elite called "stealing"). In the process, the artificial geographical unity of the Viceroyalty of the Río de la Plata became unglued.

Political Decentralization

Buenos Aires made itself the leader of revolution in the Southern Cone by virtue of the political and social changes resulting from the 1806 British invasion. The cowardly actions of Spanish officialdom at that time had given a political lift to the Creoles. The leaders of the militias, in particular, acted as the spearhead of Creole political assertiveness. They formed a tenuous alliance with their own troops, whose numbers had grown to more than three thousand in the city. These *pardo* and black militiamen now had weapons in their hands, received pay and rations that represented a considerable redistribution of income, and strutted through the city with new pride and self-importance. Not all Spaniards and Creoles were pleased. But the once powerful and wealthy Spanish merchants had fallen on hard times when Napoleon's invasion of Iberia had cut communication to their trading partners in Spain. The British and U.S. merchant ships drawing up to the city benefited Creole merchants and rural producers, with whom the Spaniards now had to compete on equal footing. So when the news arrived in 1810 that the French forces had invaded southern Spain, disbanding the very junta at Cádiz that had just appointed the new Spanish viceroy at Buenos Aires, the Creoles were ready to act.

The militia leaders forced the viceroy to call a *cabildo abierto,* an open town meeting, so that the populace could advise the viceroy on how to respond to the new political developments. Armed supporters of the Creole leaders surrounded the *cabildo* building, intimidating the Spanish delegates into staying away. On May 25, 1810, a date celebrated today in Argentina as Independence Day, the *cabildo abierto* succumbed to the pressure, voted to depose the viceroy, and appointed a ruling triumvirate of three Creoles including the Jacobin intellectual Mariano Moreno. The triumvirate, however, was not yet ready to drop the "mask of Ferdinand" and promised to return sovereignty to the Spanish king when he was released by the French. To many Spaniards, the commitment of Creole politicians to royal authority lacked sincerity.

Several factors prevented a rapid succession of Creole political revolutionaries from realizing their plan of gaining political control of the whole of the former Viceroyalty of the Río de la Plata. First of all, they bickered among themselves, intriguing, allying, and breaking up into feuding factions. Their plans, nicely formulated in endless proclamations, were quite impractical. Despite their decrees ending the slave trade at Buenos Aires and declaring Freedom of the Womb in 1813, in which children born to slave women after 1813 would be free when they reached their twenty-first birthday, the Creoles held their own *pardo* and free black followers in contempt. These leaders also had a tendency to turn on each other savagely. Mariano Moreno lost favor in 1811, and to get rid of him, his rivals sent him on a diplomatic mission to Europe, en route to which he died at sea. Others who lost favor were imprisoned. The vengeance even caught up with Santiago Liniers, hero of the British invasion and former viceroy. From his retirement in Córdoba, he voiced opposition to the arrogant manner with which the Buenos Aires junta treated the cities of the interior, for which transgression Liniers was executed. The future hero of independence, General José de San Martín, formed an altogether unsympathetic opinion of the Creole politicians at Buenos Aires. "We are being ruled by sheep, not by men!" he exclaimed.

The second reason why Buenos Aires could not effectively exert its leadership was that the Creole leaders of the other regions of the Río de la Plata desired not to be governed by their incompetent peers of the faraway port but by home rule, however ineffectual it, too, might prove to be. Across the estuary at Montevideo, the Creole gentry preferred to support the Spanish governor rather than follow the dictates of the divided politicos of Buenos Aires. In Upper Peru, the *porteños* squandered initial support by sending three "liberating" military expeditions to bring the Bolivians under political control. The *pardo* and black troops of Buenos Aires were unruly and given to riot and pillage. The Creole military leaders were no better, twice sacking the mint at Potosí and once attempting to blow it up. Besides, the social liberalism of the *porteños* also annoyed the Bolivian Creoles. The *porteños,* who had had no experience with a sedentary and subordinate native population, misunderstood the social conservatism of their peers in Upper Peru. Even though they refused to outlaw slavery back in Buenos Aires, the *porteño* invaders in Alto Peru had no second thoughts about decreeing the end to the *mita* and other labor drafts, the termination of native tribute, and equality between natives and whites. Bolivian elites were not unhappy to see Spanish forces beat back every one of the military expeditions sent by Buenos Aires in 1811, 1813, and 1815.

For the most part, the revolution in Upper Peru was to be sustained by Bolivian guerrilla bands. The rural *caudillos,* who usually came from the local white gentry or sometimes from the mestizo middle groups, organized resistance to Spanish officials. These guerrilla leaders in Bolivia, often with popular support, established local zones of domination that they liked to call *republiquetas,* "little republics." Within their bailiwicks, the *caudillos* were the law. They carried out forms of direct justice, assessing their own taxation of the peasants and tradesmen to sustain their military forces. Six major foci of such guerrilla activity emerged in the rural zones between the major cities of Bolivia early in the revolutionary period: at Lake Titicaca (led by a parish priest), the two regions on either side of Chuquisaca, at Ayopaya near Cochabamba, at Santa Cruz, and along the trade route leading toward Salta. These guerrillas fought bloody battles among themselves for leadership and power and preyed on the local populace perhaps more than they represented yearnings for freedom from Spanish rule. There was but a fine line between a patriot band and a bandit gang. Ultimately, these *republiquetas* remained vulnerable to Spanish forces coming up from the Viceroyalty of Peru and did not figure in the later consolidation of Bolivian independence.

Paraguay also resisted the political leadership of Buenos Aires. In 1811, the native-born gentry backed the Spanish intendant in defeating an expedition from the port. Afterwards, however, those same Creole landowners themselves overthrew the intendant. The Paraguayans were the first to actually gain independence from Spain, which they accomplished in gaining autonomy also from Buenos Aires. Soon one man, José Gaspar Rodríguez de Francia, consolidated power in Paraguay to guarantee Paraguayan independence. His strong-armed populism presaged one style of leadership that would bring order out of the wars of independence. To gain local political control, he made personal alliances with the humble smallholders against political competitors among his elite peers, the *hacendados* and merchants. Two congresses dominated by the popular classes voted

Francia dictatorial powers, the first in 1813 for a five-year term and the second in 1818—this time for life. From Spaniards and his political enemies, Francia confiscated property that he turned over for redistribution to his humble supporters. In other words, he purposely leveled society nearly to one class, those who were subordinate to his will; however, slavery for blacks did continue throughout his reign. Francia all but eliminated the gentry, from whose ranks he himself had been born and raised.

The isolation of landlocked Paraguay, where Guaraní remained the lingua franca among the mestizo as well as the native population, permitted Francia to militarize society. He organized a praetorian army of 3,000 regular troops and supplied them with equipment, remounts, and food from an extensive network of *estancias del estado,* state-owned ranches. The militarization of Paraguay, no doubt, was facilitated by the heritage that the mission Guaraní had developed under the Jesuits.

The independence of Paraguay came at the price of its complete isolation. Because the political powers downriver would not allow him free navigation on the Paraná River, Paraguay's lifeline to the sea, Francia sealed off the country. After 1818, British and other foreign merchants were denied entry, and others were not permitted to leave. Paraguayans became completely self-sufficient, their famous yerba maté supplanted in South American markets by poorer quality Brazilian and Argentine teas. The government restricted trade only to designated river ports and then under careful supervision. At the river port town of Itapúa, trade was conducted with Brazil partly so that Francia's troops could obtain foreign-made weapons. Thus, Paraguay secured independence as the result of a tacit agreement between one omnipotent leader, Francia, and the popular classes. Francia's policies purposely impoverished the merchant and landowner class in favor of the subsistence farmers. Although the country's isolation did not permit the creation of wealth through commerce, Francia apparently assured the population an adequate level of subsistence. He remained in power until his death in 1841. Paraguayans suffered the revolutionary chaos far less than any other national group but the Brazilians, although the popular classes were not trusted to decide their own political and social destinies.

The Popular Revolution

There is a third reason why Buenos Aires was ineffective in spreading its Creole political leadership over the Río de la Plata, and it had to do with social revolution. Given the ruinous bickering among the Creoles, the lower classes took matters into their own hands. These popular rebellions, occurring simultaneously in most regions of the old viceroyalty, radically decentralized political leadership and led to a brief but intense period of direct appropriation and redistribution of property. The landholding and merchant classes viewed these last two actions as robbery and pillage. But the rebels considered them as a just redistribution of what others had made from the labor of the popular classes during the long colonial period. It should not be assumed that these exercises of direct sovereignty of the mounted soldiers, the *montonera,* amounted to popular democracy and socialization. Among these groups, power flowed from the tip of the lance, and humble farmers and innocent girls suffered from their depredations in greater measure than the elite. After all, the old order had not prepared people of the nonelite classes for democracy and human rights. But in the process of the revolution, these popular rebellions advanced the political cause of federalism and pushed a social agenda that the Creole leadership otherwise would not have shared.

The *artiguista* movement of the Banda Oriental and the Riverine Provinces of Argentina is a perfect example of the popular rebellion at work. The *artiguistas* followed José Gervasio Artigas. He was a revolutionary *caudillo* from the Banda Oriental (today's Uruguay). In the colonial days on this rough-and-tumble frontier between Spanish and Portuguese territories, Artigas worked alternately as a cattle rustler, a landowner and cattle breeder, and the leader of mounted police forces that brought order to the countryside. Instability had abounded in the Banda Oriental, stirred up by Spanish and Portuguese conflict over control of the contraband trading port of Colonia. After Spain eliminated the Portuguese from the Banda Oriental in 1776, the area became a prosperous zone of cattle breeding and illegal trade in Brazilian black tobacco. The port of Montevideo developed as a commercial auxiliary to Buenos Aires; although Montevideo had a better port and its warehouses overflowed with hides and other pastoral products, Buenos Aires retained the commerce in silver from Potosí.

The rivalry between the two sides of the Río de la Plata estuary continued into the period of revolution. In 1810, the *orientales,* or Easterners, as they were known then, preferred to support the Spanish governor at Montevideo rather than submit to the Creole junta at Buenos Aires. However, the Spanish officials in 1811 raised their tax demands on the cattlemen—even questioning their property rights—and then invited a Portuguese expeditionary force from Brazil to help fight Buenos Aires. Although the British finally persuaded the Portuguese to leave, Artigas turned his fellow landowners against the Spaniards. He raised a gaucho army to besiege the Spaniards at Montevideo. Mutual hostility on the part of the Spaniards, Portuguese, and the *porteños* forced Artigas and 3,000 followers to make a dramatic retreat across the Uruguay River into Entre Ríos. There he quickly became the champion of the rural popular classes—made up of mulatto and mestizo gauchos, small-scale cattle raisers, and the remaining indigenous groups. In the politics of the region, Artigas represented federalism. He became the protector of the Federal League of the Río de la Plata, demanding equal status with Buenos Aires and retaining military and political autonomy within his region.

Federalism in the Río de la Plata, as in Mexico and elsewhere during the revolutionary wars, rested firmly on a popular base. Wherever social authority had eroded to the extent that the popular classes were able to act on their own agenda, a popular *caudillo* such as Artigas emerged to represent their interests. The *caudillo* himself might have been a landowner, as was Artigas, but his followers determined the content of the federalist program. In the case of *artiguismo* from 1813 to 1818, the popular followers of Artigas were very stout, indeed. Warfare had removed nearly all social authority in the countryside. The gauchos, who had been peons during the late eighteenth century, now inherited the land on which they had once worked for others. Small bands of men and women traveled in the backlands and simply helped themselves to the cattle and horses. They dried a few hides to trade for tobacco and *aguardiente,* the sugar brandy consumed by the popular classes of the region.

These were the humble folk whose cause Artigas championed in the Banda Oriental, Entre Ríos, and Corrientes. Therefore, because his control over these popular forces depended on his faithfulness to their agenda, Artigas enunciated a radical social program (see Manuscript 15.2). If he had not, he would not have had any followers at all, and a rival leader would have arisen to represent them. Artigas advocated a radical redistribution of the land. He proposed to take land from Spaniards and those Creoles who sided with Spaniards in order to redistribute it among "*pardos,* Zambos, and Indians." The banners of federalism also fluttered over the *montonera,* the mounted gangs, of other provincial *caudillos.* All the federalist bands, to a certain extent, lived off pillage. Federalists adopted political programs of regional autonomy because it was in the local arena that their followers of popular classes could more effectively carry out their social agenda of direct appropriation and redistribution of property.

It should be mentioned that the federalism of the revolutionary period contained its own contradictions of colonial origin. In all cases, the leaders were Creoles or mestizos

DOCUMENT 15.2

The Land Reforms of Artigas

As a popular military leader, José Gervasio Artigas also had to renounce the property interests of his own class—for Artigas was a Creole landowner himself—to meet the demands of his followers. In the Río de la Plata, the free blacks, mulattoes, and mestizos who made up the insurrectionary forces had come from the least privileged ranks of colonial society. Therefore, they longed for a redistribution of one of the basic economic assets that had reinforced their low status: the ownership of land. Artigas addressed these concerns during the brief time that he controlled Montevideo, the capital of the Banda Oriental in 1815. These attempts to convert the rural workers into middle-class landowners did not go into effect, because a Portuguese invasion from Brazil soon forced the popular forces of Artigas to vacate the territory known today as Uruguay. Nonetheless, the proposed reforms do articulate some of the objectives of the popular classes during the long struggle for independence.

Sixth. For now the Provincial Mayor and other officials under him will dedicate themselves to promoting vigorously the well-being of the population of the Campaign, for which they will inspect in each one of their respective Jurisdictions the available land, and the Subjects worthy of this act of grace, and with precaution, let the most miserable become the most privileged. Therefore, free Blacks, Sambos of this class, Indians, and poor Creoles, all can be favored with the good fortune of an *estancia* (cattle estate), if with their work and their honorable manhood, they advance their own happiness and that of the Province.

Seventh. Poor widows with children will be likewise favored. Married people will be preferred over single citizens, and the latter over any foreigner. . . .

Twelfth. Properties available for redistribution are all those of people who have fled to exile, of bad Europeans and worse Americans who so far have not been pardoned by the Chief of the Province so that they could possess their former Properties. . . .

Seventeenth. The Government, the Provincial Mayor, and other subordinates will keep watch to make sure that the land recipients do not possess more than the designated size of land grant [1.5 x 2 leagues]. . . .

Nineteenth. The land recipient can neither alienate nor sell these lots nor contract any debt on them upon pain of nullification, until the formal regulation of the Province in which it will deliberate over what is advisable.

SOURCE: "Reglamento Provisorio de la Provincia Oriental. . . ," in John Street, *Artigas and the Emancipation of Uruguay* (Cambridge, England: Cambridge University Press, 1959), 376–79. Translated by Teresa Van Hoy.

whose class and perspective were not the same as those of the followers. Although the *caudillo* on the rise reflected the popular agenda, the *caudillo* who consolidated political power certainly returned to the colonial legacy of disciplining the popular classes and governing them by autocratic rather than democratic means. These popular *caudillos* ultimately brought a semblance of order out of the chaos of the revolutionary period by returning to these legacies of social control. However, José Gervasio Artigas was not to be among these few. He would lose the political struggle before he was able to consolidate sufficient power to perform this conserving task.

The challenge of the *artiguistas* to Buenos Aires hegemony rose significantly when they liberated Montevideo from the Spaniards in 1815, ostensibly gaining political autonomy for the *orientales*. It was not to last. The Portuguese from Brazil returned in 1816, drove Artigas back across the Uruguay River, and blockaded Buenos Aires. Other popular *caudillos,* in the meanwhile, were operating in the interior provinces of Argentina. Francisco Ramírez became the strongman of Córdoba, Facundo Quiroga operated in La Rioja, Martín Güemes protected the autonomy of Salta, and eventually Ramírez supplanted Artigas in Entre Ríos. Because some of his erstwhile federalist allies had turned against him, notably Ramírez, the defeated Artigas requested sanctuary in Paraguay. Francia wanted no problems with the *caudillos* of the neighboring provinces, so he forced Artigas to retire permanently from politics. The federalist *caudillo,* who lived out his days in Paraguay, is considered the father of Uruguayan independence. However, Uruguay would not actually gain its independence until 1828, when Great Britain, the biggest trading partner of both Brazil and Buenos Aires, convinced these two powers to end their competition over the old colonial buffer zone known as the Banda Oriental. Although independence of the Argentine region that formed the heartland of the former viceroyalty was never in doubt after 1816, when a congress at Tucumán proclaimed it, the political system (federalist or centralist) that this region would adopt remained uncertain. The centralists formed an entity known as the United Provinces of the Río de la Plata. They attempted to rule over these provinces from Buenos Aires, but the surviving federalist *caudillos* ran their own provinces. This version of local autonomy, of course, stood in stark contrast to the centralizing program of the Bourbon Reforms.

THE CONSOLIDATION OF INDEPENDENCE

Even though the federalist *caudillos* and their followers had destroyed the colonial political order, they themselves had not been able to consolidate independence. That remained the task of three leaders who developed rather more national—even supranational—perspectives on eliminating Spanish rule in the Americas. Each of these men was a professional soldier who commanded the loyalties of the local *caudillos* in the course of determining the outcome of the revolution on national and continental scales. These men were Agustín de Iturbide in Mexico, José de San Martín in southern South America, and Simón Bolívar in northern South America. However, none of these leaders represented the popular revolution. If anything, they attempted to tame the popular revolution so as to finally eliminate all remaining vestiges of Spanish power in the Americas. They were also visionaries, as each laid plans for the governments and social relationships that should follow independence. However, Iturbide, San Martín, and Bolívar proved more successful at winning independence than at charting the future tranquility of the American nations. Each ended his career in bitter disillusionment.

Independence of Mexico

Following the capture and execution of Morelos in 1815, the royalists and insurgents settled into a relative state of equilibrium although the popular revolution would not subside. The Spaniards held out especially in the large cities and in central Mexico, protected by a conscript army of poor workers, Mexican *vaqueros* (cowboys), and peons. Spanish rule had been prolonged when the end of the European wars freed up some skilled and resolute Spanish commanders for the colonial struggle. The newly arrived officers had led the guerrillas in Spain against the French and now came to Mexico to serve as anti-insurgency commanders. These Spanish generals formulated a program of "blood and fire," putting the torch to villages thought to be supporting the guerrillas and executing those men suspected of sympathizing with the insurgency and confiscating their properties. "Your Excellency," one Spanish general wrote to the viceroy, "it is no longer possible to suffer more from this vile scum; only examples of exemplary terror will make them understand their duty." The new Spanish military officers intended to intimidate the colonials into submission—despite the fact that an identical French policy had just failed in Spain!

Many Creole military officers also participated in this brutal royalist campaign. One such officer was Agustín de Iturbide, son of an *hacendado* whose own estate had been overrun and razed by the forces of Morelos. Just like the other commanders on both sides, Iturbide condoned the summary execution of all prisoners and the confiscation of property. He even took cash and goods from royalist noncombatants, saying "The king pays for nothing." Such activity easily spilled over into outright corruption and profiteering. Royalist officers lived opulent lives, engaging openly in business, extorting customers and associates, collecting forced loans for themselves, and confiscating properties liberally. Iturbide himself became wealthy in this manner. But always he had to serve under Spanish commanders who arrived and departed while Iturbide stayed on year after year, fighting without an end in sight. Creole officers such as Iturbide seldom received promotion or recognition for their military glories and had to settle for pillage on a lesser scale than their Spanish superiors. In time, these indignities rankled the Creole officers.

However, the countryside, especially in the provinces surrounding the Valley of Mexico on all sides, belonged to the numerous insurgent bands that were, at times, indistinguishable from the bandits. These groups numbered several hundred at most, led by regional leaders fighting for local autonomy in the style of the federalists of Argentina and Bolivia. They, too, were autocratic, ruthless to prisoners and enemy sympathizers, and not above using their positions for personal aggrandizement. On the latter score, one rebel leader at Guanajuato was making 1,000 pesos a month collecting "taxes" from the local merchants. Several larger groups operated south and east of the capital. Guadalupe Victoria commanded 2,000 ragged troops in the mountains of Puebla, and 1,000 men in Oaxaca followed Vicente Guerrero. Both had been lieutenants of Morelos. Under these and other partisan commanders, the insurgency in the countryside took on the aspect of a social revolution. The rebels attacked haciendas, seized the property of the well-to-do, and put white citizens to the sword. To the east of Mexico City, in Veracruz, the runaway slaves who formed many small bands took particular pleasure in attacking the plantations of their former owners. To the west, in the provinces of Jalisco and Michoacán, landless peasants took to guerrilla warfare as a means to acquire land; no tax collectors dared visit them. To the north in Querétaro, a Spanish commander reported the haciendas were "isolated, destroyed, sacked, and ruined." Guerrilla forces everywhere intercepted commerce and forced merchants and muleteers to pay customs duties.

Even though these insurgents were unable to take Mexico City and end the conflict, neither could the royalists defeat the insurrection. The colonial state of New Spain, already near bankruptcy in 1810, increased its indebtedness from 15 to 38 million pesos during the Hidalgo and Morelos revolts. The devastation to internal commerce and to agricultural production reduced its revenue by one-half from the pre-1810 days. The once great silver mines lay in ruins.

The exhaustion of the insurgency contributed to the inevitable compromise solution. The rebels at long last had realized that they had little hope of taking Mexico City without support from the Creole elite, which the social revolution had failed to destroy. The loyalists became increasingly aware of the futility of defeating the elusive rebellion that "renews itself and grows like grass," as one royalist commander put it. The initiative for the political compromise—like the spark that set off the revolt in the first place— came from outside. In 1820, Spanish soldiers being transported to fight the unpopular colonial wars rebelled and forced King Ferdinand to accept the Liberal Constitution of 1812, which converted the Spanish government from an autocratic to a constitutional monarchy featuring a powerful Cortes. However, the Spanish liberals, who wished to impose social reforms on the colonies such as an end to native tribute and an imposition of the universal rights of man, offered little support for the conservative Creoles, who were appalled by such suggestions. And neither did the Cortes tip the balance of power in favor of the colonial rebels, for Spanish liberals utterly opposed the independence of the colonies.

At this point, the Mexican Creole military officer Agustín de Iturbide, still a colonel after 10 years of frontline service for the royalists, decided to negotiate with the Mexican guerrillas instead of continuing to fight them. He conferred with the venerable rebel leader Vicente Guerrero, and together they arrived at a compromise, the Plan de Iguala, named for the site of their meetings and also often referred to as the Plan of Three Guarantees. The first guarantee came in the form of a compromise between the monarchist Iturbide and the federalist rebels on the form of government to be adopted in the wake of Spanish withdrawal. These old Mexican adversaries chose a constitutional monarchy, promising to enlist a suitable prince from a European royal family. Secondly, both the pious rebels and Iturbide agreed that the church would retain all its privileges and powers and that Catholicism would be the exclusive religion of the realm. Finally, the rebels gave in on the third guarantee: Mexicans and Spaniards would be treated equally in the new regime. There was to be no persecution of the hated *peninsulares* in an independent Mexico, and the agreement did not mention the social concerns that had been dear to the hearts of the rebels for so long. Iturbide now became head of the Army of the Three Guarantees, which was made up of his own formerly royalist troops as well as rebel soldiers. He finally received promotion to general.

The Plan de Iguala was a masterstroke. Once Iturbide had adopted the cause of a "conservative" independence movement and succeeded in bringing in the rebels, the other Creole military officers joined him. Iturbide soon obtained the resignation of the reigning viceroy. However, the Liberal Cortes back in Spain did not agree to independence, and its members sent out another viceroy with a new Spanish army. Backed by the Mexican political consensus and the Army of the Three Guarantees, Iturbide met the Spanish viceroy-designate on the road to Mexico City on August 30, 1821, and he promptly signed a treaty recognizing Mexican independence from Spain. The number of people killed during the various insurrections cannot be calculated. Conservative estimates place the number at 200,000, whereas extreme estimates suggest 600,000, which would mean that 1 in 10 Mexicans perished in the fighting. Some were Spaniards; most were colonials. Because they bore the brunt of the fighting, nonwhites of the *gente de pueblo* suffered the greatest casualties of all.

Central America was spared the civil conflict through which the Mexicans secured their independence, although Spanish rule had not gone unchallenged after 1810. The Spanish captain-general of Guatemala, José de Bustamante y Guerra, successfully stifled Creole rebellions in El Salvador, Nicaragua, and Honduras. He prevented the enforcement in Central America of the constitutional reforms that the Cortes of Spain had established for the colonies in 1812, and the return of Ferdinand VII to the Spanish throne affirmed Bustamante's strong-arm rule. However, his successor, who arrived in 1818, dealt more moderately with the factions desiring more autonomy. The domestic elite in Guatemala and Chiapas, who oversaw large majorities of indigenous peasants, did not wish to change the political arrangements. The other Central America intendancies, nonetheless, seethed with resentment over commercial and political domination by Spanish merchants and officials in Guatemala City. Each town council, therefore, seized the initiative when the news arrived of Iturbide's Plan de Iguala. Guatemala City and most other towns quickly agreed to join the new nation of Mexico. San Salvador, Granada (Nicaragua), and San José (Costa Rica) held out for autonomy from both Mexico and Guatemala, leading to the first civil wars of the independence period. In Guatemala proper, the old pattern of white domination of the indigenous peasant majority continued just as in colonial times. In the other parts of the region where society had always been more fluid and racially mixed, the local elites began to fall away from Guatemala. Central America thus became independent of Spain—though unified securely neither unto itself nor with Mexico (see Map 15.1).

Liberation of Chile

In 1812, José de San Martín returned to the land of his birth, Argentina, after a career as an army officer fighting in Spain against the French. His father had also been a career officer in the colonies, stationed at Yapeyú on the Uruguay River, where José was born. On his return, San Martín offered his services to the various governments at Buenos Aires, which felt secure only in sending a man of San Martín's caliber far into the interior of the country. In 1816, he commanded the patriot army that stopped a Spanish invading force sent over the Andes Mountains from royalist Peru. Rather than repeat the folly of invading Upper Peru for the fourth time, San Martín decided that the surest way to eliminate the Spanish bastion at Lima lay through Chile. Therefore, he established headquarters at Mendoza, where he trained an expeditionary army composed of Argentineans and Chilean exiles. The major part of his force, especially the foot soldiers, consisted of people of color. San Martín requisitioned slaves from the local gentry, giving them their freedom on the condition that they fight for the cause of independence. Eventually, 1,500

Map 15.1   Mexico, Central America, and the Caribbean in 1825

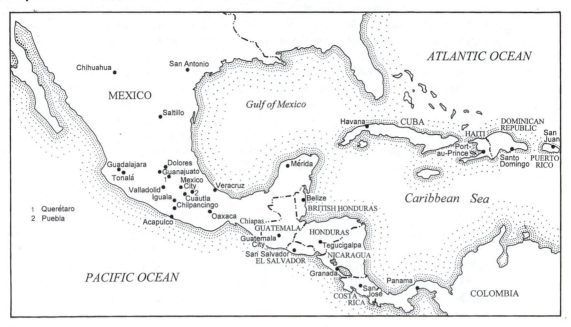

slaves entered his army. Under his command, the blacks, mulattoes, and mestizos formed a disciplined fighting force and did not engage in the sort of pillage that characterized other military units of the period. Exiled Chilean patriots led by Bernardo O'Higgins contributed another important element to this expeditionary force.

Like Argentina, Chile had also adhered early to the independence movement. Upon hearing of the acts of the *cabildo abierto* in Buenos Aires, the Spanish governor in 1810 arrested three prominent Creole aristocrats in Santiago. The outcry in Chile was so great that even the Spanish judges of the *audiencia* decided to depose the governor. But before the year was out, the Chileans held their own *cabildo abierto* and selected a junta to rule the colony, in which Creoles formed the majority of the membership. A debate then ensued as to the proper political course to take: reformism or revolution. Bernardo O'Higgins championed the cause of independence. His father had been an Irishman in the service of Spain who served as governor of Chile and viceroy of Peru. Although Chilean born, Bernardo had been educated in England, where he had met the Venezuelan precursor of independence, Francisco de Miranda. He was managing his family's hacienda in Concepción in 1810 but decided to enter politics by raising a militia to support the new junta. Among its first acts was to decree the opening of Chilean ports to ships of all neutral nations, and he collected the tariff revenues for local use only rather than sending them back to Spain. The few revolutionaries among the landowning elite made a coup d'état on the moderate junta in 1811, a move that frightened many conservative Creoles. A Spanish military expedition, manned by veteran troops of the Iberian wars, set out from Lima in 1814; it attracted moderate Creole supporters and defeated a badly prepared patriot force. O'Higgins and other leaders escaped across the Cordillera to join up with General San Martín in Mendoza, after which the victorious Spaniards miscalculated. They ruthlessly repressed those who had stayed behind in Chile, imprisoning influential Creole leaders and confiscating their properties. Guerrilla bands formed in the Chilean countryside to resist this return to Spanish rule—and to await the patriot invasion being prepared in Mendoza.

General San Martín of Argentina executed a great military feat in safely leading his 5,000 troops across the Andes Mountains. He misled the Spaniards as to his route and reassembled three columns of his troops in time to defeat a divided Spanish force at Chacabuco in February 1817. His troops then liberated the capital of Santiago. Two more battles ensued, and San Martín decisively defeated the remaining Spanish forces at Maipo in April. With Chile liberated and now ruled—firmly but not ruthlessly—by O'Higgins, San Martín laid the strategy for the next continental move. He hired a British admiral, Lord Cochrane, to organize a patriot navy for the expedition. San Martín formed a new army of Chileans, Argentineans, and Peruvian patriots. But he had no Peruvian leader of the stature of the Chilean O'Higgins. Again, slaves enlisted in his army and were subjected to military discipline in exchange for their eventual freedom. Chile levied special taxes to support the new patriot army, just as the citizens of Mendoza had supported the liberation of Chile. In 1820, 23 ships bearing the patriot army of 4,500 soldiers set sail for Lima.

From the very beginning, the campaign in Peru did not go according to expectation. San Martín landed his troops at Pisco, 200 kilometers south of Lima, and sent the fleet on to blockade the port of Callao. His patriot column then marched north, circling around the viceregal capital of Lima and setting up headquarters at Huacho. San Martín's presence sparked guerrilla activities in the sierras, but the Creole aristocracy of Lima, on whom the Argentinean general had expected some demonstration of support, sat on their hands. Nothing happened. Rather than confront San Martín in battle, the Spanish forces proceeded to negotiate. Finally, in 1821, they evacuated Lima and relocated in the highlands as San Martín entered Lima. The Creoles professed to be pleased, but they were also dismayed that the bandits and brigands, many of whom were free blacks and runaway slaves and who had made travel outside the capital so perilous, had now joined San Martín's patriot troops.

In the absence of a united Creole government, San Martín himself had to accept political leadership. The citizens of Lima may have been motivated more by public security than by making sacrifices for the liberation of Peru. They developed a widespread fear of the troops of San Martín. "Indians and guerrillas . . . surround the city and . . . , in this time of surprise, could cause many disorders," the city council reminded him, "if you do not act opportunely to prevent it." It was not lost on the local landowners that control of their slaves was undermined by the fact that many of San Martín's troops were former African slaves as well as free blacks. Moreover, San Martín levied special taxes to support his troops, which made him unpopular with the residents of Lima, the *limeños*. Here was the problem. General San Martín hesitated to risk his army in confronting the enemy, who could actually gather twice the number of troops that he could. He was receiving little assistance from the Peruvians. Moreover, as provisional governor, he alienated many Creoles by enlisting their slaves into military service, decreeing a law freeing the children born to slaves and outlawing native tribute and forced labor. The Creoles would not rise to his revolution and finally, in 1822, San Martín was ready to try another solution. The arrival of General Simón Bolívar, fresh from liberating Colombia, Venezuela, and Ecuador, gave him the opportunity. In February 1822, San Martín set sail to interview Bolívar in Guayaquil.

THE LIBERATION OF NORTHERN SOUTH AMERICA

If the young, idealist hotheads had started the revolutions for independence, it was the hard, cold realists who finished them up. Rarely were these the same individuals, except in the case of Simón Bolívar. He had experienced all the vicissitudes of the struggle. He had participated in the initial juntas, fell victim to the incessant quarreling among the Creole leadership, was undone by the rejection of nonwhites, escaped the Spanish counterrevolution, went into exile, returned to convince the nonwhites that independence was also their struggle, scaled the heights to surprise the royalists, and united the revolutionary factions under his leadership. He led the liberation of all of northern Spanish America and then expelled the Spaniards from Peru and Bolivia. No matter how great his genius for leadership, the revolutions remained larger than Simón Bolívar. He attempted to build nations from the liberated colonies, fashioning thoughtful organizations of government for the new polities. But in the end, the very peoples Bolívar helped liberate finally rejected him.

Venezuela and Colombia

Caracas was the first colonial city to learn of the breakup of the Spanish junta in 1810. A group of young Creole leaders who had been waiting for just such an opportunity shoved aside the Spanish authorities in April of that year and converted the town council into a new government for the colony of Venezuela. Of course, the town councilors all pledged allegiance to Ferdinand VII, although not all meant it. Infighting soon broke out between the autonomists, who simply wanted home rule until the king returned, and the *independentistas,* who wanted to shatter all ties to the king. Bolívar belonged to the latter group, and he secured the return of General Francisco de Miranda to assist them in gaining enough power to declare independence on July 5, 1811.

This first Republic of Venezuela, which lasted for only one year, came to be known as La República Boba, "the Foolish Republic," for the ruinous disunity among its first leaders. However, the Creole leaders actually failed because they had not taken account of the numerous nonwhites in Venezuela. Most of the leaders, Bolívar among them, had been cacao planters and slave owners, and although they outlawed the slave trade, they preserved slavery. For the numerous free blacks and *pardos* (mulattoes), the new government of independence offered equality but not suffrage, for only men of property and learning could participate in politics. Immediately, the *pardos* rebelled against the new Creole government, supported by the loyalist clergy. The African-Venezuelans rose up and committed violence, robberies, and destruction against the properties of Creole patriots. In the midst of this popular rejection, a devastating earthquake struck Venezuela, nearly destroying Caracas. It appeared to the faithful that God himself had decided against La República Boba, which fell in July 1812. Bolívar and others fled from Caracas to lead patriot military resistance in Colombia and the hinterlands of Venezuela.

The ensuing struggles in Venezuela amounted to civil war. While Spanish troops were tied down in the Iberian struggle against the French between 1808 and 1812, the American wars of independence divided the Creole aristocracy into loyalist and patriot camps. Moreover, the more important struggle raged for the hearts and minds of the nonwhites, who had been recruited as cavalrymen and foot soldiers to fight the battles of this civil war. The slaves did not play a role at this juncture—for neither side envisioned an end to slavery. However, it was the royalists in Venezuela who, at first, won the backing of the free blacks, *pardos,* and mestizos. In the expansive Llanos, the Spanish *caudillo* José Tomás Boves had organized the mestizo and *pardo* cattle hunters into ferocious cavalry-men who fought for the king. Between 1812 and 1814, his mounted troops swept the plains of all the patriot military forces and ascended into the northern Andean valleys to lay waste to the properties and lives of Creole landowners. Boves gained fame for taking no prisoners.

Victory seemed all but ensured for the royalists in 1815. King Ferdinand VII had been restored to the throne of Spain the year before and immediately dispatched veteran Spanish soldiers to secure the colonies. General Pablo Morillo arrived in Venezuela with more than ten thousand troops, who soon swept nearly all the remaining patriot forces from the field. This was Bolívar's darkest hour. While Bolívar took refuge in Jamaica and then Haiti, General Morillo and the resurgent Spanish colonial authorities proceeded to pun-ish the Creole aristocracy for the insurrection. They confiscated plantations and slaves and sold them at auction to pay for the Spanish army. Patriots were hunted down and im-prisoned; a few were executed. During this interlude, the Spaniards made it obvious that the *pardos* and other nonwhites would not receive rewards for having resisted the pa-triot forces. Slavery continued as before. Imposition of the harsh Spanish colonial regime, in fact, began to convince many whites and nonwhites alike that neutrality in the revo-lutionary struggle was becoming impossible.

Therefore, when Bolívar returned in 1816 to begin the final campaign against Span-ish rule in northern South America, both he and the Americans he was about to lead were wiser even if no closer to independence. His first task was to win over the popular classes, beginning with the *llaneros.* Bolívar set up his rebel headquarters on the Orinoco River in the heart of the Llanos region. Fortunately, his old nemesis, the Spanish *caudillo* Boves, had died in battle in 1814, and now a number of other *caudillos* were or-ganizing guerrilla bands that, in true federalist style, operated in their local regions. Bolí-var proceeded to curry the favor of these *caudillos,* bringing the greatest of them, Gen-eral José Antonio Páez, under his nominal command. While in the Llanos, Bolívar began to prepare for the political structure of the new nations, fashioning model constitutions and writing lengthy political treatises. Among the momentous social reforms he advo-cated was the abolition of slavery. Although his Creole followers rejected the notion, ar-guing that the revolution must preserve property and that slaves were property, Bolívar as general had to recruit among the slaves. Like San Martín, he held out the promise of freedom if the slaves would fight for the cause of independence. Bolívar's new policies of accepting the legitimate demands of the popular classes did enable him to recruit ef-fectively from the *pardos* and mestizos of Venezuela and Colombia—though without alienating the Creoles. Still, he was no closer to victory, as General Morillo was firmly en-sconced in Caracas with a powerful Spanish army. Bolívar needed a significant military victory to gain momentum for the cause. Bolívar decided to outflank the enemy—in Colombia, where General Morillo had left a small military force to protect the Spanish au-thorities at Bogotá.

The Creoles here, too, had had an early experience at political autonomy. In 1810, several Creole revolts broke out in highland cities, culminating in Bogotá. A *cabildo abierto* was called, the viceroy was deposed, and power was passed without bloodshed into the hands of the most prominent Creole aristocrats. But they could not agree on what to do next, as the cities (even elites within cities) divided themselves between the centralists wanting a strong central government and the federalists wanting local autonomy. The intrepid printer Francisco Nariño was called back from exile to lead the new junta as a centralist. He sent out several military expeditions from Bogotá to enforce central authority over Tunja and fought off criticism from the new congress that he was a tyrant. Nariño attempted to take the revolution to the south but was defeated and captured by the royalist inhabitants of Pasto. Bolívar arrived in 1814 to assist the federalists in subduing the centralists but fell into the trap of endless civil strife between the Creoles. He left in 1815, just before the Spanish general, Morillo, arrived with a fresh army of reconquest. The divided Colombians capitulated in city after city, but the Spaniards had not yet learned that severe repression of the Creole aristocrats did not bring pacification. The year 1816 was one of gallows, jails, and property confiscation for the Creoles as Colombia fell into a brief but exhaustive period of Spanish rule. The Creoles now paid dearly for having had their own República Boba. In 1819, however, a military victory on the plains of Casanaré by Francisco de Paula Santander revived Colombian resistance and availed Bolívar of the opportunity to return.

Bolívar's *llanero* cavalry, *pardo* infantry, and British auxiliaries joined Santander's forces at Casanaré in 1819, and together they crossed the most forbidding—thus undefended—snow-capped mountain pass into the highland valleys surrounding the viceregal capital of Bogotá. Despite having lost nearly a quarter of his men and equipment in the passage, Bolívar's army won an easy victory at Boyacá. The viceroy and the remaining Spanish troops fled, and the patriots entered Bogotá. Bolívar designated General Santander to govern the Colombian territory now in patriot hands and returned to Venezuela. While he was preparing to battle General Morillo for Caracas, the Spanish imperialists suffered a defeat on the home front. The colonial wars were not popular in Spain, and at Cádiz in January 1821, Spanish troops about to be dispatched to the Americas revolted and forced the autocratic monarch, Ferdinand VII, to accept a constitution and to share power with a new Cortes. (This was the same Spanish rebellion that provoked the compromise of Mexican independence.) In Venezuela, General Morillo was replaced, and the royalist cause lost much of its confidence. At the Battle of Carabobo, General Páez assisted Bolívar in defeating the last Spanish army. Venezuela was finally liberated. Bolívar now turned to the last territories of the former Viceroyalty of New Granada remaining in royalist hands.

Ecuador

To conquer (or "liberate," as Bolívar would have termed it) southern Colombia and Ecuador, the Great Liberator now put into motion a grand plan to create one republic out of Spanish North America. He immediately dispatched General Antonio José Sucre with 1,000 troops to take leadership over the guerrilla and federalist rebellions in Ecuador. He did not wish to lose Ecuador to San Martín and thus to a union with Peru. Bolívar himself remained in Colombia and helped organize the Republic of Gran Colombia, composed of Venezuela, Colombia, and the yet-to-be liberated Ecuador. The new constitution favored a centralist form of government, because the intellectual author of the document, Bolívar himself, had long since renounced his federalist sympathies. He became the first president of Gran Colombia. There he also utilized Colombian resources, relying on Vice President Santander to obtain the resources through confiscation of Spanish properties and simple taxation needed to build a joint Venezuelan-Colombian expeditionary army. In

Map 15.2   South America in 1828

the meanwhile, Panama on its own threw out the Spanish authorities and joined Gran
Colombia.

When Bolívar's emissary General Sucre reached Ecuador, he found yet another region that had experienced a period of political autonomy, made the worst of it, and then

General Páez and the *llaneros* of Venezuela, 1819. (Arturo Michelena, ca. 1890)

suffered a savage counterrevolution. The difference was that in Ecuador this scenario had occurred not once, as in Venezuela and Colombia, but twice. In 1809 the Creoles of Quito had been the first in Spanish America to attempt to establish home rule. It did not turn out to be a popular rebellion, for the wealthy and most powerful Creoles had organized it. Even the Bishop of Quito participated because the conservative new junta neither represented a threat to the church nor changed the status of the mass of Native Americans in any way. Nevertheless, the viceroy of Peru sent a Spanish expedition against the patriots in Quito because he did not want their example to spread; the sister cities of Guayaquil and Cuenca also assisted the royalists. But once in control of Quito, the royalist troops went on a rampage, destroying patriot property and killing 60 Creoles. When the Peruvian troops left, the *quiteño* elites took back their city and killed several Spanish officials. But even this second patriot regime was weak, as Cuenca and Guayaquil chose to stay with the royalists. The indigenous masses remained either neutral or in the Spanish camp, for the Creoles could not bring themselves to alter the status of the Native Americans in any significant manner. Therefore, a second royalist army arrived in 1812 and reestablished Spanish rule in the Andean city for the next eight years until Bolívar's army arrived from Colombia.

The final liberation of Quito consisted of a pincher movement featuring Bolívar's drive out of Colombia [from the north] and Sucre's from the south. Bolívar won a costly victory in the south of Colombia at Bombona and drew Spanish reinforcements north to help defend the royalist bastion of Pasto. To accomplish his part of the strategy, General Sucre first took Guayaquil and diplomatically glossed over the disagreements among those patriots (many of very recent vintage) who favored autonomy, those wanting union with Peru, and those desiring union with Colombia. Assisted by Peruvian patriot units, he then met the royalist force outside of Quito in a battle on the slopes of the extinct volcano of Pichincha. The victorious General Sucre then liberated a grateful Quito. (Indeed, the Ecuadorians would later name their national currency the sucre after their deliverer.) It must be concluded that in Ecuador, unlike Venezuela, the subordinate classes played no role whatsoever in the struggle for independence. The Creole elites at Quito did not have to give in at all to the indigenous agenda; in fact, they were relieved of this unsavory option by being liberated from the outside. To a certain degree, the foreign liberation of Peru would also produce the same result for the conservative native-born elites.

In the meanwhile, Pasto realized that its royalist cause was lost and submitted to Bolívar. Thereupon, the Liberator rushed to Guayaquil, annexed that port city to Gran Colombia, and prepared for the arrival of General José de San Martín.

INDEPENDENCE OF PERU AND BOLIVIA

The people of the Andean region, for reasons already outlined, had to have their independence imposed on them from the outside. The conservative Creoles simply could not sufficiently overcome their fears of an internal race war either to unite against the Spaniards on their own or even to effectively support an outside liberator such as General José de San Martín. But Peru could not be neglected, for no Spanish-American liberation was secure so long as royalist troops might be able to invade Ecuador and Chile as they had earlier. Thus, in 1822 San Martín decided that it was necessary to combine his own forces with those of Bolívar, which had just defeated the royalists in Ecuador. When San Martín went to meet Simón Bolívar in Guayaquil, the former was bogged down and discredited in Peru, and the latter had just triumphed in Ecuador. Bolívar had the upper hand in the negotiations and was not willing to share command with anyone else. General San Martín, therefore, turned over his forces to Bolívar and retired. San Martín traveled through Santiago, crossed the Andes Mountains, and departed immediately from Buenos Aires for a self-imposed political exile in France.

Not all Peruvian elites were happy at the prospect of yet another foreign army coming to "liberate" them. While Bolívar recruited and trained an expeditionary force of Venezuelans, Colombians, and Ecuadorians, bickering among the *limeños* resulted in the fall of Lima to the Spanish forces once again. When in 1824 he finally entered Peru with an army, Bolívar confronted the royalists forces in the highlands at Junín. He could not count on the local natives for assistance because many of them had mobilized to help the royalists. Bolívar still routed them in a famous cavalry battle in which his Venezuelan *llaneros,* reinforced by Argentinean gauchos and Chilean *huasos,* defeated the royalists with lances and swords. Then Bolívar descended to liberate Lima and establish a civil administration. The decisive battle of Ayacucho in December 1924 was the largest of the era, pitting 9,000 royalists against General Sucre's more mobile force of 6,000 patriot troops. Sucre won. Peruvian independence was ensured in January 1826 when the last Spanish forces at the fort of Callao finally capitulated. Liberation had to be foisted onto the Creole elites and had been regarded with indifference if not hostility by the indigenous *kuraka*s of the Andean highlands.

Upper Peru presented Bolívar with an even more royalist enclave.. The strength of the earlier federalist movements in the outlying provinces of the region drove the Creoles to the Spanish cause. The royalist troops at La Paz consisted of native Bolivians and mestizos led by Creole officers. But political factionalism had divided the royalists between those who supported the Liberal Cortes in Spain and those who favored autocracy and royal absolutism. In fact, a civil war among the Bolivian troops had prevented them from assisting the royalist forces in the great battles of Peru. But once victorious, the Bolivian reactionaries faced the task of defending Alto Peru as the last bastion of pro-Spanish rule on the entire continent of South America. Many Creoles recognized the inevitable and went over to the patriot cause in time to help General Sucre beat the weakened absolutists in the last battle of the wars of independence, at Tumusla on April 1, 1825. The epoch of civil war and independence in the former colonies of Spain had come to an end. (See Map 15.2.)

However, the problem of governing Peru and Bolivia now thrust itself upon Bolívar, who responded with characteristic confidence that his wisdom could fashion the perfect constitution for the new governments. He had long ago shed the liberal ideas of his youth and had come to design constitutions that featured strong executive powers (a hereditary president in Bolivia), aristocratic congresses, and moralistic judiciaries. However, as a troop commander, he did recognize the sacrifices and motivations of his mostly nonwhite troops. His constitutions outlawed slavery and ended native tribute, recognizing the political equality of all Americans even though countenancing the inequality of their education and property holdings. However, once the Great Liberator had departed for Bogotá, his Peruvian associates rejected the complete end to slavery, and the new Bolivian rulers reimposed native tribute.

President Bolívar found that, daunting as it was, the liberation of South America had been an easier task that governing it. As president of Gran Colombia, a hybrid nation made up of Venezuela, Colombia, and Ecuador, he ruled from the old viceroy's palace in Bogotá. But late in 1826, his former *llanero* associate, General Páez, rebelled and established Venezuela as an independent nation. Ecuador, too, fell away. Bolívar narrowly escaped an assassination attempt in Colombia, although his most faithful and able lieutenant, General Sucre, did not avoid that fate on a separate occasion. Bitter and sick of body as well as heart, Simón Bolívar renounced his shattered presidency in 1830 and traveled to the coast to follow General San Martín into European retirement. However, he took to bed in Santa Marta. Shortly before dying, he penned his final epitaph to the independence of Latin America. His reference to the social causes of instability serves as a testament to the racial and ethnic inequalities that had been nurtured during three centuries of colonial rule. "America is ungovernable," Bolívar said. "The only thing to do in America is to emigrate" (see Manuscript 15.3).

His fellow liberators would agree with Bolívar. General Iturbide survived the revolutionary period as the most important military personage of Mexico. Thus, he had a great deal of influence on the formation of the constitutional monarchy established by the Plan of Iguala. When the Mexican Congress disputed with him over public expenditures for his army, he simply dismissed them and then crowned himself as Emperor Agustín I. However, the empire lasted less than a year, as his own military subordinates organized a movement that resulted in his resignation and exile. Iturbide made the mistake of returning from exile and was quickly captured and executed in 1824. Alone among the three liberators, José de San Martín survived to survey his handiwork—though from afar. He lived out his days in Paris, disillusioned but resigned that neither he nor anyone else could have prevented the political disintegration of Spanish America. He died in 1850 as the political turmoil continued.

MANUSCRIPT 15.3

The Last Political Testaments of the Great Liberator

Simón Bolívar spent the last four years of his life attempting alternately to govern Bolivia, Peru, and especially Gran Colombia. He failed. Bolívar came to the conclusion that it was easier to liberate America than to govern it. Moreover, his personal bitterness brought out in him the prejudices of his class. Himself a former owner of plantations and slaves, Bolívar began to disparage his enemies and the rabble in racial terms. His testimony, therefore, did not express the views of Native Americans who no longer had to pay tribute after the Wars of Independence, of the slaves who had been freed in the struggle, or of Andean peasants who no longer had to work in the mines of Potosí. But the Creoles who began and ended the revolution certainly were dismayed that the political instability and economic decay did not allow them to reap the expected benefits of displacing the Spaniards in the ruling elite. In the two last years of his life, 1829 and 1830, Bolívar penned these two assessments of the revolution.

There is no good faith in America, nor among the nations of America. Treaties are scraps of paper; constitutions, printed matter; elections, battles; freedom, anarchy; and life, a torment. Such, Fellow-Americans, is our deplorable situation. Unless we change it, death is to be preferred. Anything is better than endless conflict, the indignity of which appears to increase with the violence and the duration of the movement. Let us not delude ourselves—this evil, which increases revolts and mutinies in the armed forces, will eventually compel us to reject the very first constructive principles of political life. We lost all individual rights when, in an effort to obtain them in perfect form, we sacrificed our blood and all that we cherished most, prior to the war—for, if we look back at that time, who will deny that our rights were then more respected? Never were we as badly off as we are at present. At that time we enjoyed positive and tangible benefits, whereas today we have dreams bordering upon illusion, hope feeding upon the future, and disillusionment forever tortured with the bitterness of reality. . . .

America is ungovernable. Those who have served the revolution have plowed the sea. The only thing that one can do in America is emigrate. These countries will surely fall into the hands of the unbridled masses, in order only to later come under the control of almost imperceptible little tyrants of all colors and races, devoured by all the crimes and extinguished by ferocity. Europeans perhaps will not deign to conquer them. If it were possible for part of the world to return to primitive chaos, this would be America's final era.

SOURCES: Simón Bolívar, *The Political Thought of Bolívar: Selected Writings*, ed. Gerald E. Fitzgerald (The Hague, Netherlands: Martinus Nijhoff, 1971), 127; and José Manuel Groot, *Historia eclesiástica y civil de Nueva Granada* (Bogotá: Casa Editorial de M. Rivas, 1889–93), 5:368. Translated by Teresa Van Hoy.

SLAVERY AT THE CROSSROADS

Alone among the former Iberian colonies, those that depended on plantation slave labor avoided the massive popular rebellions that convulsed the rest of Latin America in the second decade of the nineteenth century. The plantation owners in these countries were just too conservative. Cuba and Puerto Rico had a few conspiracies among the elites, but they were minor affairs. In this regard, the two slave societies of the Caribbean were not unlike the Andean societies: The existence of a large mass of nonwhite, underprivileged, and servile workers motivated the Creole elites to temper their political aspirations and to take refuge in the colonial state's commitment to the status quo. The memory of the Haitian slave rebellion was just too fresh. Moreover, both the Cuban and Puerto Rican sugar economies were booming during the second and third decades of the nineteenth century. The collapse of Spanish trade did not affect them because commerce with Great Britain and the United States, tolerated by the colonial authorities, more than made up the difference. Slaves continued to be imported into both Caribbean islands.

Unlike in Peru, the revolution could not be imposed on Cuba and Puerto Rico from without by patriot armies of adjacent countries. The Caribbean islands were too remote from Mexico and Venezuela to be accessible to Iturbide and Bolívar's armies, and neither did they become launching points of colonial reconquest, as Peru had been in the Andean region. In other words, the internal disputes of the Creole elites in Cuba and Puerto Rico never did reach the point of setting off popular rebellions as in Haiti, Mexico, Argentina, and Venezuela. What was true for Cuba and Puerto Rico in the 1810s applied equally to the other sugar islands of the Caribbean. Planter elites refused to experiment politically with home rule, lest their feuding set off slave rebellions. And neither was there to be independence for the other French, Dutch, and British possessions in the Caribbean. Even the Guianas remained faithful to the imperial powers.

Of the important Caribbean slave societies, only Santo Domingo became independent, which was largely due to the fact that the Haitian invasion and occupation from 1806 to 1808 had shattered the institution of slavery and scattered the local Creole elites. The Spaniards were just too preoccupied by the French invasion of the Iberian Peninsula and the wars of independence elsewhere in the colonies to reconstitute their oldest colony of Santo Domingo. In time, the eastern part of the island of Hispaniola became the independent, but impoverished, Dominican Republic. However, one important American slave society departed from this pattern and did successfully achieve independence by the third decade of the nineteenth century: Brazil.

Brazil

Despite its conservative, slave-owning planter elite and the absence of a popular rebellion, Brazil achieved political independence. Moreover, Brazilian independence came without being imposed by an outside army of liberation. The reason is simple: Its political circumstances were opportune. The Brazilian planter elite could have independence without any reference whatsoever to slavery or to social change. In this regard, political history may be seen as the result of accident as well as intention; the student of history can ponder how Brazilian history would have been different if Napoleon had not invaded Portugal and if the royal family of the Braganças had not subsequently escaped to Brazil. But these events did occur.

Once the incapacitated Queen Maria I and her son, the Prince Regent João, reached Brazil in 1808, they set up court in Rio de Janeiro. Brazil then became the seat of imperial rule over Portugal's vast seaborne empire, which stretched through Africa into the lands bounded by the Indian Ocean and the China Sea. The prince regent grew to love his new home, and the colonial planters were proud to have the royal family safely in Brazil, despite the fact that the Portuguese couriers who had accompanied the royal party dominated the imperial government in Brazil. Some Brazilians did come to hold important portfolios in the imperial government, and planter control of local politics and town councils did not come into question. The Braganças wisely acquiesced to expanded British trade in Brazil, and the planter class was satisfied with the buoyancy of export markets and the continuing import of slaves from Portugal's African possessions. They experienced few economic downturns that would cause them to question the legitimacy of royal power. In fact, Brazil was technically no longer a colony at all but had a political status equal to that of Portugal itself—that of a kingdom. There were no liberal movements back in Portugal after Napoleon's troops left that seriously questioned the social order in Brazil.

However, a degree of political uncertainty did arise. Taxation and political centralization increased due to the presence of the Braganças, and the Brazilian northeast still chafed under the political control of Rio de Janeiro to the south. A rebellion by military officers and planters at Pernambuco in 1817, although readily crushed, did remind João, now the king, that regional sentiments remained very powerful in Brazil. The royal court's need for revenues compounded greatly as it became embroiled after 1815 in the independence wars in the Banda Oriental (Uruguay). The court mobilized militias from throughout the kingdom to undertake a prolonged campaign against the federalist forces of Artigas and the centralist troops from Buenos Aires. A final political crisis began in 1820, when a military uprising in Portugal overthrew the king's representatives and demanded the return of King João to Portugal. Portuguese army officers in Rio de Janeiro also pressured the king to return. João did return to Portugal, albeit reluctantly. His rule in Portugal was to be subjected to a constitution, and he was to share power with a Côrtes (as in Spain at the time). His son, Dom Pedro, remained in Brazil as prince regent.

Sure enough, what some colonial royalists feared eventually did come to pass. In 1822 the Côrtes in Lisbon wished to strip Brazil of its status as a kingdom, to reimpose its colonial standing, and to recall Prince Regent Pedro. By this time, Pedro had surrounded himself with a number of important Brazilian ministers who wanted to avert a political crisis at all costs because of the social dangers of a breakdown of authority. Therefore, in region after region of Brazil, local political forces rose up in defiance of the Côrtes, in favor of Dom Pedro staying in Brazil, and in support of local autonomy. The planter class of each region agreed not on central rule from Rio de Janeiro and not on celebrating the nationhood of Brazil (which had yet to exist) but only on the political legitimacy of the prince regent. The 22-year-old Dom Pedro unified elite opinion in Brazil. Therefore, in April 1822, when he declared the independence of Brazil from Portugal and claimed the throne as emperor, he was actually acting to resolve the political crisis rather than to create one.

This act amounted to independence by default compared with the torturous process by which Mexico and Venezuela became independent. Brazilian elites did not come to a breakdown of consensus. The masses did not arise to fight either for the royalists or for Creole caudillos; they did not have an opportunity to express their demands for an end to slavery and a more equitable distribution of property. Prince Regent Pedro did, however, provide his future subjects a dramatic moment of glory suggesting that the accomplishment of Brazilian independence, nevertheless, did amount to a triumph over adversity. "Friends, the Portuguese Cortes wishes to enslave and persecute us," Pedro proclaimed in the Grito de Ipiranga, where he was traveling at the time. "As from today our bonds are ended. No ties join us anymore. . . . Brazilians, let our watchword from this day forth be *¡Independência ou Morte!'*" Despite the political hyperbole of these stirring words, independence meant little to the Brazilian masses. The lives of slaves, free blacks, frontier natives, and poor peasants continued much as before.

CONCLUDING REMARKS

The colonial elites survived economically and politically wherever the struggle for independence had been relatively painless and free from popular mobilization. Cuba, Puerto Rico, and Brazil represent the best examples of this. The elites of Cuba and Puerto Rico enjoyed the Spanish colonial sanctions of sugar exports and slave imports, the rising prosperity and danger of slave rebellions preventing the Creoles from challenging Spanish political hegemony. Brazil retained slavery and sugar exports through a simple political solution that prevented a breakdown of consensus among the elite: It adopted the Portuguese monarchy as its own. Prince Regent Pedro of Portugal became Emperor Pedro I of Brazil and, despite a crisis in 1830, would eventually pass the crown along to his Brazilian-born son. The expansion of trade with Great Britain in the nineteenth century underwrote the economy and preserved the social order. Brazil did not splinter into feuding, Portuguese-speaking republics.

Certainly, the Brazilians did not have to fight to gain their political independence, as did the Mexicans, Venezuelans, and Argentineans—and fighting made all the difference. Social change was more drastic in those parts of Latin America where the process of independence involved armed struggle. There the Creole leadership had had to enlist the military assistance of the popular classes, thus permitting them to bring their agendas into the public forum. Rebel leaders such as Morelos and Artigas and even Bolívar and San Martín had to contradict the interests of their own class and grant social reforms to fill their ranks. The mestizos and mulattoes, the blacks and the Native Americans, and the workers and the peasants, after all, were not willing to risk death just so the Creoles could supplant the Spaniards. Thus, the liberators issued proclamations and decrees ending slavery, advocating free elections for peasant villagers, terminating forced labor and native tribute, and pushing for federalism. Moreover, once under arms, the popular forces of the revolution attacked those institutions of their past subjugation: the haciendas, plantations, and mines. The old export economies had collapsed, as sugar and cacao plantations lay in ruins and the great silver mines were abandoned.

The conservative victories of the 1820s preserved the Creole elite in Spanish America, even though the social revolution had effected permanent gains for the popular classes. With the economic underpinning destroyed, the victorious Creole leadership was unable to resume business as usual in 1826. They had not begun the revolution to free the slaves or to end native tribute. But when the battle finally ended and an impoverished peace ensued, the Creoles lacked the economic wealth to reinstate their domination of the subordinate classes in the old manner. Therefore, the Creoles fell to bickering among themselves over the meager spoils of political office. They did not demobilize their troops but, during the five decades following independence, engaged in civil wars and political coups and countercoups. The four Spanish viceroyalties were thus broken down into 23 different republics. Bolívar was speaking only for his class when he pronounced, before his death in 1830, that "America is ungovernable."

Political unrest prevented any easy revival of the export economies, despite the new freedom to trade legally with England and other North Atlantic powers. Only gradually would the Creole elites organize themselves to rebuild their nations, encourage export-led development, and resume a measure of control over the popular classes. In the meanwhile, political authority became decentralized, the Creole elites fell to fighting among themselves, the mines and haciendas lay in ruins, and the popular classes gained a great measure of freedom from labor exactions. In the Spanish-American republics, the slave trade ended, slavery itself fell into disuse, and the *mita* and *repartimiento* were inoperable. Peasant autonomy and subsistence agriculture flourished. For many parts of the Spanish Americas, the process of nation building would not be perfected until the latter quarter of the nineteenth century.

The Spanish Americas had avoided a Haitian-style social revolution, it is true. But neither did most of them achieve a purely political revolution on the model of the United States. The conflicts between the races, ethnic groups, and classes formed during the colonial period were to continue into the next two centuries. Just as the Iberians had built their American colonies over the vestiges of the ancient American civilizations, so modern Latin Americans would construct their new nations upon colonial foundations—which is another history unto itself.

Additional Reading

Anna, Timothy E. *The Fall of the Royal Government in Mexico City*. Lincoln: University of Nebraska Press, 1978.

———. *The Fall of the Royal Government in Peru*. Lincoln: University of Nebraska Press, 1979.

Arnade, Charles. *The Emergence of the Republic of Bolivia*. Gainesville: University of Florida Press, 1957.

Barman, Roderick J. *Brazil: The Forging of a Nation, 1798–1852*. Stanford, Calif.: Stanford University Press, 1988.

Bethell, Leslie, ed. *The Independence of Latin America*. Cambridge, England: Cambridge University Press, 1987.

Collier, Simon. *Ideas and Politics of Chilean Independence, 1808–1833*. Cambridge, England: Cambridge University Press, 1969.

Dominguez, Jorge. *Insurrection or Loyalty: The Breakdown of the Spanish American Empire*. Cambridge, Mass.: Harvard University Press, 1980.

Graham, Richard. *Independence in Latin America: A Comparative Approach*. 2d ed. New York: McGraw-Hill, 1994.

Guardino, Peter F. *Peasants, Politics, and the Formation of Mexico's National State: Guerrero, 1800–1857*. Stanford, Calif.: Stanford University Press, 1996.

Hamill, Hugh M., Jr. *The Hidalgo Revolt: Prelude to Mexican Independence*. Gainesville: University of Florida Press, 1966.

Hünefeldt, Christine. *Paying the Price of Freedom: Family and Labor among Lima's Slaves, 1800–1854*. Berkeley: University of California Press, 1994.

Kinsbruner, Jay. *Independence in Spanish America: Civil Wars, Revolutions, and Underdevelopment*. Albuquerque: University of New Mexico Press, 1994.

Lynch, John. *The Spanish American Revolutions, 1808–1826*. 2d ed. New York: W. W. Norton, 1987.

Masur, Gerhard. *Simón Bolívar*. 2d ed. Albuquerque: University of New Mexico Press, 1969.

Rodríguez O., Jaime E . *The Emergence of Spanish America: Vicente Rocafuerte and Spanish Americanism, 1808– 1832*. Berkeley: University of California Press, 1975.

———, ed. *The Independence of Mexico and the Creation of the New Nation*. Los Angeles: UCLA Latin American Center Publications, 1989.

Russell-Wood, A. J. R., ed. *From Colony to Nation: Essays on the Independence of Brazil*. Baltimore, Md.: Johns Hopkins University Press, 1975.

Szuchman, Mark D., and Jonathan C. Brown, eds. *Revolution and Restoration: The Restructuring of Power in Argentina, 1776 to 1860*. Lincoln: University of Nebraska Press, 1993.

Tutino, John. *From Insurrection to Revolution in Mexico: Social Bases of Agrarian Violence, 1750– 1940*. Princeton, N.J.: Princeton University Press, 1986.

Williams, John Hoyt. *The Rise and Fall of the Paraguayan Republic, 1800– 1870*. Austin: University of Texas Press, 1979.

White, Richard Allen. *Paraguay's Autonomous Revolution, 1810– 1840*. Albuquerque: University of New Mexico Press, 1978.

In Spanish and Portuguese

Arze Aguirre, René Danilo. *Participación popular en la independencia de Bolivia*. La Paz: Organización de los Estados Americanos, 1979.

Bonilla, Heraclio, ed. *La independencia en el Perú*. 2d ed. Lima: Instituto de Estudios Peruanos, 1981.

Flores Caballero, Romeo. *La contrarrevolución en la independencia: Los españoles en la vida política, social y económica de México (1804– 1838)*. Mexico City: El Colegio de México, 1969.

Halperín Donghi, Tulio. *Revolución y guerra: Formación de una élite dirigente en la Argentina criolla*. Buenos Aires: Siglo Veintiuno, 1972.

Sala de Tourón, Lucía, Nelson de la Torre, and Julio C. Rodríguez. *Artigas y su revolución agraria, 1811– 1820*. Mexico City: Siglo Veintiuno, 1978.

Tavares, Luis Henrique Dias. *A independência do Brasil na Bahia*. Rio de Janeiro: Civilização Brasileira, 1977.

Torre Villar, Ernesto de la. *La independência de México*. 2d ed. Mexico City: Fondo de Cultura Económica, 1992.

GLOSSARY

All words are Spanish except as otherwise noted as Port. (Portuguese) or as one of the indigenous languages.

aguardiente—literally, "fire water;" a rum made from sugarcane popular among the *gente de pueblo* of Colombia and Argentina

alcabala—sales tax

alcaide—Port., chief constable of a town or city

alcalde—chief constable of a town or city

aldeia—Port., "village," especially a native American village under Jesuit control

alhóndiga—a grain exchange, municipal granary, or storage warehouse

almud, pl. **almudes**—measure of grain equal to 4.625 liters

alpaca—a small, domesticated Andean camelid; source of fine wool

altepetl—Nahuatl, the regional native states covering the central Mexican countryside, each of which was composed of two to four *calpolli*.

Altiplano—the high intermontane plateau southeast of Lake Titicaca in Bolivia

Alto Perú—Upper Peru; colonial name for Bolivia, a province of the Viceroyalty of Peru and after 1776 of the Viceroyalty of the Río de la Plata

amarista—a partisan of the Túpac Amaru rebellion in highland Peru, 1780–83

Amazonia—vast, low-lying basin of the Amazon River and its numerous tributaries, covering much of north central South America and lying mostly in Brazil but also including the eastern portions of the Andean countries

arroba—a unit of weight equal to 11.4 kilograms

artiguismo—the reformist political movement of José Gervasio Artigas

artiguista—of or pertaining to José Gervasio Artigas; a follower of Artigas

asiento—a long-term contract granted by the Crown to a company or individual for a near monopoly on sale of slaves in the colonies

atlatl—Nahuatl, a leverlike device for throwing spears with more accuracy and striking power than would be obtainable manually, used in Mesoamerica

atole—Nahuatl, a corn gruel used widely in Mesoamerica

audiencia—high court and advisory body in colonial Spanish America, consisting of a president and judges *(oidores)*

auto-da-fé—"act of faith"; a public event of the Inquisition in which the convicted were punished for immoral behavior or blasphemy

aviador—a supplier of goods and credit to miners

avío—mining supplies or cash credit provided by an *aviador*

ayllu—Quechua, an Andean native community composed of localized kindred or larger localized groups self-defined in kinship; social group, often localized, self-defined as ancestor-focused kindred

Aymara—a language and indigenous Andean people of the Lake Titicaca area

Bajío—an agricultural region located northwest of Mexico City in the states of Guanajuato and Jalisco

Banda Oriental—literally, the "East Bank," for its location east of the Río de la Plata estuary; the colonial name for Uruguay

bandeira—Port., a Brazilian expedition to capture native slaves

bandeirante—Port., a participant in slaving expeditions against Brazilian natives, usually based at São Paulo

barretero—a skilled mine laborer employed in cutting ores underground with a *barra,* or crowbar

barrio—an urban neighborhood or district within a city or town

batab—Maya, a native chieftain in the Yucatán

batea—Aruak, a wooden bowl used by native peoples to pan for gold in streams

boçal—Port., a slave newly arrived from Africa who lacked knowledge of Portuguese language and customs

bolas—short for *boleadoras*; a hunting weapon made of stones connected by thongs that entangle the prey's legs when thrown, used on the Pampas

bozal—Spanish for *boçal*

caballero—a knight or gentleman; the highest category of untitled nobles

cabildo—the city council of a Spanish colonial city

cabildo abierto—an open town council meeting called in cases of emergency

caboclo—Port., a person of mixed native American and European ancestry in Brazil; see also *mameluco*

cacao—the beans of the cacao tree, which is native to Mesoamerica, used to produce chocolate

cachaça—Port., rum made from skimmings in the process of Brazilian sugar milling

cacicazgo—a native polity having a single leader or *cacique*, a hereditary office of such a leader

cacique—Aruak, ruler of a native polity

calpolli—Nahuatl, the Mexica social-residential unit, or district, which had landholding, military, labor, religious, and political functions; two to four *calpolli* made up the *altepetl* native state

câmara—Port., city council, equivalent to the Spanish American *cabildo*

Cañari—a linguistic and ethnic group native to the Ecuadorian highlands, residents of Otavalo

cancho—feather weaving in Andean regions

capellanía—a private endowment given to the church in exchange for religious services

capitania—Port., "captaincy"; a large territorial division in sixteenth-century Brazil

capitâo-mór—Port., captain-major

carioca—Port., a resident of Rio de Janeiro

casa grande—Port., the big house or owner's residence on a Brazilian plantation

casta—the social group made up of those of mixed racial ancestry

castellano—the Spanish language as spoken in Castile

catarista—a partisan of the Túpac Catari rebellion in Bolivia, in 1780–83

caudillo—an informal military and political leader; a strongman of the nineteenth century whose power derived from force as well as charisma

cavaleiro—Port., a knight or gentleman; highest category of untitled nobles

cédula—decree of Crown policy issued by the king of Spain

cenote—Maya, a sinkhole in the limestone strata of the Yucatán peninsula, source of water for some city-states

chácara—sown land; a cultivated field; a small Spanish estate, usually supplying foodstuffs to local markets

Chaco—see Gran Chaco

chacra—same as *chácara*

Chan Chan—capital of Chimú society, located south of modern Trujillo, Peru

chapetón, pl. chapetones—an American term for Spaniard

Charcas—the colonial name for Bolivia; also see Alto Perú

ch'arki—Quechua, dried llama or alpaca meat

charqui—Spanish for *ch'arki*

Chavín—the name of an art style and religious cult that originated on the northern Peruvian coast in approximately 900 B.C.

chicha—Aruak, beer made from fermented maize, of Andean origin but given a Caribbean name by the Spaniards

Chichimec—Nahuatl, nomadic hunter-gatherers who inhabited northern Mexico and periodically migrated into area of Mesoamerican culture

Chichimeca—Nahuatl, northern mountain and desert lands beyond the limits of Mesoamerican civilization and inhabited by Chichimec groups; also called Gran Chichimeca

chicle—sap from the zapote tree of the Mayan lowlands, boiled down to make chicle, an ingredient in chewing gum

Chimú—a powerful culture on northern coast of Peru from A.D. 1280, famous for walled compounds and black pottery

chinampa—Nahuatl, an artificial raised plot for agriculture built up in a shallow lake; a very productive source of crops in the central valley lakes of ancient Mexico

chuño—Spanish for *ch'uño*

ch'uño—Quechua, freeze-dried, dehydrated potatoes

coca—leaf of the coca plant, a stimulant among Andean peoples, often used in religious ceremonies

cofradía—a brotherhood or sisterhood for religious and charitable purposes; a sodality

colegio—secondary school

comal—flat griddle made of pottery for cooking tortillas, developed in ancient times

comercio libre—free trade

compadrazgo—godparentage

compadre—ritual coparent; relationship between the true parent and the godparent

comunero—a citizen of the king's community, or *común*

Comunero—partisan of the citizens' revolts of Paraguay in the 1720s and of Colombia in 1781

congregación—"congregation;" forced resettlement of indigenous people to achieve greater nucleation and control

conquistador, pl. conquistadores—Spanish conquerors, especially the followers of Cortés in Mexico, Pizarro in Peru, and others who subdued native American empires and resistance

conselho—Port., a council

consulado—the merchant guild and its court

converso—a convert to Christianity, usually applied to a converted Jew or a New Christian

Cordillera—the Andes Mountains; commonly used by South Americans to denote the Andes

corregidor, pl. corregidores—Sp. & Port., a royal official in charge of a native district who had authority similar to a governor; in Brazil, a superior crown magistrate

corregimiento—the administrative district of a *corregidor*

Cortes—the parliament of Spain

Côrtes—Port., the parliament of Portugal

Creole—*criollo*; a person born in the Americas of Spanish ancestry

criollo—Creole; a person born in the Americas of Spanish ancestry

cruzado—Port., a monetary unit equal to 400 réis

cuadrilla—a group of workers, especially in mining

curaca—for *kuraka*

curanderos (-as)—religious specialists dedicated to curing with herbs; folk healers

diezmo—a church tithe of 10 percent

dízimo—Port., a church tithe of 10 percent

doctrina—a parish of native Americans

doctrinero—the priest of a *doctrina;* also an unordained native American religious assistant

dom—Port., a title attached to the first name of a male, like "Sir" in English

don—a title attached to the first name of a male, like "Sir" in English

doña—a title attached to the first name of a female, like "Lady" in English

donatário—Port., a person of sixteenth-century Portugal who was "donated" a large portion of land to settle a capitania and exploit along the coast of Brazil

Dorado, El—"the Golden One," a mythical indigenous lord rich in gold who was supposed to have reigned somewhere in northern South America during the time of the Conquest

encomienda—colonial trusteeship over the native population, conferring tribute and carrying responsibility for religious conversion

encomendero—holder of an *encomienda*

engenho—Port. a sugar mill; by extension, the plantation that supports that mill

español, pl. españoles—Spaniards, either Peninsular or Creole

estancia—a private landholding, most often devoted to livestock

estancia del estado—state-owned stock ranches, especially of early nineteenth-century Paraguay

fanega—a bulk measure equaling about 1.6 bushels or 58 liters

fazenda—Port., rural property, a ranch or farm; also the treasury

fazendeiro—Port., the owner of a *fazenda*

fidalgo—Port., a nobleman or gentleman

flota—the fleet that sailed from Spain to Havana, Veracruz, Cartagena, and Portabelo

forastero—a native living as a resident alien in a native community other than that of his or her origin

frota—Port., the fleet that sailed between Portugal and Brazil

fuero eclesiástico—special judicial privileges enjoyed by persons of religious affiliation

fuero militar—special judicial privileges enjoyed by persons of military affiliation

funcionario—a bureaucrat

gaucho—a cowboy, usually of mixed ancestry, in the Río de la Plata

gaúcho—Port., a cowboy of southern Brazil

gachupín, pl. **gachupines**—derisive term for "Spaniard" in late colonial Latin America

gente decente—well-born people of Spanish descent

gente de pueblo—the lower ranks of society, whose members work with their hands; members were white artisans as well as people of color

glyph—English, a drawn symbol in the ancient writing systems of Mesoamerica that stood for a syllable, a sound, an idea, or a word

gobernador—governor, especially an indigenous leader of the *altepetl* or *ayllu*

Gran Chaco—a flat, low-lying region east of the Andes Mountains in Paraguay, Bolivia, and Argentina, characterized by dry winters and summer floods

gremio—a guild

hacendado—the owner of an hacienda

hacienda—property of any kind but especially a large landed estate; also the government treasury

hermandad—a brotherhood, sodality

hidalgo—a nobleman or gentleman

hieroglyph—English, depictive, art-related systems of writing such as developed among the priestly class in ancient Mesoamerica

huaca—Spanish for *wak'a*

Huari—Spanish for Wari, a powerful culture that spread its authority over the Peruvian Andes from A.D. 600 to 800 prior to the Inka

huaso—a cowboy, usually of mixed ancestry, in Chile

Huitzilopochtli [Weet-see-low-POCH-tlee]—the patron deity of the Mexica, a war god whose name translates as "Hummingbird of the South"

illa—Quechua, an Andean amulet or persons believed to have magical powers, such as twins

Inca—Spanish for Inka

indio—a term applied to all indigenous Americans, who did not use it themselves

indio ladino—a derisive term by which Spaniards identified those indigenous leaders who adopted some European behavior and cultural affectations

ingenio—a sugar mill or plantation

Inka—Quechua, an Andean ethnic group whose ancient capital was Cuzco; also title of the rulers of Inka Empire from A.D. 1438 to 1532

inquilino—a rural worker based on tenancy common in Chile; a service tenant

intendente—an intendant; the chief administrator of an intendancy

irmandade—Port., a brotherhood, sodality

judaizante—"Judaizer," one who observed or professed the Jewish faith

khipu—Quechua, a mnemonic record, usually numerical, made of knotted cords

kuraka—Quechua, a native lord and leader of an Andean community or *ayllu*

ladino—a native person or sometimes an American-born black well versed in Spanish language and culture; in modern usage, a native American or mestizo who uses the Spanish language and culture

lavrador—Port., a farmer, owner, or renter of small property

letrado—a university graduate, synonymous with "lawyer"

libranza—a bill of exchange, a promissory note

licenciado—a licenciate degree or its holder

limeños—residents of Lima, Peru

limpieza de sangre—the purity of blood necessary to hold many privileges and public offices; the absence of Jewish or Muslim ancestors

llama—a domesticated South American camel, source of meat, wool, and some carrying of burdens

llanero—a cowboy, usually of mixed racial ancestry, in Venezuela and Colombia

Llanos—the southern plains of Venezuela and eastern plains of Colombia formed in the basin of the Orinoco River

macehualli (pl., **macehualtin**)—Nahuatl, a member of the Mexica class of free commoners who belonged to the clanlike *calpolli*

mestre de campo—Port., a military officer of a rural district

maguey—the agave plant, source of the drink pulque

mameluco—Port., a person of mixed native American and European ancestry in Brazil, a *mestiço;* also see *caboclo*

manioc—a starchy root that is the staple crop of South American lowlands in Paraguay, Brazil, and Venezuela

mayeque—Nahuatl, native Americans of a subordinate class, roughly equivalent to a serf

mazombo—Port., a white person born in Brazil

merced—a grant of land usually given in name of the king

Mesoamerica—the area from central Mexico south to Guatemala in which arose several advanced ancient American cultures

mestiço—Port., a person of mixed native American and European ancestry in Brazil

mestizo—a person of mixed native American and European ancestry in Spanish America

metate—trough-shaped stones used in ancient Mesoamerica to grind corn by hand with a *mano,* a loaf-shaped stone, in food preparation

milícias—Port., militias formed by colonial subjects at the level of the captaincy in Brazil

milréis—Port., 1,000 réis; a seventeenth-century coin worth 12 English shillings

minga—a voluntary wage laborer in the Andean region, especially in the silver mines

mita—the cyclical labor obligation of the natives to Spanish mines and other public works during the colonial period, from Quechua antecedents

mit'a—Quechua, the obligatory labor of Andean antecedents; corvée labor used for public works, infrastructure construction, and military service

mitayo—an Andean native fulfilling periodic obligatory service

mitimaes—Quechua, colonists sent to live next to ethnic groups known to rebel against the Inka

mitmaq—Quechua, "colonizing;" the practice of the Inka state of sending one ethnic people to settle among others to pacific the district

Moché—a powerful society of Peru's northern coast known for its crafts and religion of sacrifice and bloodletting

montonera—a troop of *montoneros*

montoneros—mounted irregular soldiers, especially in early nineteenth-century Argentina

morador—Port., a colonist, citizen householder

morisco—one who observed or professed the Islamic faith, more common in Spain than in the Americas

mulato—a person of black and white parentage (in English, mulatto)

muscavado—Port., a lower grade of sugar

naborío—Taíno, a Native American of intermediate status between slave and free man who worked as a personal servant

Nahua—the native peoples of central Mexico who spoke Nahuatl

New Christian—a convert to Catholicism, especially applied to Jewish converts

New Spain—the large Spanish jurisdiction centering on Mexico City and embracing much of present-day Mexico and the southwest United States

obraje—a factorylike shop for the manufacturing of textiles

oidor—"judge"; a member of the *audiencia*

oriental, pl. **orientales**—"of the east"; a resident of the Banda Oriental (today Uruguay)

ouvidor—Port., a judge or crown magistrate

Pacha-Mama—the Quechua goddess of the earth

padre—"father"; a Catholic priest

palenque—a fortified hamlet of runaway slaves in Spanish America

Pampas—the rolling, expansive grasslands or semi-arid plains areas of South America, lying to the south, east, and west of Buenos Aires

pardo—a mulatto

Patagonia—the semi-arid, windswept plateau in southern Argentina that runs from the Andes Mountains down to the Atlantic Ocean

patria chica— "little fatherland"; native district

patronato real—royal patronage of the church, with the right to nominate church officials and supervise church administration

paulista—Port., a resident of São Paulo

peninsular, pl. **peninsulares**—a Spaniard born in the Iberian Peninsula

pepenas—the ore that workers were permitted to extract from mines for their own use

peso—a monetary unit, the equivalent of eight reales, the basic unit of colonial silver coinage

petate—a mat woven of reeds and used in the ancient Americas for floor covering and sleeping

población, pl., poblaciones—a native settlement or town

pochteca—Nahuatl, the long-distance merchants of Tlatelolco

poderosos da terra—Port., the owners of large *fazendas,* local potentates

porteño—a person born in or resident of a port, especially of Buenos Aires

presidio—a frontier garrison, especially in northern Mexico

principal—a native noble acting as the leader of a subunit

povo—Port., "people," especially the common folk

pueblo—a town or village; *pueblo de naturales,* a native town or village; also people

pulpería—a small shop serving as a combined grocery store, delicatessen, and tavern

pulpero—the operator of a *pulpería*

pulque—an alcoholic drink made from the maguey or agave plant

pulquería—a tavern where pulque is served, mainly to commoners and workers

Puno—the dry high-altitude grassland region with frequent nocturnal freezes in the southern Andes west of Lake Titicaca

puypu—Quechua, an Andean macaw-wing ornament

Qhechwa—Quechua, indigenous word for Quechua

Quechua—the official language of the Inka state, still spoken by millions in the Andes

Quetzalcóatl [Kayt-zahl-KOH-ahtl]—Nahuatl, the god of culture or creativity, also associated with agriculture, whose name translates as "Plumed Serpent"

Quichua—a Quechuan dialect spoken even today in Ecuador

quilombo—Port., a fortified hamlet of runaway slaves in Brazil

quinoa—a midaltitude grain with high protein content, developed by ancient agriculturists

quiteño—a resident of Quito, Ecuador

quinto—"a fifth"; the royal tax levied on silver and gold; the Quinto Real

quipu—Spanish for the Quechua *khipu*

raised field—an agricultural technique used in swampy areas in which mud is dug from canals and deposited on adjacent banks, building a field above water level

ranchero—the owner of a rancho, a small farmer

rancho—a small landed property; sometimes a rude dwelling on that land

real, pl. reales—a Spanish coin, one-eighth of a common peso

real, pl. réis—Port., the smallest monetary unit, used only as money of account

Recôncavo—the area of rich alluvial soils surrounding Bahia's Bay of All Saints

reducción—a Spanish-style village into which natives were forcibly resettled, especially ca. 1570-90

regidor—a councilman, member of the *cabildo*

relaciones geográficas—geographical reports about Andean parishes and *corregimientos* sent to Spain in reply to Crown questionnaires

repartimiento—a system of temporary labor procurement; draft rotary labor from native American villages

repartimiento de efectos—the forced sale of goods to native Americans by a Spanish official

republiquetas—"little republics"; an extreme form of federalist home rule

requerimiento—the requirement to offer native Americans conversion to Christianity and allegiance to the Castilian Crown before making war on them

rescate—barter, sometimes pillage

residencia—exit hearings to which major Crown officials were subjected before leaving office to detect and remedy abuses

Río de la Plata—"River of Silver," the name given to the estuary of the Paraná River system of South America and sometimes referring to the entire region encompassing Argentina, Paraguay, and Uruguay

ruana—a woven woolen poncho worn by both native and nonnative plebeians in Colombia

Sabana—the highland savannah below the city of Bogotá

sacbe—Maya, raised causeway roads constructed in and around ancient Maya cities

Sacsahuaman—an ancient complex appearing to be a fortress on a hill north of Cuzco, Peru

saladero—a meat-salting plant, especially in the Río de la Plata

Santidade—Port., a religious movement focusing native American resistance against the Portuguese

selva—a tropical rain forest

senhor de engenho—Port., a plantation owner

senzala—Port., a slave hut or quarter on a Brazilian plantation

serrano—a resident of the sierras, or mountains

Sertão—Port., the bush, interior, back country; the backlands of western Bahia and Pernambuco

sesmaria—Port., a grant of land

sierras—"mountains," specifically those in eastern and western Mexico and those of Peru

sistema de castas—"caste system"; social ranking based on race created by the colonial elite and ratified by Spanish law

stela, pl. stelae—Latin, an erect stone monument, often sculptured; used by the ancient Olmec and Maya cultures

swidden—English synonym for the slash-and-burn system of agriculture

taco—Nahuatl, a dish made of spicy meat or vegetables rolled into a tortilla

Taki Unquy—Quechua, the native resistance movement of the sixteenth century, which was based on traditional pre-Hispanic religious rituals and beliefs

tamale—Nahuatl, a Mesoamerican dish made of chopped meat encased in cornmeal dough and steamed in a corn shuck

tambo—small settlements along the Inka highway used as inns for travelers

Tawantinsuyu—Quechua, Inka term for its vast empire, dating from A.D. 1438 to 1532

tienda—shop, store

Tláloc [TLAH-lokh]—Nahuatl, the god of rain

Tonantzin [Toe-NONT-zheen]—Nahuatl, the mother of the gods whose name translates as "Our Mother"

tortilla—Nahuatl, a flat, thin cake of corn flour; a staple food item in Mesoamerica since ancient times

tratante—a peddler; small trader

vaquero—a cowboy, usually of mixed ancestry, in Mexico

vaqueiro—Port., a cowboy, usually of mixed ancestry, in Brazil

vara—a unit of linear measure; roughly 84 centimeters

vecino—a Spanish head of household in colonial towns; citizen

vicuña—a wild camelid, relative of the domesticated llama and alpaca, found in the Andes highlands

visita—an official inspection into the conduct of bureaucrats, usually unscheduled and unexpected; a tour of inspection, especially to investigate an officeholder; a detailed field study of native settlements made for the purpose of fixing tribute quotas

Viracocha—Spanish for Wiraqocha

wak'a—Quechua, sacred Andean spirits or personages; a superhuman person; also sacred places

Wari—Quechua, see Huari

Wiraqocha—Quechua, the Andean creator god; sometimes applied to the Europeans after the Conquest of 1532

Xipe Tótec [SHEE-pay TOH-teck]—the god of spring or vegetation whose name translates as "Our Lord of the Flayed One"

yanakona—Quechua, the servant of a native noble, treated as a dependent and receiving goods for his or her services; also used in colonial times to refer to native servants in the fashion of Andean tradition, a nominally paid dependent

yanca—an Andean *huaca* priest by hereditary title

yerba maté—an herbal tea indigenous to Paraguay made from the leaves of the *yerba* tree

zambos—persons of African and Native American ancestry

INDEX